A GUIDE TO
GREEK THOUGHT

A GUIDE TO GREEK THOUGHT

Major Figures and Trends

Edited by Jacques Brunschwig and Geoffrey E. R. Lloyd
with the collaboration of Pierre Pellegrin

Translated under the direction of
Catherine Porter

THE BELKNAP PRESS OF
HARVARD UNIVERSITY PRESS
CAMBRIDGE, MASSACHUSETTS
LONDON, ENGLAND
2003

First published as *Le Savoir Grec: Dictionnaire Critique*,
copyright © 1996 by Flammarion

Library of Congress Cataloging-in-Publication Data
Savoir grec. English. Selections.
A guide to Greek thought / edited by Jacques Brunschwig and Geoffrey E. R. Lloyd;
with the collaboration of Pierre Pellegrin ;
translated under the direction of Catherine Porter.
p.   cm.
Includes bibliographical references and index.
ISBN 0-674-02156-8 (alk. paper)
1. Greece—Intellectual life—To 146 B.C.   2. Greece—Intellectual life—146 B.C.–323 A.D.
3. Intellectuals—Greece.   4. Thought and thinking—History—To 1500.
I. Brunschwig, Jacques.   II. Lloyd, G. E. R. (Geoffrey Ernest Richard), 1933–
III. Pellegrin, Pierre.   IV. Title
DF78.S23313   2003
180—dc21   2003052248

CONTENTS

TRANSLATORS' NOTE

An informal group of translators based in Ithaca, New York, we agreed in the fall of 1996 to translate the portions of *Greek Thought* originally written in French and Italian. Working largely in bilingual pairs, we met regularly to share problems and search for solutions. A broad group of willing collaborators made our task much easier. We wish to express our gratitude first and foremost to Jacques Brunschwig and Geoffrey Lloyd, coeditors of the original French edition, for their generous assistance and support. We also offer thanks to all the authors who graciously read our drafts, answered questions, and made invaluable corrections and suggestions as needed. Other specialists and consultants helped us at many points along the way: thanks in particular to Charles Brittain, Terence Irwin, Mark Landon, Philip Lewis, Culver Mowers, Pietro Pucci, Hunter Rawlings, Geoffrey Rusten, and Daniel Turkeltaub for their collaboration. The unfailingly helpful staff allowed us to use the excellent collection housed in Cornell's Olin Library with maximum efficiency, and the Department of Classics at Cornell University kindly shared its own well-stocked library. Finally, we are indebted to Jennifer Snodgrass and the editorial staff at Harvard University Press for overseeing this complex project with exceptional patience and professional acumen.

RITA GUERLAC
DOMINIQUE JOUHAUD
CATHERINE PORTER
JEANNINE PUCCI
ELIZABETH RAWLINGS
ANNE SLACK
SELINA STEWART
EMORETTA YANG

INTRODUCTION: ON HOME GROUND IN A DISTANT LAND

Alpha, beta, and the rest, all the way to omega: most of us, on first acquaintance with the Greek alphabet, have toyed with writing our own names with its characters, so close and yet so remote from our own. Their attraction for us is unequaled. Roman inscriptions are lofty and admirable: their letters decorate the pediments of our civic buildings as well as commercial signs. At the extremes of the graphic spectrum, Egyptian hieroglyphics look down upon us from the pinnacle of their forty centuries; Chinese ideograms fascinate us by their symbolism and by the complicated enigma of their design. The Greek alphabet, halfway between the strange and the familiar, is at the perfect distance from our own—of which it is a remote ancestor. It is unfamiliar enough to let us know we have left home. Yet it welcomes us with signals clear enough to avoid complete illegibility. Better than a new dissertation on the eternal modernity of ancient Greece, or one more warning against the myths that nourish such dissertations, the paradoxical kinship of the alphabets offers a limited but illuminating metaphor for the complex relation that ties our present to a past that is also ours, and that continues to inhabit our present, visibly or invisibly.

What we have just said about the Greek alphabet could be repeated, even more justifiably, about everything that has been written with those letters. Despite severe losses, the Greek alphabet has transmitted to us countless texts: poems, myths, histories, tragedies, comedies, political and legal discourses, formal speeches, dialogues, treatises on philosophy, cosmology, medicine, mathematics, zoology, and botany; through direct action, indirect influence, polemical reaction, rereading, and reinterpretation, these texts inaugurated and have nourished the whole tradition of Western thought. Here again, the feelings of familiarity and distance are interwoven. We are on home ground in a distant land; we are traveling without leaving our own room. All our thinking, in one way or another, passes through reflection on the Greeks.

The key to the unparalleled originality of the Greeks may be that their culture, by definition, did not have the Greeks behind it. Of course it did not spring up out of nothing, any more than their alphabet did (its basic elements were borrowed from the Phoenicians); we need not regret that today's historians and scholars, with increasing conviction, are replacing the celebrated "Greek miracle" with unmiraculous Greeks. But however important the

Greeks' debt to preceding civilizations, they quickly made their borrowings their own and turned them against their creditors, who represented in their eyes either a civilization turned upside down (the prestigious and astonishing Egypt) or the opposite of civilization (the despotic and barbaric Mesopotamia). Like all those who have followed, the Greeks reflected on the Greeks; but their reflections were like no one else's, simply because they themselves were the Greeks. Their thinking, like God's thinking according to Aristotle, was thinking about thinking.

The Greeks' culture of self-awareness predated the Socratic "Know thyself." Very early, their mythology, newly codified by Homer and Hesiod, gave rise to its own critics (Xenophanes, Heraclitus) and its own interpreters, allegorists or not. The Milesian cosmologies carried on a dialogue; each was intended to resolve a difficulty posed by its predecessor. The intimidating Parmenidean challenge, which threatened to smother physics, elicited almost immediate responses by Empedocles, Anaxagoras, and the Atomists. Socrates, disappointed by the physics of his forerunners, kept his distance from things and turned toward discourse. Plato transposed the ancient myths; he interpreted Socrates, constructing the conditions that made Socrates possible and that would have made his condemnation impossible. Aristotle criticized Plato, as he criticized most of his predecessors, even while he strove to retain what deserved preservation. Epicureans and Stoics, from their own moment in history, mustered enough distance to seek their own masters in a remote past before Plato and Aristotle, in Democritus and Heraclitus. Plato's heritage was diffused and dispersed in a gamut that ranged from skepticism to Neoplatonic metaphysics. Commentary, the critique of texts and the accumulation of glosses, which began astonishingly early, flourished at the beginning of the common era.

But even more striking than the critical turns taken by Greek culture in its successive stages is the work that each of its artisans performed on himself. It would have seemed impossible for Greek scientists, historians, or philosophers to do their work without knowing, or at least without wondering, under what conditions (intellectual as well as moral and political) it was possible to do science, history, or philosophy. To judge by their works, it is clear that the same thing was true for sculptors, architects, musicians, and dramatic poets: their style is manifestly not the result of rote practice or of an empirical tradition based on natural ability. Even shoemaking was taught; even cooks claimed to be conscious auxiliaries of philosophy. Every activity, every perception, every direct relation to an object raised seemingly simple questions that are as disconcerting as those addressed by Socrates to his interlocutors— questions that interpose distance and require the mind to adjust its relation to everything it encounters: "What is it all about?" "What are you really looking for?" "What exactly do you mean?" "How do you know what you have just said?"

The work from which this volume was drawn is titled *Greek Thought*. If it had one central ambition, it was to call attention to this fundamental reflexivity that seems to us characteristic of Greek thought, and which gives it even today a formative value and a capacity to challenge. The essays drawn from that book do not address "Greek science," or "Greek philosophy," or "Greek civilization." Excellent works, both introductory and comprehensive, exist on these subjects, works with which we do not propose to compete. We have not sought to explicate, or even to summarize, the whole of what the Greeks knew, or thought they knew; nor do we tally up what they did not know, the gaps in their knowledge. Similarly, we have not wanted either to repeat or to summarize histories of Greek philosophy; and nothing will be found here that touches directly on Greek art, Greek literature, or Greek religion. Instead we have sought to step back from the products to the processes that gave rise to them, from works to actions, from objects to methods. Of foremost interest to us is the typically Hellenic aptitude for raising questions that are at once "second-order"—in ways that correspond to our modern use of that term—and "first-order." They are second-order in that they relate not to substantive questions that bear immediately on the world, the beings that populate it, the events that take place in it, and the activities that transform it, but rather to the status of those questions and how they should be discussed. At the same time they are first-order or "primary" in a different sense, namely that in the view of many of the most prominent philosophers they must logically be raised first and solved or resolved in one way or another before the substantive issues are addressed. The term "Socratic fallacy" has sometimes been used to designate the idea that one could not say whether a given individual was courageous or not, so long as one was unable to say universally what courage is. Fallacy or not, Greek thought finds in this quest for lucidity its most radical task. Classical knowledge, in the sense in which we are using the term, is not the knowledge indicated by expressions like "knowing that Socrates was condemned to death" or "knowing that the diagonal of a square is incommensurable with its side." It represents, rather, the knowledge denoted in expressions such as "knowing what one is saying," "knowing what one is doing," "knowing what one wants."

In the essays assembled for this volume readers will find a series of articles on the major Greek philosophers and scholars, as well as on the principal schools and lasting currents of thought. Among so many glorious and singular individuals, the choice was necessarily a difficult one. Our selection is certainly more restrained than that of Diogenes Laertius in his *Lives and Opinions of Illustrious Philosophers*; but it goes further forward in time, and it makes room for scientists and historians as well as for philosophers. Anticipating our own second thoughts, some may find that we have been unjust toward certain figures such as Xenophanes, Sophists other than Protagoras, the Cyrenaics or the Megarians, Eudoxus of Cnidus, Theophrastus, or Philo of

Alexandria. Still, we had to make choices, and any selection reflects judgments that can always be contested. Most of the thinkers or scholars to whom it was not possible to devote a separate section are mentioned, along with their works, within one article or another, and can be traced through the index. The bibliographies and index also help make up for the inevitable disadvantages of choice and dispersal.

Finally, a word about the choice of contributors. As general editors responsible for the overall project that resulted in the original *Greek Thought* volume, the two of us who sign this Introduction are pleased and proud that our association can modestly symbolize the alliance between two major centers of research on the history of ancient thought, Cambridge and Paris; we are even more pleased and proud to have worked all our professional lives, each in our own way, in the conviction that the differences between the Anglo-Saxon and Latin worlds in traditions, methods, and instruments of analysis and research in no way prevent contact, exchange, productive discussion, and the production of a common work. This book bears renewed witness to that shared conviction.

The authors to whom we turned, British or American, Italian or French, have all contributed to the considerable progress that has been made, over the last several decades, in the knowledge and understanding of the intellectual world of ancient Greece. They all have their own personalities, which we have not asked them to suppress; their freedom of opinion and judgment has been intentionally respected. As we have said, the gaze of the moderns looking upon the Greeks looking upon themselves remains obviously, and deliberately, our own gaze, and it measures distances, proximities, gaps, and debts from this standpoint. But this gaze of ours can never be entirely unified: contemporary scholars, sometimes because of the particular fields in which they work, sometimes because of the diversity of their overall approaches, do not all necessarily interpret or appreciate our relation to Greek thought in the same way. No one is in a position to dictate that all these scholars subscribe to the latest trend, or conform to the next-to-latest fashion; if we somehow had such power, we would surely have refrained from using it.

We thank our collaborators for agreeing to write their articles in a style that is not always the one they are accustomed to. We know how wrenching it is, for academics conscious of their scholarly responsibilities, to give up footnotes and erudite references. But we deliberately chose to call upon authors for whom that renunciation would be painful, rather than those whose habits would not have been particularly disturbed.

Finally, we want to thank all those without whom the long and difficult enterprise of producing the original *Greek Thought* volume would have run aground on one or another of the countless reefs that threatened it. Louis Audibert, the literary director at Flammarion, had the initial idea; he followed its realization from beginning to end with incomparable vigilance and care.

Pierre Pellegrin played a very effective role in the revision process; he provided the liaison and the coordination that our geographic distance from each other, and from many of our authors, made particularly necessary. And we do not want to fail to thank the technical team at Flammarion, which supported us as much by its high expectations as by the help it offered us toward meeting them.

Jacques Brunschwig, Geoffrey E. R. Lloyd
Translated by Catherine Porter and Dominique Jouhaud

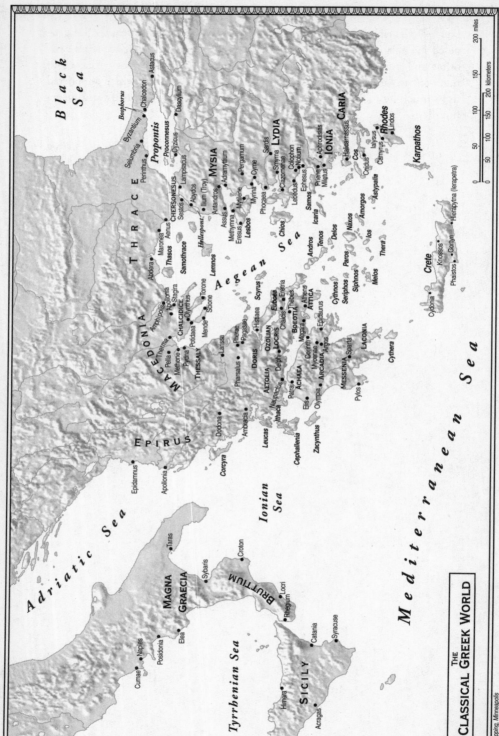

Black Sea

Bosphorus
Byzantium
Selymbria
Perinthus
Chalcedon
Astacus
Dascylium
Cyzicus
Propontis
Proconnesus
Lampsacus
Abydos
CHERSONESUS
Sestos
Maronea
Aenus
Thasos
Abdera
Samothrace
Lemnos

THRACE

Antandros
Illum (Troy)
Assus
MYSIA
Adramyttium
Pergamum
Cyme
Sardis
LYDIA
Smyrna
Colophon
Notium
IONIA
Ephesus
Priene
Miletus
Halicarnassus
CARIA
Aphrodisias
Cnidus
Cos
Rhodes
Ialysus
Camyrus
Lindos
Karpathos

Methymna
Eresus
Mytilene
Lesbos
Phocaea
Clazomenae
Lebedus
Chios
Samos
Icaria
Astypalaia

Hellespont

Aegean Sea

Amphipolis
Acanthus
Stagira
CHALCIDICE
Olynthus
Potidaea
Scione
Mende
Torone
Therma
MACEDONIA
Pella
Methone
Pydna
THESSALY
Larissa
Pherae
Pharsalus
Pagasae

Andros
Tenos
Delos
Naxos
Amorgos
Paros
Ios
Scyrus
Cynthos
Seriphos
Siphnos
Melos
Thera

Euboea
Histaea
Chalcis
Eretria
DORIS
LOCRIS
Delphi
Thebes
BOEOTIA
AETOLIA
OZOLIAN
LOCRIS
Naupactus
Chalcis
Megara
ATTICA
Athens
Epidaurus
Eleusis
Corinth
Mycenae
ACHAEA
Argos
ARCADIA
ARGOLIS
Olympia
Ellis
Patra
Sparta
LACONIA
MESSENIA
Pylos
Cythera

Ithaca
Leucas
Cephallenia
Zacynthus

EPIRUS
Dodona
Ambracia

Epidamnus
Apollonia

Corcyra

Adriatic Sea

Ionian Sea

Taras
Sybaris
Croton
MAGNA GRAECIA
BRUTTIUM
Locri
Rhegium

Cumae
Naples
Posidonia
Elea

Tyrrhenian Sea

Himera
SICILY
Acragas
Catania
Syracuse

Mediterranean Sea

Crete
Cydonia
Knossos
Gortyn
Phaistos
Hierapytna (Ierapetra)

| 0 | 50 | 100 | 150 | 200 miles |
| 0 | 50 | 100 | 150 | 200 kilometers |

THE CLASSICAL GREEK WORLD

Meridian Mapping, Minneapolis

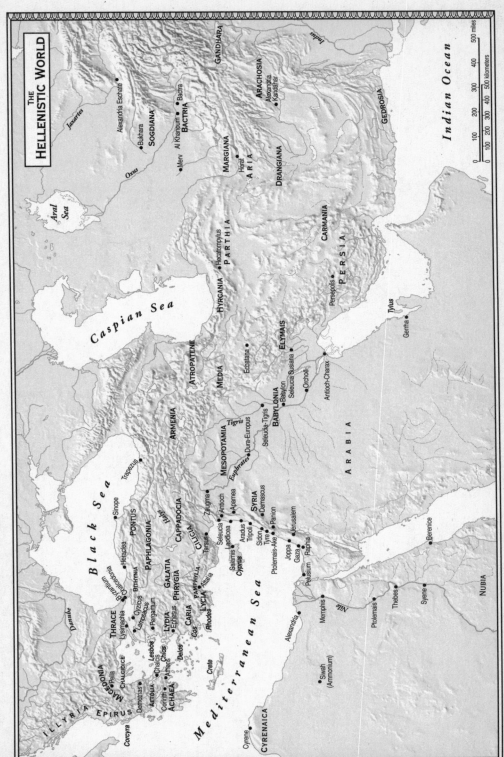

THE
HELLENISTIC WORLD

Indian Ocean

500 miles
100   200   300   400   500 kilometers
0   100   200   300   400

Jaxartes

Alexandria Eschate

Oxus

•Bukhara
SOGDIANA

•Al Khanoum
•Bactra
BACTRIA

•Merv

MARGIANA

Herat
ARIA

GANDHARA

ARACHOSIA
Alexandria-
Kandahar

DRANGIANA

GEDROSIA

Aral
Sea

Hecatompylus•
PARTHIA
HYRCANIA

CARMANIA

P E R S I A

•Persepolis

Caspian Sea

ATROPATENE

MEDIA

•Ecbatana

ELYMAIS

•Seleucia-Tigris
BABYLONIA
•Babylon
•Seleucia Susiana
•Orchoë
•Antioch-Charax

Tylus

Gerrha•

ARMENIA

Tigris

MESOPOTAMIA
Euphrates•Dura-Europus

A R A B I A

•Trapezus

B l a c k   S e a

•Sinope

Halys

PONTUS
PAPHLAGONIA

CAPPADOCIA

Zeugma•
Antioch•
Laodicea• Apamea•
CILICIA   SYRIA•   •Damascus
Tarsus• Seleucia•   Pahion•
Aradus•
Tripoli•
Sidon•
Tyre•
Ptolemais-Ake•
Joppa• •Jerusalem
Gaza•   •Raphia
Pelusium•

•Heraclea
Nicomedia
•Byzantium
Chalcedon
Cyzicus• BITHYNIA
•Lampsacus •Pergamum
THRACE   LYDIA   GALATIA
Lysimachia   •Ephesus PHRYGIA
Lesbos   CARIA   PAMPHYLIA
Chios   •Cos   LYCIA   •Attalia
•Delos   •Rhodes
Salamis•
Cyprus

MACEDONIA
•Pella
Demetrias•
AETOLIA •Chalcis
Corinth• Athens•
ACHAEA

ILLYRIA
EPIRUS

Corcyra

Crete

M e d i t e r r a n e a n   S e a

•Alexandria

•Siwah
(Ammonium)

•Memphis
Nile

•Ptolemais

•Thebes

•Syene

NUBIA

•Berenice

•Cyrene
CYRENAICA

Danube

Indus

Meridian Mapping, Minneapolis

MAJOR FIGURES

ANAXAGORAS

Anaxagoras was born around 500 b.c.e. in Clazomenae in Asia Minor. But he spent a great part of his life in Athens, and in a sense it is thanks to him that philosophy became the Athenian specialty it would thereafter remain. A friend of Pericles, who had gathered around him a prestigious group of artists and intellectuals, Anaxagoras was the target of political attacks. The adoption in 438/437 of a decree proposed by the soothsayer Diopeithes allowing charges to be brought against "those who deny divine things or who in their teaching spread theories about celestial phenomena" (Diels-Kranz, A16) was directly aimed at Anaxagoras, and led to his prosecution in 437/436. Condemned, he was forced to leave Athens, and he passed the last year of his life in Lampsacus, on the Hellespont, where he died in 437/436.

Since antiquity, Anaxagoras has represented the enlightened rationalist struggling against superstition (Plutarch, *The Parallel Lives* 3.IV.4), and he is remembered for predicting the fall of a meteorite at Aigospotami in 467/466. But because he took Mind (Nous, a term that was also used as his nickname, according to Diogenes Laertius) as the basis for his philosophy, he also embodied better than anyone the type of the contemplative philosopher. The same Anaxagoras whom Aristotle criticized for holding that it is owing to his hands that man is the most intelligent of animals was also said to have declared that man was born to contemplate the heavens (Diogenes Laertius, II.10; cf. Plato, *Phaedrus* 269e).

Anaxagoras is the author of a single treatise which, according to a well-known episode in Plato's *Phaedo* (97b), was the object of a public reading in Athens, in the presence of Socrates (we can date the event to around 450). Like numerous other Presocratic writings, the work is known only from fragments (a little more than twenty), almost all preserved by Simplicius in his commentary on the first book of Aristotle's *Physics*, and by an important series of testimonies (117 entries in the Diels-Kranz collection). Since the treatise was probably a short one, our information is less incomplete than it might seem. In any event, it is not at all certain that, had we more texts at our disposal, we would be in a better position to resolve the formidable problems of interpretation posed by a complex system of thought—the first to have exploited, if not explored, the paradoxes of infinity.

Anaxagoras's philosophy, in accordance with its geographically mediating position, has sometimes been presented as an attempt at synthesis between a physics of the Milesian type and Parmenides' (Western) ontology. It would probably be more accurate to see it as an attempt, prompted by Parmenides' poem itself, to overcome the scandal represented, in the latter, by the leap from the sphere of being and truth (in the first part of the poem) to that of becoming and opinion (in the second part). Still, such a story hardly accounts for the central role played by the Mind in Anaxagoras's system. Heraclitus's universal reason is sometimes cited in this regard, or Xenophanes' god. But these links are too loose to be really enlightening, even if we were to acknowledge their pertinence. To understand the function of Mind in the harmonious arrangement of the treatise, we must start with what is known, following Aristotelian terminology, as the Anaxagorean doctrine of "matter."

In this domain, the Eleatic heritage seems self-evident. Like Parmenides, Anaxagoras dismisses the use that men—or, as he writes, "the Greeks"—make of the terms *birth* and *destruction*. To come into being is just as impossible as to be annihilated, for nothing arises from nonbeing, nor does being return to nonbeing. This first principle nevertheless does not exclude local change, as it does for Parmenides. The "things that are" are not born, nor do they die, but they reunite *(sunkrisis)* and dissociate *(diakrisis)* themselves. Anaxagoras can thus conceive of the history of the world not as the faded reflection of ontological discourse but as the very site of its deployment. His treatise, of which the beginning has been preserved, starts right out describing the original state, characterized by indistinction: "All things were together, infinite in regard both to number and to smallness; for the small too was infinite. Since all things were together, nothing within was clear because of smallness" (Diels-Kranz, 1). From this primordial mix, which seems to be not a state of fusion but of juxtaposition (whence the infinity of "smallness"), visible things emerge by a process of "separating off," which, from another point of view, is also a process of "mixing"—for the "decomposition" of the primitive mass coincides with the "formation" of composite entities.

From the point of view of a strict Eleatism, such a redistribution represents a major concession to the world of the senses. But being, in Anaxagoras, gains in extension what it loses in intension. In Parmenides, *nothing* of what constitutes the world of opinion *is* in the strict meaning of the term (not even the two fundamental components, fire and night); for Anaxagoras, on the other hand, *everything* that constitutes the world, by the same token, *is*. It follows that every existing thing preexists and survives itself. If we do not see this and fall under the illusion of births and destructions, it is only because, disseminated, things remain indistinct, as they were in the primordial mix.

The problem, then, is to enumerate and define the members of the primitive ontological population. Nothing in principle precludes reducing fundamental entities to a small number of elements. In Empedocles, for example, whose argument coincides up to this point with that of Anaxagoras, only four elements, called "roots," are necessary to account for the totality of things that have come into being (subject, of course, to a definite "organization," whose role is more important to the extent that the elements by themselves are more amorphous). In Anaxagoras, the "things that are" are numerous and disparate, already much closer to the world that will eventually result from them; bones and blood, for example, two typical creations of Empedocles' artisan Aphrodite, are already present in the primordial mix. Even if it seems difficult to maintain that Anaxagoras, anxious to leave the least possible space for nonbeing in a world that already presupposes local change, abolished every distinction between "ingredients" and "composites," the fact remains that his position combines a stricter interpretation of Parmenides' interdict than that of Empedocles; hence his incomparably more generous ontology.

It is very difficult to set up an exhaustive list of the "things that are." In the succession of fragments, we find first air and aether (these are more abundant than the other ingredients in the primordial mix), then the moist and the dry, the hot and the cold, the bright and the dark (the "opposites" of Aristotle's doxography, *Physics* 187a); then the earth, isolated; and finally a mysterious category of seeds *(spermata)*, which are said to be infinite in number. This list is manifestly open-ended: one should probably add to it, on the basis of other fragments or accounts, the "dense" and the "rare," the sweet and the salty, as well as organic composites such as hair or flesh. (According to one possible reading of some very controversial passages, it is this last group of substances that Aristotle calls by the technical name *homoiomeres*; however, this term, which certainly does not go back to Anaxagoras, ended up referring in post-Aristotelian doxography to Anaxagoras's principles in general.) Finally, Mind should certainly be counted among the things that are, since it is, in Anaxagoras's terms, "the finest" and "the purest" among them (Diels-Kranz, 12).

The profile of the series depends in great part on the extension one gives the term *seeds*. If we take the term literally as referring to seeds of organisms, we must acknowledge that animals and plants are already included in the primordial mix. Such a view fits an interpretation that seeks to minimize the difference between ingredients and composites (an extreme version would even include in the primordial mix all the individuals that would ever come into existence). As its defenders realize, this concept is not unproblematic: organisms, in fact, do not develop through the addition of substantially identical parts. Two options seem to arise at this juncture. We may suppose that organic development is subject to more complex mechanisms than the terms of association and dissociation suggest. This approach would highlight the fact that, in addition to the vocabulary of association and dissociation, Anaxagoras uses a terminology of organic differentiation *(apokrisis)*. Alternatively, we may suppose that the term *seeds* is used here metaphorically to refer to nonorganized entities, whether we take it as a general term or, more narrowly, as corresponding to the Aristotelian *homoiomeres*. In support of the latter hypothesis (and likewise of the second option), one can emphasize that natural substances are unquestionably part of the primordial mix.

Moreover, only a limitation of the primitive population to nonorganized substances allows us to give an acceptable meaning to the formula—fraught with difficulties in any event—of universal inherence ("in everything there is a portion of everything"), which appears in several fragments. It is generally thought that this second principle, from which Mind alone is excluded, as is revealed in the course of the treatise, derives from the application of the initial principle of conservation of being to biological phenomena, and in particular to nutrition, which unquestionably interested Anaxagoras. Observing that blood, hair, bones, and so forth come from the food we eat, Anaxagoras would have concluded that "in everything there is a portion of everything." The conclusion, however, does not follow. What the phenomenon of nutrition allows us at most to claim is that *certain* things are contained in others. To be able to affirm on the basis of an empirical observation that "everything" is in "everything," it would be necessary for everything to come from everything. Such is in fact the argument that Aristotle lends to Anaxagoras in *Physics* (187b). But this is so manifestly contrary to observation that we may wonder whether it is not a rather desperate reconstruction on Aristotle's part.

Two paths open up here once again. We can try to weaken the scope of the formula "everything comes from everything," by supposing it to be true only under certain circumstances that we can try to specify; or we can admit that the principle "everything is in everything" is not based on a simple empirical observation. The first solution was adopted by Simplicius; trying to justify Aristotle even more than Anaxagoras, he suggests that everything comes from everything not in the sense that everything could at any moment come from anything whatsoever, but in the sense that, granted a certain number of steps, one could start from any entity whatsoever and arrive at any other (according to Anaxagoras [Diels-Kranz, 16], stones derive from clouds through the intermediary of water and earth, at the end of a process of progressive solidification).

However, in worrying about realism we run the risk of considerably reducing the range of a thesis that really seems to be above all "metaphysical." Taken literally, the second principle reverses the meaning of the very thesis from which it derives. While for Parmenides the predicates of being are so many aspects of self-identity, forms that his poem progressively unfolds up to the point where the homogeneous "sphere" of being is constituted, Anaxagoras's beings are characterized by their radical heterogeneity. Universal inherence in fact implies an infinite regression in the search for an ultimate identity: the earth contains gold, which in turn contains earth, which contains gold, and so on. This self-embedding structure, which defies all representation, becomes even less comprehensible as the size of the initial population increases. We can see why his interpreters devoted considerable energies to "saving" Anaxagoras from his own doctrine, whose consequences appeared logically unacceptable.

Thus some have tried to show, on the one hand, that Anaxagoras's "things" must have been pure after all (which is true in a certain sense, as we shall see) and, on the other hand, that their fundamental ingredients included only opposites. As a general rule, the basis for these solutions, which are often technically complicated, goes back to antiquity. Simplicius draws a distinction between quantitative divisibility, which alone could be pursued to infinity, and qualitative indivisibility, which permits the isolation of an ultimate element; he also remarks that Anaxagoras's fragments mention only the separation of opposites.

However, the principle of universal inherence (in other words, the thesis according to which there is no such thing as an element, properly speaking), repeated in the fragments in different ways, seems to be a fundamental tenet of the system. Even if its only value is indicative, the comparison with Leibniz (*Monadology* 67s) can help us overcome the uneasiness aroused by its paradoxical consequences. Anaxagoras was perfectly capable of measuring the resources inherent in the notion of the infinite, even though he obviously lacked the conceptual apparatus needed to resolve the logical difficulties the system produces (it requires, for example, that certain infinites be larger than others). It is important to stress, in this context, that Anaxagoras's qualitative infinite is not on the same footing as Zeno's quantitative infinite. One essential consequence of the principle of universal inherence is that, in some sense, the world in its present state does not differ from the initial mix: "Just as in the beginning now too are all things together" (Diels-Kranz, 6). It is in this sense that one might argue that there really exists in Anaxagoras a general principle of "homoiomery," each part of the primitive constituents, as Aristotle puts it, being a mix similar to the whole (*Physics* I.iv.187a). What differentiates the actual state from the initial state is not the existence of the mix but rather the internal equilibrium of its distribution, governed by the principle of domination.

By virtue of the first principle, "separation" from within the mix produces not things themselves, but their visibility. Still, this visibility is deceptive, for the thing separated off is no less mixed, or "impure," than the mixture from which it is detached. Instead of all things being invisible, it is now the mixture that has become so, as it were. The illusion of identity comes from the fact that in every detached thing, one thing, or rather a series of things, "predominates" over the other ("of things of which there is the greatest quantity, every one of these things is most manifestly these things, and was so," says Anaxagoras; Diels-Kranz, 12, end of frg.). Thus one can say of an entity that it is hot, heavy, or white because it contains a greater quantity of the hot, the heavy, or the white.

It follows from the principle of domination that the characteristics we predicate of things, useful as they may be pragmatically, are the source of a categorical illusion: in fact, they turn simple quantitative superiority into a criterion of ontological identity. A number of specific explanations in Anaxagoras's treatise can be interpreted as attempts to restore to the mix, and especially to their contrary, all those constitutive entities of our world that seem to have escaped it and to which we give a definite name: thus Anaxagoras maintains that snow is no less black than white, and that every sensation is painful, tracking down in every phenomenon what it is not *manifestly;* or else, in Anaxagoras's paradoxical language, one can say that "the visible existence is a sight of the unseen" (Diels-Kranz, 21a)—a formula Democritus praised, although he understood it differently. As for the senses, of which linguistic predication is an accomplice, they are limited, on their own, to establishing surface identities. Thus it is not surprising that Anaxagoras criticized our sensory faculties, incapable as they are of *distinguishing* between two closely related phenomena (like two shades in a gradation of colors).

The principle of domination exacerbates the logical difficulties already raised with regard to universal inherence, so much so that it has given partisans of the elementary character of ingredients one of their best arguments. The problem clearly arises from the example by which Simplicius illustrates the principle: "What has much gold in it appears to be gold, though there are numerous things in it." If it is really impossible to isolate a pure state of gold, one in which gold would be nothing but gold, the description of a piece of gold as "that which contains the most gold" seems to be circular: by virtue of the principle of the mixture, the *definiens* is neither more nor less gold than the *definiendum.* The difficulty is real. There is no solution for it compatible with the principle of universal inherence unless we are willing to distinguish between inherence in fact and independence in principle, where the status of the latter can be explained only in relation to the role of Mind in the dissociation of the original mixture.

We learn about the cosmogonic process through a long fragment of about thirty lines (Diels-Kranz, 12), the oldest example of continuous philosophical prose that has come down to us. We may be struck by a certain hieratic quality in the expression, owing to the abundance of paratactic relations, the repetition of the same terms, and, in the first lines, a "hymnic" character (as Deichgräber calls it) in the enumeration of the attributes of Mind (which Anaxagoras, however, does not appear to have called a god). We can see why the ancients must have been sensitive to the beauty and grandeur of this style. While the writer's effort to produce a syntax of justification is unmistakable, interpreters have insisted on the obscurities of the text's form, which is better suited to the expression of a dogmatic "archaic wisdom" than to the needs of argumentation. However, the fact remains that Anaxagoras's argument, taken in conjunction with the principle of universal inherence to which he explicitly refers, contains all the elements necessary for an adequate understanding of the function of Mind.

The primordial mix seems to have been held in place at first by the domination of air and aether (which suggests perhaps a natural but thwarted tendency on the part of matter toward movement). Mind gave it the initial thrust, imparting to it a rotary motion that was at first restricted in amplitude, then gradually expanded, and it will continue to expand—perhaps until the world in which we live is destroyed. Although the term signifying rotation (perichōresis) means nothing more than circular movement (it applies to the course of the stars today as well as to the initial disturbance), it is likely that the crucial stages of the formation of the world were explained by a physics of whirling movement. The first separation out of the primitive mix was that of air and aether, which are opposed, as cold and wet are to hot and dry; this separation must have been accompanied by the concentration, at the center, of the heavy mass of the earth, which as a result of rotation itself would presumably have taken the form of a flat disc. The action implies a force capable of liberating the enormous mass of opposing "elements" from their own "weight." The existence of incandescent stars, carried along by the celestial rotation, also proves the violence of a process that, in a second phase, tore enormous masses from the earth and projected them into the aether, where they burst into flame (thus the stars are stones, not gods). Anaxagoras derived this force (explicitly called violence, bia) from the extreme rapidity of the circular motion. Thus we see here how, through the intermediary of rotation, Mind made of its own constitutive weakness (it is the "finest" of all things in this sense too) the very instrument of its domination (kratos). Other aspects of the cosmogonic process are more difficult to grasp. We know that the universe tilted, probably owing to the effect of an imbalance created by the play of concentrations once living beings emerged from the earth, surely because of the effect of heat acting on a mass still damp in the center.

Like the other Presocratics, Anaxagoras went into the details of cosmology and zoology. His explanation of eclipses and meteors, in relation to the thesis of the stony nature of the stars, must have been striking to his readers' minds. We are thus informed about rainbows, the flooding of the Nile, and the sensory mechanisms of living beings. In all these cases, it would be interesting to speculate about the extent to which the particular explanations illustrate the great systematic principles of universal inherence or the phenomenal visibility of hidden things. This task, which remains to be carried out, would develop, with very different presuppositions, an approach of which the doxography has left us a few traces, when it inquires, for example, whether the tilting of the universe might not be attributable to providence (pronoia) rather than to mechanical factors, "so that certain parts of the universe are uninhabitable and others habitable" (Diels-Kranz, A67).

This last, typically Stoic interpretation of a cosmogonical episode raises the central question of the status of Mind within the system. We are indebted to Plato, in *Phaedo*, for providing a strong formulation of the problem in the famous intellectual autobiography of Socrates (96a6–100a7). On hearing one passage of the treatise (which we can identify with confidence as the beginning of frg. 12), Socrates is said to have conceived the "hope" of having discovered in Anaxagoras a philosopher of the final cause; breaking radically with the characteristic mechanism of traditional cosmogonies, Anaxagoras would explain everything through the principle of the best. Is Mind not in fact determined, from a Platonic point of view, by an end that can only be the good? It was all the more disappointing to find, in reading the rest of the treatise, that Anaxagoras was in fact appealing only to material pseudocauses, the very ones that the elevation of Mind to the level of "cause of everything" ought to have at least subordinated to the action of the final cause—a program that *Timaeus*, which is outlined in this passage of *Phaedo*, will undertake to realize.

This schema determines the whole history of the interpretation of Anaxagoras. Depending on which aspect of the Platonic reading we stress, Anaxagoras will be thought either to have provoked a decisive break in the history of philosophy or else to remain within the frame of a traditional physics—however original in other respects his views may be. While the first position is dominant in antiquity (see Aristotle, *Metaphysics* 984b11–21), modern interpreters tend rather to adopt the second (which Aristotle also mentions, in *Metaphysics* 985a18–21). Still, the opposition is henceforth situated less between Mind and the mechanism of elementary masses, following the presentation in *Phaedo*, than at the core of Mind itself, between a cognitive-intentional function, on the one hand, and a kinetic function, on the other. This duality, which Aristotle addresses again in the doxographic section of the treatise *On the Soul* (405a17), does create a tension within fragment 12 itself. While possessing understanding and will (two aspects intimately blended in the archaic usage of the word Nous), Mind is not conceived in Anaxagoras in an anthropomorphic manner, on the model of the artisan, but as a simple principle of movement. Kurt von Fritz has sought to provide a historical explanation of this strange conflation of two antithetical perspectives, seeing in it an ultimate and, so to speak, uncompromising compromise between two major evolutions of Presocratic philosophy: one tends to make Mind the supreme organ of knowledge and deliberate organization, while the other tends to explain the cosmogonic and cosmological processes in terms that leave very little room indeed for teleology.

Nevertheless, it seems that the very structure of Anaxagoras's treatise, entirely determined by the theme of mixture and separation, justifies a different approach. The first step is to recognize that the cosmogonic process is not only one of mixture and separation but also, and perhaps above all, the material projection of what is the activity of a mind, an intelligence—essentially a "critical" activity, like the process of dissociation that it initiates.

It is indispensable, in this regard, to understand the privileged bond that unites (according to a schema that was to prove enormously successful) Mind with circular movement. The relation can be analyzed on two levels. First, the setting into rotation of a point in the primordial mix can be seen as resulting from a vast hypothetical syllogism: *if* a vortex is created in the mass of mixed things, *then* the things will dissociate in such a way as to reproduce the world we know. Between conception and realization, there is room for something that we may call a scientific law, by virtue of which a foreseeable set of effects (including our world) will follow by a process enmeshed in defined conditions (those of the primordial mix). From this point of view, Anaxagoras's Mind is indeed a teleological power, not in the sense that it organizes the world and its parts in view of the Good (according to the Platonic expectation), but in the sense that it is capable of drawing the maximum effect from a minimum of means (rotation). We have already seen how the intelligence of Mind consisted in giving itself all the strength it needed.

Then—and this is the most important feature—the cosmic rotation tends, by dissociation from the primordial mix, to form identical entities. Of course Mind creates nothing (except the "composed things," if we acknowledge that they have to be excluded from the initial ontological population), since everything exists prior to Mind. And the identities that it "assembles" are never complete, precisely by virtue of the principle according to which "in everything there is a portion of everything." (If the end of our universe were the same thing as the wholesale dissociation of primitive identities, henceforth identified in their purity, our sources would probably have mentioned it.) One of the fascinating aspects of Anaxagoras's system consists precisely in the fact that, contrary to what Plato's criticism in *Phaedo* might lead us to expect, this double limitation finally brings Anaxagoras's system fairly close to the Platonic cosmogony of *Timaeus*.

The existence of affinities between the systems of Anaxagoras and Plato, beyond the pretense of teleology, has occasionally been noted. One can stress, for example, in an epistemological perspective, that the notion of the integral "inherence" of everything in everything was a first expression of the problem of predication (this reading probably goes back to the Platonic Academy: see Aristotle, *Metaphysics* 991a6ff). But still more striking is the fact that the Anaxagorean entities, which exist before Mind's intervention, combine the functions that, in *Timaeus*, are those of the paradigmatic Forms and of the principle of disorder (the *chora*). The Anaxagorean ingredients, which have been there forever, are in principle identifiable by Mind, which "knows" them. By this token (insofar as they are intelligible, one might say), they should be able to be conceived in their "purity." In this noetic sense, they are then indeed separable. But the fact remains that, unlike the Platonic Forms, they always exist in a mixture, as if a force of resistance analogous to the one the *chora* opposes to the demiurgic ordering of the universe prevented the "critical" work of Mind not only from ever reaching completion but even from making real progress. It is worth noting that, while allowing us to see the results of separation in the realized cosmos, Anaxagoras's treatise emphasizes this incapacity. Even the keenest knowledge, that of the cosmic Mind, is unable to inscribe into the world the ideal identity of things.

ANDRÉ LAKS
Translated by Rita Guerlac and Anne Slack

Bibliography

Texts and Translations

Anaxagoras. *Anassagora: Testimonianze e frammenti*. Ed. Diego Lanza. Florence: La Nuova Italia, 1966.

———. In *Die Fragmente der Vorsokratiker*, 6th ed., vol. 2. Ed. Hermann Diels and Walther Kranz. Berlin: Weidmann, 1952. Pp. 5–44.

———. *The Fragments of Anaxagoras*. Ed. David Sider. Meisenheim am Glan: Anton Hain, 1981.

———. In *Die Vorsokratiker*. Ed. Jaap Mansfeld. Stuttgart: Reclam, 1987. Pp. 482–555.

Aristotle. *Physics*. Trans. Philip H. Wicksteed and Francis M. Cornford. Loeb Classical Library.

Plutarch. *The Parallel Lives*. Trans. B. Perrin. Loeb Classical Library.

Studies

Babut, Daniel. "Anaxagore jugé par Socrate et Platon." *Revue des études grecques* 91 (1978): 44–76.

Deichgräber, Karl. "Hymnische Element in der philosophischen Prosa der Vorsokratiker." *Philologus* 42 (1933): 347–361.

Fritz, Kurt von. "Der Nous des Anaxagoras" (1964). In *Grundprobleme der Geschichte der antiken Wissenschaft*. Berlin and New York: W. de Gruyter, 1971. Pp. 576–596.

Furley, David. "Anaxagoras in Response to Parmenides" (1976). In *Cosmic Problems*. Cambridge: Cambridge University Press, 1989. Pp. 47–65.

Laks, André. "Mind's Crisis: On Anaxagoras' Nous." *The Southern Journal of Philosophy* 31 (supplement, 1993): 19–37.

Lanza, Diego. "Il pensiero di Anaxagora," *Memorie dell'Instituto Lombardo* 29 (1965): 223–288.

Mansfeld, Jaap. "The Chronology of Anaxagoras' Athenian Period and the Date of His Trial." *Mnemosyne* 32 (1979): 39–69.

Schofield, Malcolm. *An Essay on Anaxagoras.* Cambridge: Cambridge University Press, 1980.

Strang, Colin. "The Physical Theory of Anaxagoras" (1963). In *Studies in Presocratic Philosophy,* vol. 2. Ed. R. E. Allen and David J. Furley. London: Routledge and Kegan Paul, 1975. Pp. 361–380.

ANTISTHENES

ANTISTHENES, SON OF AN ATHENIAN and a Thracian slave, is said to have used his own social status as the impetus for critiquing the ideology of the "well-born" *(eugeneia)*. (His polemics were probably directed against the Athenian democracy: under laws established by Pericles in 451–450 and reestablished in 403, Athens granted citizenship only to children of two Athenian parents.) Antisthenes' status as illegitimate may account for the place he chose to do his teaching, the Cynosarges gymnasium: according to one of the many a posteriori explanations provided by the ancients, the gymnasium, which was reserved for illegitimate children and dedicated to Heracles, gave its name to Cynicism. This piece of information, like the other biographical elements that have been handed down largely in anecdotal form, is not easy to assess. In particular, the reports that establish a master-pupil succession from Antisthenes to Zeno the Stoic by way of Diogenes of Sinope and Crates have been called into question many times, for good reason. But whatever their historical accuracy may be, these reports show that the ancients—who, unlike ourselves, read Antisthenes' works—found in them significant features indicative of affinity with the Cynico-Stoic tradition. Socrates' reported praise of Antisthenes' actions in the battle of Tanagra (426), a witty remark about the battle of Leuctra (371), and the fact that Diodorus of Sicily thought that Antisthenes was still alive in 366/365 lead us to place his life span roughly between 445 and 365 B.C.E. Moreover, he is described as one of Socrates' faithful followers in Xenophon's *Symposium*, set in 422. Thus we cannot accept the idea that his life was divided into two phases, in the first of which he practiced rhetoric under the influence of Gorgias, while in the second he became one of Socrates' disciples. The "Gorgian phase" is a construct of the Hellenistic period, apparently based on little more than the "rhetorical character" of some of Antisthenes' works. However, we can credit Diogenes Laertius's report that Antisthenes "heard" Gorgias (who came to Athens as an ambassador in 427): the few remaining examples of his style (in particular the fictional discourses *Ajax* and *Odysseus*, the only texts by Antisthenes that have survived intact) are full of stylistic figures such as antitheses, parisoses (parallelisms among parts of sentences), and homeoteleutes (similarities in grammatical endings), and they do in fact betray the influence of the artistic prose associated with Gorgias.

Diogenes' catalogue of Antisthenes' works (*Lives of Eminent Philosophers* VI.15–18) seems to point to an authentic critical edition paralleling editions of Democritus's and Plato's works. It confirms what other accounts also suggest: among the Socratics, Antisthenes' importance in ancient culture was second only to Plato's. The list of the titles of his works, grouped in ten thematically unified volumes (with some exceptions possibly attributable to distortions introduced in the transmission process), constitutes the most important trace we have of his activity and interests, given the almost complete disappearance of his writings and the small number of surviving fragments. In the 3rd century, Timon of Phlius defined him as a "chatterbox who produced everything," alluding to the "countless books" St. Jerome would mention later, and also to the variety of topics addressed. Alone among all the Socratics, Antisthenes earned the praises of the anti-Platonician Theopompus, in the 4th century. Cicero admired him, and his works continued to be read into late antiquity. From the philosophical point of view, he is much more present in the writings of Dion of Prusa or of Epictetus than the infrequent mentions of his name might suggest; these writings bear witness to Antisthenes' impact on the Cynico-Stoic tradition. In the 4th century c.e., Julian and Themistius knew and cited his writings; in the imperial era, grammarians (Demetrius, Fronton, Phrynichus, Longinus) compared him to Xenophon and Plato as a model of stylistic purity.

Antisthenes' highly regarded writing style may account for the fact that, of all his immense production, the two texts that remain are fictional orations: they have been preserved in a manuscript that also includes orations by Lysias, Alcidamas, and the pseudo-Demades, along with Gorgias's *Encomium of Helen*, confirming that Antisthenes figured among the authors read in schools. He cultivated literary genres other than dialogue, but his best-known works (*Truth, Protreptics, Heracles*, among others) were written in that form. Socrates must have played an important role in them, since Panaetius unhesitatingly included Antisthenes among the authors of authentic *logoi sōkratikoi*. Unfortunately, the traces of Antisthenes' Socrates are extremely sparse, and one must be very cautious in attempting to reconstruct what has been lost on the basis of Xenophon's *Memorabilia*, or later works whose authors might have had access to Antisthenes' writings. Antisthenes takes on sharply contrasting contours in modern reconstructions: he is sometimes extravagantly praised, as a result of an extensive and often overly casual use of the sources, and he is sometimes harshly disparaged, as if the obliteration of his works over time sufficed to prove his philosophic insignificance. The vicissitudes he has undergone in these reconstructions are presented clearly and evaluated judiciously in the notes Gabriele Giannantoni prepared to accompany the most recent collection of fragments, and they warrant careful attention by future scholars in the field.

The titles of his works, to which we can link only a few fragments with certainty, point, significantly, to a number of themes frequently encountered in the culture of the second half of the 5th century. In addition to Homeric exegesis, to which Antisthenes applied himself in a systematic way, writing commentaries on numerous episodes in the *Iliad* and *Odyssey*, he also took up themes from the mythological and historico-biographical traditions (Heracles, Cyrus the Great). From a social background quite unlike that of Plato or Socrates' other followers, Antisthenes had to win prestige and fame through a socially recognized and remunerated pedagogical enterprise, although his self-portrait (Xenophon, *Symposium* IV.34ff; see also Isocrates, *Against the Sophists* 3) indicates that he did not use his teaching to build wealth. He may have earned his reputation by offering a philosophical reinterpretation of the familiar figures of the Greek *paideia*, such as Heracles and Odysseus, rereading the Homeric poems in the light of Socratic teaching and thus entering into competition with a diffuse but well-established tradition.

Antisthenes seems to have possessed the art of "knowing how to deal with men" to the fullest; he undertook to teach through dialogue and example, drawing on dialectical gifts reinforced by a refined rhetorical technique and great moral rigor. His polemics against Lysias and Isocrates, on the one hand, and against Plato, on the other, which are explicitly attested by other titles, outline the cultural space he sought to occupy. Typically Socratic themes appear in the titles of works devoted to virtues (courage, justice), goodness, law, liberty, and slavery; other works, such as *Aspasia, Alcibiades*, and *Archelaos*, also refer to ongoing discussions in the Socratic circle. An important group of writings was centered on logico-linguistic and gnoseological themes: *Truth* (a title that, after Parmenides, had been adopted by Protagoras and Antiphon); a text on dialectical argument; a work whose title, *Sathon*, involved a play on Plato's name; five volumes called *On Education, or On Names;* and still other works on the use of names, on the art of questioning and responding, on opinion *(doxa)* and science *(episteme)*, to mention just a few of the subjects addressed.

Diogenes Laertius's life of Antisthenes (*Lives* VI.1–19.103–105), to which we owe the preservation of the catalogue, is constructed and oriented in such a way as to highlight the elements of continuity between Antisthenes, Cynicism, and Stoicism. Diogenes refers primarily to *Heracles,* from which he excerpts statements in a form that quite manifestly reveals the influence of Hellenistic terminology. Even though in most cases we have no justification for rejecting them, the choice of these particular excerpts and the way they are formulated clearly tend to project Antisthenes into a period that is not his own; the way he may have responded to the questions and problems of his own day remains obscure. We are told—to cite only the most important themes—that for Antisthenes, the sovereign good is life lived according to virtue; virtue can be taught; once achieved, it cannot be lost; virtue suffices for happiness and requires only the Socratic "force"; it is manifested in actions and can dispense with speeches and theories. Heracles' saga and Cyrus's vicissitudes illustrate the idea that "effort" *(ponos)* is a good thing and leads to virtue; at the same time, pleasure is to be avoided (but perhaps less drastically than we are led to believe by the celebrated dictum, "I would rather go mad than experience pleasure"). Antisthenes the sage has many features in common—perhaps too many—with the Stoic sages. Antisthenes is also said to have been the first to define *logos* as "that which shows what things were or are" (Diogenes Laertius, *Lives* VI.3), but even that isolated assertion may reflect the Stoics' desire to establish a link with Socrates via his intermediary, since Alexander of Aphrodisias considers Antisthenes' use of the imperfect as a precedent with respect to the Stoics *(Stoicorum veterum fragmenta* II.228).

In any event, the Antisthenian doxography seems to indicate that Antisthenes had taken the Socratic message in a direction of his own, propounding an ethics based on exemplary action, relegating dialectics to marginal status, and rejecting the study of the sciences. However, in addition to the anecdotes that show the importance he attached to reasoning, the intellect, and *phronesis* (which is not practical wisdom but the instrument that makes it possible to construct a rampart of unassailable arguments), the very titles of Antisthenes' works preclude accepting this image: we must be careful not to confuse the models of virtue he proposed with the arguments intended to justify the choice of those models or with the method he used in his teaching.

Comparing him to Socrates, Epictetus *(Discourses* I.17.10) tells us that Antisthenes thought the basis of education was the study of names; we may assume that this expression designates, in the first place, the study of the meaning of terms pertaining to moral life. However, there are few surviving accounts of this aspect of Antisthenes' thinking, which must have resulted from his personal interpretation of Socratic methodology and philosophy, and these accounts are so difficult to interpret that the conclusions drawn from them have been quite divergent and often unfounded. The adequately documented facts are the following: Antisthenes was engaged in a polemic against Plato's Forms, declaring that he could perfectly well perceive a horse, but not "horse-ness," or, more abstractly, he could perceive what was "qualified" *(poion)* but not the "quality" *(poiotes)*. This amounted to rejecting Plato's ontology; Antisthenes (or perhaps his disciples: Aristotle refers to the "followers of Antisthenes"; *Metaphysics* VIII.iii.1043b) rejected the possibility of defining essence *(to ti estin),* because the definition is nothing other than an extended *logos;* however, he acknowledged the possibility of teaching "how a thing is" *(poion ti estin):* from the context, it is clear that this aporia concerned only simple substances, and, indirectly, that the predicates constituting the definition were understood as part of the *definiendum,* namely, as that *of which* a thing is constituted. Aristotle uses the example—on the whole a rather unclear one—of silver: one cannot say what it is, but only that it is similar to tin. Antisthenes also denied the possibility of contradicting *(ouk estin antilegein)*, with the argument (strongly criticized by Aristotle, *Metaphysics* V.xxix.1024b26) that nothing can be said except with the proper *logos*, and that there is only one *logos* for each thing *(tōi oikeiōi logōi, hen ephhenos)*; consequently, it is impossible to contradict, and it is virtually impossible even to say untruths. Proclus justifies this view, perhaps wrongly, as follows: "Every *logos* says the truth; for whoever speaks says something; whoever says something says what is; whoever says what is says the truth" *(In Platonis Cratylum commentaria* 37). To this we must add the previously mentioned definition of *logos* (Diogenes Laertius, *Lives* VI.3), a term that, given the way it is presented, must have had a technical value—if not the Aristotelian sense of "definition," which seems presupposed by Alexander Aphrodisias *(Stoicorum veterum fragmenta)*, then surely at least the restrictive sense of the "proper" *logos*, the only one that expresses the object in accordance with its own intrinsic nature, and that is therefore not open to contradiction.

Whatever meaning one may attribute to these scattered fragments (which appear, for the most part, in highly polemical contexts), a few facts seem reasonably certain. A fundamental theme of Antisthenes' investigations was reflection on being, truth, and language; his primary reference was to Parmenides. Yet the centrality of the ethical theme and the methodology that the fragments allow us to glimpse lead us back to Socrates as well; the latter thus remains the chief reference point for any reconstruction. Furthermore, it is illegitimate to interpret the term *logos*, which recurs repeatedly in the fragments, as an equivalent of "name," on the basis of the obscure passage in *Metaphysics* (VIII), and thus to identify Antisthenes with the thinkers who recognized only judgments of identity; in reality, Antisthenes' name never comes up in conjunction with them. This is a crucial point, because this presupposition, an overconfident use of Diogenes Laertius's doxography, and the underestimation of the attention Antisthenes paid to problems of language, dialectical argument, and rhetoric, have led to a widely accepted historiographical schema (one only recently subjected to revision, on the basis of rigorous analysis of the sources). According to this schema, Antisthenes, who was confined within the bounds of a tautological logic that was deprived of the Platonic metaphysical referent and unable to ground itself in any other way, had to fall back on an ethics based on action, setting aside all "logico-scientific" problematics (even in the sense these expressions may have had before Aristotle).

This position reintroduces, in terms that are more veiled in form but analogous in substance, the old idea according to which the figure of Antisthenes can be understood only if it is split into two phases or aspects. The first phase is oriented toward the past, dominated by rhetorical interests and by attempts at logico-dialectical analyses confined within bounds that were archaic, potentially self-destructive, and at all events incapable of responding to the great Socratic problem of the scientific foundation of ethics. In the second phase, Antisthenes is represented as committed to "living" according to virtue, seeking to outline the model of a "path toward virtue" that, inspired more than embodied by Socrates and by Antisthenes himself, took as its reference—not coincidentally—Heracles, a hero admitted among the gods after he had conquered the "tasks" (ponoi) that had tested, and proved, his virtue, and Cyrus, who rose from obscure origins to supreme royal power.

However, while these figures were indeed the protagonists of some of the works that contributed most prominently to Antisthenes' fame, we must not forget his other works if we are to avoid a distorted perspective; even in the few fragments that remain to us, we find traces that complicate the foregoing picture and make it relatively unconvincing. In particular, there is the Odysseus figure, about which, fortunately, we have information from sources independent of the biographical and philosophical tradition: the discourse attributed to Odysseus in his conflict with Ajax over Achilles' weapons, and a scholium in the first line of the *Odyssey*, preserved by Porphyrius, constitute invaluable testimony. Here Antisthenes defends the thesis according to which the adjective Homer used to characterize Odysseus, *polytropos*, "the man of a thousand tricks," has a positive meaning. He supports his argument with a complex analysis that starts with the double meaning of *tropos*, an attitude of character and a form of discourse. These two meanings are analyzed separately to begin with; later, their combination gives rise to the idea that the distinctive feature of wise men who are skilled at speaking and conversing (*dialegesthai*) is that they know how to express the same concept in many different ways, and that this ability is necessary if they are to act effectively on their diverse listeners. Only such differentiated use of *logoi* can lead the multiplicity of the listeners' *tropoi* back to unity, because "only one thing is proper to each" (*hen gar hekastōi oikeion*). This theory presupposes a subtle reflection, applied here to a specific case, on the relations between the one and the many and on the art of *dialegesthai*; it also refers to the art of "dealing with men," in which Antisthenes excelled. It lets us glimpse the complexity of the path leading to the discovery of the "proper *logos*" belonging to each thing, which transforms multiple truths into a single truth; by means of a well-conducted dialogue, this *logos* will tell us the nature of the object (which, in a Socratic inquiry, manifests its nature as good or evil).

By becoming the common patrimony of master and disciple, *logos* is in a position to transform our lives, as an effective medicinal drug might do; it allows us to distinguish between what belongs to us and what does not (rejecting anything evil as "foreign"), and thus to attain true freedom. This inner freedom supports the praise Antisthenes offers of his own wealth in Xenophon's *Symposium;* it is based, on the one hand, on tireless inquiry into the nature of things, thanks to an adequate use of the instrument of language governed by reason, and, on the other hand, on the Socratic force that prevents the body from asserting its hegemony over the rational soul and over truth.

FERNANDA DECLEVA CAIZZI
Translated by Catherine Porter and Jeannine Pucci

Bibliography

Texts and Translations

Antisthenes. *Antisthenis fragmenta.* Ed. Fernanda Decleva Caizzi. Milan: Cisalpino, 1966.

Aristotle. *Metaphysics.* Trans. Hugh Tredennick. 2 vols. Loeb Classical Library.

Epictetus. *Discourses.* Book I. Trans. Robert F. Dobbin. Oxford: Clarendon Press, 1998.

Giannantoni, Gabriele, ed. *Socratis et socraticorum reliquiae.* 4 vols. Naples: Bibliopolis, 1990.

Paquet, Léonce, ed. *Les Cyniques grecs: Fragments et témoignages.* Ottawa: Editions de l'Université d'Ottawa, 1975, 1988; Paris: Le Livre de Poche, 1992.

Stoicorum veterum fragmenta. Ed. Hans Friedrich August von Arnim. 4 vols. Leipzig: B. G. Teubner, 1903, 1924.

Xenophon. *Symposium.* In *Anabasis, Books IV–VII, and Symposium and Apology.* Trans. D. J. Todd. Loeb Classical Library.

Studies

Brancacci, Aldo. "Dialettica e retorica in Antistene." *Elenchos* 17 (1996): 359–406.

———. *Oikeios logos: La filosofia del linguággio di Antistene.* Naples: Bibliopolis, 1990.

Decleva Caizzi, Fernanda. "Antistene." *Studi urbinati,* n.s. 1–2 (1964): 48–99.

Diogenes Laertius. "Antisthenes." In *Lives of Eminent Philosophers,* vol. 2, book 4. Trans. R. D. Hicks. Loeb Classical Library. Pp. 2–23.

Eucken, Christopher. "Der schwache und der starke Logos des Antisthenes," *Hyperboreus* 3 (1997): 251–272.

Gillespie, G. M. *The Logic of Antisthenes: Archiv für Geschichte der Philosophie* 19 and 20 (1913 and 1914): 479–500 and 17–38.

Goulet-Cazé, Marie-Odile. "L'*Ajax* et l'*Ulysse* d'Antisthène." In *Chercheurs de sagesse: Hommage à Jean Pépin.* Paris: Institut d'études augustiniennes, 1992. Pp. 5–36.

Höistad, Ragnar. "Cynic Hero and Cynic King: Studies in the Cynic Conception of Man." Thesis, University of Uppsala, 1948.

Luzzatto, Maria Tanja. "Dialettica o retorica? La *polytropia* di Odisseo da Antistene a Porfirio." *Elenchos* 17 (1996): 275–357.

Natorp, Paul. "Antisthenes." *Realencyclopädie* 1 (1894): 2538–2545.

Patzer, Andreas. *"Antisthenes der Sokratiker: Das literarische Werk und die Philosophie, dargestellt am Katalog der Schriften."* Dissertation, Marburg, 1970.

Rankin, H. D. *Antisthenes Sokratikos.* Amsterdam: Hakkert, 1986.

Romeyer Dherbey, Gilbert. "Tra Aiace e Ulisse: Antistene." *Elenchos* 17 (1996): 251–274.

ARCHIMEDES

GEOMETERS IN THE 16TH AND 17TH CENTURIES, in aspiring to the title of the "new Archimedes," revealed a major source of their technical endeavor. It was hardly different in antiquity, when geometers in the generation immediately following Archimedes engaged in research directly modeled on his, while the impact of his achievement remained evident even centuries later, in works of Hero, Pappus, Eutocius, and Anthemius.

At the same time, Archimedes emerged as a figure larger than life in the popular imagination, legendary for the seeming miracles he performed through his mechanical inventions. Referring to the (apocryphal) tradition of Archimedes' use of gigantic burning mirrors for destroying the Roman fleet, the Byzantine mechanician Anthemius of Tralles (early 6th century), while voicing his skepticism about its possibility, nevertheless is compelled to admit that "one cannot gainsay the reputation of Archimedes," and so contrives some way by which "the most divine [theiotatos] Archimedes" could have done it.

On the life of Archimedes we are better informed than about any other figure of the ancient exact sciences, for it happens that military devices of his invention, including catapults and ship haulers, as well as fortification designs, proved significant in the defense of his native city, Syracuse, when it was besieged by the Romans during the Second Punic War (215–212 B.C.E.). Accordingly, from the historians Polybius, Livy, and Plutarch we learn of Archimedes' dealings with his patron, King Hieron of Syracuse, of the fearsome impression his siege engines made on the Roman attackers, and of the honor in which he was held by the Roman general Marcellus, against whose orders Archimedes was slain by a Roman soldier during the final sack of the city.

A substantial body of Archimedes' writing is extant through collections assembled in the 9th and 10th centuries during the Byzantine revival. The principal codex (lost in the 16th century but represented by a half dozen copies derived from it) includes the five treatises addressed to Dositheus at Alexandria (*Quadrature of the Parabola;* the two books of *On the Sphere and Cylinder; On Spiral Lines;* and *On Conoids and Spheroids*), plus *Dimension of the Circle, Sand Reckoner,* and the two books of *On Plane Equilibria.* In the 13th century Willem of Moerbeke prepared a literal Latin translation from this codex, collated with a second one that also included a text of the two books *On Floating Bodies.* Heiberg exploited this in his second critical edition (1910–1915), in which he also made valuable use of the evidence from yet a third codex (then at Constantinople), a palimpsest whose Archimedean underwriting was first identified by Heiberg at the beginning of the 20th century. In addition to most of the works already known in Greek, the newly identified codex provided most of the Greek text of *On Floating Bodies,* as well as texts of *Method* and *Stomachion.* This codex passed surreptitiously into private hands during the 1920s and has been inaccessible for scholarly examination ever since. A few minor works, held in other codices or in medieval versions, or attested in fragments, are included in Heiberg's second edition. Since then, studies of the Arabic tradition of the corpus have revealed an additional work, *Construction of the Regular Heptagon,* and alternative versions of works extant in Greek (*Dimension of the Circle, Sphere and Cylinder,* and fragments of *Floating Bodies*).

From Archimedes' writings we learn a few additional personal details. In *Sand Reckoner* he cites his father, Pheidias, as an astronomer. This same tract, addressed to "King Gelon" (apparently then coregent with his father, Hieron, at Syracuse), seems to be a popular lecture for the court. Archimedes takes as his theme a certain misconception about the infinite—that, for instance, the number of grains of sand is infinite—and proceeds to show how one can express a number that greatly exceeds the grains of sand, that would even fill the entire cosmos. Along the way, Archimedes alludes to his own system of nomenclature for large numbers (expounded in a tract now lost), and to his invention and use of a special sighting instrument for measuring the angular width of the sun. Archimedes here also provides our sole substantial testimony of the heliocentric cosmos of Aristarchus (cited for its being vastly larger than the conventional geocentric systems).

From the prefaces to his works, we learn that Archimedes maintained collegial contact with several scholars in Alexandria, notably Conon of Samos, an eminent astronomer in the court of Ptolemy III Euergetes; the geometer Dositheus; and Eratosthenes of Cyrene, noted for his contributions to geometry and other sciences, for literary scholarship, and for his directorship of the Alexandrian Library. "Publication" in the case of most of Archimedes' writings consisted of their being forwarded to Alexandria, with an explanatory preface addressed to one or another of these men. Hints of their personal relations emerge: that Archimedes held Conon in high esteem for his mathematical acumen, that he was impatient over Dositheus's insistence on fully elaborated proofs, and that with Eratosthenes he perceived (rightly or wrongly, we do not know) a potential for making his own geometric discoveries. It becomes clear that for Archimedes himself the *heuristic* effort to expand the domain of known results in geometry takes precedence over the criticism of proofs, but in this respect he seems already to be confronting a certain scholastic temperament among his Alexandrian colleagues.

At a few places Archimedes provides hints of his views on the nature of mathematics. In the preface to *Sphere and Cylinder,* for instance, he distinguishes between the properties of figures per se and our knowledge of them: remarkable results, like Eudoxus's theorems on the pyramid and cone or his own on the sphere, however simple in form, might long evade recognition even by most acute intellects. In *Method* he separates heuristic strategies, like his own "mechanical method," from rigorous demonstrations. The latter are obligatory if one is to claim the right actually to know or to have established a result. Nevertheless, informal methods have an indispensable role to play, for they bring to light results that might not otherwise be evident and offer guidance in the working out of proofs. To the extent that such statements may seem obvious to us, they define how deeply the Archimedean conception of research is engrained in the Western tradition of mathematical science.

The core of Archimedes' work builds directly on the "exhaustion" technique first developed by Eudoxus. Indeed, Archimedes' citations provide valuable testimony to Eudoxus's work. They suggest that Archimedes could refer firsthand to Eudoxus's writing, rather than through an intermediary version, but that Eudoxus's methods are generally well represented by the formulations in Euclid's *Elements*, Book XII.

Archimedes' most elementary geometric effort is his study of the circle, as presented in the short tract *Dimension of the Circle*. The version of this tract that survives in Greek cannot represent the original version, for commentators—among them Hero, Pappus, and Theon—cite the work according to a significantly different text form. In fact, it appears that the medieval Arabic translation (made in the 9th century) is founded on a Greek prototype superior to the extant Greek version, although even that text is at best an adaptation. Nevertheless, collating the extant versions with citations in earlier commentaries, we can piece together with reasonable confidence the content and technique of Archimedes' treatment.

Its two essential results exploit the Eudoxean method of polygonal approximation to establish measures for the area and circumference of the circle. By the first, in proposition 1 (as stated in the Greek and medieval versions) Archimedes demonstrates that any circle equals a right triangle whose two legs equal, respectively, the radius and the circumference of the circle. As cited by Hero and Pappus, however, an alternative phrasing is used: that the area of the circle equals half the product of its radius and circumference. The technique of proof follows the model of Eudoxus's theorem on the circle, as given in *Elements* XII.2, that circles are as the squares on their diameters.

Archimedes' proof falls into two cases, in accordance with an indirect mode of reasoning: if this product (Z) does not equal the circle (C), then it is either less than it or greater. If less, we can construct, via continued bisection of arcs, beginning from the square inscribed in the circle, an inscribed regular polygon P such that the difference $C - P$ is less than the difference $E = C - Z$. That this is possible is known from the Eudoxean bisection principle: since the procedure of forming the octagon from the square, for instance, diminishes the remainder from the circle by more than half, and this applies in each subsequent stage of the construction, the remainder can be made arbitrarily small (cf. *Elements* X.1, as invoked in XII.2), and thus, in particular, less than the hypothesized difference E. Thus, *P* must be greater than *Z*. But the perimeter of the polygon is less than the circumference of the circle, while its apothem (the line drawn from the center perpendicular to any side) is less than the radius. Thus, the area of the polygon, equaling half the product of its perimeter and apothem, must be less than *Z*. This contradiction thus excludes that *Z* can be less than *C*. Similarly, if *Z* is supposed greater than *C*, a contradiction is inferred by considering a sequence of regular polygons circumscribed about the circle. Thus, since *Z* can be neither greater nor less than *C*, it must equal *C*.

By the same process of polygonal approximation, in proposition 3 Archimedes calculates that the ratio of the circumference to the diameter of the circle (namely, the constant we represent by π) is less than $3\frac{1}{7}$ but greater than $3\frac{10}{71}$. The computation is among the finest specimens of arithmetic procedure from ancient mathematics outside the astronomical literature. To derive the upper bound, Archimedes works out the sequence of circumscribed polygons, from the hexagon to the dodecagon and so on, ending with the 96-gon; for the lower bound, he takes the corresponding inscribed figures. The values for the initial hexagons require estimates of $\sqrt{3}$, for which Archimedes cites, without explanation, $\frac{1351}{780}$ as upper bound and $\frac{265}{153}$ as lower bound. An extensive literature supplying possible reconstructions has arisen among modern commentators, tantalized by these odd-looking but extraordinarily good approximations (for instance, they are optimal values within the sequence of continued fraction approximations to the root). Each subsequent polygon requires application of the equivalent of a trigonometrical rule for half-angles, namely, $\tan(\emptyset/2) = \tan\emptyset/(1 + \sec\emptyset)$, which is here proved in a geometric form. Applying the rule requires the taking of irrational square roots; although the text does not explain how its cited values are derived, they appear to depend on applications of the so-called Heronian rule: $\sqrt{A} < (a + A/a)/2$, for any convenient initial estimate *a*. Thus, Archimedes' computation displays not only geometric ingenuity in its basic organization but also considerable arithmetic ingenuity in its execution.

With this effort, the estimate $3\frac{1}{7}$, which Archimedes here derives as an upper bound, enters the history of mathematics for the first time. Through the geometric manual by Hero of Alexandria (1st century C.E.), if not earlier, it becomes a fixture in practical geometry. But Archimedes is reported to have improved these estimates in another writing, now lost, which is also mentioned by Hero. One possible reconstruction of his result (for the stated figures are corrupt) leads to a lower bound of $3\frac{15}{106}$ and an upper bound of $3\frac{17}{120}$, which could be obtained via inscribed and circumscribed 640-gons. By a simple averaging technique, these bounds suggest an intermediate estimate of

$3\frac{16}{113}$. This value, which was derived independently by the Chinese geometer Tsu Ch'ung-chih in the 5th century and in the Renaissance by the Flemish computist Adriaen Anthoniszoon, as cited by his son Adrian Metius (1625), exceeds the true value of π by less than $\frac{3}{10}^7$, and would require polygons of no fewer than 10,000 sides to be established rigorously.

The Eudoxean procedure also underlies Archimedes' measurement of the parabolic segment, as being equal to $\frac{4}{3}$ the triangle having the same altitude and base as the segment (*Quadrature of the Parabola*, prop. 24). Archimedes forms a sequence of polygons inscribed in the segment *(S)* via successive bisection of the base and shows that these tend arbitrarily close to the segment. Since, further, the inscribed triangles, constituting the successive increments from each polygon to the next, decrease in the ratio 1 to $\frac{1}{4}$, each inscribed polygon is the sum of the initial triangle *(T)* plus its 4th, 16th, 64th, and so on. Archimedes shows that the sum of finitely many parts in this ratio is always less than four-thirds of *T* by an area equal to one-third the last term in the series. Since that term can be taken as small as desired, the polygonal sequence (which converges to the segment) must also converge to $\frac{4T}{3}$. By a standard two-part indirect proof, Archimedes then shows that either hypothesis—that *S* is greater than $\frac{4T}{3}$ or less than $\frac{4T}{3}$—leads to contradiction. One observes that the basic plan of this argument lies completely within the Eudoxean manner, employing only inscribed polygonal figures converging to the limit from below.

As Archimedes himself observes, his measurement of the parabolic segment marks the first case where a curved figure in the class of the circle or the conics has been found equal to a rectilinear figure. The problem of circle quadrature, whose history among the Greeks extends back at least to Hippocrates of Chios, some two centuries before Archimedes, seems to have attracted Archimedes' attention. While, as we now know through researches by Lindemann in the 19th century, no quadrature by means of algebraic functions (hence, by constructions via circle and straightedge) is possible, nevertheless a quadrature is possible by means of transcendental curves. One such is the Archimedean spiral, whose first definition appears to be due to Archimedes' mentor Conon. In the treatise *On Spiral Lines*, Archimedes establishes the condition for drawing the tangent to a spiral, which, conversely, provides a solution for the circle quadrature: the intercept of the tangent with the line drawn at right angles to the radius vector through the point of tangency equals the arc of the circle subtended by the angle lying between the initial position and the radius vector and having as its radius that same radius vector.

A natural extension of these measurements of plane figures is the consideration of curvilinear solids. One result is so remarkable in this context that Archimedes is said to have commanded its diagram to be engraved on his tombstone: a sphere inscribed in a cylinder, representing his discovery that the two solids, both in volume and in surface area, have to each other the ratio of 2 to 3.

In his *Sphere and Cylinder* Archimedes sets out the formal demonstrations of the corresponding theorems: that the surface of the sphere equals four times the area of any great circle (prop. 33); that its volume equals that of a cone whose altitude equals the radius of the sphere and whose base equals its surface area (prop. 34). Analogous results are given for the surface of spherical segments and the volume of spherical sectors and segments. Characteristic of the demonstrations of these results is the use of a variant form of convergence method, where the one-sided Eudoxean approximation is replaced by a two-sided manner. For an example one can consider the treatment of the circle in *Sphere and Cylinder* (props. 1–6), which provides an alternative to the Eudoxean manner of *Dimension of the Circle*. Archimedes shows that it is possible to construct two regular polygons, one circumscribed about the given circle, the other inscribed in it, such that their ratio is less than any preassigned ratio greater than 1 : 1. For using two lines in the given ratio as hypotenuse and leg of a right triangle, one takes the angle contained by them and constructs by successive bisection of a right angle an angle less than it; taking this as the central angle of a circumscribed and an inscribed regular polygon drawn in the same circle, one shows that the ratio of their perimeters is less than the given ratio. Similarly, one can construct two such polygons whose areas have a ratio less than any preassigned ratio greater than 1 : 1. From this it becomes possible to construct inscribed polygons exceeding any area that is less than the circle, and circumscribed polygons less than any area that exceeds the circle. Such polygons are required as auxiliaries in the indirect proofs of the measurement theorems.

This two-sided convergence typifies all the Archimedean measurements, save for the circle measurement of *Dimension of the Circle* (prop. 1) and the second of the two parabola measurements given in *Quadrature of the Parabola* (prop. 24). For these proofs Archimedes states a special principle of continuity (now sometimes called the Archimedean axiom), which, he says, fills a gap in the Eudoxean proofs, namely their assumption of a "lemma" (that any finite magnitude, on successive bisection, can be reduced to less than any preassigned finite magnitude of the same kind). This Archimedes reformulates in a manner more flexible for application in proofs, as in *Quadrature of the Parabola*, prop. 16: that of two finite homogeneous magnitudes, the lesser, by being added to itself a suitable, finite number of times, can be made to exceed the greater. This is often noted as the appropriate condition for excluding infinitesimal magnitudes, since no zero magnitude, however many times multiplied, can ever exceed any finite magnitude of its kind. But the bisection lemma provides an adequate condition for the same end. In context one sees that Archimedes' intent is to replace the bisection lemma with a more evident condition. One infers that he does not have before him the Euclidean treatment of this material, since Euclid's definition of "having the same ratio" (*Elements* V, def. 4), his proposition on the bisection (X, prop. 1), and their applications in the "Eudoxean" propositions of Book XII, would have rendered Archimedes' lemma superfluous.

Biographical anecdotes celebrate Archimedes' exploits in the practical fields of mechanics. Recognizing the principle of leverage, for instance, and deploying it in the form of compound pulleys for the hauling of ships, Archimedes is said to have extrapolated his feat, boasting "Give me a place to stand and I will move the earth." In some reports, the device associated with this earth-moving ambition is called the *charistiōn*. This heightens the audacity of the boast, as Archimedes' theory-inspired imagination outruns the physical evidence at hand, since the device is nothing other than the humble steelyard (often known as the Roman balance) used by merchants for weighing goods.

Pappus mentions an Archimedean tract *On Balances (Peri zygōn)* for a dynamic conception of the principle of leverage: that the greater circle overpowers the smaller circle when the turning is about the same center. This latter conception underlies the proof of the balance principle (that weights balance each other when they are inversely proportional to their respective distances from the fulcrum) that in certain medieval tracts forms the basis for a geometric account of the action of the unequal-armed balance (the steelyard). Although in the Arabic and Latin versions of the tract the author is named as Thabit ibn Qurra, the names employed for the balance (*garastūn* and *karaston*, respectively) and nuances in the technique of proof indicate their ultimate dependence on a Greek treatment of the *charistiōn* based on an Archimedean tradition. The key result is to show, via an indirect proof much like that used for the quadrature of the parabola, that if a section of a uniformly weighted beam in equilibrium is replaced by an equal weight suspended at its midpoint, there is no change to the equilibrium. From this one can work out the weight needed to bring into equilibrium a beam suspended off center, the theoretical correlate of the steelyard.

The medieval texts thus furnish insight into a lost portion of Archimedes' mechanical work—indeed what appears to be an early stage of his efforts in mechanics—for absent from them is the principle fundamental for Archimedes in all his extant mechanical writings, the concept of "center of gravity." No explicit definition of the barycenter is given in these works, but the commentators Hero and Eutocius, relying on other lost works, provide two formulations. In the topological sense, the barycenter is taken as that point at which a given figure or body, if supported there, will maintain its disposition relative to the horizon. Alternatively, in the quantitative sense, the barycenter of two figures is that point that divides the line joining their respective barycenters such that the weights will be inversely proportional to their distances from it. A geometric proof of the latter is given in *Plane Equilibria* I, props. 6–7. From this Archimedes determines that the barycenter of any parallelogram lies on the line bisecting its parallel sides (props. 9–10), that the barycenter of any triangle lies on the intersection of its medians (props. 13–14), and that the barycenter of the trapezium divides the line bisecting its parallel sides in a given ratio (prop. 15). In *Plane Equilibria* II, Archimedes determines the barycenter of the parabolic segment as being the point dividing its axis into segments in the ratio 2 : 3 (prop. 8).

Archimedes extends these results to the determination of barycenters of solids: e.g., that the barycenter of the cone divides its axis in the ratio 1 : 3; that the barycenter of the paraboloid divides its axis in the ratio 1 : 2; and similarly for segments of the sphere, ellipsoid, and hyperboloid. The formal demonstrations are now lost, but some of them are presented in a heuristic manner in the extant *Method*. This writing is devoted to examples of what Archimedes calls his mechanical method, a procedure for the determination of the content and center of gravity of figures by means of a conceptual weighing.

For the parabola, for instance, Archimedes considers an arbitrary section of the segment, taken parallel to the axis, and shows that since its length is to that of the section of the containing triangle as the abscissa to the base of the segment, if the base of the segment is extended and conceived as an equal-armed balance with the segment suspended along one arm, then the line in the segment, upon being transposed to the opposite end, will exactly balance the line in the triangle in its given position. Then, if all the lines in the segment are so transposed, the entire segment, now set at the opposite end of the balance, will balance the entire triangle in its position. Since, further, the barycenter of the triangle lies one-third the distance of its arm from the fulcrum, and the areas of the segment and the triangle are inversely proportional to the distances of their barycenters from the fulcrum, the segment is thus found to be one-third the triangle.

Employing the same procedure of sectioning and weighing, Archimedes shows how to find the volumes and barycenters of spherical and conoidal segments. At the end he employs it toward the measurement of two types of solid formed by sections of the cylinder. In all these cases, Archimedes insists that the method has only heuristic value, the theorem requiring its formal geometric demonstration to be considered rigorously established. In *Method* he includes such proofs for the cylindrical solids, but for the others defers to prior demonstrations. Modern critics have been especially impressed by Archimedes' application of indivisible sections, a method richly exploited by Cavalieri, Kepler, and their followers in the 17th century, and so have focused on this feature as what must disqualify it, in Archimedes' mind, from being a valid demonstration. But in the first account of the parabola in *Quadrature of the Parabola*, Archimedes replaces the indivisible sections with narrow trapezia in an indirect proof that still requires the mechanical assumptions, and he follows this with the alternative, strictly geometric treatment, involving only summations (as sketched above). This duplication of proof would hardly be called for if the first quadrature were considered adequate. Further, by naming his procedure the *mechanical* method Archimedes emphasizes that the barycentric elements are its essence, the indivisibles being merely an auxiliary feature to facilitate its execution.

Resonating far beyond the narrow domain of mathematical history is the story of Archimedes' discovery of the basic principle of hydrostatics. According to the account in Vitruvius, Archimedes was asked by King Hieron to determine whether a certain dedicatory wreath was worked of pure gold, rather than of gold alloyed with silver. Pondering over the problem, Archimedes happened to notice, as he entered the bath, how the level of the water rose higher the more deeply he immersed himself in it, and then suddenly realized the general principle involved. Elated by the discovery, he rushed out, naked, crying, *"Heurēka!"* ("I have found it!").

The more sober exposition of these principles is given in the writing *On Floating Bodies*. Postulating an incompressible fluid medium, Archimedes proves two basic properties of immersed bodies: if a solid is lighter than the fluid (that is, of a lesser specific gravity), then it will float, and the floating body will displace a volume of the fluid equal to its own weight (props. 4–6); if the body is heavier than the fluid, it will sink, such that its weight in the fluid is diminished by that of an equal volume of the fluid (prop. 7). From the latter principle one can reconstruct a method for solving the "wreath" problem. The design of an actual device, a hydrostatic balance for determining the specific gravity of bodies, is transmitted and attributed to Archimedes by Arabic writers following the authority of Menelaus (2nd century).

A miscellany of Archimedean results are attested outside the corpus. His construction of the regular heptagon by means of a sophisticated variant of *neusis* is extant in an Arabic version. A solution of the angle trisection, also by *neusis,* is reported in Arabic sources, and appears to have inspired the method via conchoid devised by Nicomedes. A method of cube duplication, this too via *neusis,* presented by Hero and related to a Nicomedean construction via conchoid, may be related to an Archimedean precedent. The rule for finding the area of a triangle from its three sides, presented by Hero, is referred to Archimedes by Arabic commentators. Pappus summarizes Archimedes' description of the thirteen semiregular solids. In a remarkable document, the epigram on the "cattle number," addressed to Eratosthenes, Archimedes sets out a deceptively simple arithmetic problem whose solutions require solving a quadratic form of the "Pellian" type and would be numbers running into hundreds of thousands of digits. It is doubtful, however, that Archimedes himself possessed the means to complete that solution.

In one account of Archimedes' death reported by Plutarch, as the Roman invaders finally breached the defenses of Syracuse, Archimedes, alone, "having given both mind and gaze" to the investigation of a certain geometric construction, failed to notice the coming of the Romans and was killed by a soldier for refusing to follow him before completing the problem and its proof. The stereotype favored by the intellectual Plutarch portrays Archimedes as possessed of "such mind and depth of spirit and richness of theorems" that despite a reputation for superhuman ingenuity, through his mechanical inventions, he saw the latter pursuits as contemptuous and base and instead devoted himself only to the beauty and precision of pure inquiry. In modern judgments, by contrast, not only Archimedes' practical inventions but also his masterful insights into the applications of geometry in mechanics and hydrostatics are esteemed as paradigms of the fruitful liaison of theory and practice that underlies great achievement in the physical sciences.

WILBUR KNORR

Bibliography

Heiberg, J. L. *Archimedis opera omnia*, 2nd ed. 3 vols. Leipzig, 1910–1915; repr. Stuttgart, 1972. The English version by T. L. Heath (Cambridge, 1897; suppl. 1912) is based on Heiberg's first edition.

Dijksterhuis, E. J. *Archimedes*. Copenhagen, 1956; repr. (with corrections and a bibliographical supplement by W. R. Knorr) Princeton, 1987.

Knorr, Wilbur. *Ancient Sources of the Medieval Tradition of Mechanics*. Florence, 1982 (supplement of the Annali dell'Istituto e Museo di Storia della Scienza).

———. *The Ancient Tradition of Geometric Problems*. Boston, Basel, and Stuttgart, 1986; repr. New York, 1993.

———. "Archimedes and the Elements: Proposal for a Revised Chronological Ordering of the Archimedean Corpus." *Archive for the History of Exact Sciences* 19 (1978): 211–290.

Schneider, Ivo. *Archimedes: Ingenieur, Naturwissenschaftler und Mathematiker*. Darmstadt, 1979.

ARISTOTLE

Many sources offer us information about Aristotle's life. Certain accounts, owing to their temporal proximity, seem to carry more weight than others. Hermippus of Smyrna, for example, an Alexandrian who lived during the 3rd and 2nd centuries B.C.E., wrote *Lives* and a work on Aristotle; he seems to be one of the chief sources for Diogenes Laertius's collected *Lives of Eminent Philosophers* (2nd or 3rd century C.E.). At the same time, like the biographies of all great men, Aristotle's is accompanied by a string of anecdotes, often unfounded and sometimes malevolent. What philosophical meaning can we grant to certain aspects of Aristotle's biography that we may reasonably consider well documented? Three of these aspects will be considered here, though not in chronological order: the influence on Aristotle of his father's profession, Aristotle's role as tutor of Alexander the Great, and his relations with Plato within the Academy.

Aristotle was born in 384 B.C.E. in Stagira, a Greek colony situated in Thracian Chalcidice. His father, Nicomachus, was physician to Amyntas III, king of Macedonia, whose grandson Amyntas IV, too young to reign, was to be supplanted by his uncle Philip II, father of Alexander the Great. Why was Aristotle born in Stagira and not in Pella, residence of the Macedonian court? Was it because Stagira was a colony of Chalcis, his mother's native town? We do not know for sure. Polybius says Stagira was a colony of Andros. Was Aristotle's father, as some suggest, on a spying mission in Chalcidice, a region coveted by Macedonia, which wanted access to the sea? His parents were both Asclepiads, members of one of the lineages that claimed descent from Asclepius, god of medicine, and that passed down a medical tradition.

Aristotle's partiality for the natural sciences is generally attributed to this family origin. Although in the 4th century B.C.E. it was possible to acquire a medical education by paying for it, medical knowledge was transmitted principally within families. Thus Hippocrates, who was born three-quarters of a century before Aristotle, was the son and grandson of physicians: he had two sons who were also physicians and who taught medicine to their own sons; they all claimed to be descendants of Asclepius through his son Podalirus. A well-established tradition discloses privileged ties between the family of Hippocrates and the court of Macedonia, since Hippocrates had attended King Perdiccas II. These ties lasted until 310, the year in which a grandson of Hippocrates was assassinated by a son of Antipater, twelve years after Aristotle's death. The historian Dionysius of Halicarnassus (1st century B.C.E.) and several other biographers maintain that Aristotle's father was a descendant of Machaon, the other son of Asclepius. But this raises two questions. Why was a Machaonite present in the king's court, when the dynasty's doctors ordinarily came from Cos and were descendants of Podalirus? And why did Aristotle not become a physician? The usual response to the second question is that he was orphaned too early to have been influenced by his father. However, such a response fails to take into account the importance of lineage, of the extended family—which, in Aristotle's case, passed along the medical tradition. As for the first question, perhaps we should minimize the medical importance of Nicomachus, and when Diogenes Laertius writes that Nicomachus "resided with Amyntas, the king of Macedon, in the capacity of physician and friend" (*Lives* V.1), we should probably stress the latter term. Moreover, if we give some credence to the testimony of the *Suda*, a 10th-century Byzantine encyclopedia that assigns two articles to Nicomachus, one on medicine, the other on physics, the image that emerges shows Nicomachus as more of a theoretician than a practitioner of the art of medicine. In other words, from this viewpoint, the intellectual breach between Aristotle and his father was considerably less profound than it is ordinarily thought to have been: Aristotle explicitly makes the healing art depend on knowledge of causes, the best physicians being also "physical philosophers" (*Of Sense and Sensible Objects* I.436a19; *On Respiration* 21.480b24).

Around 343 Aristotle was called to Mieza by Philip II of Macedonia to undertake the education of Philip's son Alexander. If this pedagogical connection between "the greatest of philosophers" and the "greatest of conquerors" has struck many as peculiar, the explanation lies chiefly in a retrospective illusion: Aristotle, then in his forties, had doubtless not yet founded his own school, and contrary to what Plutarch says in his *Alexander*, he was certainly not "the most famous and learned of philosophers" in his day (*Lives* VII.2). Alexander at the time was thirteen years old. Aristotle's tutorship seems to have lasted seven years, until Philip's death and Alexander's rise to power. Although Philip wished to give the young prince a Greek education, it is likely that for numerous reasons, mostly political, he had no desire to send the boy to Athens; we may also suppose that teachers as important as Plato or Isocrates would not have come to Macedonia to spend several years. The friendly relationship between Nicomachus and the Macedonian dynasty must have had a decisive effect on the king's choice. As to the later tradition, which shows Alexander reproaching Aristotle for having made his *Metaphysics* available to the public, asking his teacher's advice before undertaking his expeditions, and sending him specimens of exotic animals, they are all entirely without historical foundation.

All of these details finally put into even more striking relief one essential fact: of the association between Aristotle and Alexander, of the life they shared for several years, we know almost nothing. Aristotle mentions Macedonia in *Politics* only in connection with other barbarian warlike peoples, pointing out one of their strange customs: a man who had killed no enemy would wear a harness as a belt. What seems certain, however, is that relations between master and pupil deteriorated. In 327 Alexander put to death Callisthenes, a relative of Aristotle who was the historian of his expeditions. Callisthenes had ridiculed the king's pretentiousness in obliging his subjects, and also his Greco-Macedonian companions-at-arms, to prostrate themselves before him in the Oriental manner. The anecdote reveals an essential point: Aristotle shows himself reserved, to say the least, toward Alexander's grand project of merging Greek and Persian customs and characteristics under a single political system. For Aristotle, a natural difference forever separates the Greeks, who are destined to live free under *political* institutions, from the barbarians, who are fated to live in servitude under despotism and slavery. This is what Aristotle allegedly explained in a work now lost, *Alexander, or the Colonies*. The complete disruption that separates the Hellenic from the Hellenistic period, in our way of scanning history, was produced, in contradiction with Aristotle's firm convictions, by the one whom he had probably taught that the city was the natural framework for perfect political life.

When he arrived in Athens at the age of seventeen, Aristotle attended classes at Plato's Academy. It is not certain that Plato was present at that time, but later encounters must have been frequent, since Aristotle remained at the Academy for twenty years, and the Platonic school was a veritable society of philosophers and scholars leading in large part a common life. Echoing a more ancient tradition, Theodoret, a 5th-century bishop of Cyrrhus, wrote that "even during Plato's lifetime, Aristotle openly opposed him and made war on the Academy, without respect for the school of which he had been a fervent disciple." But testimony that is probably more reliable gives us an almost diametrically opposed image of the relations between Plato and Aristotle. The incontestable differences between master and disciple seem not to have spoiled Aristotle's attachment to Plato, and it appears that he did not found his own school, the Lyceum, until after the death of Speusippus, nephew and successor to Plato as head of the Academy. Perhaps he finally decided to make this institutional break when the members of the Academy chose Xenocrates as head over Aristotle himself. Aristotle seems to have remained, if not a Platonist, at least a member of the Platonist "sect" as long as he could. But his fidelity to the school proves nothing about the relationship between Plato's doctrines and his own, for within the Academy, at least in Plato's time, there was no orthodoxy to which its members were obliged to submit.

The doctrinal relations between Plato and Aristotle have also been the subject of opposing opinions. Thus the great Neoplatonist commentators on Aristotle see more continuity than rupture between the two philosophers; among the Neoplatonists of the 5th and 6th centuries C.E., Aristotelian doctrines are taught as a sort of introduction to Platonism. The fact remains, nonetheless, that tradition has had an undeniable tendency to deepen the differences between Plato and Aristotle. In Raphael's *School of Athens,* the idealist fascinated by mathematics and the realist student of biology gesture in opposite directions. The same opposition appears in every realm. In politics, for example, it was common until recently to contrast a visionary totalitarian with a pragmatic centrist endowed with good sense. Thus the problem of "Aristotle's Platonism" is generally approached by interpreters in narrow terms: on what points and to what degree has Aristotle accepted a certain Platonist doctrine? The question is a fruitful one, and it led to a recent turnabout in Aristotelian studies. But in any account of Aristotelian philosophy a larger question must be faced at the outset, and implicitly asked again at every turn. In continuing a fundamentally Platonist enterprise by other means, was Aristotle not the best possible spiritual son Plato could have had?

This turnabout was the work of Werner Jaeger and his book *Aristoteles: Grundlegung einer Geschichte seiner Entwicklung,* published in 1923. Challenging the usual presentation of Aristotelianism as a system, Jaeger offered a genetic vision of the Stagirite's thought. Although he was not the first to suggest that the contradictions in the Aristotelian corpus could be explained by further rearrangements of texts from different epochs, Jaeger pursued this research much more thoroughly than any of his predecessors, and he based it, above all, on the hypothesis that Aristotle, who had once strongly adhered to Platonism, had gradually moved away from it. Thus the Aristotelian texts could be arranged over time in terms of a decreasing "coefficient of Platonicity." Used in specific instances, this method can be productive: it is clearly significant, for example, that in *Topica* Aristotle takes the Platonic tripartite division of the soul for granted, though he disavows this doctrine in other works. But in using the method systematically as he does, Jaeger actually relies on an implicit psychological hypothesis. It seems self-evident to him that Aristotle would inevitably embrace the teaching of someone as charismatic as Plato *before* breaking free of it. However, the contrary, more Oedipean assumption—held, for example, by Ingemar During—is no less plausible: overwhelmed by a Plato at the height of his powers, the young Aristotle might well have done all he could to distance himself from his master's teaching before returning, after the master's death, to more Platonic positions on certain issues.

The very status of the Aristotelian corpus that we have at hand precludes us, doubtless forever, from choosing among hypotheses of this kind. It is often said that Plato and Aristotle, along with Plotinus, Epictetus, and Sextus Empiricus, differ from the other ancient philosophers in that they left us entire texts, whereas the Presocratics, the Stoics, and the Epicureans left little but fragments and evidence cited by later writers. In fact, the texts of Aristotle that have come down to us belong to neither category. According to a story reported by Strabo, the library of Theophrastus, which contained works by Aristotle, among others, was placed by ignorant heirs in a cave for safe-keeping. It was only at the beginning of the 1st century B.C.E. that Aristotle's texts were published by the peripatetic philosopher Apellicon of Teos, who repaired the damage done by time as best he could. Sulla had Apellicon's library moved to Rome, where it ended up in the hands of a grammarian, Tyrannion, who published Aristotle's work at least in part. Plutarch tells the same story, adding that Andronicus of Rhodes, head of the Lyceum, acquired Aristotle's works and published them, after reorganizing them in a "corpus" accompanied by "tables." This is still the form, more or less, in which we read Aristotle today.

This story is probably not without some romantic accretions. Andronicus has even been suspected of having originated it, to convince his contemporaries that the texts he published had not been published previously. Nevertheless he reports a troubling but undeniable fact: after Theophrastus, who succeeded Aristotle as head of the Lyceum, the texts of "our" Aristotelian corpus seem to have been unknown. What is more, in Cicero's day—and Cicero was a contemporary of Andronicus—a whole set of works by a *different Aristotle* was in circulation among cultivated groups: these were often dialogues in the Platonic style, and their readers gave them high marks for their literary qualities. They were intended for publication, but they have survived only in the form of citations or allusions in the works of later writers—sometimes ample enough to allow us to reconstruct their structure and content. These works may be what numerous ancient authors, and Aristotle himself, called the exoteric writings, as opposed to the treatises reserved for members of the Lyceum.

The texts that have come down to us under Aristotle's name have thus undergone a double series of interventions. In the first place, Andronicus (who may simply be the spokesman for a group) corrected, rearranged, and occasionally rewrote the texts, suppressing some passages and adding explanatory glosses to others. Such practices, which offend our sense of textual authenticity today, were in widespread use until the modern period. The "written" writings, such as poetry, or the texts that Plato or Aristotle produced for publication, may well have escaped such editorial violence, generally speaking. But what was the initial state of Aristotle's scholarly treatises as edited by Andronicus? A second intervention comes into play here. The texts of the corpus are very probably not course notes jotted down by students or handed out by Aristotle, as some have claimed. But we may have to see them as the result of a collective endeavor in which the master incorporated certain critiques and remarks offered by his assistants—who were actually colleagues rather than students. The collective character of the development of these texts must have removed the last scruples (assuming there were any) on the part of later editors when they took over the corpus that had been transmitted to them.

These basic assumptions about the texts put the chronological hypotheses of today's commentators in an inescapable vicious circle. Since the texts of our Aristotelian corpus are not, properly speaking, *from Aristotle's own hand*, they cannot be studied objectively, that is to say, according to stylistic criteria like those that have allowed interpreters to be in general agreement about the chronology of Plato's dialogues, or at least groups of dialogues. Even the rare historical allusions, as well as the internal references contained in texts that may have been revised over and over, can be used only for very imprecise dating. Chronological hypotheses must therefore depend on *doctrinal* criteria. If we judge that texts in which we think we find some Platonic resonances were written before other passages in which such are missing, it is because we are convinced that Aristotle, at first a faithful Platonist, later distanced himself from Platonism. At the same time, interpreters who think that Aristotle distanced himself from Platonism claim to rely on textual divergences attributable to the different dates of composition. The most exasperating factor in the whole affair is perhaps that it is difficult to deny that Aristotle's positions evolved over time.

The Aristotelian corpus now in our libraries thus offers a deceptively systematic form, which does not mean that Aristotle did not intend to construct such a system. The systematic order imposed from the outside on Aristotle's texts is partly canceled out by one of the fundamental characteristics of Aristotelian learning: the relative autonomy, theoretical and methodical, of the various "branches" of Aristotelian speculation. But when this autonomy is recognized for what it is, it gives us a remarkable freedom—that of beginning the exposition of Aristotelianism *at any point at all.*

Post-Andronican editors adopted the custom of putting a collection of logical and epistemological treatises, written at different times, at the head of their editions; they group these under the title *Organon*. This title bears the trace of a polemic in which Aristotle himself could have taken no part: contrary to the Stoic thesis that logic, or dialectic, was a science, and more precisely one of the three parts of philosophy along with physics and ethics, the Peripatetics—partisans of Aristotle who earned that label owing to their master's habit of philosophizing while strolling about *(peripatein)*—maintained that it was an *instrument* (the meaning of the Greek word *organon*) for the sciences and philosophy. This instrumental quality is not the only factor to justify grouping together the various treatises that constitute *Organon*. Although it is a grouping that cannot be attributed to Aristotle himself, it is nevertheless compatible with an Aristotelian perspective. Two philosophic movements, Sophistics and the Eleatic movement followed by Plato, stand out against the background of the Stagirite's epistemological enterprise.

Sophists knew how to make the weakest discourse stronger, and thus to make it prevail. *Topica*, which is probably one of Aristotle's earliest works, codifies the dialectical discussion (its last book is traditionally published separately under the title *On Sophistical Refutations*). When a topic is proposed for discussion, one of the interlocutors declares that he wishes to defend a position that the other will undertake to demolish by his questions. This confrontation takes place before one or several arbiters, whose role is to declare the winner. An examination of the different situations that each of the protagonists in the dialectical confrontation can encounter leads Aristotle to distinguish the different forms of argumentation and, more precisely, of reasoning. The most effective form of reasoning, and for the ancients the most compelling, is the scientific syllogism, which deduces from true premises a necessary conclusion that inherits the truth of the premises. But it would be mistaken to think that Aristotle has only the theory of scientific discourse in view. He means to work out the rules of argumentative discourse in general. The dialectical syllogism, for example, would not have the same "force" as the scientific syllogism, because it rests on what Aristotle calls "valid opinions" *(endoxa)*. By the term *endoxos*, which comes from *doxa* (meaning both opinion and good reputation) and means of good reputation, illustrious, Aristotle indicates opinions that have a certain weight, a certain force, because they are shared by everyone or by eminent persons—"by all, or the majority, or the most distinguished among them." Finally, deductive reasoning is not the only method through which Aristotle seeks to form a theory. What he calls *epagōge*, a term translated only approximately as induction—because it is a question of passing from particular cases to general definitions—also has its place in the Aristotelian overview of forms of reasoning.

The aim of argumentation is to persuade. Aristotle sought to codify the rules of persuasion, that is, to make them rules of an art *(techne)*: the art of rhetoric, the subject of the treatise by the same name. For Aristotle, rhetoric is not so much the art of convincing as the art of "considering in each situation what is calculated to convince." It is not a science with a definite object but an art that can be applied to all domains. Even science does not always find a way to be convincing, Aristotle tells us, and the scholar should not disdain rhetoric. Several ancient witnesses tell us that *Rhetoric,* and also *Poetics,* which presented the theory of literary "genres" and of which only one book remains, have sometimes been included in *Organon;* at all events, the problem of their inclusion in *Organon* has arisen. Ammonius, for example, a Neoplatonist commentator at the end of the 5th century C.E., thinks we should distinguish between a syllogistic component and a nonsyllogistic component in Aristotle's logic; *Rhetoric* and *Poetics* should be included in the latter.

The fact remains that, in the eyes of posterity, Aristotelian logic has been almost exclusively reduced to the theory of scientific discourse. Scientific discourse is a true discourse that bears on necessary, therefore eternal and unalterable, objects. Through Plato and his distinction between science and opinion, Aristotle is a direct heir of Parmenides on this fundamental point. Two criteria allow us to say that we have knowledge *(episteme):* when we know the cause of the thing of which we claim to have knowledge, and when we know the thing by means of demonstration *(apodeixis)* or "scientific syllogism." The articulation between these two criteria is one of the most delicate problems in the interpretation of the Aristotelian theory of cognition. We will come back to the issue of causality in discussing Aristotelian physics; for the moment, let us look at demonstration. Aristotle saw the syllogism, a form of deductive reasoning in which, once certain things are posited, others necessarily follow from the data, as the form adequate to all demonstration in the theoretical sciences, including mathematics. A syllogism is a set of propositions in which the conclusion (Greeks are mortal) is deduced from two others, called premises (all human beings are mortal, all Greeks are human beings), that have a common element (human beings), called the middle term. This definition presupposes a preliminary reduction. For Aristotle, a proposition, a statement that must be either true or false, can always be reduced to the *attribution* of a predicate to a subject by the intermediary of the copula *is:* "Socrates walks" can be reformulated as "Socrates is walking." We shall not study here the different kinds of propositions distinguished by Aristotle.

This theory of proposition presupposes an inventory and a study of simple terms. This is why, in the traditional, systematic, and nonchronological order that comes from Andronicus of Rhodes, the first treatise in *Organon* is the one we call *Categories.* Here we find what may be one of the fundamental presuppositions, and, in any case, one of the principal enigmas, of Aristotelian thought. The term *category*—from the verb *katagorein*, which means to speak against someone, to accuse, impute to, hence to attribute, predicate—is used to label what Aristotle describes as "the things that are *meant,* when we . . . speak of uncombined words" (*Categories* II); he gives the following list: substance (man), quantity (two cubits long), quality (white), relation (double), where (in the Lyceum), when (yesterday), posture or position (seated), state or condition (has shoes), action (cut), affection (be cut). But with Aristotle, categories are not only irreducible semantic units. They also express the different meanings of "being," all of which relate to the fundamental meaning of the term, which is substance *(ousia)* in the ontological sense. For Aristotle this correspondence between logic and ontology is unproblematic; the difficulties are left to his interpreters.

Thus a special way to articulate the attributive propositions among themselves is what constitutes the language of science. To be scientific, a syllogism must first be formally valid. Accordingly, in a treatise later known as *Prior Analytics*, Aristotle studied the various ways to combine different types of propositions. Thus to say, "If A is affirmed of all B and B of all C, then A is affirmed of all C" is valid, while the syllogism "A is affirmed of all B; A is affirmed of all C; therefore B is affirmed of all C" is not valid. There are 256 possible forms of the syllogism, of which only 24 are valid.

But a valid syllogism, to be scientific, must also be true, that is to say, as we have seen, it must rely on true premises that are causes of the conclusion. At the core of every science there are premises that are absolutely primary, not deduced from any anterior premise: these are the principles (*archai*, plural of *arche*). The way Aristotle intends to establish these principles is, for his interpreters, a long-standing subject of controversy. Among the different sorts of principles, Aristotle is interested above all in definitions. He devotes lengthy developments to them in his epistemological treatise known as *Posterior Analytics*. Aristotle discards two solutions: the argument according to which everything is demonstrable, including the principles, an argument that leads to an infinite regression; and the argument in *Meno* on recollection of knowledge acquired by the soul before its incarnation. The modalities of the construction of definitions in Aristotle are very complex, if only because there are several types of definitions, one of which has particular scientific importance for him, the one that posits a definition as language that "exhibits the essence" of a thing at the same time that it reveals the cause of the thing. Thus to define thunder as a noise in the clouds is to give a merely descriptive and ultimately verbal description; to define it, instead, as the noise caused by "an extinction of fire in a cloud" is to reveal its cause and its essence, at least according to Aristotle's meteorology. However rigorous and elegant the syllogism may be, one must acknowledge its sterility: the syllogism, a deductive procedure, is not an instrument of discovery or creation of information. What seems to us the main point of the scientific work accomplished in the Aristotelian framework will thus be the construction of definitions. This epistemological practice is perfectly in accord with the ontological nature of Aristotle's world; we shall see that that world is composed of autonomous entities, the substances *(ousiai)*.

Of the difficult doctrine concerning the establishment of the principles of each science, there is one thing we can remember. It is through a process of reascending from particular cases to general notions and propositions, a process called inductive (though improperly, for Aristotle does not think that a general notion necessarily emerges from the consideration of all particular cases, or even from many of them), that the spirit moves from immediate experience to abstract thought. The basic condition of our ability to constitute the general principles of the sciences is thus fundamentally rooted in a "power" that we share with the other animals, sense perception, which Aristotle then describes as "an innate faculty to discriminate." Only a difference of degree between human beings and the other animals allows the former, notably because they are endowed with superior memory permitting them to agglomerate many sense impressions from different periods into one unique idea, to undertake this kind of theoretical elaboration. Thus Aristotelian science depends on a biological reality, arranged by a beneficent Nature. Man's biological (and especially sensory) perfection is the basis for his destiny as a theoretical animal.

This bond between science and human nature leads us to consider what we might call the other face of Aristotelian science, one that has been neglected by modern interpreters. Science is both a body of doctrine (thus we speak of "physical science") and a systematic construction of which we have just given the broad outlines. But science is also a state *of the subject who knows:* Aristotle defines it in this sense as a disposition that makes one qualified to demonstrate. At the end of one of the most famous passages devoted to the definition of science (*Posterior Analytics* I.ii.71b27–35) Aristotle repeatedly associates knowledge *(eidenai)* with conviction *(pisteuein),* coordinating them by a strong tie *(te kai),* the use of which serves, in Greek, to mark the bond between two realities of the same nature. While for Plato conviction *(pistis)* is an inferior form of knowledge, when Aristotle writes that "the required condition of our knowledge or conviction of a fact consists in grasping a syllogism of the kind which we call demonstration" (ibid. I.ii.71b26–28), he is representing the two faces of knowledge as complementary and equally worthy. The learned man is one who has succeeded in giving a necessary, hence unshakable, form to what he knows. This is the aspect stressed by the Stoics: they go so far as to say that knowledge is the soul of the wise man—this soul being a body—organized in a particular way. One who knows causally or demonstratively, or both, may very well not know more things than one who knows empirically and accidentally, but he knows them in a different way. If, for example, what he knows are natural phenomena, the syllogistic formulation of his knowledge reveals nothing new to him, but it allows him to form propositions that reflect necessary connections existing in nature. Thus, speaking of the following syllogism: "all broad-leafed plants are deciduous"; "all vines are broad-leafed"; therefore "vines are deciduous" (ibid. II.xvi.98b4–11), Aristotle remarks that this syllogism should be preferred to an equally valid one that would demonstrate that vines are broad-leafed plants because vines are deciduous ("every deciduous plant is broad-leafed"; "all vines are deciduous"; "therefore all vines are broad-leafed"; I.xvi.98b11–16). In fact, the first gives the causes of the conclusion, not the second. A passage in *Generation of Animals* and some post-Aristotelian texts reveal that Aristotle thought the lack of warm humidity was what caused leaves to fall (as well as hair, and so on); one can assume that, for him, winter cold congealed warm sap. Now, a broad-leafed plant has a greater circulation of sap. The syllogism thus has no part in the *discovery* of the cause of a phenomenon: these are probably observations, as well as lines of reasoning of the at once hypothetical and generalizing sort that allowed Aristotle to arrive at his theory about why leaves fall.

In "Aristotle's Theory of Demonstration," a well-known article published in 1969, Jonathan Barnes concluded that if all Aristotle's writings on syllogisms had been lost, our idea of Aristotelian science would not have been affected; thus syllogistics had a pedagogical and not a heuristic objective. While this is true, we must be more specific: the objective was pedagogical not in the sense that syllogisms would serve to help a student acquire more knowledge, but in the sense that to relate the different objects of knowledge syllogistically with one another allows the student to re-form his knowledge (in the etymological sense of the word *reform*), that is, it gives him the form of the immutable necessity that gives knowledge some resemblance to the divine.

Aristotle occupies a primary place in the history of natural science. Taking up the torch of speculation on *physis*, which Aristotle says the Socratics had tried to extinguish, he claims to have brought the line of "natural scientists" to a close, notably through his "discovery" of the theory of the four causes. In another respect, he puts an end to research on nature *(historia peri physeos)* as an all-embracing enterprise.

The Aristotelian doctrine is a sort of recollection of earlier speculations; this is very apparent in the article entitled "Nature" published in Book V of *Metaphysics*, which is a sort of dictionary of philosophical notions. In this book Aristotle distinguishes, as he did with other ideas, several valid meanings of the word *nature*. The term *physis* describes first the growth of things that are capable of growth: the same term is used to designate the growth process itself, that from which a thing grows (the seed, for example), or that which provokes the growth process (the stock of the vine is, in this sense, the nature of the bunch of grapes). In other respects, the nature of a statue is also the bronze on which the sculptor practices his art; but the nature of a thing, as Empedocles was well aware, is also the manner, proper to that thing, in which its constituents are mixed and arranged among themselves. More precisely, the nature of a being is its *ousia*, its essence or substance, which Aristotle calls its form *(eidos)*. For Aristotle, the primary and fundamental meaning of "nature" will then be "the essence of those things which contain in themselves a source of motion" (*Metaphysics* V.iv.1015a12–14). This passage calls for several observations.

First of all, the integrative capacities of Aristotelian philosophy are manifest here in the highest degree. The old Presocratic *physis*, a bottomless reservoir from which everything comes and to which everything returns, as well as Nature itself as the set of manifold combinations of elements, is not relegated to the shadows of myth. On two conditions the ancient physics continues to tell its share of the truth. First, in Aristotle's closed, finite, and eternal world the very idea of the emergence of the total being of things from nonbeing, or of cosmic order from chaos—which Parmenides had shown we could not even envisage—disappears. Second, nature is no longer either all of being or even the most important part of being. The whole of nature, a closed system of self-propelling realities, draws its movement from outside itself. The immovable prime mover moves the "high heavens" but is itself neither moved nor material. It is *pure actuality*—that is, it contains no potentiality, nothing it has to bring about. The eternal heavenly bodies themselves are marred by a certain potentiality, which betrays itself by change, if only movement in space. According to this difficult doctrine, an incorporeal mover moves a corporeal sphere that it has not created, and in which, owing to the fact of its own completeness, it can have no interest. Aristotle's solution raises as many difficulties as it resolves: the heavens move because they are animated by a movement of desire toward the prime mover. The supernatural is thus necessary for the existence and the coherence of nature.

The heavenly bodies are composed of a special element (which was later called quintessence, because it is different from the four elements present in our region of the universe; according to later accounts, Aristotle called it "aether") that is affected by an *eternal* movement of circular translation. In contrast, in the "sublunar" region—that is, the one under the orbit of the moon, which is the nearest to us of the heavenly bodies—change is eternal, but at the same time it is more complex and less regular. By the word *change (metabole)*, Aristotle means change in terms of substance (coming to be, or generation, and disappearance), quantity (increase and decrease), quality (alteration), or place (movement in space). All natural bodies in the sublunar region are composed of four elements—Earth, Water, Fire, and Air—which eternally transform themselves into one another, each body having a *natural* movement owing to its elementary composition: heavy ones move downward (hence, if nothing prevents them, toward the center of the earth), while light bodies move upward. These movements are less regular than the movements of the heavenly bodies; in addition, the beings involved in such movements are not eternal. Accordingly, beings that have in themselves the principle of their movements are natural. A dog is a natural being; a bed is not, at least judging by its form, which is given it by the cabinetmaker—for by its matter, wood, a bed is also in a certain respect a natural reality.

Natural science, then, will be knowledge of self-propelling beings. Aristotle delimits his territory in a programmatic passage at the beginning of his *Meteorologica:* "We have already dealt with the first causes of nature and with all natural motion; we have dealt also with the ordered movements of the stars in the heavens, and with the number, kinds and mutual transformations of the four elements, and growth and decay in general. It remains to consider a subdivision of the present inquiry which all our predecessors have called Meteorology. . . . After we have dealt with all these subjects let us then see if we can give some account, on the lines we have laid down, of animals and plants, both in general and particular" (I.1.338a20–339a8).

Every attentive reader of the Aristotelian corpus will easily recognize the treatises to which the author is alluding here: *Physics, On the Heavens,* and *On Coming-to-Be and Passing-Away,* as well as *Meteorologica,* the zoological works, and the treatise on plants that is lost (or that may never have been written). In these scientific works we find no trace of the syllogistic form, one of the criteria that defined science for Aristotle. This omission confirms our idea that syllogistics had no heuristic function for Aristotle. At the same time, causality is omnipresent, in the form of a systematic account of causes in *Physics,* and actively in the other treatises that seek the causes of the phenomena they are studying.

It was certainly not Aristotle who introduced the word *cause* into philosophy (a word that translates the feminine noun *aitia,* or the neuter adjectival noun *aition*). But he gave the search for causes an unprecedented development by a triple move. First, he identified a sure understanding of science with knowledge of the cause; next, he limited interrogation about the cause to a finite number of four questions; finally, he made the theory of the four causes the secret mover of all human thought, since these are the causes that, consciously or not, his predecessors, philosophers and also "mythologists," were seeking. If we read carefully the celebrated third chapter of Book II of *Physics,* in which Aristotle examines the notion of cause in itself, we see that he turns to "manners of speaking" for the various ways to say that something is an *aition.* In Greek the adjective *aitios* means responsible, often in the sense of guilty, and *aitia* means both the responsibility accruing to a thing, and especially to a person, in a result or an action, and the accusation, the cause for complaint.

According to Aristotle, there are four ways in which something "is said to be" responsible for something else. In one sense, the responsible element in the statue is the bronze from which it is made; in another sense, a certain numerical relation is responsible for the octave; in still another sense, the one who has promulgated a decree is responsible for it; finally, the health I would like to recover is responsible for the fact that I waste my time at sports. Thus it turns out that a complete analysis of our ways of speaking furnishes us with the four causes that are actually at work in nature: taken in the order of the above examples, these are the material, the formal, the efficient, and the final.

We must say "in nature," because it is to certain physical beings that Aristotelian causality applies *completely.* God, in fact, is not really answerable to causality: without matter, nothing affects him or sets him in motion, and he has no end but himself. Perhaps a formal cause might be found for him that would be nothing other than himself. Certain natural beings are only partly dependent on causality. The heavenly bodies have as causes only the desire that connects them to the prime mover and their own nature. We must presumably resist an excessively teleological explanation of nature in Aristotle: to be sure, the meteorological phenomena obey the necessary "laws," but they exist to no purpose. As for fabricated things, one can apply causal analysis to them only indirectly: it is because there is a nature that the bed has a material cause in the natural beings that are trees, and formal and efficient causes in the mind and muscles of cabinetmakers, who are natural beings. Causality is thus the trace both of nature's grandeur and its misery. Causes are fully causes only in the case of natural beings. Paradoxically, this claim appears in Aristotle's remarks about the coalescence of the different causes. In a frequently cited passage from *Physics*, he writes: "Clearly, then, the 'becauses' being such and so classified, it behoves [sic] the natural philosopher to understand all four, and to be able to indicate, in answer to the question 'how and why,' the material, the form, the moving force, and the goal or purpose . . . But in many cases three of these 'becauses' coincide; for the essential nature of a thing and the purpose for which it is produced are often identical . . . and moreover the efficient cause must bear some resemblance in 'form' to the effect . . . for instance, man is begotten by man" (II.vii.198a22–29).

Reading such a passage shows us what Aristotle has immediately in mind when he speaks of natural beings: they are living beings, and in particular, animals. Aristotle's "biology," the supreme achievement of his natural history, constitutes such an imposing enterprise that it is hard to find anything comparable in the history of science. When he indicates that the essential nature of a thing and the purpose for which it is produced are identical—his examples could include statements such as the following: "the definition [the essence] of the lung is to be an organ intended to cool the organism" (*Parts of Animals* III.vi; cf. *On Respiration* 475b, 476a, b)—Aristotle in fact provides several of the principal keys to his biology. Far from being descriptive, his biology is explanatory. This is one of the reasons his principal object is not whole animals but their "parts"; his project is to define the functions common to all animals—respiration, for instance—and to study the variations in organs intended for these functions. Aristotle's zoology is fundamentally *teleological*.

Aristotelian teleology has often been caricatured by those who have not made the effort to appreciate its subtlety. It rests on a radical tension. Aristotle's finite and eternal world is perfect, and perfection and eternity are in a sense interchangeable, since only that which cannot improve or degrade itself can continue to be what it is for eternity. This perfection can be seen also in "our" world where, as Aristotle often reiterates, "Nature always produces the best." But we must remember that the sublunar world is a tissue of regularities that imitate the eternal and perfect round of the stars; therefore this world cannot claim absolute perfection. The presence of matter, which is indeterminate in that it is potentially the various beings, brings an irreducible element of irregularity into the sublunar world.

Thus Aristotle is the first philosopher from whom we have retained a theoretical analysis of chance—which is in itself a sort of cause. In Aristotle's phallocentric view of animal reproduction, for example, the male provides the form and the female the matter. The "resistance" of matter to being given form is the origin of "deviations," that is, of monsters, as Aristotle remarks in *Generation of Animals*, the first of these deviations being the birth of a female. Here, eternity plays the regulating role: because the reproduction of species is eternal, genetic monstrosities are drowned in a flood of "normality." In this manner, deviations cancel one another out. The image that makes Aristotelian finalism most comprehensible may be the one proposed in *Generation of Animals:* Nature is like a good head of household who arranges things for the best—one is tempted to call it a tinkerer. To take a well-known example, *it so happens* that animals of great size have a superabundance of earthy matter; thus Nature profits by it to make horns that will serve as weapons for self-defense. But since this quantity of earthy matter is not unlimited, it is impossible to provide these animals both with horns and with many teeth. That is not a problem: Nature alleviates this inconvenience by providing several stomachs—Aristotle meticulously describes the digestive system of ruminants—to convert nourishment that would otherwise be insufficiently masticated into useful food.

Nature's tendency toward perfection must also "play tricks" with the teeming abundance in the living world. Although the *History of Animals* counts more than five hundred species, Aristotle never intended to enumerate all the animals, nor to classify them as the 17th- and 18th-century taxonomists undertook to do. While he sketched out a sort of scale of living creatures, nowhere does he claim that this diversity is in itself a debased image of divine unity. For Aristotle, to be sure, man is the most perfect animal—in a remarkable formula, he refers to him as "the animal the most in accordance with nature" (*Progression of Animals* IV.706a18)—and according to him, with respect to man the other animals are "like dwarves," that is, they are ill-proportioned copies. But it is important to note that no teleological principle can account for the diversity of living things. There must, of course, be prey for predators, but that is not enough to explain this diversity. Everything happens, then, as if nature were trying out all possible organic combinations without a fixed objective. Aristotelian biology is thus far from being entirely teleological. Not only is it impossible to explain all the characteristics of living things through final causes, but Aristotle never misses an occasion to remind us that the biologist must also study the vital *mechanisms*, owing to the necessary interaction of the properties of matter.

It is then well within this domain of nature, and first in the domain of living nature, that causality functions completely. Cause, which is a cause of something, is the trace of a splitting that is itself a sign of imperfection, but it takes on its full meaning only in the domain of natural regularities. This is the image that posterity has retained of Aristotelian natural history: Diogenes Laertius, in his cursory and disappointing résumé of Aristotle's philosophy, does not fail to note that "in the sphere of natural science he surpassed all other philosophers in the investigation of causes" (*Lives of Eminent Philosophers* V.32). Aristotle's "scientific" treatises reveal an astounding desire for knowledge. Our perception of this largely neglected part of his work has been distorted for too long by a naive continuist prejudice: certain of Aristotle's "exact" observations aroused enthusiasm, but they clearly did not weigh heavily in the balance against the "errors" of a biology that is not comparable to ours in its objectives, its methods, or its theoretical or material resources.

In Aristotle, the domain of physics is thus *defined* by metaphysics, though this term was not introduced until the 1st century C.E., when Aristotle's editors used it to designate what ought to be studied "after physics," whether this "after" indicates a difference in the dignity of the objects or simply a pedagogical order of exposition. To define means both to limit and to explain. Yet Aristotle's metaphysics gestures in two directions: toward theology and toward ontology.

Aristotle speaks of God, the immovable prime mover, in quasi-mystical terms. God is pure actuality and, as such, perfect; he is alive, but he is impassible, since it is the desire that the highest heaven feels for him that makes heaven move, while God himself loves nothing and no one; it would be detrimental to his perfection to act on something other than himself, or to think of something other than himself: God is "thought thinking itself." Theology is in contact with natural science, as we have seen, through the intermediary of the celestial bodies. These share with God individual eternity, of which all the cyclical or recurrent phenomena of the sublunary world are imitations; this is the case, for example, with the specific—not the individual—eternity of animals and plants. The concept of *imitation* allows Aristotle to account for the behavior and the coherence of the sublunary world. The distance is no less great between the Aristotelian divine and sublunary, on one hand, and the Platonic intelligible and sensible, on the other. But there is, as it were, a world between the Aristotelian imitation of superior realities by sublunary beings and the Platonic participation of realities inferior to eminent realities. Weak as they are, the terrestrial substances do not have a delegated reality; they are not simply shadows cast by the ideal world, and thus they deserve to be considered in themselves. All the more so in that whatever imitates teaches us about what it imitates.

It is precisely because the universe, and especially our sublunary region, is neither an emanation nor a copy of God that metaphysics is not reduced to theology, and that we need a discourse about being *(ontology)*. The absolute simplicity of God means that he is not subject to such a discourse. But nondivine beings are characterized by division and dispersal, as the very way we talk about these things reveals. In fact, our discourse combines elements of varying status. This is something the Sophists did not realize when they affirmed that, as Plato's *Euthydemus* had already claimed, to teach Clinias was to make the ignorant Clinias disappear, thus to kill Clinias. Others were similarly unaware of this feature of discourse: this was the case with Antisthenes, and with the Eleatics, for whom every predication is necessarily tautological, and for whom to say about something anything other than "it is" amounts to saying that being is not. These difficulties, which had fascinated—that is to say, partially paralyzed—Greek thinkers prior to Plato, were resolved by Aristotle thanks to his distinction between essence and accident. In the sentence "Clinias is learned," "Clinias" signifies the essence *(ousia)*, which can be affected by different accidents, like "learned," "white," "here." Thus we rediscover the ontological side of the doctrine of categories. As for the impossibility of movement, which, according to the Eleatics, amounted to having being proceed from nonbeing, Aristotle reduced that by his distinction between act and power: the ignorant Clinias is potentially a learned man. But this distinction is accompanied by a condition, which is why Aristotle took the Eleatic objection fully into account: fundamentally, actuality is anterior to potentiality. An embryo, for instance, becomes an infant and an infant becomes an adult because the embryo has the potential to develop the characteristics that an adult has transmitted to it. "Man begets man" because there have always been men; Aristotle sometimes explains this assertion by saying that man is *by nature* anterior to the infant, even if infants are chronologically anterior to the adults they will become.

Thus, "there is a science which studies Being *qua* Being, and the properties inherent in it in virtue of its own nature" *(Metaphysics* IV.i.1003a21–22). For us, this claim presents many difficulties; let us consider just one of them. According to Aristotle, being is not a genus that can be divided into species, as, for example, the genus "figure" can be divided into rectilinear figures and curvilinear figures. In *Sophist*, Plato had already felt compelled to acknowledge this, in part by making being a sort of "transversal" genus. Now, one of the underlying features of Aristotelian epistemology is that there is one science corresponding to one genus. This means, in particular, that if form and sound are two different species, propositions concerning knowledge of forms (geometry) are not transferable to sounds (acoustics), except by analogy, as when one says that a certain sound is "sharp." Any attempt to describe the science of being in strictly "scientific" terms, then, cannot help but be inadequate. Are we encountering, here, the specter of the universal science that had up to that point claimed to be philosophy, and of which Aristotle was the first to reject the possibility?

Aristotle gave this science of being as being two different but complementary contents. In Book IV of *Metaphysics*, where he assumes its existence, he declares its object to be the great principles common to all the sciences, such as the principle of noncontradiction, which is established in the "dialectic" manner, that is to say, by remarking that even the discourse of anyone who would oppose this principle is impossible. But elsewhere in the same book and especially in the books considered to be central to *Metaphysics* (Books VII, VIII, IX), Aristotle reduces the study of being to that of the first of its categories, substance or essence *(ousia)*. This "ousiology" is the very heart of Aristotelian metaphysics. The *ousia* is characterized by three essential properties: it exists by itself; it is separate; it is "cause and principle." Several realities can, in differing degrees, claim the title of *ousia*. The universal and the species can be considered *ousiai*, but in a secondary sense, because the universal exists as a logical (intellectual) entity.

On this point, the break with Plato is very clear. In one sense, matter is *ousia*, but matter does not exist by itself, and the *ousiai* that we perceive most immediately in our concrete experience—sensible substances—are what they are more by virtue of their form than by virtue of their matter. Form alone is nevertheless not fully *ousia*, because to describe the ontological units that are natural substances only by their form is to give a schematic knowledge of them. To indicate their form, Aristotle uses the terms *eidos* (which indicates the visibility of a thing) and *schema* (which refers to its contour), for there is a complex and nonarbitrary relation between form and matter. Not just anything can be made of anything. The term *ousia* applies most properly, in the end, to what Aristotle designated in a formula that has retained a great part of its mystery: the *ti en einai*. This expression, which the medievals translated as *quiddity*, seems to be a question turned, as it were, into a substantive, as is also the case with the expression *to ti estin* (the what-it-is), used to designate the essence of a thing. But in relation to the *ti estin*, the *ti en einai* indicates a superior degree of properness. Aristotle suggests in *Posterior Analytics* that the *ti en einai*, the "essential definition of a subject," is constituted by the elements that are proper to the essence *(ti estin)*, or, following a correction proposed by a modern editor, by what is proper among the things that are in the essence (II.vi.92a7).

Nevertheless, Aristotle claims that the *ti en einai* of natural substances does not contain their matter, because matter is to a certain extent accidental. Thus the quiddity of a (sensible) natural being, while not a part of that being, is something other than the being. Let us pursue the paradox, at least that of the expression, right to the end: the *ti en einai* of a thing is, in a way, more truly that thing than the thing itself is. Thus it is with the soul, which is the vital active force of the animate body: it is more truly the living thing than the living body itself. Platonism is thus actually reversed: there is indeed something else more really "this" than "this" thing I see and touch: but the former reality is not outside or "above" the latter.

The case of the soul is an interesting one. In his treatise *De anima*, Aristotle carefully skirts the problems that the whole philosophic tradition presumably expected to see him address, particularly the problem of the immortality of the soul. The soul consists of embedded "faculties": for example, an animal that has a body adequately constituted for this purpose is able to grow and reproduce itself, to discriminate among the types of information provided by its environment, and to act in that environment. Thus the soul plays a greater role in defining the living body than does the living body itself, be-cause the soul gives the *causes* of vital manifestations, which anatomical and physicochemical knowledge of organs, tissues, and so on, does not do.

But the sublunary world is not simply the domain of living beings. It is also the domain of those animals capable of deliberation and rational choice that we call humans. The opening of Aristotle's *Politics* has a tone we would iden-tify as sociobiological: the human tendency to associate in cities is given as the result of the other natural tendencies that lead to sexual union for repro-duction, and to the association between inferior and superior beings. How-ever, the "realm of human affairs" is controlled by its own rules, and "practi-cal philosophy" does not propose to transpose laws developed in the field of theoretical knowledge into its own realm. Here, too, we are far from Plato. To grasp the peculiar characteristics of Aristotelian practical philosophy, let us confine ourselves to examining two of its key ideas, that of virtue and that of excellent constitution.

The translation of *arete* by virtue, while it has a long tradition of its own, still remains dangerous because of the connotations of the word. For Aris-totle, *arete* is the excellence of some thing. He remarks that we can speak of the *arete* of a tool or a horse. Nevertheless, he uses the term most particularly in the ethical realm. Now "ethical" comes from *ethos*—character—which, Aristotle tells us, "comes from a slight modification of *ethos*," a word that means the habitual way to be, the one that results from experience and educa-tion. If someone has acquired the habit, from childhood, of being intemperate, intemperance will become for him a habitual, almost natural, way to be. Ethi-cal virtue then will be a state of being virtuous, rooted in the human subject by long experience. But while Aristotle acknowledges that immorality and vice can procure satisfactions, he posits as the basis for his ethics the principle that virtue, which implies moderation of tendencies and self-mastery, is the principal—though not the only—element in happiness *(eudaimonia)*: no one can be happy in suffering or misery. Now happiness is every human be-ing's *natural end*. To be virtuous, then, for human beings, is to give them-selves the best opportunity to realize their human nature fully. Still, in most cases people do not spontaneously choose virtuous conduct, and the best way to lead them to conform to what is basically their nature is to constrain them to virtue by imposing "good habits" on them from childhood. But, in contrast to the Christian sinner for whom the practice of virtue does not suppress temptation, and who is, therefore, yoked to an indefinite task of self-mastery, the virtuous Aristotelian, once established in virtue, is no longer tempted by vice, since virtue gives him the happiness that is his natural end. Conse-quently, as Pierre Aubenque showed very well in *La prudence chez Aristote*, although Aristotle denies ethical relativism—good and evil really do exist—he also refuses to set absolute objective moral standards. The virtuous man, master of himself, who allows the capacities of his human nature full scope to flourish, does not conform to standards but is himself the standard. The Stoic wise man, who is always upright because there is a wise way of doing everything, including lying or killing, is not far removed; the wise man is the standard of virtuous action because he alone can determine what he should do, to whom, at what moment, and by what means.

This brief account shows the importance of education in the acquisition of virtue. For Aristotle, as for Plato, education is essentially a *political* matter. Life under good laws is what serves to anchor the good habits that lead to virtue in the minds of citizens, and especially in their children. Finally, then, public virtue, and consequently the public well-being, lie in the hands of legislators. But the practice of virtue itself, and not its mere acquisition, is political: against conventionalist theories of the social bond, Aristotle maintains that man's character is naturally political. This means that the city, in the Greek meaning of the term, is, for the individual, the place of his perfection. Hence all peoples and all individuals who cannot live in cities are excluded from this perfection.

Aristotle's political philosophy has long been distorted by interpreters. In fact, one cannot use the pretext that Aristotle separates himself from the Platonic project of the "ideal city" to conclude that he renounces political excellence. Every city, to make its citizens virtuous and therefore happy, must endow itself with an excellent constitution. For Aristotle, however, excellence is multiple. The type of constitution that can lead a city to virtue depends on the characteristics of the people involved, both psychological (these stem from a number of factors, including the climate) and historical. To a people barely emerged from a patriarchal society, royalty is acceptable, so long as it consecrates the preeminence of a man who prevails over the rest in virtue. But a good king is a king who spreads virtue and happiness throughout the social body. Consequently he digs the grave of royalty, for when virtuous people manage to form a group (a minority, to be sure, but a rather important one), it would be *unjust* for them to continue to obey a king whom they equal in virtue. It is just, however, for them to take in hand the affairs of the city and establish an aristocracy. When the majority of the citizens, owing to their virtue, deserve to exercise power, it will be necessary to establish a politeia, a word that designates in turn, in Aristotle, the constitution, whatever it is; the mere fact of living in a city; and a particular form of constitution in which a significant body of virtuous citizens holds power. This form of government could be called constitutional. It is clear, therefore, that laws correspond to constitutions and not the reverse: a given law requiring the sharing of wealth, for example, which would be just in a constitutional government, would be completely unacceptable under a monarchy. To each of these excellent constitutions there corresponds a deviant form: tyranny, oligarchy, and democracy (which we would call demagogy). Under these regimes, the man or the group in power governs to his own advantage and not "with the common advantage in view": the very purpose of politics, which is the development of virtue in the bosom of a group of free and equal citizens, is then called into question.

For Aristotle, the philosopher should no longer govern. He should not even make laws. However, he can help train legislators, who will have to establish an excellent constitution or rectify a bad one and make it excellent. It is principally to this end that Aristotle wrote his ethical and political treatises. The Platonic Academy was intended to produce kings. Aristotle's Lyceum is content to turn out professors of political virtue.

Aristotle's posterity and influence have been immense. Despite the brief eclipse that his work suffered, antiquity did not cease to consider him one of the "divine geniuses" of philosophy (Cicero). The reorganization of learning and scientific research that was accomplished in Alexandria in the 3rd century B.C.E. incontestably bears an Aristotelian stamp. While Aristotle's work was almost entirely unknown to thinkers of the Latin West from the 7th century on, it was the principal force behind the development of Arab philosophy and science, through Arabic and Syriac translations, which were translated, in turn, into Latin starting in the 12th century. The rediscovery of Greek texts by Aristotle in the 13th century, which gave birth to the Scholasticism of Albertus Magnus and Thomas Aquinas, was a revolution whose scope we have difficulty measuring even today. Modern philosophy and science have been constructed in harmony with Aristotle or in opposition to him, but never without him. But more than the survival, recognized or unacknowledged, of a given Aristotelian doctrine, what Aristotle bequeathed to following generations is a way of thinking. If it is true, as the poet Coleridge claimed, that humanity is divided between Platonists and Aristotelians, the whole history of thought might be understood as a sometimes mute, sometimes violent confrontation between Platonic thought and Aristotelian thought. The latter might be defined by several invariables: respect for concrete reality, the understanding of which is the basis of all later theoretical elaborations; the autonomy of that reality, which bears in itself the rules of its own intelligibility; a systematic articulation among different domains that retain their own rationality. The theoretical frenzy provoked by the birth of physics in the 17th century did, to be sure, impose on Aristotelianism a theoretic purgatory of three centuries. The present era, on the contrary, is auspicious for Aristotle's thought: many of today's scholars are rediscovering an Aristotelian inspiration at the foundation of their own theoretical enterprises.

PIERRE PELLEGRIN
Translated by Rita Guerlac and Anne Slack

Bibliography

Texts and Translations

Aristotle: Opera. Ed. Immanuel Becker. 5 vols. Berlin: Academia Regia Borussica, G. Reimer, 1831–1870.

Aristotle. *Works.* 23 vols. Loeb Classical Library.

Studies

Aubenque, Pierre. *Le problème de l'être chez Aristote.* Paris: Presses Universitaires de France, 1962.

———. *La prudence chez Aristote.* Paris: Presses Universitaires de France, 1963.

Goldschmidt, Victor. *Temps physique et temps tragique chez Aristote.* Paris: Vrin, 1982.

Gotthelf, Allan, and James A. Lennox, eds. *Philosophical Issues in Aristotle's Biology.* Cambridge: Cambridge University Press, 1987.

Granger, Gilles Gaston. *La théorie aristotélicienne de la science.* Paris: Aubier, 1976.

Hamelin, Octave. *Le système d'Aristote.* Paris: Alcan, 1920.

Irwin, Terence. *Aristotle's First Principles.* Oxford: Clarendon Press, 1988.

Jaeger, Werner. *Aristotle: Fundamentals of the History of His Development* (1932). Trans. Richard Robinson. Oxford: Clarendon Press, 1948.

Lear, Jonathan. *Aristotle: The Desire to Understand.* Cambridge: Cambridge University Press, 1988.

Le Blond, Jean-Marie. *Logique et méthode chez Aristote.* Paris: Vrin, 1939.

Patzig, Günther. *Aristotle's Theory of the Syllogism.* Trans. Jonathan Barnes. Dordrecht: Reidel, 1968.

Pellegrin, Pierre. *La classification des animaux chez Aristote.* Paris: Les Belles Lettres, 1982.

Robin, Léon. *La théorie platonicienne des Idées et des Nombres d'après Aristote.* Paris: Alcan, 1908.

DEMOCRITUS

THE ATOMIC THEORY OF MATTER was invented in the late 5th century B.C.E., during the lifetime of Socrates and about the time of the birth of Plato. Ancient writers attributed its invention to two men: Leucippus and Democritus. Leucippus is a mysterious figure of uncertain date and provenance. It is impossible from the surviving evidence to detach the contributions of Leucippus from those of Democritus; Democritus was better known and much more often quoted, and this article will make no attempt to distinguish the contributions of the two men.

Plato never mentions Democritus—a remarkable omission, since there is evidence in *Timaeus* that he was acquainted with Democritean atomism. Aristotle, on the other hand, frequently discusses his theories, occasionally associating him with Leucippus but usually mentioning only Democritus's name. Simplicius refers to a monograph by Aristotle entitled *On Democritus*, and books with this title are also attributed to Theophrastus, Heraclides Ponticus, Epicurus and his disciple Metrodorus, and the Stoic Cleanthes. According to the biographer Diogenes Laertius, fifty-two books by Democritus were arranged by Thrasyllus (who gave the same treatment to Plato's books) into tetralogies grouped by subject: ethics (two), physics (four), mathematics (three), music (two), and technical (two). There was also a miscellany of unclassified writings.

Not one of these books survives. The atomist tradition of Democritus and Epicurus proved to be notably antithetical to the interests of those who ensured the preservation of chosen portions of the classical heritage, especially in the period when education was in the hands of learned Christians. We are dependent for our knowledge of Democritus on quotations and summaries in other classical writers, many of them "hostile witnesses"—though it is worth noting that Aristotle himself, and Theophrastus, both treated his work with great respect, however much they disagreed with it.

Democritus was born around 460 B.C.E. and lived to an advanced old age. Several sources mention extensive travels in the course of his life—to Egypt, Persia, Babylon, "the Chaldaeans," even Ethiopia and India. He is said to have visited Athens and commented, "But no one knew me." Later sources began to give more and more stress to his cheerfulness of character, until he eventually became known and pictured as the Laughing Philosopher.

The achievement with which he will forever be associated is the theory that the universe is made of atoms and void. The arguments with which he supported the theory were metaphysical, and drew virtually nothing from sense perception, nor (of course) experiment. An *"a-tom"* is something that cannot be cut. The earliest use of the word in surviving Greek literature is as an adjective applied to the grass in a sacred meadow. If Aristotle's testimony is right, Democritus's proof of the need for atoms in physics went like this. The contradictory of the proposition "There are atoms" is "All bodies are cuttable into smaller pieces ad infinitum." Suppose, then, that a finite body is actually cut up ad infinitum. What will be left? It cannot be small bodies of finite size, since the hypothesis was that the cutting is completed ad infinitum. It cannot be points with no size, since the original body could not be composed out of points. And it cannot be cut up in such a way as to be nothing at all. The contradictory thus being proved false, it remains that there are atomic bodies—bodies of finite size that in principle cannot be cut up. (The argument, paraphrased, is attributed to Democritus by name in Aristotle's *De generatione et corruptione* 1.2.316a11ff).

There is much modern controversy about the nature of Democritus's atomism. Basically there are two irreconcilable positions. One is that the argument outlined above was intended to apply only to "body," and the kind of division in question was simply the cutting up of bodies into smaller pieces. Nothing, then, was implied about theoretical or mathematical division: one might speak about half an atom or a quarter of an atom without talking nonsense. The second interpretation takes the atom to be a theoretically minimum quantity: a point with size.

There are advantages and difficulties in both interpretations. The first has the advantage that it is easy to understand how atoms may differ in shape, as they are required to do by the theory: parts of the atom may be distinguished in thought, so that one may be shaped like an H and another like an A. What is in favor of the second is that it appears to answer the Eleatic argument from which it plainly derives, whereas the other does not; and that the argument as given by Aristotle would apply just as well to a mathematical quantity as to a physical atom. Indeed, Aristotle says in another place (*De caelo* 3.4.303a20–24) that those who talk of atomic bodies (meaning Democritus and his school) clash with the mathematical sciences. This might perhaps be regarded as conclusive, since an atom that is only physically unsplittable does not clash with mathematics; but Aristotle is in a peculiar position on this subject, since he himself held that there is no "magnitude" except corporeal magnitude.

There are some slight but ambiguous indications that Democritus may have worked out a geometry that was not based on infinite divisibility. Plutarch (*De communibus notitiis adversus Stoicos* 1079.Eff) discusses at length a problem raised by Democritus: if a cone is sliced along a plane parallel to its base, what are we to say about the surfaces of the two resultant segments? If they are equal, and this applies to every such cut, then the cone has the properties of a cylinder. If they are unequal, then the sides of the cone are not smooth but stepped, each step being one atom in thickness. Since all atoms are below the level of sense perception, the sides of the cone would appear smooth. It may be that Democritus proposed the stepped version as correct, and suggested that below the level of perception geometrical magnitudes are composed of indivisibles. There is no agreement among scholars, but the majority view now appears to be that Democritean atoms are physical bodies, and that mathematical extension was allowed by him to be infinitely divisible.

The atoms of Democritus have a strictly limited set of properties: they have shape, size, and (probably) weight, but no qualities such as color, heat, taste, and so on. There is no such thing as an atom of iron, as distinct from an atom of water. As to size, there are some texts that say that atoms may be of enormous size ("as big as the cosmos," Aëtius, in DK 68.A.47), although it is evident that all the atoms in our cosmos are below the level of perception. It is clear that they vary in shape, since the compound bodies that they form take on perceptible qualities according to the varieties of the component atoms. Indeed, we are told (Aristotle, *De generatione et corruptione* 315b8) that the perceptible varieties of compounds are infinite, and therefore the number of different atomic shapes is infinite.

Weight is a more problematic property. Aristotle and Theophrastus both report that the weight of atoms varies with their size; the doxographer Aëtius denies that Democritus's atoms have any weight, but although some interpreters accept this, and claim that weight is a property that emerges only when atoms are in some kinds of motion, Aëtius is heavily outnumbered. But it is still not an easy matter to decide what Democritus meant by weight. Aristotle defined it as a tendency to move toward the center of the universe. But Democritus's universe, being infinite, had no center. Democritus's follower Epicurus, a century later, took weight to be a tendency of all atoms to move parallel to each other in a particular direction through the infinite void. That is a theory that depends on a belief that our earth is more or less flat: the "downward" direction is simply the direction of free fall of a heavy body perpendicular to the earth's surface. Democritus too believed the earth to be flat, and it can be argued that his view of weight was the same as Epicurus's. (What other explanation did he give for the fall of heavy bodies in our cosmos?) Some scholars take the weight of Democritean atoms to be equivalent to their resistance to blows from collisions with other atoms. There is still no certainty about this.

What is certain is that Democritus described the atoms as moving in all directions, colliding and rebounding, and forming compounds whenever atoms of suitable shape and size happened to meet and join together. This is the way that worlds are formed. In the infinite void, infinitely numerous atoms are moving in all directions. Sometimes, a collection of atoms moves into "a great void," where they are caught up together in a vortex. The vortex acquires a kind of skin or membrane around its outer surface (like the embryo of an animal?), thus confining a quantity of atoms within a finite perimeter. The vortex motion brings about a sorting of atoms by size and shape (as we can observe that the churning motion of breakers on the seashore sorts pebbles into groups by size and shape), and thus the heavier atoms congregate together in the middle to form an earth, in the shape of a flat disk (though some texts report that it was not round but elongated), and the lighter and more mobile atoms are extruded so as to form the air and the heavens. This idea gives rise to a problem that troubled many of the early philosophers, and survived to Epicurus's day: if earth is heavy, and if a piece of earth when detached from the parent body and dropped from a height falls until it hits the ground, what prevents the whole earth from falling through the air beneath it? The answer given by Democritus, and most of the others, was that its breadth prevents it from falling: it floats on the air underneath it, rather as a flat plate will float on water, although it will sink if tipped up sideways.

The details of the cosmogonic process are not clearly described in the surviving literature, but there are several important features that can be regarded as being beyond doubt. Since the universe is infinite, there is no limit on the number of worlds that can be formed by this process: we must take it that there are infinite worlds. (It is probable that Leucippus and Democritus were the first to hold this view, although some attribute it to Anaximander and others of the Presocractics.) All atomic compounds, including the worlds, come into being as a result of random collisions, and perish in the course of time by the dispersion of their component atoms. The cause of creation and destruction is "necessity"—that is to say, it has to happen as it does whenever the atoms fall into the appropriate patterns. There is (and this is crucial) no plan or design.

It is particularly disappointing that none of the texts about the formation of the cosmos has survived. The pressing need for a good description of Democritus's theories in this area has led scholars to attribute a great variety of texts to him—parts of book 3 of Plato's *Laws*, the early chapters of Diodorus, book 5 of Lucretius, and so on. But convincing arguments are lacking.

Democritus proposed a system in which none of the fundamental components of the world is perceptible: we are asked to believe that all the rich variety of impressions taken in by our senses in our dealings with the physical world is missing from the "real" world, which consists only of atoms and void. The paradox is made sharper by Democritus's vocabulary: he refers to the basic components of the universe as "the full" and "the empty," or as "beings" and "not-being." This is to go back to the language of the Eleatics, Parmenides and Melissus—but with a remarkable difference. The Eleatics insisted on a strict interpretation of "what *is not*." It is equivalent to nothing, and to talk about it is to say nothing rational. Leucippus and Democritus, on the other hand, claim a kind of being for "what *is not*." It has no properties of its own except extension, it is just what separates one piece of being from another, it is contrasted with the "beings" that are atomic bodies, but nonetheless it is said to have a kind of being.

This dualism marks a retreat from the richer ontology of Democritus's predecessors. Anaxagoras classified a huge range of physical entities among the basic ingredients of the universe, and added a separate moving agent, which he called Mind; Empedocles reduced the physical substances to the four that came to be regarded by subsequent natural philosophers as the elements of all things: earth, water, air, and fire, together with the agents of change postulated in his own system, Love and Strife. Democritus banished the moving agents altogether and reduced the basic ingredients to the imperceptible pair, Being and Not-Being. The paradox that Not-Being itself has a kind of being is not explained.

There is some question about whether it is right to identify Democritus's "void" or Not-Being with space. The suggested alternative (Sedley 1982) is that it is not space itself but an occupant of space: thus there is space (for which we have no name in Democritus's terminology) that may be occupied by either "the full" or "the empty," both of which may move around and change places with each other. But Aristotle, at least (*De generatione et corruptione* 1.8.325a30), interpreted the void as the locus of the movement of "beings" (i.e., atoms)—that is, as being identified with space rather than as an occupant of space. That is certainly what the void meant to Epicurean atomists in the following century, and it is likely that Democritus had the same view of it.

The attention of philosophers has in recent years been directed at Democritus's epistemology. It is obvious that a philosopher who claims that the basic constituents of the universe are imperceptible must provide a link between human experience and his proposed ontology. There are in fact many remarks in the ancient literature about Democritus on this subject, and quotations of his own words, but they are by no means clear or unambiguous. We may begin with the most famous quotation, given in somewhat different forms by Galen and Sextus: "By convention [*nomōi*], sweet; by convention, bitter; by convention, hot; by convention, cold; by convention, color; but in truth, atoms and void" (frg. 9, cf. frg. 125). The problem is to interpret the meaning of Democritus's "by convention." The contrast between *nomos* and *physis* (convention and nature) was familiar from the teaching of the Sophists: it is a contrast between rules of behavior that have been decided on by the agreement of human beings, and those that are inevitably imposed by natural conditions such as the limits of human strength and endurance. But that contrast hardly seems applicable in this case. People do not decide by agreement whether they are experiencing heat or cold, or red or green; what they may decide is whether the object itself has these qualities. The question, in other words, is one of ontology.

Sextus—a Skeptic himself—was able to find several other remarks by Democritus to reinforce his own position. Man is "separated from reality" (frg. 6); "in reality we know nothing about anything: belief is, for each of us, a reshaping" (frg. 7). "Of knowledge there are two forms, one legitimate, the other bastard; of the bastard breed are all these—sight, hearing, smell, taste, touch; the other is legitimate, but separate from these" (frg. 11).

But there are ample indications to show that Democritus was not in any strict sense a Skeptic; he was far from advocating the "suspension of belief" characteristic of later Skeptics. The text of Theophrastus's *De sensibus*— of which we fortunately have a long consecutive portion—shows that Democritus worked out a careful causal account of sense perception. The text gives details of the sizes and shapes of atoms that according to Democritus regularly produce this or that effect *(pathos)* in the perceiver. It is true that according to his theory we cannot directly perceive the elements of reality. But we can, he thought, work out the causal relations between the shapes and behavior of atoms of different shapes and sizes, and the sense impressions caused by their impact on the sense organs.

This is a simple-minded story, based on our large-scale sense experience. Democritus works with generalizations, such as that rough surfaces are unpleasant, smooth surfaces soothing. But it is notorious that people differ in their sense impressions of the same objects; according to Theophrastus, Democritus explains this by assuming that the objects themselves are made up of atoms differing widely in shape and size, and different observers are receptive of and respond to different shapes among the collection. He avoids saying that the same atomic shapes produce different results in different people: the causal link between atomic shape and the perceiver's *pathos* seems to be preserved intact.

But how did Democritus offer a causal account of our perception of objects at a distance? He constructed a theory of "images" (*eidōla* or *deikela*), made of atoms, that flow from the surfaces of all compound objects. They produce their effect on the perceiver by direct contact with the sense organs—hence, sight and hearing are in fact a kind of touching. Democritus is quoted by Aristotle (*De anima* 419a12) as saying that if the intervening space were empty, one might have an accurate view of an ant in the heavens. There are traces in the sources of a more complicated theory of sight, too, according to which a stream passes from the eye of the beholder, meets and interacts with the stream of images from the object to produce a revised image, which is then received by the eye. The former theory is worked out and recorded in much greater detail in the Epicurean texts, especially Lucretius, *De rerum natura* 4.

To sum up, Democritus was clear that only the properties of shape, size, and weight (and we should add motion) are properties that exist at the basic level of reality; we have no direct acquaintance, by sense perception or by any other means, with the atoms and void that are alone "real." But by making analogies between our experience of the properties of large-scale objects and our perception of them, we can infer what kinds of atoms are the causes of particular sensations in us. Our inferences about the nature and behavior of atoms are not fanciful and arbitrary.

It is striking that Aristotle often quotes Democritus for his observations in the field of biology, especially in embryology. True, he has no time for Democritus's notion that the soul, the essential feature of life, is made of spherical atoms, as fire is. The reason for Democritus's choice is that spherical atoms may be thought of as especially mobile, and thus able to transmit motion to the parts of the body almost instantaneously. Aristotle objects that this is much too simple: how could spherical soul-atoms also be responsible for the body's being at rest? A completely different set of concepts is needed, such as desire and intention. But he enters into debate on terms of equality with Democritus on many embryological problems, such as the contributions of the male and female parent to the embryo, the cause of monstrous births, the infertility of mules, and so on. There are also fairly extensive references to Democritus in Aelian's *Natural History*. The random citations do not enable us to put together any body of theory.

What is most paradoxical is that Aristotle never once mentions Democritus in any of his ethical writings, and yet the vast majority of the surviving quotations of Democritus's words are on subjects that might loosely be called moral. In the anthology of Stobaeus there are 130 maxims or sayings attributed to Democritus. A work called *The Golden Sayings of Democrates* turned up in a 17th-century manuscript, and since some of them overlap with the collection in Stobaeus, they have all from time to time been attributed to Democritus, with little authority.

Most of the fragments are of the character of *gnōmai*—that is to say, short, memorable, self-contained sayings, often phrased in the form of a balanced antithesis or a telling simile, presenting a bit of moral advice. A few examples will be enough to illustrate the genre: "Fine speech does not hide a bad act, a good act is not damaged by defaming speech" (frg. 177). "There is good sense in the young and nonsense in the old; for it's not time that teaches wisdom, but seasonable education and nature" (frg. 183). "Health is the object of men's prayers to the gods, but they don't realize they have power over it in themselves. They attack it with intemperance, and become traitors to their own health through lust" (frg. 236).

The gods play no very serious part in Democritus's philosophy, either in the field of cosmology or in morality. It is no part of his intention to dismiss altogether the popular idea of the gods. Our fullest source is Sextus (*Math.* 9.19), who tells us that Democritus spoke of great "images" *(eidōla)*, some well intentioned, some not, durable but not indestructible, which come to men and foretell the future. But the absence of textual evidence makes it impossible to attribute a worked-out theory to Democritus. Shortly after the passage just referred to, Sextus quotes Democritus as deriding the men of old who attributed thunder and lightning and eclipses to the gods. At least the negative side of his theology is clear: the gods are not the makers or manipulators of the physical world.

Much of the content of the moral fragments of Democritus is strongly reminiscent of Epicurus (and to some extent suspect for that reason). The goal is "good spirits" *(euthymiē)*. It comes to men, Stobaeus reports, "through temperate enjoyment and balance in life; deficiencies and excesses tend to change around and to bring about great commotions in the soul. And souls that are extensively moved are neither in good balance nor in good spirits" (frg. 191). There are other witnesses to the demand for moderation "both in private and in public" (frg. 3). Perhaps there is a hint here of an Epicurean reluctance to engage in public life. But unlike Epicurus, Democritus was ready to offer a spirited defense of democratic institutions: "Poverty in a democracy is as much to be preferred above what the powerful call 'happiness' as liberty is above slavery" (frg. 251). "It is from consensus *(homonoiē)* that great deeds, and wars, become possible for cities to undertake; without it, not" (frg. 250). The following has been called by Eric Havelock "the most remarkable single utterance of a political theorist of Hellas": "When those in power take it on themselves to be generous to the have-nots and to help them and to please them, then there is compassion and the end of isolation and the growth of comradeship and mutual defense, and agreement among the citizens, and other good things beyond anyone's capacity to count" (frg. 255).

Is there any connection between Democritus's morality and his physics? It is certain that his theory of the soul is in harmony with his moral views. We have no detailed account of the working of the Democritean soul, such as Lucretius (books 3 and 4) gives us in the case of Epicurus. But there are fragments that indicate the power of the soul over the body (it is to have such power that the soul is made of mobile, spherical atoms), and hence the priority of thought and intention over physical needs and longings. The goal of life is sometimes expressed in almost physical terms, as "balance" and the absence of violent motion. Moral education is described in remarkable words: "Nature and teaching are akin. For teaching re-forms a person, and by reforming, creates his nature" (frg. 33). It can hardly be doubted that *some* materialist theory of moral psychology lies behind such sayings, but it is hard to be more specific than that.

No one in the history of classical philosophy has been so badly treated by tradition than Democritus (unless indeed it is Leucippus). He covered many subjects, from embryology to music to mathematics, and we know hardly anything about what he wrote. He was ignored by one of the two greatest philosophers in the next generation and opposed by the other. His great physical theory was transmitted through the medium of Epicureanism, which was received with prejudice because its morality was conceived (wrongly, but in part excusably) to be nothing more than selfish hedonism. In the Roman period, Democritus offended the Stoics; in postclassical times, his ideas were anathema to the Christians.

Yet the atomic theory is a mighty achievement, and Democritus's name has deservedly remained famous. He constructed a system that was to become the greatest challenge to Aristotelianism. He showed how worlds might occur by accident in the infinite void, how matter might be corpuscular instead of continuous, how qualities might be derived from atoms that lacked all qualities but shape, size, and weight. In vain he struggled to defend the flat earth, but in the process he demonstrated the possibility of a unified theory of motion.

DAVID FURLEY

Bibliography

Texts and Translations

Diels, Hermann, and Walther Kranz. *Fragmente der Vorsokratiker*, vol. 2, 6th edition. Berlin, 1952. (Cited as DK.)

Luria, S. *Demokrit*. Leningrad, 1970.

Studies

Alfieri, V. E. *Atomos Idea*. Florence, 1953.

Bailey, Cyril. *The Greek Atomists and Epicurus*. Oxford, 1928; repr. New York, 1964.

Barnes, Jonathan. *The Presocratic Philosophers*, vol. 2. London, 1979.

Benakis, L. G., ed. *Proceedings of the First International Congress on Democritus*. Xanthe, Greece, 1984.

Cherniss, Harold F. *Aristotle's Criticism of Presocratic Philosophy*. Baltimore, 1935; repr. New York, 1964.

Cole, T. *Democritus and the Sources of Greek Anthropology*. Cleveland, 1967; repr. Atlanta, 1990.

Furley, David J. *Two Studies in the Greek Atomists*. Princeton, 1967.

Guthrie, W. K. C. *History of Greek Philosophy*, vol. 2. Cambridge, 1965.

Havelock, Eric A. *The Liberal Temper in Greek Politics*. London, 1957.

Langerbeck, Hermann. *Doxis Epirysmiē: Studien zu Demokrit's Ethik und Erkenntnislehre*. Berlin, 1935; repr. Zurich, 1967.

Lasswitz, Kurd. *Geschichte der Atomistik* (1890). Hildesheim, 1963.

Mau, J. *Zum Problem des Infinitesimalen bei den antiken Atomisten.* Berlin, 1954.

O'Brien, D. *Theories of Weight in the Ancient World,* vol. 1: *Democritus: Weight and Size.* Paris, 1968.

Sedley, David. "Two Conceptions of Vacuum." *Phronesis* 27 (1982): 175–193.

Vlastos, Gregory. "Ethics and Physics in Democritus." In *Studies in Presocratic Philosophy,* vol. 2. Ed. R. E. Allen and D. J. Furley. London, 1975.

EPICURUS

EPICURUS WAS BORN in 342/341 B.C.E. on the island of Samos, where his father, an Athenian colonist, had settled in 352. According to Diogenes Laertius in his *Life of Epicurus*, he asserted that he had been introduced to philosophy at the (not unusual) age of fourteen, apparently by a local Platonist called Pamphilus. If we are to believe Cicero, Epicurus, whose followers were afraid of nothing so much as that they should appear to have learned anything from somebody else (*De natura deorum* I.viii.18), later referred to Pamphilus in scornful terms. The claim to autonomy, confirmed by other accounts, probably targets not only those who taught Epicurus directly but also and especially Democritus, who was incontestably his principal source of philosophical inspiration. Rather than revealing a pathological trait, the self-portrait of Epicurus as self-taught shows an original—and perhaps healthy—awareness of the difficulty raised by attempts to trace a philosophical lineage: how can borrowing be measured, when the borrower completely changes the meaning of the material used?

The fact that Epicurus weighed the question of philosophical debt does not make it any easier to interpret certain details of his intellectual biography. Thus the question of whether or not he followed the teaching of Xenocrates (who had succeeded Speusippus as head of the Academy in 338), as he would surely have had the opportunity to do during the two years he spent in Athens on his military duty (323–321), depends on how one reads the denial reported by Cicero: had Epicurus spent time with Xenocrates without learning anything from him, or did he simply ignore him?

Forced by the outcome of the Lamian War to leave Samos when he returned from Athens, he settled with his father at Colophon, on the coast of Asia Minor, a little north of Samos. It is presumably at this time (rather than before his Athenian sojourn) that he studied at Teos (north of Colophon), with an unquestionably able philosopher, the Democritean Nausiphanes. We know almost nothing of the period that preceded the foundation of an independent school in 311/310, first at Mytilene (on the island of Lesbos) then at Lampsacus on the Hellespont. We may suppose that Epicurus devoted his time primarily to reading and to the enrichment of a philosophical culture that there are good internal and external reasons to think was extensive: among all the Presocratics, Anaxagoras and Archelaus (but not Democritus) seem to have been Epicurus's favorite authors; several aspects of his physics and ethics are much clearer if we grant that he knew not only Aristotle's exoteric works but also his technical works, particularly *Physics*. This last text is mentioned, along with *Analytics*, in a fragment of a letter preserved by Philodemus (*To [the friends of the school]*, frg. 111 [Angeli]).

During Epicurus's first years of teaching, the philosophical friendships were formed that would be associated with the later development of the school. Hermarchus, first successor to Epicurus as head of the Garden, was a native of Mytilene; Colotes, Idomeneus, Leonteus and his wife, Themista, Metrodorus and his renegade brother, Timocrates, Polyaenus, and Pythocles, all well known figures in the Epicurean circle, were from Lampsacus.

Sometime around 306 Epicurus decided to settle in Athens, where, with the restoration of democracy, the law of Sophocles of Sunium controlling the opening of philosophical schools had just been abolished. Alexandria notwithstanding, Athens remained the center of philosophical activity (Zeno arrived in Athens in 312/311, and he founded the Stoa there a few years later). For twenty-four minas Epicurus acquired a small property, probably in the northwest section of Athens, which quickly became well known as the Garden. The school was not simply an institution for study and teaching, or even for "symphilosophy" (the members of the school were fond of saying they "philosophized together"). It harbored a genuine living community, based on economic solidarity, intellectual exchange, and an ideal of friendship that the doctrine exalts—a community probably unequalled in the history of ancient philosophy (as a comparison with the Pythagorean school and Plotinus's circle would show). As has often been noted, the organization of the Garden resembles in more than one respect that of a religious sect: significant in this regard are the existence of neophytes and more advanced students (the hierarchy is reflected at the beginning of *Letter to Herodotus*, which is addressed to several types of recipients), the presence of "guides," the recourse to pedagogical and psychagogical techniques based on the repetition and memorization of texts, and above all the cult of Epicurus, celebrated at a fixed date according to the traditional forms of the rite, as was done for a divinity or a hero (a surprising but essential aspect of Epicureanism). If we add that the bonds with disciples and friends in Asia Minor were systematically maintained by correspondence (Epicurus also traveled back and forth on several occasions), we can understand how it has been possible—though not without forcing the comparison—to evoke the life and missionary proselytism of the first Christian communities in connection with the Garden. One can only be struck, in any case, by the role played in the Epicurean corpus by personal address, exhortation, and more generally the defense and illustration of the behavior of the school's members. The fact is that Epicurus's teaching, emphasizing the therapeutic ambitions that animate most ancient philosophies, unquestionably sought to be the bearer of salvation.

Epicurus managed to make an emblem of his death, in 271/270, as he had of his life. The famous *Letter to Idomeneus*, which seems to have been written in agony, tells us that Epicurus's end, marked by terrible suffering, was a happy one according to the criteria of hedonism properly understood, which he had made the foundation of his teaching.

Through an exceptional set of circumstances, we are better informed about the Epicurean philosophy than about any other Hellenistic school. Several original texts by Epicurus and by certain of his disciples have in fact survived, along with the usual doxographical résumés or polemical summaries, and other citations from lost works. To begin with, Diogenes Laertius, in the tenth book of his *Lives of Eminent Philosophers*, which is devoted entirely to Epicurus, quotes in full three letters of Epicurus (to Herodotus, Pythocles, and Menoeceus), each of which represents a major aspect of his philosophy (respectively, physics, the theory of atmospheric and celestial phenomena, and ethics), as well as a collection of forty fundamental propositions or "Principal Doctrines," which complement the *Letter to Menoeceus* on the subject of moral and social theory. Finally, the eruption of Vesuvius in 79 C.E. partly charred—but by the same token partly preserved—numerous papyri belonging to the library of the Epicurean Philodemus (from about 100 to sometime after 40 B.C.E.). Badly damaged and often difficult to read, they still give us access to a number of otherwise unknown treatises that are quite varied in nature (not only philosophical but also biographical and apologetic works). Thus we possess some fairly substantial fragments of Epicurus's major work, *On Nature*, in thirty-seven books, along with important works of the second generation of disciples, like the treatise *Against Those Who Irrationally Despise Popular Beliefs* by Polystratus (Hermarchus's successor as head of the Garden, ca. 250), as well as numerous writings by Philodemus himself, writings that doubtless reflect in large part the teaching of Zeno of Sidon, a leading scholar of the preceding generation (ca. 100). Finally, *De rerum natura*, or *On the Nature of Things*, a didactic epic in six books that Lucretius, a contemporary of Philodemus and Cicero, composed to glorify Epicurus for a Latin public, constitutes a precious and sometimes irreplaceable source of information (it presents, for example, the case for the famous doctrine of atomic "declination"). Still, the properly literary ambition that animates it sometimes makes its use for the purpose of systematic reconstruction rather tricky. To this list of direct sources we could add, for the record, a collection of maxims and excerpts found in 1888 (the *Vatican Collection*) and, more surprisingly, the portico that a certain Diogenes, in the 2nd century C.E. (ca. 125 according to Smith's dating), erected at Oenoanda in northern Lycia (in what is now Turkey), and on which he had engraved the aids to salvation, for the sake of passersby—that is, for humanity in general. This public monument is probably the best symbol of the persistent vitality of Epicureanism and the extraordinary strength of its influence when the school had long before disappeared (the last great scholar we know of is Patron, at the end of the 1st century B.C.E.).

Contrary to Platonic-Aristotelian contemplation, which is an end in itself, philosophical thought in Epicurus bears the stamp of instrumentality. The individual, immersed in bodily suffering and mental fears, finds in Epicurean thought the means to attain, once and for all, a security that members of the species have been seeking from the start—for a sense of danger, which is natural at first, is nurtured above all by the exercise of spontaneous, and erroneous, speculation as to the nature of the world and our own needs. Whence the well-known maxim, whose counterfactual formulation entails a certain degree of provocation (a characteristic feature of Epicurus's philosophical style): "If we were not troubled by our suspicions of the phenomena of the sky and about death, fearing that it concerns us, and also by our failure to grasp the limits of pains and desires, we should have no need of natural science" ("Principal Doctrines" XI [Oates, p. 37]). Philosophy is like one excrescence designed to eliminate another, to reestablish the only "limits" within which a happy life can be lived.

It has often been stressed that the subordination of knowledge to the search for security did little to foster the development of theoretical sciences, mathematics for example. But, paradoxically, it also led Epicurus to examine for itself, and more systematically than any philosophy had previously done, the question of the validity of our knowledge. *Canon* (a word that denotes, in Greek, the straightedge that enables us to ascertain the verticality of a wall) may not be the first full-fledged epistemological treatise in the history of philosophy (Nausiphanes, using a different metaphor, had written *Tripod*), but it seems to have contributed in a decisive manner to the formation of a technical vocabulary on the subject. Thus the term *criterion*, which was to become so important, is a key concept of Epicurean philosophy. Faced with the infinite number of false judgments and unfounded opinions that feed our fears, criteria are the only bases that allow us to orient ourselves securely.

The doxography distinguishes two criteria of knowledge: sensations and prolepses ("affections," the third term on the list, does not have any independent value; in this epistemological usage, it refers to the internal aspect of our perceptions). Both terms, and the pair they constitute, are difficult to interpret, though for different reasons. Concerning sensation, the problem stems from the very restrictive use Epicurus makes of the word. To be able to serve as criteria, sensations must *all* be "true." This affirmation, well attested in our sources, is at first surprising. Do not the senses in fact often deceive us? However, the formula "all sensations are true" does not mean that the things of this world are, in themselves, such as one perceives them. To quote the two best-known examples, the Erinyes Orestes sees (in Euripides' tragedy, for example) are not present in person, and the fact that a tower appears short and round to me does not mean that it is not actually tall and square (Lucretius, *De rerum natura* IV.353–363; Sextus Empiricus, *Against the Mathematicians* VII.203–210 and VII.63f; frgs. 247 and 253 [Usener]). Neither the presence of the Erinyes nor the circularity of the tower forms the content of the sensation, according to Epicurus. There are, rather, inferences, in this case illegitimate, on the basis of a piece of information that is in itself incontestable. Something has gotten through to Orestes from the external world, something that has the form of the Erinyes, or is rounded. But the Erinyes themselves may be far away, and the round form may not be that of the tower. For between the experience I undergo and the world of solid objects, there is an imperceptible process by which these objects affect me. The mysterious "conjoined movement" that, paralleling the movement of the sensation, is at the source of the error, according to the *Letter to Herodotus,* now comes into play: it reflects what might be called a presumption of immediacy. This presumption is responsible not only for the error of our first-order judgments, for example about the existence of the Erinyes or the shape of the tower, but also, on the level of theory, for the destructive opinion according to which certain sensations can be erroneous.

These two illusions can be corrected only by an appropriate analysis of the sensorial process. In other words, natural science enters very early into the canonic—so early, indeed, that we can understand why the Epicureans did not generally consider it an independent discipline. Every object in the world is an aggregate of atoms from which a dense and continual flow of pellicles emanates, extremely tenuous particles that Epicurus calls images (we can call them doubles or idols, if we want to preserve the technical character of the term), and that come to strike the organs of the senses. Now these images live a life of their own, and a sometimes risky one. Exposed to injury, they can cease to correspond to the properties of the object of which they are an emanation (this is the case of the square tower that appears round); having become autonomous, they continue to act independently of the emanating source (this is the case in Orestes' vision and, more generally, of our dreams and fantasies). This in no way detracts from the truth of the feeling they provoke, but it implies that we cannot incautiously draw conclusions about the world from our sensations, if by world we mean exclusively the set of "solid" aggregates, as opposed to the (fluid) images that also fill it, and that are no less objective (nor any less numerous) than those aggregates. The truth of sensations may well be infrangible, but it probably leads us less far than we might be tempted to suppose at first glance, and in any case it leads elsewhere.

The difficulties connected with the doctrine of prolepsis are of a different sort. Here, our understanding of the term, which cannot be guided by any familiar representation (this is one of Epicurus's numerous neologisms, suggesting the idea of a "preliminary grasp"), depends on heterogeneous sources, characterized by extreme concision. The problem arises from the fact that prolepsis seems to play two completely distinct roles. On the one hand, it gives access to types of objects, or types of concepts, that do not spring from sensation. Thus it is thanks to a prolepsis that we know the divinity to be an immortal and blessed being, and that justice stipulates what is useful in the area of community relations. Given the propositional form of these contents, and their abstract character, it is tempting to see prolepsis as knowledge of an analytical and conceptual type. Yet, beyond the fact that such an interpretation does not fit well with what we otherwise know of Epicurean empiricism, it does not explain why there are also prolepses of sensible objects, whether it is a question of their form (seeing a man, we recognize him as a man on the basis of the prolepsis we have of him) or of propositional predicates (we know proleptically that the body as body is endowed with mass and the property of "resistance," or again that man is a rational animal—cf. Philodemus, *On Signs* 34.7–11). Neither does it account for the fact that Epicurus rejects the idea of a prolepsis of time while he accepts a prolepsis of cause (*On Nature* 35.26 [Sedley 1983, p. 19]).

The solution must be linked to the fact that between sensations and prolepses there is a certain dissymmetry. Although proleptic knowledge covers a realm of objects that lies outside sensorial knowledge, it is in no way defined by it. What distinguishes it, rather, is the nature of the relation it maintains with objects whose provenance can be mental as well as perceptual. For in Epicurus, along with sense perception there is a "mental perception" (the images that penetrate the mind are simply more tenuous than those that make up the sensible flow). Only its absence from the initial list of criteria— an absence that certain disciples wanted to remedy by adding to the list "the representative focusing"—accounts for the fact that some have been tempted by an intellectualist interpretation of prolepsis. If, on the other hand, we make mental perceptions an independent category, the specificity of the proleptic function stands out more clearly. Unlike perceptions, the two forms of which—sense perceptions and mental perceptions—are after all confined to the present (even if, in the texts we are considering, only sensation is viewed as "without memory"), prolepses are empirical concepts, traces that accumulated experience has deposited in us, and that guide us, as well, in the recognition of perceptible objects (the senses for men, the mind for the gods) and in understanding, at a higher level of generality, of concepts of experience such as justice or cause. We consequently understand that prolepsis possesses a linguistic function (we speak most often of things we do not have before our eyes). Interpreters have rightly recognized a reference to the criterion of prolepsis, even though the term is not used, in the first rule set forth in *Letter to Herodotus*, "grasp the ideas attached to words" (Oates, p. 3). (It is significant, moreover, that prolepsis occurs even before sensations in the order of the argument: in a certain sense, the use of words constitutes an absolute precondition for inquiry into the nature of things.)

Beyond the kernels of certitude that the criteria define, there is the whole world of "obscure" things, a world that cannot be grasped except indirectly, and through reference to what possesses immediate clarity *(enargeia)*. It is no accident that the operation of referring the invisible to the visible, the un-known to the known, plays a central role in Epicurean philosophy: philosoph-ical activity consists essentially in "relating" what we say and think, as well as what others say or may have said, and which forms the cultural horizon of our convictions, to these pockets of ultimate certainty, to see whether, or to what extent, the prevailing assumptions can be upheld, or whether they are "empty" instead. This movement of perpetual confrontation, characteristic of Epicurus's writings and often even of his sentence structure (a "form of thought" might be identified here) explains how some interpreters have been able to see Epicurean philosophy as an essentially "critical" enterprise. The critique in question can take an aggressive turn, in the face of the scandal con-stituted—given what is at stake—by the distance between the positions we take and what would justify our taking them.

The realm of obscure things, including everything that falls neither under sense perception nor under intellectual perception and thus is not the correla-tive of a prolepsis, comprises two vast domains: the set of everything that is too far distant in space for us to apprehend it directly (atmospheric and celes-tial phenomena) and the set of everything that is too minute to be grasped by the senses and thus is not the object of a mental perception either (only ag-gregates give forth images, not atoms nor, of course, the void). These are the subjects covered, broadly speaking, in *Letter to Herodotus*, devoted to basic physics, and *Letter to Pythocles*, devoted to "meteorology" (in the sense of Aristotle's *Meteorologica*) and celestial physics. But there are few subjects that are not at first "obscure," and fewer still that are not made so by the very process of clarification, with the subsidiary questions the process necessarily raises. What falls outside the temporal limits of our life, for example (past history and what will come after our death), must be just as much the object of analogical reconstruction as what is remote and what is infinitesimal. The function of the psychic faculties, and even more the exercise of our freedom, must consequently be explainable on the basis of atomic physics. *Letter to Herodotus* briefly addresses certain of these themes (along with the proposi-tions of a basic physics, it includes the outlines of a psychology and a section devoted to the theory of civilization). Detailed analysis and the treatment of more complex questions (such as that of free choice) also appear in the treatise *On the Nature of Things* (of which *Letter to Herodotus* and *Letter to Pythocles* are partial "summaries") or are developed in other specialized treatises.

Philodemus's treatise *On Signs* sheds light on the mechanism and stakes of Epicurean inference, even if the terminology and the problematics are influ-enced by the debates of the 3rd and 2nd centuries. Arguing against the Stoic critics, Philodemus aims essentially to establish that the method called "by suppression" (*anaskeue*), by virtue of which we prove the existence of an in-visible entity (the void, for example) by showing that its suppression would entail a visible phenomenon (movement, in this case), is not a process independent of an "inference through likeness," to which it can always be reduced. The most interesting case of inference through likeness is plainly that which applies only mutatis mutandis—that is, analogy. For example, it is not because—by analogy with the sensible body, where the eye distinguishes a perceptual minimum—one posits the existence of parts on the body of the atom (the so-called *minima*) that the atomic body thereby becomes divisible, as is the perceptual body. Analogy thus often leads to paradoxical results: the world of atoms and the void obeys laws foreign to the world of composite forms, laws in which the eye and the mind cannot immediately find their bearings. Atoms, whose progress nothing can impede, move at a speed that defies the imagination; in infinite space, there is neither up nor down; and so on. Epicurean physics, the physics of likeness, is based first of all on the rejection of false likenesses.

This does not mean, of course, that the propositions it establishes can ever be incompatible with the criteria, and in particular with the data of the senses. In every case, and notably in the most paradoxical among them, assertions about the invisible, which by definition cannot be the object of any direct "confirmation" *(epimarturesis)*, must be able to pass the test of "noninvalidation," or *ouk antimarturesis*. Despite what certain formulas may suggest, noninvalidation seems to have been not a method of discovery but a simple means of control, guaranteeing that a proposition established on the basis of independent considerations is actually possible.

It is therefore essential to understand the nature of the procedure that guarantees the correct use of the analogical method by imposing necessary restrictions on our spontaneous manipulation of likenesses. In this regard, David Furley is right to cast aside the idea that the ultimate propositions of Epicurean physics rely on a purely conceptual type of analysis (that is how Bailey understood the "imaginative projection of thought"). The impossibility of conceiving of a given affirmation, which Epicurus often uses as an argument, is always ultimately based on a fundamental datum provided by experience. Still, the fact remains that, once established, one proposition can lead to the rejection of other ones that likeness would nevertheless seem to suggest. If the fact that atoms include parts does not make them composites, it is because the ultimate indivisible elements, in order to account for the visible world, must contain a series of properties that can be attributed only to a resistant mass, of which a "minimum" is deprived. At the same time, the indivisibility of the atom will be explained by a new property, "impassibility," which Democritus, who saw no difference between the atom and the minimum, could dispense with. Here it is very clear how a fundamental principle has precedence over a possible and, under the circumstances, erroneous application of the principle of likeness.

Thus the order in which the propositions of physics are established is important. This is why the "pedagogical" presentation of fundamental physics under the form of a whole made up of propositional "elements," or *stoicheia* (Diogenes Laertius, X.30), also corresponds to an internal necessity. It is remarkable, in any case, that the term *stoicheiōsis* (rudimentary introduction), destined to play an important role in the mathematical sciences as well as in philosophy, is attested for the first time in Epicurus.

Physical *stoicheiōsis* consists of ten propositions (nine, according to a different breakdown) that make up the infrangible framework of the discipline, and the frame of reference which, once established, can serve as a second-degree criterion. (1) Nothing is born out of what does not exist. (2) Nothing dissolves into what does not exist. (3) The universe has always been such as it now is and will always remain the same. (4) The universe is composed of bodies and space. (5) Bodies are of two sorts, atoms and composites of atoms (the aggregates). (6) The universe is infinite. (7) The atoms are infinite in number and space boundless in extension. (8) Atoms of identical form are infinite in number, but their differences in form are indefinite in number, and not infinite. (9) The atoms are in constant motion. (10) Atoms have but three properties in common with perceptible bodies: form, volume, and weight.

These statements deviate in several respects from the ancient atomism of Democritus: for example, Epicurus acknowledges that atoms are endowed not only with form and size but also with weight. Atomic forms cannot be infinite in number, or else they would need, in order to have infinite variety, to cross the threshold of the perceptible (according to testimony as famous as it is difficult to fathom, a Democritean atom can be the size of a world). Several of these modifications can be attributed to the intention to defend the atomic doctrine against the objections that Aristotle raised, specifically in Books IV and VI of *Physics*. But they must all be understood as an effect induced by the application of the canonic rules to a theory with regard to which Epicurus turns out to be the more critical the closer he stays to it. This is particularly the case for the atom's property of deviating minimally from its trajectory. Although neither *Letter to Herodotus* nor any other work that has been preserved makes any mention of this "declination," which is mentioned for the first time in Lucretius, it is very likely that the doctrine goes back to Epicurus himself *(clinamen)*. In its cosmogonic function, it explains the fact that a world can come into being in the infinite void: atoms, which can be represented by analogy with bodies falling in parallel through space, would never meet, since they move at equal speed, if at least one did not depart from its course (Lucretius, *De rerum natura* II.216–250). But the principal object of the doctrine must have been to account for voluntary movements and human freedom, although the way it fulfills this function remains open to discussion: the unforeseeable and arbitrary deviation of an atom on the microscopic level seems ill-suited to "explain" the phenomenon of the will, which is by definition governed by an end. The idea that Epicurus could have imagined a model

of "emergent properties" (David Sedley) is not borne out by the text of Book
XXXV of his *On Nature* (our principal source of information on the subject,
along with Lucretius). Finally, the purely analogical interpretation, which sees
in the atom's "freedom" with regard to mechanical determinations the equivalent of a voluntary movement of which it would certify only the possibility
or the nonimpossibility, does not entirely do justice to the explanatory dimension of the theory, which is strongly emphasized by Lucretius (II.286).

Elsewhere we can see more clearly how the Epicurean universe is entirely
reducible to the fundamental properties of atoms and the void. In infinite
space the relatively concentrated pockets of matter are released, protected by
an envelope beyond which we find the "interworlds," where the gods live in
tranquility (at least according to accounts subsequent to Epicurus's). Inside
the perishable worlds, aggregates are formed that are no less perishable. The
cohesion that makes them "solids" at the macroscopic level results from the
constant vibration of elements that, at the microscopic level, impede each
other inside a more or less dense network; their manifest velocity is likewise
only an effect, since in the interior of the aggregate, the atoms continue to
pass through the void "at the speed of thought." A violent pulsation, which
conceals the relative stability of bodies, is responsible for the emission of the
flow of "images." Finally, the three primary properties, which are for all bodies (elementary or composite) form, size, and weight (designated by the term
Aristotle uses for accident, *sumbebekota;* in Latin, *conjuncta*), account for
the infinite variety of properties and secondary "occurrences" (*sumptōmata;*
Latin *eventa*): colors and flavors, but also war and peace, which result from
their interaction and make up the world in which we live.

The status of the gods in this physics of composition and dissolution
naturally constitutes a challenge. Their existence and their indestructibility,
known proleptically, would require a special explanation that must have been
developed, but about which we have very little information beyond a few col-
umns in Philodemus's treatise *On the Gods:* we can just begin to glimpse how
the interworld space might guarantee, beyond the absence of perturbations,
the inextinguishable renewal of the divine body. Whether and how the images emitted by the body of the gods reach us is a thornier question. The
answer depends on the interpretation of a particularly difficult account by
Cicero, who suggests, at least in the reading of the manuscripts *(ad deos),* that
the gods could, in a certain way, be nothing but the product of an abundant
flow of images projected by man's thought (Long and Sedley). If such a conception seems at first glance compatible with the presuppositions of a reso-
lutely realist doctrine, we must emphasize that for Epicurus, the mind, at
first receptive, finally succeeds in exercising all but complete control over its
own productions. The idea that the god is our own product, in a sense that
would need to be specified, should therefore not be ruled out too quickly. It is
significant in any case that Epicurus's gods are anthropomorphic, and that

Epicurus could proclaim his own divinity and have it revered. The strangeness of the doctrine converges with the strangeness of the cultic practice.

Letter to Pythocles, like the letter addressed to Herodotus, shows how the canonic allows us to filter and remodel an earlier philosophical tradition. But the data here are different. Meteorological and celestial phenomena are in effect "hidden," though not in the same sense that the ultimate constituents of the world are hidden. First, we perceive these phenomena with our senses, although at a distance. Then, the "nearby" phenomena of which we have direct experience suggest a plurality of explanatory models for the distant ones. Now the canonic, according to Epicurus, makes it impossible to choose among the various explanations, for that would amount to rejecting, in a necessarily arbitrary manner, some of the information we get from the senses, information that by definition is also all true. The seriousness of such a transgression is shown by the fact that Epicurus does not hesitate to equate the adoption of one single explanation, while sensory data suggest a plurality of explanations, with the form of "myth," itself conceived as a source of terror. Whence the formulaic constructions that punctuate the letter: "It is possible that such a phenomenon occurs for *these reasons;* it is also possible that it happens for *these other reasons.*" Thunder, for example, will result either "from the [compression] of wind in the hollows of the clouds, as happens in vessels [of our bodies], or by the [rumblings] of fire [stirred up by the] wind, or by the rending and tearing of clouds, or by the friction and bursting of clouds when they have been congealed into a form like ice" (Oates, p. 23). The vocabulary of "possibility" notwithstanding, Epicurus is not suggesting that we should welcome all possible hypotheses without distinction or preference. The thesis is a stronger one—namely, that all the possible explanations are actually true (even if not simultaneously). We more easily grasp the significance and also the philosophical foundation of such an affirmation if we acknowledge that the infiniteness of matter and of time guarantees the realization of all possibilities (Lucretius, V.526–533).

Theories about meteorological and celestial phenomena thus present a striking contrast with the propositions of elementary physics, which have an absolute value, whether they belong to the initial *stoicheiōsis* or derive from it. We may wonder whether Epicurus is justified in exempting explanations governing the realm of distant phenomena from the principles of limitation and organization at work in the field of fundamental physics: why would certain hypotheses not exclude others here too, and why would certain apparent similarities not be discarded as erroneous opinions? After all, Epicurus thought he had enough information at his disposal to affirm that the real size of the sun and stars was, if not what it appears to us to be, at least not a great deal larger or smaller. Be that as it may, the picture of the world Epicurus presents to us is not one of a unified cosmic mechanism (the equivalent of physical *stoicheiōsis*) but of a dispersed multiplicity of independent phenomena.

Such epistemological naïveté, which claims to be in the service of an ethic of tranquillity, may sound the more embarrassing at a time when contemporary astronomy was making spectacular progress, thanks to the astronomic "investigation" that Epicurus dismissed so scornfully. One fascinating aspect of the doctrine of multiple causes must be emphasized, however. Readers have long been struck by the fact that the explanations offered in *Letter to Pythocles* for each of the phenomena studied often converge with the views of the Presocratic physicists. This is understandable, since those earlier views most often rely on analogy. We must add that Epicurus could find in his contemporary Theophrastus a fully developed theory of multiple causes in the field of meteorology. The relation between the two strains of thought remains to be studied, but it is clear that the relation of Epicurean meteorology to the philosophical tradition is no different from the relation that characterizes the field of elementary physics. Here and there, the doctrine looks like a reworking of opinions already advanced by others but renewed in their content or meaning by the requirements of a canonic that is Epicurus's alone.

Despite what *Letter to Pythocles* may suggest, and despite the attitude of Epicureans toward the sciences more generally, the subordination of physics to the practical side of philosophy is not the mark of any "lack of interest" in physics. On the contrary, it situates the nature of this interest, which is deep and necessary, in refusing to see in it anything but the expression of a fundamental need. This is why the part of the doctrine that defines the nature of this need in a reflective way is not less primary than the canonic. Commonly called ethics, it bears, in fact, though in another sense, on the "choices" and "refusals" that determine the course of our life. We thus understand why *Letter to Menoeceus*, setting forth the outlines of a doctrine of human action, takes the form of an invitation to philosophize, and why, in contrast to the two other letters, its treatment is deliberately exoteric. The opening of *Letter to Menoeceus*, even though it belongs to the tradition of Aristotle's *Protrepticus*, thus perfectly expresses the universal and, so to speak, catholic aspect of Epicurus's philosophy. "Let no one when young delay to study philosophy, nor when he is old grow weary of his study. For no one can come too early or too late to secure the health of his soul" (*Letter to Menoeceus* [Oates, p. 30]).

The content of the good life is circumscribed by four fundamental propositions (again called elements), famous from antiquity on as the "quadruple remedy" *(tetrapharmakon)*. They open both the collection of *Principal Doctrines* and the *Vatican Collection*. In a modified form, so far as the last two are concerned, they also provide the structure of *Letter to Menoeceus*. A full conception of (1) the nature of the gods, (2) death, (3) pleasure, and (4) suffering are the base for a "strong" life, sheltered from harm. The fact is that the three domains of theology, eschatology, and the affections encompass the sources of all our fears, and consequently define the space wherein a serene life can be attained. The certitude that the god, minimally defined as "the blessed and immortal nature," is "never constrained by anger or favour" (*Principal Doctrines* I [Oates, p. 35]) is the first condition of human felicity, for it suppresses the fears, as well as the vain hopes, that belief in their intervention would inspire. At the same time, the life of the anthropomorphic god supplies man with his paradigm, since it is only tranquillity carried to its highest point of perfection (thus the letter promises man that he can live "like a god among men"). The terror aroused by the thought of the beyond, which feeds the fables of mythology, vanishes if death, the simple dissolution of the perceptive aggregate, "is nothing to us" (*Principal Doctrines* II [Oates, p. 35]). But the suppression of terror is also the condition for a concentration on life itself (according to a fine oxymoron in *Letter to Menoeceus*, it "makes the mortality of life enjoyable" [p. 30]). Finally, without a clear awareness of the nature of pleasure and suffering—that is, of their "limits"—we would be incapable of leading our lives as they ought to be lived. The "affections" *(pathe)* in fact guide our choices and our refusals, and serve as ultimate criteria for action.

The Epicurean theory of action is based on the Aristotelian model, common to all the Hellenistic schools (with the notable exception of the Cyrenaics), according to which all our actions tend toward an ultimate end *(telos)* called happiness. The specificity of the theory, which is also the source of its difficulty, stems from the manner in which it determines the content of happiness. On the one hand, the end, which concerns both body and soul, depends on a complex relation in which each of the two terms can claim a certain priority. On the other hand, and more important, this end is defined in negative terms: when the body is not suffering and when the soul is not tormented, "all the tempest of the soul is dispersed, since the living creature has not to wander as though in search of something that is missing, and to look for some other thing by which he can fulfil the good of the soul and the good of the body" (*Letter to Menoeceus* [Oates, p. 31]). Because pleasure, corporal and psychical, is itself defined negatively as the absence of pain (in the body) or affliction (in the soul), Epicurus can maintain that "pleasure is the beginning and end of the blessed life" (ibid.) The beginning, because even before becoming the ultimate criterion for our choices and rejections it is what the living being seeks from its birth onward. The end, because the serenity that ataraxy procures (*ataraxy* is Epicurus's term for the absence of all psychical disturbance) is a particular form of pleasure—the greatest form conceivable.

While, on the one hand, this negative conception of pleasure shields the doctrine from the accusations of vulgar hedonism that it encountered from the outset (Epicurus was already answering such charges in *Letter to Menoeceus*), on the other hand it poses the problem—which is articulated perfectly in Cicero's critique in *De finibus*—of the relation between the ordinary sense of the term *pleasure* and its Epicurean redefinition. It is not certain that the gap between them can be entirely filled in, nor even that it should be: why would Epicurus not maintain that the common concepts of the nature of pleasure are erroneous, as in the case of the gods? Still, there is every reason to think that Epicurean pleasure is not a negative state. It is not enough to recall—even though this is an important element in our understanding—that the Epicurean doctrine stands out among classic conceptions of pleasure (Platonic or Cyrenaic) in that it does not admit a median state between pleasure and suffering. Although this model implies that the absence of suffering must, ipso facto, be identical with pleasure, it does not rule out the possibility that Epicurus may have simply rebaptized as "pleasure" what others had called the "median state." Now, the disappearance of suffering certainly leaves room for a state of positive contentment or satisfaction that Epicurus occasionally describes in terms of "health," or "well-being," or even "serenity." Whether or not the comparison goes back to Epicurus, Seneca succeeds in conveying what the dissipation of the tempest implies: not the dead calm that the Cyrenaics blamed Epicurus for setting up as an end, likening it to the state of a corpse, but the pure brilliancy of a sky cleared by the disappearance of all that darkened it (Seneca, Epistle 66.45).

Underlying the "negative" definition of pleasure is the distinction between pleasure "in movement" (or kinetic pleasure) and pleasure at rest (or catastematic pleasure). While the opposition may well owe something to the Aristotelian analysis of the nature of pleasure in Book X of *Nicomachean Ethics*, it is difficult, given the nature of our information, to arrive at a firm picture of the systematic relation between the two terms. Epicurus distinguishes between two phases of pleasure that correspond to two aspects that are connected in reality but distinct in theory; more technically, they are related to an important categorial difference. Pleasure is in fact measured quantitatively by the process leading to the suppression of lack, or catastematic pleasure. Beyond this it "varies" only qualitatively, without increasing. It seems clear that the existence of an ongoing qualitative variation, once catastematic pleasure has been secured, serves to show the duality inherent in the earlier phase of repletion, when the (quantitative) pleasure of the suppression of need is inextricably entangled with "kinetic," qualitative pleasure. We may admit that this lack of distinction is responsible for an illusion equivalent to the one that taints our sensory judgments, when we think that a delicate dish brings more pleasure than bread does: the error is categorial, inasmuch as the true measure of pleasure is the satisfaction of an "objective need." The methodical concentration on the quantity and state of pleasure, to the detriment of its "variety" and movement, explains the ascetic aspects of the Epicurean doctrine, which are well attested, and which had seduced the Stoic in Seneca.

Epicurus's hedonism, however, does not in principle exclude variation. In fact it does not operate in a binary system where the necessary, with which one ought to be satisfied, would simply be opposed to the nonnecessary, which one ought to reject. The model is tripartite, as we can see from the classification of desires: these are either "natural and necessary" or "natural and nonnecessary" or "not natural and not necessary" (this is "empty"). Only the third category, that of artificial desires deriving from opinion, should be rooted out. The status of the second category, on the other hand, is more complex. Since they are natural, desires cannot be blameworthy in themselves: delicate dishes do taste good, and sex is a source of pleasure. However, the consequences stemming from the abandonment of the sphere of necessity can turn out to be alienating and even destructive, in that they give rise to false needs, which will have less chance of always being able to be satisfied, or even of remaining "within our power," in that they will be more diversified and demanding (cf. *Vatican Collection* 51). "Variation" thus falls within the province of prudence *(phronesis)*, which *Letter to Menoeceus,* if we do not amend the text, identifies with philosophy itself. The fact remains that delicate Epicureanism, which Horace's carpe diem emblematically represents, is a possibility structurally inscribed in the doctrine. Contrary to what Epicurus himself suggests, it is not on the basis of a simple misunderstanding that the enemies of pleasure condemn its philosophy.

In Epicurus himself, warning nevertheless takes precedence over authorization, and abstinence unquestionably tends to be endowed with intrinsic value. The deliberate confinement to the sphere of necessity, which could be explained by the harshness of the times (the siege of Athens by Demetrius Poliorcetes in 294), is also the result of an intellectualism profoundly anchored in the ancient philosophical tradition going back to Socrates, a tradition to which Epicurus was heir no less than the Stoics.

Here we must explore the complex relationship that, beyond the parallelism marked by their common "negativity," links pleasures of the body with pleasures of the soul. On the one hand, Epicurus admits the "superiority" of the latter over the former. This superiority, which is of a quantitative nature, is due to the exclusive connection the soul maintains with time: while the body's affections are limited to the present, the soul, which embraces the past and the future, multiplies their intensity (the Cyrenaics, on the contrary, in insisting on the qualitative difference between actual affection and affection anticipated or remembered, maintained the superiority of corporal affections over psychical ones). Consequently we find a first shift from body to soul: false opinions on death and, within the limits of life, uncertainty about the future are infinitely harder to bear than any corporal pain. Conversely, the power of serenity is in proportion to anguish, more than to pain. But at the same time, the satisfaction of psychical pleasures always depends, in the last analysis, on the satisfaction of bodily pleasures. For the psychical pleasures always refer to the bodily pleasures as their final object: certainty about the future is first of all certainty about the possibility of always satisfying one's elementary needs. It is in this sense that not being hungry, thirsty, and cold, and expecting that this will remain the case in the future, allows one to "rival even Zeus in happiness" (*Vatican Collection* 33 [Oates, p. 41]).

Thus there is no question that psychical pleasures will ever substitute for corporal pleasures. Still, some of Epicurus's assertions unquestionably point in that direction, for example when he maintains that the wise man will be happy under torture. The last of the four remedies accounts for this paradox: "Pain does not last continuously in the flesh, but the acutest pain is there for a very short time, and even that which just exceeds the pleasure in the flesh does not continue for many days at once. But chronic illnesses permit a predominance of pleasure over pain in the flesh" (*Principal Doctrines* 4 [Oates, p. 35]). The idea is that, so long as life continues, the quantity of corporal pleasure, understood here as a factor of organic cohesion, prevails de facto over the destructive force of suffering, which gets the upper hand only at the very moment when it vanishes with the dissolution of the aggregate in death (whence the opening of *Letter to Idomeneus* mentioned above). This analysis of the quantitative relation between suffering and pleasure also accounts for the central role played by reflection in the Epicurean doctrine of pleasure: only the thought of the "limits" of pleasure and suffering is capable of transforming survival in the most miserable conditions into the equivalent of life, and even a happy life, to the point of abolishing the distinction, which remains true in principle, between the desires "necessary for happiness," those necessary "for the repose of the body," and those necessary "for very life" (*Letter to Menoeceus* [Oates, p. 31]). It is just as though, now, the ultimate source of pleasure were less the satisfaction of the body than reflection on the minimal conditions for such satisfaction. Put back in this perspective, the idea that it is "easy" to satisfy the needs of the body takes on a second sense, since the absence of bread can always be compensated by the certainty that pleasure still prevails over the suffering of the stomach. Thanks to the concept of limits, everything can always virtually step down a rung on the ladder of needs, and the modest pot of cheese can become the equivalent of the greatest luxuries. A number of Epicurean paradoxes that have been found shocking, like the idea that a premature death does not diminish the quantity of lived pleasure, are also explained by this: the soul is the organ of time, but it is also, by the force of the thought that it shelters, the instrument of time's abolition.

Given these conditions, we shall be less surprised that the idea of a "natural variation" plays an even more discreet role in the case of the pleasures of the soul than in that of the pleasures of the body. It is as if the psychical energy concentrated in thinking about limits had eliminated even the pleasure linked with other intellectual enjoyments. Still, one can understand that later Epicureans (such as Philodemus) could feel entitled by the logic of the system to rehabilitate music. Besides, Epicurus himself seems to have recognized the legitimacy of certain aesthetic pleasures: the wise man takes pleasure in spectacles, and even "more than the others."

The fact remains that the life outlined by Epicurus is dominated by an idea of autonomy that is capable of confining gratifications to their proper place. The essential point—and on this, too, Epicurus is close to the Stoics—is that we must be masters of our own lives and responsible for our actions. The most serious reproach Epicurus addresses to "the destiny of the physicists," by which he means chiefly, if not exclusively, the ancient atomism of Democritus, is that, in demolishing human freedom, it was unable to give meaning either to the practice of blame and praise—two fundamental aspects of social life too obvious to question—or to the use of argumentation, which presupposes that the opponent can change his mind. Whatever the challenge to atomism raised by the obligation to account for human liberty, it is clear that Epicurus had to take it on. Epicurean man is only very provisionally a receptive being subject to the flood of images. Through the exercise of thought, the memorization of principles, and work on his own character, he is capable of developing a capacity for selection, so that he can become master of what he sees as well as of what he decides.

It is not surprising, given the role it plays in physics and ethics, that the idea of security also dominates the final aspect of Epicurean doctrine, which is devoted to the theory of society and the relation of friendship. It has long been the standard view, undoubtedly sustained by the famous injunction to "live unknown" (to which Plutarch consecrated one of his three anti-Epicurean treatises) that Epicurus was not interested in problems of social organization. Still, the rejection of political ambition as well as renown—quintessential examples of "empty," destructive desires—is perfectly compatible with an analysis of the basis of human society and particularly of justice, which is well represented in the last ten *Principal Doctrines* as well as in a long fragment of Hermarchus (cited in Porphyry's treatise *On Abstinence* 1.7–12).

Although justice is defined as a "contract," Epicurus is not a conventionalist, because the content of such a contract, according to the prolepsis of justice, is objectively defined by "utility." This utility touches essentially on the preservation of life, at the expense of animals and other men, and it does not seem that Epicurus or his disciples sought to analyze the way it was translated into the multitude of arrangements that form the specific infrastructure of societies and political systems. The central aim of the theory seems to have been to show—once again, in opposition to a precipitous conclusion—that the variability of norms of justice does not constitute an argument against the objectivity of justice. On the contrary, it is because utility is always identical to itself "from a general point of view" that institutions resulting from the accord can vary in the function of circumstances and remain open to revision. The resultant distinction between justice and laws is not without originality in the context of Greek thought, strongly marked as that thought is by conventionalism: laws are just only to the extent that they are useful. From Hermarchus's fragment we can draw a second distinction that is not attested for Epicurus himself but that allows us to cast light on an important aspect of his social theory. Laws are formulated, in a perspective that is partly pedagogic and partly prophylactic, for the sake of those incapable of understanding the usefulness of their provisions on their own. A society of wise men would thus have no need for laws. We can understand better now how Epicurus could declare that "the laws exist for the sake of the wise, not that they may not do wrong, but that they may not suffer it" ("Fragments from Uncertain Sources" 81 [Oates, p. 51]), and that he recognized the existence of an organic bond between virtues and pleasure. In particular, contrary to what Cicero suggests in *De finibus* (II.51–59), the wise man has every reason, at least under normal circumstances, not to commit injustice, independently of threats that the laws bring to bear on him. Thus we see taking shape, within the very limits of society, the program for a community ruled by the imperatives of wisdom alone. Thanks to the inscription at Oenoanda, we know that later Epicureanism developed a genuine social utopia on this basis. In Epicurus himself, the idea takes the more limited form of a community of friends who represent, at the heart of an imperfect society ruled by the constraint of law, what would be the ideal for that society.

Given the importance attached to the practice of friendship in Epicurus's philosophy, it is paradoxical that the doctrine of friendship is also the doctrine (if we except declination) whose philosophical justification raises the most difficulties: how do I move from a utilitarian concept locating the end of my actions in the acquisition of pleasure that can only be my own to an "altruistic" perspective that accords as much value to my friend's pleasure as to mine (Cicero, *De finibus* I.68)? The problem, apparently, had already preoccupied certain disciples. Cicero mentions two solutions supported within the school: either that friendship properly so called develops progressively on the basis of an original interest that it surmounts at a certain point in its evolution, or that it is based on a form of contract. Without minimizing the philosophical difficulty of the position, we can acknowledge that if Epicurus's philosophy culminates, in a way, in a paradoxical doctrine of friendship, this is because the relation of friendship combines the fundamental features of Epicurean man and brings them to their point of greatest intensity: friendship is at once the site of the greatest dependency and that of the greatest certainty.

ANDRÉ LAKS
Translated by Rita Guerlac and Anne Slack

Bibliography

Texts and Translations

Arrighetti, Graziano, ed. *Epicuro: Opere*, 2nd ed. Turin: G. Einaudi, 1973. Includes papyrological fragments.

Bailey, Cyril, ed. *Epicurus: The Extant Remains*. Oxford: Clarendon Press, 1926; repr. New York: Hildesheim, 1975.

Gigante, Marcello, ed. *La scuola di Epicuro*. Naples: Istituto italiano per gli studi filosofici, 1978–.

Long, Anthony A., and David N. Sedley. *The Hellenistic Philosophers*. Cambridge: Cambridge University Press, 1987.

Oates, Whitney J., ed. "The Complete Extant Writings of Epicurus." Trans. Cyril Bailey. In *The Stoic and Epicurean Philosophers*. New York: Random House, 1940. Pp. 3–66.

Seneca. *Epistles*. Trans. Richard M. Gummere. Loeb Classical Library.

Smith, Martin F., ed. *Diogenes of Oenoanda: The Epicurean Inscription*. Naples: Bibliopolis, 1993. *La Scuola di Epicuro*, suppl. 1.

Usener, Hermann, ed. *Epicurea*. Leipzig: Teubner, 1887. Repr. 1966.

Studies

Alberti, Antonina. "The Epicurean Theory of Law and Justice." In *Justice and Generosity*, ed. André Laks and Malcolm Schofield. Cambridge: Cambridge University Press, 1995. Pp. 161–190.

Asmis, Elisabeth. *Epicurus' Scientific Method*. Ithaca, N.Y.: Cornell University Press, 1984.

Brunschwig, Jacques. "The Cradle Argument in Epicureanism and Stoicism." In *The Norms of Nature*, ed. Malcolm Schofield and Gisela Striker. Cambridge: Cambridge University Press, 1986.

Clay, Diskin. "The Cults of Epicurus." *Cronache Ercolanesi* 16 (1986): 11–28.

———. *Lucretius and Epicurus*. Ithaca, N.Y.: Cornell University Press, 1983.

Furley, David J. "Knowledge of Atoms and Void in Epicureanism." In *Cosmic Problems*. Cambridge: Cambridge University Press, 1989. Pp. 161–171.

———. *Two Studies in the Greek Atomists*. Princeton: Princeton University Press, 1967.

Glidden, David K. "Epicurean Prolepsis." *Oxford Studies in Ancient Philosophy* 3 (1985): 175–217.

Goldschmitt, Victor. *La doctrine d'Epicure et le droit*. Paris: Vrin, 1977.

Mitsis, Philip. *Epicurus' Ethical Theory: The Pleasures of Invulnerability*. Ithaca, N.Y.: Cornell University Press, 1988.

Schmid, Wolfgang. "Epikur." In *Reallexikon fur Antike und Christentum* 5 (1961): 681–819.

Sedley, David. "Epicurean Anti-Reductionism." In *Matter and Metaphysics*, ed. Jonathan Barnes and Mario Mignucci. Naples: Bibliopolis, 1988. Pp. 297–327.

———. "Epicurus' Refutation of Determinism." In *Suzetesis: Studi sull' epicurismo greco e romano offerti a Marcello Gigante*. 2 vols. Naples: G. Macchiaroli, 1983. Pp. 11–51.

————. *Lucretius and the Transformation of Greek Wisdom.* Cambridge: Cambridge University Press, 1998.

Striker, Gisela. "Kriterion tes aletheias." *Nachrichten der Akademie der Wissenschaften in Göttingen,* Philologische-historische Klasse (1974: 2): 47–120.

Van der Waerdt, Paul A. "The Justice of the Epicurean Wise Man." *Classical Quarterly* 37 (1987): 402–422.

EUCLID

Across the centuries and up to our own day, Euclid's name has endured in the minds of thinkers and scholars as synonymous with mathematics. What exactly was his work? What has been its place in the history of science for more than twenty centuries? What problems does it raise for scholars today, and what new research has sprung from it?

EUCLID AND HIS WORK

We know very little of the life of Euclid the mathematician—who must not be confused with his homonym, the philosopher of Megara. Only by cross-checking sources can we surmise his birth and death dates. It is fairly certain that these dates place him between the mathematicians who worked at the Academy after Plato's death and Archimedes' early scientific work. His institutional position provides us with more specific information. Euclid taught mathematics at Alexandria; he was probably drawn there, along with other scientists, by Ptolemy I Soter when the Museum was founded. It is safe to say that Euclid's scientific work was carried out during the first decades of the 3rd century B.C.E.

According to ancient sources, the Euclidean corpus comprised about ten titles relating to the "mathematical sciences" as that term was used by the Greeks (including, for example, astronomy and optics). Six of these works have come down to us; however, some important texts have been lost.

Pappus of Alexandria, for example, cites Euclid's four books on *Conics*, apparently an ordered presentation of everything that had been learned about the question since the discovery of these curves (parabolas, ellipses, hyperbolas) by Menaechmus and, later, the treatment of curves as conic sections by Aristaeus (*Pappi Alexandrini*, II.672.18–678.24). This is probably the work to which Archimedes refers on several occasions. Pappus provides the most likely explanation for the disappearance of this work when he states that Apollonius of Perge (latter half of the 3rd century) completed the four books of Euclid's *Conics* and added four others, to form his own famous eight-volume treatise of the same name.

The second important work that has been lost is *Porisms*, in three volumes, mentioned by Pappus and Proclus. Its subject matter is disputed. It appears to have been a work preparatory to a theory of geometric loci. Since this theory was developed for the most part during the Hellenistic period, we may infer that its very successes led to a loss of interest in Euclid's initial work. In 1860, Michel Chasles published an attempt to reconstruct the work, based on fragments found in Pappus.

A third treatise, *Surface Loci* in two books, is also cited by Pappus as being part of a *Treasury of Analysis,* but its purpose is also a matter of conjecture. Did it deal with surfaces treated as loci of certain characteristic lines, for example surfaces in rotation limiting certain solids? Archimedes did brilliant work on these bodies, which may explain why, once again, Euclid's work itself has not survived.

According to Proclus, the corpus also included a didactic treatise intended to teach students to avoid paralogisms, entitled *Pseudaria* (Fallacies).

Of the works that have survived, the most important, and the source of its author's age-old fame, are the thirteen books of *Elements.* However, in the field of plane geometry we should not overlook the extant collection of *Data,* which provides the elementary foundation for all analytical reasoning; this text shows what can be determined about a figure when certain information is given. We must also note the treatise *On Divisions (of Figures):* the Greek text is lost, but fragments have reached us via the Arab-Latin tradition; here figures are divided proportionately by lines subject to certain restrictions.

To this collection we must add three other texts that stand apart from geometry, strictly speaking. *Phaenomena* provides a description of what is visible in the celestial sphere in motion, in other words the rising and setting of the stars, not including planetary movements. Starting from the hypothesis of visual, rectilinear rays, *Optics* determines what is actually seen of a distant object, and its argument depends in reality on perspective. The *Sectio canonis* contains the arithmetic theory of musical intervals, in the spirit of Pythagorean tradition, and is perhaps only a fragment of the more complete *Elements of Music.* These three treatises are presented in the Euclidean form that governs *Elements.*

Besides these ten titles, others attributed to Euclid include several fragments of *Mechanics* (of dubious authenticity), a *Catoptrica* that is not genuine, and an *Introduction to Harmony* that is by Cleonides, a disciple of Aristoxenes.

ELEMENTS

The tradition of composing *Elements* extends back to Hippocrates of Chio (ca. 435); the texts were revised on several occasions by geometricians who were probably from the Academy. Euclid's edition seems to be the fifth, and while the four preceding versions have been forgotten, his had no successor—a clear indication of its success.

The *Elements* were not "elementary" works, not in the sense that their mathematical content had been simplified for beginners. According to Proclus's analysis, they contained necessary and sufficient propositions for the advancement of science beyond the results obtained, and they permitted further exploration of unsolved problems. They constituted the body of the central doctrine of mathematical sciences from which all the rest could be derived. Though they gave an accounting of acquired knowledge, they adhered to essentials and were not a demonstration of all extant mathematical knowledge to date. As theoretical works, they did not introduce the art of calculation, called "logistics"; they bore instead on the two fundamental mathematical sciences, arithmetic and geometry. The composition of *Elements* was thus a matter of complex choices: specialized questions were eliminated; both prolixity and excessive brevity were avoided; a general guideline for the deductive process was provided.

Elements developed during a period of major advances in Greek mathematics, between the time of Hippocrates of Chio and Euclid, and one might expect to find traces of that period in Euclid's text. The chronological order in which knowledge was acquired was not necessarily the order adopted by the treatise in its exposition. Thus there is a large historical question about the genesis of *Elements*.

Euclid's exposition is divided into propositions, each one demonstrated by means of the preceding one, and each being either a theorem or a problem, all of which are connected according to the order of a deductive synthesis. This approach presupposes certain initial statements serving as starting points, or principles. These form three groups. First, definitions of terms appear each time new objects are introduced. Second, certain statements that are true for all mathematical sciences, called common notions, deal with the properties of equality and inequality, and correspond to what Aristotle considered "judgments of reason" (axioms), indubitable by their very nature. Finally, for geometry alone, there are hypotheses formulated as "claims" (or postulates), especially concerning the possibility of using an "ideal" ruler or compass, and—most famous of all—the meeting of straight lines the sum of whose angles with a common secant is inferior to two right angles (the Fifth Postulate).

Several theories or subtheories are distributed, in a somewhat complicated order, among the thirteen books. Book I opens with the theory of plane figures, but beginning with proposition 35 and throughout Book II, the subject is a theory of equivalence in measurements for rectilinear areas, a theory of great importance because it allows for transformation of a given figure into a different, equivalent one. This leads most notably to the so-called Pythagorean theorem on right triangles, and the solution of the problem of the squaring of a rectangular figure. Then, in Book III, the theory of plane figures resumes with the study of the circle; in Book IV the subtheory of regular polygons results in the application of the knowledge acquired in Book II to that of Book III. This collection of results is applied to the case of solids in Book XI.

Up to this point, the author of *Elements* does not allow himself recourse to the idea of proportion among geometric magnitudes. This idea is a very general one, since it applies to any ratio between magnitudes, even if it cannot be expressed numerically. The theory is developed in Book V, a pivotal book in the organization of *Elements,* for it takes the reader to a further level of abstraction. Its first application to plane figures leads, in Book VI, to the subtheory of similar figures that allows one to find, in a generalized form, the results obtained in Books I and II by means of the equivalence of areas. One should note that, in this generalized form, the arguments involving ratios between the areas of polygons lead beyond *Elements* to the theory of conics. In addition, the theory of proportions opens the way to a sophisticated method for measuring areas and volumes that prefigures infinitesimal calculus by using progressive approximations of the magnitude to be estimated; known ever since the 17th century as the exhaustion method, it does not appear, in essence, until the beginning of Book X, and it comes into its own in Book XII. Archimedes made important advances in this area and provided brilliant applications.

Books VII, VIII, and IX contain Euclidean arithmetic, the theory of whole numbers and their ratios; proportions here constitute in effect a special case, and the notion of "continuous proportion" leads to the development of a subtheory of the powers of whole numbers.

When two magnitudes of the same type have a number-to-number ratio between them, they are mutually commensurable. The case of incommensurables thus remains to be examined in Book X, where incommensurable straight lines and the rectangles that they can form are classified.

The last three books are devoted to stereology, or solid geometry. Book XI lays the foundation by generalizing plane geometry for the third dimension. Book XII treats the measurement of circles, pyramids, cones, and spheres by applying the exhaustion method. Book XIII describes the construction of the five regular convex polyhedra in a given sphere; this argument presupposes in particular some results from Book X.

The text of *Elements* is remarkable in its form. Basically, each proposition is developed according to a precise and unchanging formal process consisting of six steps, the most important being the statement, the construction, the demonstration, and the conclusion; each step has a set function, either heuristic or logical.

Elements can be seen as a treatise on the measurement of geometric objects, using only straight lines and circumferences. This metric geometry is created without recourse to the notion of rational numbers, nor real numbers; without a clearly defined notion of "operation" (despite its use) and without recourse to an algebraic form of literal and operative symbolism. Finally, we should note that in no case did Euclid employ any processes that might suggest actual infinity.

THE HISTORY OF THE WORK

Since ancient times, as we can see from any number of the great works, Euclid's *Elements* has been the object of many commentaries. The work of Heron of Alexandria has been partially preserved in Arabic; it is shaped by Heron's desire to complete and perfect Euclid's treatise. The Neoplatonist logician Porphyry of Tyre seems to have been interested in the forms of Euclid's argumentation, the precision of his propositions, and the rigor of his proofs. The mathematician Pappus of Alexandria left an important contribution to the discussion that is known through an Arabic version as his *Commentary on Book X*. The Aristotelian Simplicius examined the principles, in particular—that is, the initial propositions—and his commentary became an introduction to geometry; excerpts have been preserved in Arabic. Finally, there remains in Greek, from the 5th century c.e., the very important *Commentary on Book I* by Proclus of Lycia, the diadochus (head of the Academy); treating all aspects of the text and its historical, logical, epistemological, and philosophical context, *Commentary* remains an irreplaceable document on the position of *Elements* in Greek science, the intentions of its author, the progress that culminated in *Elements*, the criticism it encountered, and the difficulties it contained.

Elements was the chief means of transmission of basic mathematical knowledge in Hellenic and Roman times. In the 4th century c.e., the mathematician Theon of Alexandria put out a new edition, somewhat enlarged for didactic purposes, from which all the known Greek manuscripts before the 19th century were derived. The tradition continued in the Byzantine empire. For example, in the year 888 Arethas, the archbishop of Caesarea, had *Elements* copied and annotated the text in his own hand: today this codex is in the Bodleian Library at Oxford. The Greek manuscripts, actually still quite numerous in Europe, contain a total of 1,440 scholia from various periods.

Before it was resurrected during the Renaissance, Euclid's work followed a different course in the countries that had been converted to Islam. From the very beginning of the 9th century, educated people in Baghdad knew the Greek text, and the caliphs encouraged its translation into Arabic. Two traditions appeared, one from the two successive editions of the first translation by Al-Haggag, the other stemming from a work of the second half of the 9th century by Ishaq ibn Hunayn and revised by Tabit ibn Qurra. Although these translations indicate an interest in the sources and in comparing manuscripts, they made no secret of their aim to improve on the text, either for didactic purposes or for logical and mathematical ones. Starting with these versions, an entire "Euclidean" literature developed, consisting of critical analyses, summaries, précis, emendations, and, finally, commentaries on *Elements*, as a whole or in part. From the 9th century to the 13th, the greatest mathematicians and philosophers of the Arab world studied Euclid, and principally concerned themselves with the question of parallels and the Fifth Postulate, with the theory of proportions in Book V, and with the theory of incommensurable lines in Book X. These debates were important for the development of mathematical thought in the Arab world, while the translations figured in the transmission of *Elements* to medieval Latinists in the West.

The early Middle Ages knew *Elements* only through collections containing altered fragments of a Latin translation probably done by Boethius. In the 12th century a Latin translation of a Greek text appeared in Sicily but apparently had little influence. However, a translation of a manuscript from the Ishaq-Tabit school is attributed to Gerard of Cremona, who was famous in Toledo in the 12th century; in the same period, Adelard of Bath is credited with three successive versions of *Elements:* a translation, a condensed commentary, and a complete collection in the tradition of Al-Haggag, of which some fifty manuscripts survive. This was the beginning of a tradition that lasted up to the 15th century with some fifteen revisions, including the translation by Campanus of Novare, appearing in 1259, the best Latin version of the Arabic from a mathematical point of view. So it is not true that people of the Middle Ages were ignorant of Greek mathematics; in the later centuries several versions of *Elements* were available. These presented some notable differences from the Greek, since they came through the Arabic tradition, but they nevertheless allowed for comparison and discussion. Medieval scholars were interested in logic and principles, in the problems of infinity, real or potential; and thus in the question of the divisibility of magnitudes and of geometric continuity. Philosophical preoccupations outweighed mathematical inventiveness. Afterward, as Latin continued for a long time to be the language of scholars, the practice of accompanying the Greek text with a Latin version continued until the beginning of the 20th century.

Since the invention of the printing press, there have been more editions and translations of Euclid's *Elements* than of any work except the Bible. The first printed edition of Euclid appeared in Venice in 1482: this was Campanus's Latin text, which brought the work into the modern age. It was soon followed in 1505, again in Venice, by the complete Euclid of Zamberti, this time a Latin version of the Greek text. Editors and scholars were divided about the merit of these two editions throughout the 16th century, even though the first printed edition of the Greek appeared in Basel in 1530; unfortunately, this edition was based on two of the poorest manuscripts. The quarrel continued until the appearance of Commandino's Latin version in 1572 in

Pesaro. This was the first one based on an acceptable Greek original, and it served as the basis for many later works.

Besides these key facts, the 16th century stands out for the great number of publications throughout Europe; these reflected various choices, but their common goal was to provide a working instrument adapted for students. The first vernacular translations also appeared at this time: for example, the one by Pierre Forcadel in French (1564–1566). Finally, in the 16th century a whole genre of commentaries emerged that often dealt with the logical structure of *Elements*, and also with the mathematical implications of the theory of proportions in Book V. The masterful work of Christopher Clavius fell within this genre; an extremely detailed Latin review that appeared in 1574, it was frequently reissued: rewriting, notes, additions, critiques, and explanations all combined to provide an instructive and stimulating mathematical approach to the Hellenistic legacy. There is every reason to believe that it was from Clavius's Euclid that Descartes first taught himself mathematics at the college of La Flèche.

The history of the Greek text was next punctuated by Gregory's edition at Oxford in 1703; by Peyrard's discovery of the Vatican manuscript, indicating a tradition that antedates the edition of Theon, and which allowed him to publish a trilingual edition (Greek, Latin, French) in 1814–1818; and, finally, by Heiberg's critical edition, which became the authoritative modern version (1883–1916). In addition, the tradition of publishing texts for teaching purposes—the commentaries and handbooks used in schools—persisted throughout the 17th and 18th centuries, and even into the 19th in some countries, for example in England. This is the source of the view of *Elements* as an elementary pedagogical text, even though the mathematical discussions it introduces are of the first rank. At the same time, Euclid was translated into every language of Europe, and the influence of his work extended to China and India.

ELEMENTS AND MODERN MATHEMATICAL THOUGHT

The development of modern mathematics has occurred not via a rejection of *Elements* but in a dialogue permitting a better elaboration of new concepts by integrating ancient knowledge destined to be surpassed. For example, in the 17th century mathematicians drew on every possible aspect of the theory of proportions and its key ideas, including infinitesimal geometrical analyses, before the discovery of the differential calculus algorithms; one could say the same of the exhaustion method, which works in conjunction with proportion before the introduction of integral calculus.

Between the time of Henry Savile, who studied implicit postulates in 1621, and the time of Girolamo Saccheri, who tried to prove the Fifth Postulate in

1733, the work of the best commentators, such as Isaac Barrow (1655), Robert Simson (1756), or John Playfair (1795), offered a host of indicators on the means of perfecting proofs. In England in particular, until the 19th century, *Elements* remained the basis for teaching and continued to spark productive critical work. Logicians such as Augustus De Morgan studied the text closely. That England should be the home of so many innovators in modern mathematical logic is perhaps owing to research into the laws of logic in standardized discourse in search of proof, the discourse of mathematics, of which *Elements* was still the classic example.

This work, moreover, was to have an impact on mathematics itself. In effect, the logical analysis of arguments progresses naturally to axioms. Since Descartes, the epistemological status that Aristotle had given axioms developed amid differences between philosophical doctrines. Instead of relying on self-evidence, Leibniz sought to derive axioms from the principle of noncontradiction. Moreover, since Pascal's day, the discussion of definitions of primary terms that Aristotle had initiated took a different course. The 19th century was characterized by more technical reflections, in which more adequate reformulations were sought. Correlatively, the distinctions between axiom and postulate, indeed between definition and postulate, began to be questioned. The discussions of the Fifth Postulate contributed substantially to this reconsideration. Launched anew by Saccheri, the attempts to prove the famous proposition ended with the appearance of some ten equivalent propositions, assumptions implied in the so-called new demonstrations. The result is well known: the failure of the attempts to prove via the absurd led to the appearance of diverse non-Euclidean geometries. The notion of mathematical theory and that of mathematical truth changed; the status of preliminary principles changed as well. Increasingly, the logical properties were brought out that should belong to any collection of propositions that could be called axiomatic.

At the very end of the 19th century, in 1899, David Hilbert brought modern axiomatics to Euclidean geometry, completing the developments begun a century earlier. Since the presentation of the mathematical content of the other theories figuring in *Elements* had been profoundly transformed by the generalization of the idea of "number" and the growth of analysis, it is clear that, by the end of the 19th century, the debate about Euclid's work and its fecundity for the development of science was over, and its place in history was definitively established.

What this work has contributed to the history of human thought is nothing less than one form of scientific rationalism. This is characterized by applying universally recognized rules in furnishing proof. The proof of the falsity of a proposition can be obtained in two ways, either because the facts refute it, or because it can be found to be in contradiction with propositions taken as true. In the first case, the furnishing of the proof is experimental, while in the second it is entirely logical—in other words, it is linked to the structure of the standardized discourse written in technical language that the Greeks called *logos*. *Elements* furnished the signal example of this second type, one adopted by all great mathematicians since antiquity. Such a mode of rationalism corresponding to what Aristotle described as "demonstrative science" demands not only that one define the objects on which knowledge rests, but also that one specify a small number of propositions initially taken as true in reference to the universe containing these objects and that one allow oneself certain manipulations of these objects (in geometry, "constructions") compatible with the structure of that universe. It is the function of the postulates to be hypotheses assuring the applicability of Euclidean mathematics in a world where physical bodies are invariable for the group of displacements (translations, rotations, or both). This choice assured it the privilege of appearing to be "natural" for hundreds of years, well into the 19th century. Moreover, concerning what measure of "truth" came from intuition of first principles, it was permissible for mathematicians to continue to reduce the role of intuition more and more, and this tendency toward ever-increasing abstraction was the main line of historical development in mathematics. This was perfectly compatible with the type of rationalism that *Elements* offered; thus *Elements* continued to be the ideal pursued even in periods when new methods focused attention on the proliferation of results obtained by the strength of calculus more than by the rigor of the demonstration. When, under the influence of non-Euclidean geometries, reference to "the natural world" ceased to be exclusive, we saw a change in the meaning of the initial hypotheses. Mathematical theories appeared as paradigms of possible worlds, divided between the demand of noncontradiction and the demand of constructibility. Although singularly refined, *Elements'* model of rationalism endured. In the 17th century, Giles de Roberval wrote a new *Elements of Geometry;* in the 20th, the Bourbaki group entitled its great work *Elements of Mathematics.*

ELEMENTS AND CONTEMPORARY RESEARCH IN THE HISTORY OF SCIENCE

Just when *Elements* had lost its power to inspire mathematicians, a new area of interest in it began to appear. Under the influence of philological scholarship and studies in the history of universal thought after the manner of Hegel and Renan, the ancient Greek world, its culture, and its thought were the focus of attention for all those who were searching for the roots of Western civilization. Greek reason engaged the mind. The history of science began to replace philosophy in the search for the birth process of these canons of rationality in Greek mathematics that people in every century had admired. The 20th century has been punctuated by works by the historians of Greek mathematics: Zeuthen, Tannery, Heath, Becker, Loria, Mugler, Abel Rey, Van der Waerden, to name only the principal authors in the first half of the century. Thanks to their works, a more accurate vision, a deeper comprehension, of the history of Greek science has been achieved. This historical enlightenment has modified the understanding of the text itself, some of whose details can be explained only by the intellectual and linguistic practices, modes of thought, and cultural features of the period. This historical interest was entirely lacking in the classical approach to *Elements*.

Contemporary research centers on a few principal themes, which can be only briefly stated. First of all, it involves reconstituting, so far as possible, the origin of *Elements*, the mathematical advances that preceded Euclid. This project raises the extremely complex problem of determining the role of the Pythagoreans, cited by Aristotle but burdened with the weight of later legends that call for intense scrutiny. In particular, one aspect of the reconstruction is the question of the antecedents of the theory of ratios: was this theory based in ancient times on the sophisticated definition that Euclid gave it, or on a calculation procedure known as Euclid's algorithm? Linked to this question of origins is the important problem of the influence that doctrines advanced by Plato or Aristotle to define "science," which at the time constituted what we would call the epistemology of mathematics, might have had on Euclid. Bearing on this problem is also the question of the deductive structure of the collection of *Elements:* to what extent was Euclid able to complete effectively and accurately the logical outline of a perfect deductive theory and an entirely coherent technical language?

If we turn to the history of the civilizations that preceded or followed that of the Greeks, we must take into account the recent challenge to a "classical" interpretation built up by early 20th-century historians, who saw a "geometric algebra" in certain Euclidean methods for transforming areas; this question also bears on the interpretation of the codes for calculation revealed by the cuneiform tablets of Mesopotamia, as well as on the history of mathematics in the Islamic countries. Another historical question, which has been studied surprisingly little, involves the way geometricians of the Hellenistic period used Euclidean techniques and methods. Finally, owing to the recent discovery of manuscripts, a new interest in medieval Latin versions of Euclid is emerging; this returns to the forefront the need for critical editions of the Arabic translations, which are still lacking. Euclid's *Elements* remain a locus for dynamic research; in this respect, the work's career is far from over.

Maurice Caveing
Translated by Elizabeth Rawlings and Jeannine Pucci

Bibliography

Texts and Translations

Busard, H. L. L. *The First Latin Translation of Euclid's Elements Commonly Ascribed to Adelard of Bath*. Toronto: Pontifical Institute of Medieval Studies, 1983.

————. *The Latin Translation of the Arabic Version of Euclid's Elements Commonly Ascribed to Gerard of Cremona*. Leyden: Brill, 1984.

Chasles, Michel. *Les trois livres de porismes d'Euclide rétablis*. Paris: Mallet-Bachelier, 1860.

Euclid. *Les eléments*. Ed. and trans. Bernard Vitrac. 3 vols. Paris: Presses Universitaires de France. Vol. 1: *Introduction générale*, by Maurice Caveing, and *Géométrie plane* (Books I–IV), 1990. Vol. 2: *Proportions, Similitude: Arithmétique* (Books V–IX), 1994. Vol. 3: *Grandeurs et Incommensurables* (Book X), 1998.

————. *The Thirteen Books of Euclid's Elements*. Ed. and trans. Thomas Little Heath. 3 vols. Cambridge: Cambridge University Press, 1908; 2nd ed. revised and supplemented, 1926; repr. New York: Dover, 1956.

Euclidis Elementa, post Heiberg ed. Evangelos Stamatis. 5 vols. Teubner: Leipzig, 1969–1977.

Euclidis Opera omnia, ed. Iohannes Ludovicus Heiberg and Henricus Menge. 8 vols. Teubner: Leipzig, 1883–1916.

Heron of Alexandria. *Anaritii in decem libros priores Elementorum Educlidis Commentarii*. Ed. M. Curtze (an. Nayrizi). Leipzig: Teubner, 1899.

Pappus of Alexandria. *Pappi Alexandrini collectionis quae supersunt*. Ed. Friedrich Hultsch. Berlin: Weidmann, 1876–1878; repr. Amsterdam: Hakkert, 1965.

————. *The Commentary of Pappus on Book X of Euclid's Elements*. Ed. G. Junge and W. Thomson. Cambridge, Mass.: Harvard University Press, 1930; repr. New York and London: Johnson Reprint Company, 1968.

Proclus: A Commentary on the First Book of Euclid's Elements. Trans. Glenn R. Morrow. Princeton: Princeton University Press, 1970.

Thomas, Ivor. *Selections Illustrating the History of Greek Mathematics*. Vol. 1: *From Thales to Euclid;* vol. 2: *From Aristarchus to Pappus of Alexandria*. Loeb Classical Library.

Studies

Caveing, Maurice. *La figure et le nombre: Recherches sur les premières mathémathiques des Grecs*. Lille: Presses Universitaires du Septentrion, 1997.

————. *L'irrationalité dans les mathématiques grecques jusqu'à Euclide*. Lille: Presses Universitaires du Septentrion, 1998.

Hilbert, David. *The Foundations of Geometry* (1899). Trans. E. J. Townsend. 2nd ed. La Salle, Ill.: Open Court, 1971.

Knorr, Wilbur Richard. *The Evolution of the Euclidean Elements*. Dordrecht and Boston: Reidel, 1975.

Michel, Paul-Henri. *De Pythagore à Euclide: Contribution à l'histoire des mathématiques préeuclidiennes*. Paris: Les Belles Lettres, 1950.

Mueller, Ian. *Philosophy of Mathematics and Deductive Structure in Euclid's Elements*. Cambridge, Mass.: MIT Press, 1981.

Mugler, Charles. *Dictionnaire historique de la terminologie géometrique des Grecs*. 2 vols. Paris: Klincksieck, 1958–1959.

Taisbak, Christian Marinus. *Division and "Logos," A Theory of Equivalent Couples and Sets of Integers Propounded by Euclid in the Arithmetical Books of the Elements*. Odense: Odense Universitetsforlag, 1971.

GALEN

As much a philosopher as a physician, Galen was viewed by his contemporaries as garrulous, brilliant, and intolerable. For us, the image of the physician has won out over that of the philosopher. Galen lives in history as an exceptional figure distinguished by a combination of great speculative power and passionate investigation of medical phenomena. His prolixity as a writer, too, explains the influence he has exerted throughout the centuries. Handed down through the Oriental world and later in the West, his vast work—of which the twenty volumes of the Kühn edition offer only a part—remained the basis of medical teaching until the beginning of the 18th century. This success was also the reason for the decline of Galen's influence. Because his work was tied to a science, it gradually fell out of fashion, and Galenism became synonymous with a way of thinking judged both dogmatic and sterile. It was only when it could be completely detached from science and restored to history that the Galenic corpus could finally be studied in its own right. From the hands of physicians it passed to those of historians and philologists at the beginning of the 19th century. Despite their efforts, however, Galen's thought is still not fully known. The reasons for this are the very large size of the corpus, the fact that access to it is still difficult, and the problem of mastering its complexity and scope. Moreover, a good number of his writings have disappeared, as have many of the works to which Galen refers. Others survive only in Arabic or in bad Latin, and in translations of translations. In the last analysis, we know the man better than his work.

As part of Galen's work is autobiographical, we have a good deal of information about his life and career. Born in 129 C.E. in the wealthy town of Pergamum, the gifted young man was educated under the attentive care of his father, Nicon, a learned architect. A taste for mathematics and rigorous demonstration, a thorough grounding in philosophy acquired without loss of intellectual freedom, and rigorous standards on the intellectual and moral planes remained associated, for Galen, with this revered and noble paternal figure. About his mother, however, Galen says only a few harsh words. When a dream suggested to Nicon that he should let his son pursue the path of medicine, he offered the young Galen a medical education at the hands of the best masters. After his initial training in Pergamum, Galen went to Smyrna, where he could hear Pelops and also the Platonist philosopher Albinos, then to Corinth, where he arrived too late to encounter the great anatomist Numisianus, and finally to Alexandria, a major center for the study of anatomy in particular; this was the only place one could study human skeletons. His study tour completed, he returned to Pergamum, where he became a physician to gladiators, a prestigious job for a young practitioner. He saved many, by his own account. But political troubles in 166 led him to leave his native city for Rome, the imperial capital, where he stayed initially for four years (162–166). This was an exciting period. Galen built up a high-level practice and devoted himself to intense anatomical research. Nevertheless, for a number of reasons, among which he mentions the fierce jealousy of his colleagues, he left the city for his homeland, stopping along the way at various places to gather medicinal material. Pharmacology remained one of his chief interests.

He had scarcely arrived home when he had to leave again, called back by the emperors Marcus Aurelius and Lucius Verus to join them at their winter camp in Aquileia, the base for their expeditions against the Marcomans. Nevertheless Galen, who had nothing to gain from cold military stations, obtained permission to remain at Rome with Commodus, the son of Marcus Aurelius. He spent eight years there, devoting his time to intense study and writing, before Emperor Marcus Aurelius returned. Galen remained in favor at court from then on. This period was clouded, though, by a huge fire in Rome in 191; it destroyed the house in which he had stored numerous unpublished manuscripts. Despite this blow Galen, already advanced in years, had the courage to begin several of his projects all over again. He went on to write important treatises, and seems to have lived and continued writing to an advanced age.

Galen's work undeniably represents a major achievement, owing to its encyclopedic nature. It is encyclopedic in the fields it covers—medicine, of which he had explored almost all the branches—as well as logic, philosophy, philology, and so on. It is comprehensive, too, in its pedagogical interest, pointing out in what order subjects should be taken up, from the beginning to the highest level. But it is a masterwork also because Galen saw himself as continuing the entire Hippocratic and Hellenistic medical tradition; he did not view himself as an innovator, a claim he detested. Such an attitude on his part implied that he took the history of doctrines into account. In this respect, Galen was often a historian or doxographer. Even when he truncates or distorts his adversaries' thought, or interprets them in a tendentious manner, we are indebted to him for transmitting crucial accounts of medical and philosophical history, Stoic in particular—accounts that, without him, would have disappeared.

A MEDICAL PHYSICS

To analyze the essence of Galen's doctrine, we may begin with what forms the basis of his "physics," the substance of which living creatures are made, according to him, and with what animates them. Galen's thought depends, to begin with, on a theory of the constitution of matter that is presented as a holdover from the ancients. It is on them, in particular on Hippocrates, that he bases his thesis of a continuous and noncorpuscular matter, made up of four fundamental elements *(stoicheia)*. By the term *element,* he explains, he does not mean an element in itself in an absolute form (fire), or a pure quality (warmth); he is referring to what is dominant in a particular body. It is this last form that interests medicine, which is concerned with living bodies. In these bodies, the elements, or qualities, always appear mixed *(krase)*, and in proportions that make up the uniqueness of individuals. Similarly, and in conformity with the Hippocratic tradition, Galen's humoral theory is based on four humors: yellow bile, black bile, phlegm, and water, each formed of a mixture of qualities. Although it will play no role except in pathology, this humoral theory will become one of the key elements in late Galenism.

Galen's theory of the constitution of matter allows him to explain phenomena relating to health and illness. It is in fact the nature of the mixture (or temperament) that determines the performance of bodily functions and their disorders. In a general way, the state of health, or the unimpeded performance of the functions of the body, depends on a good mixture *(eukrasia)* and the good proportion of qualities. Illness, on the contrary, is principally attributable to a bad mixture, a *dyskrasia.* Galen develops these notions, which he sees as essential for the vital processes and their disorders, in the two treatises that set forth the bases of this medicophilosophical physics, *On the Elements according to Hippocrates* and *On Temperaments.* He adds the Aristotelian notion of quality, active (warm) or passive (cold), in the tradition of physicians who attribute an important role to innate heat and to "breath" or *pneuma,* especially in the process of generation. Moreover, at the end of his long career, Galen continued to posit these notions as the foundation of a knowledge of nature that he considered absolutely necessary for any good doctor.

The second theoretical stage, in which medicine and philosophy are still allied, is that of the dynamic properties issuing from the mixtures of elements or humors. The notion of faculty *(dynamis)* is complemented by that of activity *(energeia)*, or function. Physiology as a whole depends on two types of faculties: those that preside over involuntary or "natural" functions, and those that rule over voluntary or "psychic" movements. The issue of the natural faculties raises the essential problem of finalism in nature. For Galen, the natural functions—which can ultimately be summed up under four headings: attraction, assimilation, retention, expulsion—are each attributed to an innate faculty required by nature and inscribed in bodies. For example, the attraction that allows the body to draw nourishment essential for its growth is an innate faculty. Here, Galen opposes any corpuscular or mechanistic vision, or any vision that is simply less goal-oriented than his own, one that would depict digestion, for example, as the result of a pulverizing of the elements, and filtering and urinary excretion as a purely mechanical process. On this point, he never stops taunting his favorite adversaries, the Alexandrian Erasistratus and especially Asclepiades (1st century B.C.E.).

The other faculties, the so-called psychic ones, also bring Galen into some of the basic arguments of his day: debates over the place of sensations and the role of the heart and brain. The problem touches on the question of the soul in its nature, its parts and their localizations. Galen adopts an unwavering position: he chooses not to take a stand on questions he deems unanswerable through physiological investigation and useless to medicine. Conversely, the concrete question of the hegemonic seat of the soul, responsible for sensation and movement, remains a fundamental issue for him. In this realm Galen, like Plato, locates the hegemonic soul and its activities in the brain, or rather in the psychic *pneuma*, which allows for their realization and which fills its ventricles (let us recall that the cavities of the brain are thought more important than its substance, during this period). The heart plays a secondary role: through the carotid arteries, it supplies the brain with the aeriferous blood that contributes to the formation of the psychic *pneuma*, the one that belongs to the higher functions. Whence the idea of ligating the arteries to see what damage is done.

Just how, then, are sensation and movement produced? The example of the electric ray, which transmits a shock to the fisherman through an iron-tipped harpoon, is an example of a "qualitative transmission" from the brain to the muscles via the nerves. The hypothesis of the transmission of *pneuma* through the nerve canal, adopted by other physicians, applies for Galen only to the optic nerve, the only one that appears to be hollow. In his treatise *On the Doctrines of Hippocrates and Plato*, in which he does his best to show that Plato and Hippocrates are in agreement on the soul, he sharply attacks the belief of Chrysippus the Stoic, who saw the heart as the seat of the *hegemonikon*, especially in its function as producer of the voice and of discourse. Galen shows that, on the contrary, the voice is tightly linked to respiration and that respiration is achieved by muscles moved by the nerves themselves, under the direction of the brain. In the course of his ongoing arguments with his adversaries, Galen used his favorite tactics: he liked to point out the way an author contradicted himself (Chrysippus on the soul) or the way he habitually "denied the evidence." For Galen, failing to acknowledge what is self-evident means falling into error or skepticism.

ANATOMY AND PHENOMENA

The importance attributed to visible facts, or "phenomena," explains the preeminent role of anatomical knowledge for Galen. Here again he sees himself as his masters' heir, continuing the work of Hippocrates. Against all reason, he even goes so far as to consider Hippocratic anatomy an infallible source of truth—all the while claiming credit for himself, to be sure, for some important discoveries, such as his famous recurrent laryngeal nerve.

Anatomical knowledge overall has, for Galen, several goals. It is indispensable for practice, whether that involves surgery or a simple bleeding; it is necessary for physiological knowledge; and finally, it offers access to the understanding of nature in general, and to natural philosophy. These various levels of interest are reflected in specific works. At the beginning of his career Galen wrote short works for strictly pragmatic purposes, such as a treatise for midwives on the anatomy of the uterus and several treatises intended for beginners. These useful studies of anatomy are designed to prevent physicians from making serious mistakes not only in their actions but also in their diagnoses. In this regard, Galen defends the theory of "affected spots" in pathology, a theory that attributes local causes to many ailments, and that therefore requires sound anatomical knowledge. Whether it remains situated in a precise spot or affects other structures through "sympathy," the ailment will be the more curable if its place of origin is treated. This brought Galen many therapeutic successes: for example, he cured a man with paralyzed fingers by working on the spinal column and not—as did his more ignorant colleagues—on the fingers themselves.

Aside from its practical value, Galen saw anatomy as the chief means of access to an understanding of physiological processes. Nevertheless, the step from structures to functions remains tricky. Not everything is as simple as demonstrating that the hand is perfectly adapted for grasping. In any case, Galen discarded the oversimplistic principle of "anatomical deduction," that is, the direct deduction of function from form, and he also rejected the topological argument that draws on the organ's position in the body. Moreover, he took advantage of the opportunity to attack the "anatomical indolence" of the Stoics once again. Nevertheless, in his writings the form and the other characteristics of organs (texture, density, composition, relations, and so on) are inseparable from their functions, because they have been perfectly adapted to them by a provident Nature. And an understanding of functions, even the most complex, such as respiration or digestion, will in turn permit an advance in the understanding of particular structures. Thus it is clear that Galen refers to anatomy at every turn. We find in anatomy the most visible sign of Nature's providence, Nature having chosen the best possible forms and dispositions for the accomplishment of the functions in question. The great treatise in fourteen books *On the Use of Parts* spells out this functional and providential anatomy for each part of the body.

The principal means of acquiring anatomical knowledge is dissection. Galen devoted a magisterial work, *Anatomical Procedures*, to animal dissection—the only kind he envisaged and practiced. This treatise also contains an account of practical experiments on animals or, better, "still living" animals—swine, monkeys, and other animals whose suffering did not trouble him inordinately. Galen's most famous experiments, which go back to much of his teachers' repertory, concern the neurological and vascular system: compressions of the cerebral ventricles, serial section of the spinal nerves, experiments on thoracic nerves and muscles responsible for respiration and the voice, ligatures or sections of vessels such as the carotid artery and an experiment with a tube in the femoral artery, and many experiments performed in embryology. These are all aimed at proving the existence of phenomena that are not directly accessible to the senses: the responsibility of the brain and not the heart for movement and sensation, the production and function of the pulse, and so forth. The strength of his experiments, for Galen, lies precisely in their demonstrative power. As a matter of fact, he performed many of these experiments in public sessions during his first stay in Rome, playing on the curiosity and surprise of the spectators.

The understanding of complex phenomena, such as those having to do with major bodily functions, implies not only observation but also other means that are theoretical in nature. Galen refers to a variety of concepts, and especially to the Aristotelian type of causality (the Stoic causal system turns out to be useful to him in pathology). He also resorts to many other notions, such as balance, proportion, and exchange, or "sympathy." The more difficult the function is to understand—for example, the exchange between blood and *pneuma* through the pulmonary vessels—the stronger the presence of these models becomes. They sometimes lead Galen to go beyond observation, as when, from the pores visible on the lining separating the two cardiac ventricles (interventricular septum), he infers the existence of passages allowing the blood to pass directly from the right ventricle to the left. Later acknowledged as an intangible truth, this "error" was hard to refute because it was linked to a coherent explanatory system and to the implacable principle that Nature does nothing in vain. This explains the minimal importance Galen gave to quantitative measures. In this regard, scholars have long been intrigued that Galen "missed" the circulation of the blood when he had all the elements necessary to understand it. The only real example of quantitative measurement was the production of urine, which was measured and compared to the quantity of liquid ingested, a model in which Owsei Temkin saw a possible source of inspiration for Harvey. Actually, Galen had no need to know objective quantities, since his system was based on a balance of exchanges that he judged satisfactory. And he attached much more importance to the demonstrative method.

THE THEORY OF DEMONSTRATION

Even if Galen uses many ad hoc arguments whenever the need arises, he gives his developments a character that is at least formally rigorous, so persuaded is he that the discovery of truth comes through sound methodical reasoning. A major treatise entitled *On Demonstration*, which has disappeared, attested to the importance Galen attributed to the art of logical demonstration. He sought to provide an accesssible explanation of it for specialists as well as a broader public, including the medical profession in particular. For Galen, as for Aristotle, the basis of knowledge rests on principles *(archai)* that are facts or axioms recognized by everyone and accessible through evidence. From that starting point, truth lies in deducing, from general but more specific statements, "theorems," which can comprise empirical or practical elements. Logical operations also call for definitions and divisions. The question of definition and nomination holds little interest for Galen. He says he cares nothing for designations, so long as they are clear and understood by everyone, and that what is interesting is the esssence of the "thing." And nothing irritates him more than sterile discussions with the "sophists" or "logickers" he often meets on his way. Of his abundant logical work, nothing remains but *Logical Education*, a manual of elementary teaching. In this field Galen is particularly exacting in the choice of propositions. Among the classes of premises discussed in his treatise *On the Doctrines of Hippocrates and Plato*, he follows Aristotle in considering scientific premises the only acceptable ones. And on that point he once again vents his dislike of the Stoics, who use the most common phenomena, gestures, and ordinary expressions in their deductions. Galen's competence extends to other areas such as language and the various forms of error in expression: he devotes an entire work to linguistic ambiguity. A preoccupation with logic, in the larger sense, pervades all of Galenic medicine. And he uses this competence as a criterion of excellence and a "war horse" against his adversaries, whether they are ignorant, like the Stoics, or negligent, like the Empiricists.

THE THERAPEUTIC AND PHARMACOLOGICAL METHOD

Pathology and therapeutics offer more propitious terrain than physiological knowledge for observing Galen's stance between speculation and empiricism. He makes an initial choice, which is not to follow the Empiricists, who refuse to know or even to name maladies, on the pretext that to do so is of no use. Second, he rejects any theoretical element that might have an explanatory function, and he even renounces any inductive or deductive procedure linked to theoretical notions. A first sign of this attitude is that Galen sees pathology as the opposite of physiology and considers it necessary to know the latter to understand any pathological issue. Next, he applies logical procedures to pathology as he has done for physiology: definitions and divisions like those of genus and species and the proper use of differences are indispensable instruments for the physician in this area as well. Thus pathology is anchored in theory, as the method of healing will be.

Speculation alone can grasp causes. As a matter of fact, for Galen, all pathology comes down to two generic causes, breaks in continuity and *dyskrasiai*. Ruptures are wounds or ailments, such as ulcers that destroy the skin. *Dyskrasiai* are an excessive predominance of one of the four qualities in the tissues or homoiomerous bodies, or in the *pneuma* or innate heat. The result is damage to the functions, which only work thanks to a good *eukrasia* of the body and its parts. This is why Galen defines pathology in general as damage occurring to a specific function (vision, stride, digestion) or to the whole body. The same explanation holds good for the soul and certain of its ailments. In his treatise *That the Habits of the Mind Follow the Temperaments of the Body*, certain psychological disorders, like delirium and melancholy, are attributed to a poor bodily temperament.

Therapeutics, for Galen, is directly derived from this principle: an illness gives the "instructions" for its own treatment. In its generality, these instructions are of a logical nature, like the reasoning one follows to establish that a person who suffers from a rupture will be cured by the renewal of continuity. Nevertheless this "theorem" must be completed by others to lead to particular therapeutic acts. For example, to treat an open wound, rules must be considered for the replacement of flesh, that is, the mechanism of its formation, its duration, the supplementary effects (formation of residues that make the wound damp and unclean), the age and constitution of the patient, and so on. The same approach is to be followed in the case of defective "diathesis." The choice of treatment, its strength and duration, is then a function of many specific considerations drawn from the general principle. This constitutes the "therapeutic method," a logical approach radically distinct from that of the medical empiricists. But it is clear that, in actual practice, experience is of prime importance for Galen.

This is particularly the case in pharmacology. Knowledge of the actual effects of a medicine on the patient seems to Galen still more important than knowledge of the nature of the medicine itself. In extreme cases, pharmacology can dispense with theory, especially when compound medicines are involved. All the same, the pharmacologist should not ignore the test results, whether he does the testing himself or profits by others' experience. Galen did a number of experiments on himself, such as burning his skin in several places to find the best remedy for burns. As for experiments with dangerous products, it was safer for him, he admits, to have them tried by some country doctor, on sturdy peasants. A respected doctor should take certain precautions. Whenever he could, Galen went off to gather vegetal, mineral, or organic substances with local uses or those handed down by the pharmacological tradition. Thus he built up huge reserves of substances of superior quality, in which he took pride. His pharmacological works are full of picturesque accounts: how he found a given medication by chance or used certain others, such as animal or human excrements he recognized as having remarkable efficacy. But he expresses with horror his revulsion for the use of "vile and shameful" substances, especially if they are dangerous, of which he found many examples in the pharmacological tradition. In this field we inevitably touch on the outer frontiers of science. Local beliefs, true or mythic accounts, symbolic materials, social distinctions are all part of this body of knowledge. And the dividing line between what is rational and what is irrational, despite all Galen's efforts, is not always easy to perceive. Nevertheless, pharmacology was the principal route by which the name of Galen spread throughout the Occident.

ETHICS AND RELIGION

Being a good doctor depends on paying close attention to things and ideas. But for Galen, the ideal also explicitly entails a moral dimension. When he states that *A Good Doctor Must Also Be a Philosopher* (the title of one of his treatises), he is indeed using the term in the moral sense. In the first place, rigorous training of thought and work give the practitioner a general aptitude to distinguish what is true from what is false. The excesses and lies of the "sophists" are detected by authentic learning. The trained physician thus avoids wasting his time, avoids talking nonsense, and can concentrate on his art. Better still, study itself strengthens him against corruption. The asceticism it imposes is incompatible, for Galen, with the striving for wealth and patronage that characterize his contemporaries. Conventional as this type of social diatribe against the luxurious life in Rome may be, we cannot discount the strong connections that Galen established between education, practice, and virtue. Constant practice is the surest guarantee of an upright life devoted to learning and virtue.

Nor is Galen's medicine detached from all religiosity. For him, as for the Hippocratic doctors, science goes hand in hand with piety. It does not exclude the intervention of the gods in cases where, for example, the doctor is helpless before the severity of the disease. Among the gods, Galen feels a particular devotion to Asclepius. He believes in his revelations during dreams, even when they conflict with his scientific activity. Thus Galen accepts certain medical prescriptions that come to him through dreams, such as performing a bloodletting through an artery in the hand. In his experience, the god generally approves or confirms rational medicine, or informs it, conferring on it a supplementary supernatural element. Moreover Galen acknowledges that temple medicine constitutes a specific form of medicine. He expresses neither skepticism nor irony with regard to it, as certain doctors of his time seem to have done, such as his contemporary Aelius Aristides. He remains halfway between the skeptics and the devout.

Galen manifests a more intellectual veneration for the divine power that sometimes he calls the Demiurge, sometimes Nature, the source of a very strongly teleological representation of nature. Galen's Demiurge, who in certain ways very much resembles Plato's in *Timaeus*, willed that the entire body, like its parts, should have the best possible predisposition. But this teleology is not without restrictions or hierarchy, and Galen explicitly opposes the conception, which he attributes to Jews and Christians, of an all-powerful divinity capable of extracting anything from nothing, while his god takes into account natural constraints such as the separation of species or the existence of organic materials. Nevertheless, the action of Nature retains a certain mystery for him, as he acknowledges in particular, concerning the process of generation, in his treatise *On the Formation of Fetuses*; in his intellectual testament *On My Own Opinions*, Galen himself acknowledges that in this field he sometimes has no answers.

GALEN THEN AND NOW

Galen was much concerned with the transmission of medical knowledge. He annotated Hippocrates copiously, and worked to ensure the future of his own work. In this transmission, the role of the second school of Alexandria (4th to 6th century C.E.) was of prime importance; it made possible the diffusion of this work among scholars who came to study in Alexandria from all parts of the empire. Translated into Syriac, then into Arabic, Galen's work never ceased to be taught and studied in the course of the brilliant centuries of Arab domination in Baghdad and Ispahan, by scholars such as Rhazes, Haly Abbas (al-Magusi), or Avicenna, and in Muslim Spain. In Córdoba, Averroës played a critical role in the transmission of Galen's work; his own work, translated into Latin, was to exercise a lasting influence. Even after the Christian reconquest, the city of Toledo continued to be a great center of teaching, manuscript copying, and translation. In the Latin Occident the tradition had been weak in antiquity and had been passed on through bad translations. But Galen resurfaced in the Middle Ages, owing to new translations made from the Arabic by such scholars as Constantine the African at Monte Cassino in the 11th century, or Gerard of Cremona at Toledo in the following century. Along with the works of Arab doctors, Galen's works made a definitive entrance into the curriculum of medieval universities. In the Renaissance, the rise of Hellenism meant a new departure for the history of the Galenic corpus, marked by the *princeps* edition of the Greek text of his complete works. The Aldine edition of 1525, the result of considerable work by humanists, was greeted by contemporaries with indescribable enthusiasm as a return to the pure sources of antique knowledge, and as a means of liberation from a barbarous period for thought. New Latin translations, made directly from the

Greek, were to result in a diffusion of Galen's work in various European countries. Thus his work became known by great scholars such as Vesalius and Harvey, who were nourished by this rediscovery before they brought their own decisive renewal to medicine.

Modern interest in Galen is marked, on the contrary, by the retreat of the medical perspective, if not its disappearance. Even if medical doctors like Charles Daremberg, in the 19th century, were interested in Galen for apparently practical purposes, as Littré was in Hippocrates, the enterprise ceased to have the slightest practical value. Approaches to Galen were nevertheless not uniform; they varied according to national traditions in the history of medicine, philology, and science. Until the middle of the 20th century, the principal studies of Galen's work were undertaken in the fields of anatomy and physiology (notably on the question of pulmonary circulation). But within the past twenty years, a renewal of Galenic studies has led to a rediscovery of this great figure. Preoccupied at first with shedding light on the least known aspects of Galen's work, such as its clinical, epistemological, and religious aspects, recent research has concentrated on two principal fields: Galen's historical environment and his philosophy. Placing Galen back in his own time, the better to know his life, his contemporaries, the position of medicine, and the medical customs of the period, among other things, helps draw him out of his splendid isolation and helps integrate him better into the society and the cultural milieu of the Second Sophistics, and the very diverse practices of his era. Studies on Galen's epistemology and various other aspects of his philosophy not only help reveal in a precise manner the importance of this aspect of his work, but also help counter the image of his eclecticism or, worse, of his philosophical syncretism, that had prevailed earlier. Whether causality, logic, empiricism, or doxography is at issue, we discover what Galen, and thereby also medicine, contributed to ancient thought. This revised view has the additional effect of giving new meaning to certain notions, including eclecticism; it invites speculation about the transmission of Plato or Aristotle; it helps clarify Galen's importance in the formation of commentary as a genre, and it allows us to look at empiricism in a new way. In fields other than philosophy, too, the revised approach to Galen opens up unexpected paths. For historians of science, medicine, and philosophy, as for historians in general and philologists, the Galenic lode is still full of treasure.

ARMELLE DEBRU
Translated by Rita Guerlac and Anne Slack

Bibliography

Texts and Translations

Galen. *Opera omnia.* Ed. and Latin trans. C. G. Kühn. 20 vols. Leipzig: 1821–1833; repr. Hildesheim: Olms, 1964–1965.

———. *Oeuvres anatomiques, physiologiques et médicales de Galien.* Trans. Charles Daremberg. 2 vols. Paris: Baillière, 1854–1856; partial repr. A. Pichot, Paris: Gallimard, 1994. 2 vols.

———. *Scripta minora.* Ed. Johann Maquardt, Ivan Müller, and Georg Helmreich. 3 vols. Leipzig: B. G. Teubner, 1884; repr. Amsterdam: Harrert, 1967.

———. *On Anatomical Procedures.* Trans. Charles Singer. London and New York: Oxford University Press, 1956.

———. *Galen on Anatomical Procedures: The Later Books.* Trans. W. L. Duckworth. Cambridge: Cambridge University Press, 1962.

———. *On the Doctrines of Hippocrates and Plato.* Ed. and trans. Phillip De Lacy. Berlin: Akademie Verlag, 1978–1984. *Corpus medicorum graecorum* 5, 4, 1–2.

———. *Three Treatises on the Nature of Science. On the Sect to Beginners. An Outline of Empiricism. On Medical Experience.* Trans. Richard Walzer and Michael Frede. Indianapolis: Hackett Publishing Co., 1985.

———. *On Semen.* Ed. and trans. Phillip de Lacy. Berlin: Akademie Verlag, 1992. *Corpus medicorum graecorum* 5, 3, 1.

———. *On the Therapeutic Method,* Books I and II. Trans R. J. Hankinson. Oxford: Clarendon Press, 1994.

Galen. *Selected Works.* Trans. and annotated P. N. Singer. Oxford: Oxford University Press, 1997.

Moraux, Paul. *Galien de Pergame: Souvenirs d'un médecin.* Paris: Les Belles Lettres, 1985.

Studies

Debru, Armelle. *Le corps respirant: La pensée de la physiologie chez Galien.* Leiden: Brill, 1996.

Haase, Wolfgang, ed. *Aufstieg und Niedergang der Römischen Welt,* Series 2, vol. 37, books 1–2. Berlin: W. de Gruyter, 1993, 1994 (numerous articles on Galen).

Harris, Charles Reginald Schiller. *The Heart and the Vascular System in Ancient Greek Medicine from Alcmaeon to Galen.* Oxford: Clarendon Press, 1973.

Kollesch, Jutta, and Diethard Nickel, eds. *Galen und das hellenistische Erbe.* Proceedings of the 4th International Galen Symposium at Humboldt University in Berlin, September 1989. Stuttgart: F. Steiner, 1993.

Kudlien, Fridolf, and Richard Durling, eds. *Galen's Method of Healing: Proceedings of the 1982 Galen Symposium.* Leiden: Brill, 1991.

Lloyd, Geoffrey E. R. *Greek Science after Aristotle.* London: Chatto and Windus; New York: Norton, 1973.

López-Férez, Juan Antonio, ed. *Galeno: Obra, pensamiento e influencia.* Colloquio internacional celebrado en Madrid, March 22–25, 1988. Madrid: Universidad Nacional de Educación a Distancia, 1991.

Manuli, Paula, and Mario Vegetti. *Cuore, sangue e cervello: Biologia e antropologia nel pensiero antico.* Milan: Episteme Editrice, 1977.

————. *Le opere psicologiche de Galeno: Atti del terzo Colloquio galenico internazionale.* Pavia, September 10–12, 1986. Naples: Bibliopolis, 1988.

Nutton, Vivian, ed. *Galen, Problems and Prospects: A Collection of Papers Submitted at the 1979 Cambridge Conference.* London: The Wellcome Institute, 1981.

Temkin, Owsei. *Galenism: Rise and Decline of a Medical Philosophy.* Ithaca, N.Y.: Cornell University Press, 1973.

HERACLITUS

HERACLITUS OF EPHESUS lived at the end of the 6th century B.C.E. Nothing is known of his life (the ancient "biographies" are fiction). There is no sign that he ever left his native city, which at that time was part of the empire of the Achaemenid dynasty of Persia. (Iranian influences on his thinking have sometimes been suggested.)

The book written by Heraclitus was famous in antiquity for its aphoristic obscurity. About a hundred sentences survive. The obscurity is a calculated consequence of Heraclitus's style, which is usually compact and often deliberately cryptic. He believed that what he had to say went beyond the limits of ordinary language. Combined with the meagerness of other testimony, this obscurity is a formidable obstacle to understanding.

Interpretation of Heraclitus has been a controversial matter since at least the late 5th century B.C.E. Both Plato and Aristotle attempted to fit Heraclitus into the mold of Ionian "natural philosophy" and accepted the view of Cratylus, who attributed to Heraclitus his own doctrine of "universal flux." Later ancient interpreters, notably Theophrastus and the Stoic Cleanthes, influenced (and clouded) the later testimony; but Cleanthes at least took a broader and more sympathetic view of Heraclitus than Aristotle had done. It is probable that Heraclitus intended and anticipated some of the difficulties of his interpreters, since the understanding of language, cryptic or otherwise, is itself a guiding theme in his thinking.

Since he was "rediscovered" at the end of the 18th century, and rescued from crude misunderstandings, Heraclitus's appeal has grown, in spite of his obscurity. Hegel explicitly acknowledged his indebtedness; Heidegger gave a lengthy exegesis. Wittgenstein's *Tractatus* is rather similar to Heraclitus in style and perhaps partly in method.

There are certain requirements that necessarily constrain and guide any serious attempt to interpret Heraclitus. First, one must keep in mind the intellectual context within which Heraclitus found himself. The new so-called natural philosophy of the Milesians, with its abstract approach, claimed to make the universe intelligible as a whole. It had already given rise to problems both epistemological (how could anything be known or plausibly conjectured about matters far beyond human experience?) and systemic (how was it possible convincingly to account for the variety of the experienced world in terms of only one or two fundamental components?). Xenophanes of Colophon, earlier in the 6th century, can be seen already grappling with these problems, and though Heraclitus speaks slightingly of Xenophanes, he may have learned from him.

Second, one must respect the systematic unity of thinking that lies behind the aphoristic form and is implicit in the correspondences of language and meaning by which the individual remarks are tied together. It is clear that Heraclitus's book was meant to form a comprehensive and systematic whole, covering every aspect of human experience, of which each part was connected with every other. Hence, as in a jigsaw puzzle, each statement of Heraclitus must be compared and contrasted with many others, in order that something like a map of his thinking can be constructed, within which each remark can then be located. One must also take note here of the difference between the examples drawn from everyday experience and the generalizations expressed in more abstract terms.

Third, one must be sensitive to the linguistic clues given by the fragments. These are of many different kinds. There is ambiguity of meaning in single words and phrases, and ambiguity of construction in sentences. Words, by their form or associations, carry deliberate allusions to other senses. Passages of Homer and Hesiod are implicitly referred to. In some cases it seems that Heraclitus's statements are intended to be self-applicable: their linguistic form exemplifies the very structure of which they speak.

Fourth, one must be guided by what Heraclitus himself says and implies about the business of interpreting difficult statements, and about all understanding as consisting of interpretation. "The prince to whom the oracle at Delphi belongs neither speaks nor conceals: he gives a sign" (frg. 93, Diels-Kranz). Another remark (frg. 56) tells how Homer was "deceived" by the terms of a riddle that he could not solve; just so are human beings generally "deceived" in their attempts to understand what is given in their own experience. For "bad witnesses to men are eyes and ears, if they have souls that do not understand the language" (frg. 107); they will not even be given what they need, for their very eyes and ears will distort their testimony to accord with their mistaken presuppositions, just as we misread and mishear the words of a foreign language to accord with our mistaken expectations. Therefore, "If one does not expect it, one will not discover it, undiscoverable as it is and unreachable" (frg. 18). Deciphering the "account" *(logos)* of Heraclitus himself is, for Heraclitus, the same operation as deciphering the meaning of experience, for both consist of the very same statements. One must listen to the *logos*, but it is equally "not understood" by most hearers.

A GENERAL HYPOTHESIS: THE INWARD TURN

The hypothesis on which the present account is founded is as follows. Heraclitus's thinking resulted from the turning-in on itself, the self-application, of the abstract theorizing invented by the Milesians. This introjection of the theoretical enterprise was a response to the problems encountered in trying to discover the nature of the universe as a whole. By this "turn" Heraclitus hoped to transform and to solve the original problems.

The inward turn was not in any way intended as a retreat from the immediate realities of ordinary experience. On the contrary, Heraclitus insists on the primacy of these realities: "All of which there is seeing, hearing, learning: those things I rank highest" (frg. 55). This programmatic statement is supported, most obviously, by his repeated appeals to familiar situations of ordinary experience, and by the direct and vivid language in which they are described. Ordinary experience includes, also, what is experienced by the mind when it inspects reflexively its own contents and operations. This, for Heraclitus, is not a separate realm of experience but an area continuous with the rest.

Immediate experience has an inherent structure and meaning, which it is Heraclitus's concern to explore, and which is identical to the structure and meaning of the universe. Language has a special place as the vehicle of both.

STRUCTURE: THE UNITY IN OPPOSITES

The abstract notion of structure is omnipresent, sometimes explicitly (in the word *harmoniē*), more often implicitly. In general, the structure that is indicated is one that may conveniently be described as "unity in opposites." This appears in the surviving fragments in many shapes.

In the first place, there are many examples drawn from everyday life, with no comment or elaboration. "People step into the same rivers, and different waters flow onto them" (frg. 12). "A road, uphill and downhill, one and the same" (frg. 60). "Sea is water most pure and most polluted: for fish drinkable and life-giving, for human beings undrinkable and deadly" (frg. 61). These, and the other such remarks, are not meant to infringe the law of noncontradiction. They rely for their first impact on the appearance of a contradiction, which is removed when we have recourse to our own experience to add the necessary qualifying phrases. But the paradox remains: how is it that these oppositions cohere so closely that they are mutually inseparable in thought or in experience, that they need one another? The traditional approach to representing opposites (e.g., Day and Night) in Homer and Hesiod was to make them separate persons in a state of mutual enmity or avoidance. Heraclitus explicitly rejects such a representation: Hesiod "did not know Day and Night: they are one thing" (frg. 57).

But at the same time, Heraclitus does not, as it might at first seem from these words, proclaim the identity of opposites. It turns out that Day and Night "are one thing" only in the sense that they are different temporary states of one and the same thing. To each pair of opposites, Heraclitus supplies an "underlying unity" in which the opposites are present.

In the case of Day and Night, the opposites are successively but not simultaneously present in the unity. In many other cases the opposites are simultaneously present. It is therefore clear that the unity in opposites does not depend on time and change: rather, the temporal aspect of things is for Heraclitus only one among many aspects that allow the manifestation of the fundamental structure. This is the first indication that (as will be seen later) the temporal dimension, though not denied by Heraclitus, becomes in effect of limited interest, because the cosmos and the soul pass through repeated cycles of change. "Beginning and end are together on the circle" (frg. 103). Each unity, then, exhibits in these examples a systematic ambivalence, as between the two opposites; it is an ambivalence that belongs to its essential nature. And in each pair of opposites there is typically one "positive" and one "negative" term.

Besides the examples drawn from everyday life, explicit generalizations, containing more abstract statements of the same structure, also appear. "People do not understand how what disagrees comes to agree: back-turning structure like that of the bow and the lyre" (frg. 51). "Comprehensions: wholes and not wholes, agreeing disagreeing, consonant dissonant; and from all things one and from one thing all things" (frg. 10).

These generalizing statements apply to all examples and therefore also to themselves, if we may regard sentences, and particularly statements containing opposed predications of the same thing, as examples of unity in opposites. This is an example of the self-reference in some of Heraclitus's remarks, and it is a particularly interesting one, because it suggests the infinite regress generated by generalizations that try to encompass everything, or by theories that try to explain everything, including themselves. Another remark says that "the soul has a *logos* which increases itself" (frg. 115), which again suggests awareness of the infinite regresses engendered by self-reference.

The notion of unity in opposites appears also to be used by Heraclitus as a theory-guiding idea, for yet another class of remarks contains examples of unity in opposites that are manifestly not derived directly from ordinary experience. They are rather to be understood as parts of a theory: of the physical transformations of the cosmos, or of the parallel transformations of the soul.

REASON, KNOWLEDGE, UNDERSTANDING

It has often been recognized that for Heraclitus there is a parallelism or structural identity between the operations of the mind, as expressed in thought and language, and those of the reality that it grasps. This parallelism implies that understanding any part of reality is like grasping the meaning of a statement. The "meaning," in this case, like that of a cryptic statement in words, is not obvious but yet is present in the statement, and can be worked out provided one "knows the language." Human reason has the power to know the "language of reality," precisely because its own operations are conducted in the very same way.

A prominent place is given by Heraclitus to what he calls "this *logos*" or "the *logos*." It is evident that he is here starting from the most basic and familiar sense of the word: "this *logos*" is his own account, what he has to say. It is what is given by his own words. Yet it is also evident that, characteristically, Heraclitus packs much more meaning into the word *logos*. "Of this *logos* which is always people prove to have no understanding" (frg. 1). "When one listens not to me but to the *logos*, it is wise to agree *[homologein]* that all is one" (frg. 50). "While the *logos* is public *[xunou]*, the many live as though they had a private source of understanding" (frg. 2). "Those who speak with sense *[xun nōi]* must affirm with what is public *[xunōi]* for all, as a city does with law, and much more firmly" (frg. 114).

These remarks, and the extension of sense of the word *logos*, fall into place if we note that here it is the *logos* that supplies the independent authority to which Heraclitus appeals. In attacking traditional beliefs and the authority of sages, Heraclitus, like the other 6th-century thinkers, was implicitly setting up and appealing to a standard independent of tradition and personal authority. What could this be? It could not be the empirical standard of immediate experience, as suggested by Xenophanes. Heraclitus prized experience, but (as we have seen) he knew that it needed interpretation. For this, "insight" *(noos)* was needed. The *logos* provides a *public* test of insight: it can only, therefore, be something like reason. And in fact the sense "reason" is well attested for the word *logos* in the next hundred years.

Having appealed to reason as something to which all have access, Heraclitus has to explain why it is that the fruits of reason are (in his opinion) gathered by so few: why, in fact, his teaching has so far not been accepted by others, let alone independently discovered.

It is first of all clear that the acceptance of the *logos* as such is not something automatic. On the contrary, "of this logos which is always people prove to have no understanding, both before they have heard it [they do not discover it independently] and when once they have heard it [they do not accept it from Heraclitus]. For though all things come to be according to this *logos*, they are like inexperienced people though they experience the words [Heraclitus's sayings] and the deeds [the facts of experience] such as I set forth, as I take apart each thing according to nature *[kata phusin]* and show how it is. But other people do not notice what they do when awake, in the same way as they do not notice all the things that they forget about when asleep" (frg. 1).

The image of sleepers, who "forget about" the public world of shared experience, shows that the mistake of most people consists in "living as though they had a private source of understanding." They do in some sense experience things, but they force on their experience some private interpretation, just as a dreamer distorts in his dream the external stimuli that impinge on him. Several other images suggest the same conclusion. Most people are like children (frgs. 70, 74, 79); like dogs (frg. 97), and perhaps other animals; like fools (frg. 87); like deaf people (frgs. 19, 34).

The process of "waking up," of becoming conscious of one's reason and deliberately exercising it, is also far from automatic. It requires strenuous self-exertion to get any distance. Besides, "the nature of things likes to lie hidden" (frg. 123). To free oneself of error is presumably just a matter of self-discipline, though hard and painful for those who are not used to it. But to attain positive understanding is a matter of solving enigmas, for which a guide or an unforeseeable insight is needed.

"Human character does not have knowledge, but divine character does" (frg. 78). This remark may seem to put an unbridgeable gulf between human beings and any worthwhile insight. But at a closer view it can be read encouragingly. "Character" (ēthos) is not what is essential but what is determined by habit. To shake off all-too-human habits is to move halfway toward acquiring "divine character." What exactly may be implied by that must be left at present in suspense, but at least it is clear that the divine intelligence in the cosmos is named by Heraclitus "the wise" or "the only wise."

THE INTERPRETATION OF EXPERIENCE: THEORIES OF COSMOS AND SOUL

Reason has to be applied to immediate experience. This implies the existence of general principles of interpretation. What these may be, Heraclitus does not tell us explicitly. But a reconstruction of them can, with due caution, be attempted. We have to be guided by (1) the general analogy of understanding with interpretation of language; (2) the results of the interpretation as evidenced by what we know of Heraclitus's cosmology and his theory of the soul.

These guides lead us to suppose that Heraclitus followed two principles: "No Cancellation" and "No New Sensibles." These may already have figured in the epistemology of Xenophanes. The principle of No Cancellation requires that no part of immediate experience may be discarded; everything that is experienced must be accounted for in theory, and must appear in the theoretical account exactly as experienced. This is analogous to the demand that every part of a sentence must be interpreted, and the interpretation must account for it as it functions in the sentence and not otherwise. The principle of No New Sensibles sets limits to what may be added to experience by the interpretation. It requires that nothing extra may be postulated as existing but not experienced unless it is not the sort of thing to be an object of experience at all. This corresponds to the requirement of interpretation of language, that we must not postulate unspoken or unwritten words in addition to the ones that are expressed.

The result of applying these two principles to sensory experience of the world is a characteristically parsimonious empiricism, like that of Xenophanes. The observed cosmos is all there is. The physical constituents are the obvious ones: earth, sea, atmospheric vapor, fire. Their transformations are governed by the characteristic physical opposites: hot-cold, wet-dry. The sun is not even a persisting object but a regularly repeated process, in which a container of modest size is carried up into the heavens by the power of fire after its contents have ignited.

There are indications that for the individual soul there was a parallel theory. In the physical theory, two pairs of opposites (hot-cold, wet-dry) give a system of transformations between four states or stages of the underlying fire, which must be thought of as a process rather than as a "material." In the more cryptically expressed theory of the soul the pair wet-dry reappears, but there are also the oppositions alive-dead and awake-asleep.

The reconstruction is in both cases controversial, and the nature of the analogy between the two systems still more so. One fundamental question concerns the nature of the "measures" or "proportions" that are said to be preserved throughout the transformations of fire. Do these represent an equilibrium between actual amounts of physical opposites in the cosmos? Or do they indicate the conservation of some quantity less closely tied to observation? In the latter case, it is possible that the cosmos goes through long-term cyclical oscillations of state, as the Stoic interpretation asserted.

In any case, though, the interest, for Heraclitus, lies not so much in the theory itself as in subsumption of these aspects of experience under the general structure of unity in opposites. Unlike Xenophanes, Heraclitus insists that the cosmos (and analogously the individual soul) is something that makes sense as a whole. (Understanding is literally "putting together," *xunienai*, the creating of a unified whole.) It remains, therefore, to see how cosmology and psychology were intended to be subordinated to Heraclitus's general metaphysical concerns. This depends on the identification of the underlying unity in both cases with "fire" in the sense of an intelligent process: the divine intelligence.

MEANING, STRUGGLE, AND THE DIVINE IN COSMOS AND SOUL

It follows from the principles already explained that the key to understanding the nature of the world is *introspection:* "I went looking for myself" (frg. 101). The human self ("soul," *psukhē*) is variously occupied: it is combatively active, physically, emotionally, and intellectually; it is reflectively self-discovering and self-extending; and it is constantly self-reversing in the swings of circumstances or passion or thought. Yet it needs firm frameworks (objective truths, fixed rules of conduct) to be at all, or to make sense of its own existence. For Heraclitus, all this is true of the world too. Here also there is no sharp line between what it is and what it means. As already mentioned, the behavior and structure of the world and of the soul are seen as closely analogous, if not the same.

In fact there is good reason to suspect an underlying identity. In the series of physical changes between opposites, fire (in the sense of a cosmic process that is also a self-transforming force) is given as the underlying unity. "All things are got in exchange for fire, and fire for all things; just as all goods are got in exchange for gold, and gold for goods" (frg. 90). "This cosmos . . . an everliving fire which is kindled in measures and is quenched in measures" (frg. 30).

In the soul, too, wet and dry appear as the important opposites, with negative and positive values: "Dry beam of light is soul at its wisest and best" (frg. 118), while the stumbling drunkard "has his soul wet" (frg. 117). The underlying unity is not named, but the association with light, and some other slight indications, might suggest that here, too, it is seen as fire. What adds force to this suggestion, and completes the chain of links, is that the divine intelligence controlling the cosmos is certainly identified as a kind of fire. "Thunderbolt steers all things" (frg. 64); the traditional attribute of Zeus is given as a name for the divine intelligence, elsewhere "the wise." "For one is the wise to be versed in the knowledge of how all things are steered through all" (frg. 41). "The one only wise is unwilling and willing to be called by the name of Zeus" (frg. 32). The traditional role of Zeus—to be the cunning supreme governor of the cosmos—is taken over by "the wise."

If these identifications are right, it follows that the divine intelligence is not something remote from human understanding; on the contrary, it is, at least qualitatively, the same as human intelligence itself. True, Heraclitus emphasizes that it is different in nature from anything else: "Of all those whose words I have heard, none has got so far as to recognise that the wise is separated from all things" (frg. 108). It is in fact the underlying unity of "all things" that are given in experience, and therefore necessarily different in nature from them. But "the wise" is a term that can be applied to both human and divine intelligence, and there are indications that Heraclitus saw no essential difference between them. This is intelligible if they are both, in the best state, fire.

But human intelligence is often unable to function at its best, as it is impeded by "wetness." It is possible for human beings to take possession of their inheritance of intelligence; otherwise Heraclitus's preaching would be pointless. It needs, however, a choice, and a struggle, for a human being to become truly wise, as Heraclitus claimed to be. The same should therefore be true of the divine intelligence; that, too, must have its moral struggles, and its periods of "death" and "sleep" produced by the excess of moisture, followed by renewed vigor. We can understand of both soul and cosmos the cyclic process implied in this remark: "The same thing is present inside as living and dead, as sleeping and awake, as young and old; for these change to become those and those change to become these" (frg. 88).

This hypothesis, that the cosmos, too, goes cyclically through processes of decay and renewal, and that these are accompanied by struggles, is confirmed by various evidence. The Stoic reconstruction of Heraclitus contained long-term oscillations between the extremes of cosmic conflagration and cosmic deluge. Even if this cosmic cycle is doubted, the oscillations of day and night, winter and summer play the same role. That the cosmos is the arena of "war" or "strife" is stated explicitly. "War is the father of all things and the king of all things" (frg. 53). "One must know that war is shared in by all, and that strife is justice, and that everything comes to be according to strife and necessity" (frg. 80).

It seems to be this struggle, in the individual soul and in the cosmos, that for Heraclitus gives meaning to both. Certainly there are some remarks reminiscent of the heroic ideal of Homer. "The best choose one thing in place of all: glory ever-flowing of mortals; but the many are glutted like cattle" (frg. 29). "Those slain in war are honoured of gods and men" (frg. 24). It seems even possible that for Heraclitus the individual struggle to achieve (and to spread?) the use of intelligence may be a contribution to the cosmic struggle on the side of the hot and the dry. Certainly war and peace are mentioned as cosmic as well as merely human opposites. And the actors on the human stage are, though mortal (because subject to periods of being dead), just as mortal and just as immortal, too, as the actor or actors on the cosmic stage. "Immortals mortals, mortals immortals: alive in the others' dying, dead in the others' living" (frg. 62).

IMAGES AND GENERALIZATIONS

Heraclitus, in spite of his deliberate obscurity, was a lucid and ambitious thinker. We may expect that he would have been aware that a system of thought, such as has been outlined, raises certain crucial questions. How, above all, are we to understand the equation of strife or war, on the one hand, with justice (and perhaps necessity) on the other hand? It is reasonable to suppose that this is one more example of the structure of unity in opposites, but saying that is not enough for understanding. We need also some sort of explanation—*how* such opposites are capable of forming a genuine unity. (The difficulty is deepened if we accept as genuine the remark: "For the god, all things are fine and good and just; but men suppose some things to be just and others unjust" [frg. 102]. In fact, there are independent reasons for doubting the authenticity of this fragment.)

In the same way, we wish to have better insight into how it is possible for the underlying unity, the cosmic intelligence, to conduct strife against itself. It may be that Heraclitus took the fact of such internal strife to be immediately acceptable as a possibility, on the model of "the mind divided against itself." Yet that does not make it any more intelligible.

As indications for dealing with such crucial questions, Heraclitus provided not explicit statements but images. Some of the remarks drawn from everyday life may have been intended also to serve as thought-guiding images of a general kind. The remark about rivers (the river persists though the waters change) is capable of being taken, and has often been taken, as an image of the permanence through change of the cosmos or the individual soul.

As the supreme image of the coexistence of justice and strife, Heraclitus describes a child playing both sides of a board game. "*Aiōn* ["Lifetime" or "Time everlasting"] is a child playing, playing at tric-trac; a child's is the kingdom" (frg. 52). The child pits his wits against themselves, by alternately playing both sides in the game. The game is thus a genuine struggle, though conducted by only one person. And it is conducted according to rules; the lawlike moves are the conflict. The outcome is determined perhaps by the chances of war in any one case, but in the long run, if the child plays equally well on both sides, the honors will be even. The image captures the opposites that stand at the highest level in Heraclitus's thinking and helps us to understand their fundamental coexistences: those of conflict and law, of freedom and regularity, of intelligence and its lapses, of opposition and unity.

EDWARD HUSSEY

Bibliography

Diels, Hermann, and Walther Kranz. *Die Fragmente der Vorsokratiker.* Berlin: Weidmannsche Verlagsbuchhandlung, 1956.

Dilcher, Roman. *Studies in Heraclitus.* Hildesheim and New York: Olms, 1995.

Heidegger, Martin. "Logos (Heraclitus Fragment B 50)." In *Early Greek Thinking.* Trans. D. F. Krell and F. A. Capuzzi. San Francisco: Harper and Row, 1984. Pp. 59–78.

Hölscher, Uvo. "Heraklit." In *Anfängliches Fragen.* Göttingen: Vandenhoeck and Ruprecht, 1960. Pp. 130–172.

Hussey, Edward. "Epistemology and Meaning in Heraclitus." In *Language and Logos: Studies in Ancient Greek Philosophy Presented to G. E. L. Owen.* Ed. Malcolm Schofield and Martha Nussbaum. Cambridge: Cambridge University Press, 1982. Pp. 33–59.

Kahn, C. H. *The Art and Thought of Heraclitus: An Edition of the Fragments with Translation and Commentary.* Cambridge: Cambridge University Press, 1979.

Kirk, G. S. *Heraclitus: The Cosmic Fragments.* Cambridge: Cambridge University Press, 1962.

Vlastos, Gregory. "On Heraclitus." In *Studies in Presocratic Philosophy*, vol. 1: *The Beginnings of Philosophy*. Ed. D. J. Furley and R. E. Allen. London: Routledge and Kegan Paul, 1970. Pp. 413–429.

HERODOTUS

HERODOTUS WISHED to rival Homer; what he became, ultimately, was Herodotus. In other words, he drew from the epic the courage, or the temerity, to begin. Like the epic, the recording of history always starts with conflict, with war. Herodotus set out to do for the Persian Wars what Homer had done for the Trojan War. As the famous opening sentence of *Histories* begins, "What Herodotus the Halicarnassian has learnt by inquiry is here set forth: in order that the memory of the past may not be blotted out from among men by time, and that great and marvellous deeds done by Greeks and foreigners and especially the reason why they warred against each other may not lack renown" (Herodotus, *Histories* I.1).

Of Herodotus the man (roughly 480–420 B.C.E.) we know very little. He came originally from Ionia, the birthplace of the earliest Greek thinkers (such as Anaximander, the creator of the first map of the world, and Hecataeus of Miletus, sometimes considered the first historian). Herodotus traveled throughout the Mediterranean, experienced exile, learned what it meant to be an outsider (at least until he arrived at Thurii, the new colony that Pericles wished to make Panhellenic), and spent time in Athens. Some traditional sources present him as a lecturer, visiting the great centers of Greece and collecting speaker's fees. Thus he appeared as an itinerant historian, a peddler of stories, not unlike the rhapsodes who traveled from contest to contest, or those other, better-known travelers, the Sophists. However, at that time "history" did not refer to a sphere of knowledge, nor was it regarded as a profession.

The life of Herodotus unfolded between two major conflicts. The Persian Wars (which he had not known firsthand but which he chose to relate) were a period of threats to, and consolidation of, the polis, and the Peloponnesian War, inextricably linked to Thucydides' account, was also a perilous time of profound questioning. The period Herodotus describes in his work (550–480, with several additional flashbacks) saw important changes. To the east, the Persian empire arose and prospered; in Greece, first Sparta and then Athens came to prominence. Politically, the ancient ideal of "eunomy" was replaced by that of "isonomy" (equality of political rights for all citizens), and finally by an entirely new notion, that of democracy.

Histories is divided into nine books, but these divisions were introduced much later. Herodotus himself spoke only of his "account" or "accounts." The last five books are largely devoted to the history of the Persian Wars proper, starting with the revolt of Ionia against the Persians (500 B.C.E.) up to the capture of Sestos in Chersonese. The Persians were defeated, the Ionians liberated, and the bridges that the overambitious Xerxes built across the Hellespont were destroyed. The first four books, in contrast, deal with the barbarians: Lydians, Persians, Babylonians, Massagetes, Egyptians, Ethiopians, Arabs, Indians, Scythians, Libyans. However, these books are not so much ethnographic or geographic notes as they are an account of the emergence of these various peoples as they were confronted by the advancing power of the Persians (or of the still earlier Medes), for the Persians, as Herodotus describes them, were incapable of staying put. Thus *Histories* is also a meditation on the drive for conquest and the destiny of the conquerors.

THE INVENTION OF THE BARBARIAN AND THE INVENTORY OF THE WORLD

When *Histories* opens, the barbarians were already situated geographically, forming, with the Greeks, a pair of opposites. To Herodotus, the division between them is obvious: there was no need to explain or justify it, although it was absent from Homer's poems. The distinction had appeared between the 6th and 5th centuries, starting with the Persian Wars, which territorialized the barbarians geographically (opposite Europe, in Asia) and gave them a face: first of all, that of the Persian. In *Histories* Herodotus bore witness to this phenomenon and actively contributed to it. He went even further, however, in constructing a political rationale for distinguishing between Greeks and barbarians, which also offered a political perspective on the Greek past. As a result, the word *barbarian* came to signify not primarily, or necessarily, barbarism (cruelty, excess, laxity) but political difference; it separated those who chose to live in city-states from those who never managed to get along without kings. The Greek is "political"—in other words, free—while the barbarian is "royal," meaning submissive to a master *(despotēs)*.

Between the world of the barbarian and the city-state stands the tyrant. It was in opposition to this Greek figure of power, typical of the end of the archaic period, that the "isonomic" city-states were developed. Herodotus's account establishes the ties that link king and tyrant: by highlighting the overlap of the two images (each borrowing from the other), the representation of despotic power appears barbarian. The king is a barbarian and the tyrant is a king; thus, the tyrant is a barbarian, or barbaric.

The despot (king or tyrant) exercises excessive power. Prey to hubris, which Herodotus borrows from the lexicon of tragedy, he is incapable of moderation and is guilty of every transgression: spatial transgression, in that a king always overreaches his space, and transgression against the gods (who, according to Themistocles, "deemed Asia and Europe too great a realm for one man to rule" [*Histories* VIII.109]). He violates the *nomoi* (laws and customs) not only of other cultures but of his own as well. In *Histories*, three despots vie for first place: Cambyses, the mad king; Periander, the tyrant of Corinth; and Cleomenes, the king of Sparta, who was also mad. One Persian and two Greeks: are we to conclude, then, that the distinction between Greek and barbarian is no longer pertinent? No, on the contrary, for the great kings, tyrants, and ordinary kings spring from a common ground (that of despotic power) or lean toward barbarism. In contrast to this world of the outsider, and also, from this point on, to the past, stands the city-state. Between the Greeks and the "other," *Histories* tells us, the new frontier is above all political. This frontier separates Asia and Europe, but it also cuts across Greece itself, shaping and explaining the brief period when tyranny flourished and the isonomic city-state was established (it perhaps even stigmatizes the city-state that later became democratic and that, in the years around 430, was accused of behaving in a "tyrannical" fashion: Athens?).

The "political" division proposed by Herodotus is consistent with a worldview in which the fundamental categories of Greek anthropology are still at work (divisions between animals, men, and gods, as they were set down in the stories of Homer and Hesiod). Herodotus, the curious traveler, like a Lévi-Strauss of his time, presents a broad canvas on which all the different cultures are arranged systematically. The concept that best expresses this attitude of openness toward the world is *theōria*, traveling in order to see. The Athenian legislator Solon appears in *Histories* as a thinker and a traveler, for whom the project of "seeing" the world and the effort to "philosophize" (the first use of that word) are linked. King Croesus greets him with those words and questions him in the name of that knowledge. In a larger sense, wise men (of whom the best known are the Seven Sages) undertake travel as a way of life, even if they generally do so more to teach than to learn. In fact, *Histories* represents a time in Greek culture that is both confident and curious: Herodotus travels less to construct his representation of the world than to confirm it.

Once he has established the Otherness of people and places, he uses a variety of narrative strategies to reveal his grasp and mastery of the subject. He exploits a whole series of expressions and figures of speech that I have referred to elsewhere as "the rhetoric of Otherness": the category of the *thōma*, or marvelous; play on symmetry, oppositions (hot/cold, courage/cowardice, and so on), and inversions (a useful form that transforms the difference of the other into the inverse of the self); the omnipresent concern for counting and measuring; the use of analogy; validation of the notions of "blending" and "center." This rhetoric allows him to speak the Other, or rather to write it, and to encompass it as he depicts the cultures and draws a map of the known world. Mindful of his limits, the investigator intends to expand his story as far as possible, up to the point where extreme heat or cold prohibits his going any farther and learning more. But up to that point he makes it his task to investigate, to enumerate customs, to name peoples, to define space, constructing in the process, *more geometrico,* so to speak, a representation of the world.

If Herodotus, quoting Pindar, declares that custom is the queen of the world, his ethnology shows just as clearly that all customs are not equal (and that in all cases, absence of laws or of rules is a sure criterion of inhumanity). Above all, *Histories* reminds us constantly that around the notion of *nomos* there is always something essentially and inherently Greek. The famous dialogue between Xerxes, the barbarian king, and Demaratus, the exiled Spartan king, is a perfect demonstration: Spartans, Demaratus says, are at once free and submissive to a "master," the law. The laughter with which Xerxes greets this declaration indicates his total lack of understanding. Whereas this Spartan "contract" clearly shows that, while non-Greeks may have their *nomoi* (sometimes very fine ones), the Greeks alone have "politicized" their *nomos.*

THE BEGINNINGS OF HISTORY

Did the writing of history begin in Greece? For many years the answer from scholars of the ancient civilizations of the East has been an emphatic no, expressed with the impatience of those who have had difficulty making themselves heard, so strong was the habit of regarding Greece as the place of all beginnings. To take just one important example: Mesopotamian historiography, linked directly to royal authority, is as ancient as it is rich. The Greeks did not invent history; in fact, they rediscovered writing rather late, borrowing the Phoenician alphabet. However, it was with the Greeks, beginning with Herodotus, that the historian as a subjective figure first appeared. In the service of no particular power, with his very first words he begins to define and claim the narrative form that begins with the use of his own name: "Herodotus the Halicarnassian . . ." He is the author of his "account," and it is this account *(logos)* that establishes his authority. The paradox lies in the fact that, at the same time, this newly claimed authority has yet to be fully constructed. Such a narrative strategy, characteristic of this moment in Greek intellectual history, marks a break with the Eastern historiographers. If the Greeks were inventors of anything, it was less of history than of the historian.

This new form of discourse and this singular figure did not emerge from a vacuum. Both the epic and the bard were still present, close at hand and yet very old, in the prologue to *Histories,* which answered, for the most part, the question: How can one be a bard in a world that is no longer epic? The answer: by becoming a historian. Like the bard, the historian deals with memory, oblivion, and death. The bard of old was a master of glory *(kleos),* a dispenser of immortal encomia to the heroes who died gloriously in war, and the organizer of the collective memory. Herodotus sought only to ensure that the traces and the markings of men, the monuments that they produced, would not disappear (like the colors of a painting that fade with time), would not cease to be recounted and celebrated (he used the term *aklea,* stripped of glory). The shift from *kleos* to *aklea* indicates that the historian refers continually to the epic, but also that he makes more modest claims than the bard. It is as if he knew that the ancient promise of immortality could never again be uttered except as a negative: as the promise to delay oblivion.

Similarly, where the bard's area of expertise covered "the deeds of heroes and of gods," the historian limits himself to the "deeds of man," in a time that is itself defined as "the time of man." He adds one principle of selection: to choose what is great and elicits astonishment *(thōma).* Thus he gives himself a means of measuring difference in events and of ordering multiplicity in the world.

"Tell me, O muse, of the man of many devices" (*Odyssey* I.1) was the inaugural pact of the epic. The Muse, daughter of memory and source of inspiration, was the guarantor of the poet's song. With the first history, the realm of the spoken word is over. Prose has replaced verse, writing dominates; the Muse has disappeared. In its place we find a new word and a new narrative economy: "What Herodotus the Halicarnassian has learned by inquiry *(historiē)* is set forth." This emblematic term took hold, little by little (although Thucydides, for his part, took pains never to use it). It was Cicero who gave Herodotus the lasting title "father of history." *History* is an abstract word, formed from the verb *historein,* to inquire, originally in the sense of judicial inquiry; *historia* is derived from *histōr* (which itself is related to *idein,* to see, and *oida,* I know). The *histōr* is the I, the "one who knows by having seen or learned." Thus the *histōr* is present in the epic, where he appears, always in a context of dispute, as arbiter (never as an eyewitness): he has not seen with his own eyes, but, in terms of the process, it is he who will reveal what has happened, or, still more probably, who will be the guarantor of the decision made.

Herodotus is neither bard nor arbiter. He lacks the natural authority of the latter (he is not, like Agamemnon, a "master of truth"), and he does not benefit from the divine vision of the former (the bard is an inspired seer); he inquires. He has only *historiē,* a certain method of inquiry, which I offer as the starting point of his practice of historiography. Produced as a substitute, this inquiry operates in a way analogous to the omniscient vision of the Muse, who was able to know because her divine nature allowed her to be present everywhere and to see everything. The historian, acting on no authority but his own, intends from this point to "go forward with my history, and speak of small and great cities alike [we remember what was said about Odysseus in the *Odyssey:* "Many were the men whose cities he saw"], for many states that were once great have now become small" (*Histories* I.5).

If the historian's inquiry (thus defined) both evokes the wisdom of the bard and breaks with it, Herodotus also appeals to a second register of knowledge:

that of prophecy. He investigates, but he also "signifies," *sēmainei:* he "designates," "reveals." The term *sēmainein,* for example, is used for someone who sees what others do not, or could not, see and makes his report. The verb specifically designates oracular knowledge. In the epic, the seer, who knows present, future, and past, is already portrayed as a man of knowledge. Epimenides of Crete, a famous seer, was reputed to apply his gift of prophecy not to what ought to be but to what, having happened, still remained obscure. We are also reminded of Heraclitus's formula, according to which the oracle neither says nor hides, but "means" *(sēmainei).*

Thus, beginning with the prologue, at the very moment when Herodotus speaks for the first time, saying "I," he signifies *(sēmainei):* drawing on personal knowledge, he reveals who first took offensive action against the Greeks: Croesus, the king of Lydia. The first to subjugate the Greeks, Croesus is "designated" as "responsible," or "guilty" *(aitios).* By assigning responsibility in this way, Herodotus appeals to a level of knowledge that is inherently oracular.

The verbs *historein* and *sēmainein* form the junction where ancient and contemporary knowledge come together and intertwine, as attested by the work of Herodotus himself. These verbs—both functions of "seeing clearly," of seeing further, beyond the visible, into space and time—characterize the style of the first historian. He is neither bard, nor prophet; he is between bard and prophet: he is Herodotus.

François Hartog
Translated by Elizabeth Rawlings and Jeannine Pucci

Bibliography

Texts and Translations

Herodotus. *Histoires.* Ed. and trans. Philippe-Ernest Legrand. Paris: Les Belles Lettres, 1932–1954.

———. *Histories.* Ed. and trans. T. E. Page. Loeb Classical Library.

———. *L'enquête.* Ed. and trans. Andrée Barguet. 2 vols. Paris: Gallimard, 1985.

———. *Libro I: La Lidia e la Persia.* Ed. David Asheri. Trans. Virginia Antelami. Milan: Mondadori, 1988.

Studies

Burkert, Walter. "Hérodote et les peuples non grecs." In *Entretiens sur l'antiquité classique,* vol. 35. Geneva: Vandoeuvres, 1990.

Corcella, Aldo. *Erodoto e l'analogia.* Palermo: Sellerio Editore, 1984.

Darbo-Peschanski, Catherine. *Le discours du particulier: Essai sur l'enquête hérodotéenne.* Paris: Editions du Seuil, 1987.

Hartog, François. *The Mirror of Herodotus: The Representation of the Other in the*

Writing of History. Trans. Janet Lloyd. Berkeley: University of California Press, 1988.

———. "Myth into Logos: The Case of Croesus, or The Historian at Work." In *From Myth to Reason: Studies in the Development of Greek Thought.* Ed. R. Buxton. Oxford and New York: Clarendon Press, 1999. Pp. 183–195.

"Herodotus and the Invention of History." *Arethusa* 20 (1987):1–2.

Hunter, Virginia. *Past and Present in Herodotus and Thucydides.* Princeton: Princeton University Press, 1982.

Marincola, John. *Authority and Tradition in Ancient Historiography.* Cambridge and New York: Cambridge University Press, 1997.

Meier, Christian. "An Ancient Equivalent of the Concept of Progress: The Fifth-Century Consciousness of Ability." In *The Greek Discovery of Politics.* Trans. David McLintock. Cambridge, Mass.: Harvard University Press, 1990. Pp. 186–221.

Momigliano, Arnaldo. "The Herodotean and the Thucydidean Tradition." In *The Classical Foundations of Modern Historiography.* Berkeley: University of California Press, 1990. Pp. 29–53.

Nagy, Gregory. *Pindar's Homer: The Lyric Possession of an Epic Past.* Baltimore: Johns Hopkins University Press, 1990.

Payen, Pascal. *Les iles nomades: Conquérir et résister dans* l'Enquête *d'Hérodote.* Paris: Editions de l'Ecole des Hautes Etudes en Sciences Sociales, 1997.

Sauge, André. *De l'épopée à l'histoire: Fondements de la notion d'historié.* Frankfurt: Peter Lang, 1992.

Thompson, Norma. *Herodotus and the Origins of the Political Community.* New Haven: Yale University Press, 1996.

HIPPOCRATES

HIPPOCRATES, often called the father of medicine, represents a semilegendary figure for many people, just as Homer does. In fact, he was a real historical figure who lived in Pericles' time; he was famous even in his own day, as his contemporaries attest. If he was not the founder of Greek medicine, strictly speaking, he gave it an influence it had never had before, probably owing to his personality and to his teaching. What helped in particular to assure his lasting fame, from antiquity to the present, was the existence of an important collection of medical texts attributed to him and designated today by the title *Hippocratic Collection* or *Hippocratic Corpus*. Although they could not all have been written by Hippocrates himself, these texts nevertheless allow us to discover Hippocratic thought in the broadest sense and to measure the decisive influence of his legacy on the history of Western medicine and, more generally, on how we think about science and about human beings.

What we know about Hippocrates' life we owe to a variety of sources of unequal reliability. The oldest account (and the most interesting) is that of his young contemporary Plato, who refers to Hippocrates on two occasions: first, in *Protagoras*, as the exemplar of a great physician whom Socrates' interlocutor should approach if he wishes to learn the art of medicine, just as he might go to Polyclitus of Argos or Phidias of Athens to learn the art of sculpture. The second reference is in *Phaedrus*, where Socrates (ambiguously) praises Hippocrates' thought. Some forty years later, Aristotle, himself the son of a doctor, refers to Hippocrates in his *Politics*—somewhat incidentally, to be sure—as an example of a man who is great because of his medical science and not because of his size.

Besides these important, although allusive, references, we find more detailed biographical data in a variety of texts. The *Letters* purported to be by Hippocrates (or to him) in the *Collection* are certainly apocryphal, if not fictional; still, they may contain a certain amount of authentic information. Similarly, the *Ambassadorial Speech*, or *Presbeutikos*, which also appears in the *Collection* (a speech that Thessalos, the son of Hippocrates, is believed to have given before the Athenian Assembly toward the end of the 5th century) contains some information on Hippocrates' family—information confirmed, in part, by recent epigraphic discoveries. Besides the *Collection*, there are two *Lives* of Hippocrates, one by Soranus of Ephesus (a physician of the 1st and 2nd centuries C.E.), the other by the so-called Pseudo-Soranus (this

Vita Hippocrati is in fact anonymous and incomplete); both draw on earlier sources. Finally, the immense work of Galen of Pergamum (2nd century C.E.), a great admirer of Hippocrates and an authority on his work, contains numerous allusions to the physician from Cos, who was a role model for the physician in Pergamum. All these sources enable us, after a critical examination, to extract a few proved or probable facts about Hippocrates' life. This information is divided fairly distinctly into two periods, before and after his departure from Cos.

In ancient cities there was no organized, public instruction such as we have today, nor were there titles authorizing the practice of medicine; thus the teaching that took place in the city-states was still clearly organized along familial and aristocratic lines. Hippocrates is a perfect case in point. Born around 460 B.C.E. on the Dorian island of Cos, close to the coast of modern Turkey, he descended on his father's side from the Cos branch of the Asclepiades family; another branch had settled just opposite Cos, at Cnidus, on a promontory of Asia Minor. Doctors in general were sometimes called "Asclepiades," and Hippocrates actually was born into a great aristocratic family that claimed direct descent from Asclepius and, more significantly, from the latter's son Podalirius, who is mentioned in Homer along with his brother, Machaon. This family played an important role on the island of Cos in both politics and medicine. Hippocrates, far from being the "inventor" of medicine, actually belonged to a long line of physicians who passed down their medical knowledge from father to son. One of Hippocrates' ancestors, Nebros, became famous as a doctor at the time of the first holy war (600–590 B.C.E.). Hippocrates' grandfather and his father, Heraclides, were also doctors, and in his turn, Hippocrates passed down to his sons, Thessalus and Draco, the knowledge that he had acquired within his family. Hippocrates was actually a link in a long family tradition, rather than the founder of the "school of Cos."

We know that he remained in Cos during the early years of his career, married there, and had three children (two sons, Thessalos and Draco, and a daughter who married one of his students, Polybius). The *Letters* link two anecdotes to this period, anecdotes that bear witness to Hippocrates' renown in both Greek and barbarian lands. He is supposed to have been summoned by the inhabitants of Abdera to tend to the mad philosopher Democritus, who laughed at everything for no apparent reason, and Hippocrates found that, far from being a sign of madness, Democritus's laughter showed the philosopher's wisdom. True or false, the anecdote enjoyed great popularity even beyond antiquity, as attested by one of La Fontaine's fables *(Democritus and the Abderians)* and by an allusion Stendhal makes in his *Life of Henry Brulard.* In another, the king of Persia, Artaxerxes I, is said to have made Hippocrates a magnificent offer to employ him at a time when a plague was devastating his country; however, Hippocrates spurned the king's offer, for he was unwilling to aid the enemies of Greece. This second story, already well known to Plutarch in the 2nd century C.E., survived for centuries, as we know from a painting by Girodet housed in the Ecole de Médecine in Paris.

But Hippocrates' fame would not have been what it was had he not left his native island for continental Greece. The career of a physician in antiquity was different from that of his modern counterpart who, once established in an office, rarely leaves it. A Greek doctor could, by contrast, practice in different city-states throughout his career, either as a public doctor or in private practice. Like the great Sophists, important doctors traveled to perfect their medical training, and also to profit financially from their reputation abroad. The most famous example before Hippocrates is that of Democedes of Croton, whose brilliant and eventful career is reported by Herodotus. It is in the context of this type of medical career that we can understand Hippocrates' departure from Cos for Thessaly, where he spent the second part of his life surrounded by his sons and his disciples (his practice probably extended throughout the north of Greece). Certain geographic indications preserved in a few of the Hippocratic treatises identify areas of activity of the Hippocratic school after Hippocrates' departure for Thessaly.

In the treatises entitled *Epidemiology,* for the first time in the history of medicine we find individual case studies that track the course of a disease day by day. The geographic origin of the patients is sometimes mentioned, which allows us to trace on a map the places where Hippocrates himself, or a doctor associated with his school, must have practiced. In a few of these cases, the patients lived in the cities of Thessaly (Larissa, Melibeus, Crannon, Pharsale, Pheres), but they are also found in cities of the Propontis (for example, Cyzicus and Perinthus), Thrace (Abdera and Thasos), and Macedonia (Pella).

Hippocrates' biographers link two events to his Thessalian period. The first relates to Macedonia: called to the bedside of Prince Perdiccas II of Macedonia, who was thought to have consumption after the death of his father, Alexander I, Hippocrates is said to have diagnosed him as lovesick for one of his father's courtesans. While the story may not be entirely believable, one can see in it some traces of the bonds of hospitality between the Asclepiades family and the kings of Macedonia that are found in the *Ambassadorial Speech.*

The second event is mentioned only in the *Ambassadorial Speech:* at some time during the years 419–416, Hippocrates apparently refused (again) to help the barbarian princes in the north of Greece (Illyris and Paeonia) combat the plague; however, thanks to the information he had gained from them on the nature and course of the disease, he was able to alert the Greek regions threatened, and to treat those already afflicted. This attitude won him compensation from various city-states, including Delphi; inscriptions found at Delphi indicate that Hippocrates paid a visit there, and that special privileges were extended to the Asclepiades of Cos and of Cnidus.

Hippocrates died at an advanced age in Larissa, perhaps around 377 B.C.E.

His biographers disagree as to his age at the time of death: he may have been 85 years old, or perhaps 109. Buried near Larissa, he became a legendary healer after his death, and at Cos he became the object of a public hero cult. He is figured on coins from Cos as a bald and bearded old man, sometimes in association with Heracles.

If Hippocrates' name became so famous that he was called the father of the art of medicine, it is chiefly because he made the school of which he was a product known far and wide. The school's influence was undoubtedly due in part to its expansion during Hippocrates' lifetime. A true revolution in medical training occurred at a moment that is difficult to date: the family training program in Cos was opened to students from outside the island, for a fee. It was at that point, according to Galen, that the art of medicine spread beyond the Asclepiades' line. Did this revolution occur before Hippocrates' arrival, or was he in fact responsible for it? We do not know, but it is certain that the change took place during his lifetime, since Plato, in *Protagoras*, suggests to a young Athenian that he pay Hippocrates to teach him medicine; and we know that Hippocrates had such students, since his son-in-law, Polybius, although not a direct male descendant of the Asclepiades, was nevertheless a student in Cos. The *Oath* itself confirms this dramatic change: while the second part contains the well-known code of medical ethics, the entire first part reveals that there was in fact a partnership agreement to which only the new students outside the Asclepiades family had to subscribe. The disciple agreed, under oath, to accept his teacher as a father, and eventually to offer free medical training to his teacher's sons. The biographies then name a dozen or so students, some of whom ensured the school's reputation over that of Cnidus, its neighbor and rival, even after Hippocrates' departure.

What contributed more than anything else to the fame of the Cos school and of Hippocrates are the written medical treatises in which the medical teaching was recorded. Here, however, we have to proceed with caution: although tradition has handed down to us some sixty treatises under Hippocrates' name, they are not the work of a single man, nor of a single school, nor even of a single epoch. We cannot go into the "Hippocratic question" in detail here; it is just as thorny and debatable as the Homeric question. We must refrain from unequivocally attributing any particular treatise to Hippocrates himself; but, by the same token, we must not be unduly skeptical. An important core subset of these treatises is undoubtedly the product of Hippocrates himself or his immediate followers; to this original core other treatises were added from outside Cos, often from a later period.

The central core traditionally linked to the school of Cos includes a number of well-defined groups. One group, the "surgical treatises," offers carefully edited texts describing with precision either various head injuries and their treatment—there is an especially detailed description of trepanation (*Head Wounds*)—or different methods for reducing dislocations and fractures; the search for effective treatment is based on respect for the natural conformation of the limb rather than on sensational effects *(Fractures and Articulations).* These treatises, while technical, are the work of a strong personality, remarkable for both his human and his scientific qualities, and it is perfectly possible that this figure was Hippocrates himself. These works, apparently intended for publication, are associated with others, edited in a rather terse style, that may simply be notes: for example, *Mochlicon* (the title comes from the Greek word for the "lever" used in surgery), which is a reworked summary of *Fractures and Articulations,* and *Doctor's Dispensary,* which spells out the rules for dressings and operations in the doctor's office.

Another important group consists of *Epidemics,* texts linked, as we have seen, to Hippocrates' and his disciples' Thessalian period of activity. Actually, this collection of seven treatises brings together texts written at different times, and it also artificially breaks up some obvious groupings. Three groups can be reassembled (*Epidemiology* I and III, *Epidemiology* IV and VI, and *Epidemiology* V and VII), extending from the last decade of the 5th century to the middle of the 4th; of these, only the first group can credibly be attributed to Hippocrates himself. Another well-known treatise, *On Airs, Waters, and Places,* also focuses on the activity of the itinerant doctor. Its first, scientific section explains the various external factors the physician must observe when he moves into an unfamiliar city, in order to anticipate the local diseases and treat them successfully (wind direction, water quality, climate). A second, wholly original section shifts from medicine to ethnography and explains the differences between Asians and Europeans through differences in climate and soil, and secondarily in political organization (Montesquieu will echo this argument in *Spirit of the Laws*). The importance attributed to climate reappears in a brief but remarkable treatise, *Sacred Disease,* probably by the same author, which strongly suggests that the disease in question (epilepsy) is no more sacred than others and can be explained, like any other disease, by natural causes. This treatise offers a vigorous polemic against doctors who attribute a divine origin to epilepsy and claim to treat it with magic.

Whether the physician was itinerant or stationary, to provide the best treatment he had to know how to interpret symptoms and predict the course of a disease: this is the object of the famous *Prognostic,* some of whose descriptions are canonical, for example that of a face transformed by illness and announcing imminent death (the "Hippocratic facies"). The therapeutics of acute diseases is treated in *Regimen in Acute Diseases,* a large part of which is devoted to the use of a barley brew, but it also contains prescriptions concerning the use of drinks and baths, and warnings against abrupt changes in diet. In addition, the treatises whose aphoristic style ensured that Hippocratic learning would circulate very widely are also linked to the Cos school. The collection called *Aphorisms* is the most widely read, cited, published, and discussed of all the Hippocratic treatises (the best-known being the first, "Life is brief, art is long," echoed in a verse by Baudelaire, "Art is long and time is short"). *Coan Prenotions* also received wide circulation. It constitutes a sort of critical encyclopedia of Hippocratic diagnosis. To this by no means complete list must be added, lastly, the famous *Oath*, attesting to the time when the Cos school was opened to include students from the outside, and a treatise—which Aristotle tells us is the work of Polybius, Hippocrates' son-in-law—called *The Nature of Man*, which contains the famous theory of the four humors that was subsequently attributed to Hippocrates himself.

The school of Cnidus, Cos's rival, also left some writings that have come to be included in the *Hippocratic Corpus*. They are referred to in the polemic that the author of *Diet in Acute Diseases* develops against a now lost Cnidian work entitled *Cnidian Lines;* in it he addresses some specific criticisms to the authors (he viewed it as a collective work): their list of diseases was too specific and too limited; their cursory treatments placed too much emphasis on purges like milk and whey, and they neglected the issue of diet. These charges allow us to identify, within the *Corpus*, the texts that meet these criteria. They include the nosological treatises such as *Diseases* II, *Diseases* III, and *Internal Conditions*, to which we may also add the treatises on gynecology, *Nature of Woman* and a complex group on *Female Diseases* (I, II, and III). These treatises can be identified not only by their content but also by their consistent expository style. They generally consist of a sequence of notes about different diseases or types of disease considered according to an ordering principle called *ad capite ad calcem*, from head to toe. Each note contains three main parts: symptoms, diagnosis, and treatment; the very sentence structure in the notes appears to follow an established pattern. These treatises preserve a medical tradition that seems not to have been shaped by the experience of an itinerant doctor nor to have been enlivened by any general reflection on the art of medicine, as was the case at Cos. This is not to say that the Cnidian tradition is without merit: its description of symptoms is very detailed, and in it we find for the first time in the history of medicine a description of the procedure for direct auscultation.

Over time, other treatises independent of Cos and Cnidus came to enlarge the *Corpus*. The most important are the medical treatises with a philosophical bent, like *Winds, Weeks, Flesh*, and *Diet*. In these works man appears as a microcosm reflecting the universe and composed of one or more fundamental elements: air in the case of *Winds*, fire and water in the case of *Diet*, ether, air, and earth in the case of *Flesh*, and up to seven elements in the case of *Weeks*. Two doctors in the *Corpus* argue vigorously against this sort of cosmological medicine. One is Hippocrates' disciple and son-in-law, Polybius, who, in a famous preamble, takes on the philosophers who believe that human nature is made up of a single primordial element. The other is the author of *Ancient Medicine*, who denounces the "modern doctors" who oversimplify notions that cannot explain diseases such as hot, dry, cold, or humid, and declares that all true knowledge about human nature must come from medicine.

The texts called Hippocratic thus form a complex and heterogeneous corpus (some additional texts, not discussed here, were clearly written much later). However, despite their differences, and even in the polemical texts, a certain unity of thought emerges, whether in medical practices or in the rational approach to disease and its treatment. In this respect, one can speak of "Hippocratic thought" in the broad sense. Moreover, it was the originality and strength of this thought that earned for Hippocrates, over the course of centuries, the title "father of medicine."

The primary concern of all the Hippocratics clearly was the practice of medicine, and their goal was to cure the patient. In the interest of the best possible practice, they combined examination, classification, and treatment. The Hippocratic doctor can be characterized first of all by his need to observe. Observation was subject to limitations, of course. Since dissection was not practiced, knowledge of internal anatomy was very vague. Polybius's description of the blood vessels in *The Nature of Man* was well known in its time, as attested by Aristotle's reference to it; however, it does not even mention the heart. The difference between veins and arteries was not recognized, nor was the difference between tendons and nerves. Diagnosis by taking the pulse was unknown. All those developments came later, particularly during the Hellenistic period in Alexandria. One of the more unusual opinions concerned gynecology: the uterus was thought to be subject to strange displacements within the body, moving all the way from the head to the feet. In terms of physiology, doctors were left to imagine internal processes (such as the flow of the humors) whose functioning was thought to be analogous to that of external processes (organs shaped like suction cups, such as the head and the uterus, attracted the humors). Despite these obvious obstacles, the observations doctors made were often remarkable. Hippocratic doctors, in whom all the senses were called into play, accumulated in their descriptions of diseases and patients a host of concrete and precise observations about the symptoms and the course of diseases, observations that continue to command the respect of modern medicine.

Certain descriptions are still famous, particularly the description already mentioned of what we call the Hippocratic facies—the face of a patient just prior to death—provided in the treatise *Prognostic*. Another observation still linked to the name of Hippocrates is the "Hippocratic finger," which refers to the curved nails associated with certain respiratory diseases. Some Hippocratic physicians practiced direct auscultation in cases of respiratory ailments by putting their ear to the patient's chest, and they described hearing a "leathery sound," their term for the pleural rubbing in dry pleurisy; modern medical texts still speak of the rubbing as sounding like "new leather."

Laënnec, to his credit, in his famous treatise *De l'auscultation médicale* (1819), drew attention to the practice of listening directly to the chest as the Hippocratic doctors had done, a practice that had been forgotten by their successors. The examination of symptoms was essential to making a diagnosis (which was the high point of the medical consultation, able to make or break a doctor's reputation).

The diseases observed in this way were classified by Hippocratic physicians either according to the old principle—preserved by the Cnidians—of localization, from the head to the heels, or, in the case of the Cos school, according to more elaborate principles that could vary from one treatise to another. Thus we find internal diseases contrasted with others, generalized maladies contrasted with localized ones, and acute illnesses contrasted with what have come to be known as chronic ones. Doctors tried to anticipate who would be likely to develop a particular disease on the basis of constants like the seasons or the nature of a geographical location, and on the basis of variables like the patient's age, sex, or lifestyle.

Ultimately, illnesses had to be treated. Treatment was essentially allopathic; it consisted in fighting the disease by a variety of means. The same attempt at classification and synthesis used in diagnoses was also applied to treatments. Physicians used three types of treatment, regarded as increasingly effective: purges (oral and other), incisions (especially bleeding), and cauterizations: "Whatever cannot be cured by fire," said one aphorism, "is considered incurable." But to this traditional therapeutic intervention, the Hippocratics added a new treatment: the patient's regimen. By this was meant not only diet but also lifestyle, the practice of regular physical exercise, and even the use of baths: a long treatise, entitled *Regimen*, is chiefly devoted to these considerations.

It should not be assumed that the Hippocratic physician saw his patient as only a theoretical case to study. On the contrary, the *Hippocratic Corpus* consistently reveals the doctor's humanity toward the patient. There are frequent recommendations indicating how to make the patient more comfortable, from using a pillow to choosing a less harsh treatment or designing a diet to suit the patient's tastes. Moreover, the Hippocratic doctor showed a strong sense of duty to his profession. The most famous provision in medical ethics is found in *Epidemiology* I: "Help, or at least do no harm." In taking the oath, the physician promises never to abort or to poison, never to disclose anything he has seen in the home of a patient, and to refrain from any kind of seduction. Several other treatises also contain allusions to the duties of the physician (as well as those of the patient!): *Law,* the treatises on surgery, and such later works as *Medicine, Precepts,* and *Propriety.*

The originality of Hippocratic medicine lies in the fact that it concerns not only practice but also thought and theory. Medicine did not escape the great movement of scientific and intellectual ferment that originated in Ionia in the

6th century with the thinkers of Miletus (Thales, and Anaximander and his disciple Anaximenes) and Samos (Pythagoras, who later emigrated to Croton in southern Italy) and continued in Athens with the brilliant "age of Pericles," which saw the birth of rationalism, humanism, and arts and science *(technai)*. Like other thinkers of their time, physicians reflected on their art and about science in general.

Hippocratic medicine is characterized above all by its rational approach to illness. Even if we can detect here and there the legacy of the archaic mentality that held disease to be an external demonic force, Hippocratic thought vigorously denied any divine intervention in the progress of illness, and rejected magical treatment by prayer, incantations, or purification. Many doctors reacted forcefully against seers and charlatans who attempted to act as healers. This fact is all the more remarkable because popular belief in Hippocrates' day held that disease was caused by the gods, and because religious medicine as practiced in the temples of Asclepius—and in particular in Cos—had experienced unprecedented growth. However, the rationalism of the Hippocratic doctors was not a form of atheism. The *Oath* and other pointed remarks in several treatises all acknowledge a notion of the "divine," but with a new definition: all the essential elements of the universe were considered divine, independent of man and capable of influencing both health and illness. The divine is thus called on to explain a pathological phenomenon, but it lacks any anthropomorphic content. It is a sort of rational divinity that looks very much like nature.

In this respect, Hippocratic rationalism approaches that of Thucydides: the concept of nature *(phusis)* is a central one for Hippocrates, as it is for the historian. The art of medicine, like the understanding of historical facts, is based on knowledge of the laws of human nature. But for the doctor there is the added notion that "human nature" varies according to the external environment. For example, according to the author of *The Nature of Man,* every humor in the body increases or decreases as a function of the season. For the author of *Airs, Waters, and Places,* the physical characteristics and intelligence of human beings vary as a function of the climate and the winds to which they are exposed. The doctor even becomes an ethnographer, comparing the characteristics of Europeans and Asians; he offers in passing an original depiction of the lacustrian villages of Phase (today's Rioni) and describes their inhabitants as indolent, soft, and thick, like their environment, which is swampy, hot, humid, and foggy. In this treatise we also find for the first time the opposition between *phusis* (nature) and *nomos* (custom, law): it is offered not to support the subversive theories that Callicles would develop later in order to undermine the law, but to explain how something acquired by usage—for example, the elongated head of a macrocephalic, an artifact of birth—can come to modify nature.

Greek doctors did not stop at defining the place of human beings in their environment when they reflected on the causes of disease. They also reflected on the art of medicine and on the place it occupied in human history. The author of *Ancient Medicine*, for example, regarded the doctor's art as a civilizing force thanks to the discovery of dietary principles, following on the introduction of cooking. Cooking was a process of adapting raw food to human nature by a sequence of operations, primarily heating and mixing; it was medicine that showed how cooked food could be adapted to the diets of both healthy and sick people. Thus cooked food was the mark of a superior humanism, and one that was not shared by everyone, since certain barbarians continued to feed themselves after the fashion of savages. But medicine was also seen as an art that could be called the model for all other arts. For the author of *The Art*, medicine is an elevated art, a fact only professional skeptics would dispute. In defending his argument, he launches into a reflection that might qualify as the earliest general epistemological essay left to us by antiquity. Not only does the author affirm, in the style of Parmenides, that it is impossible for science not to be, and for nonscience to be, but he also bases his arguments on both a philosophy of language and a theory of knowledge (opposing science and randomness, chance and necessity) that bring to mind the well-known Sophists and Plato. Other treatises, however, are vehemently opposed to this confusion of medicine with philosophy, and the *Hippocratic Corpus* offers valuable testimony to the identity crisis that medicine experienced at the end of the 5th century, at the moment when the art of medicine began to affirm its independence from philosophy. This independence was so fully achieved in medicine that it served in turn as the model Plato would use to define authentic history or authentic politics. And Galen later associated Hippocrates' reflection with Plato's to describe the ideal physician.

Hippocrates has shaped medical thinking for more than twenty centuries; his influence can be compared to that of Aristotle on philosophical thought. Sometimes disputed, often admired, and very often twisted to suit individual purposes, the work of the Hippocratics remained a constant reference in Western medicine from antiquity to the 19th century.

JACQUES JOUANNA
Translated by Elizabeth Rawlings and Jeannine Pucci

Bibliography

Texts and Translations

Hippocrates. *Oeuvres complètes d'Hippocrate*. Ed. Emile Littré (Greek text with French translation). 10 vols. Paris: J. B. Baillière, 1839–1861.
———. *Works*. 8 vols. Ed. and trans. W. H. S. Jones, E. T. Withington, Paul Potter, Wesley D. Smith. Loeb Classical Library.

Studies

Ayache, Laurent. *Hippocrate*. Paris: Presses Universitaires de France, 1992.

Bourgey, Louis. *Observation et expérience chez les médecins de la Collection hippocratique*. Paris: Vrin, 1953.

Di Benedetto, Vicenzo. *Il medico e la malattia: La scienza di Ippocrate*. Turin: G. Einaudi, 1986.

Duminil, Marie-Paule. *Le sang, les vaisseaux, le coeur dans la Collection hippocratique: Anatomie et physiologie*. Paris: Les Belles Lettres, 1983.

Grensemann, Hermann. *Knidische Medizin*. Vol. 1, Berlin and New York: Walter de Gruyter, 1975. Vol. 2, Stuttgart: F. Steiner Verlag, 1987.

Grmek, Mirko. *Diseases in the Ancient Greek World*. Trans. Mireille Muellner and Leonard Muellner. Baltimore: Johns Hopkins University Press, 1989.

———. *Les maladies à l'aube de la civilisation occidentale*. Paris: Payot, 1983.

Grmek, Mirko, ed. *Western Medical Thought from Antiquity to the Middle Ages*. Trans. Antony Shugaar. Cambridge, Mass.: Harvard University Press, 1998.

Joly, Robert. *Le niveau de la science hippocratique*. Paris: Les Belles Lettres, 1966.

Jouanna, Jacques. *Hippocrate*. Paris: Fayard, 1992; 2nd ed., 1995.

———. *Hippocrate: Pour une archéologie de l'école de Cnide*. Paris: Les Belles Lettres, 1974.

Lloyd, Geoffrey E. R. *Magic, Reason and Experience: Studies in the Origin and Development of Greek Science*. Cambridge: Cambridge University Press, 1979.

———. *Science, Folklore and Ideology: Studies in the Life Sciences in Ancient Greece*. Cambridge: Cambridge University Press, 1983.

Pigeaud, Jackie. *Folie et cures de la folie chez les médecins de l'antiquité gréco-romaine: La manie*. Paris: Les Belles Lettres, 1987.

Smith, Wesley D. *The Hippocratic Tradition*. Ithaca, N.Y.: Cornell University Press, 1979.

Thivel, Antoine. *Cnide et Cos: Essai sur les doctrines médicales dans la Collection hippocratique*. Publications de la Faculté des lettres et des sciences humaines de Nice 21. Paris: Les Belles Lettres, 1981.

PARMENIDES

Among the earliest Greek thinkers, it was Parmenides who gave philosophy the object that has remained central to it ever since, namely, being. He thus inaugurated the history of what is called ontology, or the science of being.

According to Diogenes Laertius, biographer of the ancient philosophers, Parmenides reached his "acme" (one's culminating point, traditionally located around the age of forty) in the sixty-ninth Olympiad (504–501 B.C.E.). This observation, based on the *Chronicles* of the chronologist Apollodorus (a text generally considered reliable), thus indicates that he was born between 544 and 541. However, that chronology appears incompatible with the account Plato gives in the *Parmenides* dialogue (127a). According to Plato, Parmenides, accompanied by his disciple Zeno, came to Athens when he was sixty-five years old, and met Socrates when the latter was still quite young. Socrates was born in 469, so the meeting Plato imagined could have taken place around 450; in that case, Parmenides would have been born about 515. But most specialists tend not to take Plato's account literally; they are inclined to credit Apollodorus's chronology instead.

Also according to Diogenes Laertius, Parmenides, son of a certain Pyres, was born in Elea, a Greek colony founded by the Phocaeans in southern Italy about 540. He is said to have given his fatherland excellent laws (this information comes from Speusippus, and it is confirmed by Strabo and Plutarch). These details have come into sharper focus since the finding in 1962, in Elea (Velia in Latin), of a headless herm dating from the first half of the 1st century C.E. and bearing the following inscription: "Parmenides, son of Pyres, Ouliades, physician." Scholars hold that "physician" means doctor here, and "Ouliades" means a descendant of Apollo Oulios, that is, Apollo the Healer, viewed as the father of Asclepius, the mythical inventor of medicine.

According to Aristotle, Parmenides was a student of Xenophanes of Colophon (*Metaphysics* I.5.986b22), while Diogenes Laertius borrows another detail from Sotion: Parmenides was a student of Ameinias, the Pythagorean. The two assertions are not incompatible: Parmenides probably had contacts with Xenophanes, who is said to have participated in the foundation of Elea, as well as with the Pythagoreans, whose school was flourishing in southern Italy at the time. At all events, Parmenides' philosophy is wholly original with respect to the teachings of his supposed masters. According to Plato, as we have seen, Zeno was one of his disciples; others claim that Empedocles of Acragas was also among his pupils.

All the ancient doxographers agree that Parmenides wrote a single work, a poem in hexametric verse entitled *On Nature*. Owing above all to citations by Sextus Empiricus and Simplicius (the latter relying on Theophrastus), about one hundred sixty verses from this poem, spread over some twenty fragments, have survived, and we have good reason to consider them authentic, since, beyond the guarantee conferred by metric analysis, they are often confirmed by citations in Plato and Aristotle. In addition, we also have some fifty statements by ancient authors attesting to Parmenides' life and his doctrine.

THE PROEM

Parmenides' poem begins with a proem of thirty-two verses (frg. I), in which the author, speaking in his own name, tells how he has been transported on a chariot drawn by docile mares and driven by young girls, identified as the daughters of the Sun, on a "many-voiced way" *(hodos poluphemos)*. This road, characterized also as "the resounding road of the goddess" and as able to lead "the man who knows" everywhere, is said to proceed from "the realm of the night" to the light, that is, to "day," while the author claims to have encountered along the way "the gate [separating] the ways of day and night." The keys to this door are said to be held by a goddess called Justice. Persuaded by the words of the daughters of the Sun, the goddess is said to have unlocked the door, thus allowing the traveler, his chariot, and his horses to enter the "high road"—the path of day.

The proem goes on to say that the goddess, presumably the same Justice, then greeted the traveler cordially, rejoicing with him that he had arrived on a road so little traveled by men but one in conformity with divine law and justice; and she described in advance the path followed by that road: "You must hear about all things, both the still heart of persuasive truth and the opinions of mortals, in which there is no true conviction. But even so, these things too you shall learn: how the things that appear would have to have real existence" (frg. I.28–32).

This narrative is manifestly inspired by the mythical tradition, in particular by travel myths, which are common in ancient epics. But there is no opposition here between myth and *logos,* or reason; Parmenides presents the myth as a true discourse, as the divine revelation of a truth. At the center of the myth is the image of the path, a trajectory leading from darkness to light, and this is presumably the symbol of the trajectory of human knowledge moving toward truth. This image subsists in later Greek philosophy: the "way" *(hodos)* becomes the "method" *(met-hodos),* the trajectory of knowledge. The content of the revelation, which is prefigured in the proem and will constitute the body of the poem as a whole, entails first a presentation of the "truth," through the description of the way things really are, then a presentation of the "opinions of mortals," that is, of what men believe (but which is false), and also an explanation of the way "the things that appear would have to have real existence."

The meaning of these last words, which clearly allude to the final section of the poem, is controversial; some recent studies (Couloubaritsis; Reale and Ruggiu) suggest that the phrase presents the final section not as an uncovering of what is false but as a valid explanation of appearances—that is, the reconnecting of physical phenomena, beyond all the erroneous opinions of mortals, with their true origin, which is a blend of two opposing principles, light and darkness. This interpretation appears to be supported by the fact that Aristotle views the last part of Parmenides' poem as an authentic expression of his thought; he even seems to appreciate it, since he discovers in it on two occasions an allusion to the discovery of the source of motion (*Metaphysics* I.3.984b2; 4.984b25).

THE REVELATION OF TRUTH

According to the unanimous interpretation of the scholars, fragments II–VIII (1–49) of Parmenides' poem contain a revelation of truth, and these fragments include more than half of the lines that have been preserved, doubtless because the ancient doxographers thought it was less important to cite the poem's last part. In the opening lines, which seem to come directly after the proem, the goddess formulates the following revelation: "I shall tell . . . just what ways of enquiry there are, the only ones that can be thought of. The one <way, which tells us> that 'is' [hopōs estin], and that it is not possible not to be, is a path of persuasion, for <persuasion> accompanies truth. The other <way, which tells us> that 'is not' [hōs ouk estin], and that it is necessary not to be; this I tell you is a road of which we can learn nothing. For you could hardly come to know what is not—for <what is not> is not accessible—nor could you tell <it to others>" (frg. II.1–8).

Here, the paths designated earlier as "the way of day" and "the way of night" seem to reappear in the form of an alternative, the one that separates the thought "is" from the thought "is not." Of the two alternatives, however, only the first, namely, the thought "is," is in conformity with truth. The second, the thought "is not," does not make it possible to learn anything; on the contrary, it even amounts to thinking nothingness, that is, to not thinking. This does not mean that the second path is absolutely impossible to follow: it is devoid of truth, and that is why all those who find themselves on it—as was doubtless the case for Parmenides himself before he was brought into the presence of the goddess—are in a state of ignorance or in error.

The fragment that comes immediately afterward seems to express the same doctrine as well: "For there is the same thing for being thought and for being" (frg. III). This does not mean that being is reduced to thought, after the manner of idealism, which is a concept foreign to the most ancient Greek philosophy and whose application would thus be totally anachronistic; it means that to think is the same thing as to think being, or else that to be is the same thing as to be thought. Indeed, the fragment is sometimes translated as follows: "To think and to be are in fact the same thing," or even: "The possibility of thinking and the possibility of existing are in fact the same thing." In any case, however the fragment is translated, the meaning indicated above is accepted more or less unanimously.

By identifying the first way, that is, the way of truth, with the thought "is," Parmenides was probably referring to all the thoughts expressed by true affirmations and containing the verb "to be," whether that verb is in the position of copula or predicate. It would be anachronistic indeed to suppose that he clearly conceptualized the distinction between a copula and a predicate, or the distinction between a predicate of the simply attributive type, a predicate of the existential type, and a predicate of the so-called veritative type (x is = x is true). Furthermore, if we may judge by the reason he gave for declaring the second path impossible to follow, Parmenides considered that such thoughts or statements were equivalent, respectively, to thinking and to expressing "being" *(to eon)*. In this way, the copula or the predicate *is* turned out to be transformed, so to speak, into indications of an object existing in itself, or of an objective reality—that is, precisely, being, which became in turn the subject of the verb *to be*.

We can see this clearly in a later fragment, in which Parmenides declares: "See <them>, though they are absent, as firmly present to the mind *[noōi]*. For <the mind> will not cut off what is from holding onto what is: <what is will not cease to hold onto what is> either by <its> scattering in all directions everywhere across the world, or by <its> coming together" (frg. IV.1–4). In short, even what is not present to the senses is thought of as being, inasmuch as it is an object of thought, and thought can think only that it is; in other words, it cannot separate being from its own being, it cannot say that being is not. Here thought, or mind *(noos)*, is viewed as true thought, capable of guaranteeing the existence of its object, even in the absence of other attestations stemming, presumably, from the senses.

The same doctrine is affirmed once again further on, when the goddess declares: "It is necessary to say this, and to think this, <namely> that there is being *[eon emmenai]*; for it is possible to be, while it is not possible for <what is> nothing <to be>" (frg. VI.1–2). Here, thinking and saying "is" become thinking and saying that "there is being," where "being" or "existent" is that which is, i.e., it is the subject about which being, as predicate, understood as a verb, is affirmed. If one must think and say that being is, the reason for this is the impossibility of thinking and saying nothingness—i.e, nonexistent, nonbeing—or better, the impossibility of thinking and saying that nothingness is. The idea is repeated in yet another fragment, one that is famous because both Plato and Aristotle cite it verbatim: "For never shall this <wild saying> be tamed, <namely> that things that are not, are" (frg. VII.1). It is not clear what "tamed" may mean here: we may understand it as "imposed by force," or else "made acceptable." In any case, the overall meaning of the sentence is that it is impossible for nonexistents to be.

Why did Parmenides consider the verb *to be* the only one capable of expressing the truth, and thus as being the sole possible object of thought? Probably because this verb is the only one that makes it possible to express, in Greek, all truths as predicate or copula. Indeed, Aristotle indicates later on that expressions such as "the man walks" or "the man cuts" are perfectly equivalent, respectively, to expressions such as "the man is walking" or "the man is cutting" (*Metaphysics* V.7). This function of universal vicariousness, so to speak, with respect to all verbs, a function belonging to the verb *to be*, must have been a phenomenon already known to Parmenides.

What is striking, nevertheless, in Parmenides' doctrine is not only that discovery—the discovery that to think and speak truly always means to think and express being—but also the affirmation, immediately linked to the preceding one, that the truth of thinking and speaking is always and only a necessary truth; in other words, thinking and expressing being not only to affirm how things are but also affirm that they are that way necessarily, that they cannot be otherwise. In fact, for the philosopher of Elea the first path, the only way endowed with truth, consists in thinking "is" and also in thinking "it is not possible not to be." If such a thought is expressed in the formula "it is possible to be" (frg. VI), by virtue of the preceding declaration this formula also signifies that "it is not possible for <what is> nothing to be," i.e., that there is necessarily being. In short, at the very moment when he is discovering being, Parmenides conceives of it as necessary, whether what is in question is copulative being, existential being, or veritative being. For Parmenides, all true knowledge is what Plato and Aristotle will later call science (*episteme*), that is, knowledge endowed with necessity.

What is the reason for this conception? What led Parmenides to think that being—everything that is, or everything that is something—is necessary, cannot not be, or cannot not be what it is? The answer is not clear. Some have found an explanation in the fact that the verb *to be* in Greek, like the equivalent verbs in the Indo-European languages, possesses a meaning—perhaps arising from a contamination of its various roots—that could be synthesized around the idea of enduring presence, permanence, which would contrast it with becoming (Aubenque). Perhaps the very opposition that Parmenides established between being and nonbeing led him to believe that being cannot in any way not be, that is, to use post-Parmenidean terms, that a being is a being by essence, which has as its unique essence being itself.

Immediately after affirming the necessity of saying that being is, the goddess adds: "For this is the first way of enquiry which *I hold* you *back* from *[eirgō]*, and then next from the <way> which mortals fabricate, knowing nothing, double-headed" (frg. VI.3–5). And right afterward, she characterizes the position of these latter as consisting in admitting that being and nonbeing are identical and nonidentical, and that for all things (or for them all), the way is "one that turns back upon itself" *(palintropos)*. In fact, the expression "hold back" is not found in any surviving manuscript; it was inserted by Diels on the basis of the so-called Aldine edition, which probably drew on manuscripts that are no longer available. The expression presupposes that that "first way" is not the one that has just barely been mentioned, the one that says "is," but the one that has remained implicit in the fragment, the one that says "is not." Furthermore, it implies that the goddess holds the traveler back from not just one but two paths, and thus that she is speaking of three paths, whereas earlier she mentioned only two paths between which the traveler had to choose.

That is why some interpreters (Cordero, for example) have preferred to introduce another expression, "you will begin" *(arxei)*, meaning that the traveler has to begin by learning the way of truth, and then must learn the way of error as well. In this view, the ways of which the poem speaks would remain two in number. However the text might best be completed (and there is unquestionably a gap here, as the metric structure proves), the consensus among contemporary scholars is that the ways mentioned by the goddess are only two in number, that of being and that of nonbeing; a possible third path, which affirms at the same time being and nonbeing, can be reduced to the second, inasmuch as the second affirms that being is not, and thus is condemned by the goddess as devoid of truth.

The same fragment raises another difficulty: who are the "double-headed" men? Some scholars have identified them with Heraclitus, a contemporary of Parmenides, by virtue of the fact that the Ephesian speaks of a harmony "that turns back upon itself" *(palintropos, frg. VIII)*; others associate them with the earlier philosophers (Ionians, Pythagoreans, and so on); still others equate them with the common man, influenced by sensations. Whoever the "double-headed" men may be, however, it seems clear that Parmenides condemns their way as an erroneous interpretation of perceptible appearances; in the second section of the poem, he presumably reserves for himself the right to supply what he deems to be the best explanation of these appearances.

The condemnation recurs in the subsequent fragment, in which the goddess declares, referring precisely to the affirmation that "things that are not, are": "But do you turn away your thought from this way of enquiry. Let not habit <too> full of experiences, drag you along this way <and force you> to exercise an aimless eye, an echoing ear and tongue; but judge by reason *[logōi]* the refutation that has been uttered by me, <a refutation> arousing much controversy *[poluderin elenchon]*" (frg. VII.2–3, frg. VIII.1). Here the senses, the eyes and ears, the source of error, and reason *(logos)*, the source of truth, are clearly contrasted; the exposition of reason is presented as a refutation *(elenchos)* of the opposing way, even if the refutation in question seems to have to be repeated several times.

After ruling out the way of error, the goddess moves on to present the path of truth, the one that says "is": on this path, she declares, are found numerous "signs" *(semata)*, that is, signals indicating direction, expressing an equivalent number of characteristics of being. These are listed in advance: unborn *(ageneton)*, imperishable *(anolethron)*, whole of limb *(oulomeles)*, unshaking *(atremes)*, unendable *(ateleston)*, one *(hen)*, continuous *(suneches)* (frg. VIII.1–6). The reason for being to be unborn and imperishable is that it cannot have an origin: if it had one, it would have to have gotten it either from nonbeing or from being; but nonbeing is not, it is neither thinkable nor expressible; and being is already, thus it cannot be that from which being takes its origin. This is why, according to the goddess, being is firmly bound up, as it were, in the chains of Justice (frg. VIII.6–15).

Of being, then, one can say neither that it was nor that it will be, but only that it "is now, all <of it> together." If in fact one were to say that it was, one could no longer say that it is, and also if one were to say that it will be, one could no longer say that it is. In short, being is eternal; it subsists in a sort of timeless present. Furthermore, it is one and continuous in the sense that it is not divisible, because it is not more in one place and less in another: it is the same everywhere, and there is nothing that can prevent it from being unified, because it is entirely full. In short, "Since staying both the same and in the same <place>, it lies by itself and stays thus fixedly on the same spot" (frg. VIII.29–30).

Finally, the goddess continues, being is limited: "for <a> powerful Necessity holds <it> in the chains of a limit *[peiratos]* which shuts it in all around," because it lacks nothing; it is complete, perfect. By virtue of the limit that encloses it, it is complete in all respects: thus it is like the mass of a well-rounded sphere, equal in all its parts, starting from the center throughout its limits (frg. VIII.30–49). Here we can clearly see the emergence of the typically Greek concept according to which limitation is not a flaw but a form of perfection, because it is synonymous with completeness. The limited nature of a sphere is only an image, which makes it possible to emphasize the perfection and the homogeneity of being without any connotation of materiality. It is probably because of this doctrine that Aristotle, though he is one of

Parmenides' harshest critics, nevertheless credits him with having conceived of being as one "in concept" *(kata ton logon)*, not "according to matter" *(kata ten hulen)*, as did Melissus *(Metaphysics* I.5.986b18–21); Aristotle approves of Parmenides for conceiving of being as limited, and he will reproach Melissus for having conceived of it as unlimited *(Physics* III.6.207a15–17).

If being is eternal, immobile, one, undifferentiated, then any expression such as "coming into being and passing away," "being and not <being>," "changing place and altering <their> bright color"—in other words, any expression indicating change, alteration, difference in place and quality, any expression created by a "mortal" in the belief that it was true—is merely a "name" *(onoma)* devoid of truth (frg. VIII.38–41). Thus Parmenides denies the reality of change and of difference, or else he relegates change and difference to the level of simple appearances, which "mortals," that is, all those who follow the path of error, are incapable of explaining in a satisfactory way.

Given these characteristics, we can understand how Parmenides' being was viewed—by his disciples Zeno and Melissus as well as by his critics Plato and Aristotle—fundamentally as "one," even if Parmenides does not place particular emphasis on this feature and stresses instead the eternal and homogeneous nature of being. Some interpreters have even explicitly denied that Parmenides' text contains the term *one (hen),* so far as the "signs" of being are concerned; they lean toward a manuscript variant that speaks only of its homogeneity (Untersteiner). Still, it is undeniable that this homogeneity rules out the existence of true differences at the heart of being: such differences would imply differing degrees or modes of being, and that is something Parmenides quite clearly disallows.

THE EXPLANATION OF APPEARANCES

The second part of Parmenides' poem is presented by the goddess herself as the account of the "opinions of mortals"; nevertheless, these latter must be learned in the proper order. According to the goddess, mortals "have set their minds on naming two forms, one of which is not right <to name>; <that is> where they have strayed <from the truth>. They separated <the two forms, so as for them to be> oppositely <characterized> in body, and they set up signs independently one from the other" (frg. VIII.50–56). Whatever the precise translation of line 54 may be, it is clear that for Parmenides it is a mistake to posit two opposing realities, and that, on the contrary, it is necessary to posit only one.

The two forms posited by mortals are fire (designated later also as light), which is tenuous and light in weight, identical to itself and opposed to the other, and night, which is dense and heavy, it, too, identical to itself and opposed to the other. "This division and ordering <of the cosmos> I tell you looks good enough, in every way [eoikota panta], for no mortal ever to be able to overtake you in the conclusion he has come to" (frg. VIII.60–61). This phrasing seems to entail an affirmation that the opinion presented by the goddess, although false (because of the opposition it establishes between two realities), remains the best of all explanations that mortals can offer for perceptible appearances.

The central thesis of the second part is then stated by the goddess in the following terms: "All is full alike of light and of night invisible, both of them equal, since <there is> nothing <that> falls to the lot of neither" (frg. IX.3–4). Here it appears clearly that the true explanation for perceptible things, that is, for appearances, is that they are all the result of a mixture between two opposing principles, one positive and the other negative, and that neither one can do without the other.

The goddess then announces an explanation of the origin, and thus of the nature (phusis), of the aether, which seems to be the element that constitutes "the sky which embraces all," the stars, the sun, the moon, and all the other heavenly bodies (frgs. X–XI). But this explanation has been preserved only in a very fragmentary fashion: the text speaks in fact of certain things that the doxographers designate as rings or "coronas," that is, circles or spheres; some are narrower, full of pure fire; these are followed by others, full of night mingled with fire; amid these spheres there is a divinity who governs all things and who presides over all unions, such as that of the male and the female toward the end of reproduction (frg. XII). This divinity would have conceived, as the firstborn of all the gods, the god of love and of generation, Eros (frg. XIII).

According to the doxographers, these entities are precisely concentric coronas, formed alternatively of light (that is, of fire) and night (earth), between which are interposed coronas made up of a mixture of both elements; on the outside there is a solid corona, and in the center there is a solid body surrounded by fire. Among the mixed coronas, the central one is the cause of movement and generation; it is a divinity known as Justice and Necessity. At all events, we encounter a grandiose cosmology that conceives of the universe as a system of concentric spheres formed by two opposite realities, a system governed by a divinity that presides over all generation by uniting and blending opposites.

Parmenides must have dwelt at length on the idea of mixture as exemplified by sexual union, for other fragments describe in detail the mixture of male and female seed, specifying that if this mixture produces a true union, well-constituted bodies result, while if the mixture gives rise to conflict, the bodies that result are tormented (frg. XVIII). Some doxographers report as one of Parmenides' doctrines the idea that if the female seed comes from the right side of the uterus, the offspring will resemble its father, whereas if it comes from the left side, it will resemble its mother; according to others, the two seeds, male and female, will struggle against each other, and the offspring will resemble the parent who produced the victorious seed.

In this context, the soul and its faculties, thought and sensation, also had to be mentioned. One fragment asserts, in fact, that thought (*noos*) is arranged in men in the same way the mixture of members takes place, "for what there is more of is thought" (frg. XVI.4). The doxographers, for their part, report that for Parmenides the soul, too, consists of a mixture of fire and earth; the soul coincides with intelligence; sensation and thought are the same thing; and knowledge is achieved through resemblance. We may conclude from this, apparently, that the soul, or thought, is constituted by a mixture of the two opposing principles, and that this is why it is capable of knowing the various realities, which are constituted by the same mixture.

Finally, in what must have been the last fragment of the poem, we read: "That then, I tell you, is how these things were born to be and now are and shall from this <time> onward grow and die, in the way that <people think of them and that> they appear <to them to be>. To them men have assigned a name, peculiar to <and distinctive of> each <and every> one" (frg. XIX). This seems to confirm that the account just produced has to do with opinions held by men: what is at issue, in other words, is not real truth but the world of perceptible appearances. At the same time, the goddess repeats that what is in question is the most plausible explanation of the origin and the nature of these appearances, and thus also of the names that men have given them. In short, it seems that, in the second part of his poem, Parmenides intended to offer us what would later be called a physics, the best physics possible, even while he remained convinced of the purely illusory character of perceptible appearances.

PARMENIDES' LEGACY

Parmenides' doctrine had an enormous influence over all of ancient philosophy. His disciples, Zeno of Elea and Melissus of Samos, left the second part of the poem completely aside; they abandoned the effort to produce a theory of nature, and they interpreted the first part of the poem as the assertion of a being that is essentially one and immutable. Zeno set out to refute multiplicity and becoming, with his celebrated arguments by way of the absurd; that is why Plato and Aristotle view him as the founder of dialectics. Melissus, in contrast, interpreted being as a unique mass of matter, and consequently conceived of it as infinite in space as well. That is why Aristotle saw Melissus as a crude thinker.

The other philosophers of nature, Empedocles, Anaxagoras, and the Atomists Leucippus and Democritus, fell under Parmenides' influence to a similar extent. At the base of all things, they posited realities (respectively, the four elements, the "seeds" of all things, the atoms) that were permanent, although multiple. Moreover, in their opposition between plenitude and multitude, the Atomists reproduced the Parmenidean opposition between being and nonbeing. Parmenides' doctrine was contested later in a thoroughgoing way by the Sophist Gorgias, who affirmed what being is not, that it is not thinkable and not communicable. Among his various arguments, one in particular stands out: being, since it is uniquely identical to itself, has nothing more than nonbeing, which is also identical to itself; for this reason, one cannot say that it is, that it is thinkable, and that it is communicable, any more than nonbeing is.

Reference to Parmenides is a central feature in Plato's writings. Plato describes Parmenides as "one to be venerated" and also "awful" (*Theaetetus* 183e); he gives his name to one of the dialogues, presenting Parmenides above all as a proponent of oneness; and he refutes him in *Sophist*, where he presents his critique of Parmenides as a form of parricide. This critique consists in positing nonbeing alongside being, but nonbeing understood not as absolute nonbeing (after the fashion of the void introduced by the Atomists), but as an "otherness" that belongs to every being, together with "sameness." In this way Plato paves the way for Aristotle's critique, which accuses Parmenides of having conceived of being in only one sense, namely as univocal, and Aristotle opposes his own conception of being as plurivocal, as something that has several meanings (*Physics* I.2–3).

In modern and contemporary philosophy, because Parmenides said that being is identical to itself, he has been viewed as having discovered what is called the principle of identity, according to which every existent is identical to itself; and because he said that being cannot not be, he has been viewed as having discovered the principle of noncontradiction. In reality, the latter principle, formulated by Plato and Aristotle, simply says that each existent cannot have opposite characteristics at the same time and under the same aspect. The most appropriate modern interpretation may remain Hegel's: because Parmenides took as his object the philosophy of being, which is the first of all concepts, he is, for Hegel, the true initiator of all Western philosophy. Hegel nevertheless also took up Gorgias's critique, by observing that being, by being simply identical to itself, that is, devoid of all determination, has nothing more than nonbeing and is thus reduced to the latter, thereby giving rise to becoming. More recently Parmenides was exalted by Heidegger, who interpreted the identity of being and thought, affirmed by the philosopher from Elea, as an opening of being to thought, and thus as truth (*aletheia*) in the original sense of nonconcealment, a truth that precedes the logical form of the proposition and all the representative thought based on that form (*Introduction to Metaphysics*, 1953).

ENRICO BERTI
Translated by Catherine Porter and Jeannine Pucci

Bibliography

Texts and Translations

Parmenides. *Fragments: A Text and Translation.* Intro. David Gallop. Toronto: University of Toronto Press, 1984.
———. *The Fragments of Parmenides: A Critical Text.* Trans. and ed. A. H. Coxon. Assen: Van Gorcum, 1986
———. *Le poème de Parménide: Texte, traduction, essai critique.* Trans. and ed. Denis O'Brien. Vol. 1 of *Etudes sur Parménide.* Ed. Pierre Aubenque. 2 vols. Paris: Vrin, 1987.
———. "The Proem." In G. S. Kirk, J. E. Raven, and M. Schofield, *The Presocratic Philosophers: A Critical History with a Selection of Texts.* 2nd ed. Cambridge: Cambridge University Press, 1983.

Studies

Allen, R. E., and David J. Furley. *Studies in Presocratic Philosophy,* vol. 2. London: Routledge, 1975.
Aubenque, Pierre, ed. *Etudes sur Parménide.* 2 vols. Paris: Vrin, 1987.
Barnes, Jonathan. *The Presocratic Philosophers,* 2nd ed. London: Routledge, 1982.
Beaufret, Jean. *Le poème de Parménide.* Paris: Presses Universitaires de France, 1955.
Conche, Marcel. *Parménide: Le Poème: Fragments.* Paris: Vrin; Brussels: Ousia, 1996.
Cordero, Nestor-Luis. *Les deux chemins de Parménide.* Brussels: Ousia, 1984.
Couloubaritsis, Lambros. *Mythe et philosophie chez Parménide.* Brussels: Ousia, 1986.
Dumont, Jean-Paul. *Les présocratiques.* Paris: Gallimard, 1988.
Guthrie, W. K. C. *A History of Greek Philosophy,* vol. 2: *The Presocratic Tradition from Parmenides to Democritus.* Cambridge: Cambridge University Press, 1965.
Heidegger, Martin. *An Introduction to Metaphysics.* Trans. Ralph Manheim. New York: Doubleday, 1961.
Kirk, J. S., J. E. Raven, and M. Schofield. *The Presocratic Philosophers,* 2nd ed. Cambridge: Cambridge University Press, 1983.
Mourelatos, Alexander. *The Pre-Socratics: A Collection of Critical Essays.* Garden City, N.Y.: Anchor Press, 1974.
Reale, Giovanni, and Luigi Ruggiu. *Parmenides: Poema sulla Natura: I frammenti e le testimonianze indirette.* Milan: Rusconi, 1991.
Reinhardt, Karl. *Parmenides und die Geschichte der griechischen Philosophie.* Bonn: Cohen, 1916.
Tarán, Leonardo. *Parmenides: A Text with Translations, Commentary and Critical Essays.* Princeton: Princeton University Press, 1965.
Untersteiner, Mario. *Parmenide: Testimonianze e frammenti.* Florence: Nuova Italia, 1958.

PLATO

PLATO OF ATHENS (429–347 B.C.E.) descended from a wealthy and distinguished Athenian family; on his mother's side he had Solon, the great lawgiver, as an ancestor. His family, like many, was divided by the disastrous political consequences of the Peloponnesian War. Plato's stepfather, Pyrilampes, was a friend of Pericles and a democrat who even called his own son Demos; but two of Plato's uncles, Critias and Charmides, became members of the Thirty Tyrants, infamous for their reactionary, antidemocratic, and lawless rule. Plato probably grew up expecting to play a prominent role in public life, but so far as we know he did not do so either under the Thirty or under the restored democracy.

At some point in his life Plato decided to devote his life to philosophy, and he took two steps that decisively detached him from his family and political context. He rejected marriage and the normal duty to family and clan of producing citizen sons. (To the performance of this duty one's personal sexual preferences were irrelevant, so we cannot ascribe this rejection to Plato's being homosexual in temperament, something that seems evident from much of his writing.) He also founded a philosophical school, called the Academy after the public gymnasium where it held its discussions and instruction. The Academy, something new in the Greek world, soon became famous and attracted many students, the most noteworthy being Aristotle. We have almost no evidence as to its organizational structure, but the founding of this new institution, inward-looking and "academic" by comparison with the public activities of the Sophists, marks an important point in the history of philosophy. Thenceforward, philosophical schools would be distinguished by different doctrines, approaches, and arguments.

Ironically, the motivation for this momentous step came in large part from the influence on Plato of Socrates of Athens, someone who himself wrote nothing and founded no organized school. Socrates was a charismatic figure of undistinguished background, and by the end of his life he was poor because of his devotion to philosophical activity; earlier he had served as a heavily armed soldier, or hoplite, a duty requiring substantial financial means. Socrates attracted a great variety of pupils and became the ideal figure of the philosopher. Many of his followers wrote dialogues including him; the later dominance of Plato's dialogues should not make us lose sight of the fact that many different writers and philosophers claimed Socrates as the inspiration and symbol of their ideas. He was regarded as the "patron saint" of ascetic

Cynics, hedonistic Cyrenaics, Stoics, and Skeptics, as well as of the ideas that Plato presents in his works. Socrates' deep influence on Plato is clear from the fact that most of Plato's works take the form of dialogues between Socrates and other people, even where, as in some later dialogues, this is plainly unsuitable and the actual role of Socrates shrinks. Also influential, of course, was the fact of Socrates' execution by the restored democracy, on the vague and inflammatory charge of introducing new divinities and corrupting the young men. It has always been suspected that the charge was politically motivated and stemmed from Socrates' association with some of the political leaders who had destroyed the democracy during the closing years of the Peloponnesian War. But whatever the truth of this, Plato was certainly moved to spend much of his own philosophical activity defending the memory of Socrates.

The ancient biographical tradition about Plato offers much romantic detail to fill in the sparse outline I have given of a life lived teaching philosophy, mainly in Athens. The ancient accounts of Plato's life ascribe to him, for example, extensive travels. Scholarly study of the accounts' sources, however, should incline us to suspend judgment about most of what they contain, for much of the detail is tailor-made to fit with aspects of the dialogues. In *Laws*, for example, Plato discusses Egyptian art and its high degree of stylization (656–657), and the ancient biographies tell us of a trip to Egypt. We may suppose that the latter is historical fact that explains the former. But we may equally well suppose that it is an example of a common tendency to explain something in Plato's writing by giving it a personal reason or association.

Part of this reconstructed biography, of uncertain date, took the form of alleged "letters," a recognized literary genre that probably did not originally intend to deceive. One of them, the seventh, which gives an account of Plato's relationships with Dionysius II of Syracuse and his relative Dion, has been accepted by many scholars and even turned into an account of historical fact explaining Plato's political writings, particularly *The Republic*. This is surely unsafe; the authenticity of the "Seventh Letter" remains controversial, and it is regarded by many as created later to illuminate *The Republic*.

The tendency to accept "biographical" background about Plato has been particularly strong in the 20th century. However, it has also been influenced by a constant desire to find *something* that straightforwardly expresses, or explains, Plato's views on a topic. For Plato differs strikingly from most philosophers: deliberately spurning the standard format of the prose philosophical treatise, he chose to use the form of dialogues, in none of which he appears as an interlocutor, thereby formally distancing himself from what is expressed in any of his works. The desire for a "Life and Letters of Plato" undoubtedly springs in part from the frustration that many readers feel at this detachment.

In the Academy Plato probably did some oral teaching, and he gave one unsuccessful lecture, "On the Good," but his only preserved works were a number of dialogues. Since the 19th century, great effort has been expended on establishing the chronology of their composition, but in spite of much computer-based analysis, no stylistic test serves to establish any precise order. However, there is a general consensus on three roughly marked groups: (1) the short "Socratic" dialogues, in which Socrates is the main figure, questioning others but putting forward no philosophical theses himself; (2) the "middle" dialogues, notably *Phaedo, The Republic*, and *Symposium*, marked by large, confident metaphysical schemes; (3) the later dialogues, in which the dialogue form is used merely for exposition, Socrates retires as the chief figure, and Plato deals with philosophical issues in a way that is more piecemeal and more "professional," paying serious attention to other philosophers' views. Some dialogues are difficult to place; *Theaetetus* and *Euthydemus* seem, in different ways, to postdate *The Republic*, but both return to the Socratic format and examine Socratic method. *Timaeus* and its unfinished companion, *Critias*, belong thematically with *The Republic* but fit stylistically with later dialogues, such as *Laws*. Plato is a skilled and versatile writer whose works cannot be listed chronologically by any simple stylistic criteria.

The dialogues are not only bewilderingly varied but are also more interpretatively open than other ancient philosophical works. From antiquity onward there has been an unceasing debate as to whether Plato put forward any systematic positive ideas. Arcesilaus (315–240 B.C.E.), who became the head of the Academy, initiated a period during which Plato's philosophical legacy was taken to be one of debate and argument, not doctrines. This "skeptical" or investigative way of reading Plato gave great emphasis to *Theaetetus*, the dialogue in which Socrates compares himself to a barren midwife who draws philosophical ideas out of others and criticizes them, but puts forward none himself. On this conception, it is all right for the philosopher to hold positions, as Socrates emphatically does, but these are not advanced to be argued for, nor as the basis for further argument. The philosophical impulse is to "follow the argument where it leads," to destroy the ill-conceived views of others, as Socrates does, not to put forward a system of one's own.

However, while the skeptical reading of Plato can account excellently for the Socratic dialogues and *Theaetetus*, it does not seem to do as well with the confident positive pronouncements of dialogues like *The Republic* and *Laws*. It can, of course, regard these as mere presentations of positions for argument, but from antiquity onward this reading has had to compete with the "dogmatic" reading, according to which the dialogues should be read as presenting pieces of doctrine that the reader is encouraged to put together in systematic ways. The dogmatic reading has, historically, been by far the more popular one, and most of the discussion of Plato's thought has taken the form of arguing about how, not whether, it should be systematized. In the 1st century B.C.E. we find the writer Arius Didymus insisting that "Plato has many voices, not, as some think, many doctrines" (*ap.* Stobaeus, *Eclogae* II.55.5–6). The dogmatic reading has to cope with the diverse and unsystematic nature of the dialogues, with some conflicts between passages in different dialogues, and with the changing role of Socrates. In the 20th century, few interpreters have doubted that Plato's thought undergoes development, but for the most part this has been traced as a development of doctrine. Often it is assumed that in the early dialogues Plato is reproducing the thought of the actual Socrates, while in the middle and later dialogues he goes on to develop his own ideas.

As is clear by now, there is no uncontroversial way of presenting Plato's thought. Some aspects of his thought invite the reader to open-ended investigation of the philosophical issues. Others present the reader with worked-out positions. These can always, of course, be regarded as *merely* presentations of positions for argument, but still they are substantial enough to characterize a number of views as distinctively "Platonic." Any brief introduction to Plato risks losing either the emphasis on continuing investigation and argument or the importance of adopting certain positions and rejecting others. In what follows I shall focus on certain prominent themes and their development in Plato's writings, rather than either presenting Plato's ideas as finished doctrines or merely listing the arguments without systematizing their conclusions.

Much of Plato's discussion clusters around two recurring themes: knowledge and the conditions for it (and, concurrently, claims about the metaphysical nature of what is known) and the importance of morality in the best human life (and the proper conditions for society to produce the best life). I shall follow through these themes in turn, seeking to bring together, in mutually illuminating ways, a number of Plato's most central arguments. Inevitably this approach is selective and omits much of independent interest—for example, Plato's view of *eros*, his differing positions on art, and his views on the soul and its afterlife. But with Plato, even more than other philosophers, a listing of his concerns misses the point of his activity as a philosopher, something that a selective discussion can bring into sharper focus.

In the early dialogues, Socrates is constantly in search of knowledge. He supposes that his interlocutors have it but discovers by questioning that they do not. Sometimes the supposition is patently insincere, and provides comedy (often rather cruel) at the interlocutor's expense. What is immediately striking is that Socrates is not afflicted with modern epistemological doubt about ordinary knowledge claims; he shows no hesitation in claiming to have knowledge about a variety of ordinary matters, but this is seen as irrelevant to his need for a kind of knowledge that he frequently calls wisdom *(sophia)*. When he disclaims knowledge, it is this kind that he disclaims, so that there is no inconsistency with his retaining ordinary knowledge claims. (Nonetheless, this sets up a somewhat awkward situation in which there are two standards for knowledge, the ordinary and the higher.)

Wisdom is not a lofty or meditative state; the people who have it, Socrates agrees, are simple craftspeople. They are cobblers, weavers, ordinary working people whom Socrates is scornfully accused of constantly dragging into the discussion. What Socrates admires as a paradigm of knowledge is *expert* knowledge, *techne* or expertise. Right from the start, therefore, Socrates assumes that knowledge of the kind he seeks can be found, for everyday examples of it exist. There is no attempt to meet the skeptic who denies that there is knowledge. Socrates' complaint is rather that actual experts are insufficiently aware of the limits of their expertise; his own goal is a global expertise over one's life as a whole, a knowledge of how best to live. Such knowledge has ethical implications and, as we shall see, is taken to be the essential aspect of virtue.

An expertise extends over its field as a whole; it is not an aggregative knowledge of matters of fact. When Ion says that he has expert knowledge of poetry, but only of Homer, Socrates takes it as obvious that if he lacks knowledge of other poets, he also lacks (expert) knowledge of Homer. This point, untrue of our familiar notion of knowledge, shows that expert knowledge is a unified understanding. It also involves a grasp of principles rather than just memory of facts. A plausible comparison might be understanding a language; if one knows the indicative but not the subjunctive, then one just does not know Latin. Also of great importance is the characterization of expertise offered in *Gorgias*. Socrates sharply distinguishes "experience," our ordinary way of getting by unsystematically on the basis of memory and observation, from expertise, a unified intellectual grasp based on *logos*, reasoning, enabling the expert to say what it is that he knows, and to justify his judgments in particular cases. The expert, unlike the person who proceeds unsystematically on the basis of experience, has something that he understands, and can explain and justify what he understands.

This is an attractive model of knowledge. The basic demand is for the explanation and justification that only the person with understanding can provide; a different model from the post-Cartesian demand for certainty and absence of doubt that has dominated modern discussions of knowledge. A problem arises, however, in that Socrates' method for achieving his goal, the famed Socratic "testing," or elenchus, does not seem a promising way to achieve it. In dialogues like *Laches*, Socrates declares that what is being sought is expertise, but what he then proceeds to do is to argue negatively against his interlocutors' suggestions. When Laches and Nicias offer answers to the question, What is bravery? Socrates draws them into committing themselves to other theses, and then points out that these conflict with the original suggestion. All that has been shown, of course, is that the interlocutor is committed to inconsistent premises; he could reject any of the theses that lead to the problem. In fact, however, the discussion is always focused on the original suggestion, and the result of the elenchus is that the interlocutor, and Socrates, end up knowing more about what bravery or friendship or piety is not, but no nearer to knowing what it is.

Not only is the elenchus an irritating procedure that makes several interlocutors lose their temper, but also it is hard to see how it could get Socrates any nearer the goal of expert knowledge. As a technique, it is appropriate to the investigative, "skeptical" Socrates, concerned to destroy ignorant pretension. But it does not have the potential to produce expert knowledge of the required kind. There is a systematic mismatch between Socrates' goal and his method of achieving it. In one dialogue, *Gorgias,* the elenchus appears in a somewhat different light, and Socrates makes rather different claims about it. It is characterized as a way of uncovering a person's real beliefs: argument forces you to admit what you really believed all along, although before the argument with Socrates you rejected it—usually because the thesis in question is counterintuitive, even absurd to most people. This much stronger conception of the role of argument goes along with increased claims by Socrates that the argument has *forced* the interlocutor to a conclusion, and that the arguments are as unbreakable "as iron and adamant" (508e–509d). But no grounds are given for these increased claims about the elenchus, and they are most implausible, and not repeated in other dialogues.

The mismatch between goal and method is at its most striking in the dialogues of "Socratic definition," where the goal is to answer the question, What is X (bravery, etc.)? Socrates is not concerned with definitional questions as such, and it is misleading to think of these dialogues as concerned with meaning; the question What is X? applies where there is, in Socrates' view, expert knowledge to be had. From *Laches,* where the preferred answers turn out to be either too broad or too narrow, we find increasingly more stringent initial conditions on an acceptable answer. In *Euthyphro* and *Hippias Major* we find that the answer to the question, What is piety (etc.)? has to be in some way explanatory of our claims that certain kinds of things or actions are pious. Further, we find that grasping such an answer is described metaphorically as "looking toward the form" of the notion in question, "form" (*eidos,* idea) being the ordinary Greek for the appearance of a thing. And an acceptable answer to the question What is F?, we find in *Hippias Major,* has to meet two more conditions: it must be itself F, and it must be in no way the opposite of F. The demand that what explains particular cases of being F must be itself F comes from a generally accepted conception of explanation: only something that is itself F could do this job. The demand that it be in no way the opposite of F comes from a desire to evade counterexamples. Plato is concerned that things that are F by some standard turn out to be the opposite of F by some other standard; faced by even a well-established example of justice, or piety, an opponent can show it to be unjust or impious by clever counterexamples appealing to some other standard. We do not have to look far for the source of this worry; it is the sophistic practice of producing arguments on both sides of an issue, illustrated dramatically for us in *Double Arguments (Dissoi logoi)*. Plato is convinced that where expert knowledge is possible, its object cannot be the object of this kind of counterclaim. Taken together, these conditions push Plato away from accepting empirically based claims as knowledge, since such claims are always open to counterexamples of the kind he produces. But this point is not made explicitly.

In *Meno*, elenchus is dramatically replaced by a new idea—knowledge is really "recollection." For the person to acquire knowledge is for his soul to recollect what it already knew before incarnation. This new account of knowledge is tailored for the acquisition of a priori knowledge, and is introduced by an example in which Socrates gets an uneducated slave boy to understand a mathematical proof. Since the proof requires the introduction of a counterintuitive idea, Plato is also introducing a basis for his demand that knowledge of some topics requires revision or discarding of everyday empirical beliefs. Plato's demands on knowledge have got him to raise the standards so that now only intellectually graspable objects, like mathematical proofs, meet them. However, he develops one feature of the *techne* conception of knowledge: knowledge, characterized as understanding, is something that each knower has to achieve for him- or herself: it is only when the boy can do the proof for himself that he will know it.

Further, it is in *Meno* that Plato, having raised the standards for knowledge, clearly distinguishes it from true belief, a status to which he now relegates what were previously taken as everyday-level knowledge claims. Later in the dialogue he distinguishes knowledge from true belief with the condition that the knower can "tie down" the true belief by "reasoning out the cause," a plausible development of the explanatory side of the expertise model. However, although this process is said to be recollection, Plato unambiguously produces an example of empirical knowledge—knowledge of the road to Larisa. Scholars have been much exercised by this seeming slip—for what can my soul be recollecting when I come to know the road to Larisa? It seems that Plato is working with a broad conception of knowledge, for which the conditions are that the knower come to understand what is known *for himself*, and be able to justify and explain his knowledge claims; but at the same time he is drawn (doubtless under the influence of mathematics as an example of an undisputed body of knowledge) to the thought that knowledge proper is to be found only in fields where this kind of justification can be found entirely from within the knower himself—that is, entirely a priori.

In the well-known "middle" dialogues *Phaedo* and *The Republic*, we see the convergence of Plato's different lines of thought about knowledge and its objects, and the formation of a grand, ambitious conception of both, one that has dominated interpretation of Plato, perhaps excessively. Two lines of thought hitherto developed separately are brought together. On the one hand, *Meno* argues that some knowledge, at least, must be a priori, obtained "from within" the person by use of his or her mind, without reliance on the empirical world; but the only examples of this knowledge are mathematical proofs. On the other hand, Socratic dialogues such as *Euthyphro* and *Hippias Major*, which call the desired objects of expert knowledge "forms," set up conditions for their achievement that seem to rule out ordinary empirical access (since any empirical account we can give of justice, piety, and so on, seems vulnerable to empirical counterexample) but leave the reader in the dark as to how actually to get knowledge of such forms, especially since the only available instrument, the elenchus, seems to be inadequate in principle. In the middle dialogues we find that the objects of knowledge are forms, and that they are taken to be nonempirical.

At the end of the fifth book of *The Republic* Plato gives us an argument to show that knowledge has forms as objects. He claims that, since the person with knowledge cannot be wrong, the objects of knowledge must be "fully" or "purely" what they are; otherwise knowledge would not be "of what is, to know it as it is." This idea is clarified by means of the same kind of example as in *Hippias Major:* everyday instantiations or characterizations of what is just, pious, good, and so on, all have the defect that they also turn out to be unjust, impious, bad, and so on. The examples of forms are familiar from early dialogues in their search for accounts of moral terms; here, and in the analogous passage of *Phaedo*, they are joined by mathematical and quantitative examples (half, double, straight, equal) reflecting the new confidence in mathematics as a field of knowledge.

Plato's argument falls far short of showing that *only* forms can be objects of knowledge, for the condition is that what is known be "fully" what it is, in a way that precludes error and precludes its being called the opposite of whatever it happens to be. The cases Plato has in mind are clearly disputable ethical terms, and mathematical terms like *equal*. Plato does not acknowledge the point that the problems arise when there is an opposite to the term in question and do not apply to terms with no opposites. Since, as Aristotle was later to observe, substance has no opposite, substances such as people, horses, and the like would seem to be possible objects of knowledge. And they could be, so far as Plato's actual arguments go, although he undoubtedly writes, in the middle dialogues, as though he had consigned the entire world as we perceive it to the realm of belief rather than knowledge.

It remains a large problem for Plato's position on forms that the only argument for forms in the middle dialogues is the "argument from opposites," which cannot be extended to other terms. In the tenth book of *The Republic* Plato talks of a form of bed, but this is generated by the framework of the argument, which represents artworks, artifacts, and forms as all being examples of things made (either by skill or by copying). It is unclear how serious this argument is, and likewise unclear how Plato believes himself entitled to think, as he sometimes does, as though forms corresponded to all the terms we use, not just terms with opposites. Nor is it easy to see how he could do this without trivializing the grounds for introducing forms. (A passage in *The Republic*, 596a, sometimes thought to introduce a form for every general term, is in fact quite controversial, and the Greek has been construed in very different ways.) It is not surprising that in a presumably later dialogue, *Parmenides*, Plato has Socrates express doubt as to whether there are forms for substance terms and shrink from commitment to forms of hair and mud, while having no doubt as to forms for the kinds of terms to which the argument from opposites is applied in the middle dialogues.

The knowledge that Plato envisions in *The Republic* is, as we shall see, practical. However, it is also theoretical, bringing to a culmination Plato's increasing interest in mathematics from *Meno* through *Phaedo*. The two strands are not brought together very convincingly. Plato insists that his ideal rulers will direct practical matters in a way that is based on unified insight into principles, as the doctor and the navigator do. Yet he insists that this insight must be based on lengthy abstract intellectual training, founded on mathematical reasoning, which decreases dependence on the senses and encourages the person to rely on abstract thinking.

Mathematics gives us confidence that there is knowledge that is not dependent on sense experience. However, it also serves as a model in its methods and structure. Plato takes from mathematics the notion of hypothesis, a protean idea that figures rather differently in *Meno, Phaedo*, and *The Republic* and, more important, develops the idea that the understanding that knowledge involves has the structure of the understanding that someone would have who had mastery of the relations holding in a field where results are obtained deductively using a set of primary principles. Given the evidence for interest in mathematics in Plato's Academy, it is likely that he would have in mind an embryonic form of what was to become Euclidean geometry. Knowledge, in *The Republic*, has the form of mathematics (geometry, that is) writ large; to have knowledge is to have the understanding that someone has of an abstract field and the relations of derivation and dependence holding within it. Nothing less counts as knowledge; anything short of this is mere true belief. Few accounts of knowledge have been as ambitious.

But we have more surprises yet. Because Plato is insistent that the knowledge that concerns him, however abstract, must issue in practical directions, he holds that the ultimate ground of the whole system, the basis for all the abstract derivation, is the form of the Good, which is the source of everything, not merely intelligibility but the very being of things (509a–b). Plato leaves this suggestive thought, deliberately, at the metaphorical level. It does not seem to solve the potential tensions between the theoretical and practical aspects of this grand conception of knowledge.

Finally, there remains a constant element at the heart of Plato's grand synthesis. The philosophers in his ideal state will do mathematics as a preparation for philosophy proper, the intellectual discipline that comes to understand everything in the light of the form of the Good. Although Plato's account is sketchy, we get some idea of the method to be employed at this crucial point. And it is the same as the philosophical method visible since the early dialogues—argument.

In dialogues that are traditionally regarded as later than *The Republic*, we find that its grand metaphysical and epistemological synthesis has fallen apart. We do not find trenchant criticisms of it, but we do not find it recurring either. Plato no longer has one concern with knowledge and its objects, but several. One striking development is that the practical and theoretical strands in Plato's account of knowledge become separated. In *Statesman* we find, unchanged, the view that directive practical knowledge has the structure of a *techne*, but its abstract and mathematical underpinnings have disappeared. Plato has not lost interest in the distinctive nature of mathematical thinking. In *Laws* the capacity for mathematical thinking is what distinguishes those who have a serious claim to intellectual activity from those who do not, and in *Philebus* the mathematical method is contrasted sharply with the empirical. Mathematics continues to be important to Plato for its potential for improved effectiveness in skills and techniques, and because it represents for him a way of thinking intrinsically superior to any that relies on the empirical world. But, deprived of its place in the grand synthesis, mathematical thinking shrinks in significance; in *Laws*, for example, there is a tension between the continued praise of mathematical thinking and a new, more Aristotelian stress on the importance of learning from experience.

The nature of Plato's continued interest in forms is more elusive. Partly because of the dominance of *The Republic* in Plato studies, forms have been far more prominent in Plato interpretation than they are in Plato, who says strikingly little about them and presents a few arguments without ever trying to bring them together in a connected theory. The one passage of Plato devoted to sustained discussion of forms is wholly negative: the first part of *Parmenides*, where various powerful arguments are brought against forms, and no answers are supplied. Whatever Plato's opinion of these arguments (some bear a strong resemblance to arguments in early Aristotle), forms in the later dialogues revert to a role more like their earlier one. Plato takes it that some kinds of things have an objective nature, and that the way to discover it is to bring the mind actively to bear on the data of experience. His attention has shifted, however, from the problematic moral and mathematical concepts of the early dialogues to a more general concern with the definition of natural-kind terms. Large parts of the later dialogues *Sophist* and *Statesman* are devoted to the search for definitions that will mark out the objective divisions of reality. Plato calls this process "collection and division"; his char-

acterizations of it are difficult and contentious, as is the question of its relation to basic philosophical discussion and argument.

Further, Plato is now inclined, sometimes in a rather professorial way, to
stress the need for pedagogical practice before embarking on important topics,
and so spends large amounts of time on illustrative definitions of subjects like
weaving. However, one central point remains the same: Plato still holds that
there are, in the world, objective natures and real divisions between kinds, and
that to grasp these requires active thought and inquiry, not just passive reliance on phenomena. Any idea that forms might correspond to general terms
is exploded by a passage that declares that language can be misleading; Greeks
like to divide the world up into Greeks and barbarians, but this is merely the
projection of Greek prejudice: there is no form of barbarian, since the word
simply means "not Greek," and this is not a unifying characteristic. Which of
our words do, then, pick out real kinds? We cannot say in general; there is no
single method, only the use of inquiry in each case *(Statesman)*.

Plato's concern with knowledge continues, and is shown in one of his finest
dialogues, *Theaetetus*, but in a way that bypasses rather than explores the
conceptions of knowledge brought together in *The Republic*. *Theaetetus*, by
raising the question, What is knowledge? brings into question the assumptions of the early dialogues, and pursues difficulties in the everyday notion of
knowledge, leaving mathematics and higher philosophical flights aside. One
aspect of this pursuit is that Plato's concern, in much of the dialogue, is to argue for the existence of objective knowledge, against various forms of relativism and subjectivism represented by Protagoras. The other is that he has expanded his view of knowledge to include types that have hitherto interested
him not at all. Right at the end of the dialogue we find some examination of
the idea that knowledge might be true belief *plus* some extra factor, which he
calls "an account." He explores different construals of this, without success.
This notion of knowledge, that it is some kind of improved true belief, is otherwise glimpsed only at the end of *Meno*, and is in general upstaged in Plato's
thought by the idea of knowledge as some kind of expertise. It is an indication
of the continued fertility of Plato's thought that he should at this point raise
an essentially fresh view of knowledge—one that lays more weight on the
justification for particular knowledge claims. We find this further developed
in the Hellenistic period, as well as in much of modern epistemology.

Plato's concerns with knowledge and its objects thus display a pattern: in
the Socratic dialogues a number of lines of thought are developed separately,
brought together in the grand synthesis of *The Republic*, and later developed
separately once more. In this, as in other areas, the dominance of *The Republic* can distract attention from the interest and subtlety of Plato's treatment of
the distinct strands.

Plato's concern with morality and the good life likewise shows continuity
of concern coupled with dramatic shifts of interest from the early to the mid-

dle and from the middle to the late dialogues. Plato shifts on the relation of individual and social morality, and on issues like the relation of happiness to pleasure, but on the importance of morality in the individual's life, and insistence on the objectivity of values, he is consistent from beginning to end.

In a passage in *Euthydemus* Socrates undertakes to show to a young boy why wisdom is worth pursuing; he recommends a serious commitment to learning, and to argument as an intellectual tool, as opposed to the shallow, and ultimately naive and clownish, arguments of the Sophists with whom he is confronted. It is not merely a matter of intellectual fashion whether one follows Socrates or the Sophists. The choice between them is presented as a choice between ways of life: on the one hand there is trivial competitiveness; on the other, Socrates' wisdom, a wisdom that in recognized worldly terms constitutes pathetic failure—failure to achieve wealth, success, even to save his own life—but that the thoughtful can recognize as true virtue. Socrates' search for knowledge is also a search for virtue; knowledge is not taken to be a purely cognitive state isolated from the rest of one's life.

Socrates begins from the assumption that everyone seeks happiness. Given the ancient notion of happiness, a vague and capacious one, this is taken to be trivially true. It is not itself a Socratic thesis but a commonplace that Plato relies on as late as *Laws*. Plato never spells out for us, as Aristotle would do later, the structure of this initial thought: we all seek an overarching final end in all we do, and we agree that this is happiness (since happiness is the only end that, intuitively, we seek for its own sake and not for the sake of any further end) though we disagree as to what happiness is. Nonetheless, it is reasonable to see Plato as working intuitively with the basic structure of eudaemonistic ethics, which Aristotle was the first to articulate. But since Plato does not articulate it, and he tries out several variations within the basic structure, it is difficult and hazardous to extract a "Platonic" or even a "Socratic" ethics understood as a fixed system of doctrines.

Socrates does not rest content with an ethical commonplace but shows that, rightly understood, the idea that we all seek happiness has important implications. For happiness comes from good things, but a little thought shows us that the things themselves, just sitting there, do nothing for us; it is from using them that we benefit. Thus we find that the only thing that is really good, and that really benefits us, is the knowledge that ensures right use of the other conventionally respected goods. It is not health or wealth that we should be seriously aiming to get, but the wisdom that enables us to make a right use of health and wealth. This wisdom, moreover, is virtue—for it is essential to virtue, the other, emotional or dispositional aspects of virtue being likewise regarded as so much raw material that can be put to good or bad employment (*Meno* 87d–89a).

This argument prefigures rather strikingly a central thesis in Stoic ethics, but whereas the Stoics develop the theory fully, Plato leaves it at a suggestive stage. Nothing is said, for example, to meet several points that arise at once if virtue and other things have different kinds of value: why should we, for example, value other things except insofar as they contribute to our virtuous activity? Plato does not face this problem, but he makes Socrates reiterate the point in *Apology,* his speech defending his life: ordinary people's values are completely wrong, since they most value things like money, and value virtue and knowledge only insofar as they produce things like money. This is to get it the wrong way round, he says: "Virtue does not come from possessions; it is from virtue that possessions and all the rest become good for people, both in private and in public."

In the Socratic dialogues Socrates is constantly trying to get people to rethink their priorities. He does this in a variety of ways, something that may reflect the protean quality of the historical Socrates' own ideas (they inspired both hedonism and asceticism) as well as Plato's own dissatisfaction with the various ethical ideas he works out. In *Apology* Socrates urges the jury to consider him not a subversive wrecker of established values but the gods' gift to Athens, someone whose actions deserve public support. In *Gorgias* he stresses that he has no idea how to perform the simplest administrative task, but that he is nonetheless the only person in Athens who has knowledge of how politics should be carried out. In *First Alcibiades* he urges the young politician to forget about making his way in public life until he first comes to understand himself. The two *Hippias* dialogues are scathing in their portrayal of a person who is the epitome of fashionable success as being really a pompous and empty fool, someone whose ideas are contemptible beside those of Socrates, who is, in worldly terms, unattractive and a failure.

We should rethink our values and priorities, then, and the message of the early dialogues is that we shall do so only if we achieve the wisdom that can give us a correct assessment and use of everything else. As we have already seen, there is a built-in problem with Socrates' pursuit of this wisdom. What he has, to achieve it, seems to be merely the elenchus, which does not seem capable of achieving the desired positive goal. The wisdom he seeks has the structure of a skill—a unified grasp based on the principles defining the field, enabling the person to explain and justify her particular decisions and actions. We do not see Socrates claiming that he does in fact have this skill; nor could he, given the repeated failure of his attempts to achieve answers to questions about the nature of bravery, piety, and other controverted moral notions. However, we do find Plato developing some aspects of the idea of moral knowledge, considered as a skill.

In one very striking dialogue, *Protagoras,* we find Socrates claiming that the skill that will preserve and improve our lives is a skill of a calculating kind—and we find that it is purely instrumental to achieving pleasure. Moreover, in a somewhat Benthamite fashion, pleasure is construed as something that can be measured in an entirely quantitative way. We always aim at getting the most pleasure, it is assumed, and the major problem in our lives comes from faulty perspective: we imagine future pains, because they are future, to be less than they in fact are, and so on (354e–357a). It is, to say the least, surprising to find such a mechanical and crude conception of the role of moral reasoning in Plato, and those who dislike it are fortified by the fact that we find, in *Phaedo*, strong rejections of the idea that our final aim could be pleasure, or that moral reasoning could be limited to calculating amounts of it.

The solution to this apparent contradiction seems to be more complicated than Plato's simply changing his mind, being a hedonist in *Protagoras* and an antihedonist in the other two dialogues. The theory in *Protagoras* is not put forward as Socrates' own; it is a theory that Socrates examines in an inquiring spirit. But it is not ascribed to Protagoras either, and it is not definitively rejected. And in Plato's last dialogue, *Laws*, we find strikingly hedonistic passages, enough to make a 1st-century B.C.E. author compare Plato with Democritus as a kind of hedonist. It seems, then, that Plato is tempted toward a form of hedonism at times, perhaps for the reason that is aired in *Laws*: it is trivially true that we all seek happiness, and surely this must involve a search for pleasure in some form. Plato gives several accounts of pleasure in different dialogues (*The Republic*, most of *Philebus*) and seems to have been exercised throughout his life by the question of its role in the good life. Whatever the reasons for his trying out the hedonist theory in *Protagoras*, he shows himself willing, on that occasion, to cast wisdom in the role of minister to pleasure. But it is possible that the reason that this form of hedonism is not more widespread in Plato's work is precisely that it forced on him an unacceptable role for moral reasoning.

There is some wavering, then, as to the instrumental and noninstrumental roles for moral reasoning. There is also a tendency for Plato to expand the scope of moral reasoning from the agent's own life to the lives of others. The eudaemonist appeal is to the structure of the agent's own life. However, we find that the skill of dealing well with one's own life will also be the skill of excellently managing the lives of others *(Lysis)*. The skill of living well thus comes sometimes to be characterized as *politikē technē*, the "political skill" or skill exercised in political activity. We find this in *Euthydemus:* later in the dialogue we return to the theme of the protreptic passage, and a problem is found in it, but in the process this skill is casually identified as the "kingly" skill and the skill of directing and ruling. The same wholly casual identification of personal virtue with justice, understood as the virtue of ruling over others, characterizes *Alcibiades* and *Lovers*. In *Gorgias*, Socrates treats the question of individual virtue as being essentially the same as the question of what is the best state for someone to be in who is to exercise political power. Plato seems to feel no need for argument to make this identification; this is part of a general cluster of attitudes that we shall turn to, about the organization of society and the relationships of people within it. By the time of the later *Philebus* and *Laws* he has shown that he can separate the questions of how best an individual should live and how best political power should be exercised, but earlier he shows no concern to separate them, and indeed in *The Republic* he provides one of the most famous of the theories that take the two issues to be necessarily interconnnected.

Plato's treatment of what we would call social or political matters is always marked by a tension between two strands in his thought. One is his conviction that what most matters is the exercise of expert judgment: just as in an individual life it is an overall grasp based on understanding that is crucial, so in a community what is required is an overall direction based on an understanding of what is in the common good. Plato also, however, is alive to the dangers of relying on expert insight in running society and thereby undermining the rule of law. There are disadvantages, but also advantages, in being able to rely on the stability provided by obedience to law. Plato's position changes dramatically in several respects, but we can trace a continuing engagement with the problem of obedience to law.

In *Crito* the laws of Athens are introduced, telling Socrates why he should not, as his conventionally minded friend Crito suggests, evade his unjust condemnation to death. The laws stress two grounds for this, grounds that, on their face, have very different implications. One is that a citizen's obligation to his laws and government is like his obligation to his parents; he is bound by a relationship that he has not chosen but may not reject. Further, it is a notably asymmetrical relationship: the laws may inflict punishment on you, or make demands, while you are not entitled to respond in kind; in this context the relationship is even likened to that of master and slave. (Like any Greek, Plato is ready to see a relationship where one side exercises power and the other has no control over it as one of master and slave.) The laws, however, also stress that Socrates will be breaking his "agreements" with them. They regard him as having made an implicit agreement to obey the laws by his having undergone the *dokimasia,* or vetting, when admitted to the citizen body, and by having stayed in Athens when it was open to him to go elsewhere. Having shown his satisfaction with Athens, they claim, by staying and raising a family, he has shown himself satisfied with its laws. The conflict between these two grounds for compliance is patent: one set appeals to obligations that one has not chosen to have, the other appeals to obligations that one has chosen to have. Socrates' obligation to obey the laws of Athens can hardly be both of these things at the same time—not, at least, without further argument, which is lacking here.

Crito also creates a well-known problem when taken together with the passage in *Apology* where Socrates says that if the court releases him on the condition that he stop practicing philosophy, "I will obey the god rather than you." The laws in *Crito,* however, demand obedience; Socrates must "persuade them or obey." This has been taken to mean that one must obey the law unless one succeeds in changing it; more realistically, it could mean that one must obey unless one persuades the jury. Either way, Socrates has clearly failed to persuade; how can his resolve in *Apology* not conflict with the demands of the laws in *Crito*? If the laws were *ideal* laws, there would be no problem; Socrates could not then be in the right in defying them. But how the unideal laws of Athens can make the claims that the laws do, remains obscure. In *The Republic* Plato moves on to considering an ideal state in which the rule of law is considerably reduced. He does not return to the *Crito* situation until *Laws*, when he finally gives the laws a better answer to Socrates.

The Republic begins with the question, starkly posed, of why I, the individual agent, should be just, but here Plato sees an adequate answer as requiring an entire sketch of a just society. *The Republic*'s double focus, which has led to widely different types of interpretation, is the culmination of Plato's previous tendency to conflate individual moral reasoning with the skill of ruling over others. But at the end of Book 9 he suggests firmly that it is the individual that is his primary concern: the just state, Socrates says, may well be merely a pattern laid up in heaven, but it is still possible for the person who is determined to become just to think about it, and develop his character accordingly. (As against this, the suggestion that one could start off an ideal state with people under the age of ten may be merely a vivid way of saying that it is not a practical possibility.) Still, to know what it is to be just, we need to know what it would be for a state to be just.

Plato's state, it is important to stress, is not a utopia; it is an ordinary Greek city, transformed so as to become just but otherwise subject to normal Greek conditions such as the assumption of warfare with other states, dependence on slavery, and normal economic processes. It is within this context that Plato develops his idea that a just city is one in which our inevitable interdependence is organized in a rational way, so that conflicts are eliminated.

Conflict is to be eliminated by ensuring that people are educated, and function, only in ways appropriate to their nature. This will come about, it is claimed, if there are three classes in the state: the Guardians, who rule in the general interest; the Auxiliaries, who help to put that rule into practice; and the Producing Class, who have no unifying characteristics but are just normal citizens of a Greek state, pursuing their private business, but with no political power. These three classes must function together in such a way that the Producing Class obey the political directives of the Guardians, whose exercise of power in the common interest is institutionally unconstrained. Plato is somewhat ambivalent about the attitude of the Producing Class. At times he is confident that they have enough sense of the general good to appreciate that it is best for them to go along with what the Guardians think, and they are presented as deferential. At other times, however, Plato seems to think that resentment and lack of cooperation on the part of the Producing Class are inevitable, given their inability to understand what is in the general good, and will have to be repressed by the Guardians.

The Republic is based on the idea that the individual soul will exhibit the same sort of three-part relationship as the state: reason, which seeks the truth and realizes overall good; spirit, which provides the energy for rational considerations to be acted on; and the desiring part of the soul, marked by no unifying factor other than the fact that all desires aim merely at their own satisfaction, without regard for overall good. People will fit into one of the three political classes according as reason, spirit, or desire dominates in their souls. But all are alike in having all three parts of the soul, and the unified and harmonious state that results from all three parts' "doing their own," as Plato puts it, will differ in members of the three different classes. In the Guardians reason dominates, and so those people will have love of truth and devotion to the common good as their major aims; their spirit and desires have been reformed and restructured by these priorities. Similarly with the Auxiliaries. The members of the Producing Class are dominated by their desires, and so reason and spirit function in them mostly as instrumental to the achievement of their desires, though (in a way parallel to the political problem with the Producing Class) their reason is sometimes taken to have enough implicit grasp of the general good to approve of what the Guardians do.

Plato, against all Greek intuitions, identifies this state of harmony of soul with the virtue of justice. It is a radical redefinition, and his solution as to how to produce justice is a radical departure from any strategy hitherto envisaged. It can be understood only in terms of his desire to make reason paramount in political organization. Just government is to be brought about by putting people in charge whose souls are ruled by reason. Plato sneers at the idea of improving states by modifying laws or institutions; this is, he thinks, a useless waste of energy. True improvement can come only by trying to conform ourselves to the rational pattern "laid up in heaven" and accessible only to those who use their reason. Hence Plato relies entirely on the Guardians' education (first of character, then of intellect) to ensure the correctness of their reasoning. Laws serve a limited and pragmatic function and do not constrain the results of the Guardians' reasoning.

Reason in its capacity as what discerns the general good demands much that is outrageous by both Greek standards and our own. The Guardians will have no property, no private life, no lasting personal relationships. Women as well as men will be Guardians, since the demands of reason overrule convention. Reason in its capacity as what aims at the truth turns out to require similarly radically revised standards. For the Guardians to be entitled to rule, they must *know* what is right, and Plato now conceives of knowledge, as we have seen, in a way depending on mathematical method. To rule, the Guardians must spend several years perfecting their techniques of philosophical thinking. And Plato faces the paradox that results: by the time they are fit to rule, the Guardians are unwilling to rule, because they alone appreciate the overwhelming value of philosophical study for its own sake. The only truly just people, then, will not want to rule the just state and will have to be in some way "compelled" to do so.

The Republic represents the most thorough working-out ever attempted of the principle that knowledge is what entitles rulers to rule. Plato accepts the extreme consequences both for the rulers and for the ruled, although later he comes to have doubts about both aspects. In The Republic Plato is alive to the corrupting power of money and ambition but ignores the corrupting force of power itself. Later he allows that it is not a possibility for human nature to have absolute power and remain selfless (Laws). And he comes to rethink the role that absolute, knowledge-based rule assigns to its subject. Rulers are constantly compared to experts, such as doctors and pilots. But people are not like a craftsman's material; in a political community, each citizen is a distinct person with needs and desires that should be given a hearing, if they are to consider themselves members of a genuine community rather than slavelike subjects whose labor is exploited. In Laws Plato comes to hold that "masters and slaves can never be friends" and so cannot, as he thought in The Republic, form a community together. In Laws the doctor who treats free people, as opposed to the doctor who treats slaves, has to convince his patient to undergo the treatment and argue with him by rational means, persuading him and not merely threatening him (Laws 719e–720d, 857c–e).

Laws thus presents a considerably changed ideal state from that of The Republic. But it would be a mistake to ascribe this simply to the increased pessimism of old age (despite the many rather tedious references in Laws to the wisdom of the old). Rather, Plato's final thoughts about politics are marked by a more profound treatment of themes that were previously treated in too simple a way. Over a number of areas he shows himself ready to recognize the necessity of compromise and complexity.

The most immediately striking is the question of the status of law. While earlier Plato had given expertise total priority over law, he comes to appreciate the advantages of the sovereignty of law. A long passage in Statesman develops this. Law is a blunt instrument, falling far short of the precision of expertise, but if the expert is not available, his prescription is a lot better than nothing, or guesswork. In the world as it is, in which an ideal statesman is not a realistic prospect, we should make use of the stability and rationality that laws offer. Hence, in Laws, we find Plato producing an ideal state by drawing up a legal code.

Plato is in fact surprisingly empirical in his second great political work. Rather than sketch a fundamentally new form of life, he takes an existing institution and modifies it in the light of a new, moral aim he takes to be achievable by it. (Unafraid of ridicule, he claims that drinking parties can be transformed to achieve an educational, moral goal, and tries to transfer the public honors and glamour of military heroes to aged public officials who have served the state in undramatic ways.) In particular, he takes over many existing Athenian laws, aiming to make them coherent and rationally acceptable to the citizens by prefacing them with philosophical preambles giving their rationale. Many of these laws frame democratic institutions, and the ideal city of *Laws*, Magnesia, is in many ways, and quite deliberately, like Athens. However, it also retains the feature insisted on earlier, that all citizens be educated in a way appropriate to their capacity. Now this has a far more egalitarian result than previously, but there is still a heavy emphasis on the common good and shared community goals. Indeed, in some respects Plato goes further than ever: pregnant women have to do daily exercises; everyone must be trained to be ambidextrous; and, most alarmingly, all citizens must get up early and get used to as little sleep as possible.

Laws stresses both the communal education that instills in the citizens a strong consciousness of the common good and the democratic institutions that give them a space for individual political activity. *Laws* can be read as authoritarian, but it can also be read as developing a far more individualistic and egalitarian strand than hitherto seen. The virtue characteristic of the citizen is "self-control" *(sophrosune)*, the virtue of recognizing the dominance of the common good over one's own good. But Plato proposes here a "mixed" constitution: the principle of "monarchy," or obedience to authority, must now be constrained by the principle of "democracy," each citizen living according to his own plan of life. Democratic institutions are taken over, but they are modified in ways that in ancient terms bring them closer to oligarchy— though we should note that the result is often much closer to democracy in the modern sense of the term than is ancient democracy. Plato, for example, removes most direct political decision making from the assembly, which functions instead more like a modern electorate, electing officials and ensuring that they are responsible to it for their actions.

The increase in Plato's willingness to use empirical method in ethics and politics is remarkable; it comes out most strikingly in his attitude to history. While *The Republic* is totally ahistorical, *Statesman* makes use of collective memory to develop the truths in folktales and myths about the past. *Critias*, an extension of the frame-dialogue of *Timaeus*, contains an extraordinary kind of unfinished historical fiction about the cities of ancient Athens and Atlantis, designed to teach political morals about the superiority of land-based cities over sea-based ones, and the importance of abiding by the law. And the third book of *Laws* is an extended exercise in drawing political lessons from history. Although Plato's actual history is selective and biased, it is recognizably a first step toward the study of political history that we find in Aristotle's *Politics* and the studies of constitutions that lie behind it.

The increased empiricism of *Laws* is reflected in different ways in the other late dialogues. In *Timaeus*, Plato constructs a strange and elaborate cosmology, showing a remarkable degree of interest in issues that had previously been dismissed as trivial. In *Statesman* he is on the way to a pragmatic interest in political institutions, although he retains an interest in the idea of the ruler with knowledge. Whereas earlier Plato had used the dialogue form to begin discussion of philosophical issues from a fresh point of view, one owing little or nothing to the state of the contemporary debate, *Sophist, Philebus,* and *Theaetetus* are occupied in answering problems, or furthering debates, initiated by other philosophers, while *Parmenides* is partly occupied with problems that Plato himself has produced. Again Plato is moving in a direction that will be followed further by Aristotle, who begins from problems that are already philosophical and positions himself in a debate that has already begun.

In these later dialogues Plato makes less use of the figure of Socrates, as though recognizing that the anachronism is too striking. He also seems to realize the distance that he has come from the new beginnings that Socrates makes in the early dialogues to the far more developed and academic discussions of the late ones. Plato never abandons the dialogue form; to the last he retains the position of the person who puts forward the arguments without committing himself to them or their premises. But in the later dialogues this position makes less and less sense; we do not really feel a distance between the author and the arguments of *Sophist* or *Timaeus.* These dialogues are, however, strikingly difficult to fit into any overall account of "Plato's thought." This is because in them we find Plato going down avenues opened up by the work of others—cosmology, Parmenides' problem of being and not-being, Protagoras's account of truth and knowledge. In recent years much energy has been spent in trying to determine whether and how Plato is being self-critical in the late works. A more fruitful approach, however, is probably one in which we see Plato as moving, in the late works, toward a different way of doing philosophy, one to which the dialogue form is increasingly irrelevant, a problem-based approach to philosophy that takes account of the work of others—a way of doing philosophy recognizably like Aristotle's.

Owing to these features of the later dialogues, their appeal has been primarily to philosophers. Some of the middle dialogues, like *Phaedo* and *The Republic,* have had a literary life of their own, and the Socratic dialogues have always been an attractive introduction to philosophy; few but philosophers will get through *Sophist* or *Parmenides.* Because of this, they resist brief summary or evaluation; each deals with a difficult philosophical issue in a complex but focused and complete way. Also, because they are relatively independent from the set of concerns that dominate the early and middle dialogues, they have fitted less well into overall accounts of Plato's thought; from antiquity to the 20th century, an account of "Plato's ideas" is bound to feature *The Republic* more than *Critias* or *Philebus.* It would, however, be wrong to think that a fine system of ideas peters out into academic detail in the late dialogues; to think that is to undervalue the practice of philosophical investigation and argument that we see in these works. They will always be less attractive to nonphilosophers, and more compelling to philosophers, than works like *Phaedo* and *The Republic*.

Plato is possibly the most original philosopher who ever lived. He begins by adopting a radically new way of doing philosophy, one which consciously makes a break with previous approaches to the subject. We also find him, over the course of a long lifetime, gradually traveling a long road back to more conventional ways of doing philosophy. Throughout, however, he never wavers in certain respects, such as in formally distancing himself from the argument by the dialogue form. Even the last works maintain an elusive quality that distinguishes Plato from other great philosophers. It is this combination of daring ideas presented in elusive form—locally clear but globally fragmented and disjointed—that makes Plato perennially frustrating, challenging, and fascinating.

JULIA ANNAS

Bibliography

Annas, Julia. *An Introduction to Plato's Republic*. Oxford: Oxford University Press, 1981.

———. *Platonic Ethics Old and New*. Ithaca: Cornell University Press, 1999.

Canto-Sperber, Monique. *Les paradoxes de la connaissance: Essais sur le Ménon de Platon*. Paris: Editions Odile Jacob, 1991.

Chatelet, François. *Platon*. Paris: Gallimard, 1965.

Goldschmidt, Victor. *Platonisme et pensée contemporaine*. Paris: Aubier-Montaigne, 1970.

———. *Questions platoniciennes*. Paris: Vrin, 1970.

Irwin, T., ed. *Classical Philosophy: Collected Papers*, vol. 2: *Socrates and His Contemporaries;* vol. 3: *Plato's Ethics;* vol. 4: *Plato's Metaphysics and Epistemology*. New York and London: Garland Publishing, 1995.

Kahn, Charles. *Plato and the Socratic Dialogue*. Cambridge: Cambridge University Press, 1996.

Kraut, R., ed. *The Cambridge Companion to Plato*. Cambridge: Cambridge University Press, 1992.

Schuhl, Pierre-Maxime. *L'oeuvre de Platon*. Paris: Vrin, 1954.

Vlastos, Gregory. *Platonic Studies*, 2nd ed. Princeton: Princeton University Press, 1981.

Vlastos, Gregory, ed. *Plato: A Collection of Critical Essays*. 2 vols. Garden City, N.Y.: Doubleday, 1971.

PLOTINUS

PLOTINUS WAS BORN IN EGYPT about 205 C.E. and is rightly regarded as the founder of Neoplatonism. The first of these statements he would have found trivial, the second puzzling. His biographer Porphyry, whose *Life of Plotinus* supplies almost all our information about his career, begins by telling us that "Plotinus was ashamed to be in the body." That attitude may have led to some reticence about his life, even if it is to be understood as a manifestation of the philosopher's concern to avoid more than the necessary involvement with either his own body or the sensible world of which it is a part; it is in any case not unparalleled at this period. Nevertheless, Porphyry gives us a series of invaluable stories about the philosopher's life and teaching—and even about his illnesses.

As for Neoplatonism, it is important to realize that the word does not exist in ancient Greek; it was invented by English and French writers in the fourth decade of the 19th century. It is important because Plotinus, like all the Neoplatonists who came after him, regarded himself simply as a Platonist. From Plotinus in the first treatise of the fifth *Ennead* through to Proclus in his massive *Platonic Theology*, the Neoplatonists claimed that everything they said was already there, even if not explicitly, in the text of Plato. Here it should be said that it was the text of Plato as it is accessible to us, and not some alleged esoteric Platonic doctrine, that they took as the basis of their philosophy. It was not, of course, a reading of his texts that Plato would have understood. Plotinus may have learned at least some of his approach to Plato from the mysterious figure of Ammonius Saccas, who Porphyry tells us was the first teacher of philosophy whom Plotinus found satisfactory after much searching in Alexandria, and with whom he stayed for some eleven years. Porphyry reports that Plotinus brought the mind, or the thinking, of Ammonius into his own philosophy. Unfortunately we can only speculate about what that thinking was, and in spite of many attempts to discover facts about Ammonius or reconstruct his ideas, we know nothing further about him.

Apart from his standpoint as a Platonist, two other points about Plotinus's philosophy should be borne in mind. The first is that he was a metaphysician rather than a mystic. Though he has for long and often been thought of as a mystic, and had certainly had mystic experiences, these appear only rarely in his writings and do not control his philosophy. Indeed one of the few texts in which he has been thought to refer to them, the beginning of *Enneads* IV.8, has recently been recognized as having to do with Intellect rather than with the One. The other point is that, like all Greek philosophers, his philosophy was not disinterested enquiry but a search for the way to achieve the best life for the individual. A consequence of this was that it could be seen as a kind of religious practice, though it would be misleading to think of it as a "religious philosophy," an expression that embodies a distinction that neither he, nor Plato or Aristotle before him, would have been able to appreciate. This remains true even if strictly ethical discussion occupies a relatively small proportion of Plotinus's output that survives in its entirety. His philosophy is represented by the *Enneads*, so called because they consist of six groups of nine treatises, arranged by his pupil, colleague, biographer, and editor, Porphyry. These fifty-four treatises are not, however, fifty-four separate works by Plotinus: they have been forced into this numerologically significant framework by the dismemberment of some of the longer treatises, such as that on the soul, which appears as IV.3, 4, and 5, or the one on issues raised by Plotinus's conflict with the Gnostics, which has been distributed over three *Enneads* as III.8, V.8, and V.5 and II.9, and occasionally the amalgamation of short pieces to form others such as III.9. The six *Enneads* group treatises mainly concerned with ethics, physics, the physical world and our life within it, Soul, Intellect, and the One, but this is only roughly true, since many works do not fit well into these categories, and in any case Plotinus is notorious for tending to introduce large parts, or even all, of his philosophy into many of his works that are ostensibly directed to a single topic, a direction that is only rarely followed. This is probably a result of his method of practicing philosophy by discussion, against a background of philosophical reading, a method described for us in the *Life*, rather than a conscious attempt to follow this tendency as it is already manifest in the writings of Plato.

Being a Platonist, Plotinus did, however, follow Plato in dividing his world into sensible and intelligible, or material and immaterial, forms of existence. He differed from Plato in having a more complicated structure for his intelligible world and a different status for his material one. The structure and operation of both, moreover, were heavily dependent on ideas that Plotinus, following the tradition of one tendency in Hellenistic and later Platonism, had adopted, and often adapted, from Aristotle. These were particularly important in the construction of the second hypostasis, Intellect, and also in his exposition of the functioning of the human soul.

Apart from the mysticism, what most people who know anything about Plotinus are aware of is his division of the intelligible world into three hypostases, namely One, Intellect, and Soul. Though the boundary between the latter two was sometimes blurred and transgressed, and though some have found a fourth, in which nature *(phusis)*, as a lower form of soul corresponds to the higher form *(psukhe)*, which is the third, Plotinus is firm about there being no more than three and, equally important, no fewer. In this he may be contrasted with his Platonist predecessors who, with the possible exception of

Numenius, had no One above their Intellect. Plotinus's One is the basis and origin of the whole system. Both these terms must be understood in an unusual sense, because the One is "above" rather than underlying, and it is the origin only in the sense that all else depends on it, for in Plotinus's philosophy there can be no question of any beginning in time. Thus any expressions suggesting temporal succession must be understood as referring only to causal sequence or stages of exposition. Though some Platonists did—as do an increasing number of modern scholars—understand Plato's account of the genesis of the world in *Timaeus* in a chronological sense, Plotinus followed what was always the majority view, that the succession of events in it was merely an expository device.

With these cautions we may consider the status and characteristics of the One, always bearing in mind that, strictly speaking, there is nothing that can be said about it: it is, as most translators have it, ineffable *(arrhēton)*. That is because it transcends Being and can be defined only by the negation of all the characteristics of Being that, however, derive from it, or by the use of words applicable to Intellect prefixed with "super-" *(huper-)*, for example superintellection *(hupernoēsis)* or "superexistently" *(hyperontōs)*. The common description of it as "beyond Being" goes back to Plato's description in *The Republic* of the Form of the Good as being on the far side of the things that exist *(epekeina tēs ousias)*, but while Plato used this as an indication of the position of the Good at the head of the hierarchy of the Forms, which were for him what truly has being, for Plotinus and all Neoplatonists it meant that it was something transcending, and other than, the Forms. Nevertheless Plotinus's One, which he also calls the Good, has this in common with the Platonic Form, that it is responsible for the being and, though Plotinus has less to say about this, the intelligibility of everything in the intelligible realm. One of the most difficult problems about Plotinus's philosophy is how the One relates to everything else and, in particular, whether or not it can be said to take any interest in its products. The view that it can has been advocated mainly by Christian interpreters who have perhaps wished to assimilate Plotinus's thought to their own, but the more austere interpretation, according to which the One is responsible for the existence of the others and their various levels of unity but has no other relation to them except insofar as it is an object of aspiration, is probably correct. This problem is connected with others about the nature of the One and its role as the source of all else. The most important is why there should be anything else at all, and it can be argued that this is a fundamental defect in Plotinus' philosophy, notwithstanding the fact that the philosophical reason for positing a One will have been the wish to have a completely simple unitary first principle for the soul and intellect, which were part of the now Aristotelianized Platonic heritage. The next problem is whether the One can be said to have will, a question to which Plotinus devotes the long and difficult treatise VI.8, and whether, if it does, that will is involved in its causation of the others. This question tends to be answered positively by those who think that the One is somehow personal, like a Judeo-Christian God, and negatively by those who deny this, inter alia, on the grounds that to equip the One with will, or self-knowledge, would infringe its unity. For them what is "below" the One emerges automatically as a consequence of its supreme power and intrinsic infinity. A further problem, which relates to the others rather than to the One, is how the atemporal process by which they arise is to be described. The word *emanation* has often been used for this purpose, indicating that the others flow from the One as from an inexhaustible spring, but though commonly used by writers on Plotinus, the relevant words are far less common in the text of Plotinus himself.

The first product of this coming into being of other things is the second hypostasis, Intellect. Though it is essentially Form and Being, at its first appearance it is unformed and indeterminate, and so preexistent. It acquires its characteristics by turning back to the One and contemplating it. Thereby it acquires the Form and Being that the One bestows without itself having them. This acquisition of characteristics from the One by means of contemplation is based on a piece of Aristotelian rather than Platonic thought, namely the notion that in thinking, the intellect, be it human or divine, is assimilated to its objects, a notion that is a crucial element in the structure of Intellect itself and of the relationship, on more than one level, of what is below with what is above. It might be as well to state that above and below are merely metaphorical, if frequently utilized, ways of talking about the hierarchical or causal relationship of things that are conceived, qua immaterial, as not being in place at all. Another way of describing the relationship is to talk about lower entities being in higher ones: here Plotinus follows a suggestion in Plato's *Timaeus*. Intellect falls short of the unity of the One by virtue of the duality that Plotinus insists exists between what knows and what is known. With that qualification the Intellect is a unity insofar as its contents are not only Forms with the enhanced characteristics of Form as described in a famous passage of Plato's *Sophist* (248–249), but also intellects that have each other as objects and, by virtue of the Aristotelian theory of intellectual cognition, are thereby identified, and identical, with each other. A problem about the genesis and structure of the hypostasis Intellect lies in whether its Being, or its being Forms, is in any way prior to its being Intellect or intellects. It can be argued with adequate support from the texts that Being must come first for there to be an object of the intellects, but an equally good case can be made for its intellectual aspect's being prior, insofar as it is necessary for the as yet unformed Intellect to receive its being by contemplation of the One. The best solution is that neither is prior since both are eternal.

As Intellect corresponds to the model used by the Demiurge, or divine maker, in *Timaeus*, it should contain Forms of everything that exists in the sensible world: "Everything that is here comes from there, and exists there in a better way." In fact Plotinus was not entirely sure about the universality of this principle, which receives lengthy discussion in a late and rightly admired treatise titled, "How the Multiplicity of Forms Came into Being, and the One" (VI.7). Though he argues, for example, that even though there is no conflict in the intelligible world, the Forms of animals require the parts necessary for conflict, since they will be part of the world that these Forms produce, he does not introduce forms of undesirable things nor, a fortiori, of evil though, strictly speaking, Intellect should include them in some appropriate form. This is only one of the problems and inconsistencies relating to evil that will be discussed below. These difficulties, just like the principle that Intellect should contain everything that appears in the physical world, are a result of Plotinus's strict monism, which allows no room for matter as an independent principle such as most would find in Plato. The amalgamation of Platonic Forms and Aristotelian Intellect to produce a new kind of Platonic intellect had been made by certain so-called Middle Platonists of the preceding period, who saw this as a solution to the notorious problem about what would be the object(s) of the eternal intellection of the self-thinking Intellect that is Aristotle's supreme principle. They thus added to the Aristotelian description of its activity that it thinks itself "and its own thoughts," which are the Forms. For Plotinus this solution required special care to avoid importing duality into the unity of Intellect, and we learn from Porphyry that much time was spent in his circle on showing that the intelligibles, namely the Forms, are inside the Intellect, a matter that is the subject of treatise V.5. This was one of a number of questions on which Plotinus's Aristotelian solution was prepared by the precisions brought to Peripatetic thinking by the commentator Alexander of Aphrodisias, the best known of those whose work was studied in Plotinus's philosophical group. The unity of the Intellect was encapsulated in a description drawn from Plato's *Parmenides*, namely that it was a one-many or one and many, to be distinguished from the third hypostasis, which was many and one. In most, though perhaps not all, of Plotinus's work, where the question arises, the human individual may be part of this unity by having the highest part of his soul permanently at this level. This was one of the points on which most later Neoplatonists were not prepared to follow Plotinus, who by his own admission in IV.8 was taking a line that was unorthodox. A problem that is connected with our presence in Intellect, and that has received much discussion recently, is whether or not there must therefore be a Form of each individual. In general those who favor a personalizing interpretation of the nature of the One tend to accept the existence of Forms of individuals on the grounds that they are a reflection of the high value Plotinus placed on the individual. Those who do not, and who find that Plotinus's writings appear to be inconsistent on this point, would say that this was a matter on which he did not come to a final decision. Certainly some of the later treatises suggest, even if they do not prove, that Plotinus then thought that the highest part of the individual existed at the level of Soul rather than Intellect. This interpretation has the further advantage that it fits with a new way of looking at Plotinus—not so much, as has been the custom, as a systematic philosopher, but as one who was prepared, in the manner of Aristotle, if to a lesser degree, to put forward ideas tentatively and then reconsider them later if and when a better solution came to mind.

The hypostasis Soul is the link between the intelligible and sensible worlds. Soul, as Plotinus puts it, stands on the boundary. It is in the middle, having the intelligible in the fullest sense on one side, the sensible on the other. As with the generation of Intellect, so with the generation of Soul it is difficult to explain why it should happen at all. Again one must resort to the explanation that the infinite power of the One requires the existence of everything else. If, moreover, the world is to exist, then there has to be some part of the intelligible that both proximately gives it form and controls it. The difficulty of the controlling function increases as one descends from what all Platonists and Aristotelians regarded as the higher kind of physical existence to be found in the heavens to the lower kind that exists on earth. Thus Soul's function of governance is exercised effortlessly in respect of the heavens but not in respect of what is on earth, where it risks being affected, in some sense, by the unsatisfactory nature or behavior of what it controls.

Soul "comes into existence" by a process similar to that which lies at the origin of Intellect—though occasionally Plotinus will attribute a personal motive in the form of boldness or daring *(tolma)*, a concept possibly acquired from Gnostic opponents that recurs in other contexts, such as the descent of the human soul, but that he does not seem to have taken very seriously. But just as Intellect falls short of the unity of the One, which it contemplates to finalize its own existence, so Soul falls short both of the unity and the level of being to be found in Intellect. Thus all its formal elements exist at a greater level of diffusion than they do in Intellect. Another way of expressing this disunity is to say that the contents of Soul are not all simultaneously present in and to each other, as are those of Intellect by virtue of the reciprocal identity of intellects and intelligibles.

Related to the difficulty of justifying the coming into being of Soul is another, well known to students of Plotinus and also his pupil Porphyry: the problem of keeping the two hypostases separate and distinct. At times when Plotinus is concerned to stress the tripartite nature of the intelligible world and the existence of neither more nor fewer than three hypostases, he distinguishes Intellect from Soul in some or all of the following ways: Intellect is a one-many, while Soul is a many and one. In Intellect all cognition is simultaneous and immediate, whereas in Soul there is transition *(metabasis)* from one component to the next, as in reasoning from premise to conclusion. Intellect is characterized by eternity, whereas in Soul there is time, which is generated along with Soul itself—an anomalous position insofar as Soul qua hypostasis is no less eternal than Intellect itself. Soul stands to Intellect as an unfolding or unraveling of what exists in a more compact form there, a relationship that Plotinus, at this and other levels, describes by calling the lower form of being the *logos* of the higher, meaning it is a representation of it in a lower mode—an unusual use of *logos*, but one frequently found in Plotinus. Soul is also causally dependent on Intellect, which in itself makes it different by virtue of a Plotinian principle, stated in the early treatise VI.9, that the cause is other than the effect. In addition Soul has the responsibility of being involved with, and in charge of, what is below, a responsibility that Intellect does not share because, when it is considered as being responsible for the existence of the world, it has assigned to Soul the duty of maintaining it. These distinctions include some in which Soul is defined by not being Intellect, and when Plotinus on one occasion says that the two differ by otherness alone, without defining what this otherness might be, we must assume that he himself saw the philosophical difficulty of having two entities that are immaterial but required to differ from each other. At times this difficulty is too much for him, and we find that he has removed the distinction between the two, tending to import characteristics of Soul into Intellect when he wishes to emphasize its dynamic and even creative nature, and conversely attributing characteristics of Intellect to Soul when he is concerned to stress its transcendence above the material world, or the contrast between immaterial and material existence—as, for example, in his treatise "The Simultaneous and Identical Omnipresence of What Is" (VI.4–5)—or even the untroubled nature of Soul's control of the world. At such times he also denies to Soul the discursive and progressive nature of thought by which he normally distinguishes it from Intellect; when he makes this distinction he will say that when we have finished with discursive thinking and arrive at immediate intuition of its results, we have passed from Soul to Intellect.

Another context in which similar language to that used of Intellect is applied to Soul is when Plotinus is trying to show that Soul remains unaffected by its involvement with body. Here we have reached the level of existence at which we are talking not about the intelligible hypostases on their own, but about Soul's function of organizing and controlling the body, be it the superior body to be found in the heavens or the ordinary kind found below. Before we look at how Soul functions in this capacity, we must look at the distinctions Plotinus makes between different kinds of soul. While he asserts that all souls are one, the subject of one of his earlier treatises, IV.9, this assertion applies only to two of the three kinds of soul he distinguishes: Soul as a hypostasis, the World-soul, and the souls of individuals. Though it sometimes appears that all these are coextensive "parts" of one single Soul, closer inspection reveals that the hypostasis is not a part of this unity but stands above it, differing precisely by its having no direct involvement with matter or body.

Those souls that do, and that may be seen as a reflection or image of Soul it-self, just as Soul is sometimes seen as a reflection or image of Intellect, are to be seen as one. World-soul differs from the individual souls only by having a better body to govern and so being exempt from the problems that may trouble any one of the souls of individuals—that is, human individuals, since Plotinus takes no great interest in the souls of other kinds of living beings. Inevitably he will have problems in explaining how the theoretically identical souls of different individuals are not the same.

With this problem we move into the area where Plotinus's monism causes difficulties. Since everything has its being from above, with what is above causing what is below to be such as it is, different individuals should be identical, insofar as they are caused by souls. And yet Plotinus explains their differences as being due to body rather than matter, which has no characteristics until it is informed by a soul and thereby becomes a body. Though he sometimes speaks in terms of a soul's being short of informative and controlling power by virtue of its distance from its origins, and so unable fully to control a body, or even matter, which can influence a soul as it descends to them, a basic inconsistency remains. Plotinus on occasion tries to alleviate this inconsistency by treating bodies as if they were part of a whole preformed by Soul so that individual parts of Soul can become embodied in parts of that whole.

Plotinus's account of the human soul is another area where Platonic and Aristotelian ideas are fruitfully combined. As a Platonist, Plotinus believed that the soul was separate from and superior to the body, which it used as an instrument. How it did so, or, from another point of view, how the individual functioned, was explained on lines that generally follow Aristotle's account of the soul in *De anima*, omitting only the crucial concept of the soul as the formal element in a single substance for which body provides the matter. Only at the level of the intellect, to which Aristotle was at least prepared to give a separate existence, did the two philosophers' views virtually coincide. Given his Platonist and dualist approach to psychology, Plotinus naturally found it difficult to explain how the soul related to the body at all. After examining various possibilities in his long treatise *On the Soul* (IV.3–5), once again in the light of Alexander's treatment of Aristotelian ideas, Plotinus concludes that the soul is present to the body, rather than in it, after the manner of heat in air: heat may affect the air, by warming it, without itself being affected. Though he envisaged the nerves as somehow transmitting instructions from the soul and sensations to it, Plotinus never gave a clear account of how soul and body act on each other. That he did allow body to act on soul, in spite of his principle that it was inferior to and controlled by it, is clear on more than one occasion, for he was sufficiently realistic to see that some explanation of other than ideal behavior needed to be given. In holding that the unsatisfactory condition of the body, or excessive attention to it, could drag down at least the lower "part" of the soul, Plotinus again allowed matter and body a degree of autonomy that realism requires but strict adherence to his own principles would forbid. It was partly to avoid these difficulties that Plotinus, like all the later Platonists, divided the soul into a lower and a higher part, which they generally but he less often referred to as irrational and rational. The higher was generally immune to affections from the body, and the individual who succeeded in not concentrating on the body and its demands lived at the level of the higher soul; whether that level was the discursive reason, or the intellect, which transcended the individual and had a permanent place in the intelligible, is not always clear. To preserve this immunity from corporeal interference, and also to make it possible to have reincarnation for the "respectable" part of the soul only, Plotinus doubled the imaginative (or representative: *phantastikon*) faculty that lay on the border between the two, thus allowing to each part of the soul the appropriate kind of memory, since memory was a function of the imagination. An important addition to traditional Greek views about perception and memory was the idea that unconscious memories could be stronger and longer-lasting than conscious ones. This, combined with the notion that our personality is formed by what we have seen and remembered, is one of the clearest anticipations of modern thought in ancient psychology.

We have already seen that it is desirable for the human to turn his attention away from the body. The immediate result of this is that he may live at the level of higher rather than lower soul, thus embarking on that process of aspiration to higher reality that is shared by everything in Plotinus's hierarchy. In this way, contemplation, which focuses on what is above and results in assimilation to it, is the most important activity for a philosopher: the Greek word for contemplation was the same as one of the terms for philosophical enquiry. The term of this process is normally the Intellect, but on rare occasions the One itself, which can be known only by means of a sort of touching.

From all this, matter stands apart, since the creative processes that have produced it are by then so weak that matter is devoid of all the formal and other characteristics that might have caused it to join in the upward aspiration of everything else. It is described as sheer negativity, being as devoid of features as the One itself. Somehow this negativity is the cause of evil, thus making evil a metaphysical rather than a moral problem; in a few texts, however, it is explained in moral terms as due to weakness in the soul.

Though later Platonists differed from Plotinus in numerous ways, their systems were a development of his, so that all Neoplatonism to a greater or lesser extent absorbs his influence. In the West, Plotinus, or his pupil Porphyry, provides the Platonic elements in the Latin philosophical tradition of late antiquity, both pagan and Christian. In the East it was generally mediated by later Platonists like Proclus and the Aristotelian commentators. More directly influential was the work known as the *Theology of Aristotle*, which appeared to provide the missing theology for Aristotle's metaphysic but actually consisted of selections from Plotinus, possibly first organized by Porphyry, but in any case known only in Arabic. Through Syriac and, later, Arabic translations of Neoplatonic works, Plotinus's thought became a crucial part of the Islamic, and the Jewish, philosophy that was written in Arabic and through Latin translations found its way back into the Western tradition in the Middle Ages. It is now generally recognized that much of the so-called Aristotelianism of the later Middle Ages was strongly influenced by Neoplatonism, and in particular the Platonizing interpretations of the Greek commentators of late antiquity mediated by Averroës and other commentators of the Arabic tradition. Similarly the Platonism of the Augustinian tradition owed much to Plotinus, either directly or through Porphyry. Thereafter Plotinus was more influential in art and literature than in philosophy, this influence receiving its greatest impetus from the 1492 Latin translation by the Florentine Marsilio Ficino. The Greek text of Plotinus remained unpublished for nearly another century, and it was not till 1973 that the first edition on modern principles was completed.

HENRY BLUMENTHAL

Bibliography

Texts and Translations

Plotinus. Ed. A. Hilary Armstrong. 7 vols. Loeb Classical Library.

————. *Enneads.* Ed. Paul Henry and Hans-Rudolf Schwyzer. 3 vols. Oxford: Clarendon Press, 1964–1982.

Studies

Armstrong, A. Hilary. "Plotinus." In *The Cambridge History of Later Greek and Early Medieval Philosophy.* Ed. A. H. Armstrong. Cambridge: Cambridge University Press, 1967. Pp. 195–268.

Blumenthal, Henry J. *Plotinus' Psychology: His Doctrines of the Embodied Soul.* Amsterdam: Nijhoff, 1971.

Bréhier, Emile. *The Philosophy of Plotinus.* Trans. Joseph Thomas. Chicago: University of Chicago Press, 1958.

Emilsson, Eyjólfur K. *Plotinus on Sense-Perception: A Philosophical Study.* Cambridge: Cambridge University Press, 1988.

Gerson, Lloyd P., ed. *The Cambridge Companion to Plotinus.* Cambridge: Cambridge University Press, 1996.

Hadot, Pierre. *Plotinus, or, The Simplicity of Vision.* Trans. Michael Chase. Chicago: University of Chicago Press, 1993.

Himmerich, Wilhelm. *Eudaimonia: Die Lehre des Plotin von der Selbstverwirklichung des Menschen.* Forschungen zur Neueren Philosophie und ihrer Geschichte n. F. 13. Würzburg: Konrad Triltsch Verlag, 1959.

Igal, Jesús. *Porfirio, Vida de Plotino; Plotino, Enéadas I–II.* Madrid: Editorial Gredos, 1982. Pp. 7–114.

O'Meara, Dominic J. *Plotinus: An Introduction to the Enneads.* Oxford: Clarendon Press, 1993.

Rist, John M. *Plotinus: The Road to Reality.* Cambridge: Cambridge University Press, 1967.

Schroeder, Frederic M. *Form and Transformation: A Study in the Philosophy of Plotinus.* Montreal and Kingston: McGill–Queen's University Press, 1992.

Trouillard, Jean. *La procession plotinienne.* Paris: Presses Universitaires de France, 1955.

———. *La purification plotinienne.* Paris: Presses Universitaires de France, 1955.

Wallis, Richard T. *Neoplatonism.* London: Duckworth, 1972. Pp. 37–93.

PLUTARCH

For anyone interested in Greek learning, Plutarch is an obvious reference, so rich and varied is the prolific work left us by this Pico della Mirandola of antiquity. Modern scholars rely heavily on him for information about lost authors or obscure periods of the Hellenistic and Roman epochs. Still, to portray him as a "guardian of the temple," or even to limit his Hellenism to mere learning, would give too reductive an impression of a man who explored tradition for an answer to the questions of his time, drew vital strength from that tradition, and sought to revive it. In this sense, Plutarch is an exemplary representative of the period in which Trajan tried to revitalize the former city-states and Hadrian worked to restore the Temple of Delphi.

A DOUBLE ANCESTRY: CHAERONEA AND PAIDEIA

Plutarch was born around 45 C.E. in Chaeronea, in the region of Boeotia, near the two great historic poles of Hellenism, Athens and Delphi. In his youth, he went to Athens, storehouse of the classical intellectual heritage, to study philosophy with the Platonist Ammonios; later, he returned frequently to see his friends and to take advantage of the "many books and all manner of discussions" (*Moralia, The Epsilon at Delphi* 384e). He was even made an honorary citizen of the Leontian tribe. Toward the end of the 90s he became a priest at Delphi, which had remained the major center of the religious tradition, despite the decline of its oracle. In this favorable geographical setting, Plutarch's moorings in the tradition were reinforced by his immense learning. In addition to the knowledge of rhetoric and literature a classical education implies, and in addition to philosophy, he himself tells us of his youthful passion for mathematics. He displays his knowledge in a variety of other fields as well: in music (even though the treatise *On Music* preserved under his name is spurious), in the physical and biological sciences (largely drawn from the Aristotelian school), and in medicine, which he may have studied during his stay in Alexandria. Following the custom of the time, he effectively completed his education while traveling throughout the Roman empire before giving the successful lectures that brought him to Rome toward the end of Vespasian's reign (69–79) and probably again when Domitian was in power (81–96). Nevertheless, around the year 90, before the expulsion of the philosophers in 93–94, he chose to return to Chaeronea, where he served as magistrate and where he taught philosophy. The major portion of his work dates from this second part of his life, during which he continued to travel to see his friends. The very form of his work gives us some idea of the way he and his circle must have lived.

The prefaces to Plutarch's treatises not only introduce us to members of that circle, distinguished Romans and eminent Greeks to whom the works are dedicated, but they also echo these men's concerns and the debates that informed Plutarch's writing. Once allowances are made for the literary shaping that minimizes controversy and suppresses anything that is not of intellectual interest, the learned banquets of *Table-Talk* show us, more than anything else, the ideal of urbane sociability that prevailed in Plutarch's cultivated milieu, the varieties of fields of knowledge in which he and his interlocutors were interested, and the spirit in which they approached those fields. So when each guest in turn is prevailed upon to develop a personal theory, he makes a point of respecting the categories of the probable *(eikos)* and the credible *(pithanon)*, in the spirit of the line by Xenocrates with which Ammonius liked to punctuate his accounts: "Let this be our opinion, with the look of truth" *(Moralia, Table-Talk* IX.14.746b). Here, as in so many passages in Plutarch's work, we find the spirit of the New Academy, anxious to refrain from manifesting "excessive confidence" *(to agan tes pisteōs)*, and this encouragement of probabilism—but not of skepticism—partly accounts for the polyphonic form of philosophic dialogues like *The Oracle at Delphi No Longer Given in Verse* and *On the Sign of Socrates* (which are quite different in this respect from Plato's dialogues), as well as the difficulty commentators sometimes have in appreciating the interest of every contribution.

One other feature is evident in *Table-Talk* and characteristic of imperial paideia: a taste for learning and commentary. This feature underlies works like *The Roman Questions* and *The Greek Questions*, which deal with the customs of various peoples, and, in the realm of philosophy, it inspires *Platonic Questions;* more curiously, it also turns up in *Parallel Lives*. The biographer does not hesitate to interrupt his account to detail his sources, retrace a history of mechanics, or comment on the attitude of his heroes. While this procedure appears quite natural, it is also very revealing of the way Plutarch looks at the past and at history.

THE LESSONS OF HISTORY: POLITICS ACCORDING TO PLUTARCH

It is remarkable that Plutarch should have composed *Parallel Lives*, about a Greek and a Roman; it is a sign that, for him, Greeks and Romans shared a common moral universe in the framework of a single civilization. This is clear in the priority he gives to moral values, and in his manifest desire to discern the nuances of virtue or to look in the mirror of the history of great men "to try to rule his [own] life and make it conform to the image of their virtues" ("Aemilius Paulus," *Parallel Lives* VI.1.2). This effort brings to mind the passage in the treatise *How a Man May Become Aware of His Making Progress in Virtue* where we are invited to wonder: "What would Plato have done in this case? What would Epameinondas have said? How would Lycurgus have conducted himself, or Agesilaus?" (*Moralia* I.85.15b). Plutarch's emphasis on morality and virtue reveals the profound unity that links the moral treatises and the *Lives;* the works are distinguished from one another only for the convenience of classification. Moreover, the word *Bios* (life) may apply, as it does in *Gorgias* and the Myth of Er, to the "way of life" that everyone must choose, or it may designate the literary genre of Peripatetic origin that is used to describe the "way of life" chosen; but in both cases, the idea belongs to the philosopher's domain, not the historian's.

Writing as a moralist, in numerous prefaces Plutarch affirms the exemplary quality of great men, but he does not deceive himself about the imperfection of man in general and of his heroes in particular. While he claims not to dwell on the latters' defects, his *Lives* do not become hagiography any more than they become indictments when he chooses such antimodels as Demetrius and Anthony, stressing that there is no moral conduct without knowledge of good *and* evil. Instead, Plutarch sets out to enumerate the myriad "struggles of virtue *[arete]* pitted against fortune *[ta syntynchanonta]*" (*On the Sign of Socrates* VII.575c), and in the guise of a chronological account, he develops a fragmented narrative in which a historical fact is stripped of its properly historical substance and treated the way orators treat literary quotations taken out of context, using them in support of a particular feature or idea. Thus historical facts tend to turn into exempla: using a mimetic style, Plutarch allows them to speak for themselves, or else he comments on them the way he comments on literary texts in the treatise *How the Young Man Should Study Poetry.*

He claims to arrive in this way at an instructive portrayal of the character of a statesman, since, in keeping with his own choice of lifestyle, he considers only "practical" and not "theoretical" lives, even if he never fails to emphasize his heroes' philosophical training and affinities. He does not conceal his partiality to his compatriot Epaminondas, who knew how to combine politics and philosophy. In Plutarch's portrayal of a statesman, the first characteristic called for is absolute devotion to the city-state, and we have to understand the amount of space Plutarch gives to wartime exploits in this context. At first glance, this emphasis seems out of keeping with the reality of the imperial city, and it contradicts even the *Precepts of Statecraft,* where Plutarch advises speech makers to avoid recalling past victories and encourages them rather to extol the virtues of peace. However, his stress on valor in war allows him to give contemporary leaders examples of men who were ready to serve the city everywhere and under all circumstances, ready to sacrifice their lives, their interests, and their personal attachments, even their honor and their principles, to their community.

But many dangers lurk in the struggle *(agōn)* we know as political life, and in all epochs (which he often neglects to differentiate), Plutarch finds the passions that he denounces in the *Precepts of Statecraft:* ambition *(philotimia)*, a necessary spur to action but which can degenerate into party strife *(philoneikia)* and thirst for power *(philarchia)*, and jealousy *(phthonos)*, a sword of Damocles suspended over the head of the powerful, who need prestige and popularity in order to act.

This is why the politician must follow Pericles' example and combine the teacherly qualities of firmness and persuasiveness. He must be able to resist the attractions of the crowd, and he must be aware of his responsibility as a leader whose duty it is to ensure the safety of those he governs. If he wishes to have followers, he must also persuade people to like him, and Plutarch attaches the greatest importance to the contacts the hero establishes with his fellow citizens or subjects. Smiling and affable, shunning the ostentation of a luxurious style of living that would alienate others, accommodating and accessible to all, he remains very much a man of the city, even if Plutarch's text occasionally resonates with Plato's theory of the philosopher-king, or with Pythagorean reflections. We see evidence of Plutarch's ideals in his discomfort with the Hellenistic kings, whose arrogance, greed, and perfidy he stigmatizes. His heroes fully deserve to be called *politikoi*, that is, both "belonging to" and "befitting" the city-state, because in fact they both serve the city-state and respect its values of humanity and tolerance.

THE LESSONS OF PLATONISM: REASON AND ANCESTRAL FIDELITY

Devoted to Chaeronea, Plutarch is also the servant of philosophy and of the god of Delphi. These two elements are indispensable for understanding a body of thought that is often difficult to grasp. In the first place, Plutarch's thought is never presented systematically; the variations inherent in the needs of the subject under consideration lay it open, accordingly, to accusations of incoherence. In the second place, while Plutarch repeatedly proclaimed his attachment to Platonism and assailed Stoics and Epicureans in his polemical works, and while his disciple and friend Favorinus chose to give his name to a defense of the New Academy's method, against Stoic assaults, we do not know for sure whether there was still a New Academy school in Plutarch's day, nor do we know what is implied by the fuzzy term "Middle Platonism." Some scholars even deny Plutarch the label Platonist, charging him with an eclecticism for which he is sometimes blamed and sometimes praised, but it is difficult to determine how much he himself contributed and how much he received from a philosophic tradition that had been nourished on five centuries of reflection since Plato and Aristotle.

Some critics, too, are willing to see Plutarch only as a moralist, a sort of Greek Seneca who, like the Roman writer, drafted advice on how to control anger or attain spiritual tranquillity. And the *Lives*, which, like Plutarch's pedagogical and moral treatises, manifest great psychological refinement, undoubtedly offer strong evidence of his qualities as a moralist. Still, in his eyes, if philosophy is to be truly the "mistress of life," it cannot neglect the beginning and the end of life. Thus the thought of God is at the heart of his reflection, and it underlies his differences with the other schools of thought. He is no more willing to accept the immanence of the Stoic *logos* than he is to accept Epicurean "atheism": the transcendence of the divine being is an essential truth that he has his teacher Ammonius proclaim in the discussion on the Epsilon at Delphi. The letter *epsilon* is pronounced *"ei"* (thou art); this votive offering to God should remind us that He alone possesses the plenitude of being, since He escapes the vicissitudes of time (*The Epsilon at Delphi* 392e). On the contrary, the precept "Know thyself," which the god confers on us, reminds us of the fragility of our nature and our inability to comprehend God in a consistent way (cf. *The Oracle at Delphi No Longer Given in Verse, Moralia* V.409d, or *On the Delays of the Divine Vengeance, Moralia* VII.549e). This transcendence precludes our bringing the divine being at random into our human world, and reason, like respect for divinity, condemns the excesses of superstition. But the limits of our knowledge in turn mean that we must not reject traditional faith in heavenly signs for the sake of a narrow rationalism, or scoff at the prerogatives of Providence. Providence can inspire us to action, but only by way of representations that stimulate the active and volitional part of our soul; it does not make our arms and legs move. To see Providence at work, a crucial distinction is required, one that Plutarch attributes to Plato: the distinction between the final or higher cause and the material or natural cause (*The Obsolescence of Oracles, Moralia* V.435e–436e). Pericles' unicorn ram offers a striking illustration of this: the anomaly had physical causes that Anaxagoras brought to light, but it also revealed that its owner would become the sole master of Athens, as the soothsayer Lampon saw.

This general framework helps us situate two highly debated points, Plutarch's dualism and his demonology. Inspired by *Timaeus*, Plutarch's cosmology deviates from Plato's precisely through the role attributed to the divine being. Instead of conceiving a demiurge intermediary between form and matter, Plutarch identifies God with the paradigm and develops the idea that "universal nature, disordered before, became a 'cosmos'; it came to resemble after a fashion and participate in the form and excellence of God" (*On the Delays of the Divine Vengeance,* 550d). But once Ideas are left aside and the world has become a reflection of the *Nous* (eternal mind), what about evil? Must one make God its cause—an intolerable blasphemy—or deny its existence against all evidence?

The preexistence of anarchic matter—which a temporal interpretation of *Timaeus* implies—lets us escape from this dilemma and suppose the existence of a precosmic and disordered evil soul (*On the Generation of the Soul in the Timaeus, Moralia* XIII.1.1014f–1015f) whose strength could not compare with divine power (*Isis and Osiris, Moralia* V.371a); this evil soul is more like a resistance to order and intelligence than a maleficent will. Apart from this theologico-physical analysis, there still remains the question of evil spirits, which is the focus of some recent studies on Plutarch's religion. But any consideration of evil spirits in isolation is unfaithful to a much broader demonology, which has to be put back within the framework of the destiny of the soul as it is treated in three great myths (*Concerning the Face Which Appears in the Orb of the Moon; On the Delays of Divine Vengeance; On the Sign of Socrates*). In his commentaries on *Timaeus*, Plutarch distinguishes between the irrational principle in the soul, a remnant of primordial disorder, and the divine *nous*. In *On the Sign of Socrates*, he reserves the term *soul* for the part immersed in the body and makes *nous* the term inappropriately applied to the part inaccessible to corruption, which is the *daimōn* (VII.591e). Once liberated by death, depending on whether vice has weighed it down or virtue lightened it, the *daimōn* can rise to unite itself with pure Intelligence, according to *Concerning the Face Which Appears in the Orb of the Moon*. It is no longer a matter, as in Plato, of contemplating Ideas, which have already been separated from cosmological speculations, and so demonology brings an answer to eschatological questions and the anguish of salvation. In certain cases, demonology also allows us to preserve the transcendence of the divine being in a plausible manner: thus, by assuming the intervention of demons in the operation of oracles, one can avoid the dilemma of "[making] the god responsible for nothing at all" (*On the Obsolescence of Oracles* V.414f), or seeing divine intervention in everything, and one can exonerate divine goodness from responsibility for human sacrifices by considering that sacrifices are demanded by demons that have not yet been purified of their evil worldly sentiments.

Owing in part, but only in part, to his monumental learning, Plutarch embodies the essential features of the Hellenic tradition: service to the city-state, the virtues of civilization, the requirements of reason introduced by Socrates, ancestral faith, and respect for divine grandeur. The man Montaigne celebrated for holding opinions that were "Platonic, mild, and accommodated to civil society" reminds us that the classical ideal put no distance between learning and life.

FRANÇOISE FRAZIER
Translated by Rita Guerlac and Anne Slack

Bibliography

Texts and Translations

Plutarch. *Moralia*. 15 vols. Loeb Classical Library.

———. *Parallel Lives*. Greek-Italian ed. Mondadori, in progress.

———. *Plutarch's Lives*. Trans. Bernadotte Perrin. 11 vols. Loeb Classical Library.

Studies

Aalders, Gerhard J. D. *Plutarch's Political Thought*. Amsterdam and New York: North-Holland Publishing Co., 1982.

Aalders, Gerhard J. D., and Lukas de Blois. "Plutarch und die politische Philosophie der Griechen." *Aufsteig und Niedergang der Römischen Welt (ANRW)* II, 36, no. 5 (1992): 3384–3404.

Babut, Daniel. *Parerga: Choix d'articles 1975–1993*. Lyon: Collection de la Maison de l'Orient Méditerranéen, 1994.

———. "Plutarque et le Stoïcisme." Dissertation, Paris, 1969.

Boulogne, Jacques. *Plutarque: Un aristocrate grec sous l'occupation romaine*. Lille: Presses Universitaires de Lille, 1994.

Brenk, Frederick E. "An Imperial Heritage: The Religious Spirit of Plutarch of Chaironeia." *ANRW* II, 36, no. 1 (1987): 248–349.

———. *In Mist Apparelled: Religious Themes in Plutarch's Moralia and Lives*. Leyden: E. J. Brill, 1977.

Dörrie, Heinrich. "Le platonisme de Plutarque." *Actes du VIIIème Congrès de l'Association Guillaume Budé*. Paris: Belles Lettres, 1969. Pp. 519–530.

———. "Die Stellung Plutarchs im Platonismus seiner Zeit." In *Philomathes: Studies and Essays in the Humanities in Memory of Philippe Merlan*. Ed. Robert B. Palmer and Robert Hamerton-Kelly. The Hague: Nijhoff, 1971. Pp. 35–36.

Frazier, Françoise. *Histoire et morale dans les Vies Parallèles de Plutarque*. Paris: Belles Lettres, 1996.

Hershbell, Jackson P. "Plutarch and Epicureanism." *ANRW* II, 36, no. 5 (1992): 3353–3383.

———. "Plutarch and Stoicism." *ANRW* II, 36, no. 5 (1992): 3336–3352.

Jones, Christopher P. *Plutarch and Rome*. Oxford: Clarendon Press, 1971.

Montaigne, Michel de. *The Complete Essays of Montaigne*. Trans. Donald M. Frame. Stanford, Calif.: Stanford University Press, 1958.

Mossman, Judith, ed. *Plutarch and His Intellectual World*. Oxford: Clarendon Press, 1997.

Panagopoulos, Cécile. "Vocabulaire et mentalité dans les Moralia de Plutarque." *Dialogues d'histoire ancienne* 3 (1977): 197–235.

Pavis d'Escurac, Hélène. "Périls et chances du régime civique selon Plutarque." *Ktèma* 6 (1981): 287–300.

Pelling, Christopher. "Aspects of Plutarch's Characterization." *Illinois Classical Studies* 13:2 (1988): 257–274.

———. "Plutarch's Adaptation of His Source Material." *Journal of Hellenic Studies* 100 (1980): 127–140.

———. "Plutarch's Method of Work in the Roman *Lives*." *Journal of Hellenic Studies* 99 (1979): 74–96.

Puech, Bernadette. "Prosopographie des amis de Plutarque." *ANRW* II, 33, no. 6 (1992): 4831–4893.

Stadter, Philip A. "Life of Pericles." *Ancient Society* 18 (1987): 251–269.

———. "The Proems of Plutarch's *Lives*." *Illinois Classical Studies* 13, no. 2 (1988): 275–295.

Van der Stockt, Luc. *Twinkling and Twilight: Plutarch's Reflections on Literature.* Brussels: Paleis der Academien, 1992.

Vernière, Yvonne. *Symboles et mythes dans la pensée de Plutarque.* Paris: Les Belles Lettres, 1977.

Ziegler, Konrat. *Paulys Realencyclopädie der classischen Altertumswissenschaft.* Stuttgart: J. B. Metzler, 1894–1972. XXI.1, col. 639–961.

POLYBIUS

POLYBIUS EXEMPLIFIES one of the crowning achievements of classical historiography. His importance is the product of several factors: Polybius's moment in history, during which the end of the autonomy of Greek city-states
coincided with the onset of the *pax romana;* his exceptional role as witness to
the events he recounted; the object of his work—to explain Roman expansion
and Rome's domination of the Mediterranean world; his experience as someone destined to exist between two worlds, Greek and Roman, which enabled
him to adopt a clear and somewhat detached point of view of both. Moreover,
he had a distinctive approach to the writing of history, and he maintained
throughout a reflective and critical view of the meaning of his work.

Polybius was born around 208 B.C.E. at Megalopolis in Arcadia, and spent
his youth in the Achaean Confederacy. The son of a high-ranking politician,
he served as Hipparch of the Achaean Confederacy in 170. The Greek world
was torn by factions at the time, and the confederacy did not align itself decisively enough with the Roman side in the struggle against Perseus of Macedonia. After the victory of Pydna (168 B.C.E.), between 167 and 150, the
Romans deported to Italy some one thousand Achaean hostages suspected of
treachery; Polybius was among them. While living in Rome, he became a
friend of the young Scipio Aemilianus. His circumstances there were ambiguous: he was both a hostage and a member of an important philhellenic society
(the "Scipionic circle"), and he enjoyed a privileged position from which to
observe Roman civilization, its institutions, the role of religion in maintaining cohesion within the state, and the organization of the army. Having become a trusted ally of the Romans, Polybius accompanied Scipio in 147–146
B.C.E. during the siege of Carthage. He continued to play an active role in the
political life of the Greek world, especially in the context of the administrative
reorganization that followed the sack of Corinth. It seems likely that the major part of his *Histories* was written during the last twenty years of his life.
Polybius is also the author of a *Life of Philopoemen,* a treatise on tactics, and
a work on the Numantine War.

Polybius's intention was to answer the question, "Who is so worthless or
indolent as not to wish to know by what means and under what system of
polity the Romans in less than fifty-three years have succeeded in subjecting
nearly the whole inhabited world to their sole government—a thing unique
in history?" (*Histories* I.1.5) A dual objective is thus set forth: he sought to

understand the unfolding of events that led first to the pursuit of world supremacy and then to its realization (from 223 to 168 B.C.E.); basing his research on a comparison between Greece and Rome, he also looked at their political systems and institutions, in search of a key to understanding this great historical process and the military success of the Romans. Starting with Book III of *Histories*, Polybius broadened his chronological scope to include the period immediately following the sack of Corinth and the destruction of Carthage (146 B.C.E.).

It is a dizzying panorama: in Greece, there were chronic conflicts among Achaeans, Aetolians, and Spartans, and the city-states were powerless to form a coherent policy in the face of the rising power of Rome and the Macedonians, whose Panhellenic ambitions led first Philip V and then Perseus to confront the Romans (in the three Macedonian wars that ended in the defeat of Persia at Pydna in 168 B.C.E.). There was also the conflict with Carthage, which took place in the western Mediterranean (Sicily, Spain, and Italy) before concluding in Africa. Last, there were conflicts with the eastern kingdoms, including Pergamum, Seleuceia, and Ptolemaic Egypt, and the Roman war against Antiochus III.

Polybius's work was written with the advantage of hindsight and was constantly revised, even during the final phases of editing, when the author further modified the early books. Polybius had by then returned to Greece, where, according to legend, he died after 118 B.C.E. following a serious riding accident. By that time, his very readable history had already been completed.

A project such as his demanded a particular form of historiography. Clearly, in choosing to limit himself to the events of the recent past, and in emphasizing politics, Polybius adhered to the tradition of Thucydides, Xenophon, and Theopompus. His history is an exercise in memory, made up of his interpretation of events experienced firsthand, testimony taken from participants (from the preceding generation as well as his own), archival research, and critical readings of earlier historians.

In contrast with his predecessors, however, Polybius sought to write a universal history; his project went beyond the formal framework of a historiography centered on the Greek world and Greek history. As a result, he could not conform to Thucydides' strict chronological principles. He had to find a connecting thread that would allow him to organize the whole and that was consistent with his ambitions, stated in the opening lines of the work: to reconstruct the course of historical process in a condensed time frame, but encompassing the entire Mediterranean world. It was less a matter of retracing a chain of events than of providing the reader with an overview of the whole that would include those events and reveal their underlying relationships. To do that, Polybius had to reconcile the chronology of events—from one Olympiad to the next—with the broad geographic framework: in other words, he had to relate the continuity of a particular event, its causes, and its consequences, to the simultaneous outbreak of events, the playing out of the same action in different parts of the world. Such a writing of history aims at total isomorphism with the dynamics of the events that it recounts.

This spatial dimension is evident not only in the purpose of *Histories* but also in the form and organization of the text. Rome was undertaking to unify the world under its authority. To do so, it had to operate on several fronts and to impose its law on distant regions over a period of time. Polybius sought to retrace the process by which history is fulfilled through an organic unification of space (I.1.3). In choosing the 140th Olympiad (220–216 B.C.E.) as his starting point, he points to the dawn of a period when "the affairs of Italy and Africa have been interlinked with those of Greece and Asia, all leading up to one end" (I.1.3). The history repeatedly attempts to show how the sequence of local events contributes to this final end; in other words, it tries to reveal the connections between what appear to be separate events and the consequences of those linkages. Polybius chose to write a universal history, rejecting a method that juxtaposes regional monographs in favor of one that aims at grasping the interconnectedness of events. The universality of the work derives not from a history that reaches into the distant past and continues up to the present time (like those of Ephorus or Diodorus Siculus) but from an ecumenical dimension, and, embedded in this, from the exposure of links between events that had previously appeared unconnected.

Keeping in mind this goal, which is restated at several key points in *Histories,* and also Polybius's unflagging interest in geography (to the point that he dedicated Book XXXIV to "continental topography"), we may reflect on the almost cartographic organization of a work that articulates many disjointed parts within an organic whole, and constantly refers regional information to the overall structure. Starting with the 140th Olympiad, Polybius covers the inhabited earth according to a determined order: Italy, Sicily, Spain, Africa, Greece, Macedonia, and Egypt. As the organizing principle of his narration, he adopts the form of a journey around the Mediterranean. Like a cartographer, Polybius seeks to construct a synoptic point of view, from which it would be easy to see the coherence and profound unity of an action "with a recognized beginning, a fixed duration, and an end which is not a matter of dispute" (III.1.5). Also like a cartographer, he has to draw out the correlation among distant places or phenomena. Here, synchronicity is the equivalent of the relations of commensurability established by means of the Euclidean grid of parallel and perpendicular lines that organized Eratosthenes' Alexandrian map. Polybius's conception of historical action ultimately converges with the theory of tragic action outlined in Aristotle's *Poetics:* unity and coherence as criteria, the body as metaphor.

The narrative challenge before Polybius is to reconcile chronology and topology: in other words, to situate each event in its proper place, and yet to respect the antithetical demands of describing the connectedness and continuity of events. The divisions by Olympiad and the method of describing events year by year (XIV.3.12) have to be adapted to a narrative that covers events occurring in different theaters of action—Greece, Asia, Africa, Spain, and Italy. This necessity sometimes leads Polybius, depending on the geographical progression, to relate the outcome of an event before describing its beginning (XV.3.24). The general rule lends itself to a variety of adjustments, made to avoid breaking the flow of events by fragmenting the account (for example, XXXII.C.2.ll). Such a principle of composition assigns an active role to the reader, who has the task of tying up the threads of this rhapsodic tale and restoring continuity: "But I myself, keeping distinct all the most important parts of the world and the events that took place in each, and adhering always to a uniform conception of how each matter should be treated, and again definitely relating under each year the contemporary events that then took place, leave obviously full liberty to students to carry back their minds to the continuous narrative and the several points at which I interrupted it" (XXXVIII.1.6). The form of the work and the evolution of a principle of composition thus had to reflect the very dynamics of history, in which theaters of action that seem independent at first become progressively interrelated within a universal configuration (IV.1.28). The discontinuity of the narrative, a consequence of the universal dimension of the particular historical process being investigated, while posing a difficulty for the reader against which Polybius defends himself in advance, also establishes an aesthetic of diversity (XXXVIII.1.5–6).

Another aspect of Polybius's work is the combination of historical narrative with continuous reflection on the task of the historian. The writing of history itself is accompanied by epistemological and ethical reflections on the issues at stake in this practice, the principles to be respected, and the pitfalls to be avoided.

Histories highlights Polybius himself, as both actor and author. He speaks of himself sometimes in the third person, sometimes in the first, to introduce some variety and to keep the reader interested; he even refers to himself by name, since "no one as far as I know, up to the time in which I live at least, has received from his parents the same proper name as my own" (XXXVI.12.5). He does not fail to recall his own political activity and the carefully argued support that he gave the Roman policy in Greece. More broadly speaking, his military and political experience give Polybius an essential advantage as a historian. As he notes (XII.13.25g and h), it is quite impossible to retrace these kinds of incidents if one has not been personally involved in the events themselves. History is done well, he adds, only when politicians themselves undertake to write it (XII.14.28).

Instructed by his fieldwork, Polybius takes every opportunity to reinforce his account by recalling the circumstances of his investigation and his sources of information. Very often these involved site visits (in Italy, Gaul, Spain, and Africa: most notably, following Hannibal's itinerary across the Alps) and personal encounters with people who had made history. Polybius's travels, which recall those of the polymath Ulysses, come across as the way he substitutes truth for the approximations and errors of armchair historians (III.2.48 and III.2.59, for instance). Examples include his interviews with Massinissa about Hannibal and with Laelius about Cornelius Scipio. However, it was his friendship with Scipio Aemilianus in particular that placed him at the center of events.

Polybius also inserts himself into the picture as the author of *Histories*, commenting frequently on the progression of his narrative, underlining the connections between cause and effect and crucial moments, and justifying his choices. Throughout the account he defines the objective of history, what it is that he must construct in his narrative: not the tedious detail of the actions, but their general features and the effects they produced (I.1.57, II.1.l). He does not hesitate to rank events or to restore chronological continuity when it has been interrupted by the shift from one theater of action to another.

One of the means Polybius adopts to affirm his conception of history is critical reading; at times he even corrects his predecessors. Underlying these controversies we see Polybius engaged in drawing a negative portrait of the ideal historian, that is, of Polybius himself. The reader is the final judge: often directly challenged, he is ultimately the only one in a position to determine the reputation and the future success or failure of the work.

Polybius's critiques of earlier historians define, in contrast, his own conception of history. On several occasions Polybius distances himself from the tradition of historical pathos that seeks to excite emotion in the reader by fueling the imagination with spectacular images (II.3.56) or even supernatural events. He aims his criticism at a form of history influenced by the rhetorical effects of tragedy, even though he himself resorts at times to the same stylistic expedients. Book XII devotes a lengthy argument to a critique of Timaeus of Tauromenium in which Polybius is attempting as much to reestablish the facts as to undermine the reputation of an author who might be called, with some justification, the first great Greek historian of the West and of Rome. Polybius severely criticizes Timaeus's factual errors, and also his systematic lies, his lack of historical ethics, the uncritical acceptance of witnesses that leads him to introduce unbelievable elements, and his propensity for polemic. Polybius also denounces the emotion that led Timaeus to present a partisan portrait of certain individuals, without a balanced dose of praise and blame. But the opposition is most clearly stated where it contains the two authors' conception of history. Polybius reproaches Timaeus for basing his research

entirely on books, for visiting libraries instead of sites (XII.14.27): "But to believe, as Timaeus did, that relying upon the mastery of material alone one can
write well the history of subsequent events is absolutely foolish, and is much
as if a man who had seen the works of ancient painters fancied himself to be
a capable painter and a master of that art" (XII.12.25e). It is impossible,
Polybius believes, to describe a battle without ever having experienced warfare. By the same token, without having personally been there it is impossible
to describe a scene of action or the configuration of a city. Truth and the ability to bring words to life are beyond the reach of the armchair historian, and
it is impossible to spark the interest of readers when one has not been personally involved in the events.

Polybius's emphasis on the reader is striking. His entire work reflects his
preoccupation with a public whose interest must be captured, readers who
must be motivated to pursue a work forty volumes long (forty papyrus
scrolls) and who must be aided by frequent summaries, by the addition of a
preface for each Olympiad, and by the inclusion of a chronological table in
the final volume (which has been lost). Polybius belonged to a world in which
books were beginning to circulate, in which the historian had to "publish" his
work by having the manuscript copied and put in circulation through libraries
(see, for example, XVI.3.20).

The presence of the reader also shaped Polybius's philosophy of history.
Unlike those authors who spared no effort to seduce their readers by resorting to anecdotes of the supernatural and appealing to a sense of pathos,
Polybius's aim was primarily practical: he wanted to inform. But he was not
pursuing knowledge for its own sake. He saw history as a storehouse of experiences, examples, and lessons that could help a reader avoid the mistakes of
the past. The lessons of history can be applied to the present (XII.2.25b), provided that one pays attention to the similarities between different situations.
Thus, he presents reading history as a means of acquiring political, military,
and ethical experience by proxy: one can draw the lessons of history without
running the attendant risks (I.1.35). In consequence, there is a gap between
Polybius's narrative itself and his ethical and political discourse, which systematically recalls the overall stakes involved in a given situation, the strate-
gic principles behind a military maneuver, and the vigilance required in interpreting human behavior. *Histories* constitutes a dissertation on the art of war
and a treatise on political science that fills in a portrait of the ideal statesman with repeated brush strokes. However, it also explores a vast range of situations—battles, sieges, ambushes, betrayals, reversals of fortune, and so
forth—all of which, if they are thoroughly learned by heart, will provide
the reader with a kind of wisdom and experience. Particularly striking are
Polybius's emphasis on commanders' mistakes, which often precipitate the
catastrophic outcome of a battle (X.5.32), and his analysis of the reasons for

success as well as failure, an analysis that transcends the pleasure of the text to extract useful lessons (XI.4.19a). In the same way, the actions of statesmen are painstakingly scrutinized: "It will be, I think, of some service to examine into the principles of the leading politicians in each place and decide which of them prove to have acted in a rational manner and which to have failed in their duty" (XXX.2.6).

At times these lessons take the form of structured developments that Polybius analyzes according to categories of Greek political philosophy (Peripatetics, Stoics), as in Book VI, for example, which is devoted to the army and to Roman institutions. The political life of a state is subject to a quasi-biological cycle of growth and decline, in which royalty, aristocracy, and democracy follow one after the other, as do their corrupted forms, tyranny, oligarchy, and mob rule. To escape this cycle, which sees a return of monarchy after a period of decadence, in the course of its political development Rome adopted a form of "mixed constitution," a synthesis of the three constitutions of the cycle, in which power is shared among the consuls, the Senate, and the people. But while Carthage, another example of a mixed constitution, left the greatest power to the people, in Rome the Senate dominated the other two components. Certain Greek states, such as Achaea, Sparta, and Crete, which possessed similar political organizations, failed to derive the same historical benefit from this break in the cycle. Polybius's account of the Roman constitution and its military organization attempted to explain the singularity of Rome to the Greeks in the framework of their own political thought, and also sought to present the Romans with a global interpretation of their institutions.

This insistence on the useful lessons of history suggests that Polybius's historical project is indeed twofold: to reconstruct the mechanism of the rise of Rome, and also to understand the reasons for the decline of Greece, a disaster parallel to that of Carthage—worse, even, since the Greeks had no extenuating circumstances to excuse their errors (XXXVIII.1). Moreover, his political and pragmatic approach to history suggests a dual readership: on the one hand, statesmen, or those who aspire to be statesmen, and on the other hand, Greeks of the city-states, to whom he offers an explanation of the principle mechanisms that brought about the final result. The unfolding of recent history is intended to enlighten his contemporaries: is life under Roman rule acceptable or intolerable? As for praise, credit, and blame, it will be for future generations to evaluate the Romans, by studying Polybius's account as well as by observing how they managed their victory (III.1.4).

Histories paints the portrait of a good leader. Such a leader adapts his decisions to an accurate evaluation of the circumstances, he shows moderation in victory, and he is honest. Among the more remarkable examples, Polybius offers Philopoemen, Scipio, Hadrusbal, and Hannibal. But one of the primary qualities of a leader is his awareness that fortune brings about unforeseeable changes, and for that reason Polybius has all the more admiration for Scipio who, at the moment of victory over Carthage, felt a certain anxiety for his own fatherland (XXXVIII.4.21).

A meditation on the responsibility of men and the role of Fortune in the unfolding of history runs throughout Polybius's work. History appears as a field where Fortune—the power that brings all events together toward a unique end (I.1.4)—can act, or even experiment; Fortune would thus be the principle of underlying order behind events. She embodies the instability of things, and can even overturn a seemingly certain outcome at the last moment, thus creating unexpected opportunities. Fortune is the only enemy that even the best generals cannot vanquish. She is also the least dependable ally, and a cautious general deserves greater credit than a lucky one who gambles. Fortune is generous in her warnings, and it is wise not to provoke her capricious moods. According to Hannibal, speaking to Scipio before the battle of Zama, Fortune "behaves as if she were sporting with little children" (XV.6.8). Nevertheless, she appears as a form of justice, punishing excess and the worst crimes—it was Fortune that brought on all the ills resulting in the defeat of Philip and the Macedonians (XXII.2.10). Fortune also urges those she favors to moderation, for fear of unpredictable outcomes. Thus she might be compared to the historian, who reads about events long after they transpired and knows how they came out. She can almost personify the unlimited inventiveness of the play of circumstances that always introduces the unpredictable into human actions.

Enlivened by the author's exceptional ability as a storyteller (his descriptions of Hannibal crossing the Alps, the battle of Cannes and the meeting between Hadrusbal and Scipio before the last battle at the gates of Carthage have become set pieces in anthologies) and by a surprising sense of portraiture, Polybius's work is a major source for historians today who seek to understand this crucial period. It has been required reading in the modern epoch, both for its instruction in the art of governing and for the political theory that emerges from its analysis of the Roman constitution—as attested, for example, by Machiavelli.

CHRISTIAN JACOB
Translated by Elizabeth Rawlings and Jeannine Pucci

Bibliography

Texts and Translations

Polybius. *Histories*. Trans. Walter Paton. Loeb Classical Library.

Studies

Ferrary, J.-L. *Philhellénisme et impérialisme: Aspects idéologiques de la conquête romaine du monde hellénistique*. Rome: Ecole française de Rome, 1988.

Pédech, Paul. *La méthode historique de Polybe*. Paris: Les Belles Lettres, 1964.

Wallbank, F. W. *Polybius*. Berkeley: University of California Press, 1972.

PROTAGORAS

Protagoras was born around 492 b.c.e. in Abdera, a Greek colony in Thrace, and died at the age of about seventy. He seems to have begun his working life by practicing a manual trade and then had the idea of teaching for fees *(misthos)*. He thus established the social status of the Sophist, someone who lived by transmitting his learning and who traveled from town to town doing so.

The Sophists' earnings seem to have depended on the results they obtained, as we can see from the suit that Protagoras brought against his disciple Euathlos, an advocate. It had been agreed that Euathlos would pay fees to his master only when he had won his first case. However, Euathlos was in no hurry to plead and hence paid nothing, and Protagoras eventually felt obliged to sue him. Euathlos then explained to the judges two possible outcomes of the suit: either he would win the trial, and that would mean that Protagoras would not be justified in demanding payment from him; or he would lose, and then Protagoras, by the very terms of their agreement, would have no grounds for claiming fees from him. If this story is true, we see that it is not quite right to call the Sophists the first teachers, since they were formally obliged to achieve results! Moreover, this explains the great difficulty the Socratics had in exonerating their master for having had as disciples two men of such questionable behavior as Alcibiades and Critias.

Protagoras came to teach in Athens, where he was a friend of Pericles, but his treatise *On the Gods* created a scandal there (rightly or wrongly; we shall try to decide), and Pythodoras brought a suit against him for impiety. Protagoras was condemned to leave Athens, and his works were burned on the Agora. This key event in his life prompts us to begin with a study of the scandalous treatise, or at least what remains of it, fragment B4.

From the famous affirmation according to which "of all things the measure is Man" (frg. B1; *Ancilla*, p. 125) the question of the existence of the gods seems to follow quite naturally, and Protagoras's agnosticism would thus follow from his relativism. In turn, the interpretation of the famous fragment B1 on man the measure *(anthropos metron)* would depend on the interpretation of the equally famous fragment B4, which deals with the impossibility of knowing the gods: "About the gods, I am not able to know whether they exist or do not exist, nor what they are like in form; for the factors preventing knowledge are many": their invisibility "and the shortness of human life" *(Ancilla*, p. 126).

This fragment was nothing other than the exordium of a book, *On the Gods*, which probably constituted the first part of Protagoras's great treatise on *Antilogies*. The general plan of this book seems to be indicated by a passage in Plato's *Sophist*, where the Sophist is defined as being essentially an *antilogikos*, a manipulator of contradictions. The Stranger invites Theaetetus to investigate the fields in which the Sophist reveals antilogies, that is to say the fields in which one finds "two contradictory discourses," as Protagoras would put it. At the end of the account, Theaetetus recognizes the allusion to Protagoras's writings.

The first of these fields was that of the invisible: the problem of the gods. Protagoras also studied the fate of the soul after death; we know he had written an essay titled *On the Underworld*.

The second field concerned the visible. Here, Protagoras explored the following. (1) Cosmology, "what the sophists call the cosmos" (Xenophon, *Memorabilia* I.1 [11]). No fragment of this text has survived. (2) Ontology (being and becoming): Protagoras opposed Parmenides and the argument for the unity of being. (3) Politics, that is to say, the study of various bodies of law. This section probably included the discussion on the death of Epitimus, who was accidentally killed by a javelin. The discussion presumably determined the responsibility for the death: was it the javelin, the thrower of the javelin, or the organizer of the games? (4) Art *(techne):* included in this part were reflections on mathematics, which for Protagoras was an art form (frg. B7 on tangents).

To understand fragment B4, it is essential to *situate* it within the totality of Protagoras's thought and not take it as an absolute. It is a fragment, and it is but one phase—the first—of Protagorean analysis. Indeed, Diogenes Laertius is careful to remind us of this: "For this *introduction* to his book, the Athenians expelled him; and they burnt his works" (*Lives of Eminent Philosophers* IX.52; emphasis added). Moreover, if we extend the context still further, we perceive that the treatise on the gods was the subject of a certain publicity: "The first of his books he read in public was that *On the Gods* . . . ; he read it at Athens in Euripides' house" (ibid. IX.54).

This last circumstance is important because fragment B25 DK, attributed to Critias by some scholars and to Euripides by others, is likely to have been written by Euripides. This fragment declares that the existence of the gods is a fable invented by a "far-seeing man" so that fear would prompt every man to respect the law of his own accord. But it is probable in other respects that a discourse that entirely rejected traditional piety could not have been the subject of a reading attended by such publicity.

We should in any case be well aware of one fact: if we had only a single passage of Descartes's *First Meditation*, we might thereby conclude that the author in question was casting doubt on the existence of the external world, whereas Descartes sought on the contrary to establish it, albeit in his own way. Similarly, in the rest of the work Protagoras too may have been establishing, in his own way, the existence of the gods. The finest fragment in the world can offer only what it contains, and fragment B4 is simply the first step in Protagoras's undertaking. Now by good fortune we also have an account of the *outcome* of Protagoras's reflection on the gods: the myth of Epimetheus and Prometheus in Plato's *Protagoras*. The fact that we are dealing with myth should not cast suspicion on its content; Protagoras in fact gives his listeners a choice as to the form of the account, scientific argument or myth, and he implies that the underlying content will be the same in either case.

Thus, having started from a position of doubt, Protagoras seems to have ended with belief in the gods. Can we trace the outline of the path the Sophist followed in his thinking? To do so we would use the general outline of Protagoras's approach, which would have allowed him, starting from the establishment of "double discourses," to end by affirming the statement of a "Truth." This outline would have three stages: the antilogies; man the measure; strong discourse.

THE ANTILOGIES

We cannot say, with respect to the gods, that "either they exist, or they do not exist." I prefer to translate the passage as "neither that they are, nor that they are not," instead of "neither how they are nor how they are not," for it is hard to find meaning in the expression "how they are not." It has been pointed out, moreover, that we should not give *eisin* (they are) an existential meaning; it would in fact be absurd, we are told, to wonder about the "appearance" of the gods while their existence remains uncertain. It is easy to answer this last remark, and Protagoras's thinking seems to be the following: even if we could prove that the gods exist, we could not know how they look (Gorgias will use a similar argument in his *Treatise on Nonbeing*: being does not exist, and even if it does, it is unrecognizable).

The expression "either they exist, or they do not exist" unquestionably puts before us an antilogical formulation. This theme of the double nature of reality and of hesitation before two divergent paths is not peculiar to Protagoras. It is first of all a tragic theme (we may think here of Aeschylus's Orestes in the *Choephorae*), and it is also a moral theme (here the example is the famous choice made in Prodicos's *Herakles*, when the hero is invited to choose between a life of pleasure and life ruled by excellence). It is an aesthetic theme as well: we may refer to an account by Pliny the Elder *(Natural History)* of a picture by the painter Parrhasios: "His picture of the People of Athens also shows ingenuity in treating the subject, since he displayed them as fickle, choleric, unjust and variable, but also placable and merciful and compassionate, boastful . . . , lofty and humble, fierce and timid—and all these at the same time" (IX.xxxv.69). This last account shows us that we are also dealing with a political theme.

But this theme of the fundamental ambiguity of reality turns out to be partially reabsorbed, in the tradition, by the reference to the gods. Here the very existence of the gods comes within the provisions of antilogy instead of making us depart from it. What is the source of this crisis in the belief in the traditional gods? It appears that we cannot attribute it to the loss of confidence in civic gods, since this crisis was brought about by the defeat of 404 (on this point, see Edmond Lévy's *La défaite de 404*), and Protagoras in fact died around 422. There is one other possible cause: at about this time people began to look closely at the texts of the poets, especially Homer, discovering contradictions and improprieties. We can see the critical spirit developing; for example, Protagoras reproaches Homer, chiding him on his language and for giving orders to the goddess in the guise of a prayer, when he began the *Iliad* with "Sing, goddess, the wrath."

The formula "nor how they look" clearly sets the stage for the gods' *invisibility*, to which it is related. The problem of the gods' visible form surprises the modern reader, who conceives of the deity rather as the Christian hidden God: the church is highly skeptical about "apparitions," while the Greek gods are manifest gods. Doubt about the existence of gods thus means, first of all, for a Greek, doubt about their perceptible manifestation. Herodotus tells us that Homer and Hesiod, who were the founders of polytheism, were concerned not only with naming the gods but also with determining their forms: "These they are who taught the Greeks of the descent of the gods, and gave to all their several names, and honours, and arts, and declared their outward forms" (*Histories* II.53). And while Plato would later protest against the liberties the poets took in their presentation of the gods, he rejected the idea that the gods were in the habit of changing their form. "A god," Plato wrote, "abides for ever simply in his own form" (*Republic* II.381c). Thus the god has a form, and that form is changeless.

In fact, as Jean-Pierre Vernant recalls in *L'individu, la mort, l'amour* ("Le corps divin"), the gods have bodies. Of course a god's body is "glorious," if I may use Christian terminology here. In comparison with the human body, the gods have a "superbody," an eternal body, according to Vernant. A god's body has blood, but a wound does not cause him to die; a special diet of nectar and ambrosia provides him with the elixirs of immortality. Gods also feed on the fumes of sacrifices; this is why the Pythagoreans will say that one can feed on odors. The body of a god is resplendent and radiant, with a strength far superior to that of a mortal. A god can intervene without becoming visible, concealing her body in a cloud (as Aphrodite did when she spirited Paris away from combat in the *Iliad*), or he can reveal himself in majesty—although an excess of light can be as obscuring as darkness.

From Vernant's analysis, then, we shall retain the notion that the gods have bodies that can be totally invisible without ceasing to be bodies. This ambiguity of the divine superbody, one of whose powers is to make itself invisible at will, is not unproblematic. Problems arise with regard to statues, for example, when it is a question of representing a god: let us recall, for instance, Phidias's statue of Zeus, a chryselephantine statue at Olympia; fifteen meters tall, it was unanimously admired for its truly divine bearing (Phidias, like Protagoras, was a contemporary of Pericles). This statue, like that of Athena, has a human aspect. Similarly, we may recall Polygnotus's paintings, with their mythological subjects. These representations perhaps contributed to reviving the criticisms of Xenophanes, who challenged their anthropomorphism as early as the 6th century: "But mortals suppose that gods are born, wear their own clothes and have a voice and body" (frg. 14). "Ethiopians say that their gods are snub-nosed and black; Thracians that theirs are blue-eyed and red-haired" (frg. 16). "But if horses or oxen or lions had hands or could draw with their hands and accomplish such works as men, horses would draw the figures of the gods as similar to horses, and the oxen as similar to oxen, and they would make the bodies of the sort which each of them had" (frg. 15). This text is a good example of a Protagorean antilogy, a century in advance, and it shows the impossibility of having *knowledge* based on the presentation of a form, so far as the nature of the gods is concerned.

The series of problems about existence and form was to take up again a question already posed, one that would be canonical in Stoicism, for example. In Cicero's *De natura deorum*, Cotta the Academician says to Balbus the Stoic, "First you designed to prove the existence of the gods; secondly, to describe their nature" (III.iii.6).

The justification for the difficulty of knowing the gods, namely that human life is short, has troubled commentators with its facile air. And yet it does not seem to harbor irony. One might explain it this way. The gods are the "immortals"; really to know the gods, to understand their nature, would require verifying this immortality. Now our life—that is, the life of a mortal—is always too short for that; we cannot measure our lifespan against that of the gods, who thus remain outside our comprehension in time as they remain in space.

But there is another possible, and perhaps more plausible, explanation of the formula about the brevity of human life. Here we are presumably dealing with a literary reminiscence in Protagoras, an allusion to a "saying" of the poet Simonides, who was in many respects Protagoras's favorite author. Indeed, if we turn to Cicero's *De natura deorum*, we will be able to understand Protagoras's allusion: "Inquire of me as to the being and nature of god, and I shall follow the example of Simonides, who having the same question put to him by the great Hiero, requested a day's grace for consideration; next day, when Hiero repeated the question, he asked for two days, and so went on several times multiplying the number of days by two; and when Hiero in surprise asked why he did so, he replied: 'Because the longer I deliberate the more obscure the matter seems to me'" (I.xxii.60).

Thus man's life is too short with respect to the extraordinary difficulty of knowing whether the gods exist and, if they exist, what they look like. With Simonides, as with Protagoras, the obscurity of the question of the visualization of the gods takes a very long time to dissipate.

MAN THE MEASURE

We must read the famous fragment B1 all the way through: "Of all things the measure is Man, of the things that are, that they are, and of the things that are not, that they are not" (*Ancilla*, p. 125).

We find once again the terms used in the fragment on the gods, on their being and their nonbeing, but we go a step further with regard to the balanced hesitation of fragment B4, "whether they exist or do not exist," since with regard to this being or nonbeing, it is man who will decide. The being or nonbeing of the gods will have man as its measure; that is without doubt the real blasphemy of Protagoras, who makes the gods depend on man, and not the reverse. That is why Plato will oppose him in *Laws*, where he writes: "The measure of all things" is God (IV.716c).

That man is the measure of the being or nonbeing of a god means that man may be either a believer or an atheist (like Diogoras or Theodorus of Cyrene), and if he is a believer, that he may have a quite different "idea" about *what* this god is. (We may recall that in his youth Protagoras had spent time with the magi of Persia, for whom the gods are personifications of natural phenomena; that is a different conception of traditional polytheism.) However, we are still left with a division of opinions, since "man" in Protagoras's formula has both an individual and a generic meaning. In the debates that this division produces over time, the adherents to one set of opinions come to outnumber the others. Thenceforth, one of the two discursive strategies used to express these divergent viewpoints (the discourses of existence and nonexistence, the discourses of "like this" and "like that") will be weak and marginal, the other powerful and majoritarian.

Now the strong discourse, that is to say the most widely accepted one, expresses a reality: it affirms the existence of the gods and sees them as the tradition of the city-state dictates.

STRONG DISCOURSE

The theory put forward by the strong discourse, though it was used, after Protagoras, for eristic ends, and though it uses rhetoric to persuade, is not the manipulation of opinion to which it will later be reduced. Instead it expresses a large *consensus*. It has been wrongly believed that Protagoras contested the tradition, while in fact he was its most ardent supporter: the existence of the gods rests entirely on tradition, which has the stability of our renewed adherence.

To this some may object that Protagoras accepts and exploits the *belief* in the existence of the gods more than the existence of the gods itself. But in fact, in his philosophy, these amount to the same thing, since Protagoras suppresses the distinction between knowledge and opinion. What is true is collective adherence, which constitutes strong discourse. Such is truth, according to Protagoras.

Of course against this Protagorean conception it will be argued that this truth is not truth at all, that it is completely relative, that it is changing and far from universal. To be sure, Protagorean truth is not justified by its absoluteness (the Absolute and, a fortiori, a transcendent absolute do not exist for Protagoras), but it justifies itself by its quality of *usefulness*. It is a useful truth, to borrow an idea applied to Nietzsche by Jean Granier. The explanation of Protagoras's thought in Plato's *Theaetetus* is clear on this point: all appearances are not of equal value; appearance has a greater or lesser value according to its degree of usefulness (167a). The symptoms of health and those of illness are both real and true, but those of health are more useful than those of sickness, which are harmful. In the same way, all opinions are not to be considered on the same level: the Sophist, that is to say, the man who knows, is more clever than other men to the degree that he is able to replace a harmful appearance by a useful one: men of the skilled professions also do this, artists, doctors, and farmers. A doctor, with his remedies, replaces the symptoms of sickness with those of health; the farmer, with his fertilizers, allows plants to thrive instead of remaining sickly. In the same way, those who have mastery of the great art of rhetoric—the Sophists—properly speaking, by their lucidity and oratorical talent, will carry a better measure *(beltion)*, that is, a more useful one *(chrestos)*, and thus triumph in the eyes of the city-state by making their discourse into a strong, unanimous one, thereby giving it the appearance of truth.

Now the discourse that affirms the existence of the gods is more useful than the discourse that denies it, especially in the field of politics, as is shown by the myth of Epimetheus and Prometheus in Plato's *Protagoras*, the myth that was part of Protagoras's text called *Truth*. This famous myth shows that while Prometheus may be able to steal fire (that is to say, *techne*) and give it to men, he nevertheless cannot steal civic wisdom *(sophian politiken)*: "This was in the possession of Zeus" (321d). And the intervention of Zeus is necessary to give men, through Hermes, the art of politics, without which men either remain dispersed and are destroyed by other animals, who are better equipped than they with natural defenses, or they gather together and destroy each other, because they are unjust, and so they still perish. The political art cannot be developed until men receive "shame and justice" from Zeus. These alone make the city-state possible, because they bring about order and the bonds of friendship. We must conclude, then, that for Protagoras not only is the existence of the gods posited but even divine Providence is restored. Belief in the gods is the necessary condition for solving the political problem, human survival. Thus, for Protagoras, a society cannot exist in which the majority of the people are atheists. The religion in question, then, is pragmatic and not mystical: it is a religion necessary for humanity if humanity is to survive.

If the existence of the gods is an appearance created by the persuasive art of the Sophist (as in the famous fragment attributed to Critias, but which is probably by Euripides, as we have seen, an echo of Protagoras's teaching in the tragic poet's work), through an immediate reaction, the organization of men in city-states—that is, political and social life—is achieved, and humanity is saved. It is only when man has created the gods that the gods can create man. That, perhaps, is what the succession of two moments suggests in the myth. After the invention of technology and before any attempts to found city-states, "man was the only creature that worshipped gods, and set himself to establish altars and holy images" (*Protagoras* 322a). Then, in a second phase, Zeus granted man the political virtues and thereby saved humanity. Belief in the simple *existence* of the gods has as a consequence the appearance of *providential* gods: thus the two degrees of Greek theology are established.

Here is a grandiose theory, a remarkable union of transcendence and immanence. Without this foundation of the divine, man cannot be man; this is why, in the myth of Epimetheus and Prometheus related by Plato, man is presented as being the work of the gods, which means that when he becomes aware that he is the work of the gods, man, by strong discourse, begins to create gods.

By quite different paths, Protagoras arrives at the same conclusion as Socrates, who says to a disciple: "And that I am speaking the truth, you, too, will know, if you do not wait until you see the shapes of the gods, but if it is enough for you when you see their works, to revere and honor the gods" (Xenophon, *Memorabilia* IV.3[13]). It is in this sense that, in Plato's *Protagoras*, impiety, with the injustice it entails, is the opposite of political virtue.

Plato, in a passage of *Laws* where the Sophists are under attack, seems to allude to the theology of Protagoras and Euripides when he writes: "The first statement, my dear sir, which these people make about the gods is that they exist by art and not by nature—by certain legal conventions" (889e). All in all, for Protagoras, the gods are the creatures of man, and if by mischance the gods do not exist, we must hasten to invent them.

GILBERT ROMEYER DHERBEY
Translated by Rita Guerlac and Anne Slack

Bibliography

Texts and Translations

Cicero. *De natura deorum*. Trans. H. Rackham. Loeb Classical Library.

Diels, Hermann, and Walther Kranz. *Ancilla to the Pre-Socratic Philosophers; A Complete Translation of the Fragments in Diels Fragmente der Vorsokratiker.* Trans. Mary Fitt. Oxford: Basil Blackwell, 1948. Cited in text as DK.

Diogenes Laertius. "Protagoras." In *Lives of Eminent Philosophers*. vol. 2. Trans. R. D. Hicks. Loeb Classical Library.

Herodotus. *Histories*. Trans. A. D. Godley. 4 vols. Loeb Classical Library.

Plato. *Laws*. Trans. R. G. Bury. 2 vols. Loeb Classical Library.

———. *Protagoras*. Trans. W. R. M. Lamb. Loeb Classical Library.

Pliny. *Natural History*. Trans. H. Rackham. 10 vols. Loeb Classical Library.

Poirier, Jean-Louis. "Les Sophistes." In *Les Présocratiques*. Coll. La Pléiade. Paris: Gallimard, 1988.

Untersteiner, Mario. *Sofisti: Testimonianze e frammenti*, fasc. 1. Florence: La Nuova Italia, 1949.

Xenophanes of Colophon. *Fragments*. Trans. and commentary by J. H. Lesher. Toronto: University of Toronto Press, 1992.

Xenophon. *Memorabilia*. Trans. Amy L. Bonnette. Ithaca, N.Y.: Cornell University Press, 1994.

Studies

Adorno, Francesco. *La filosofia antica*, vol. 1. Milan: Feltrinelli, 1991.

Bayonas, Auguste. "L'art politique d'après Protagoras." *Revue philosophique* 157 (1967): 43–58.

Bodéus, Richard. "Réflexions sur un court propos de Protagoras." *Les études classiques* 55 (1987): 241–257.

Dupréel, Eugène. *Les Sophistes: Protagoras, Gorgias, Prodicus, Hippias.* Neuchâtel: Editions du Griffon, 1948.

Granier, Jean. *Nietzsche*. Paris: Presses Universitaires de France, 1982.

Guthrie, William Keith Chambers. *The Sophists*. London: Cambridge University Press, 1971.

Isnardi-Parente, Margherita. *Sofistica e democrazia antica*. Florence: Sansoni, 1977.

Jaeger, Werner. *Paideia: The Ideals of Greek Culture*. Trans. Gilbert Highet. New York: Oxford University Press, 1939.

Kerferd, George Briscoe. *The Sophistic Movement*. Cambridge: Cambridge University Press, 1981.

Lana, Italo. *Protagoras*. Publicazioni della Facoltà di Lettere e Filosofia. Vol. 2, fasc. 4. Turin: Universita di Torino, 1950.

Levi, Adolfo. *Storia della sofistica*. Naples: Morano, 1966.

Léyy, Edmond. *La défaite de 404: Histoire d'une crise idéologique*. Paris: De Boccard, 1976.

Romeyer Dherbey, Gilbert. *La parole archaïque*. Paris: Presses Universitaires de France, 1999.

———. *Les Sophistes*, 4th ed. Paris: Presses Universitaires de France, 1995.

Romilly, Jacqueline de. *The Great Sophists in Periclean Athens*. Trans. Janet Lloyd. Oxford: Clarendon Press; New York: Oxford University Press, 1992.

Untersteiner, Mario. *Les Sophistes*, vol. 1. Trans. A. Tordesillas, preface G. Romeyer Dherby. Paris: Vrin, 1993.

Vernant, Jean-Pierre. *L'individu, la mort, l'amour: Soi-même et l'autre en Grèce ancienne*. Paris: Gallimard, 1989.

Zeppi, Stelio. *Protagora e la filosofia del suo tempo*. Florence: La Nuova Italia, 1961.

PTOLEMY

ALTHOUGH THE ACHIEVEMENTS of Claudius Ptolemaeus represent the very peak of Hellenistic astronomy, remarkably little is known of the precise way in which the subject developed during the three centuries between him and the astronomer to whom he owed most, namely Hipparchus, who died sometime after 126 B.C.E. Ptolemy himself remains a shadowy figure. His synthesis of the work of his predecessors, together with his own considerable additions, continued to influence Greek, Islamic, and Western civilizations for more than fourteen centuries after his death, and yet our knowledge of his life is slight and uncertain. We know from his principal astronomical work, *Almagest*, that he made series of observations between 127 and 141 C.E., during the reigns of the emperors Hadrian and Antoninus, and the existence of subsequent writings from his pen is compatible with the statement of a later writer that he died during the reign of Marcus Aurelius (161–180).

Ptolemy's name tells us a little about his forebears. "Claudius" indicates Roman citizenship, possibly granted to his family by the emperor of that name, or by Nero. "Ptolemaeus" shows that he was an inhabitant of Egypt, descended from Greek—or at least Hellenized—stock. His writings give many indications that he worked in Alexandria, and none suggests any connection with any other place. He promised in *Almagest* that he would list the geographical positions of towns with reference to Alexandria's meridian, but when he came to write *Geography*, he took the meridian through the "Isles of the Blest" (the Canaries), since they had the advantage of being at the western extreme of the known world.

Beyond these trifles gleaned from his name and his works, we know almost nothing about him of a personal nature. The scholarly advantages of life in Alexandria, and in particular of access to its Museum, do not need to be repeated here. The Museum had entered a period of renewed prosperity under the Pax Augusta, had been well patronized by Hadrian, and would survive two generations after Ptolemy's death before suffering under the depredations of Caracalla. Although Ptolemy must have been indebted to this institution, we know nothing of his associates there. From *Almagest* we know that he was provided with observations by a certain Theon, and several of his works are presented to a certain Syrus. These persons are no more than names to us. In the last analysis, it is through Ptolemy's works that we must know him. Numerous legends that cluster round his name in Arab and later Western sources are without value. One theme is particularly common, namely his royal ancestry. The idea stems, of course, from the fact that Ptolemy was the name of all the Macedonian kings of Egypt. By the 2nd century it had become an extremely common boy's name—just as Cleopatra was common for girls.

GREEK ASTRONOMY BEFORE PTOLEMY

Especially since the time of J.-B. Delambre (1817) it has been customary to disparage Ptolemy's contribution to astronomy and to suggest that he did no more than report on the achievements of his predecessors, in particular Hipparchus. This is unjust and is ironic to the extent that it is almost entirely through Ptolemy's personal testimony in *Almagest* that we know the foundations on which he built, and that he is supposed to have purloined. *Almagest* is the work on which his reputation chiefly rests. His writings on geometrical projection, on geography, and on optics would undoubtedly have given him an important place in history on their own account. His *Almagest* is his great synthesis, however. Its very name is from the Greek for "the greatest compilation" *(he magiste)*. The Arabs turned this phrase into *al-majisti*, which became *almagesti* or *almagestum* in medieval Latin. This summary of the whole of mathematical astronomy is presented from a very Greek standpoint, with its characteristically geometrical form, although it is now known to contain a strong Babylonian component of astronomical data—and the Babylonians had built their astronomy on what were primarily arithmetical foundations.

The first Greek attempts to represent the movement of the Sun, Moon, and planets by mathematical models used simple rotational movements that failed to account for the variations in the velocities of the bodies concerned as they move against the background of fixed stars. The planetary motion that gave the most trouble was retrograde motion, to which all planets then known (Mercury, Venus, Mars, Jupiter, Saturn) are subject. Their general drift round the sky is in a direction opposite to that of the daily rotation. However, as a consequence of the fact that we view the planets from Earth, which is revolving round the Sun just as they are, each planet appears from time to time to reverse the direction of its long-term motion. In other words, although each planet moves (with direct motion) in the general direction of the Sun, from time to time it slows down to a stationary position (with respect to the fixed stars), reverses its path for a relatively short period (retrograde motion), and then again returns to direct motion.

To explain this retrogradation, the geometer Eudoxus of Cnidos, early in the 4th century B.C.E., devised a system of spheres concentric with Earth ("homocentric spheres"). He found that he could produce a figure-of-eight motion by pivoting one sphere inside another, both of them rotating, so long as the axes were inclined to each other. To get a retrograde motion, it was necessary only to carry this figure-of-eight around the sky on yet another concentric sphere. The details of this brilliant geometrical device are less important than the fact that, as a model to predict precisely the observed motions of the planets, it can have achieved very little. It was adopted by Aristotle, who was attracted to it by the thought that it mirrored the physical workings of the universe. In the form of the Aristotelian spheres, Eudoxus's model remained in intellectual currency until the 17th century and even later—almost two millennia after it was superseded astronomically. Even Ptolemy found it physically appealing.

The great change in geometrical approach to the problem of retrogradation came with the twin concepts of the eccentric and the epicycle. The idea of the eccentric is essentially simple: if a body—and the Sun was the body for which the scheme was devised—is moving at constant speed round a circle, then its speed as seen from a point at some distance from the center of the circle will be variable over the cycle. The Sun's annual motion is known to be nonconstant—in other words, the seasons were known to be of different lengths. It was found that a simple eccentric model can give a very reasonable approximation to the Sun's annual motion, if the scale of the model is carefully chosen.

The eccentric alone will not explain the retrogradation of the planets, but there is a very simple model that may be used to do so: the epicycle. If a planet moves around a small circle, and the center of that circle moves around Earth, then the resulting apparent motion will represent appearances in a qualitatively acceptable fashion. By choosing the values of the two speeds, the starting points of the motions, and the relative scale of the two circles, it is possible to get quite respectable empirical results for the movements of any particular planet. The same model may be used to explain to some extent the notorious irregularities in the Moon's motion. (This is so even though the Moon never enters a retrograde phase. In this case the sense of rotation of the Moon on the epicycle is the reverse of that of the planets.)

With Hipparchus (2nd century B.C.E.) Greek astronomy became a more rigorously quantitative science. Hipparchus was in possession of Babylonian materials—for example, Babylonian eclipse records and lunar and planetary theories—and through Hipparchus's writings Ptolemy obtained the same invaluable material. The Babylonian theories, arithmetically based, were of a level of sophistication unparalleled in any other civilization. Hipparchus's achievement was to combine the merits of the two different mathematical outlooks, for instance in his epicyclic theories of the Sun and Moon, using Babylonian parameters. He measured the parallax of the Moon (its apparent shift in place due to the fact that we observe this relatively nearby object from places at a distance from Earth's century) and found ways of measuring the distance of the Sun and Moon. His most important discovery, however, was that the so-called fixed stars do not hold their position but seem to drift around the sky along courses parallel to the zodiac. This they do at a very slow rate: by comparing his own observations of the star Spica with those of Timocharis 160 years earlier, he found that the rate was greater than a degree per century. (It is roughly half as much again as this.)

By Ptolemy's time, the mathematical tools of the astronomer were highly developed. Although we think of trigonometry as a self-sufficient subject, at an elementary level having to do with figures in two dimensions, this is to overlook its origins. It grew out of the geometry of three dimensions, as that part of geometry that was needed for solving astronomical problems. As such, although Hipparchus had advanced it considerably, some of its most important results were made available only a generation or so before Ptolemy, by Menelaus. Ptolemy codified all this brilliantly, added a number of results of his own, and so put astronomy in his debt for more than a millennium.

ALMAGEST

Ptolemy's *Almagest* is in thirteen books, the first of which gives the necessary mathematics, including the theorems of Menelaus for solving triangles on the surface of a sphere. He uses the chord function where we would use sines, but this first book translates very easily into modern terms, and it set the pattern for future works on "spherical astronomy." He made full use of the sexagesimal notation of the Babylonians, dividing the degree into 60 minutes, each minute into 60 seconds, and so forth.

From the extremes of the Sun's declination he found a figure for one of the fundamental parameters of astronomy, the inclination of the ecliptic (the Sun's path) to the equator. His instruments were imperfect, and his figure was indifferent—in fact he probably allowed his admiration for Hipparchus to influence his judgment. In Book III of *Almagest* Ptolemy accepts Hipparchus's solar theory, and again there was little incentive to change what was a relatively successful theory. When he came to the theory of the Moon, however, in Book IV of *Almagest*, he showed his mastery of planetary theory. Starting from a careful discussion of the lunar theory of Hipparchus, he compared it with his own observations and found that it fitted well only when the Sun, Earth, and Moon were in line (at conjunctions and oppositions). He added extra elements to earlier explanations and produced a geometrical model that produced far better results for the Moon's celestial longitude than any before it. *Almagest* Book V ends with a discussion of the distances of the Sun and Moon, and includes the first known theoretical discussion of parallax, that is, of the correction it is necessary to apply to the Moon's apparent position to obtain its position relative to Earth's center. In Book VI, Ptolemy uses the solar, lunar, and parallax theories of the preceding books to construct tables for solar and lunar eclipses.

Before dealing with the planets, Ptolemy turned to the longitudes, latitudes, and magnitudes (in six classes of brightness) of the fixed stars. His catalogue of 1,022 stars in 48 constellations, and a handful of nebulae, provided the framework for almost all others of importance in the Islamic and Western worlds until the 17th century. It was based on materials by Hipparchus that are no longer extant and took into account his theory of precession, but it was more extensive than anything before it.

Books IX, X, and XI of *Almagest* account for the longitudes of the inferior planets (Mercury and Venus) and the superior (Mars, Jupiter, and Saturn). Two different arrangements of the epicycle in relation to the deferents are needed, and since Mercury gives rise to difficulties of its own, further refinements were needed in that case. He extended in important ways the epicycle principle developed by Apollonius of Perge and others. One new technique was especially important to him, and yet it gave rise to much controversy in later periods. The epicycle had always been thought to move around the deferent circle at a constant rate along the circumference. Ptolemy introduced the idea of a motion that was constant as seen from a point that was neither the center of the universe (Earth) nor the center of the deferent circle. This, his "equant" principle, was all the more commendable because it meant breaking with the traditional dogma that all must be explained in terms of uniform circular motions. The power of his method did not save him from criticism, and fourteen centuries later we find that even Copernicus found the equant distasteful. Ptolemy's final two books deal with predicting planetary phenomena, such as first and last appearances, and latitudes.

Ptolemy was concerned not only to explain observed planetary motions but also to make it easy to calculate them. His *Almagest* includes tables to this end, and other tables he issued separately *(Tables manuelles)* had enormous influence on the later progress of astronomy, for they set the style for astronomical technique, first in the Islamic world and later in Europe. Ptolemy taught posterity the art of selecting and analyzing astronomical observations for theoretical purposes, although it has to be said that in this supremely important aspect of astronomy he had no real equal until Johannes Kepler came to analyze the observations of Tycho Brahe.

TETRABIBLOS

For astrology Ptolemy wrote what also became a standard text, *Tetrabiblos*. Babylonian astrological schemes were known in Roman Egypt. Hellenistic astrology was flourishing, and astronomical methods that were easier to apply than Ptolemy's, however inaccurate, were called for. *Tetrabiblos* is a masterly book, and in many respects a scientific one. Where Babylonian and Assyrian divination had mostly concerned public welfare and the life of the ruler, the Greeks applied the art in large measure to the life of the individual. The activity had been unintentionally encouraged by the teachings of Plato and Aristotle on the divinity of the stars, and in late antiquity many astrologers regarded themselves as interpreting the movements of the gods. With the rise of Christianity this attitude was of course repressed, although it flourished as a literary device throughout Roman antiquity and has been a characteristic of Christian Europe almost until the present day. Ptolemy's *Tetrabiblos* was thus a handbook for people of many different persuasions.

It opens with a defense of astrology and is ostensibly written around the idea that the influences of the heavenly bodies are entirely physical. In the end, however, it amounts to a codification of unjustified superstition, largely inherited from Ptolemy's predecessors. Book II deals with cosmic influences on geography and the weather, the latter a popular and spiritually safe subject in later centuries. Books III and IV deal with influences on human life as deduced from the state of the heavens, but they are oddly lacking in any of the mathematics of casting the houses that so obsessed astrologers in later centuries.

OTHER WRITINGS

Ptolemy's extensive writings suggest that he was engaged in assembling an encyclopedia of applied mathematics. One work of considerable interest is his *Planetary Hypotheses*, which went a long way toward providing a more sophisticated version of Aristotelian cosmology than the original. It made use of the paraphernalia of circles—eccentrics, epicycles, and so forth—but added the requirement that there should be no empty spaces in the universe. This led to a curious model in which the planetary distances were automatically deducible. They were of course wrong, but to our eyes they were impressively large (on the order of millions of miles). Of Ptolemy's books on mechanics, only the titles are known.

Much of his *Optics* and *Planetary Hypotheses* can be pieced together from Greek or Arabic versions. *Optics* includes some important semiempirical work on refraction, and it inspired the monumental study by Ibn al-Haytham (d. 1039). Some minor works on projection (his *Analemma* and *Planisphere*), as well as the monumental *Geography*, survive in Greek, as does his great treatise on astonomy, *Almagest*. A treatise on musical theory by Ptolemy was never directly influential, but Boethius placed much reliance on it, and so at secondhand it entered the European tradition.

Geography was essentially an outgrowth of astronomy, and apart from its comprehensive lists of places and their latitudes and longitudes, covering the known world, it is noteworthy for the ingenious map projections it introduces. For his data, Ptolemy acknowledges the work of Marinus of Tyre. Ptolemy corrects many of Marinus's errors but of course leaves many uncorrected, especially in regard to India and Africa. The influence of *Geography* was considerable in the Islamic world (where it was translated into Arabaic ca. 800), but in Europe it was surprisingly slight until the 15th century. It was translated from the Greek ca. 1406, and thereafter a Renaissance interest in Greek literary works gave it a certain cachet. New exploration soon rendered it obsolete, but through the work of Mercator (1554) and others, Ptolemy's map projections greatly affected later practice.

A purely philosophical work that has survived under Ptolemy's name has the title *On the Kriterion and Hegemonikon*. By *kriterion* the author means not only judging but also analyzing the process of judging, while *hegemonikon* denotes a principle of acting, or exerting power. The aim of the work is to investigate the *kriterion* of reality, and the procedure followed makes use of an analogy with legal procedures and institutions, so that the human desire for truth, for example, is made analogous to the human desire for social harmony.

The epistemology is in no respect strikingly new. The act of judging is analyzed into sense perception, the impression and transmission to the intellect *(phantasia)*, thought (internal *logos*), and speech (uttered *logos*). Internal *logos* may in turn be mere supposition, or it may be firmly grounded knowledge and understanding. Like Plato—who is briefly mentioned—and Aristotle, the writer holds that knowledge, when clear scientific distinctions are made, is always of the universal. The work has a strong admixture of physiology and psychology, and betrays a concern to come to grips with the mind-body problem. Thus a distinction is drawn between the *hegemonikon* of the body and that of the soul, between the cause of mere life (especially the lung-heart system) and "the chief cause of living well" (the brain, "through which we direct our impulses towards what is best"). In regard to the second cause, the heart is said to be not even next in importance. The writer believes rather that the senses, in particular, sight and hearing, contribute more to "living well" than does the heart.

The brief text of this philosophical work has clarity and succinctness rather than philosophical depth. In subject matter it has scarcely any point of contact with Ptolemy's generally accepted writings, but in its didactic qualities— for instance its businesslike brevity—it does have a slight resemblance to *Tetrabiblos*, and no completely convincing grounds for rejecting it have yet been given.

All told, there are very few scientific writers, whether from antiquity or any other historical period, whose work so strongly influenced posterity as did Ptolemy's. Through him the mathematical methods of the astronomical sciences passed into the domain of the natural sciences generally, and this must be counted as one of the most significant of all events in the entire history of Western science, even outweighing in importance the technical brilliance of Ptolemy's individual results.

JOHN DAVID NORTH

Bibliography

Barker, Andrew. *Greek Musical Writings*, vol. 2: *Harmonic and Acoustic Theory, Ptolemy*. Cambridge, 1989.

Bouche-Leclercq, Auguste. *L'astrologie grecque*. Paris, 1899; repr. Brussels, 1963.

Goldstein, Bernard R., ed. *The Arabic Version of Ptolemy's Planetary Hypotheses*. Philadelphia, 1967.

Heiberg, Johan Ludwig. *Claudii Ptolemaei Opera quae existant omnia: Syntaxis mathematica*. 2 vols. Leipzig, 1898–1903.

Huby, Pamela, and Gordon Neal, eds. *The Criterion of Truth: Essays Written in Honour of George Kerferd Together with a Text and Translation . . . of Ptolemy's On the Kriterion and Hegemonikon*. Liverpool, 1989.

Lejeune, Albert. *L'Optique de Claude Ptolémée*, 2nd ed. Leiden, 1990.

Neugebauer, Otto. *A History of Ancient Mathematical Astronomy*. 3 vols. Berlin, 1975.

North, J. D. *The Fontana History of Astronomy*. London, 1994.

Pedersen, Olaf. *A Survey of the Almagest*. Odense, 1974.

Ptolemy. *Tetrabiblios*. Ed. and trans. F. E. Robbins. Loeb Classical Library.

Toomer, Gerald James. *Ptolemy's Almagest*. London, 1984.

PYRRHON

LIKE SOCRATES, Pyrrhon (ca. 365–275 B.C.E.) wrote nothing. However, he played a major role in the history of philosophy, owing to his singular personality, his eccentric way of life, and his electrifying presence as a speaker; for those close to him he held a fascination that has been transmitted to later generations through the relatively stylized accounts of his followers. He gave his name to Pyrrhonism, a term that is broadly applied to the various strains of Skepticism, even down to modern times. He owes his renown no doubt in large part to the fact that the principal formulation in which Skeptical arguments are preserved—that is, in the writings of Sextus Empiricus (2nd century C.E.), one of whose works is entitled *Outlines of Pyrrhonism*—takes him as its patron. Sextus, moreover, was writing in an older tradition, that of Aenesidemus (1st century B.C.E.), himself the author of *Pyrrhonian Arguments*.

Pyrrhon's historical position has encouraged this equation between "Pyrrhonism" and Skepticism. The period he lived in was a turning point both in philosophical history and in history as such. With his teacher and friend Anaxarchus, he joined the eastern expedition of Alexander the Great, whose tutor had been Aristotle. Some twenty years younger than Aristotle, Pyrrhon belonged to the generation preceding Epicurus and Zeno of Citium, founders of the new philosophical schools of the Hellenistic period, generally said to have begun with the deaths of Aristotle and Alexander, which occurred a few months apart (about 323–322 B.C.E.). Before that period, there had certainly been no absence of critics to point out the shortcomings of human knowledge, but it is safe to say that various triumphs in the sciences, particularly in mathematics, had enabled philosophers, when they focused their inquiry on knowledge as such, to concentrate on questions about its nature, its origin, its instruments, and its structures of research and exposition, rather than on the question of its existence or possibility. The Hellenistic period, by contrast, was a period in which philosophers, particularly the Epicureans and the Stoics, became suddenly and vitally preoccupied with establishing that knowledge is possible, that our cognitive access to the world rests on an infallible base, which they called the "criterion of truth." They attempted to identify and describe that criterion in such a way as to demonstrate the accessibility of knowledge. This preoccupation, apparently a new one, leads us to suppose that in the intervening period an unheard-of and radical challenge had been issued, aiming to deny or question the very possibility of knowledge. And if one were to ask who could have initiated this challenge, Pyrrhon, living when he did and with the reputation attributed to him, would seem to be the ideal candidate.

The scenario is perhaps too good to be true. We do not need to take the logic of Skepticism to the extremes of Theodosius, a 2nd-century physician, who reasoned that "if the movement of the mind [in someone else] is unattainable by us, we shall never know for certain what Pyrrhon really intended, and without knowing that, we cannot be called Pyrrhoneans" (Diogenes Laertius, IX.70), but we have to admit that the figure of Pyrrhon is shrouded in obscurity. His thought has been the object of many fairly divergent attempts at reconstitution. All the testimonies about his life and thought that do exist (and until 1981 these had not been collected) come principally from Book IX of *The Lives of Eminent Philosophers* by Diogenes Laertius (3rd century C.E.). This material contains biographical information about Pyrrhon and his disciples (the best known, Timon, is a satirical poet-philosopher of whose work a fair number of fragments have been preserved), about Pyrrhon's way of life and the impression he made on those who knew him. Many anecdotes—perhaps too many—about Pyrrhon are to be found there; these are often piquant, at times astonishing, always meaningful, but their historical value is clearly subject to reservation.

In these accounts we discern the beginning of a split between two images of Pyrrhon—corresponding to two versions of Skepticism—which will continue to vie with each other for a long time. According to the first, Pyrrhon is equally indifferent toward others and toward himself; he takes no care to stay out of harm's way; he finds no value in the sensory information and daily assumptions that ordinarily guide human conduct; thus he behaves as a bizarre eccentric. This image may have given credence to the idea that he had been influenced by the gymnosophists (the so-called naked sages) of India, fakirs whose exploits he had perhaps witnessed admiringly in his travels; this is also the image by which he prefigures what has been called "rustic Skepticism," the refusal to accept any belief or assumption, even of the most ordinary sort. According to the second image, which remains just as alive in the tradition, Pyrrhon is on the contrary a quiet and unassuming country man, rather conventional, living with his sister and his chickens, going about his chores, respected by his fellow citizens; this second image presages the "urbane" variant of Skepticism, which rules out any belief that could be characterized as dogmatic: the dogmata of philosophers and scholars who claim to know the true nature of things, the hidden aspect of phenomena. These two images may well come from a common root in Pyrrhon himself, and they may express a conflict between his deep desires and his awareness of the limited prospects for realizing them. According to one particularly good story, he had once fled from an attacking dog, and when he was reproached for having violated his principles of indifference, he replied that it "was not easy entirely to strip oneself of human weakness" (IX.66)—which is another way of saying both that he was striving to adhere to his principles and that he should be forgiven if he did not always succeed in his efforts.

What seems certain is that Pyrrhon aimed to find, for himself as well as for others, an infallible recipe for happiness by adopting an attitude of *adiaphoria*, or indifference, with respect to conventional values. Though it may be true that, since antiquity, some people have seen this indifference as verging on *apatheia*, a complete absence of feeling (this is the rustic slant of the Pyrrhonian ethic), and others have seen it as verging on *praotēs*, or mildness (this is its urbane slant), the end to be achieved by these various means remains the same and is of an ethical order. Timon sees his master as a guide on the path of life and exalts him, asking him for the secret of his superhuman serenity. And Cicero, finally, depicts Pyrrhon uniquely as a moralist—one of the most imperturbable ever, with respect to what men consider good or evil.

The problem posed by the necessarily conjectural reconstitution of Pyrrhon's thought lies in knowing whether to include, among the means that Pyrrhon musters toward this ethical end, a line of argument that could be considered genuinely Skeptical, in the traditional sense of the term—that is, a critique of the possibility of knowledge and a systematic development of the arguments and experience that can produce and endorse what later Skeptics will call the *epochē*, or the suspension of judgment (the impossibility or refusal to choose between yes and no) with respect to all possible assertions.

The tight interweaving of the project of happiness and the critique of our means of knowing seems to be solidly attested by a text that all historians of Pyrrhon consider fundamental because of its synthetic character, its philosophical content, and the fact that it comes, via two intermediaries, from Timon. The text is too long to be cited in its entirety here, but it is articulated clearly enough so that a summary, accompanied by a few comments, should not greatly misrepresent it.

To be happy, says Timon, three points, or questions, must be considered. "First, what are things like by nature? Second, in what way ought we to be disposed toward them? And third, what will be the result for those who are so disposed?" (Eusebius, *De evangelica praeparatione*, XIV.16.3). The order in which these three points are enumerated is already surprising: a Skeptic of the type that would become traditional would not inquire into the nature of things before having asked whether we have the means to know that nature. If he is true to the principle of the *epochē*, he will carefully abstain from any opinion about that nature, even if only to say that it is unknowable. (According to Sextus, such a "metadogmatic" statement is foreign to genuine Skepticism.)

To the first question, however, Pyrrhon has an original answer, which occurs in the only sentence in the text that Timon expressly attributes to him. His reply is that "things" are indifferent, indeterminate, and undecided, a statement that seems to imply that it is we who introduce between and among things the distinctions that apparently differentiate them for us (for example, good things from bad ones—perhaps also white things from black ones, and anything that we may in general describe as being "thus, rather than otherwise"). The text goes on to say, strangely, that "for this reason, neither our sensations nor our opinions tell the truth or lie." Unless we change the text to reverse the logical connection between the two propositions—that is, to make the fallibility of our cognitive means the cause and not the consequence of the indeterminacy of things (a correction suggested by some of the most knowledgeable commentators)—it seems to mean that our sensations and our opinions, being in some respects "things" themselves, suffer from the same indeterminacy as things in general, and such a condition means, in the case of sensations and opinions, that what they tell us is neither always true nor always false. The grammar of the text suggests that this line of thinking is spelled out not by Pyrrhon but by Timon. One could conclude that Pyrrhon's thought has been inflected in the direction of a critique of knowledge as a result of an intervention by Timon, a disciple who was undoubtedly less devoid of philosophical personality than has sometimes been believed, and whose interest in these questions, hotly debated in his own generation, is well attested elsewhere.

The second question in Pyrrhon's program, according to Timon, bears on the appropriate attitude to adopt with respect to those things that are not differentiated by their own nature. The "indifference" of the sage is a consequence that must be inferred from the "indifferentiation" of things: the correct response is to treat things as they are, and thus to be "without opinions and without inclinations and without wavering" in one direction more than another. The verbal translation of this attitude is to say of each single thing that "it no more is than is not" or else (if one must say something at all costs), to recant immediately by saying that it "both is and is not" or that it "neither is nor is not."

According to the third point of Pyrrhon's program, man will find the reward for his training in the leveling of his practical attitude toward things (he neither chooses nor rejects them) and in the balancing of his discourse about things (he neither affirms nor denies them). Timon uses two terms to describe this reward: the first condition attained by the Pyrrhonian adept will be *aphasia*, speechlessness, or at least an abstention from any assertory use of language; the next will be *ataraxia*, a complete absence of the trouble and anxiety that constitute human unhappiness. The order in which these two terms are presented suggests that the Pyrrhonian manner of speaking is only a stage on the way to a Pyrrhonian manner of living.

This analysis of a crucially significant account, which obviously leaves the door open to discussion, widens the distance that modern historians have often sought to establish between Pyrrhon and the Pyrrhonians who have claimed him as their model. The quiet reserve of Alexander's wise, taciturn companion, this enigmatic observer of the legendary Alexandrian enterprise, isolated from other philosophers by his refusal to write, by his indifference to the tumultuous relations among the various Athenian schools, and by his scorn for the rules of the dialectical game, contrasts with the tireless fighting spirit of Sextus, who packs into his voluminous writings the entire argumentative arsenal, accumulated over centuries, against "professors," scholars, and "dogmatic" philosophers of every ilk. Moreover, is it not striking to note that the main target of Sextus's attacks, the Stoics, are philosophers clearly younger than Pyrrhon?

Perhaps Pyrrhon was not the first of the Pyrrhonians; perhaps his name has only been conferred on Pyrrhonism on the basis of a more or less contrived legend. But there must have been in him, as in Socrates, the matter and the occasion for such a legend. If the only surviving accounts were those by the sarcastic and biting Timon, from whose criticism Pyrrhon alone was spared, we might already credit him with exceptional charisma, but Diogenes Laertius tells us that he had many "disciples" (if we may apply this word to followers of a master who taught nothing) who tried to rival him in their scorn for humankind's futile agitations, and who passed on to their own pupils—who were intrigued by Pyrrhon's reputation—what they themselves had been able to grasp of the man. No doubt this was how the myth of Pyrrhon was forged, from one person to the next, initially by word of mouth: a myth that finally made him, through the centuries and right up to our own day, the silent Greek hero of nonknowledge.

JACQUES BRUNSCHWIG
Translated by Emoretta Yang and Anne Slack

Bibliography

Texts and Translations

Decleva Caizzi, Fernanda. *Pirrone: Testimonianze*. Naples: Bibliopolis, 1981.

Di Marco, Massimo. *Timone di Fliunte: Silli*. Rome: Edizioni dell'Ateneo, 1989.

Diogenes Laertius. *Lives of Eminent Philosophers*, vol. 2. Trans. R. D. Hicks. Loeb Classical Library.

Sextus Empiricus. Vol. 1: *Outlines of Pyrrhonism*. 2: *Against the Logicians*. 3: *Against the Physicists; Against the Ethicists*. 4: *Against the Professors*. Trans. R. G. Bury. Loeb Classical Library.

Studies

Ausland, Hayden Weir. "On the Moral Origin of the Pyrrhonian Philosophy." *Elenchos* 10 (1989): 359–434.

Bett, Richard. "Aristocles on Timon on Pyrrho: The Text, Its Logic, and Its Credibility." *Oxford Studies in Ancient Philosophy* 12 (1994): 137–181.

Bett, Richard. *Pyrrho: His Antecedents and His Legacy.* Oxford: Oxford University Press, 2000.

Brochard, Victor. *Les Sceptiques grecs.* Paris, 1887; repr. Paris: Vrin, 1923, 1981.

Brunschwig, Jacques. "Once Again on Eusebius on Aristocles on Timon on Pyrrho." In *Papers in Hellenistic Philosophy.* Trans. Janet Lloyd. Cambridge: Cambridge University Press, 1994. Pp. 190–211.

Conche, Marcel. *Pyrrhon ou l'apparence.* Paris: Presses Universitaires de France, 1994.

Dal Pra, Mario. *Lo scetticismo greco.* Milan, 1950; repr. Rome and Bari: Laterza, 1975.

Flashar, Hellmut, ed. *Die Philosophie der Antike, Bd. 4: Die Hellenistische Philosophie. Zweiter Halbband* (W. Görler, *Älterer Pyrrhonismus*). Basel: Schwabe, 1994.

Giannantoni, Gabriele, ed. *Lo scetticismo antico.* 2 vols. Naples: Bibliopolis, 1981.

Hankinson, R. J. *The Sceptics.* London: Routledge, 1995.

Long, Anthony A. "Timon of Phlius: Pyrrhonist and Satirist." *Proceedings of the Cambridge Philological Society* 204, n.s. 24 (1978): 68–91.

Robin, Léon. *Pyrrhon et le scepticisme grec.* Paris: Presses Universitaires de France, 1944.

Stopper, M. R. "Schizzi pirroniani." *Phronesis* 28 (1983): 265–297.

SOCRATES

SOCRATES' NAME ALONE suggests an image of the philosopher. Yet nothing that contributes to his reputation today applies to philosophic activity. Socrates wrote nothing, nor did he teach. He spent most of his time on the Agora, endlessly questioning his fellow citizens. The philosophers who came after him did write or teach, for the most part; they appear to owe him nothing. Plato was the author of the first philosophical opus ever written, the founder of the first school of philosophy; thus in his life and his philosophic activity he had little in common with Socrates. Yet Plato promoted Socrates as the embodiment of the philosopher.

This paradox reveals Socrates as the model—however inimitable—for philosophic life and thought, and it shows how hard it is to isolate the historical figure of Socrates, an Athenian citizen of the 5th century B.C.E. about whom we have a limited amount of relatively solid information, from Socrates the first philosopher, acknowledged by Plato and by the Cynics, the Skeptics, and the Stoics as their philosophic hero. Determining who Socrates really was is not just a modern concern: the question was being asked as early as the 4th century B.C.E. Addressing it twenty-four centuries later, we are not unduly handicapped, since we can benefit from the rigorous critique to which the various source materials offering testimony about Socrates have been subjected. A presentation of "the problem of Socrates" presupposes a preliminary portrait of the individual as he emerges from the points of agreement among the four major sources available to us, each more or less contemporaneous with Socrates' life.

The oldest—and also the most hostile—source, which gives us the only portrait of Socrates known to have been written during his lifetime (at least twenty-seven years before his death) is Aristophanes' *Clouds*. Two other major contributions, from Plato and Xenophon, came later; their accounts are more detailed, and vastly more favorable to Socrates. Plato knew Socrates during the final years of the philosopher's life, while he himself was in his early twenties. His earliest dialogues, doubtless written after Socrates' death, are called the "Socratic" dialogues; they include *Apology, Crito, Lysis, Laches,* and *Gorgias.* In these texts, Plato seems bent on reproducing his master's philosophical approach and ideas. Xenophon's testimony is quite different: in *Memorabilia, Economics, Apology* ("Socrates' Defense to the Jury"), and *Symposium,* Xenophon shows us Socrates arguing about concrete questions with a common sense that is often quite conventional. For a long time, moreover, the very ordinariness of the character Xenophon presents was taken to confirm the authenticity of his portrait. Last, in *Metaphysics* and *Eudemian Ethics* Aristotle provides information that is not derived from direct knowledge of Socrates; its value is based on Aristotle's close dealings with the Academy in his youth. While these four sources are sometimes difficult to reconcile, and do not allow us to draw an entirely coherent picture of Socrates the philosopher, we still need to acknowledge the many areas of agreement, especially regarding Socrates' intellectual biography.

SOCRATES, CITIZEN OF ATHENS

Socrates was born in Athens around 469 B.C.E. His father, Sophroniscus, was a sculptor, born in the deme of Alopece. His mother, Phaenarete, is said to have been a midwife. Although Socrates may have been trained as a sculptor in his youth, no evidence indicates that he practiced any craft at all. This does not mean he was idle: on the contrary, he spent his days carrying out the task a god had prescribed for him "through oracles and dreams and in every way in which any man was ever commanded by divine power to do anything whatsoever" (Plato, *Apology* 33c). His responsibility was to examine every human being he encountered, "young and old, foreigner and citizen," to incite them "not to care for [their] persons or [their] property more than for the perfection of [their] souls, or even so much" (ibid. 30a). As Socrates makes clear in addressing his fellow citizens, such an examination bears first on "the manner in which [they] now spend [their] days, and . . . the kind of life [they have] lived hitherto" (*Laches* 187e–188a), but it also allows him to test the reality of some knowledge that his interlocutor claims to possess, some quality with which he credits himself or some behavior of which he boasts. As he reminds his fellow citizens, he is "a gadfly . . . I go about arousing, and urging and reproaching each one of you, constantly alighting upon you everywhere the whole day long" (*Apology* 30e–31a). Xenophon's testimony is even more explicit: Socrates "was always visible . . . he used to go on walks and to the gymnasia"; he was prepared to spend the day "where he might be with the most people" and where all those who wanted to hear him could do so (*Memorabilia* I.i.10). Socrates' philosophic activity thus was a form of systematic interrogation applied to whoever agreed to submit to it, whether out of bravado, conviction, or a desire to save face. Plato's first dialogues capture the public essence of these conversations perfectly: we see Socrates confronting an interlocutor, but the two are surrounded by attentive listeners. Even if the exchange is protreptic—that is, even if it is intended to transform the respondent's soul—its goal is not so much to teach as to supply a model for any listener capable of profiting from it. This condition justifies Socrates' claim that he was never anyone's master, for, he says, "if any man says that he ever learned or heard anything privately from me, which all the others did not, be assured that he is lying" (*Apology* 33b). Such a passion for the improvement or elevation of souls is no doubt the principal form of the love that Socrates said he felt toward young people (*Memorabilia* IV.i.2).

The divine injunction that assigned Socrates the task of constant examination is frequently confused with the inner signal that Socrates often called his *daimonian*, or demon: "It is a sort of voice that comes to me, and when it comes it always holds me back from what I am thinking of doing, but never urges me forward" (*Apology* 31d). This form of divine inspiration (which can incite as well as dissuade, according to Xenophon's texts) has remained one of the most popular features of the Socratic persona; it has also helped shape the image of a Socrates inspired by the god. But it may be advisable to think of the "demon" as a form of moral awareness that came to be attached, especially in Plato's account, to the divine forms of delirium and inspiration.

Apart from this philosophic occupation, we know very little about Socrates' life. At the time of his death, he was married to Xanthippe, with whom he had at least two sons. He may have been married earlier to the daughter or granddaughter of Aristides. He fought courageously during the Peloponnesian War, at Potidaea, at Amphipolis, and at Delium, where he served as a hoplite. This detail is important, for the citizen hoplites, who had to pay for their own arms, belonged to the first three classes of the census. The poverty to which Socrates so often referred was thus relative to the wealth of others of his class and to that of the Athenians who kept him company; it must by no means be mistaken for the destitution of a cynical sage. Socrates' frugal and modest way of life, his legendary ability to withstand cold and hunger, his temperance, his indifference to physical discomfort, and his deliberate asceticism (Diogenes Laertius tells us that "he used to say . . . that he was nearest to the gods in that he had the fewest wants," "Socrates" 27) must have been thought more plausible when credited to extreme poverty. It may be, too, that the modest antecedents traditionally attributed to Socrates (at first glance hardly compatible with the fact that he served as a hoplite) were depicted as humbler than they really were for the same reason.

Socrates boasted, it seems, that he had never left Athens, except when he was participating in a military campaign and when he attended the Isthmic Games (just once). He accepted the political assignments that fell to him as a citizen, although he did not have much taste for them (as he recalls in *Gorgias:* "When I was elected a member of the Council and, as my tribe held the Presidency, I had to put a question to vote, I got laughed at for not understanding the procedure," 474a), nor did he have any ambition to hold power. But when Socrates disapproved of the Assembly's decisions, he seems to have opposed them without hesitation. Two incidents bear witness to this. In 407, as a member of the Council and while his tribe held the presidency, he objected to the Assembly's illegal move to pass collective judgment on six generals who had succeeded with great difficulty in disengaging the Athenian fleet from Sparta's blockade in the battle of Arginusae, but who had failed, after the battle, to retrieve the corpses and shipwrecked sailors from the sunken boats, as religious law required (*Apology* 32b; Xenophon, *Hellenica*). And a few years later, summoned with four other citizens by the Thirty Tyrants and ordered to bring Leon back from Salamis so he could be put to death, Socrates refused to obey and returned home, leaving his companions to carry out their grim task. These acts demonstrate his resolution "not to do anything unjust or unholy" (*Apology* 32d). During his trial, Socrates in fact recalled that he had preferred to take the side of "law and justice" (ibid. 32c) rather than support the Athenians and their unjust designs "through fear of imprisonment or death" (ibid. 29a). It is easy to understand how he could have credited the repeated interventions of his "demon," aimed at deterring him from political action, for the fact that he could live in Athens until the age of seventy without ever betraying his resolution to act justly.

Socrates' personality cannot be evoked without mention of the friends that surrounded him, friends whose fidelity was especially apparent during the events leading up to his death. Socrates referred to the value of friendship in many contexts, and he described the model of excellence that two friends eager to improve their souls can represent for each other. Socrates doubtless never had such a perfect friend, but the devotion and admiration of Crito, a rich landowner, and of his son Critobulus, the loyalty of Chaerephon, exiled among the Thirty as a "friend of the people," the fidelity of Hermogenes, Callias's brother, and of Aeschines, called the Socratic, all attest to the outstanding character of Socrates' personality. These men admired Socrates without reservation and imitated his behavior, to the point that Aeschines of Spettos, who later became a philosopher, was accused of stealing texts supposedly written by Socrates. Several foreigners were also devoted to Socrates (Simmias and Cebes of Thebes, Euclid and Terpsion of Megara, Aristippus of Cyrene); some of these men later founded schools (the Megaric school, the Cyrenic school) in which the Socratic influence was pronounced. Finally, another, less stable element of the "Socratic circle" consisted of a group of well-to-do young men closely associated with the most dramatic events in Athenian politics at the time. They must have felt a similar fascination with Socrates, and they sought his company over a period of several years. Among their ranks were the immensely wealthy Callias, Agathon, Critias, and Charmides, who later figured among the Thirty Tyrants, and most notably Alcibiades, who may have sought to seduce Socrates through his beauty, his noble birth, his powerful intelligence, and the force of his personality. The praise he offers at the end of Plato's *Symposium* attests to Socrates' clearly exceptional influence: Alcibiades says that when he is in Socrates' company he cannot keep from being ashamed of himself.

The major event in Socrates' life was the trial of which he was the victim in 399, at the age of seventy. An accusation of impiety was lodged with the archon-basileus by three Athenian citizens: Meletus, a mediocre poet; Anytus, a politician; and Lycon, an otherwise unknown orator. Anytus was the real instigator of the trial. A moderate democrat from Theramene's entourage, he had been forced into exile under the Thirty before rejoining Thrasybulus. He then became one of the most powerful men in Athens in the period following the restoration of democracy. The hatred he felt for Socrates was probably fanned by personal motives (rivalry for Alcibiades' love, rancor owing to the influence Socrates had had for a time over his own son) as well as political ones. The principal accusation against Socrates, as reported by Diogenes Laertius (who in turn is citing Favorinus of Arles, a historiographer from Hadrian's time), was worded as follows: "Socrates is guilty of refusing to recognize the gods recognized by the state, and of introducing other divinities. He is also guilty of corrupting the youth" ("Socrates" 40; we find a different formulation in Xenophon, "Defense" 10). The trial was conducted by the Heliaea, a popular tribunal made up of 501 judges. Plato seems to have been present, as well as all of Socrates' friends, among them Hermogenes—who may have been Xenophon's informant, for the latter was absent from Athens at the time.

After Meletus had developed the main points of the accusation, Socrates probably spoke out in his own defense. Considering that he had no proof of his innocence to supply, beyond a life totally devoted to justice, Socrates rejected the services of the orator Lysias, according to Diogenes Laertius. It is highly unlikely that the dialogue Plato reports in *Apology* between Socrates and his official accuser, Meletus, actually took place, but it is certain that Socrates sought neither to win the judges' pity nor to justify himself. After he made his plea, Meletus and Anytus, fearing that the judges might have been persuaded, apparently intervened to reiterate their accusations. On the first ballot Socrates was condemned by a vote of 281 to 221. Given the unusual nature of the complaint, the accused and the accuser were urged to propose the penalty themselves. Meletus asked for death, but Socrates, considering the services he had rendered the city-state, asked that he be given his meals in the prytaneum or, short of that, that he pay a small fine. The judges decided in favor of death. Before the sentence was carried out, Socrates was detained for about a month in the prison of the Eleven. He could easily have escaped, but he apparently refused to do so. His friends came to visit daily (*Phaedo* 59d); they were with him when he drank the hemlock. As the poison was beginning to take effect, Socrates raised the veil that covered him and spoke what, according to Plato, were his last words: "Crito, we owe a cock to Aesculapius. Pay it and do not neglect it" (118a).

THE PROBLEM OF SOCRATES

A critical examination of the accusations brought against Socrates brings us to what is conventionally called "the problem of Socrates." This term actually covers several problems having to do with Socrates' role in Athens, the specificity of his philosophic thought and practice, and the question of whether there exists an authentic Socratic philosophy. As it happens, the solution to this problem is closely tied to the critique of the sources of the information we have about the Socratic persona.

The charge that Socrates corrupted youth was in part inspired by the portrait Aristophanes drew of him in *Clouds.* In the play Socrates is perched in a gondola suspended in the air, his head in the clouds; arguing like a Sophist, he persuades tne young Phidippides that it is legitimate to beat one's father. But the accusation can also be explained by the fact that the young people who sought Socrates' company, most of them idle and wealthy, found it entertaining to hear him examine the Athenians, and they tried to imitate him by subjecting their relatives and friends to the same sort of examination. As Socrates recalls in *Apology,* it is understandable that "those who are examined by [the young people] are angry with me, instead of being angry with themselves" (23c). The hostility toward Socrates that such exchanges reveal also betrays the uneasiness felt by the upper reaches of Athenian society at the idea that the city's traditional values were being subjected to rational examination, criticism, and evaluation. Moreover, in this regard Socrates was often confused with the Sophists, who had also carried out a form of critical reflection while professing to teach virtue.

However, another, more aggressive reproach accuses Socrates of leading a life unworthy of a citizen of Athens. Here is Callicles accusing Socrates in *Gorgias:* "This person . . . is bound to become unmanly through shunning the centres and marts of the city . . . he must cower down and spend the rest of his days in a corner whispering with three or four lads" (485d). The examples Socrates uses (he speaks of "pack animals, blacksmiths, shoemakers, and tanners" [*Symposium* 221e], since they always seem to be saying "the same things with the same means") also appear contemptible; Hippias remarks that they are "mere scrapings and shavings of discourse" (*Greater Hippias* 304a). Ridicule and scorn of this sort helped transform Socrates into a comic character.

Finally, a third complaint, more difficult to appreciate today, tended to depict Socrates as a sorcerer who, by asking questions that were at once simple and unexpected, left his interlocutors paralyzed, reduced to confusion or silence; in short, he bewitched them *(Meno).* This charge may account in part for the accusation of impiety, which is otherwise hard to explain, given what is known of Socrates' conformity in religious and ritual matters. Rather than reproaching him for introducing new divinities (toward whom the city of

Athens was actually fairly tolerant) or for believing in his demon as if it were a new god, the accusation of impiety expresses disapproval of Socrates' critical attitude toward the values of the city. Even if it was not aimed at religion, Socrates' critique was probably perceived as antireligious. The same accusation of impiety was regularly brought against philosophers: Anaxagoras was subject to it, and perhaps also Protagoras and Euripides.

While each of these accusations at least confirms that in the eyes of the Athenians, Socrates "was doing something other than most people" (*Apology* 20c), another motive for hostility, not mentioned in the official charges, has been offered in several recent critical works as the real reason for his death: out of hatred for democracy, Socrates is alleged to have favored tyrants and tyranny. Socrates was unquestionably opposed to several of the principles and aspects of Athenian democracy as it was actually practiced (for example, the drawing of lots, or majority rule). The power acquired by rhetoric in the place of knowledge, the contempt in which real competence was held, the ignorance of those in power, the practice of pandering to the demos are indeed characteristic of all those who "manage the city's affairs" (Plato, *Alcibiades* 119b). But Socrates' criticisms are aimed more at the new men of democracy (rhetoricians and socially ascendant artisans) than at the regime itself. Probably exaggerated in the accounts of Plato and Xenophon, who were both rather hostile to democracy, Socrates' criticisms did not express a condemnation of the democratic regime as such, still less a declaration of faith in the oligarchy. His praise of the Spartan regime in *Memorabilia* and *Crito* bears only on minor questions and hardly allows us to deduce that he really admired the way Sparta was governed.

The proponents of the thesis that accuses Socrates of being a friend of tyrants are thus reduced to a single argument, based on Socrates' friendship with Critias and Alcibiades and the influence his teaching had on them. Xenophon himself explains that the Athenian democrats condemned Socrates because of his friendship with tyrants, an accusation that could not be included explicitly among the official charges because of the amnesty of 403. But such friendship, even though it may explain the circumstances of Socrates' trial, could in no way prove that he was sympathetic to the oligarchy; one could counter with the long friendship between Socrates and the democrat Chaerephon, and, even more tellingly, with the fact that Socrates did not turn away any listeners and that he taught no one anything that he did not teach everyone. If the lives of Critias and Alcibiades cannot be used as an argument in favor of the master who trained them, Socrates, who refused to be anyone's master, cannot be held responsible.

As for the other pieces of evidence presumed to prove Socrates' antidemocratic leanings (Polycrates' pamphlet against Socrates, published several years after his death, and the end of *Gorgias*, where Plato seems to be justifying Socrates against Polycrates' attacks), they emerged for the most part from the enterprise of justifying and critiquing the Socratic persona that helped form the legend of Socrates; it would be imprudent at the very least to use such indications to assess the reality that those same pieces of evidence seek to inflect in one direction or another. To be sure, Socrates was condemned to death by a democracy, but that does not suffice to establish that he was condemned as an enemy of democracy. Nor does the hatred that a good number of democrats felt toward him prove anything. That hatred was doubtless directed at all intellectuals, and it attests most of all to the conformity that reigned in the years following the Athenian defeat. Since Socrates himself recognized that he would not have been able to live as long under any regime other than democracy (and since he himself was not the philosophical reformer in political matters that Plato was to become), he must have thought that, despite its failings in practice, it was no doubt the least undesirable of regimes.

Thus we have moved gradually toward an examination of Socrates' thought. This aspect, too, of the problem of Socrates is tied to the critique of sources, for our four major sources differ widely as to the definition of the objects or theses of Socratic thought. Aristophanes speaks of a Socrates who speculates about "the things in the air and the things beneath the earth" (*Apology* 23d), but such a characterization has a somewhat predictable cast, and, since other accounts contradict it, we can readily abandon the image of a chiefly "meteorological" Socrates. Aristotle's indications, on the other hand, have given credence to the thesis according to which Socrates was concerned only with "human things," morality and politics; they confirm the portrait that emerges from the earliest Socratic dialogues. As for Plato's and Xenophon's accounts, they disagree both on the conceptions found in Socrates' philosophy and on its style.

If the Socrates we see in Plato's first dialogues deals only with moral notions (justice, piety, the beauty of men and actions) and human affairs, Xenophon's Socrates, on the contrary, speaks of theology or theodicy and seeks to prove the existence of a divine spirit. In other respects, if Plato's Socrates opposes the ordinary morality of the era (in which virtue is conceived as the capacity to fulfill one's role as man and citizen and in which justice consists in part in returning evil for evil and good for good), Xenophon's Socrates basically expresses the moral values of his day. Furthermore, this Socrates implacably wins over his adversaries and always seems to accomplish the protreptic function that Socrates advocated for philosophy. In contrast, however conclusive the arguments of Plato's Socrates may be, they rarely persuade: Polos, Callicles, Thrasymachus, and Meno seem briefly troubled but do not abandon their own convictions. Finally, Plato's Socrates wields irony and double meaning; for example, after a long and wholly vacuous presentation by Hippias, he exclaims: "Bravo, bravo, Hippias!" (*Greater Hippias* 291e). This Socrates, who constantly plays on a two-pronged way of understanding utterances (in their everyday sense and in philosophical terms), is absent from Xenophon's account. Xenophon defends a Socrates who is so conventional and whose responses are so predictable that one wonders how such a character could ever have troubled the Athenians.

Where, then, is Socrates the philosopher to be found? Hegel was one of the first to attempt to show that the real Socrates could not be the one Plato used as the main character in most of his dialogues. However, he did not succeed in establishing that the real Socrates is Xenophon's, for the Socrates of *Memorabilia* in no way resembles the philosopher we have legitimate reasons to seek. Still, it is not very plausible that in his dialogues Plato would have created a Socrates very different from the one all his contemporaries still remembered vividly. In addition, starting with *Meno, Phaedo,* and *The Republic* a new thematic cluster appears (the interest in mathematics, the conception of Forms) that seems to belong to Plato himself (and that cannot be attributed to Socrates, contrary to the views of Burnet and Taylor). The presence of these new themes and the implementation of new methods give us, within Plato's thought itself, a way of differentiating between Socratism and Platonism. Thus we shall end up with a solution that closely resembles the conventional definition.

It is perfectly plausible that the critique of the Sophists or the rhetoricians should belong to the historical Socrates. We can readily grant that the irony of the Socratic persona bears Plato's mark. But there is a body of Socratic thought that includes a set of theses in moral and political philosophy, that carries out the search for meaning and truth according to a certain protocol (which Aristotle's account describes reasonably well, as does Xenophon's, on occasion), and that can be fairly clearly differentiated from the set of "Platonic" theses. Whether this set of theses belongs to the historical Socrates (as is probable) or whether it expresses the first state of Plato's thought, influenced in varying degrees by that of Socrates (a hypothesis that cannot be ruled out), is a dilemma that, in the current state of affairs, remains intact. What I shall proceed to present is the core of this thought, conventionally called Socratic, whose primary methods are dialectics and maieutics.

SOCRATIC DIALECTICS: *ELENCHOS* AND MAIEUTICS

His refusal to allow himself to be credited with any knowledge is one of the most striking features of the Socrates who appears in Plato's early dialogues. Socrates reports in *Apology* how astonished he was to learn that the oracle of Delphi had designated him the most learned of men. It was out of a desire to understand the oracle, he says, if not to put it to the test, that he undertook to interrogate learned fellow citizens: politicians, poets, authors of tragedies, and artisans. At the conclusion of these conversations, which he himself calls "Herculean labours" (*Apology* 21a), he had to admit that what these men know masks an ignorance that is unaware of itself; he also had to recognize, as he put it in *Apology,* that "what I do not know I do not think I know either" (21d). The connection between his systematic examination of others and the task assigned by the god is self-evident. But the fact remains that examining the lives and beliefs of one's fellow citizens and showing the vanity of the political or "technical" knowledge they claim to possess are two different enterprises. In the one case, it is a matter of refuting ill-founded or unfounded moral beliefs and of showing the connection between moral knowledge and moral behavior. In the other, it is a matter of critiquing the major forms of knowledge to show that they do not represent, or do not adequately represent, true knowledge.

This last Socratic critique is all the more astonishing in that it seems to be conditioned on setting aside several areas of knowledge (such as mathematics and astronomy) that Socrates, like Plato after him, might have recognized as models. Yet it seems that Socrates took no interest in that sort of knowledge. As Xenophon notes: "He did not converse about the nature of all things in the way most of the others did—examining what the sophists call the cosmos: how it is, and which necessities are responsible for the coming to be of each of the heavenly things" (*Memorabilia* I.i.11). No doubt he had good reasons to dismiss studies leading in that direction as vain occupations, even though he himself had undertaken such studies in considerable depth. ("He said that one should learn geometry up to the point of being competent" in measuring, but "he disapproved of geometry as far as the diagrams that are hard to comprehend. For what benefit these might have, he said he did not see," *Memorabilia* IV.vii.2–3.) But it is regrettable that the critique to which Socrates chose to subject politicians, poets, and artisans does not really tell us what reservations he had regarding mathematical or astronomical knowledge. Socrates indicates that the forms of knowledge he is criticizing do not satisfy the *kata ton theon* examination, an examination that is conducted in conformity with the order of the god and that undoubtedly aims to identify the conditions that make a body of knowledge authentic. These conditions seem to select for the only form of knowledge that Socrates does not deny possessing, a form of *anthropine sophia,* a human science or a science having to do with humankind. That such a science does not bear on any specific content, however, could explain why Socrates sometimes calls it nonknowledge.

It is important to stress that Socrates' interlocutors never interpret his profession of nonknowledge as indicating real ignorance; on the contrary, they continually solicit his advice *(Laches).* It is true that in a famous passage of *Memorabilia* Xenophon attributes specific objects of investigation to Socrates: "He himself was always conversing about human things—examining what is pious, what is impious, what is noble, what is shameful, what is just, what is unjust" (I.ii.16), but the essential element in this account is still the idea of examination. The fact that "human things" are the proper object of

Socratic study must not be interpreted, then, in the strictly anthropological sense of "human affairs."

The autobiography Socrates gives us in *Phaedo*, when he recalls his own interest in the "investigation of nature" (96a), and his disappointment with explanations using matter as a cause, seems to suggest that he could have conceived a theory of the soul in connection with a cosmological representation (to which the last myth in the same dialogue may also refer). There remains essentially no trace of such a conception, the expression of which is influenced in *Phaedo* by Platonic philosophy, but one may suppose that it shored up the Socratic conception of the immortality of the soul, of retribution after death, and of the possibility of knowing. If Socrates' philosophical contribution remains particularly closely tied to morality and politics, the hypothesis that he sketched out a theory of the soul makes it possible to explain how "human knowledge" in the sense in which Socrates understood it relates to criticism and the establishment of certainties, which is the proper object of dialectics.

In Plato's early dialogues, dialectics is defined as the art of questioning and answering. But this definition is accompanied by a well-defined procedure for questioning, *elenchos*, or Socratic refutation, which helps to make dialectics an art and to determine its capacity for truth. *Elenchos* starts from a thesis affirmed by an interlocutor who believes it to be true; the technique consists in showing that the thesis is in contradiction with a set of beliefs held by the same interlocutor. *Elenchos* thus proves to be particularly well suited to assessing the coherence of individuals' moral beliefs, and it helps bring to light the links between the various moral qualities that stem from virtue. But this form of refutation cannot really contribute to the conceptual definition of the notion being studied, nor can it help define the characteristic differences between the various virtues. Furthermore, the truth of the conclusion of an *elenchos* has no guarantee except the validity of a generally accepted formula (for example, all men desire happiness) that represents the starting point for the procedure. *Elenchos* thus can reach only moral certainty; it does not manage to achieve the foundation in truth that Plato's later philosophy will find in the intellectual apprehension of Forms.

The same requirement of consistency among the beliefs of a given individual allows maieutics, or the art of giving birth to minds—in *Theaetetus* Socrates says he learned the art from his mother, a midwife—to distinguish true conceptions from those that are merely illusory. The beliefs brought to light form a true conception when they are linked together in a coherent whole, one that can confront established certainties or moral "axioms" without contradiction and that entails no contradictory consequences. However, maieutics, which is a discovery procedure, cannot suffice to establish the truth of the set of beliefs thus disclosed.

Socrates usually begins his questioning, which shapes the material of his refutations, by requesting a definition. "What is courage?" in *Laches*. "What is beauty?" in *Greater Hippias*. "What is virtue?" in *Meno*. But however celebrated the request for a definition may be—to the extent that it is referred to as the question "What is X?"—it still remains somewhat obscure. The definition Socrates asks for is not a lexical definition (which would give equivalents for the term and conditions for its correct use). It is not a causal definition either, but rather an essential definition aiming to exhibit a real essence endowed with the same sort of being as the particular phenomena to which it belongs and which are known by its name. This property, called *eidos* or idea, is probably the object of the "universal" definition, which, as Aristotle reminds us, Socrates was believed to have sought *(Metaphysics)*.

In another account, Aristotle assures us that these real properties, which belong to a collection of individuals, have no independent existence. This is an additional reason not to attribute to Socrates a theory of Forms similar to the one Plato will propose (Forms as permanent, independent, nonperceptible realities, the only ones available to knowledge); Aristotle, removing Socrates from the picture, will attribute the origin of the theory to a systematization of Heraclitus's legacy. But from another standpoint, the Socratic definition is not universal in the sense that it would proceed from a conceptual inquiry (Socrates is often content with a characteristic mark), or in the sense that it would provide a procedure allowing the justification of beliefs and the establishment of bodies of knowledge. In fact, the definition of a thing cannot be constructed from knowledge of its properties; on the contrary, as *Meno* teaches, one must first know the essence of virtue before determining whether it possesses the property of being teachable. This is the main reason one would hesitate to acknowledge a Socratic epistemology. A related reason is that, as a procedure for seeking certainty, *elenchos* seems limited to the specific domain of moral objects.

MORALITY

The Socratic conception of morality has remained famous because of the radical form of intellectualism it defends. Indeed, not only does it reserve to reason (rather than to conventions or desires) the task of defining the goals of human action, but it also defines the goals themselves as forms of knowledge. Aristotle, whose opposition to this Socratic thesis is well known, formulates one of its consequences clearly: "Socrates . . . thought that the End is to get to know virtue . . . he thought that all the virtues are forms of knowledge, so that justice and being just must go together" (*Eudemian Ethics* I.15).

Socrates' conception takes its validity from the paradigm of technical activity. Happiness, to which all human beings aspire, is generically defined as the goal of human action. But such a certainty, which figures in the Socratic conversations as a practical axiom, applies not to happiness conceived as internal satisfaction or beatitude, but rather to happiness conceived as a form of accomplished action *(eupragia)* or success *(eutykhia)*. The import of one of the best-known "Socratic paradoxes" (it suffices to know the good in order to do good, and no one does evil knowingly) is easier to understand if one compares moral action to technical action. Like the artisan who is concerned with carrying out his task to the best of his ability and who commands the means for doing so, the moral agent, whose desire for happiness is also a desire for *eupragia,* for straightforward successful action, and who knows that knowledge, intrinsically defined as virtue, is the only means for achieving his goal, cannot deliberately choose to act badly.

Socrates repeatedly stresses the sovereignty of virtue and the fact that it is a component of happiness. Virtue is knowledge, for the good of the soul that it represents can only be knowledge; it is at once the principle of internal order and the means for correct usage, success, and accomplishment. Socrates does not spell out the aspects or the objects of such knowledge, but one may suppose that virtue represents, first of all, the exercise of a certain cognitive activity whose effect is to maintain within the soul the optimal state that corresponds to its good and inspires actions destined to consolidate that good. Such an identification of virtue with knowledge frees the latter from goods that depend on the body and also from external goods (such as wealth, honor, or power, which are essential to the practice of political virtue). Socrates sometimes seems to want to assign an object to this knowledge, one that would represent the content common to all the moral qualities, but it is hard to see what kind of common knowledge would make true virtues of the various virtues—piety, justice, courage—that designate optimal forms of action under specific circumstances. Socrates seems to indicate that such knowledge has to do with good and evil *(Charmides),* but he does not specify in what way it allows each of the virtues to be characterized. It is true that Socrates helped introduce a certain requirement of universality in virtuous behavior by detaching it from the circumstances or from consideration of its beneficiaries, but that requirement results more from the conception of virtue as "successful action" than from an ethical demand. In addition, detachment from conventional morality is also the consequence of an increased requirement of reflexivity. Above all, Socrates does not depart at all from Greek morality conceived as exclusively centered on the agent.

The Socrates of Plato's early dialogues defends a fairly explicit conception of human motivation. On the basis of the thesis that reason defines goals and motivates agents, Socrates is commonly credited with a bipartite conception of the soul in which a rational component and an irrational component (which incorporates desires of all sorts) are in opposition, along with a mechanistic moral psychology in which motivation results from a power relation between reason nourished by knowledge and by desire. But this conception does not correspond very well with what is implied by the Socratic thesis of virtue as knowledge. For while Plato's moral psychology seems to recognize an irreducible set of desires, Socratic psychology tends instead to depict the rational soul as the true nature of the human soul. Ignorance of the passions and of the importance of moral character justifies the Socratic certainty that the improvement of moral knowledge would lead to the improvement of moral character.

The impossibility of acting against one's better judgment stems from the commensurability postulated among all the elements of the soul that contribute to human motivation. Socrates shows that *akrasia* (weakness of the will) does not exist, because one cannot be "overcome by pleasure" *(Protagoras)*. While pleasures may promise satisfactions, they yield, if need be, to considerations that demonstrate their uncertain or ephemeral character and weigh them against other more stable satisfactions. Virtue is then identified with an activity of assessment that compares the claims of the various pleasures without actually distinguishing them according to their origin. More than the reality of a Socratic hedonism, as it is presented in *Protagoras* in particular, this conception attests to the sovereignty of reason and to the specifically moral value of rational deliberation. A similar tendency to define moral behavior through rational deliberation—as Socrates said of himself, "I am not only now but always a man who follows nothing but the reasoning *[logos]* which on consideration seems to me the best" (*Crito*, 46b)—is precisely the object of Aristotle's criticism in *Nicomachean Ethics*. The same use of rational argument also justifies the belief in a future life and the immortality of the soul, even though Socrates acknowledges that he has no arguments to prove it. Still, even if the soul is not immortal, Socrates insists on the necessity of improving it, for the improved soul allows one to live with a better self, and the prospect of future pleasure is a good reason to prefer virtue.

SOCRATIC POLITICS

The foregoing conceptions lie behind Socratic politics. Socrates repeatedly emphasizes that he has not participated a great deal in the political life of the city, and he evokes the dangers he would have incurred had he been more active. But he also reminds us that, despite his remoteness from the political scene, he is the only man in Athens who is truly devoted to politics and concerned with the affairs of the city. How are we to understand the fact that Socrates saw his mission—that of questioning his fellow citizens and exposing their ignorance—as a plausible reason for declaring that he was "the most political" man in Athens? A study of *Crito* and *Apology*, along with part of *Gorgias*, allows us to suggest an answer.

The improvement of the soul, which is the goal of Socratic conversation, has political implications. Its result, a better state of the soul as a form of order or harmony, is in the first place the product of rational deliberation and choice. It is also the true work of the art of politics, or the art "that has to do with the soul" (*Gorgias* 464b), since rational persuasion, intended to convince citizens to take care of their soul and to be just, can exist on a broad scale and in an effective way only in the framework of a city-state. Thus the moral quality of individuals is the very object of politics. When a just government, concerned not with enriching the city but with improving it, uses such persuasion as the foundation for political consensus, it "accomplishes" justice in a way that no one could with private exhortation alone. Socrates' moral intellectualism, or the conviction that if citizens have access to knowledge of the justice that the government is meting out, they will act justly, supports this hope.

Since political competence is comparable to any other technical competence, those who possess it should be entrusted with the governance of human affairs. Xenophon's Socrates defends the same idea, although the knowledge he speaks of consists largely in knowledge of the city's income and expenses, the military forces at its disposal, or its problems of provisioning and resources. Such a "scientific" conception of politics must have been surprising in an Athens in which people justified democracy by stressing that the essence of political community lay in the institutionalization of public discussion. But in Socrates' eyes, such discussion, unless it is illuminated by knowledge of the public good, consists merely in pandering to citizens' desires by means of political rhetoric.

Socratic "politics" can also be credited with proposing one of the first formulations of political obligation. In *Crito*, when one of his friends suggests to Socrates that he should avoid death by escaping from prison, Socrates insists on submitting the proposition to rational examination. If flight is just, he will flee; if it is not, he will stay in prison and accept his punishment. The Laws of Athens then come on stage to remind Socrates of his civic responsibilities. The duties of citizens toward the state are similar to those of children toward their parents; there exists no "right" to dissent or to disobey; Socrates' flight would thus be an injustice. Sufficiently convinced, Socrates then gives up the idea of escape. This decision seems hard to reconcile with the passage in *Apology* where Socrates informs his judges that if they want to let him live on condition that he will no longer practice criticism, he will be compelled to disobey. But this latter case in fact makes the limits of the duty of civic obedience quite clear; its benefit will be devoted in this instance to convincing the state of its injustice and its error. The duty of the individual toward the state stops at the point where the accomplishment of that duty threatens to alter the quality of his soul. In all other cases, the individual is obliged to submit to the punishment prescribed by the state, even if that punishment is unjust, for in fact it is never just to mistreat those under whose protection we have agreed to live. Political obligation results from a form of "tacit consent" that is freely given and confirmed by the mere fact of living in the city. On this point, nothing is more contrary to Socratic politics than the theses presented in *The Republic* and *Laws*. There, improvement of citizens remains the ultimate political goal, but Plato no longer sees moral autonomy, to which each individual could accede through rational persuasion, as the way to reach that goal. For him, specifically political resources (the definition of a constitution, the organization of society, coercion), of which Socratic politics makes no mention, are what will make it possible to achieve justice in the city-state.

SOCRATES IN HISTORY

This brief evocation of Socrates' political thought will perhaps help nuance the conventional image of untrammeled confrontation between the philosopher and his city, an image that is still attached to the Socratic legend. For even though it is commonly believed that Socrates' trial and death at the hands of the Athenians account by and large for his fame, we must recall that virtually no mention of the event can be found either in the works of contemporary dramatic authors or in those of the orators Lysias, Andocides, or Isocrates, even though the latter were intimately involved in the political events of the early 4th century. Diogenes Laertius's remark ("Not long [after Socrates' death], the Athenians felt such remorse that . . . they banished the other accusers but put Meletos to death," *Lives of Eminent Philosophers* II.43) is of dubious accuracy, and it already belongs to the constitution of the Socratic legend.

Xenophon and Plato were the first to give Socrates' death the exemplary sense of the execution of a courageous man, a victim of his city's injustice. After them, Cicero calls the Athenian judges "scoundrels," and Marcus Aurelius labels them "vermin." In the Renaissance, the image of Socrates as a free spirit and a victim of intolerance is definitively forged. Rabelais, Montaigne, and Erasmus see in him a "perfect soul," a "great light of philosophy" whose attachment to truth and independence of spirit led to his death. But the myth of Socrates' martyrdom is constituted during the Enlightenment: "The death of Socrates," Condorcet says, "is an important event in human history. It was the first crime that marked the beginning of the war between philosophy and superstition, a war which is still being waged amongst us between this same philosophy and the oppressors of humanity" (*Sketch*, p. 45). Likewise Rousseau and Diderot (who, when he is locked up in Vincennes, calls himself a prisoner of the Eleven) see Socrates as a victim of intolerance and fanaticism. Moses Mendelssohn makes him the figurehead of the Enlightenment. The history of philosophic interpretations of Socrates culminates with Hegel (who stresses the "tragic" character of Socrates' death, the unfortunate outcome of the conflict between the legitimacy of the state and that of philosophy) and Kierkegaard. At the end of the 19th century—indeed, with the development of Greek history as a discipline and the more general understanding of the intellectual world of democratic Athens—interpretations of the Socratic persona change in nature, becoming less "philosophic," and relying more closely on the critique of sources.

Socrates' philosophic posterity is found first of all in the groups known as "the Socratics" (Megarics, Cynics, Cyrenaics). Our knowledge of their thought is fragmentary, owing to the disappearance of many of the writings of those who were influenced by Socrates (Aeschines, Phaedo, Antisthenes), authors of "Socratic speeches" *(logoi sokratikoi)* or erudite dialogues that have come to constitute an authentic literary genre.

There remains Plato, whose thought developed in close contact with that of Socrates. Far from being a Socratic author himself, he is perhaps the one whose creative power did the most, involuntarily, to conceal Socrates' own thought, or to make it hard to disentangle. The effort to pinpoint the theses that constitute Socratic thought is an enterprise of modern criticism, begun in the 19th century; it is still basically a question of looking for Socrates behind Plato. The enterprise is nevertheless undoubtedly less hopeless than it would be in the case of the Sophists or Antisthenes, for Plato's philosophy and Socrates' are similar, in a way: they have in common the freedom and the isolation that Plato described as philosophy's share in unforgettable pages of *Theaetetus.*

MONIQUE CANTO-SPERBER
Translated by Catherine Porter and Dominique Jouhaud

Bibliography

Texts and Translations

Aristophanes. *Clouds.* In *Clouds; Wasps; Peace.* Trans. Jeffrey Henderson. Loeb Classical Library.

Aristotle. *Eudemian Ethics.* In *Aristotle,* vol. 20: *Athenian Constitution; Eudemian Ethics; On Virtues and Vices.* Trans. H. Rackham. Loeb Classical Library.

———. *Metaphysics.* Trans. Hugh Tredennick. 2 vols. Loeb Classical Library.

———. *Métaphysique.* Trans. J. Tricot. Paris: Vrin, 1953, 1970.

Condorcet, Antoine Nicolas de. *Sketch for a Historical Picture of the Progress of the Human Mind.* Trans. June Barraclough. London: Weidenfeld and Nicolson, 1955.

Diogenes Laertius. "Socrates." In *Lives of Eminent Philosophers,* vol. 1. Trans. R. D. Hicks. Loeb Classical Library. Pp. 148–177.

Plato. 12 vols. Loeb Classical Library.

———. *Lettre VII.* Trans. Luc Brisson. Paris: Flammarion GF, 1987.

Socrates: A Source Book. Compiled by John Ferguson. Open University Set Book. London: Macmillan, 1970.

Socratis et Socraticorum Reliquiae. Ed. Gabriele Giannantoni. 4 vols. Naples: Bibliopolis, 1990.

Xenophon. *A History of My Times (Hellenica)*. Trans. Rex Warner. London: Penguin Books, 1979.

——. *Memorabilia*. Trans. Amy L. Bonnette. Ithaca, N.Y.: Cornell University Press, 1994.

Studies

Benson, Hugh H., ed. *Essays on the Philosophy of Socrates*. Oxford: Oxford University Press, 1992.

Canto-Sperber, Monique, ed. *Les paradoxes de la connaissance: Essais sur le Ménon de Platon*. Paris: Odile Jacob, 1991.

Finley, Moses I. "Socrates and Athens." In *Aspects of Antiquity*. London: Chatto and Windus, 1968. Pp. 58–72.

Grote, George. *Plato and the Other Companions of Socrates*. London: J. Murray, 1865.

Guthrie, W. K. C. *Socrates*. Cambridge: Cambridge University Press, 1971.

Humbert, Jean. *Socrates et les petits socratiques*. Paris: Presses Universitaires de France, 1967.

Magalhaes Vilhena, V. de. *Le problème de Socrate: Le Socrate historique et le Socrate de Platon*. Paris: Presses Universitaires de France, 1952.

Mossé, Claude. *Le procès de Socrate: A Collection of Critical Essays*. Notre Dame: University of Notre Dame Press, 1971.

Vlastos, Gregory. *Socrates: Ironist and Moral Philosopher*. Cambridge: Cambridge University Press, 1991.

Wolff, Francis. *Socrate*. Paris: Presses Universitaires de France, 1985.

THUCYDIDES

THUCYDIDES OBLIGES READERS by supplying all the information on his own life that he considers relevant for this purpose. What he volunteers is, from our point of view, sparse. It is confined to his opening statement, that he was an Athenian and began writing on the Peloponnesian War as soon as it broke out in 431 B.C.E.; that he lived to see its end, and that he was mature enough at the time to understand what was going on; that he was in Athens and afflicted by the plague in 429 B.C.E. (*History of the Peloponnesian War* II.48.3); that he was a general in 424/423 B.C.E., serving in the vicinity of Thasos and Amphipolis, where he had some interest in gold mines and thus considerable influence among the local upper classes; and that he spent twenty years in exile after his service at Amphipolis. We learn his father's name, Olorus, only incidentally, when he identifies himself by his full name in connection with his generalship. In short, Thucydides tells us just enough to establish his credentials as a historian—or more precisely, as an accurate reporter of the events of his own time—specifically because he personally experienced the Peloponnesian War in its entirety. We know the date of his birth only by inference from the date of his generalship: since it is likely that a general had to be at least thirty years of age at the time of his election, Thucydides cannot have been born later than 454 B.C.E. Similarly, he will have died after the end of the Peloponnesian War (404/403 B.C.E.), since he tells us that he lived through the whole of it. For other data about his life—that he came from an aristocratic family related to that of Miltiades and Cimon, which had Thracian connections, and that he belonged to the deme Halimous (not far from the modern airport of Athens)—we depend on what later biographers, especially Marcellinus (4th to 5th century of our era), have preserved for us. Thucydides himself apparently did not consider these details relevant to his enterprise.

Although Thucydides is more forthcoming with biographical data than is Herodotus, many aspects we should have liked to hear about remain unaddressed in any credible fashion even by later authors. What kind of education did he have? Who were his friends? Was he married, and if so, to whom? Did he have children? What did he do before the Peloponnesian War broke out? What did he do between his recovery from the plague and his generalship? What mechanism sent him into exile? What were his movements during his twenty years of exile? Who were his major informants?

A question that has occupied modern scholars for a long time is the chronology of the composition of his work. Even a superficial reader will notice that Thucydides' opening statement, namely that he began his work as soon as the war broke out, cannot mean that he wrote what he did at the time that each event happened and in the sequence in which it has come down to us: statements such as those about the Sicilian Expedition and the end of the war, which are appended to his estimate of Pericles (II.65.11–12) or appear at the opening of the so-called second preface at V.26, presuppose that he out-lived some of the events he described. At what time did he write these sections? When did he compose the introductory section on past events, the *archaiologia*, through which he wishes to prove the greatness of the Peloponnesian War? When was the so-called *pentekontaēteia* written, which describes the growth of Athenian power? All we can know is that he must have revised at least part of his work before he reached the end point he had envisioned for it but never attained: his account breaks off abruptly in the middle of a sentence in his narrative of events of 411 B.C.E. and is taken up precisely at that point by Xenophon's *Hellenica*. Intensive research has shown us what passages must have been inserted at certain points, but it has not been and cannot be definitively established at what period larger sections were composed. Moreover, attempts at detecting changing historical perspec-tives, which might help differentiate earlier strata from later, have not been successful, since it is difficult to demonstrate that Thucydides ever changed his mind on fundamental historical principles.

Unlike his only major predecessor, Herodotus, Thucydides selects as a theme not the recent past but the history of his own time, as he and his con-temporaries experienced it. What prompted him to do this can be reliably in-ferred from his insistence on accuracy and precision in his own account of the Peloponnesian War and his protestations that these criteria cannot be ex-pected of a study of the past. This suggests that the present was the only pe-riod on which it was possible to get precise and controllable information. That he was an Athenian is as important as the fact that the Athenians exiled him: it explains any bias—for Athens as well as against it—that a reader might detect in his writing. Moreover, he treats his exile not as the hardship it un-doubtedly was, as it would have been for anyone in antiquity, but as an opportunity, in his quest for accuracy, to gain access to both sides in the Peloponnesian War. For apparently no other reason than to establish his cred-ibility, he emphasizes his intellectual maturity at the outbreak of the war and the fact that he lived to see its end twenty-seven years later. He offers no apology for his failure at Amphipolis despite his military experience and his standing among Thracian tribes, even at the risk of giving his political or per-sonal enemies ammunition for censure. There is no complaint and no self-pity; the information is given to supply his reader with a clue to his compe-tence. Similarly, his statement that he succumbed to the plague bolsters his authority to speak about that. In short, Thucydides refers to only those of his vital statistics that establish his credentials as an accurate reporter; the data he regards as important are given without concern for their consequences on the reader's estimate of Thucydides' personal culpability.

Consistent with this penchant for dry objectivity is Thucydides' statement of his aim and methods. He discusses his method under two headings, speeches and narrative. What he has to say about his narrative is more easily understood than his statement about speeches: "As for the factual side of what happened in the war, the right thing to do seemed to me to base my report not on information gathered from just any witness, nor on my own impressions; but to follow up with all possible accuracy in every detail both what I myself witnessed and what I learned from others. This procedure was laborious, because those present at any given event did not say the same thing about the same points, but their statements were colored by sympathy or memory favoring one side or the other" (I.22.2–3).

The speeches are more problematic because the modern reader is unaccustomed to having so much importance attached to a direct report of public utterances. Moreover, accuracy in reporting speeches was infinitely harder to attain in an age without radio, television, and tape recorders. Thucydides was aware of this problem: "It was as difficult for me to remember accurately the language used in the speeches I myself heard delivered as it was for those who reported to me from elsewhere" (I.22.1). Why, then, did he find it important to include speeches in his work at all? There is no explicit answer to this question anywhere in his eight books, suggesting that he took the importance of including them for granted. Accordingly, we must try to find our own answer by combining his methodological statement on speeches with his practice in the body of his work.

"I have included in my work how each speaker seemed to me to come to grips with the issues that faced him, keeping as closely as possible to the general thrust of what he actually said." This constitutes a disavowal of verbatim accuracy and claims merely (a) that a given speech in the written text accurately reflects the attitude of a speaker toward the course of action he advocated; (b) that it was addressed to the situation that is its context in Thucydides; and (c) that it adheres as literally as possible to the spoken text of the speaker. But what are we to make of the phrase *"seemed to me to come to grips"*? Is this not an admission on the part of Thucydides that it was ultimately he who composed the speeches he put into the mouth of others? And if so, what objective historical value can we attach to them?

The response to these fundamental questions is decisive for our estimate of Thucydides as a historian. A partial answer emerges from his usual (but not universal) practice of presenting speeches in antithetical pairs: when the point has been reached at which a major decision needs to be taken, he frequently has a representative of one of the interested parties look at the situation from his vantage point, to be followed at once by a speech presenting the counterarguments raised by the opposing interested party. A few examples will help to illustrate the point.

The first pair of speeches in his work (I.31–44) sheds light on the problems facing the Athenians as a result of Corcyra's request for an alliance against Corinth in 433 B.C.E. Interestingly enough, no Athenian speech is reported. The first speech (I.32–36) is attributed to unnamed Corcyreans, who not only air their grievances against Corinth and argue that by complying Athens would help an injured party, but also hold out as a lure the advantages that an alliance with the second most powerful navy in the Greek world would bring to Athens, without violating the terms of the Thirty-Years' Peace. The complementary speech (I.37–43) is given by unnamed Corinthians. After refuting the Corcyreans' charges against them, they point to the dire consequences an Athenian alliance with Corcyra would have on Athens's relations with Corinth. They impress the Athenians sufficiently that they accommodate the Corcyreans by agreeing to only a defensive alliance with them, which, in the immediate sequel, leads to a naval encounter between Athenians and Corinthians at the Sybota Islands (I.54), but ultimately leads to the outbreak of the Peloponnesian War.

Are these two speeches historical? Although there is no external evidence to confirm or refute Thucydides, there is no reason to reject their historicity. Similarly, we have no way of checking whether the arguments Thucydides attributes to the speakers here were actually made by them. But it is clear that the Corcyreans make out the best possible case to tempt the Athenians with their offer, and that the equally cogent counterarguments of the Corinthians are borne out by the events that followed. Furthermore, no narrative could have depicted the Athenian dilemma as graphically as these two speeches.

There are two further points. First, the decision on what speeches to insert into his narrative from among the many that were given can only have been Thucydides' alone, and his choices must have been motivated by considerations other than the desire to be complete as well as accurate in his account. Evidently his view of "accuracy" included making as precise a presentation as possible of a situation whose full significance could be communicated only by having the living arguments of both sides involved supplement his own narrative. By proceeding in this way he also isolates the issues in each situation, but—and this is important—it is the situation as seen through the historian's eyes.

The second point is: why did Thucydides choose the speeches of the Corinthians to oppose the Corcyreans when he could equally well have chosen, for example, the speech of an Athenian opposed to foreign entanglements on the ground that they would ultimately lead to war with Sparta? Thucydides may have chosen the Corinthians not only to remain faithful to historical reality but also to demonstrate how a local quarrel between two states on the periphery of Spartan-Athenian relations could lead to the general conflagration that it did. The fact that he motivates the presence in Athens of the Corinthians merely by their awareness of the possible consequences of an Athenian-Corcyrean alliance stresses the urgency of an issue that the Athenians themselves did not fully recognize. In addition, the two speeches enable Thucydides to make an indirect "philosophical" statement on the general historical truths he sees embedded in the concrete situation: momentous results may come from small local beginnings.

All paired speeches in Thucydides serve similar purposes. The proper treatment of allies, for example, presents a fundamental problem of imperial policy to the Athenians after the suppression of the revolt at Mytilene: would a harsh treatment of subdued rebels or a more compassionate one be more conducive to deterring recurrence? The former course of action had already been voted by the Assembly when it was decided to reconsider the issue. Thucydides reports none of the speeches that must have been delivered at the first debate; although he tells us that "different views were expressed by different speakers" at the second debate (III.36.6), he reports only those of the influential demagogue Cleon and of Diodotus (otherwise unknown) at the second Assembly meeting, even though both had already presented their opposing views in the earlier debate. Why he did this can only be guessed; presumably the second debate established a sharper contrast between their opposing views than the first had done. Cleon, maligned by Thucydides as "the most violent citizen," attacks excessive discussion and argues that only the fear of harsh treatment can teach the allies to accept Athenian rule. Diodotus welcomes deliberation and discussion as a prelude to intelligent action; no law, he argues, and not even the death penalty, has ever inhibited human nature from pursuing its impulses. A peaceful solution, he suggests, will not deprive Athens of its future revenue from Mytilene, and a policy of generosity toward the lower classes, the demos, who, he claims, are sympathetic toward the Athenian democracy in all the states of the empire, will prevent the upper class from any future attempts at rebellion.

By choosing these two speakers, Thucydides achieves a multiple effect. In the first place, he pinpoints the issue as centered on the question of the politically most effective way of handling rebels. Second, by excluding other speeches made on this occasion, some of which will doubtless have pleaded for a gentler treatment of the captured Mytileneans on humanitarian grounds, he shows that Cleon's motion could be refuted and defeated only by another tough argument based on the rebels' usefulness to the state. Third, by branding Cleon as "violent" before reporting his speech and by presenting him as opposed to discussion, he reveals his own sympathy for the rational argument of Diodotus against the blind emotionalism of Cleon. Fourth, at the same time he also wistfully notes the tragic aspect of the human condition, which has to hide its nobler moral impulses behind a curtain of political usefulness in order to prevail. In other words, a debate on a practical political problem is manipulated in a way also to yield a "philosophical" statement on human nature, which remains impervious to conventional laws or penalties, and on the human condition, which permits moral action only when it is also politically advantageous.

Issues have no objective existence. They have reality only once they are recognized as issues by an intelligent observer. The observer in this case is, of course, Thucydides, who has his identification of an issue confirmed by two of the agents involved in it. Since it would have been impossible as well as undesirable for Thucydides to report any and every speech delivered during the Peloponnesian War, his activity compelled him to select the events that he regarded as crucial enough to be presented as issues. To the extent that he has to work under this constraint, an element of subjectivity is bound to appear in his report.

Moreover, what applies to speeches also applies (in a way not explained by Thucydides) to the narrative. However good Thucydides' own memory may have been, and however accurately he may have checked it as well as the information he received from others, the decision on which facts to include as relevant to the whole can only have been his. This means that, as modern readers, we depend for our knowledge of the past on the judgments of a historian who experienced it, and the relevance of what is to be included is subject to his choice; only rarely can we check his judgment against external sources. The great merit of Thucydides lies in his serious effort to stay within the limits of objective historiography and his recognition of the subjective element necessarily inherent in his enterprise. The sum total of issues identified and the observations made on them in speeches enables us to isolate the view of history taken by the historian. His selection of facts, the way he relates them to one another, the occasions he selects for the insertion of speeches, and the persons he selects for delivering arguments, which, though partly their own, nevertheless bear the historian's stamp—all these factors enable Thucydides to convey to the reader what significance he sees in the historical process.

This leads us to the question of what significance Thucydides saw in his history. While he is explicit in his estimates of such men as Pericles, Cleon, Brasidas, Hermocrates, Nicias, Antiphon, and some others, most of his views are so firmly embedded in his narrative of events or in the words he attributes to the speakers that the facts themselves speak more powerfully than the interpretation an outsider living centuries later can give to them. What can interpretation say about the significance of the plague, described at II.47.3–53? How can we express the meaning of civil discord (stasis) beyond what we read about it in Corcyra, at III.82–83? The meaning is unequivocal, even though it is communicated only through a statement of the unadorned facts. It is different with other questions he seems to address, and to which only close interpretation or juxtaposition of different passages and contexts can give an uncertain answer. To what factors does Thucydides attribute the outbreak of the Peloponnesian War? Could it have been avoided? Could it have ended differently than it did? To what extent is man master of his fortune? Does Thucydides believe that human morality declined as the war went on? What role does reason play, and what role do emotion and passion play, in human affairs? Is democracy reconcilable with empire?

We know from Thucydides' own opening statements that he sensed from the beginning that the Peloponnesian War would be the most momentous disturbance the Greek world had ever seen, and he spends the first nineteen chapters of his work proving the point. Moreover, he censures past historians for having been too cavalier in not ferreting out facts from reliable evidence, and for having shown more concern to make their tales arresting and entertaining (I.20). Against them he maintains that he has meticulously sifted what evidence he found, to present an account that may indeed be less enjoyable but nevertheless useful to those "who will wish to gain a clear view of the events of the past and, in future, of the events which, human affairs being what they are, will again be like or very similar to them" (I.22.4).

He does not imply that history has a circular movement but merely suggests that the immutability of the very humanity of man will guarantee that future generations can learn from the experiences of his own. Some of Thucydides' general observations are unremarkable, e.g., that man is fallible, that life takes many unexpected turns, that hardships will always beset men in times of civil strife, that men have the tendency to exaggerate their assets. But there are some interesting views on the parameters that limit human existence. No human inventiveness, he tells us, could cope with the plague; the fall of Torone could not be explained in human terms; and he has Hermocrates brand as "beyond human power" the realization of the desire of some Sicilians to see Syracuse both humbled and preserved. It is in these passages, if in any, especially in his description of the fall of Torone, that Thucydides comes close to recognizing the existence of a transcendent power against which human efforts are of no avail. Other human limitations are inherent in the biological nature of man: the plague is said to have been too severe for "human nature" to endure, and Nicias's troops, "having achieved what humans can, have suffered what they cannot endure."

By far the most momentous use of the "human" element in history, however, is in the explanation of the development of empire. The locus classicus is the Athenians' defense of their empire in their address to the First Lacedaemonian Congress: "We have done nothing extraordinary or different from the way men act, if we have accepted an empire that was given to us, and if we did not give it up under the pressure of the [three] most potent motives: prestige, fear, and self-interest. We were not the first to display this attitude, but it has always been a rule that the weaker must be kept down by the greater power. At the same time, we regarded ourselves as worthy and were so regarded by you, until in calculating your interests you are now using the argument from justice, which no one has ever advanced to inhibit his lust for more when he had the chance of gaining his ends by force. Those men deserve praise, who once they have made use of human nature to establish control over others, follow justice more than the power at their disposal requires" (I.76.2–3).

The Athenians thus ground imperialism in a force that is ineradicably given as a constant element in the human animal. Since prestige, fear, and self-interest are ingrained in human nature, we expect them to explain not only Athenian imperialism or even imperialism as such, but also all personal and social human conduct. This raises the question of whether Thucydides means his readers to take the convictions articulated to be only those of leading Athenians as filtered through his mind, or as convictions of his own that he regarded as objectively true, and that he used the Athenians to express. Obviously Thucydides gives no explicit answer to this question. But the frequent reappearance of prestige, fear, and self-interest, and related expressions, as mainsprings of personal and political action and reaction in the bulk of his work leaves little doubt that he has the Athenians at the First Lacedaemonian Congress expressing something of the truth of which he was himself convinced.

To prove this point philologically is made difficult not only by Thucydides' indifference to a strict technical vocabulary but also by the consideration that he is not and does not pretend to be a philosopher whose aim is to offer to his readers a coherent and consistent theory of historical development. If he has such a theory, we find it embedded in the details of his narrative and in the arguments he attributes to his speakers; and we do find it embedded so deeply that it is fair to say that these motives formed a pattern in Thucydides' thinking. Appeals to all three motives, jointly or separately, pervade the entire work, from its opening account of early history (archaiologia) to the aftermath of the oligarchical revolution of 411 B.C.E. at its end, in speeches as well as in the narrative. Fear (deos, phobos) is the most common, and references to it range from the emotion felt on the field of battle to Thucydides' own statement of his own deepest conviction about the cause of the Peloponnesian War: Athenian expansion and the fear it engendered in the Lacedaemonians made its outbreak inevitable, but the Athenians also fear the Spartans (I.91.3). Mutual fear of the use the other side might make of the captured island of Sphacteria determines the policies of both Athens and Sparta. The actions of the Plataeans against the Thebans are prompted by fear (II.3.1,4), and fear makes the Sicilian cities resist Athenian expansion and prompts the Syracusan attack on Messana. But fear also prevents Nicias from attacking Syracuse immediately after landing in Sicily.

Self-interest enters Thucydides' argument as ōphelia (benefit), kerdos (gain), pleonexia (greed), to xymphoron, to chrēsimon, to lysiteloun (advantage), and similar expressions. Together with fear, self-interest appears as a motive in the attempt by the Corcyreans to persuade the Athenians to become their allies, and in the Corinthian argument at the Second Lacedaemonian Congress, that the Greek cities will rally to the Peloponnesian cause; Hermocrates looks on Sicilian fear of Athenian aggression as "useful" *(chrēsimon)* to effect a united Sicily, and a similar argument is used by Gylippus when he warns his men that the Athenians will not reap any advantage *(ōphelia)* from the size of their navy if the Sicilians do not fear them.

Prestige *(timē)* is somewhat harder for us to understand. It includes a sense of personal or national "dignity," the esteem or honor in which a person or state is held by another person or state *(doxa, axiōsis, axiōma)*. As a motive in interstate affairs, it is the sense in which a more powerful state feels that it cannot afford to yield to the claims, demands, or interests of a weaker state in matters where it believes its own vital interests affected. Together with fear *(phobos)*, it enters the Melian Dialogue at several places in the Athenians' argument that they have to assert themselves among their allies, and that they cannot project an image of weakness or fearfulness in dealing with them.

Of special relevance are four passages in which fear, self-interest, and prestige combine to explain the complex dynamism of a given situation. The first of these is the revolt of Mytilene. What the Athenians most resent about it is that the Mytileneans had occupied a privileged position among Athens's allies and that Mytilene had respected Athens. But at the same time, the Athenians feared the strength of Mytilene's fleet, just as Mytilene feared the Athenian navy. The combination of these two motives goes some way toward explaining the narrow vindictiveness with which Cleon proposes to handle the situation. Against him, Diodotus argues that discussion is beneficial *(ōpheleitai)* and fear *(phobos)* detrimental to the city, and that a good citizen ought not to be dishonored *(atimazein)* for giving the city the benefit of his advice.

A second passage has Hermocrates argue for Sicilian unity at the Congress at Gela on the grounds that "no one is compelled to go to war by ignorance, or prevented by fear from going into it, if he thinks he will gain anything by it; in some cases, the gain appears greater than the danger; in other cases, people are willing to undertake risks rather than face an immediate humiliation. But if both sides miss the right moment for acting, the advice to come to terms is profitable" (IV.59.2–3, cf. 61.6, 62.2). A similar confluence of the three motives is found in the third passage, Euphemus's defense of Athenian policy at Camarina. He begins by reminding his audience of Athenian prestige *(axioi ontes)* won by her past leadership of the Greeks; he affirms that the presence of the Athenians will be advantageous *(xympheronta)* for Sicily; and he asserts that they have nothing to fear *(phoberōteron, perideōs, deos)*.

The fourth passage shows that Thucydides believes (as, indeed, he has Diodotus suggest at III.45.3) that this triple motivation applies to individuals as well as to states. All three motives enter his description of Alcibiades' character: "Desirous to be general and hoping to be instrumental in capturing Sicily and Carthage, and, if successful, to profit personally in wealth and reputation [chrēmasi te kai doxēi ōphelēsein]. For the prestige [axiōma] he enjoyed among the citizens made him gratify desires greater than the means he had allowed, both in keeping horses and in his other expenditures. This became later a considerable factor in bringing Athens down: fearing [phobēthentes] the extent of his lawlessness in his personal lifestyle and in the design pervading every single action of his, most people became his enemies, convinced that he wanted to be tyrant" (VI.15.2–4, cf. 17.1). As a contrast, Pericles' power is earlier attributed to his prestige (axiōma, axiōsis), through which he could bring an overconfident populace back to reality by instilling fear in it (kateplēssen epi to phobeisthai) (II.65.8–9).

The preceding is only a very small part of the evidence that shows how the three factors adduced by the Athenians to explain their empire pervade the whole of Thucydides' History. To interpret this evidence, as is still fashionable, as explaining Thucydides' fascination with imperialism is only partly true. He leaves no doubt that he sees fear, prestige, and self-interest as the mainsprings of all human action, anchored by an inescapable necessity (anankē) in human nature.

Thucydides defines his fascination with the unprecedented dimensions of the Peloponnesian War as his motive for writing its history, and he spends the first nineteen chapters of Book I demonstrating that it was indeed the "greatest movement that ever shook the Greek and part of the non-Greek world" (I.1.2). It is tempting to see this greatness less merely in terms of imperialism than as affording Thucydides a large canvas to explore the actions and reactions of the human animal in extreme situations. As to what benefit future generations will be able to derive from his accurate account, the only possible answer is knowledge. But not the kind of knowledge that will enable a person to prevent the mistakes of the past: if Thucydides is convinced that fear, prestige, and self-interest are ingrained in the nature of man, nothing will ever free human beings from the necessity that this unholy trinity lays down for them. What knowledge can do is alert future generations to the workings of fear, prestige, and self-interest, so that when they observe these or similar symptoms in the future, they can recognize what is in store for them and, if possible, initiate measures to soften the blow that is sure to come.

One example of this is Thucydides' description of the plague. He introduces his painstakingly detailed and precise account by saying: "All speculation as to its origin and its causes, if causes can be found adequate to produce so great a disturbance, I leave to other writers, whether lay or professional; for myself, I shall simply set down its nature, and explain the symptoms, which will enable an observant student, if it should ever break out again, to know what is coming and not be ignorant. This I can the better do, as I had the disease myself, and watched its operation in the case of others" (II.48.3, trans. adapted). Thucydides makes clear his doubts that future generations will be any more successful than his own at discovering the cause of the disease (and, perhaps, in that way finding a cure). He is content if he can describe the symptoms—and not merely those that he experienced himself—accurately enough to enable members of future generations "to know what is coming and not be ignorant."

Thucydides' celebrated comments on the civil upheaval in Corcyra corroborate that this is his purpose: "Many hardships befell the cities in the course of civil war, things which have been happening and will always be as long as the nature of man remains the same; but changing in form from severe to mild, depending on the changes of fortune that determine them. In peace and prosperity states as well as individuals have better judgement, because they are not faced with conditions they cannot control and that are not of their own making. But war, in removing easy provision of daily needs, is a violent schoolmaster and brings most people's tempers to the level of their situation" (III.82.2). Again the purpose of a detailed and gruesome description, here of the events in Corcyra, is not to prevent a recurrence (which is impossible inasmuch as it is determined by human nature) but "to know what is coming and not be ignorant." It is no accident that this same insight characterizes such great statesmen in Thucydides' account as Themistocles and Pericles (I.138.3; II.65.5–6, 13).

The conviction that human actions are primarily motivated by fear, prestige, and self-interest gives Thucydides a hard-nosed, "realistic" attitude toward the events he so graphically describes. Nothing relieves his stark description of the plague; nothing embellishes the partisan attitudes and actions rampant during the Corcyrean revolt. No considerations of humanity or compassion enter into the debate about the prisoners from Mytilene, either on Cleon's side or on the part of Diodotus. The *raison d'état* alone governs all interstate relations.

This comes out most unequivocally in the Melian Dialogue (V.85–114). According to Thucydides, the Melians, though ethnically related to the Lacedaemonians, had remained neutral in the war until the Athenians decided to incorporate them into their empire as the only islanders who were not yet part of it. In other words, the Athenians felt that their own prestige as a superpower demanded their incorporation of a small island that might possibly be used as a base against them and that refused to surrender voluntarily. In the debate that follows, the Athenians rule questions of right and wrong out of order and deprecate appeals to past achievements or to Spartan kinship for help; they invite the Melians to consider nothing but the hard fact that their survival depends on surrendering without bloodshed to the more powerful enemy: "You know as well as we do that what is right is a criterion in human calculation only when both sides are equally powerful to enforce compliance; but a preponderant power exacts what it can and the weak have to concede" (89); "In the case of the divine it is our opinion and in the case of humans our clear conviction that by a constraint inherent in nature they rule wheresoever they have the power" (105.2). This seems to be the underlying principle in the historical process that Thucydides sees at work not only in the passages just discussed but throughout his *History*. That its recognition constitutes a landmark in cultural history is beyond question, and is the basis on which some modern scholars have called him a "scientific" historian who, like Machiavelli or Marx, has contributed to discovering the dynamics of human history.

But this is not the whole story: Thucydides did not see himself in this light alone. What we regard as his principles are for him mainsprings of particular actions embedded so deeply in the nature of man that they will of necessity shape whatever man does. But the effect they have on the human condition is nothing short of tragic. Since, in facing them, man is subject to a necessity inherent in his own nature, they inhibit the exercise of free choice: where self-interest *(to xympheron)* asserts itself, the voice of morality *(to dikaion)* is stilled. Again and again Thucydides makes a point of showing that moral stirrings, which also animate human thought and aspiration, are suppressed by the overriding demands of fear, prestige, and self-interest. From the arguments of the Corcyreans at Corinth we may glean that arbitration of disputes rather than resorting to war constitutes one set of moral desiderata, and the Corinthian speech at Athens suggests that adhering to the terms of a treaty is another. We learn from the Melians and from the list of Athenian allies who joined the Sicilian expedition that kinship ought to be a motive for states to help each other in an emergency, and that the decision to go to war should be taken by autonomous states on the basis that it is morally right to do so. Statements by the Athenians at Sparta as well as at Melos, that arguments from justice are eclipsed when one side is stronger than the other, suggest that moral considerations ought to carry more weight than considerations of relative strength and weakness. That judicial proceedings, even if they result in injustice, are preferable to violent treatment and that gentle treatment of allies is preferable to harshness are implied by the Athenian speech at Sparta and by Alcibiades' justification of the Sicilian campaign.

Moral considerations dominate especially what is normal in personal (as opposed to collective) behavior. This is shown most vividly in Thucydides' account of civil discord in Corcyra: morality is suppressed as soon as fear, prestige, and self-interest appear on the scene. Thucydides regrets that partisanship imported foreigners to interfere in internal matters, and that vindictiveness, atrocity, greed, and personal ambition prevailed. What emerges as desirable is a situation in which daily needs are satisfied, in which words retain their normal meaning and are not perverted into slogans, and in which kinship counts for more than partisan loyalty. He values obedience to laws and respect for the sanctity of oaths; public interests should have a higher priority than private; verdicts must be just; violence must be shunned; gods and parents must be respected; and unsophisticated openness must not be ridiculed.

The impression that this list does not significantly differentiate Thucydides' values from those of a conventional Greek is confirmed by an inquiry into his views on religion. In his account of the settlement of the Pelargikon with evacuees from the Attic countryside he mentions an oracular injunction that prohibited its settlement. Thucydides attacks the interpretation of the oracle current at the time, which attributed the disasters befalling Athens to the unlawful occupation of the place, by asserting that "the war constituted the necessity of settling it; though the oracle did not name the war, it knew in advance that its habitation would never bode any good" (II.17.1–2). This shows that he regarded the inviolability of religious injunctions as desirable; while he questions the interpretation of an oracle, he does not reject its basic veracity. Similarly, in the dispute between Athenians and Boeotians about the sacred water that the Athenians had used for mundane purposes during their occupation of the Temple of Apollo at Delium, the fact that the Athenians defend themselves by saying that they had disturbed the water not in wanton disregard of its sanctity but prompted by necessity, and that, accordingly, their act does not constitute a transgression (IV.98.5), shows that religious sanctions ought normally to be respected, regardless of one's own opinions about them.

There has been a tendency in recent scholarship to emphasize Thucydides' more humane side and to see in him a moralist who views with regret how the pursuit of self-interest leads to the eclipse of human values. This interpretation seems to be as one-sided as its opposite, the view that he was first and foremost an exponent of hard-nosed realpolitik. To regard both views as aspects of the same person seems to me closer to the truth. Their combination gives us a Thucydides who knew and felt the tragic side of the human condition: man has the power to recognize the forces that shape human behavior, but his knowledge does not enable him to change their course; he has to ride roughshod over the more conventional social values that make life civilized.

If we were to interpret Thucydides only on the basis of what we learn from him about the moral social values of his time, he would at best be a polemicist who put his great artistic gifts into the service of preaching how the horrors of war barbarize the human animal, and whose own values differ little from those of his fellow citizens. But this would ignore the much greater and more profound dimension of Thucydides the intellectual. His respect for conventional values does not conceal the fact that intellectually Thucydides accepts the antithetical principles of realpolitik, which he sees as pervading the entire Peloponnesian War, from the Athenians' defense of their empire in Book I to the Melian Dialogue in Book V, the speeches of Hermocrates and of Euphemus in Books IV and VI, and the oligarchical maneuverings in Book VIII. It informs his method, his passion for accuracy and precision, his chronological

division of the year into summers and winters, his use of (usually antithetical) speeches, and his constant search for deeper realities behind the events.
These preoccupations, in addition to his disinclination to accept the transcendent explanations of human events found in Herodotus, suggests that he had
been exposed to the sophistic teaching that had captured the minds of young
Athenians in the second half of the 5th century, and which favored an enlightened, rational view of the world over an older more religiously informed
attitude.

This assumption also explains certain Thucydidean attitudes and apparent
contradictions that have baffled modern scholars. How can an author whose
avowed aim is accuracy and precision in reporting so consistently denigrate
Cleon? He describes him at his first appearance as "the most violent citizen
and far more trusted by the people at this time than anyone else" (III.36.6;
IV.21.3). Cleon's spectacular success at Sphacteria is presented as the result
of intrigue and prevarication because his own motives for opposing peace
were under suspicion, and even his death in battle in Thrace is attributed
to cowardice and lack of judgment. But how popular can Cleon have been,
if, as Thucydides tells us, his offer to resolve the Pylos affair within twenty
days was met "with laughter at his irresponsible talk, while serious persons
greeted it with delight, reckoning that they would gain either way, either in
getting rid of Cleon (which was their greater hope), or in unexpectedly reducing the Lacedaemonians" (IV.28.5)? Is popularity a bad thing in a democracy?
Or is democracy itself a bad thing in the eyes of Thucydides? A number of
narrative passages—that is, passages in which Thucydides speaks in his own
name—might suggest as much: the fickle "crowd" reelects Pericles as general
after just having fined him; the "mob" eggs on Nicias to surrender his generalship to Cleon while Cleon prevaricates; the people are crazy with emotion as
the ill-fated campaign against Sicily is launched; panic-stricken, they hear of
the desecration of the Herms (VI.60); the "mob" at Syracuse gets overconfident when an expected Athenian attack does not materialize. At the same
time, democracy is extolled in Pericles' great Funeral Oration (II.36–46, esp.
37), and Diodotus praises, as Pericles had done, "democratic" discussion as a
prelude to action.

The assumption that Thucydides was influenced by sophistic teaching implies what is also implied by his service as general. He must have been a
member of the upper class; as a beneficiary from gold-mine concessions, he
could well have afforded the fees charged by the sophists for their instruction.
His training and his social class, together with his personal temperament,
would have made him sympathetic to rational political discourse, freed from
emotionalism as far as possible, regardless of the political orientation of those
who used it. Therefore, he would have favored the intellectual attitude of a
Pericles, a Diodotus, or a Hermocrates to the rabble-rousing of a Cleon and
the unreasoning sentiments with which the common people reacted to events.

This stance does not characterize Thucydides' attitude to democracy alone: he is equally averse to the machinations and strong-arm methods with which the oligarchs established their regime in 411 B.C.E. But there, too, Antiphon, "the person who had organized the method by which the whole affair should come to this issue," is praised as "second to none of the Athenians of his time in excellence and most forceful in conceiving ideas and in communicating his conclusions"; this despite (or because of?) the fact that "his formidable talent rendered him suspect in the eyes of the masses" (VIII.68.1).

This would suggest that Thucydides was indifferent to what kind of regime prevailed in a given state, so long as it gave the state intelligent leadership that governed in the interest of all. This is perhaps also the reason why the only regime that elicits his unqualified praise is the short-lived government that briefly ruled Athens after the overthrow of the oligarchy of the Four Hundred: "It was a judicious blend geared to the interest of the few and the many, and this fact first buoyed up the city after the wretched condition into which it had fallen" (VIII.97.2).

Thucydides' view, embodied in his account of the Peloponnesian War, cannot be translated into partisan politics. What he favors is a politics of human intelligence, a product of human rationality, operating without appeal to transcendent powers but open to an understanding of what the limits of rationality are, and also aware of the obstacles that stand in the way of attaining it.

MARTIN OSTWALD

Bibliography

Texts and Translations

Thucydides. *History of the Peloponnesian War.* Trans. Richard Crawford. Everyman Library. Citations in the text are to this edition.

———. *History of the Peloponnesian War.* Trans. C. F. Smith. 4 vols. Loeb Classical Library.

Studies

Adcock, F. E. *Thucydides and His History.* Cambridge, 1963.

Cochrane, C. N. *Thucydides and the Science of History.* Oxford, 1929.

Cogan, M. *The Human Thing: The Speeches and Principles of Thucydides' History.* Chicago, 1981.

Connor, W. R. *Thucydides.* Princeton, 1984.

Cornford, F. M. *Thucydides Mythistorichus.* London, 1907.

De Romilly, Jacqueline. *Histoire et raison chez Thucydide.* Paris, 1956.

———. *Thucydides and Athenian Imperialism.* Trans. Philip Thody. Oxford, 1963.

Finley, J. H. *Thucydides.* Cambridge, Mass., 1946.

Gomme, A. W., A. Andrewes, and K. J. Dover. *A Historical Commentary on Thucydides.* 5 vols. Oxford, 1945–1981.

Hornblower, Simon. *Thucydides.* London, 1987.

Ostwald, Martin. *Anankē in Thucydides*. Atlanta, Ga., 1988.

Parry, Adam. Logos *and* Ergon *in Thucydides*. Salem, N.H., 1981.

Rood, Tim. *Thucydides: Narrative and Explanation*. Oxford and New York, 1998.

Schwartz, Eduard. *Das Geschichtswerk des Thukydides*. Bonn, 1919.

Stadter, P. A., ed. *The Speeches in Thucydides*. Chapel Hill, N.C., 1973.

Stahl, H.-P. *Thukydides: Die Stellung des Menschen im geschichtlichen Prozess* (= *Zetemata* 40). Munich, 1966.

Strasburger, H. "Die Entdeckung der politischen Geschichte durch Thukydides." *Saeculum* 4 (1954): 395–428.

XENOPHON

XENOPHON THE ATHENIAN (ca. 430–after 355 B.C.E.) was a brilliant military strategist, an accomplished man of letters, and a devoted follower of Socrates. Xenophon could be called the first journalist: he recorded his personal adventures in wartime, and expressed himself on the leading moral, social, and political issues of his day.

Xenophon's intelligence was more practical than theoretical. He was not interested in abstract philosophical argument for its own sake, but he had a keen practical interest in many of the questions raised by Socrates, such as what is justice, and how might the good life be reliably secured, not only for an individual but also for a household, a city-state, or an empire. On these topics Xenophon has much to say that is interesting and even wise. Thus, although Xenophon is not a major figure in the history of philosophy, if philosophy is viewed (as Plato viewed it) as a comprehensive and professionalized theoretical discipline, he is nonetheless a major figure in the history of social thought. To use a modern parallel, Xenophon is more a Camus than a Sartre.

Opinions of Xenophon have varied greatly through the ages. To some, Xenophon has seemed like a dull and boring pious old uncle, a man far too unphilosophical to have understood Socrates. To others, Xenophon's rival Plato appears to be a dangerously alienated intellectual, a man who is a genius at abstract philosophy but who has very little concrete understanding of ordinary human life. Xenophon, by contrast, is sensible and insightful and wise.

Although Xenophon was not a professional philosopher, his works are permeated with philosophy. Here is one example. Xenophon repeats many times the traditional Greek view that one should help one's friends and harm one's enemies. By contrast, Plato's Socrates insists that it is never right to harm anyone. Here it may seem that Xenophon is resting content with prephilosophical common sense, but this is not truly the case. Xenophon's Socrates also holds the philosophically grounded views that good people should be friends to good people and enemies to bad, and that it is in everyone's interest to become good. When combined with those views, the traditional maxim, Help your friends and harm your enemies, is transformed into a thoroughly moral principle. It now signifies roughly the same as Promote the good and oppose evil.

Over the centuries, Xenophon's works have served as models of the "simple" style of Attic prose. From ancient times down to 20th-century Europe, generations of schoolchildren have been taught to imitate him. Fluent, lucid, and unpretentious, Xenophon's style of writing can seem easier and less carefully crafted than it is. Underneath the apparent casualness of Xenophon's prose there lies a skilled and intelligent author who chooses words with great care and organizes each work with a deliberate, though subtle, plan.

The most controversial aspect of Xenophon's significance is the value of his testimony concerning Socrates. In antiquity his portrait of Socrates was quite influential, for example on the Stoics. Leading scholars, especially in the last century, have argued that Xenophon is our most reliable source for the historical Socrates, since Plato was too creative to be a good historian. Other equally prominent scholars have argued that Xenophon was too dull or unphilosophical to understand the real Socrates. No scholarly consensus concerning "the problem of the the historical Socrates" exists today.

Plato and Xenophon were not the only authors of Socratic dialogues. Many of Socrates' followers contributed to this genre. The conventions of the genre seem to have allowed authors considerable freedom to reshape Socrates, idealize him, and put their own views in Socrates' mouth. Therefore the cautious and reasonable view is that certainty about the historical Socrates is lost to us—and, in a way, not very important. The most important fact about Socrates was his influence: the extraordinary fertility of his ideas and the moral example he set for his followers. The richness of the Socratic movement is a fascinating subject for which we do have good evidence, and Xenophon's Socratic writings are a precious resource.

The variety and literary originality of Xenophon's works are remarkable. He wrote, among other things, a history, a military memoir, Socratic dialogues, a biographical novel, and technical treatises on horsemanship and hunting. In fact Xenophon's main contribution to Greek thought is not any set of doctrines but rather the many literary genres that he either created or to which he gave a new impulse.

The *Cyropaedia,* or *Education of Cyrus,* is a biographical novel or historical romance about the life and character of Cyrus the Great, founder of the Persian empire. Xenophon's chief aim is to use Cyrus as a vehicle for portraying the ideal ruler. Thus the work does not aim at historical accuracy but is a kind of utopia—Xenophon's counterpart to Plato's *Republic. Cyropaedia* is Xenophon's longest and most comprehensive work, incorporating ideas from all his other writings. It covers not just Cyrus's boyhood but his entire career, thus implying that education is a lifelong process. *Cyropaedia* is perhaps the most influential of all mirrors of princes. It had great influence in Roman times, and again in the Renaissance, for example on Machiavelli. As the first historical romance, it has affected the history of Western imaginative literature, particularly influencing the ancient Greek novel and literature in the 16th and 17th centuries.

Whereas in *Memorabilia* Xenophon portrays Socrates as the ideal example of one who does not seek to rule others, in *Cyropaedia* he portrays Cyrus as the ideal example of one who has a large or unlimited desire to rule others. (In between these complementary opposites lie Ischomachus of *Oeconomicus*, the ideal ruler of a household, and the fictionalized Agesilaus of *Agesilaus*, who is the ideal ruler of a kingdom.) The problem Cyrus faces is that human beings, unlike sheep or cattle, by nature resist those who try to rule them. Cyrus's solution is to rule justly, i.e., to rule over willing subjects in accord with law. He persuades people to follow him through two main methods: the display of his own virtue, and benefaction—treating his subjects well and making them better off. Thus Cyrus is merciful and kind to those he conquers, to convert them into loyal subjects. Part of Cyrus's virtue as a leader is his great skill at manipulating other people for his own ends.

Xenophon opens *Cyropaedia* by declaring that a central problem of politics is instability, the tendency of people to overthrow their government. Xenophon was no democrat: the solution he offers to this problem is monarchy by a brilliant and virtuous leader like Cyrus. But the limits of this solution are revealed when, after Cyrus's death, the empire breaks up due to his sons' inadequacies. Just as the famous question Is virtue teachable? inspires the beginning chapters of *Cyropaedia*, so its corollary, Why do virtuous fathers so often fail to pass on their virtue to their sons? haunts the end.

Memorabilia, or *Recollections of Socrates*, is Xenophon's major Socratic work. *Memorabilia* 1.1–2 presents a formal defense of Socrates, who was condemned to death by Athens, against the charges lodged against him at his trial. These chapters present a revised and expanded version of Xenophon's independent work, *The Apology of Socrates*. The rest of the *Memorabilia* continues this defense by showing that Socrates' words and deeds were beneficial to his companions and to Athens. Plato's Socrates claims to know nothing. If that were true, then Socrates would be acting immorally in spending so much time with young people, as he would not know whether his influence on them was bad or good. Xenophon's Socrates has a great deal of moral wisdom, which he generously shares with his young associates, thereby improving their lives. *Memorabilia* is a rich and episodic work, portraying Socrates in conversation with a great variety of people on a great variety of subjects.

For the historian of philosophy *Memorabilia* can be frustrating, since Xenophon has Socrates discuss or assert many interesting philosophical theses, but—in contrast to Plato's dialogues—the arguments for these theses are often entirely missing or else condensed or weak. The interpreter's difficult but rewarding task is to reconstruct the philosophical arguments and outlook that underlie the claims.

According to Xenophon, Socrates benefited his companions in large part by his outstanding moral example. But in addition, by means of argument and advice, Socrates made his young associates more pious and just, and he discouraged overambitious and ignorant young men from seeking power. Xenophon stresses more than Plato does Socrates' concrete practical wisdom and his intense interest not only in abstract definitions of moral concepts but also in helping the people around him live better lives.

Symposium, or *Dinner Party,* is Xenophon's most polished and enjoyable Socratic work. Whereas the *Symposium* that Plato wrote is magnificent and profound, Xenophon's *Symposium* is light and charming, but with the serious purpose of presenting philosophical views on love, virtue, and education. Of those present at the dinner gathering, Socrates has the most *kalokagahia*—an untranslatable Greek term meaning something close to virtue or nobility of character. Nobility of character is a central concern in all of Xenophon's Socratic and political writings, but *Symposium* highlights an underappreciated feature of Socrates' noble character: his urbanity. Socrates displays the exact mixture of humor and seriousness, irony and tact, and frivolity without a hint of coarseness that make for an ideal dinner companion. Other more familiar Socratic themes are also stressed. What one should love in another person is not money or power or physical beauty but rather virtue and nobility of character. In the case of the young, one should love their *potential* for nobility of character. The sexual urge behind ordinary Greek homosexual attraction is spiritualized by Socrates into a force for moral education.

Although overshadowed by Plato's, Xenophon's *Symposium* was greatly admired in antiquity, as it has been admired by others since. A work of philosophy, it also has historical value in giving us a more realistic picture than Plato's does of what an actual Athenian dinner party might have been like.

Oeconomicus, or *Estate Manager,* is not about economics in the modern sense but rather household or estate management. Its moral and political importance is obvious: relations between husband and wife, parents and children, and (in ancient Greece) master and slave all fall within its scope. *Oeconomicus* was thus pathbreaking as the earliest work devoted to this vitally important branch of practical philosophy. The dialogue shows Socrates in the unusual role of student: Ischomachus, a perfect country gentleman, teaches Socrates the basic principles of managing or ruling a country estate. While the historical Socrates spent all of his life in the city of Athens, Xenophon had considerable experience as an estate manager. Toward the end of the 390s, perhaps because of his pro-Sparta activities, Xenophon was banished from Athens. He then settled down at an estate near Olympia, where he led the life of a country gentleman, farming, hunting, and also writing. Just as Plato put his own ideas into Socrates' mouth in *The Republic,* so in *Oeconomicus* Xenophon puts his ideas into the mouth of Ischomachus.

A basic theme of the work is that the art of ruling others begins with the art of ruling oneself. Xenophon and Plato agree on this thesis. They also agree, against Aristotle, that the art of ruling oneself, the art of ruling a household, and the art of ruling a city are fundamentally the same.

The section of the work in which Ischomachus describes how he taught his young wife her domestic duties is the longest and most detailed classical Greek portrayal of the role of women in the household. Although written from the point of view of a man, it is an important source for women's history.

From a literary point of view, Xenophon's *Anabasis*, or *March Up Country*, is his most successful work. *Anabasis* is a "good read," combining entertaining narrative with vivid and colorful details. In 401 Xenophon decided (ignoring advice from Socrates) to join a Greek militia accompanying Cyrus the Younger on an expedition to overthrow Cyrus's brother Artaxerxes, ruler of Persia. *Anabasis* recounts these experiences. At Cunaxa near Babylon, Cyrus was killed and his army collapsed. The Greek mercenaries (the Ten Thousand) found themselves far from Greece and surrounded by powerful enemies. Xenophon played a chief role in rallying the dispirited troops, eventually leading them on their march through 1,500 kilometers of unknown and hostile territory until they reached the Black Sea. The chant of the troops as they sighted shore has become famous: *"Thalatta! Thalatta!"* ("The sea! The sea!")

This successful retreat was a brilliant military exploit. It was also a significant turning point in world history, since it demonstrated the weakness of Persian military power in the face of superior Greek tactics and discipline. The success of Xenophon and his band of mercenaries gave grounds for hope that the Greeks might conquer Persia—a dream realized three-quarters of a century later by Alexander the Great.

Generations and generations of schoolmasters assigned *Anabasis* to generations and generations of schoolboys, partly to teach them Greek, but also to teach them virtue. As Xenophon recounts the military adventures of the Ten Thousand, the virtues of the ordinary Greek soldier shine through: courage, determination, piety, independence of spirit combined with a capacity for teamwork. These are just the virtues that schoolmasters aimed to teach their charges. Historians of military strategy have also always valued *Anabasis* highly. The tactics of retreat fighting and techniques for commanding a rear guard that Xenophon described (and presumably helped to invent) were major and enduring contributions to military science.

Xenophon's *Hellenica* is a history of Greek affairs from 411 to 362 B.C.E., although the chronological limits are accidental to the narrative. Thucydides died before completing his great history of the Peloponnesian War, so Xenophon began his history where Thucydides' history ends. In *Hellenica* Xenophon writes the political and military history of his times. It is valuable as the only surviving complete, contemporary account of the period. Xenophon's narrative is highly selective, however, and shows marked pro-Sparta and anti-Thebes bias. It is therefore important to supplement and correct Xenophon's history with such other sources as *Hellenica oxyrhynchia* and the works of the later authors Diodorus Siculus and Plutarch. Overall, *Hellenica* is one of Xenophon's least successful works. As a product of the historian's craft, *Hellenica* is dramatically inferior to the works of his predecessors Herodotus and Thucydides, and also to his own *Anabasis*.

DONALD MORRISON

Bibliography

Texts and Translations

Bowen. A. J., ed. and trans. *Symposium*. Warminster: Aris and Phillips, 1998.

Marchant, E. C. *Xenophontis opera omnia*. Oxford: Oxford University Press, 1900–1920 (in Greek).

Xenophon. 7 vols. Loeb Classical Library.

Studies

Anderson, John K. *Xenophon*. New York: Scribner, 1974.

Breitenbach, Hans R. *Xenophon von Athen*. Stuttgart: Druckenmuller, 1966. (Published separately and as vol. 9, A2 of *Pauly's Realencyclopädie der classischen Altertumswissenschaft*.)

Gera, Deborah. *Xenophon's Cyropaedia: Style, Genre, and Literary Technique*. Oxford: Clarendon Press, 1993.

Gil, Juan, ed. and trans. *Economico*. Madrid: Sociedad de Estudios y Publicaciones, 1966.

Gray, Vivienne. *The Framing of Socrates: The Literary Interpretation of Xenophon's Memorabilia*. Stuttgart: Steiner, 1998.

Guthrie, W. K. C. *A History of Greek Philosophy*, vol. 3: *The Fifth-Century Enlightenment*. Cambridge: Cambridge University Press, 1969.

Morrison, Donald R. *Bibliography of Editions, Translations, and Commentary on Xenophon's Socratic Writings, 1600–Present*. Pittsburgh, Pa.: Mathesis Press, 1988.

Patzer, A. *Der historische Socrates*. Darmstadt: Wissenschaftliche Buchgesellschaft, 1987.

Pomeroy, Sarah, ed. and trans. *Oeconomicus: A Social and Historical Commentary, with a New English Translation*. Oxford: Oxford University Press, 1994.

Strauss, Leo. *On Tyranny*, rev. and expanded ed. New York: Free Press, 1991.

———. *Xenophon's Socrates*. Ithaca, N.Y.: Cornell University Press, 1972.

Tatum, James. *Xenophon's Imperial Fiction*. Princeton: Princeton University Press, 1989.

Vander Waerdt, Paul, ed. *The Socratic Movement*. Ithaca, N.Y.: Cornell University Press, 1994.

ZENO

Zᴇɴᴏ ᴏꜰ Eʟᴇᴀ ɪꜱ ʀᴇᴍᴇᴍʙᴇʀᴇᴅ ᴛᴏᴅᴀʏ thanks to a fairly large number of accounts. Those of Diogenes Laertius, Diodorus Siculus, Plutarch, Clement of Alexandria, and Philostratus are limited to unverifiable biographical events. In addition to these, there are a few maxims attributed to Zeno. The sources for his contributions to philosophy are Plato, Aristotle, and Simplicius, who in turn cites Alexander of Aphrodisias, Eudemus of Rhodes, and Porphyry of Tyre, as well as Themistius and Philoponus, who simply reiterate Simplicius. Clearly, on this front, the Aristotelian tradition prevails.

According to the doxographers, whose accounts differ slightly, we can estimate that Zeno reached maturity around 460 B.C.E. and surmise that he rarely left his native Elea in southern Italy. Although the *Suda* credits him with four works, only one was known in antiquity, between Plato's time and Simplicius's. Proclus describes this text as a dry collection of forty "arguments." Of these, Aristotle discusses six, at times only through allusion and without citing the texts; Plato may refer to one. Simplicius, however, quotes passages of Zeno's book treating two additional arguments, and Diogenes Laertius adds another. We can therefore recreate, with more or less precision depending on the case, roughly ten of Zeno's arguments.

Plato's account is found in *Parmenides* (127e6–128d6, 135d8–136b), where he confirms that Zeno, as a supporter of the philosophy of Parmenides of Elea, conceived all of his arguments for the purpose of refuting the existence of "plurality," and claimed success. Although their works were not organized according to the same principle (Parmenides argued for monism and Zeno against pluralism), they were both defending the same thesis, and Zeno sought to demonstrate the absurdity in the position of those who found Parmenides' monism absurd. Skeptical though we may be about the scenario described in Plato's dialogue, where Parmenides, Zeno, and Socrates all meet in Athens, we may nevertheless accept Plato's interpretation of the doctrine in the light of the very learned discussion that has taken place among specialists on this point. It is plausible that a passage from a different dialogue (*Phaedrus* 261d6–8) gives a very brief summary of the aporias (paradoxes) that Zeno derived from the hypothesis of plurality: if one wants to refute a thesis by reducing it to an absurdity, one must show that, taken as a hypothesis, it leads to contradiction. Popular tradition has held, for example, that Zeno denied the existence of motion. This is an oversimplification that ignores the meaning that this negation had in the context of his work in its entirety. I propose to examine those of Zeno's arguments that have come down to us, grouping them thematically.

THE ARGUMENTS AGAINST THE PLURALITY OF BEINGS, ACCORDING TO SIMPLICIUS

If, like the Greeks, we agree to make a substantive of the present participle of the verb *to be*, to designate that which is permanent by itself and identical to itself, as opposed to changeable and unreliable appearance, then we can say that "being" is properly what Parmenides wanted to characterize in his doctrine. He did this in the negative, by excluding "what is not": in other words, becoming (for how can something become without ceasing to be, or without not yet being?), difference (for how can something be other without yet ceasing to be the same?), and division (for how can something be divided if nothingness and emptiness do not exist?). Thus being, or what exists absolutely, is immutable and permanent, one and identical to itself, indivisible, all of a piece, a fullness of being that is motionless and unique.

If the adversaries of the doctrine reject as absurd the affirmation of a unique being beyond appearances, they also have to deny that it is all of a piece and indivisible; and if it is divisible, then it is in fact divided, since any gap between the possible and the actual would imply a "becoming" that is excluded from being. Thus, in this hypothesis, there is a plurality of beings, each one existing absolutely, each one immutable and permanent, each one all of a piece and identical to itself, each one indivisible, for if it were divisible, then it would in turn be divided, and so on. Zeno set out to test the consistency of this thesis of a plurality of indivisible beings.

Zeno and his contemporaries doubtless knew that every segment of a straight line is divisible into two at its midpoint (which they probably knew how to determine with a ruler and compass): each half can also be divided in half, and so on, indefinitely; in addition, while a geometric magnitude is divisible in this way, the same word, *magnitude*, is applied in Greek to a physical body as well, to designate not only its size but also the body itself.

Once this had been posited, according to texts quoted by Simplicius, Zeno then raised two questions about the plurality of beings, the first concerning their number and the second their size, leading us to suppose that the adversaries he was addressing took pride in mathematics. With regard to number, if the existent is reduced to a multitude of indivisible beings, how many will there be, for example, in a given length? It is logical, on the one hand, that there should be twice as many in its entire length as there are in half of its length: thus there will be just as many beings as there must be, in each part of the length, and therefore the total number of beings will be finite. But, on the other hand, since what exists is not indivisible, it is therefore divisible everywhere. Thus the dichotomy of the length at its midpoint can be repeated on each half, and so on to infinity, so that between two beings there will always be others, and consequently beings will be infinite in number. Thus, if beings are a plurality, they will be, at the same time and in the same object, both finite and infinite in number, which is a contradiction.

Next, from the standpoint of size, nothing indivisible can have any parts, for if it did, it would be divisible; thus indivisibles can have no size, for everything that has size has parts. But even an infinite number of indivisible entities without magnitude, which are therefore nothing, could never constitute something of finite magnitude. Thus it is necessary for each of the ultimate products of infinite division to have magnitude; that means that each one contains at least two parts exterior to one another, contiguous, and with no point in common; hence these parts are in contact at at least two points, and these points are not without magnitude, since otherwise they would be nothing. Now, what we have said about an indivisible entity having magnitude will also be true about each of the parts mentioned above, and so on to infinity. To put it in more modern terms, each being contains at least a double infinity of points of contact that are not without some measure and is therefore infinite in magnitude. All finite magnitude, being made up of an infinity of such "indivisibles," is formed of an infinite number of infinite magnitudes, which is absurd. If this were the case, then the same things could be at the same time without magnitude and of infinite magnitude, which is a contradiction.

What Zeno shows is that the thesis of the plurality of beings contains an intrinsic incompatibility. It implies both the actual infiniteness of the division of a fixed magnitude (for once the indivisibility of the whole is rejected, division cannot be stopped) and the additive composition of this magnitude by means of the ultimate indivisible parts (for the physical composition of existing things is conceived by means of the mathematical additivity of magnitudes).

Another of Zeno's arguments seems to deal with the question of plurality as well (Aristotle, *Physics* VII.5.250a19–25; Simplicius, 1108.18): if a bushel of millet spilling creates noise, then a single grain or a tiny fraction of a grain must also make a noise, if it is true that the ratio of noises to one another is the same as the ratio that exists between the objects. Such an argument is directed against an adversary who maintains that facts that are sense-data are in themselves mathematical facts, arithmetical in this case, and that things form a divisible, physical reality, so that the elements that make up this real plurality are always additive and constitute, by their addition, physical magnitudes. This supposed adversary thus rejects the Eleatic distinction between being and appearance and grants an ontological meaning to arithmetic by allowing a plurality of beings whose magnitude or physical effect must add up in every case.

Finally, Plato's argument, succinctly reported in *Parmenides* (127d6–127e4), also concerns plurality: if beings are a plurality, they cannot fail to be both alike and unlike at the same time, which is impossible and contradictory. In fact, if beings are the ultimate and shared constitutive elements of tangible things, they must all be the same, identical, for otherwise they would not be ultimate but could be broken down into more fundamental elements. But if tangible things are varied—and if there is no distinction between appearance and being—then beings are necessarily dissimilar, for otherwise they could not account for this diversity. Those who seek to relate the diversity of appearances to an ontological plurality transform into a rigid, absolute, and irreparable contradiction an opposition that, in the world of appearance, differing from being, fades into the relativity of different points of view.

"KINEMATIC" ARGUMENTS ACCORDING TO ARISTOTLE

In *Physics*, Aristotle echoes four of Zeno's aporias concerning movement, aiming to prove that despite what the senses tell us, movement is impossible.

The first of these asserts the impossibility of movement, on the ground that the moving object must arrive first at its halfway point before reaching its final goal (Aristotle, *Physics* VI.9.239b9–14; cf. VI.2.233a21–32; VIII.8.263a4–11 and 263a23–263b6). We are back to the midpoint that divides a distance to be covered into two equal parts; this argument is known in English as the "Racecourse" or the "Dichotomy." Obviously, in the elliptical form the argument is given by Aristotle, it is important to understand that the same reasoning process is applied to the first half of the course, and so on. Thus the argument embraces infinity. It goes as follows: if you actually divide a continuous line in half, the point of division is used twice, once as the end point of the first half, and again as the starting point of the second; thus the moving object must both reach this point and depart from it. Since the dichotomy repeats itself ad infinitum, the moving object has to cross an infinite number of actual points, achieve an infinite number of contacts, or, rather, accomplish an infinite number of tasks of the arriving/departing type. Now, this is impossible in a finite amount of time, since each task, when it is actually carried out, requires a constant amount of time, however short, and an infinite number of tasks requires an infinite amount of time.

Hence we can see that if motion is impossible, it is so under particular hypothetical conditions similar to those of the preceding arguments. The distance to cover (as a physical object) is viewed as made up of indivisible beings all actually given, separate and therefore contiguous. The length of the trajectory results from an additive process of composition, starting with real, indivisible "elements," and at the same time the infinite divisibility of a finite magnitude is recognized. Hence the contradiction: a finite distance demands an infinite amount of time to be covered.

The second kinematic argument reported in Aristotle is well known as the "Achilles" (Aristotle, *Physics* VI.9.239b14–29): the faster of two runners

(Achilles) can never overtake the slower (the tortoise) for the faster must first reach the point from which the slower left, and so on, in such a way that the latter will always have a head start. We must keep in mind that the aporia does not concern the lengths of the intervals, the infinite number of which introduces a limit that ancient Greeks could calculate very easily once Achilles' handicap and the ratio n of the distances covered in the same time were known: the ratio of Achilles' total distance to the handicap, is $n/(n-1)$, the well-known *epimorphios* ratio. Commentators who assert that Zeno did not know how to compute geometric progression are missing the point. The question once again concerns the points Achilles must cross, and it is quite true that the point at which the faster moving object actually catches up with the slower is none of those belonging to the infinite sequence of points defined by the argument, points that the faster object must cross one after another: if the points are actual physical entities, Achilles must indeed complete an infinite task before even reaching the point that "closes" the line, where he would overtake the tortoise. In substance, therefore, the argument is identical to the Racecourse paradox and it obeys the same implicit hypothesis: it would take Achilles an infinite amount of time to complete all the steps that make up this infinite sequence.

Besides the fact that, to divide the course, the Racecourse argument employs the ratio $1/2$, and the Achilles the ratio of $1/n$, where n can be any whole number, we can imagine that the Achilles answers the following objection to the Racecourse dichotomy: if one repeats the division as often as necessary, one must be able to reach a segment of the distance so small that to cover it a moving object—even a very slow one—would take only an instant, and therefore the entire distance would be covered in a finite number of instants. This objection misses the point of the argument; it is possible only because the intervals considered successively in producing the dichotomy, if taken in the direction of the moving body's motion, are *overlapping* intervals: if the moving object manages to cover an interval of a given length "in an instant," however small that length may be, it will have succeeded in beginning its race, and it will have before it only a finite number of tasks to accomplish, whatever they may be. Thus, if only for didactic reasons, Zeno had to show successive intervals that did not overlap but that were juxtaposed in succession, and that is what the Achilles manages to do. Moreover, the Achilles argument divides time as it does space, and rejects the "instant" at the end of the indefinitely repeated division. The structure of the argument does not allow for the problem to be resolved by "forcing" the matter, a "final" interval crossed "in an instant." The presumed adversary is compelled to agree that one and only one "point" on the trajectory must correspond to one and only one "moment," and to recognize that in a single moment one can cross only a single point.

Zeno then counters with his third argument: the "Arrow." Aristotle summarizes it by saying that the arrow in its flight—a moving object, we notice, even faster than Achilles—is stationary (*Physics* VI.9.239b29–33; cf. 239b5– 9). This conclusion is reached by considering time as made up of instants, that is, by extending to time one of the implicit hypotheses that we have identified with respect to space. This argument can be compared to a proposition that several accounts attribute to Zeno: "A moving body moves neither [in a place] where it is nor [in a place] where it is not" (Diogenes Laertius, *Lives of Eminent Philosophers* IX.72). As a whole, the argument most probably took the following shape: everything is at rest whenever it is in a space equal to itself, and everything is, for a given instant in time, in such a space; now, at any instant, a moving body is in the moment and consequently the arrow—in mid-air, flying—is immobile.

Attaching a single instant of time to every point in the trajectory, and vice versa, is pointless if time is "composed" of instants—in other words, if these instants are consecutive, and if the points are contiguous. At every instant, the "moving object" can be located in one point of its trajectory, where it is at rest, and no real movement is produced by juxtaposing immobilities. The argument applies whether the indivisibles of time and space are finite or infinite in number.

There is only one recourse left to the adversary attempting to defend the idea of movement: to argue that, in a moment in time, a moving object passes from one point to another one immediately next to it. Called the "Moving Blocks," or the "Stadium," Zeno's last argument is his response: the term *stadium* proves useful for talking about rectilinear and parallel trajectories (Aristotle, *Physics* VI.9.239b33–240a18). Let us imagine three such trajectories, A, B, C, and on each of them are "blocks" arranged in rows. Each block is treated as though undivided; each is equal to every other; all are identical in shape; and each row has an equal number (an even number), which we shall call $2n$. Row A remains immobile in the middle of the stadium; B and C move in opposite directions passing A; the first block of each row, at the start, is lined up with the middle of row A. Then let us suppose that at the end of the movement, the first B has reached one end of row A while the first C has simultaneously reached the other end, and the first B has thus passed before n A, the first C before $2n$ B, so that the time of one is half the time of the other, but, at the same time, the first B has passed before $2n$ C, so that the time of the first B is equal to that of the first C, even though it is only half of it. Consequently, a given time is the same as its double, which is absurd.

It has been said that Zeno had no concept of relative speed; the question is, rather, the following: what structure of space and time is necessary to make the notion of relative speed intelligible? As Aristotle emphasized, the validity of the argument rests entirely on the following axiom: the time it takes for a B to pass every A and for a C to pass every B is the same. But this axiom itself presupposes that the blocks are treated as indivisible—in other words, that space is made up additively of contiguous points and time of successive instants. The Stadium argument "stages" the cost of imagining for every point another point that is immediately contiguous in space, and for every instant another instant that follows it immediately in time, and motion as the passage from one element to the next: the instant of a B passing an A splits into two "instants," in which the B passes 2 C's (as well as from one C to another). Now, contiguity and the additivity of constitutive elements are what we get if we presuppose magnitudes and physical bodies that can be reduced to indivisible entities that really exist: the beings in the arguments summarized by Simplicius.

Another of Zeno's arguments, mentioned by Aristotle, illustrates this point well (*Physics* IV.1.209a23–26 and IV.3.210b23–37; cf. Simplicius, 562.3–6 and 563.17–19). It involves "place," and it can be understood as follows: if a "place," for example the trajectory of the moving body, is made up of "points" existing in reality, in short, of beings, and since every being is in a place, there must be a place of the place, and so on indefinitely, which is absurd; consequently, "space" constituted in this way does not exist.

All of this corroborates Plato's claim that all of Zeno's arguments were directed against the plurality of beings. In his "kinematic arguments" Zeno shows that if those who argued for the existence of motion (as anything other than mere appearance) thought they could base the argument on the thesis of plurality as opposed to Parmenidean immobility, they failed, and that ontologically, in any case, motion, change, and becoming are impossible.

RESOLUTIONS OF THE APORIAS

Zeno reasons within the framework of a physical world where there exists in actuality an infinite number of real and distinct "points," in pairs, a world that is actually ontologically plural. This framework is characteristic of the thesis that he means to refute as absurd, it being, a contrario, out of the question that the Parmenidean being should contain in actuality an infinity of distinct elements, since it is not divisible.

From a modern point of view, the aporias are resolved in the following way. We can consider the (ideal) points that divide a continuous line, such as a straight segment, according to a given iterative law; hence, they are separate from one another and form an infinite, enumerable sequence that we can number. The set of these points can be ordered as the set of whole numbers can, but it is not measurable; all we have left to do is to add up the series of lengths of intervals, producing a sum limited to the length of the segment. Alternatively, we can consider the totality of points of the segment that form an infinite and nonenumerable set, but then the set is not ordered like a set of whole numbers: there are no two contiguous points (the points cannot be numbered, or no point has an immediate successor), and there is no question of considering the length of the line as resulting from some sort of addition of all the points-elements. What is true of points in a line is also true of instants in time. The paradoxes developed by Zeno result from the assumption of the double hypothesis: there is an infinite set of elements, the end result of repeated division, and there is a possibility of adding the magnitudes of the indivisible entities together to obtain the magnitude of the segment of the continuum under consideration.

Aristotle saw very clearly that he had to accept the infinite divisibility of a continuum, even a physical one, of time on the same pattern as space, as the "Achilles" argument had shown. But he rejected the second premise of the aporias, repeating that a line is not "composed" of points, nor time of moments. What, then, would prevent one from "composing" a finite line by adding an infinite number of points? Aristotle's reply consists of eliminating actual infinity. Never is the totality of points of one section of a continuous line given in actuality and simultaneously. Only certain specific points, the ends, the middle, and so on, are given in actuality. The others exist only potentially, for division is never achieved and will never reach the ultimate element; it is infinite to be sure, but only potentially infinite. It suffices for a continuum to be indefinitely divisible, in other words, for division always to be capable of being taken beyond the point it has reached. Continuity does not boil down to contiguity of elements: in a continuum, these exist only potentially, blended together in some way. The doctrine of potential infinity has in fact been found by mathematicians to be sufficient. It was not until the end of the 19th century that infinity became conceivable as actual infinity through concepts developed by modern mathematics.

However, the Aristotelian distinction between the actual and the potential, beginning with actual infinity and potential infinity, came after Zeno's time. Starting from premises that his contemporaries took for granted in an attempt to understand the measurement of distance and time in motion, and more generally the texture of a physical continuum, Zeno, as a faithful Eleatic, could show only their intrinsic contradictions.

ZENO AND THE HISTORY OF PHILOSOPHY

Diogenes Laertius reports, and Sextus Empiricus confirms, that Aristotle viewed Zeno as the inventor of dialectics (Diogenes Laertius, *Lives* IX.25, VIII.57; Sextus Empiricus, *Adv. Math.* VII.6). Dialectics, he explained, takes accepted beliefs as premises to deduce consequences and to submit the beliefs to debate by examining whether or not the consequences were coherent. Already in Plato's work, the testing of a hypothesis by examining the non-contradiction of its consequences was part of dialectical training, as seen in *Parmenides* in the example of Zeno himself. This process of refutation by showing the absurdity of the opposite thesis would be rightly a technique of logic whose invention we owe to Zeno.

What, then, were the "accepted ideas" that Zeno took as targets in defending the Eleatic doctrine against its detractors? Many answers have been proposed, some maintaining that these targets concerned merely "common sense," which grants the plurality of things and the existence of movement as an immediate given, based on the senses, while others maintain that the targets were one or another of the various "pluralist" theories that predated the Eleatics or were contemporary with them. But an analysis of the set of arguments themselves suggests that Zeno sought to refute an idea that was still quite foreign to the distinctions between the perceptible and the intelligible, between the physical and the mathematical, between the physical and the ontological, between the potential and the actual, between arithmetic unity and the ultimate element of the division of magnitudes. This idea grew out of syncretic, archaic thought. Now, the confusion among ontology, physics, geometry, and arithmetic is quite obvious in Aristotle's summary—which shows signs of perplexity, moreover—of the old Pythagorean doctrine prevailing in southern Italy during the period when Zeno was defending Parmenides. Moreover, it is most likely that the Pythagoreans were critical of Parmenidean monism. However, this historical interpretation has largely lost the credit it had gained from the work of Paul Tannery. While it is not possible to go into the details here, the debate is worth recalling.

After Zeno, it was hard not to take into account the aporias to which he had drawn attention. Some aspects of doctrines from later times seem designed to avoid those questions. For example, Democritean atomism rejects the infinite divisibility of physical magnitudes: it posits atoms as unbreakable and varying in shape and size, and it conceives of the continuum as a vacuum in which the movement of atoms nevertheless exists. Platonism, for its part, makes a radical distinction between mathematical entities and the things of the perceptible world, by positing the former as ideals; this may be no more than a partial response, but it is nevertheless a decisive first step. Aristotle maintains this distinction by presenting mathematical entities as abstractions of the physical world, and his doctrine of potential infinity, valid for both the geometrical continuum and the physical continuum (Aristotle is no atomist), resolves for good—as we have seen—Zeno's aporias. The Aristotelian and even the Scholastic traditions were content to adopt this position; however, it entails a distinction between the actual and the potential that has been challenged in modern times.

If we set aside the misunderstandings that we can attribute to lack of knowledge of the historical doctrinal context, all the greatest thinkers have kept Zeno's arguments in mind. We see this, for example, in Spinoza, in the "Letter to Louis Meyer" (April 20, 1663), in which he explains that time, measure, and number exist only in the mind, as modes of thought; we see it in *The Principles of Descartes's Philosophy* (II, VI, scholia) in which Spinoza contests the existence of a minimum of time. There is also Pascal, who criticizes the indivisibles in depth at the end of the first section of the treatise *On the Geometrical Mind;* and there is Kant, who evokes Zeno with regard to the "cosmological conflict of reason with itself," a conflict linked to the assumption that the world is an entity in itself (*Critique of Pure Reason* I, II, 2.2.7). At the end of the 19th century and in the 20th, discussion of Zeno of Elea regained its vigor, owing to the influence of neo-Kantianism, to mathematical theorizing on the actual infinite, and to the development of the history of Greek science. Those debates have not always shed any new or relevant light on the topic, and they have led some to conclude that the famous aporias constitute an eternal defiance of human reason. I hope to have shown that that is not at all the case.

Maurice Caveing
Translated by Elizabeth Rawlings and Jeannine Pucci

Bibliography

Texts and Translations

Diels, Hermann. *Die Fragmente der Vorsokratiker.* Ed. Walther Kranz. Berlin: Weidmann, 1968.

Lee, H. D. P. *Zeno of Elea: A Text, with Translation and Notes.* Cambridge: Luzac, 1936.

Simplicius. *In Physica.* Ed. Hermann Diels. 2 vols. Berlin, 1882–1895.

Untersteiner, Mario. *Zenone: Testimonianze e Frammenti.* Amsterdam: Hakkert, 1967.

Studies

Brochard, Victor. "Les arguments de Zénon d'Elée contre le mouvement." *Comptes-rendus de l'Académie des sciences morales* 29 (1888): 555–568. Repr. in *Etudes de philosophie ancienne et de philosophie moderne.* Paris: Alcan, 1912; Vrin, 1974.

——. "Les prétendus sophismes de Zénon d'Elée." *Revue de métaphysique et de morale* (1893): 209–215. Repr. in *Etudes de philosophie ancienne et de philosophie moderne.*

Caveing, Maurice. *Zénon d'Elée: Prolégomènes aux doctrines du continu.* Paris: Vrin, 1982.

Fraenkel, Hermann. "Zeno of Elea's Attacks on Plurality." *American Journal of Philology* 63 (1942): 1–25, 193–206.

Fritz, Kurt von. "Zenon von Elea." In *Paulys Realencyclopädie der classischen Altertumswissenschaft.* 2nd ser., 19.2. Stuttgart: Metzler, 1972. Pp. 53–83.

Grunbaum, A. *Modern Science and Zeno's Paradoxes*. London: George Allen & Unwin, 1967.

Koyre, Alexandre. "Remarques sur les paradoxes de Zénon." Trans. from *Jahrbuch für Philosophie und Phänomenologische Forschung 5*. Halle, 1922. Repr. in *Etudes d'histoire de la pensée philosophique*. Paris: Gallimard, 1971. Pp. 9–35.

Lachelier, Jules. "Note sur les deux derniers arguments de Zénon d'Elée contre l'existence du mouvement." *Revue de métaphysique et de morale* 18 (1910): 345–355.

Raven, J. E. *Pythagoreans and Eleatics*. Chicago: Argonaut, 1967.

Solmsen, Friedrich. "The Tradition about Zeno of Elea Reexamined." *Phronesis* 16, no. 2 (1971): 116–141.

Tannery, Paul. "Le concept scientifique du continu: Zénon d'Elée et Georg Cantor." *Revue philosophique de la France et de l'étranger* 20, no. 2 (1885): 385ff.

Vlastos, Gregory. "Plato's Testimony concerning Zeno of Elea." *Journal of Hellenic Studies* 95 (1975): 136–162.

———. "Zeno of Elea." In *The Encyclopedia of Philosophy*. Ed. P. Edwards. New York and London: Macmillan, 1967. Vol. 8, pp. 369–379.

CURRENTS OF THOUGHT

THE ACADEMY

THE HISTORY OF THE ACADEMY seems better suited than that of any other school to illustrate the creative freedom that is a hallmark of Greek thought. For this reason, the bond of tradition is particularly difficult to discern when one seeks to define an Academic. From an institutional point of view, the matter is a simple one: an Academic philosopher is someone who belonged to the school founded by Plato, a school that functioned without significant difficulties under a series of scholarchs, or heads, up to the 1st century C.E. But if we want to bring even a modicum of philosophical coherence into correspondence with this historical unity, we find ourselves with a real problem. What type of continuity could there have been, for example, between Plato, the inventor of the theory of Forms, and Speusippus, who denied their existence? How can we include in the same lineage the dogmatic philosopher Xenocrates, whom the ancients credited with inventing the tripartite division of philosophy (physics, ethics, logic), and Arcesilaus, who preached suspension of judgment in all circumstances?

INSTITUTIONAL HISTORY

Even in antiquity, some writers attempted to solve the problem just raised: preferring to emphasize differences rather than commonalities, they distinguished among several Academies. The most complete classification is that of Sextus Empiricus. Referring to sources he does not cite, Sextus identifies three distinct Academies: the Early, that is, Plato's; the Middle, that of Arcesilaus; and the New, that of Carneades and Clitomachus. He even points out that others added a fourth, that of Philon, and a fifth, that of Antiochus of Ascalon. Despite its apparent rigor, this classification has no absolute value: it is confirmed neither by Cicero, who knew the Academy from the inside, as a pupil of Philon of Larissa, nor by Plutarch, who identified with the Academy and knew it well. Sextus's account proves only that the ancient historians of philosophy had dwelt on genuine differences to justify the discontinuity in their presentation of the Academy. But what Sextus does not make clear is that these philosophical changes never disturbed the institutional unity of the school.

We know that at the age of twenty-eight, after Socrates' death, Plato traveled through various regions in the Mediterranean Basin; when he returned to Athens he began to teach in a gymnasium located in a zone outside the walls. This site was named after the hero Hecademus, whose legend, passed down in various versions, is connected with the account of the arrival of the Dioscurides in Greece. Some time later Plato set up his school in a small garden near the gymnasium. The Academy was founded in 387, and it was long believed that this institution had the status of an association. However, such a status did not exist under Athenian law, nor was the school defined by Plato's ownership of the property. Institutionally, then, the Academy existed only through the selection of a scholarch; by this means, an Academic chosen by his peers was designated a successor to Plato. The first succession seems to have been arranged by Plato himself, who chose his nephew Speusippus as scholarch. The election, if there was one, was merely a ratification of the master's choice. After Speusippus's death, however, a real electoral process was adopted. One might have expected that the choice would be Plato's most brilliant student, Aristotle, but whether by chance or as the result of some maneuvering, Aristotle was traveling in Macedonia at the time. Xenocrates just barely won the election over two other candidates who, after their defeat, chose to found other schools rather than remain in the Academy. Xenocrates was not the most brilliant philosopher: Plato himself had said that Aristotle needed a rein and Xenocrates a goad. The election seems to have been based on a moral criterion, Xenocrates having qualities in this realm that Speusippus was said to have lacked. Was the selection of other scholarchs the object of such close competition? The sources are silent on this point. We may suppose, in any case, that no scholarch tried to impose his own successor himself, even though some let their personal preference be known: according to Diogenes Laertius—but how credible is he?—Crates and Arcesilaus were made scholarchs because they were special favorites of Polemon and Crantor.

According to the most rigorous chronology, the dates of election of the principal scholarchs of the Academy were as follows: 348/7, Speusippus; 339/8, Xenocrates; 314/3, Polemon; 270/69, Crates; 268/264?, Arcesilaus; 244/3, Lacydus; 167/6, Carneades; 127/6, Clitomachus; 110/9, Philon of Larissa.

Until fairly recently, it was generally thought that the Academy had functioned without interruption from Plato's day until the Athenian schools were closed by Justinian. In fact the history of the school founded by Plato ends in 88 B.C.E., the year in which the last scholarch, Philon of Larissa, sought refuge in Rome, fleeing an Athens besieged by Mithridates. This date marks a break in the institutional line, and the efforts of Philon's dissident disciple, Antiochus of Ascalon, to substitute what he believed to be philosophical legitimacy for institutional legitimacy proved vain. At various times, philosophers claimed to be representing the Academy—Plutarch, for example—or founded Platonic schools. However, these thinkers were never Academics in the historical sense of the term.

THE EARLY ACADEMY

The designation Early Academy was of course given a posteriori to the scholarchs in the line from Speusippus to Crates, to emphasize the importance of modifications introduced after their time by Arcesilaus. It is only recently that the Early Academy has been studied in depth, and these efforts have run into considerable difficulty. No works by the scholarchs of the Early Academy have survived, and Aristotle, our most complete source for an understanding of their thought, is by no means an objective historian. Committed to refuting Plato and the Academics, he proceeded with his demonstration without troubling to give precise references. Speusippus, for example, while very important in *Metaphysics*, is cited only twice. It is thus difficult to know what can be attributed to each of the philosophers of the Early Academy. An additional difficulty arises in connection with learned controversies over Plato's "oral teaching." The group of exegetes known as the Tübingen school (Konrad Gaiser, Hans Joachim Kramer) used some passages from Aristotle to construct the theory according to which Plato's oral teaching was more important than his writings; an understanding of that teaching was indispensable, according to the theory, for an analysis of the philosophy of Speusippus and Xenocrates.

Speusippus

The Early Academy was characterized from the outset by one fundamental feature: the abandonment of the theory of Forms as Plato had conceived it, and the search for what we may call a "substitute transcendence." Indeed, although Speusippus remained faithful to the Platonic dogmas, according to Diogenes Laertius, a reading of Aristotle's *Metaphysics* suggests that Plato's first successor did not maintain the doctrine of Forms, which had evolved over time in its conception but which the master had never completely renounced.

Why did Speusippus dissociate himself from Plato on such an essential point? We have no information about his motivations, but we may suppose that this decision did not merely express a desire to affirm his philosophical originality after the disappearance of Plato's overpowering personality. It probably resulted above all from a reckoning with all the objections to the Platonic Forms raised within the Academy. Does Aristotle not say that the school of Speusippus "abandoned Ideal number and posited mathematical number because they perceived the difficulty and artificiality of the Ideal Theory"? (*Metaphysics* XIII.9.1086a.3–6). These objections are analyzed by Plato himself in *Parmenides;* they are presented differently in the critiques formulated by Aristotle in *Metaphysics*, which takes up the themes already expressed in his book on ideas, prior to the founding of the Lyceum. In the

Platonic dialogue that bears his name, old Parmenides shows Socrates what difficulties await him when he considers the multiple world of the sensible as the copy of these Forms, which are absolute realities situated apart from the things that belong to them. Without going into the details of a very complex demonstration, we can recall some of the arguments here. If sensible things belong to separate Forms, do they belong to form as a whole? This would assume that each Form, present in each of its representations, is separate from itself. But if we abandon this hypothesis and assert that a sensible thing participates in only one aspect of Form, Form loses the essential unity that was presented as one of its characteristics.

Just as serious a difficulty arises with the argument that Aristotle calls the "third man." As expressed by Parmenides, the objection goes as follows: when we look at a collection of objects that appear great, there is in them a common characteristic by which we infer that greatness is one thing. But when we include in our thought at the same time greatness and things that appear great, there will also appear a greatness in relation to which all these appear great. Accordingly, as Parmenides tells Socrates, "each of your ideas will no longer be one, but their number will be infinite" (*Parmenides* 132b). It is quite likely that, in Aristotle's day, the objections expressed in *Metaphysics* were also debated in the Academy. In that text, the Stagirite condemns what he calls *ekthesis,* the Platonic separation between the world of Forms and the world of sensible realities, in which he sees the source of insuperable contradictions. For example, if each Idea constitutes a separate reality, this reality is impossible to define, for the definition will be made up of common nouns, and this implies that the definition will apply equally to other things. Moreover, how could Forms be, as Plato would have it, the cause of movement and change? By virtue of their immutable nature, they must rather be causes of repose. And if we seek to define the relation between a sensible object and the equivalent Form, we still find ourselves in a quandary: if a Form is identical to a thing both by nature and by name, it constitutes a useless doubling of the thing; and if a Form has nothing in common with a thing but a relation of homonomy, in what sense can the two belong together, given that there is an essential difference between the two realities? It is also possible that for Speusippus the theory of Forms was incompatible with the method of division *(diairesis)* by which Plato had believed he could surmount the objections put before him.

Speusippus thought he was escaping these difficulties by equating the absolute that Plato had found in the Forms with mathematics. His recourse to mathematics was not made ex nihilo, for mathematics already had an important place in Platonic philosophy. But whereas Plato viewed mathematical objects as intermediary beings between Forms and sensible things, Speusippus saw in numbers the characteristics that Plato attributed to Ideas.

According to Aristotle, Plato recognized three substances: Ideas, mathematical objects, and sensible things. For him, then, mathematical objects were intermediary between Numbers and ideal Figures, which did not differ essentially from any other Form, on the one hand, and the numbers and figures of the sensible, on the other. For example, between the necessarily imperfect circles of the sensible and the Idea of a circle, there exists the circle insofar as it is a mathematical object, defined by its perfect roundness. This intermediary status of mathematical objects explains the difference that Plato establishes in *The Republic* between mathematicians and dialecticians: the former reason from hypotheses, for which they seek verification, while the latter seek to attain an unconditional *(anhypotheton)* that will guarantee them absolute knowledge.

We know for certain from Aristotle that Speusippus rejected the theory of Forms: he believed neither in absolute numbers nor in absolute figures. If numbers and figures constituted for him the only absolute realities, this was not insofar as they were Forms but insofar as they were mathematical entities. It would be too simple to suppose that Speusippus reserved for numbers and figures the status that Plato assigned to all Forms. The matter is much more complex, for it is in the very conception of number that he expressed his difference in relation to his predecessor. For Plato, each ideal number, by virtue not of its nature as number but of its status as Form, constitutes a unity that is separate both from the numbers of the sensible world and from the other ideal numbers. Speusippus, on the contrary, defines each number not as a unique entity but as a set of units, since he derives them from two principles: One and multiplicity. The Speusippean number is, like the Platonic Ideas, an eternal reality, separate from the sensible world, and the figures are derived from it by analogy, the analogy of the point being number one, the line number two, and the plane number three. One of the principal problems that arise here is the status of the One: has it a substance different from that of the other numbers, or is it only the first of numbers? Aristotle writes: "Speusippus assumed still more kinds of substances starting with 'the One,' and positing principles for each kind: one for numbers, another for magnitudes, and then another for the soul" (*Metaphysics* VII.ii.1028b). Taken literally, the text implies that One is of a different nature from the other numbers, but in another context the same Aristotle says that, for Speusippus, mathematical numbers are the first entities. The explanation of this problem may lie in the ingenious solution proposed by Leonardo Tarán, who stressed the difference between Aristotle and Speusippus with regard to One. For Aristotle who, like Plato, begins the series of numbers with two, One is not a number but the principle of numbers. For Speusippus, on the contrary, One is identical with the number one, and it is for this reason that it is the principle of numbers. The contradiction that can be discerned in Aristotle concerning the Speusippean One can thus be explained by interference on this point between his own thought and that of the Academic.

As far as the second principle of number, multiplicity, is concerned, there is a paucity of evidence, and it is quite possible that Speusippus himself was not very explicit on this point, since Aristotle reproaches him for not having stated precisely how number can be composed of One and of Multiplicity. In any event, it is especially important to know how Speusippus moved from numbers, which he saw as the primary entities, to sensible objects. As we have already seen, he established a relation of likeness between figures and mathematical numbers. But according to Aristotle's account, Speusippus identified several substances: in addition to numbers and figures, the soul—which he claimed to be immortal—and others he did not specify, until he came to sensible objects, which he also apparently construed as a substance. Thus Aristotle criticizes him for representing the universe as a series of episodes lacking any relation one to another. This charge has to be assessed in relation to the fact that Speusippus did not equate the One with the Good; he asserted that for plants and animals the beautiful and the perfect did not meet in the seed but in the products derived from it. In thus refusing to give an essential status to the Good, he diverged from Platonism on a fundamental point of doctrine. According to Aristotle, in so doing he sought to avoid the difficulties involved in identifying the One and the Good—for example, the resultant need to equate Evil with Multiplicity. But how is one to conceive of this universe, which is made up of different substances and which reveals its perfection only at the end of its course?

For Aristotle, numbers cannot be the cause of anything, and that is one reason he viewed the Speusippean universe as a discontinuous series of "episodes." But we know that Speusippus himself established a relation of similarity, or *homoiotes,* between the different levels of reality. This concept is unquestionably inherited from Plato, for whom a thing is defined by a relation of similarity to the corresponding Form. But its use by Speusippus poses at least two problems. On the one hand, what can this similarity be when the first entities are no longer Forms, but numbers? On the other hand, if we recall that similarity goes hand in hand in Plato with causality, since *Phaedo* indicates that Ideas are at once models and causes of being and becoming, what does this really mean for Speusippus?

On the first point, Tarán emphasizes that each individual object turns out to be, for Speusippus, the center of a network of relations, the set of which constitutes its essence. If knowledge of numbers, which are the only eternal and immutable entities, is direct, knowledge of sensible realities requires that we allow concepts of similarity and difference to come into play, for these concepts are derived from this direct knowledge of number, and they allow us to determine the relation of the object in question to other objects. The classification of sensible objects thus presupposes a dichotomy, which arises when we establish whether two things are alike or unlike, and Speusippus applied this method to the classification of words, plants, and animals.

As for the second problem, that of the unity of the Speusippean universe, the volume of criticisms formulated by Aristotle show that this was the locus of a cluster of quite significant difficulties. As Léon Robin justly writes: "Speusippus, preserving the One as principle, considered it not as something real and actually in existence, but as an imperfect and indeterminate principle that is itself gradually determined and enriched" (p. 510). In considering that One is all in potentiality and nothing in actuality, the Academic left himself open to the objection formulated in *Metaphysics:* if One is not a substance, how could number exist as an independent reality? Aristotle also reproached the Platonists in general and Speusippus in particular for failing to define with adequate precision how numbers derive from principles. Finally, he rejected the Speusippean theory of similarity, which he criticized for confusing genus and species. As even the exegetes most favorable to Speusippus emphasize, it is hard to see how his system can end up with concepts such as "man" or "plant."

Another aspect of Speusippus's philosophy warrants mentioning precisely because it is responsible for a great deal of confusion, and that is its relation to Pythagoreanism. Speusippus was unquestionably interested in this philosophical doctrine, since according to Iamblichus he had written a "nice little book" on numbers, inspired by Philolaus's writings, a good half of which was consecrated to the decade. The question of just what in Iamblichus's account really comes from Speusippus is controversial. However much influence Pythagoreanism may have had on Speusippus, an essential divergence between these two philosophical beliefs persists: for the Pythagoreans, numbers were inherent in matter, while for Speusippus, they had a transcendent status.

The philosophy of Speusippus, who claimed to have gotten around the difficulties of Platonic idealism, itself drew numerous objections. Thus it is not surprising that Xenocrates did not maintain the same positions, and that he developed a system that he undoubtedly thought allowed him to avoid the contradictions with which his two predecessors were charged.

Xenocrates

Xenocrates' attempt at renewal found no favor in Aristotle's eyes. In fact the Stagirite seems to have thought that Xenocrates, instead of producing a satisfactory solution, had developed the most erroneous doctrine of all, since he combined the incoherent aspects of both Plato and Speusippus. Speusippus had been charged by Aristotle with "episodism." Xenocrates, for his part, placed special emphasis on the articulations of philosophic thought and on the definition of the nature of relations between the different levels of reality.

According to Sextus Empiricus, Xenocrates was the first to divide philosophy into three parts: physics, ethics, and logic. To be sure, Sextus, reclaiming a tradition that was to be echoed again in a passage of Cicero's *Academica*, says that this tripartite division was already implicitly present in Plato. The fact remains that Xenocrates was the one who provided a clear definition of this method, which played an important role in the constitution of the great Hellenistic documents, notably those of Stoicism.

Concerning the way reality is organized, several sources show us with what care Xenocrates sought to eradicate the Speusippean doctrine of a world made of mutually independent substances. Sextus Empiricus—whose testimony does seem to be contradicted by a much more allusive text by Theophrastus—tells us that Xenocrates identified three substances, the sensible, the intelligible, and the mixed, and that he situated the first inside heaven, the second outside, and the third in heaven itself. According to Sextus, Xenocrates had at least one thing in common with Speusippus: he affirmed the existence of intelligible realities external to the world. But while Speusippus identified these intelligible realities with numbers, Xenocrates went back to the theory of Ideas, which must have struck him, all things considered, as less subject to difficulties than the doctrine of his immediate predecessor. As further evidence of a tendency toward systematic simplification, one can point to the fact that Xenocrates criticized the multiplicity of Aristotelian categories and affirmed that all realities could be encompassed within the categories of the in-itself and the relative.

Relying on the testimony of Theophrastus, Léon Robin points out that Xenocrates was the first of the Platonists to pursue deduction from principles to its logical end, "and to determine, by their means, everything in the Universe" (p. 297, n. 272). This systematic use of deduction explains why Xenocrates has been viewed as the one of the Academics who most clearly foreshadowed Neoplatonism.

We actually know very little about the way Xenocrates conceived of principles. Aristostle refers at some length in *Metaphysics* to the various ways the Academics named the principle opposed to the One, but he does so without identifying the philosophers by name, and this allows for divergent interpretation on points of detail. We know from other sources that he opposed the *aenaon* to the One *(en)*; ancient Pythagoreanism, for which the *aenaon* was an important concept, interpreted it as "not-one," whereas the meaning was probably "always fluid." Did Xenocrates define this principle of multiplicity in terms of the Platonic dyad of the Large and the Small? This is entirely possible, but the anonymous character of Aristotle's discussion rules out any certainty on this point.

Nor do we know how Xenocrates explained the derivation of Ideas, which Plato said escape becoming, on the basis of the principles of the One and the Multiple. In contrast, we are better informed about the way he conceived of these Ideas, which were restored under his scholarchate after Speusippus's mathematical approach. Xenocrates defined the Idea as being "the exemplary cause of all the things that always subsist in the order of nature" (Proclus, *In*

Plat. Parm. IV.888). This definition, considered suspect by certain commentators owing to the fact of its inclusion in one of Proclus's texts (several passages of which are indeed foreign to the Early Academy), seems, on the contrary, characteristic of the Xenocratean effort to avoid the objections that had been raised to Speusippus. Indeed, the definition of the Idea as being inextricably model and cause constituted a display against the Aristotelian reproach of episodism. The reference to "things that always subsist in the order of nature" can be understood in opposition to the products of technology, which for their part are not included in this narrow relation to ideas and, beyond these, to principles. But Xenocrates' return to idealism does not mean that he is confined to an attitude of Platonic orthodoxy. His mature innovation in the domain of Ideas was in fact to develop more fully an alternative that Aristotle called "the worst" (*Metaphysics* XIII.viii.1083b), namely, the equation of ideal Number with mathematical number. For Aristotle, this way of thinking involves arbitrarily attributing to mathematical number properties that do not belong to it, and encountering anew all the difficulties of the ideal Platonic Number. Aristotle also reproaches Xenocrates for constructing magnitudes on the basis of matter and ideal Number, each geometric figure deriving from a Number-Idea. What is the status of these magnitudes? he inquires. Are they Ideas, and in what way will they contribute to establishing the existence of sensible things? As Margherita Isnardi Parente has rightly remarked, Aristotle criticizes Xenocrates both for his mathematical concept of Ideas and for endowing these with a kind of "intrinsic capacity for dynamic deployment in the spatial dimension" (*Senocrate,* p. 346). This was the point of view from which Aristotle and the Peripatetics vigorously criticized the Xenocratean theory—already present in Plato, according to certain scholars—of the indivisible line. Xenocrates, who, contrary to Speusippus, did not conceive of every number as deriving from the One (at once principle and first number), defended the thesis of indivisibility of all the magnitudes, each of them referring to a Number-Idea.

So far as cosmology is concerned, Xenocrates affirmed that in *Timaeus* Plato had evoked a creation of the world to clarify his thought, and he compared this method to the construction of a geometrical figure designed to make clear what the essence of a triangle is, for example, even if the triangle itself does not correspond perfectly to this transcendent reality. With regard to this interpretation, Aristotle critizes Xenocrates for seeking to "come to Plato's aid," and this concept of "aid" *(boetheia)* does not necessarily have a polemical origin; it can be interpreted as demonstrating genuine historical solidarity between the Early Academy and Plato. This solidarity left a great deal of room for interpretation (the little we know of Xenocrates' cosmology reveals significant differences from that of *Timaeus*), but it can be defined as the determination not to leave the last word to Aristotelian criticism on fundamental points. This dual aspect, original creation against a background of faith in the Platonic inspiration, appears with particular clarity in Xenocrates' definition of the soul as being a "number moving by itself" (*On the Soul* I.ii.404b27–28). In this definition we find both a Platonic element—the soul is defined in *Phaedrus* as self-moving—and the mathematical idealism characteristic of Xenocrates. Following the lead of Aristotle, who had criticized this definition, Simplicius claimed to demonstrate that the soul, for Xenocrates, was an intermediary between the Idea and the sensible, but there is every reason to believe that Xenocrates, who like Plato proclaimed the immortality of the soul, did not establish any difference between the soul and the ideal Number. Moreover, the fact that an entire doxographic tradition, perhaps inaugurated by Xenocrates himself, attributes this definition of the soul to Pythagoras changes nothing so far as the equivalency of this definition with the general orientation of the Xenocratean philosophy is concerned. After all, a text by Plutarch shows how the Academic—who had abandoned the tripartite division of the soul described in *The Republic* for the bipartite division of Pythagorean origin (reason, passion)—could invoke *Timaeus* in support of this definition, by interpreting in a very personal manner the passage in which Plato explains how souls are constructed.

But Xenocrates was also particularly careful to explore all the possible articulations between philosophy and theology, and this aspect of his thought had a lasting influence; Varro (116–27 B.C.E.) drew on it when he sought to give the Roman religion a philosophical foundation. We know that Xenocrates, who attributed a certain notion of the divine even to irrational animals, had explained that the One and the Dyad are gods, the first corresponding to Zeus, king of heaven, the second to Hera, mother of the gods, sovereign of all things under heaven and soul of the universe. In the same way he identified heaven and the stars with the fire of the gods of Olympus, and he declared that the sublunary world is peopled with invisible demons, intermediaries between gods and men. Using a mathematical metaphor, he compared the gods with an equilateral triangle (a symbol of the invariable), man with a scalene triangle, and demons with isosceles triangles. Through his reflection on religion, Xenocrates seems thus to have preceded the Stoics in their identification of the mythological gods with philosophical concepts. Still, no source attributes explicitly to him, as do certain exegetes, the invention of the theme—so present in Middle Platonism—of ideas as thoughts of God.

The Ethics of the Early Academy

In the realm of ethics, too, Xenocrates asserted his own strong philosophical personality, opening the way for Stoicism with his reflection on happiness. A number of accounts of his moral thought bear the mark of the rereading of his work by Antiochus of Ascalon and should thus be interpreted with great prudence, but the presence in Xenocrates of pre-Hellenistic themes, and most particularly pre-Stoic ones, is difficult to contest: the search for inner serenity as the ultimate end of ethics, the importance of voluntary submission to the law, the invention of the category of indifferents, a reflection on virtue in its relation to nature and happiness. Now the little we know about Polemon, his successor as head of the Academy, has to do almost exclusively with the field of ethics. Polemon stressed moral action and criticized those who devoted themselves to logical speculation, comparing them to people who might have learned a manual of harmony by heart but would be incapable of putting it into practice. Polemon defined the sovereign good as a life in conformity with nature, and he seems to have strongly influenced his student Zeno, who was to be the founder of Stoicism. We find this same priority granted to ethics in Crantor, another Academic who was the author of a commentary on *Timaeus* (of which only a few fragments have survived), but who was especially well known in antiquity for his *Consolation*, addressed to a friend after the death of his child, in which he urged the distraught father not to fight suffering in a radical way—as the Stoics would do later on—but rather to moderate it. In this work, Crantor developed the theme of the survival of the soul after death, proof that the Early Academy's stress on the natural foundations of ethics had not cut it off from Platonic transcendence.

THE SKEPTICAL ACADEMY

It has long been a commonplace of the history of ancient philosophy to affirm that, with Arcesilaus, the Academy passed from dogmatism to Skepticism. This dualist vision of the history of the Platonic school is justified: Arcesilaus claimed to be unable to know anything, and he made the universal suspension of judgment *(epoche peri pantōn)* the key to his philosophy. Moreover, unlike the scholarchs of the Early Academy, who had written a great deal, those of the Middle and New Academies most often restricted themselves to the oral practice of philosophy, which had its origin at least partly in the Socratic model. Nevertheless, to characterize this period of the Academy as Skeptical is problematic, inasmuch as this does not correspond to the genealogy of the concept of Skepticism. Indeed Skepticism, in the sense in which we understand it today, does not appear as an autonomous philosophy until the 1st century B.C.E., when Aenesidemus criticized the New Academy, too dogmatic in his eyes, for quoting Pyrrhon—and recent research has shown that Pyrrhon did not correspond very well to the common image of a Skeptic.

The Neopyrrhonism of Aenesidemus is the philosophy that, by way of Sextus Empiricus, is at the origin of the skeptical ideas that have proliferated from antiquity to our day. However, it would never have occurred to Arcesilaus to use the term *skepticism* in connection with himself; the word was not applied to him until much later, and there is every reason to believe that he described himself first and foremost as an Academic. Here much more than a label is at stake. Indeed, even though Arcesilaus preceded the Neopyhrronians in the universal suspension of judgment, this suspension occurred in his case against the background of his Platonic philosophical identity; this is the principal difficulty for those who study his thought. We may even wonder whether Aenesidemus's decision to take Pyrrhon as an emblematic figure of Skepticism—a Pyrrhon of whom the only traces were the memory of a moralist indifferent to everything that was not the moral good—was not the result of the difficulty inherent in professing a philosophy of universal doubt while attempting to integrate oneself, if only by institutional tradition, with the posterity of Plato.

This problem of the coexistence in the same line of thought of the suspension of assent and the reference to Plato was already intriguing to the ancients. Some, evidently not very happy with the course the Academy had taken under Arcesilaus's direction, explained the mutation by proclaiming the existence of an esoteric teaching: according to them, the Academics concealed the positive side of Plato's philosophy, revealing it only to a small number of students. Thus their skepticism was only a tactical maneuver, intended to counter the development of the dogmatism proper to Hellenistic schools and notably to the Stoics. St. Augustine himself, in *Contra Academicos*, comes to the defense of this thesis, but it appears chiefly as the caricature of an unquestionable reality: in the Academy of Arcesilaus and Carneades, Plato continued to be studied, and even to serve as a source for universal doubt. But precisely what of Plato's was being read? Although the thesis of a selective reading, retaining only the dialogues in which Plato claims he himself had arrived at no result, may be immediately attractive, it is not confirmed by any source, and several indications allow us to suppose, on the contrary, that the New Academics had taken over the entire Platonic corpus. While they clearly could not claim that Plato had come up with the theory of the suspension of judgment himself, they announced that they had found in him a refusal of certainties, a universal questioning in which they saw the anticipation of their own intellectual undertaking.

Arcesilaus

Arcesilaus's complex personality is too often muddled by the fact that we refer almost exclusively to the account of Sextus Empiricus, who, while not recognizing Arcesilaus as a genuine Skeptic, still speaks of him in the framework of Neopyrrhonism. Now, in seeing Arcesilaus only as the philosopher of the *epoche,* we neglect important aspects of his thought. Thus we are too often unaware that this philosopher, to whom we generally attribute the responsibility of a real break in the history of the Academy, was seduced in his youth by a very dogmatic Platonism, since he compared the school of his master, Polemon, to a place that would have provided refuge for survivors of the

Golden Age. A few traces remain of his attachment to this teaching: we know from Tertullian that he worked out—it would be nice to know at what period in his life—a theology in which three types of divinities derived from heaven and earth. In any case, the importance that this "Skeptic" saw in the articulation between philosophy and religion, in the tradition of the Early Academy, is confirmed for us by the fact that, in interpreting a verse from Hesiod in a very personal way, replacing the word *bion* (life) with the word *noon* (mind), he liked to repeat that the gods concealed intelligence from man. All this shows that Arcesilaus's aporetic philosophy still retained something of the transcendental orientation of Platonism. There is even a late but on the whole well-informed text, *Prolegomena in Platonis philosophia*, in which we are told that among the arguments raised by the New Academy to justify its philosophy of doubt there was a reference to *Phaedo*, a dialogue in which it is said that the soul can never reach truth so long as it is intertwined with the body. But whereas Plato, in the most famous of his myths, compared the life of men with that of prisoners who perceive only shadows on the walls of the cave, Arcesilaus declared that the world was entirely covered with darkness, and he claimed to go further than Socrates, who had at least the certainty that he knew nothing.

Arcesilaus's aporeticism, which led him to claim that the senses, and also reason, are incapable of reaching any certain knowledge, and that the wise man should suspend his judgment under all circumstances, gave rise to very different interpretations. Some have found Pyrrhonian or Peripatetic influences, though these are not very likely. Much more interesting is the thesis advanced by Pierre Couissin in 1929, for whom the fundamental concepts of Arcesilaus's thought resulted from the dialectical subversion of Stoic concepts. The Stoics maintained that most representations are "cataleptic," that is, that they correspond to at least part of reality and produce assent almost automatically. In proclaiming that man lives in a world of darkness, Arcesilaus thus transformed into a rule what was the exception for his dogmatic adversaries; in this way he made *epoche* the very essence of wisdom. Similarly, the concept of the probable *(eulogon)*, which he advocated as a guide for the wise man's action, resulted from the ironical generalization of a concept that, for the Stoics, characterized "middle" morality, precisely that of the man who has not attained wisdom. Couissin's thesis accounts for many aspects of Arcesilaus's philosophy, but it does not reckon with all the sources, especially those that tell us that he based suspension of assent on the principle of isosthenia, that is, the equal force of opposed discourses.

Thus there really was in Arcesilaus a personal philosophy of the impossibility of knowing that could not be reduced to his anti-Stoic dialectics, even if the struggle against Stoicism was his major cause, as it was of the scholarchs who followed him. Yet Arcesilaus did not claim originality: we know from Cicero and Plutarch that he had built up a genealogy of the philosophy of doubt that included not only Socrates and Plato but also such Presocratics as Parmenides, Heraclitus, Democritus, Anaxagoras, and Empedocles. It would be a mistake to see in this enumeration nothing but a confused amalgamation. In bringing together in a single tradition thinkers whose profound divergences he could not have failed to recognize, Arcesilaus was trying above all to emphasize an old way of philosophizing that was exempt—whatever dogmatic aspects were manifested by one philosopher or another—from the criticisms he directed at the Hellenistic, and especially the Stoic, philosophies, namely, the claim to absolute certainty, the obsession with a perfect system, the exaltation of the sage, who was equated with a god. This is especially clear in the way in which he elaborated the criticism of "cataleptic" representation. In the Stoic system, this has three characteristics: it is actual—that is, it derives from a real object; it is in conformity with that object; and it is such that it could not be the same if it came from anything other than that object. In concentrating his whole dialectic on this last provision, which he himself—if we can believe Cicero—obliged the Stoic Zeno to formulate, Arcesilaus was not merely attacking the sensualism of the Stoics. Indeed, when he strove to demonstrate that to every representation there may be a corresponding one that is in every respect identical to the first and that derives from a different object (this is what happens when twins are confused with one another) or from a nonbeing (dreams, hallucinations), he called into question a whole system that was based on the instinctive trust in fundamental ideas about nature and that established a continuity of certainty, from initial confidence in the senses to the perfect and unshakeable reason known as wisdom.

Carneades

Arcesilaus's inspiration was perpetuated, and in certain respects modified, by Carneades. One of the few things we know about Carneades is that he took part in an embassy sent by Athens to Rome in 155 in an attempt to lower a fine that had been imposed as a result of the sack of the village of Oropos. This embassy was unusual in that it consisted of three philosophers: in addition to Carneades, scholarch of the Academy, it included Critolaus and Diogenes of Babylon, scholarchs of the Lyceum and the Stoa, respectively. Carneades fascinated the Roman public with his oratorical virtuosity in defending, then in criticizing, the virtue of justice, or rather its diverse philosophical definitions. The Roman episode was a diplomatic success: Cato the Censor, fearing that the philosophers would turn Roman youth away from their ancestral virtues, asked the Senate to settle the affair as quickly as possible, and this was done to the benefit of Athens. Yet for a long time the embassy of 155 gave credence to the idea that Carneades was close to the Sophists, since he shared with them the quite undiplomatic practice of antilogy.

Considerable recent research has established that, despite some superficial resemblances, Carneades had nothing in common with the Sophist Gorgias.

From the standpoint of epistemology, Carneades is presented as the founder of probabilism, a system of hierarchization of representations in terms of their degree of resemblance, since he judged that one cannot state with certainty about any representation that it is true. However, the term *probabilism* should be used with caution, for it possesses all the modern connotations, mathematical connotations of probability in particular, whereas Carneades reasoned solely on the basis of the feeling of truth that representations produce in us. The term *probable* comes to us from Cicero, who created the philosophical language used in Latin, and who chose a term he had already used a good deal in his reflections on rhetoric. But with *probable*, Cicero was translating both *eulogon* and *pithanon*, and these terms corresponded to different phases in the philosophy of the New Academy. It has long been remarked that in sources dealing with Carneades, in place of the concept of *eulogon*, which Arcesilaus used, we find *pithanon* (literally, persuasive), a term that referred directly not to the activity of reason but to the feeling of truth that one experiences in the face of most representations. Carneades returned to Arcesilaus's critique of "comprehensive" representation and developed it further, pointing out in particular that no criterion for the truth of representations exists, since representation, which should simultaneously reveal the condition of the subject and the reality of the external object, is often a source of error. But he also called into question the capacity of reason to arrive at truth and claimed to doubt the very principles of mathematics. His dialectics used *sorites* as its privileged instrument, that is, the sophism making it possible to pass imperceptibly from a thing to its contrary. However, this radical refusal to recognize the existence of a criterion for knowledge elicited from the Academy's adversaries the accusation that all life was being made impossible. Thus Carneades defined a practical criterion based on the feeling of truth that representations produce, and also on the capacity of reason to carry out the task of verification. He thereby established a hierarchy, placing at the top the representation that gives a feeling of truth, that is not contradicted by any other, and that has been subject to verification.

Did Carneades himself espouse probabilism, or should his probabilism be interpreted only in terms of anti-Stoic dialectics, since the concept of *pithanon* also belonged to the gnoseology of that school? To tell the truth, the two aspects of Carneades' thought are inseparable. Dialectically, he certainly wanted to prove to the Stoics that at the very heart of their system they possessed elements that allowed them to do without a dogmatism that was impossible to espouse, since it was regularly contradicted by experience. But beyond this anti-Stoic dialectics, the Academic probably also wished to rehabilitate, at a point when philosophy was heavily dogmatic, a concept of the act of thinking in which uncertainty no longer appeared as a defect, but on the contrary as the sign of a requirement and as the condition of progress.

Carneades was not only a philosopher of knowledge. His reflection also bore on the other two parts of philosophy, ethics and physics. In the first of these fields, he struggled unceasingly to show the contradictory consequences that resulted from the Stoic claim to base morality on the natural impulse that makes every living thing seek from birth to persevere in being. For the Stoics, ethics was nothing but the passage from an instinctive harmony with nature to a harmony grounded in reason. Carneades responded, from within a certain Platonic tradition, that this natural tendency is not the source of wisdom but of self-centeredness and violence. Similarly, where physics was concerned, he demonstrated that if the Stoics were as rigorous as they claimed to be, they would start from their own premises—the observation of nature, a reckoning with beliefs about nature and the gods—and would cease to believe in the existence of a universal reason governing the world for man's benefit, reaching the conclusion that God does not exist and that everything is made and unmade through a straightforward dynamics of forces. For Carneades, the Stoic rooting of reason in feeling and instinct led to the negation of any really rational order. Though no source notes any dogmatic reference to Plato on the part of the Academic, it is certain that the systematic questioning of the Stoics' immanent rationalism left as a possible way out the recourse to a philosophy of transcendence. In this sense, one might say that Middle Platonism, which began to develop in the 1st century C.E., situates itself within a certain continuity in relation to the New Academy.

Carneades' Successors

The very long duration of Carneades' scholarchate and the philosopher's exceptional dialectical power were bound to lead to divergences as to the interpretation of a teaching which, like that of Arcesilaus, was exclusively oral. Clitomachus, Carneades' third successor as head of the Academy (we know nothing about the first two, and their scholarchates were very brief), abandoned this tradition of orality and indeed proved to be quite a prolific writer: he is credited with more than four hundred works. Comparing Carneades to Hercules, Clitomachus expressed his gratitude to his predecessor for liberating the human soul from what he considered a monstrosity, namely, assent, a source of opinions and lack of reflection. He gave a highly detailed presentation of his master's thought, insisting particularly on the absolute character of the suspension of judgment and on the viability of *pithanon* as a practical criterion. Clitomachus, some of whose writings have been passed along by Cicero, declared that, contrary to his adversaries' claims, the Academy in no way suppressed sensations. "The Academic school holds that there are dissimilarities between things of such a nature that some of them seem probable and others the contrary; but this is not an adequate ground for saying that some things can be perceived and others cannot, because many false objects are probable but nothing false can be perceived and known" (Cicero, *Academica* II [*Lucullus*], xxxii.103).

Clitomachus has been described as standing in the same relation to Carneades as Xenophon did to Socrates: as an attentive disciple, but lacking significant originality or depth. The fact is, despite the importance of his written work, he did not succeed in convincing the majority of other Academics that he had given an irrefutable representation of his master's thought. In particular, Metrodorus of Stratonicea, who had gone from the Epicurean school to the Academy, claimed that he had been the only one who understood Carneades' teaching, and he expressed his differences with Clitomachus on two essential points. While Clitomachus placed absolute value on suspension of judgment, Metrodorus claimed that it had been only a weapon against Stoicism. Moreover he maintained that, contrary to Clitomachus's assertions, Carneades had acknowledged that in certain cases the sage himself gives his assent to an opinion. How can we assess these Metrodorean interpretations? The relativization of the suspension of judgment contained at least a partial truth, in that the Skepticism of the New Academy was principally a form of anti-Stoicism. As a matter of fact, Metrodorus posed a problem that has been given new currency by Pierre Couissin's research, and which contemporary specialists of this period of the Platonic school continue to debate: how is the game of dialectics, in which one only pretends to accept the adversaries' positions in order to draw contradictory or absurd consequences from them, articulated with personal beliefs in the thinking of the New Academics? So far as the problem of the sage's assent is concerned, Metrodorus's exegetical position expresses the same wish to define a New Academic thought independent of the fascinating Stoic model. Indeed, in the "orthodox" interpretation of Clitomachus, the New Academic sage is the mirror image of the Stoic sage: in admitting that the wise man sometimes does gives his assent by mistake, the scholarch departed from the Hellenistic conception of the *sophos* to return implicitly to the figure of the philosopher, a seeker of wisdom who thus accepts his own fallibility.

Metrodorus was never a scholarch, so his original position, which he pronounced with a certain arrogance, could be considered that of one of the dissidents who were regularly churned up by the system of philosophical schools. The conflict of interpretation between Clitomachus and Metrodorus would thus have assumed much less importance if Philon of Larissa, who was the last institutional scholarch of the Academy, had not adopted a position close to Metrodorus's. Despite the affirmations of some, no source authorizes us to suppose that it was in Athens itself that Philon, who had at first been in Clitomachus's camp, changed his opinion. He was already acquainted with Metrodorus's theses, but if he had accepted them while he was still scholarch at Athens, the books he wrote after his arrival in Rome, where he went into exile after the siege of Athens by Mithridates, would not have astonished his friends as well as his adversaries. On this point, Cicero's account in *Academica* is devoid of ambiguity: the Roman books of Philon scandalized his old pupil Antiochus of Ascalon, who had seceded from the New Academy to recover what he insisted was the authentic inspiration of the Early Academy, as well as Heraclitus of Tyr, who had remained faithful to Carneades' philosophy insofar as Clitomachus had understood it. Unfortunately Cicero's *Academica* has come down to us in mutilated form, and the exact content of the Philonian innovations are the subject of debate among specialists. These innovations were of such importance that, in antiquity itself, some scholars saw Philon as the founder of a fourth Academy. More recently, Harold Tarrant has sought to give this philosopher an importance that he had never before had in philosophical research, by presenting him as the real promoter of the passage from Academic Skepticism to Middle Platonism. This is probably an excessive magnification of the role of someone who did no more than give official sanction to an evolution that would have taken place without him. What points did he develop in his Roman books? Certainly he insisted much more than his predecessors had on the unity of the Academy, from Plato to himself. This stress on the theme of unity does not mean that Arcesilaus and Carneades considered themselves foreign to the Platonic tradition, and we have seen that the former, in any case, had included Plato and Socrates among the inspirations of his philosophy. But in their day it was simply not as crucial to affirm the historic unity of the Academy as it was at a time when the philosophical and institutional continuity of the Academy might appear to have been shaken by the break with Antiochus of Ascalon and by the fact that, for the first time, a scholarch of the Platonic school found himself in exile, far from Athens.

It is in the field of epistemology that it is hardest to pinpoint the Philonian innovations. One thing at least is certain: he continued to fight the Stoic doctrine in this field, using the dialectical tools forged by his predecessors. There is no doubt that, even in his Roman books, there were sections in which he went back to the Academy's arguments against the Stoic criterion of knowledge, the "cataleptic" representation. But this criticism, traditional in its form, was no longer integrated into a vision of the world in which all certainty was considered impossible. Philon declared, in effect, that if the Stoic criterion does not allow knowledge of reality, the latter is none the less knowable by nature. Thus with Philon the skeptical arguments of the New Academy took on new meaning. They no longer expressed aporia, but instead reflected prudence and the need for truth in a cognitive process presented as conforming to the very nature of things. The problem that confronts the historian of the Academy is that the accounts that have Philon as their source do not tell us how he conceived of this knowledge, whose possibility he clearly affirmed.

Reading Cicero, in particular, leaves the impression that Philon, after giving the Academy this new orientation, had chiefly devoted himself to perpetuating the anti-Stoic dialectics that had prevailed since Arcesilaus. Certain recent research has nevertheless emphasized the concept of evidence (enargeia), which would constitute Philon's personal contribution to Academic epistemology. Yet if we take into account the fact that he pugnaciously pursued his criticism of the criterion of self-evidence, and if we also recall that Carneades had already constructed his hierarchy of probability on the basis of the feeling of self-evidence, we must conclude that Philon was not being truly innovative in the appreciation of sensorial knowledge. In reality, he seems not to have been capable of giving a concrete content to the theoretical revolution that his Roman books expressed. Although no account credits him explicitly with a return to Platonic idealism, it is likely that he gave a more positive interpretation of Plato than Carneades had done. Having limited Academic Skepticism to a form of anti-Stoicism, he could demonstrate without contradicting himself that the Platonic corpus had contained something other than aporias concerning knowledge. Perhaps it was he who began to emphasize a theme that was starting to arise in Cicero and that flourished notably in Middle Platonism: "to become like God, so far as this is possible," which Plato develops in the digression in Theaetetus (176b). I would add that, in the area of relations between rhetoric and philosophy, Philon also showed his capacity to establish a new spirit. While Clitomachus had perpetuated only the Platonic tradition of hostility to rhetors, Philon introduced a radical innovation by offering his own courses in rhetoric alongside his teaching of philosophy; we may suppose that in this enterprise he drew on a personal interpretation of Phaedrus.

Antiochus of Ascalon

Even before Philon's exile in Rome, the Platonic school had undergone a significant schism with the departure of Antiochus of Ascalon. Antiochus claimed to have recaptured the inspiration of the Early Academy, over and beyond that of the New Academy, which he ended up considering an aberrant parenthesis in the history of Platonism. Things would have been relatively simple for the Academics if Antiochus had been content to comment on the works of Speusippus or Xenocrates. But his aim was not simply to reestablish a dogmatic interpretation of Platonism. His ambition was actually to restore the Academy's preeminence over the Hellenistic schools, primarily the Lyceum and the Stoa, by demonstrating that they had by and large contributed nothing but terminological innovations. The consensus on these schools, which Antiochus had made a key point of his philosophy, corresponded to goals that were hardly innocent: it meant reducing Aristotle and Zeno to talented and rather unruly successors of the unsurpassable Plato. This strategy was not foolproof: Antiochus himself risked being viewed as more of a Peripatetic or a crypto-Stoic than a real Academic. In fact, Cicero, who held him in high regard, but who in *Academica* revives the arguments of the New Academy against him, did Antiochus no favor in characterizing him as an "authentic Stoic"; the theme has been repeated by many scholars interested in him. Now the least one can say is that such a formula does not account for Antiochus's philosophical personality.

In the field of ethics and physics, his method consisted in demonstrating that the Peripatetics and the Stoics had been satisfied to offer a new presentation of what already existed in Plato and in his successors in the Early Academy. Antiochus did not hesitate to claim as discoveries of the Academy concepts that were foreign to the Platonic school, such as *oikeiosis*, the immediate adaptation of the living being to its own nature. In the same way, his presentation of the physics of the Early Academy contains a good number of propositions derived much more from Zeno than from Speusippus or Xenocrates. But Antiochus, allegedly close to Stoicism, carried on an implacable polemic against the Stoics on all the points of doctrine that he could not really attribute to the Academy. For example, Book IV of Cicero's *De finibus* shows how relentlessly he attacked the specifically Stoic idea that the happiness of the wise man is totally independent of his external environment.

In the field of knowledge, our perception of Antiochus's philosophy is somewhat blurred by the fact that, to combat the Skepticism of the New Academy, he used the arguments of the Stoics themselves. This has led certain historians of philosophy to think that, on this point, Antiochus had completely gone over to the Stoic doctrine, judging that this doctrine really represented progress with respect to the Early Academy. Taken all together, our sources inspire more caution. Antiochus gave a sympathetic account of Platonic idealism, and he attributed to the Early Academy the idea that certainty should not be sought in the senses independently of reason, an implicit condemnation of the Stoic theory of "comprehensive representation." There is thus reason to believe that, in this field too, Stoicism was for him only an instrument in an overall strategy that he thought would incontrovertibly demonstrate the superiority of Platonism.

Antiochus, who purported to have recovered the true doctrine of the Academy, was never recognized as head of the Platonic school, because the institutional bond that, above and beyond any doctrinal changes, had connected the scholarchs from Plato to Philon of Larissa, was broken with Philon's departure for Rome. The school founded by Antiochus in Athens survived for a time after his death; then, for more than a century, no source mentions any Academic philosophers in Athens. During this whole period Middle Platonism was spreading in various parts of the Roman world; one of its features was that it functioned without the central core constituted by the Hellenistic schools. Was the Academy restored in the 2nd century C.E. thanks to Ammonius, Plutarch's master? The question is controversial, and the fact remains that with the departure of Philon of Larissa, a certain mode of organization of philosophical reflection disappeared once and for all.

We can now try to respond to the initial question: what, notwithstanding the changes that occurred in the Academy, distinguishes an Academic from any other Greek philosopher? Part of the answer lies, first of all, in the reference to Plato. This is apparent in the Early Academy. It is a little more problematic in the New Academy, insofar as there is still a scholarch—and not least since the scholarch in question is Carneades—for whom no source indicates any loyalty to the figure of the founder. There is even a passage (whose source is open to question) in Cicero's *De republica* in which we are told that Carneades criticized the Platonic conception of justice. These difficulties must not be underestimated. Still, the fact that Arcesilaus and Philon of Larissa explicitly claimed a relationship to Plato, and the reference in *De oratore* to the study of *Gorgias* under the direction of Charmadas, one of Carneades' disciples, allow us to suppose that the Platonic corpus remained, from the beginning of the Academy's history to the end, a living source of inspiration.

If admiration for Plato and the sense of being the legitimate repository of his work constituted the basic elements of the Academy's identity, these factors were never understood as implying a duty of adherence to any point of doctrine whatsoever. All the same, Platonic thought—so diverse, so difficult to establish—preserved from the beginning for the Academics the almost religious respect for a body of doctrine that was commonly found in the Hellenistic schools. That this freedom of inquiry has been perceived as essential to the tradition of the Academy was never in doubt. But in the Early Academy this inquiry seems often to have been oriented by the desire to "come to Plato's aid"—reserving the right to contradict him—on questionable points of his thought. It is also important to stress that the Academy's thinking was always dialectic, in the sense that it always developed in confrontation with a privileged adversary: Aristotle for the Early Academy, Stoicism for the New. Yet in each case, the interlocutor is a philosopher not radically foreign to the Platonic tradition but a product of that tradition, someone who won his own autonomy by using criticism of Plato to define himself.

Is it possible to find in the history of the Academy not a dogma but a philosophical orientation common to all the scholarchs? The reference to transcendence is very clear in the Early Academy—if we except Polemon (about whom we know very little), who was concerned with expressing the extra-universal character of essential realities. In contrast, there is only marginal reference to transcendence in accounts of the New Academy. Still, we may imagine that transcendence made itself felt through its absence, for if on the one hand the New Academy carried on an unremitting battle against Stoic immanentism, on the other hand it never criticized the Plato of the Forms. For this reason, idealism remained an outlet for the aporias that the Academics denounced in the Stoic confusion over the nature of reason.

The extreme complexity of the evolution of philosophical systems makes it difficult to draw up a "balance sheet" for the Academy. Let us simply recall that the Early Academy, which we might think had been forgotten after Arcesilaus and Carneades, was one of the sources of inspiration for Neoplatonism, which itself strongly influenced Christian thought. And the concepts developed by the New Academy were useful to Neopyrrhonism, whose role was so important in the history of Western thought—especially in the Renaissance—and also, to a lesser degree, in Middle Platonism, that is, among authors as diverse as Philon of Alexandria, Apuleius, and Plutarch. The inability of the Platonic school to settle on a body of doctrine could seem a disadvantage in the era of the great Hellenistic dogmatisms. Over time, this drawback has turned out to be a source of richness and variety.

CARLOS LÉVY
Translated by Rita Guerlac and Anne Slack

Bibliography

Texts and Translations

Aristotle. *Metaphysics.* Trans. Hugh Tredennick. 2 vols. Loeb Classical Library.
———. *On the Soul.* In *On the Soul; Parva naturalia; On Breath.* Trans. W. S. Hett. Loeb Classical Library.
Cicero. *Academica.* In *De natura deorum; Academica.* Trans. H. Rackham. Loeb Classical Library.

Studies

Barnes, Jonathan. "Antiochus of Ascalon." In *Philosophia togata.* Ed. Miriam Griffin and Jonathan Barnes. Oxford: Clarendon Press; New York: Oxford University Press, 1989. Pp. 51–96.
Burnyeat, Malcolm, ed. *The Skeptical Tradition.* Berkeley: University of California Press, 1983.
Cherniss, Harold. *The Riddle of the Ancient Academy.* New York: Russell and Russell, 1962.
Couissin, Pierre. "L'origine et l'évolution de l'*épochè*." *Revue d'études grecques* 42 (1929): 373–397.
———. "Le Stoïcisme de la Nouvelle Académie." *Revue d'histoire de la philosophie* 3 (1929): 241–276.
Dorandi, Tiziano. *Filodemo: Storia dei filosofi Platone e l'Academia.* Naples: Bibliopolis, 1991.
Gaiser, Konrad. *Platons ungeschreibene Lehre.* Stuttgart: E. Klett, 1968.

Glucker, John. *Antiochus and the Late Academy.* Göttingen: Vandenhoeck and Ruprecht, 1978.

Inwood, Brad, and Jaap Mansfeld, eds. *Assent and Argument: Studies in Cicero's Academic Books.* Leiden: E. J. Brill, 1997.

Ioppolo, Anna Maria. *Opinione e scienza.* Naples: Bibliopolis, 1986.

Isnardi Parente, Margherita, ed. and trans. *Senocrate-Ermodoro, Frammenti.* Naples: Bibliopolis, 1982.

———. *Speusippo-Ermodoro: Frammenti.* Naples: Bibliopolis, 1981.

———. *Speusippo: Frammenti.* Naples: Bibliopolis, 1980.

Kramer, Hans Joachim. *Platonismus und hellenistische Philosophie.* Berlin: De Gruyter, 1971.

Lévy, Carlos. *Cicero Academicus: Recherches sur les "Académiques" et sur la philosophie cicéronienne.* Rome: Ecole française de Rome, 1992.

Mette, Hans Joachim. "Philo von Larissa und Antiochus von Askalon." *Lustrum* 28–29 (1986–1987): 963.

———. "Weite Akademiker heute . . . von Lakydos bis zu Kleitomachos." *Lustrum* 27 (1985): 39–148.

———. "Zwei Akademiker Heute: Krantor von Soloi und Arkesilaos von Pitane." *Lustrum* 26 (1984): 7–104.

Robin, Léon. *La théorie platonicienne des Idées et des Nombres d'après Aristote.* Paris: Félix Alcan, 1908.

Tarán, Leonardo. *Speusippus of Athens: A Critical Study with a Collection of the Related Texts and Commentary.* Leiden: E. J. Brill, 1981.

Tarrant, Harold. *Scepticism or Platonism?* Cambridge: Cambridge University Press, 1985.

ARISTOTELIANISM

THE HISTORY OF PERIPATETIC PHILOSOPHY after Aristotle falls into two phases, divided by the renewal of interest in the works we now possess after their publication by Andronicus in the 1st century B.C.E.

Initially, Aristotle's own associates in the Lyceum and their successors carried on the work of the school. When Aristotle left Athens for Euboea at the news of the death of Alexander the Great in 323 B.C.E., the scholarchate passed to Theophrastus of Eresus, who had collaborated with Aristotle at least since the latter's stay in Assos in Asia Minor in 347–345 B.C.E. When Theophrastus died in 288/7 or 287/6 B.C.E., he was succeeded by Strato of Lampsacus, who remained head of the school until his own death eighteen years later.

The early activity of the school was characterized, as it had been in Aristotle's lifetime, by the collection and interpretation of information in every field, and by the raising and attempted resolution of theoretical difficulties. Two very different examples of the collection of information are provided by the best-known of the surviving works of Theophrastus. The first example, *Characters*, is a series of sketches of more or less imperfect personality types; it has been variously interpreted as material for a study of comedy, for the presentation of character in rhetoric, or for that study of character that the ancients called "ethics," but that we might rather classify as psychology; these purposes are not mutually exclusive. The second example is found in Theophrastus's botanical writings, which are the earliest systematic botanical texts to survive. The botanical subject matter calls some aspects of the Aristotelian theoretical framework into question; what is unnatural, Theophrastus says, may become natural with time, and the way in which art helps nature in the cultivation of plants prompts consideration of whether the true end of a tree's growth is to produce fertile seed or edible fruit (edible by humans, that is, and Theophrastus is prepared, in discussing wild and cultivated species, to speak about natural kinds in a flexible way, describing reversion from cultivated to wild varieties as changes of kind [genos]). But Theophrastus does not—in the extant texts anyway—explicitly present his approach to natural history as different from that of Aristotle.

The Lyceum was also active in collecting the views of earlier scholars: Eudemus compiled a history of mathematics, Menon of medicine, and Theophrastus the opinions of earlier philosophers about the natural world and about sense perception. Theophrastus's concern with earlier writers was not, however, purely historical; like Aristotle himself, he discussed their views as a basis for establishing his own, though he does seem to have gone into more detail than Aristotle, and some interest in historical detail for its own sake cannot be excluded.

It has often been held that Theophrastus, and to an even greater extent Strato, changed the emphasis of Peripatetic philosophy, placing a progressively greater emphasis on empiricism and materialism. There is some truth in this view, but it has been overstated. For our knowledge of much of Theophrastus's activity and all of Strato's, we are dependent on fragmentary reports by later writers. Writers like Plutarch, a Platonist, and Cicero, emphasizing the differences between philosophers of the same school in the interests of neo-Academic skeptical debate, may not be the best guides to whether or not Strato is a good Aristotelian. Plutarch presents Strato as denying any purpose in nature, but the sense in which Aristotle himself admits it has not been uncontroversial either.

To show that there is a basis in *some* passages of Aristotle for a position adopted by Theophrastus or Strato does not establish that it is not in some sense un-Aristotelian; divergence can take the form of selective emphasis and omission as well as of straight contradiction. But such divergence may be unconscious and unintentional, and since selective emphasis of particular aspects of Aristotle's thought is not confined to Theophrastus and Strato, or even to Plutarch and Cicero, but is found among modern interpreters as well, we need to be aware of the standpoint from which a modern judgment of what is or is not Aristotelian is being made. Those who regard metaphysics as the central philosophical issue, and theology—in the sense of the study of incorporeal principles—as central to metaphysics, may well regard not only Theophrastus and Strato but later ancient Peripatetics too as neglecting what *they* regard as Aristotle's chief contributions. In a recent masterly short account of Aristotle, Jonathan Barnes devoted just two pages out of eighty-eight to Aristotle's theology and the theory of the Unmoved Mover. This might have surprised Thomas Aquinas; Theophrastus and Strato might have found Barnes's Aristotle more familiar than Aquinas's.

One of the Theophrastean works to survive is his so-called *Metaphysics*. This has often been described as a "fragment"; it seems in fact to be complete, but it comes to no conclusions and raises questions rather than answering them. In questioning the explanation of natural phenomena in terms of purpose and the theory of the Unmoved Mover, it can easily be seen as indicating Theophrastus's rejection of central Aristotelian doctrines—especially when Theophrastus can be seen as paving the way for Strato. However, Glenn Most has shown that some (but only some) of the examples of purpose in nature apparently rejected by Theophrastus are ones equally rejected by Aristotle himself, and he has suggested that Theophrastus's discussion is aimed not against Aristotelian teleology but against a more thoroughgoing Platonist version. And though Theophrastus's treatise has no definite conclusions, it does have a positive message, which is that the universe is an organized system in which the same degree of purposefulness and goodness should not be expected at every level—a theme we shall find recurring in later Peripatetics too.

That Theophrastus did reject Aristotle's Unmoved Mover seems probable enough; but Aristotle did not accept the theory of the Unmoved Mover throughout his career, and in any case, raising objections is a thoroughly Aristotelian way of proceeding. Critics have been too ready to forget the problematic and exploratory nature of much of Aristotle's own surviving works, and too ready to interpret his successors as abandoning supposedly crucial features of Aristotelianism rather than as continuing Aristotle's enquiries (or sharing in them, for there is no reason to suppose that Theophrastus's *Metaphysics* was not written in Aristotle's lifetime). Even where Aristotle's own position can be easily stated, it is not always clear how we should interpret his successors' relation to him. Theophrastus certainly begins his surviving treatise *On Fire* by raising general questions about the Aristotelian theory of the elements, but, characteristically, he then turns aside from the general questions to investigate particular phenomena. Some of his remarks about these do seem to reveal un-Aristotelian assumptions. At this point we may suppose that Theophrastus did indeed develop a distinctive theory of his own, and look for other reports of Theophrastus's views that seem to confirm this; or we may suppose that Theophrastus couples a general adherence to an Aristotelian framework with a flexibility and readiness to speculate on particular details.

One reason why the question of Theophrastus's and Strato's loyalty to Aristotelianism has received attention has yet to be mentioned. After Strato, the Lyceum, and with it Peripatetic philosophy, rapidly fell into decline. Strato's successor Lyco (head of the school for forty-four years, from 270/69 or 269/8 B.C.E.) was notable for his oratory, social standing, and love of luxury rather than for science or philosophy; his successor Ariston of Ceos was noted chiefly for his biographical studies. (It is probably to Ariston that we owe the preservation of the wills of Aristotle and Theophrastus, and perhaps the list of Aristotelian titles in Diogenes Laertius.) In the 2nd century Critolaus, who accompanied the Academic Carneades and the Stoic Diogenes of Babylon on their visit to Rome in 156/5 B.C.E., was philosophically active, chiefly in defending Aristotelian positions (the eternity of the world, the fifth heavenly element, and the inclusion of external goods as a constituent of happiness) against the Stoics. Those for whom the most important aspects of Aristotelianism are those that they see Aristotle's immediate successors as questioning, rejecting, or neglecting have tended to see the decline of the Peripatetic school as a natural consequence of the change of emphasis. Others, themselves favoring an empiricist approach to the natural world, have seen

Theophrastus and Strato as advancing scientific inquiry where Aristotle's attitudes hindered it; this equally seems to overstate the contrast between Aristotle and his successors.

The real reasons for the decline of the Lyceum may be harder to recapture. Certainly the special sciences in the Hellenistic period developed an impetus of their own in institutions other than the Lyceum—notably medicine in Ptolemaic Alexandria—but this does not explain why zoology and botany, the sciences Aristotle and Theophrastus had made their own, declined in the Lyceum without developing elsewhere. Where philosophy in a narrower sense is concerned, the answer may be easier. Aristotle's own thought is guided indeed by clear structures and assumptions, but within that framework it is characteristically questioning, open-ended, and provisional. Moreover Aristotle explicitly stressed, against Plato, the relative independence of the different branches of philosophical enquiry. For those who were attracted by comprehensive and dogmatic philosophical systems, the Lyceum had nothing new to offer that could compare with Epicureanism or the Stoa, while for those who rejected dogmatism, the tentative and questioning approach of Aristotle's "unpublished" writings, such as *Metaphysics*, proceeding within the context of an assumed general framework and clearly supposing that there were answers to be reached, must have seemed a poor second best to the aggressive skepticism introduced to the Academy by Arcesilaus in the middle of the 3rd century B.C.E. Strato's successors emphasized those aspects of the school's activity—present indeed from the outset—that related to the general literary and rhetorical culture of the period, and this too may have lessened the distinctive appeal of the school. There is nothing un-Aristotelian in paying attention to the views and concerns of people in general, as a glance at the *Nicomachean Ethics* will show, but for Aristotle himself it was only the foundation on which he built.

To speak of how Aristotle's "unpublished" writings might have seemed to Hellenistic readers assumes, indeed, that those who might have wanted to read them could have done so. (I use "published" and "unpublished" as equivalents for the traditional "exoteric" and "esoteric," respectively; the latter, in particular, could have misleading connotations.) The decline of the Lyceum is linked by Strabo and Plutarch with the story that Aristotle's and Theophrastus's writings, left by Theophrastus not to Strato but to Neleus of Scepsis in the Troad, passed from Neleus to his descendants. They, having no interest in philosophy, hid the works in a cellar to preserve them from the kings of Pergamum, who wanted to create a library to rival the one in Alexandria and were not too scrupulous about their methods of acquiring materials. Thus, according to the story, the unpublished works of Aristotle—those which we now have, the published works having been lost later in antiquity—were inaccessible until rediscovered in the 1st century B.C.E., and the Peripatetics were unable to "do philosophy in a systematic way" without them. The manuscripts were eventually recovered by the bibliophile Apellicon, who took them to Athens and published them, but inaccurately; they were then seized by the Roman general Sulla when he sacked the city in 86 B.C.E., and taken to Rome, where they were copied by the grammarian Tyrannio. From his copies a new edition, which established the arrangement of Aristotle's writings that still exists today, was produced by Andronicus of Rhodes; this also included some works of Theophrastus.

It is true that the revival of Aristotelianism dates from Andronicus, and that it is different in character from what had preceded; where the earlier Peripatetics had sought to continue Aristotle's work, later writers essentially look back to it and comment on it. It is significant that Strabo supposes that one *could not be* a Peripatetic philosopher without access to the texts of Aristotle himself. Concentration on the study of canonical texts was not a development confined to Aristotelianism; it was characteristic of the imperial period. What is much less certain is that Aristotle's works were ever as inaccessible as the story suggests. It is unlikely that even the unpublished works existed in only one copy; we know that different, and differing, copies of Aristotle's *Physics* existed in the lifetime of Theophrastus, and Strato left to Lyco "all the books, apart from those I have written myself" (Diogenes Laertius, 5.62). H. B. Gottschalk suggests that the books inherited by Neleus may never have left Athens and speculates that Apellicon may have stolen the books and made up the whole story to conceal the fact. If Aristotle's works were little read in the Hellenistic period, this may be not because they were unavailable but because—however strange this may seem to modern interpreters, for whom Aristotle is a central figure in the whole history of philosophy—they were not considered of great interest. Aristotelian doctrines were still discussed and referred to, but characteristic of the Hellenistic period is not the study of Aristotle's own works but the compilation and use of summaries of the sort that underlie Cicero's knowledge of Aristotle and the accounts of Areius Didymus and Diogenes Laertius.

The writing of such summaries of Aristotelian doctrines did not cease after Andronicus's edition. Nicolaus of Damascus, a courtier of Herod the Great, compiled, in addition to historical and ethnographical writings, a summary of Aristotle's philosophy, including the biological works, which survives in a Syriac summary and in other fragments. This brought together material on similar topics from different Aristotelian texts edited by Andronicus. Nicolaus also made use of Theophrastus's *Metaphysics,* unknown to Andronicus, and other material from Theophrastus and later Peripatetics. A treatise by Nicolaus on plants, possibly part of the compendium, was translated from Syriac into Arabic in the 9th century C.E., thence into Latin in the second half of the 12th century, and thence back into Greek. In the process it became misattributed to Aristotle himself, and it is this retranslation that appears as *On Plants* in modern editions of Aristotle, though the falsity of the attribution was already realized in the Renaissance.

Areius Didymus, a Stoic and "court philosopher" to the emperor Augustus, wrote summaries of the teachings of the various schools. Of his treatment of the Peripatetics we possess the section on ethics, quoted at length by Stobaeus, and fragments of the section on physics. Areius sometimes used the Aristotelian texts, but the terminology and emphases reflect Hellenistic preoccupations; with regard to the section on ethics in particular, while the doctrine is basically Aristotelian, it appears in a guise and with emphases that owe more to Hellenistic preoccupations and to Areius's own concern to stress the similarities between Peripatetic and Stoic ethics.

Other scholars, however, directed their activities toward the writing of commentaries on the newly popular Aristotelian texts. The earlier commentaries are now lost except for scattered quotations, having been replaced by later, often Neoplatonic commentaries. Andronicus and his pupil Boethus commented on *Categories* and other works; so too did Alexander of Aegae, teacher of the emperor Nero. The earliest surviving complete commentary is that of Aspasius (first half of the 2nd century C.E.) on *Nicomachean Ethics*. But the earliest author from whom a considerable number of commentaries survives is Alexander of Aphrodisias, described as "*the* commentator" by his successors, though even of his works only a part survives, much having been superseded by later commentaries. Interest in Aristotle's published works declined as that in the unpublished works in Andronicus's edition developed; for Cicero, who either did not know of or was not interested in the texts published by Andronicus, Aristotle still meant the Aristotle of the published works, but he is perhaps the last major writer for whom this is true.

It is possible that the Lyceum ceased to exist as an institution at the time of Sulla's sack of Athens. But Athens continued to be a center for philosophers of all schools. In 176 C.E. Marcus Aurelius established posts there for teachers of the four principal philosophies (Platonic, Aristotelian, Stoic, and Epicurean), and it may be to an appointment in Athens that Alexander refers in the dedication of his treatise *On Fate*, written between 198 and 209. The institution of the imperial appointments only confirmed a situation that already existed; philosophers of the different schools were teaching in Athens—and engaging in lively polemic against each other's schools—throughout the 2nd century.

Alexander's commentaries do not yet show the adaptation to a context of formal teaching apparent in the later, Neoplatonic commentaries. They are discursive and open-ended, presenting alternative interpretations without always indicating a preference between them. We also possess some collections of short discussions attributed to Alexander; once there were more, but they are now lost. Some of these take the form of problems in Aristotelian doctrine, or in the interpretation of particular texts, followed by solutions; others are expositions of particular passages, or summaries of texts or doctrines, which seem to derive from a teaching context. Whether they were written by Alexander himself has to be considered text by text; it is unlikely that they all were. Since many of these texts are connected with themes dealt with in Alexander's commentaries or in monographs by him, it is natural to assume that they at least originate from his school. But it has recently been suggested that some of them may be considerably later in date, though still concerned essentially with Aristotelian issues. This highlights a problem: that of the *second* disappearance of Aristotelianism in antiquity, or rather its absorption into Neoplatonism.

We know the names of Alexander's teachers and can identify some of their doctrines and his reaction against them. But we do not know the names of any of his pupils; with one exception, all ancient commentators on Aristotle after Alexander whose writings are known to us are Neoplatonists. There had long been a tendency on the part of Platonists to incorporate Aristotelian ideas into their expositions of Plato; some, notably the 2nd-century Platonist Atticus, rebelled against this, but they were in the minority. Plotinus himself had the works of Aristotle and the commentaries of Alexander, among others, read in his school. Subsequently, with the formalization of the Neoplatonic philosophical curriculum, selected works of Aristotle were studied as a preliminary to the reading of Plato. The emphasis was on the logical and physical treatises and the work *On the Soul*; this explains why Aspasius's commentary on *Ethics* survived and why we have to wait until the 12th century for commentaries on *Parva naturalia* or any of the zoological works, and on *Rhetoric*.

The exception to the general dominance of Platonists after Alexander is Themistius, who in the 4th century combined epideictic rhetoric with the production of explanatory paraphrases of Aristotle's works. But Themistius's Aristotelianism has no clear heritage; we cannot trace either its immediate antecedents or his successors. There are occasional references to other individuals as Peripatetics, but none of this amounts to the continued existence of a distinctive Aristotelian tradition.

Before considering the reasons for this second decline of Aristotelianism, it will be convenient to consider developments throughout the period of five centuries separating Aristotle from Alexander in each branch of Aristotelian philosophy in turn, following the order of topics in the standard arrangement of Aristotle's writings that goes back to Andronicus.

LOGIC

Theophrastus and Eudemus continued and developed the study of formal logic that Aristotle had instituted in *Prior Analytics*. There are two areas in which they made a particular contribution. The first is modal logic, the logic of necessity and possibility. Aristotle had utilized a notion of possibility according to which "possible" excludes not only what is impossible but also what is necessary; while this is intuitive (it is not natural to say, "It is *possible* that 2 + 2 = 4," for example), it removes the expected parallelism between statements of possibility and statements of fact. For with this type of possibility, "It is possible that all B are A" implies "It is possible that no B are A," and "It is possible that no B are A" does not imply "It is possible that no A are B" (for it may be that all B have the possibility of being A or not being A, but that there are some other A that cannot be B at all). Moreover, while it may seem natural to suppose that a conclusion cannot be stronger than the weakest of the premises from which it follows—the "weakest link in the chain" principle, or, as medieval logicians put it, *sequitur conclusio partem deteriorem*—for Aristotle it made a difference which premise was concerned; he regards as valid that "Necessarily all B are A" and "All C are B" yield "Necessarily all C are A," while "All B are A" and "Necessarily all C are B" yield only "All C are A" and not "Necessarily all C are A."

On both these issues Theophrastus and Eudemus, who are regularly cited together, adopted the opposite view; and in both cases the effect is to make modal logic simpler and tidier. Statements of possibility now behave like statements of fact, and the modality of the conclusion in all syllogisms is determined by a simple rule. If Aristotle was influenced in taking the view he did by extralogical considerations (for example, that being as a matter of fact a member of a group implies possessing necessarily the properties that all members of the group possess necessarily), the changes made by Theophrastus and Eudemus may indicate a move from logic conceived in terms of its applications in the real world to logic as a purely formal system. It is, however, one thing to assert this with hindsight and quite another to claim that Theophrastus and Eudemus would have seen the change in these terms.

Theophrastus also developed the study of argument forms mentioned by Aristotle but not fully discussed by him. It seems highly probable that these included the forms of argument with conditional, conjunctive, and disjunctive premises that were to form the basis of both Stoic logic and modern propositional logic. But it also seems likely that Theophrastus did not realize the significance of what he had discovered, and did not see that propositional logic was actually more fundamental than the Aristotelian logic of terms.

The contribution of Aristotelian writers after Theophrastus and Eudemus to the development of logic was not great. The innovations came from writers outside the school, such as Galen (even though it is not true, as once thought, that Galen discovered the fourth figure of the "Aristotelian" syllogism). Alexander of Aphrodisias wrote an extensive commentary on *Prior Analytics* and a separate monograph, now lost, on *Syllogisms with Mixed Premises* (that is, premises of differing modalities); characteristically, he endorsed Aristotle's view on the latter topic against that of Theophrastus and Eudemus.

PHYSICS AND METAPHYSICS: FATE AND PROVIDENCE

Aristotle defined time as the numbered aspect of motion (*Physics* 4.11.219b5) indicated most clearly by the movement of the heavenly sphere, though not to be identified with it (*Physics* 4.14.223b23). Theophrastus and Eudemus followed Aristotle's view, but Strato rejected it on the grounds that motion and time are continuous whereas number is discrete, and defined time as quantity or measure both in motion and in rest, thus giving it an existence independent of motion. He was followed on the latter point by Boethus (Simplicius, *In Cat.* 434.2ff). Alexander explicitly rejected such a theory, attributed to Galen; indeed, Alexander identifies time as the number of the motion of the outermost heavenly sphere more definitely than Aristotle himself had done. Aristotle had suggested that there could be no time without soul, as without soul there could be no numbering (*Physics* 4.14.223a21ff); Alexander argues that time is in its own nature a unity and is divided by the present moment only in our thought. This suggests that time itself can exist without any actual *numbering;* and Alexander appears to identify time in this sense with the continuous *numerable* movement of the outermost heavenly sphere. Characteristically, Alexander's approach combines a claim to be simply setting out the Aristotelian position, and an attempt to defend it, with a new development and emphasis of his own.

Though Theophrastus did not challenge Aristotle's view of time, he assembled a whole series of difficulties for Aristotle's definition of place as the innermost unmoved limit of what surrounds a thing. We do not, however, know whether these difficulties led Theophrastus to reject the Aristotelian conception of place altogether. The Neoplatonist commentator Simplicius, after outlining the view of place held by his predecessor Damascius, mentions in passing that Theophrastus seems to have anticipated this, interpreting place as the proper position of a part in a complex whole. What is not clear is whether Theophrastus, like Damascius, already extended this concept to the place of things in the universe as a whole. Strato certainly rejected Aristotle's view of place and defined it as the interval or extension delimited by the outermost surface of what is contained or the innermost surface of what contains it—which amounts to saying that the place of a thing is not, as for Aristotle, what contains it, but the space that it occupies.

For Aristotle, sublunary things are composed of the four elements, earth, air, fire, and water (which can be and are transmuted into each other), while the heavenly spheres are composed of ether, the fifth element, which has the capacity for movement but for no other kind of change. It has been argued that Theophrastus both rejected the fifth element and maintained that fire requires a substrate in a way that the other elements do not. It is true that in the opening section of *On Fire* Theophrastus draws attention to the fact that terrestrial fire needs a constant supply of fuel, which might be thought to conflict with its status as a primary element; and he also speculates over whether the sun, if not fire, may not be at least hot. Such thoughts might indeed lead to a world picture radically different from Aristotle's; but it is not clear that they did so for Theophrastus. The introductory discussion in *On Fire* ends inconclusively and, as already mentioned, Theophrastus turns to more specific questions, but not before pointing out that the need for replenishment applies not just to fire but to all the sublunary elements. As for the fifth element, Philoponus suggests that Theophrastus retained it. Strato certainly rejected the fifth element and held that the heavens are composed of fire, and the Stoics rejected the fifth element and gave a major role to fire and—later, with Chrysippus—*pneuma* as embodiments of the active principle in the universe.

It has also been suggested that Theophrastus emphasized the role of heat, especially that of the sun, in causing physical change, and that he modified the Aristotelian theory of the dry and moist exhalations, reducing the dry one to mere reflection of the heat of the sun. But both Theophrastus's *Meteorology* and his *De igne* suggest less divergence from Aristotle's views than this interpretation supposes. And, once again, there is the question of Aristotle's own consistency. Theophrastus treated fire as active and the other three elements as passive, and both this and his distinction between the generative heat of the sun and terrestrial fire develop themes that are already present in Aristotle's physiological and biological writings, as opposed to his general physical theory.

Although Theophrastus denied the existence of the Unmoved Mover, he continued to hold, like Aristotle, that the heavens are ensouled. (That the heavens are ensouled was later the belief of Alexander of Aphrodisias, and of his teacher Herminus.) Theophrastus, like Aristotle, upheld the doctrine of the eternity of the world, and engaged in polemic against the Stoic Zeno on this issue—if we can trust an early work of Philo Judaeus.

Aristotle maintained the infinite divisibility of matter and the absence of any void. Scholars have drawn particular attention to contexts where Theophrastus, in the explanation of physical processes, makes use of the notion of passages or pores. There is, however, no inconsistency between this and Aristotelian physical theory, unless we are to suppose that the pores contain a vacuum; they may well be thought of rather as containing more tenuous matter than what surrounds them. Strato, but not, it seems, Theophrastus, was prepared to allow the temporary existence of completely empty voids within material bodies. Theophrastus *did* apparently employ the principle of "nature abhorring a vacuum" in the explanation of winds. But all this is still far removed from the Atomist conception of discrete particles of matter moving within an otherwise empty space. A tendency toward materialistic explanations can be seen in Theophrastus's introduction of material effluences into the explanation of odor, which Aristotle had interpreted as the propagation of a change in the intervening medium.

On issues of physical theory such as these, the Peripatetics of the Roman empire, concerned as they were to explain the Aristotelian texts, returned to orthodox Aristotelian positions. But on other aspects of the organization of the natural world, later Peripatetics found themselves constrained to develop "Aristotelian" positions on issues to which Aristotle himself had devoted little or no direct attention. The Stoics, in particular, had made fate and divine providence central topics of philosophical debate. Aristotle himself had little to say about the former, and his account in *Metaphysics* XII of the Unmoved Mover as engaged in self-contemplation, causing movement as an object of desire without itself being affected, seems like a complete denial of divine providence, though there is evidence to suggest that in his published works he may have taken a less uncompromising view.

The nature of divine involvement with the universe forms the climax of the treatise *On the World (De mundo)*, attributed to Aristotle (and contained in our standard editions) but probably in fact a composition of the Roman period. In it God is likened to the Persian king, ruling by delegated authority; divine influence is present in the world, but God himself is remote in a way that is appropriate to his dignity. Other interpreters, however, took a harsher line, and the standard view attributed to Aristotle in both pagan and Christian sources—among them, Areius Didymus and Diogenes Laertius—is that the heavens are the objects of divine providence while the sublunary region is not. The Platonist Atticus attacked Aristotle vehemently for holding such a view (and also for denying the immortality of the soul); Aristotle's views, he argued, are really no different from those of Epicurus, but at least Epicurus had the courage of his convictions and denied providence altogether, whereas Aristotle allows its existence, but only in a context where it cannot directly benefit us.

It was apparently in reply to Atticus that Alexander of Aphrodisias developed an alternative "Aristotelian" theory of providence, preserved in part in his treatise *On Providence,* which survives in two Arabic versions, and partly in various of the short texts attributed to him. Providence is located in the heavens, he argues, in the sense that it is exercised from the heavens over the sublunary region, which is subject to coming-to-be and passing-away, and so is the only part of the universe that actually needs providential care. However, providence extends to the sublunary only in preserving the eternity of natural kinds; there is no involvement of providence in the lives of individuals (as contemporary Platonists, for example, were arguing). By adopting this position Alexander can account for the occurrence of misfortunes in the lives of individuals, and also avoid an involvement of the divine in things that would be beneath its dignity—something for which he repeatedly criticizes the Stoics.

Alexander's theory of providence is a reworking of authentically Aristotelian materials in a new guise. That the movements of the heavens, and especially the seasonal movements of the sun, preserve the continuity of sublunary coming-to-be, and hence of natural kinds, is argued by Aristotle himself in the penultimate chapter of his *De generatione et corruptione,* and the eternity of natural kinds had been used as an argument for that of the world by Critolaus (frg. 13, Wehrli). Moraux, before the Arabic text of *On Providence* was known, criticized Alexander's theory of providence for being "mechanistic." In fact the Arabic text makes it clear that Alexander does want to assert that the divine is aware of its beneficial effects on the sublunary, though how he reconciled this with *Metaphysics* XII we do not know.

Similarly, where fate is concerned, Alexander's position is an adaptation of Aristotelian themes. For Aristotle, what is natural applies for the most part but not always; and Alexander, in his treatise *On Fate,* argues that individuals' fate is their nature or, quoting Heraclitus, their character, which for the most part determines what happens to them, but not always. Alexander may not have been the first to put forward this view; certainly one of the texts attributed to him endeavors to read such a notion of fate back into Aristotle's own two uses of the adjective *fated,* into Theophrastus, and into an otherwise unknown Polyzelus.

What Alexander's view of fate emphatically rules out is the Stoic concept of fate as inexorably determining everything. The unity of the universe, he argues, is preserved not by the chain of causes and effects, but by the regular movement of the heavens; as in a household, so in the universe, minor variations in matters of detail do not affect the orderliness of the whole (Alexander, *On Fate,* chap. 25). The similarity to Alexander's theory of providence is apparent; so too is the recurrence of the idea, already encountered both in Theophrastus's *Metaphysics* and in *De mundo,* of the Peripatetic universe conceived as a hierarchy in which the same degree of order, goodness, and perfection is not to be expected at every level. It is tempting to see the remoteness of God in *De mundo,* and Alexander's attacks on the Stoics for involving God in every detail of the management of the world, as reflecting the increased remoteness of earthly rulers when the Greek city-state was replaced, first by the Hellenistic monarchies and then by the Roman empire, but the fact that the hierarchical picture is already implicit in Aristotle (*Metaphysics* XII.10) may argue for caution here.

Theophrastus and Strato devoted little attention to such problems of general metaphysics as the status of universals. With the revival of Aristotelianism and the placing of *Categories* at the beginning of the whole sequence of Aristotle's works, the status of universals became a central issue. Once again the thinker on whose views we are most fully informed is Alexander, though his views were anticipated by Boethus, and some of the evidence comes from short texts that may not all be by Alexander himself. Definitions, it is argued, are of specific or generic forms, which do not include any of the pecularities of individuals, such as Socrates' snub nose—these being due to matter—and yet they are not universal in themselves; the nature of human being would be the same even if only one human being existed. Socrates exists because "human being" exists, and not the other way round; yet "human being" would not exist if no individual human being at all existed. It seems reasonable to suppose that each human being has the same nature or form, the form of the species human being, but that my form and yours are the same only in kind (or "form"; the Greek is the same), not numerically; or, putting it another way, to speak of "the same form" does not mean that there is a single numerically individual form that you and I share. The first way of putting it suggests a doctrine of individual forms (not, of course, in the sense that each person's form will include individual *peculiarities*, just that my form and yours are two tokens of the type "form of human being"); the second, that a form is the sort of thing to which questions of numerical identity or difference do not apply. The question of whether *Aristotle* believed in "individual forms," and if so in what sense, has been a major topic of contemporary debate.

Alexander's position has been criticized both in ancient and in modern times for being nominalist and hence un-Aristotelian. Some of those criticisms come, however, from a Platonist standpoint, and thus are suspect so far as the assessment of what is and is not Aristotelian is concerned. For Aristotle as well as for Alexander, universals have their existence as *post rem* mental constructs; but it is important that those mental constructs are not arbitrary but reflect the fundamental reality of the specific forms. The latter are indeed the product of the abstracting power of intellect, but that does not mean that it is up to us which features we abstract. On the contrary, the important thing about every human being, as it were, is that he or she is a *human being*, the various accidents due to matter being secondary to this. This explains why texts attributed to Alexander can say that the universal is prior to any *particular* individual; and while it may be questionable whether we should use ideas from one area of Alexander's philosophizing to settle an issue in another, the emphasis in his theory of providence on the preservation of the species agrees with an emphasis on the reality of specific form.

Alexander has also been regarded as un-Aristotelian in diminishing the role of form in comparison with that of matter. But this is chiefly in the context of his doctrine of soul, to which we shall now turn.

SOUL

Aristotle defined the soul as the form of the living creature. It is thus neither a separable immaterial entity (as Plato had supposed) nor a distinct material ingredient in the whole creature (as Epicurus, for example, was to argue). But neither is it, for Aristotle, simply a product of the arrangement of the bodily parts and thus reducible to the latter; body is to be explained in terms of soul, and in general, compounds of matter and form are to be explained in terms of form. A human body has a certain structure to enable the human being to function in the way that human beings do.

However, that body is to be explained in terms of soul and not vice versa need not mean that a certain arrangement of bodily parts is not a necessary condition for the existence of a certain type of soul. In the case of perceptive soul, indeed, the bodily organ that relates to a particular soul-faculty is evident: the eye in the case of sight, the ear in that of hearing. It is less obvious how we are to relate the soul to the body in general—both in terms of how soul and body interact, and in terms of whether some part of the body plays a particularly vital role. Aristotle had seen "connate spirit" *(pneuma)* as the physical means by which soul operated, and the heart as the particularly vital organ, the first to develop in the embryo. He had also asserted that intellect, alone of the soul-faculties, was not correlated with any particular organ, and had spoken, in the notorious chapter 3.5 of *De anima*, of a distinction in intellect between "that which makes everything" and "that which becomes everything," apparently presenting the former as imperishable in a way in which the latter was not. The history of subsequent Peripatetic discussion of the soul is largely that of attempts to clarify these issues, attempts that were affected to varying extents by contemporary attitudes and the positions of other philosophical schools. It will be convenient first to discuss the nature of the soul as a whole and its relation to the body, and then to consider the question of intellect separately.

Among Aristotle's immediate pupils, Dicaearchus is said to have regarded the soul as a "harmony," or mixture of the four elements in the body, a view that some reports present as equivalent to denying the existence of the soul at all. Aristoxenus, too, is said to have regarded the soul as simply a harmony or attunement of the body.

Strato emphasized the role of *pneuma*, breath or spirit, in the functioning of the soul. Aristotle and Theophrastus had used *pneuma* to explain bodily processes, and for Strato soul-faculties were explained by *pneuma*'s extending throughout the body from the "ruling part," which he located not in the chest (as both Epicurus and the Stoics did) but in the head, or more precisely in the space between the eyebrows. Tertullian illustrates Strato's theory with the analogy of air in the pipes of an organ (the Stoics were to use that of the tentacles of an octopus). Strato was influenced here by developments in contemporary medicine and anatomy. All sensation, he held, was felt in the ruling part of the soul, rather than in the bodily extremities, and all sensation involved thought. Some have drawn a contrast between Strato's views on thought itself and those of Aristotle, emphasizing Strato's view that all thought is ultimately derived from sensation; but the contrast sometimes depends on attributing to Aristotle himself a belief in intuition as a mode of cognition distinct from the senses, and this is at best questionable.

Lyco's successor Ariston of Ceos may have stressed the distinction between rational and nonrational soul, against the Stoics, but perhaps in an ethical rather than a psychological context. Critolaus described the soul as made of ether, the fifth element. Cicero says that Aristotle himself identified the soul with ether, but this may reflect a misunderstanding, aided by the familiarity of materialistic theories of soul in other schools.

Andronicus defined the soul as the power arising from the mixture of the bodily elements, and he was followed in this both by Alexander's teacher Aristoteles of Mytilene and by Alexander himself. Alexander has been criticized for interpreting Aristotle in a materialist way, treating soul as form, indeed, but making form secondary to matter. His treatment of soul as the culmination of an analysis that starts from the simple physical elements and builds up through successively more complex structures does suggest that he sees form in general, and soul in particular, as the product of material arrangement. However, it is not un-Aristotelian to say that a certain bodily arrangement is a *necessary condition* for the existence of soul. Indeed, Alexander may have intended to defend an authentically Aristotelian position against more materialist interpretations. Alexander's view does indeed exclude any personal immortality, but so does Aristotle's own, with the possible exception of his cryptic remarks in *De anima* 3.5 about the Active Intellect. Alexander compared soul as a principle of movement with the nature of the simple bodies, for example the weight of earth. It was by appeal to this conception of nature (itself Aristotelian enough; Aristotle, *Physics* 2.1.192b21) that Alexander explained the application to the simple bodies of Aristotle's claim that everything that moves is moved by something (Aristotle, *Physics* 8.4.254b24), defending it against Galen's attack in a treatise surviving only in Arabic. Alexander's view can be seen as an ancestor of the impetus theory used by Philoponus to explain the forced motion of projectiles (on which Alexander holds the orthodox Aristotelian view that it is caused by the transmission of movement through the air behind the projectile) and passed on by him to medieval science.

INTELLECT

Discussion of Aristotle's theory of intellect begins with Theophrastus. A major difficulty was how intellect—which can have no nature of its own if it is to be able to receive all intelligible forms—can ever begin to perform the task of abstraction by which it separates forms from their matter (cf. Theophrastus, frgs. 307, 309, 316–317; Fortenbaugh et al.). Alexander (*De anima* 84.24–27) later expresses the point by saying that our intellect, at birth, is not so much like a blank wax tablet as like the blankness of the wax tablet, and Xenarchus, an Aristotelian in the Augustan period, suggested, whether seriously or as a reductio ad absurdum, that potential intellect was to be identified with prime matter. It was natural to see Aristotle's remarks in *De anima* 3.5 about an Active Intellect that "makes all things," contrasted with the passive intellect that "becomes all things," as indicating some solution to this problem.

In the treatise *De generatione animalium*, moreover, Aristotle refers, in passing and with no very clear explanation, to intellect, alone of our soul-faculties, as entering into the father's seed "from outside" (2.3.736b27). At some point this was linked with the Active Intellect of *De anima*. One of Alexander's predecessors, possibly his teacher Aristoteles of Mytilene, is recorded in one of the minor works attributed to Alexander, *De intellectu (On Intellect)*, as answering the objection that such an intellect could not "come from outside" since, being immaterial, it could not change place at all.

Before answering the objection, the author of *On Intellect* first explains the role of the Active Intellect. For him, it is not an element in the soul of each individual separately; rather, it is identified with the supreme intelligible, the Unmoved Mover, and acts on our intellect to develop its potential through our thinking of it. The objection concerning movement is answered by the argument that the Active Intellect is present everywhere throughout the world, but can produce intelligence only in those parts of matter that are suitable—i.e., human beings (and any superior intelligences there may be). To this the author of *On Intellect* himself replies with objections similar to those that Alexander elsewhere brings against Stoic pantheism, complaining that involvement of the divine in the sublunary world is inconsistent with the divine dignity.

The author of *On Intellect* does, however, retain the basic explanation of the way in which the Active Intellect acts on our intellect: it is by our becoming aware of it so that it becomes, as it were, a paradigm of the intelligible for us. The difficulty with this is that it suggests that God is the first thing we actually think of, whereas it would be more plausible for awareness of him to be the culmination of our understanding. And in Alexander's own certainly authentic *De anima* we find two other explanations of the role of the Active Intellect; being the supreme intelligible itself, it must be the cause of other things' being intelligible, and it is also the cause of things' being intelligible because, as Unmoved Mover, it is the cause of their having being in the first place. Neither argument, however, indicates *how* the Active Intellect causes us to have intelligence; they simply provide ingenious grounds for asserting that it does so. Such concentration on solving the immediate problem is typical of Alexander, naturally enough for a commentator. An explanation would indeed be available if we were to suppose that the divine intellect already contained within itself the thoughts that we can come to apprehend, but that is essentially the position of Plotinus, and while he may be indebted to Alexander's account of intellect, there is no indication that Alexander himself took this step.

It has been debated whether Alexander's *De anima* is an attempt to improve on *On Intellect,* or the reverse. Both accounts, by identifying the Active Intellect with God rather than with a part of the individual's soul, deny personal immortality. Since thought, for Alexander as for Aristotle, is identical in form with its objects, and the Unmoved Mover is pure form without matter, our mind in a sense becomes the Unmoved Mover while it thinks of it, and can thus achieve a sort of temporary immortality; but that is all. Whether such a claim is to be seen in mystical terms, or whether it is simply the by-product of Alexander's undoubted ingenuity in attempting to clarify Aristotelian doctrine, is debatable. It is also questionable as exegesis of Aristotle; Aquinas was later to argue, against Alexander and against Averroës (who adopted Alexander's interpretation of the Active Intellect but differed from him in holding that the passive or potential intellect, too, was one and the same for all individuals), that Aristotle *had* intended the Active Intellect to be a personal element in each individual's soul and had thus intended a personal immortality. Alexander's interpretation became a focus of discussion of the question of immortality in Renaissance Italy.

ETHICS, POLITICS, RHETORIC

Throughout the period under discussion, Peripatetic ethics are characterized by a contrast with the paradoxical extremes of Stoicism. Rhetorical contrast may play a part; Cicero repeatedly portrays Theophrastus as weakening virtue by recognizing external goods, subject to fortune, as necessary for happiness. Theophrastus's position is not that far removed from some aspects of Aristotle's; after all, Aristotle had said that to call someone being tortured happy is absurd (*Nicomachean Ethics* 7.13.1153b19).

The claim that happiness is "completed" by the three classes of goods—of the soul, of the body, and external—is attributed also to Critolaus, though he argued that if virtue were placed on one side of a balance and bodily and external goods on the other, the former would far outweigh the latter. The account of Aristotle's views in Diogenes Laertius agrees with Critolaus in regarding bodily and external goods as *parts* of virtue (Diogenes Laertius, 5.30). Areius Didymus, however, seeking to reconcile Peripatetic and Stoic ethics, explicitly rejects Critolaus's view and regards bodily and external goods as *used by* virtuous activity.

Opposition to extremist Stoic ethical views played a part in the renewed interest in Aristotelianism on a popular level in the imperial period. It is particularly notable in the treatment of *pathos*, or "emotion," which Aristotle had regarded as fundamental to ethics. The Stoics confined the term to emotional reactions that went beyond right reason, and therefore regarded *pathé* as such as uniformly bad (though also recognizing a class of good feelings, *eupatheiai*, such as watchfulness by contrast with fear). The Peripatetics characteristically recommended not the absence of passions, *apatheia*, but *metriopatheia*, moderation in the passions. As Aristotle himself had taught, failure to show anger when anger is due is a shortcoming.

According to Areius Didymus, Aristotle regarded *pathos* not as an excessive movement of the soul but as an irrational movement *liable* to excess. Andronicus shared with the Stoics the view that all *pathos* involves a supposition that something is good or bad, and Boethus held that it was a movement possessing a certain magnitude. Aspasius rejected both these points, distancing the Peripatetic position further from the Stoic one. Aspasius's role in the development of Aristotelian ethics as a subject of study has been a topic of recent debate. His commentary on *Nicomachean Ethics* includes the "common books" that are transmitted both as part of *Nicomachean Ethics* and part of *Eudemian*. It has been shown that it is from the time of Aspasius that *Nicomachean Ethics*, rather than *Eudemian*, has been the work regularly studied and cited (as in the *Ethical Problems* attributed to Alexander, for example). Given the immense influence of the study of *Nicomachean Ethics* on ethical discussion up to and including the present century (it and Plato's *Republic* were the two works of ancient philosophy that were for a long time central to the Oxford philosophy curriculum, for example), the significance of this change can hardly be overstated.

The Stoics based their ethics on the appropriation *(oikeiōsis)*, or recognition, by living creatures of their own selves. The most fundamental impulse was that to self-preservation, which developed in two ways in human beings as they grew older, first by the person's coming to recognize virtue and reason as true self-interest, and second by the recognition of other people as akin to oneself. Attempts have been made to trace the origin of this Stoic doctrine to the post-Aristotelian Peripatos. It was indeed attributed to Aristotle by Areius Didymus, Boethus, and Xenarchus, but this may simply reflect Stoic influence and, in the case of Areius at least, a desire to assimilate Stoic and Aristotelian thought to each other. Theophrastus spoke of affinity *(oikeiotēs)* between all human beings and animals, but this is not really the same as the process of appropriation described by the Stoics. Some, however, have argued that a major part of Cicero's *On Ends*, including the account of moral development in terms of appropriation at 5.24–70, derives from Theophrastus, though book 5 as a whole represents the views of Antiochus of Ascalon.

Dicaearchus in his *Tripoliticus* set out the doctrine of the mixed constitution, a combination of monarchy, aristocracy, and democracy superior to each of these. The concept was already present, applied to Sparta, in Plato (*Laws* 4.712d) and Aristotle (*Politics* 2.6.1265b33); it was later to be applied to Rome by Polybius (6.11.11) and Cicero (*Republic* 1.69–70, 2.65), and it appears in Areius Didymus. Theophrastus developed Aristotle's study of rhetoric, elaborating from Aristotelian materials a doctrine of the four virtues of style (correctness, clarity, appropriateness, and ornament) that became standard for later writers, and dealing with rhetorical delivery, a subject Aristotle had neglected. Subsequently, however, the study of rhetoric became a subject in its own right and grew apart from Peripatetic philosophy.

The history of Aristotelianism as a separate tradition in the ancient world comes to an end with Alexander and Themistius. It has already been suggested that one reason for the first decline of Aristotelianism, in the Hellenistic period, was that it lacked a clear program to rival the attractions of Stoic or Epicurean dogmatism, on the one hand, and Pyrrhonian or Academic skepticism on the other. It is tempting to suppose that the reason for the second decline of Aristotelianism was the reverse of the first; the revived Aristotelianism of the empire was too closely tied to the exposition of texts, and lacked the scope and appeal of revived dogmatic Platonism. More might indeed have been made of the Aristotelian texts: Alexander's discussion of intellect might have shown the way here, whether he realized it or not. But further development of his ideas would have led to a position not unlike that of the Neoplatonists themselves. And this may indicate a further reason for the decline of the Peripatetic tradition.

Some scholars assess Alexander in terms of a tension between naturalism and mysticism. Indeed it has been suggested that the whole history of the Peripatetic tradition in antiquity can be seen in terms of an uneasy oscillation between a materialism insufficiently distinct from Stoicism and a belief in immaterial principles insufficiently distinct from Platonism. The school declined because it lacked a distinctive enough position of its own.

The end of a purely Peripatetic tradition was not, however, the end of Aristotelianism, in two ways. Aristotle's works continued to be studied by the Neoplatonists, although they were interpreted as applying to the sensible world as opposed to the higher, intelligible realm, and where that higher realm was concerned, the influence of Aristotelian doctrines and concerns, transmitted through the Peripatetic school, was felt. The placing of the Platonic Forms within the Divine Intellect may well go back to Xenocrates, the third head of Plato's Academy; but the way in which the theory of intellect was developed by Middle Platonists and Plotinus owes not a little to the Aristotelian doctrine of the Active Intellect and the interpretation of God as self-thinking immaterial thought. The Neoplatonic commentators did not all adopt the same approach to Aristotle's works—Philoponus, in particular, was ready to reject Aristotelian positions—but even a critical reaction reflects a type of influence.

It may also have been the type of reaction Aristotle would himself have welcomed. For the second legacy of ancient Aristotelianism to subsequent thought is a problem-solving approach to philosophy, structurally in texts like the *quaestiones* attributed to Alexander and the medieval format of responses to objections, and more generally in a certain cast of mind and way of proceeding. It is a thoroughly Aristotelian approach, for it is Aristotle himself who says that it is an advantage in any inquiry to "state all the difficulties well" (*Metaphysics* III.1.995a28). What we will never know is how definitive he regarded his own achievement as being, and how he would himself have regarded the ways in which his successors continued the process he had begun.

R. W. SHARPLES

Bibliography

I would like to acknowledge my considerable debt to the writings of Paul Moraux and Hans Gottschalk. A longer version of this article appeared in the *Routledge History of Philosophy*, vol. 2 (1999).

Texts and Translations

Aspasius, Alexander of Aphrodisias, and the Neoplatonic commentators on Aristotle: *Commentaria in Aristotelem Graeca (CAG)*. Berlin: Reimer, 1883–1909. Alexander's minor works in *Supplementum Aristotelicum* 2.1–2 (ibid., 1887–1892); annotated English translations in the *Aristotelian Commentators* series edited by R. Sorabii (London: Duckworth, 1987–).

Theophrastus. *De causis plantarum*. Ed. B. Einarson and G. K. K. Link. Loeb Classical Library.

———. *Historia plantarum*. Ed. S. Amigues. 4 vols. Paris: Budé, 1988–.

———. *Metaphysics*. Ed. W. D. Ross and F. H. Fobes. Oxford: Oxford University Press, 1929.

———. *Theophrastus of Eresus*. Ed. W. W. Fortenbaugh, P. M. Huby, R. W. Sharples (Greek and Latin) and D. Gutas (Arabic). 2 vols. Leiden: Brill, 1992; commentaries, 1995–.

Wehrli, F. *Die Schule des Aristoteles*, 2nd ed. Basel: Schwabe, 1967–1978.

Studies

Barnes, Jonathan. *Aristotle*. Oxford: Oxford University Press, 1982.

Fortenbaugh, W. W., et al., eds. *Rutgers University Studies in Classical Humanities*. New Brunswick, N.J.: Transaction, 1983–.

Gottschalk, H. B. "Aristotelian Philosophy in the Roman World." In *Aufstieg und Niedergang der römischen Welt (ANRW)*, II, 36, no. 2. Berlin: De Gruyter, 1987.

Hahm, D. E. "The Ethical Doxography of Arius Didymus." In *ANRW*, II, 36, no. 4.

Lynch, J. P. *Aristotle's School*. Berkeley: University of California Press, 1972.

Moraux, Paul. *Der Aristotelismus bei den Griechen*. Berlin: De Gruyter. Vol. 1, 1973; vol. 2, 1984; vol. 3, forthcoming.

Regenbogen, Otto. "Theophrastos." In *Paulys Realencyclopädie der Classischen Altertumswissenchaft*, suppl. 7. Stuttgart: Metzler, 1940. Pp. 1354–1562.

Repici, Luciana. *La natura e l'anima: Saggi su Stratone di Lampsaco*. Turin: Tirrenia, 1988.

Wehrli, Fritz. "Der Peripatos bis zum Beginn der römischen Kaiserzeit." In Friedrich Ueberweg, ed. Hellmut Flashar, *Grundriss der Geschichte der Philosophie: Die Philosophie der Antike*, vol. 3. Basel: Schwabe, 1983. Pp. 459–599.

CYNICISM

CYNICISM was an antiestablishment philosophical movement that arose in Greece in the 4th century B.C.E. around Diogenes of Sinope, called the Dog, and his disciples. It lasted until at least the 5th century C.E.; the last known Cynic philosopher, Sallustius, was connected with the circle of the Neoplatonist Proclus. Acting in all realms—political, moral, religious, literary, and philosophical—to contest traditional values in a radical way, Cynicism offered a "shortcut" to happiness: physical asceticism in pursuit of a moral end. In a period when speech was an instrument of power, Cynicism preferred the power of acts and testimony to the subtleties of discourse and, in this respect following the path opened up by Socrates, it gave priority to the existential experience of the wise man.

Study of this movement is hampered by a lack of documentation. Virtually nothing remains of ancient Cynic literature. We know these philosophers principally through anecdotes and sayings (passed down by Greek tradition but also by Arab gnomologies) whose historical value is impossible to verify. Some Cynic *Letters* have been preserved; unfortunately, they are pseudepigraphical. Moreover, the sources on which we depend are not unbiased: these include not only opponents of Cynicism, such as the Epicureans or certain Church Fathers, but also figures such as Epictetus and Julian, whose idealized views of Cynicism were shaped by their own personal convictions. Moreover, even when we have no reason to suspect bias, it is difficult to determine to what degree we can depend, for an understanding of Diogenes, on late sources like the five very substantial discourses (IV, VI, VIII, IX, and X) in which Dio Chrysostom presents the philosopher. Finally, because of the very nature of this movement, texts with doctrinal content are quite rare, and this is aggravated by the fact that our principal source, Book VI of Diogenes Laertius's *Lives of Eminent Philosophers* (in particular the doxographic sections 70–73 and 103–105), has been influenced by a Stoic outlook that has unquestionably distorted some of the theoretical aspects of Cynicism.

We must nevertheless try to discover behind the anecdotes, apothegms, and slogans not a system—for nothing is more contrary to the spirit of Cynicism—but at least a guiding thread, a homogeneous philosophical inspiration expressed in a coherent manner.

HISTORICAL SURVEY

We cannot speak of Cynicism without first exploring the meaning of this label. Two explanations were already available in antiquity, based on two different etymologies. The first, which certainly derives from a need for similarity with the Academy, the Stoa, or the Lyceum, links the movement to a place well known to Athenians of the period, the Cynosarges gymnasium, which housed a temple dedicated to Hercules and was where Antisthenes, one of Socrates' disciples, taught. This gymnasium was reserved for *nothoi*, that is, sons of an Athenian father and foreign mother, as well as for illegitimate children and freedmen. The etymology of the word *cynosarges* is itself uncertain: it may mean dog food, white dog, or fast dog. Partisans of this explanation of the word *cynicism* maintain that Antisthenes was the founder of the movement. The second explanation comes from a jest that compared the cynics to dogs *(kunes)* owing to the freedom and simplicity of their behavior and the shamelessness and impudence of their lifestyle, which led them to declare that acts ordinarily judged morally shameful were "unimportant": masturbation or copulating in public, eating in the public square, sleeping in empty earthenware jars or on street corners. The name "Dog" perfectly suits our philosophers, who took pains to "bark" loud and long; they would not only have accepted it, they would have adopted it proudly.

Cynicism was never a school. Is it even reasonable to speak of Cynicism or Cynics? This philosophical movement indeed readily located itself outside the traditional framework of school life: it had no fixed place of teaching, no succession of famous scholars, no courses or lectures; instead, it hurled disruptive "barkings" into the street, in squares, at temple doors, at the entrance to the stadium while the games were on, voiced by strong personalities who knew how to give weight to their message by flaunting their actions and their way of living.

Who was the founder of the movement? Was it Antisthenes, who, after studying with the orator Gorgias, became one of Socrates' well-known disciples, and was nicknamed *haplokuōn* (perhaps "plain dog," in an allusion to cynical frankness, or "dog with a plain coat," because of his *tribōn* [worn cloak], or else "natural dog," that is, one whose behavior was based on natural requirements and not on social conventions)? Or was it perhaps Diogenes of Sinope (412/403–324/321), the man in the tub who, while sunning himself in the Craneum gymnasium in Corinth, calmly asked an astounded Alexander to "stand out of [his] light" (Diogenes Laertius, *Lives* VI.38), and who used a lantern to look for men in broad daylight? The ancient tradition leans toward Antisthenes, but the sources on which it is founded are late (Epictetus, Dio Chrysostom, Aelian, Diogenes Laertius, Stobaeus, and the *Suda*), and the moderns suspect, perhaps rightly, that some Stoics in search of a Socratic lineage forged a pedigree extending through Socrates to Antisthenes, Diogenes, and Crates to Zeno, one that the authors of *Successions* would hasten to adopt, since it made their task so much easier. In fact the chronological and numismatic data are not unanimous, and we still do not know for sure whether Diogenes, exiled from Sinope, spent time with Antisthenes in Athens. Whatever role Antisthenes may have played (and he did play one, if only through the decisive influence his writings were to have on the earliest "Dogs"), there is no doubt that it was Diogenes who launched Cynicism as a movement and who determined its principal directions.

How could such a philosophy arise in 4th-century Athens and develop in the Hellenistic period? The society in which Diogenes lived was acquainted with all the refinements of luxury, as attested by the numerous anecdotes that show the philosopher castigating the behavior and gluttony of his contemporaries; we may conclude that Athenian society was in need of harsh censors. But we should not see Diogenes as an ignorant and unpolished man, inclined by his social origins to scorn the effects of civilization. He was the son of a banker, born in Sinope, a Greek city-state on the Euxine Sea in the Pontus region. Sinope was very active in the commercial realm and very advanced, owing to the numerous contacts it maintained with other centers. Diogenes apparently received a solid education there, to judge by the works he produced, whose titles Diogenes Laertius has preserved.

But 4th-century society was also one of contrasts. Around the edges of a brilliant civilization that was responsive to luxury, a world of the disadvantaged was growing: impoverished citizens, slaves, exiles, the victims of pirates, and so on. In such a context, an individual really was prey to terror; compelled to face Tuche, or Fortune, the only active divinity in this troubled world, with only his own resources, he felt helpless, condemned to individualism and a personal search for happiness. Thus we can imagine the effects of the vociferous Dog, exempt from complacency but extremely bracing, on individuals whose everyday existence was precarious. Like the other Hellenistic philosophies, but with extraordinary vigor, Cynicism thus set itself the goal of securing individual happiness.

Two major periods in the history of the movement have to be distinguished: the ancient Cynicism of the 4th and 3rd centuries B.C.E. and the imperial Cynicism of the 1st to 5th centuries C.E. The first period is dominated by the exceptional figures of Diogenes and his disciple Crates. The former was intransigent and in many respects heroic; he had chosen to shock, both by his way of life and by his caustic language. The latter was just as committed but perhaps more humane and more approachable in his manner. People admired Diogenes, the "heavenly dog," but they also feared him; they admired Crates, the "dear hunchback," and they liked him, too. We know that Diogenes left Sinope and took the path of exile after a murky adventure involving counterfeit money about which we shall never know the true story, or even whether it really happened. He went to Athens, where he may have frequented Antisthenes; captured by pirates on a sea voyage, he was sold as a slave to one Xeniades of Corinth, who made him his children's teacher. Diogenes had the chance to prove his never-failing frankness when he met Philip of Macedon, and later Philip's son Alexander. The numerous stories that circulated about his death attest to his wish to conform as much as possible to rules dictated by nature. Among his disciples, Crates of Thebes, born to a rich family, deliberately gave away all his resources to dedicate himself to Cynicism and live a real dog's life with his wife, Hipparchia of Maronea, even going so far as to make love in public. Crates, too, had his disciples, notably Metrocles of Maronea (Hipparchia's brother), Monimus of Syracuse, who began as the slave of a banker, and the famous Menippus of Gadara, also a slave, whose literary influence on writers such as Varro, Seneca, Petronius, Apuleius, and of course Lucian was very important.

In the following century, two people who were atypical, but who were unquestionable strong personalities, turned to the Cynic movement: Bion of Borysthenes (ca. 335–245 B.C.E.), son of a freed merchant of salting equipment and a courtesan, whose completely eclectic philosophical education led him in turn to the Academy, the Cynics, the Cyrenaics, and finally the Peripatetics; and Cercidas of Megalopolis (ca. 290–217 B.C.E.), a friend of Aratus of Sicyon, who was at once a statesman, a general, a legislator, and a poet. In addition to these colorful figures, thanks to Stobaeus we can mention Teles, a modest professor of philosophy who lived in Athens and Megara and who appealed to a circle of young people. We are indebted to Teles for passing on to us, in his *Diatribes* (the oldest testimony we have on the Cynico-Stoic diatribes), some sayings by several Cynic philosophers, including Crates, Metrocles, and especially Bion, the model Teles preferred.

During the next two centuries, Cynicism seems to have undergone a certain eclipse. In Greece, one can cite only the poet Meleager of Gadara (ca. 135–50 B.C.E.) and the *Pseudepigraphical Letters* of the Cynics, some of which date from this period; among the Romans, we see almost no one but the senator Marcus Favonius, an intimate of Cato of Utica, whose bearing and speech conformed to the Cynic style. However, beginning with the 1st century of the Christian era, that is, during a period when Rome was experiencing an economic prosperity that fostered the development of wealth and luxury, we see such an extraordinary revival of Cynicism that Diogenes' philosophy became the popular philosophy par excellence in Rome, Alexandria, Constantinople, and Athens. To be sure, exceptional personalities emerged: Demetrius of Corinth, a friend of Seneca and of Thrasea Paetus, was banished from Rome by Nero, then by Vespasian, and remained faithful to the short path of asceticism; Demonax of Cyprus professed a milder Cynicism that appealed to his laudatory biographer, Lucian. The latter adopted a very different tone, in contrast, with regard to Peregrinus Proteus, who professed both Cynicism and Christianity; with crudely slanderous insinuations, Lucian relates many piquant but unedifying anecdotes about Peregrinus that can be held quite suspect, thanks to the very different and even contradictory testimony left by Aulus Gellius. In the 2nd century we encounter Oenomaus of Gadara, whose highly audacious opinions would be criticized harshly later on by the Emperor Julian. Among other works, Oenomaus wrote one that we know under two titles: *Against the Oracles* and *Charlatans Unmasked,* in which he launches attacks of a rare violence against gods whom he pronounces unjust, against soothsayers whom he treats as ignorant charlatans, and above all against oracles whose fraudulent character he delights in stressing.

Peregrinus was not the only example of a Christian Cynic. In the 4th century we also know Maximus Hero of Alexandria, a friend of Gregory Nazianzus who became the latter's worst enemy when he surreptitiously got himself named bishop of Constantinople one night (Gregory had hoped to assume that office himself). Maximus Hero practiced frugality, made use of Cynic frankness, wore the *tribōn,* the rough little cloak characteristic of Cynic dress, and claimed to be a citizen of the entire universe. Finally, in the following century, the figure of Sallustius stands out. Damascius tells us that after studying law, Sallustius attended the rhetorical schools of Alexandria and devoted himself to Cynicism, practicing a rigorous and austere asceticism. He succeeded in diverting one member of Proclus's circle, Athenodorus, from philosophy; later, Sallustius quarreled with Proclus himself.

But the Cynicism of the imperial period was not confined to these prominent figures. It was above all a popular philosophy that attracted its adepts from the most disadvantaged regions of the large cities, from among poor citizens and slaves. It was also a philosophy practiced collectively, yet outside of any school framework; in fact, along with those who, like Oenomaus, produced literary texts, groups of Cynics roamed the streets of Rome and Alexandria, begging on street corners and taking up stations where the crowds were thickest: on squares swarming with people, in ports, or outside the stadiums. These beggars harangued an undefined public that changed from day to day. We can imagine that charlatans, relying on the principle that clothes make the philosopher, were not in short supply; they were the targets of the criticisms leveled by Epictetus, Lucian, and Julian. All the same, imperial Cynicism on the whole remained faithful to the tradition of the Dogs, to the extent that it remained faithful to the practice of asceticism.

The Cynics have often been compared to members of the most rigorous Christian sects, such as the Encratites and the Apotactites. It is certainly easy to see the resemblances between these two movements: they both defended poverty, criticized false values, vaunted the universality of their message, and, although their ultimate goals were different, they shared the same aspiration to self-abnegation. Nevertheless, while Peregrinus and Maximus Hero were

Christians, it was Crescens, a Cynic, who was responsible for the martyrdom of Justin in 165, and Church Fathers such as St. Augustine and Sidonius Apollinaris did not hide the fact that they were shocked by the Cynics' impudence and their rejection of the most widely shared moral values.

Cynicism did not disappear with the Roman empire. It aroused great interest, and it has even undergone an occasional resurgence in the modern period and in our own era. Thus the reader of Montaigne's *Essais* often comes across a reference to Diogenes, a Diogenes whom Montaigne came to know through Diogenes Laertius. But it was in the 18th century, in the atmosphere of the Enlightenment, that Cynicism came back into prominence most compellingly. In 1770, in Germany, Christoph Martin Wieland, an Enlightenment philosopher, published a work titled *Sokrates mainomenos oder die Dialogen des Diogenes von Sinope (Socrates out of His Senses, or Dialogues of Diogenes of Sinope)*; it was a great success. In France, Rousseau was nicknamed "Diogenes," quite to his own disliking, by a number of his contemporaries—with respect by Kant and Wieland, with sarcasm and spite by Voltaire. The latter used this appellation to make fun of him yet again: under his pen, Rousseau became "Diogenes' monkey," a "little would-be Diogenes who hides the soul of a scoundrel under the cloak of Diogenes," and even a "Diogenes without a lantern," which was the ultimate insult in a period when everyone aspired to Enlightenment. D'Alembert, for his part, thought that every age, and especially his own, had need of a Diogenes. However, it is unquestionably with the Diderot of *Le neveu de Rameau* that we can best measure the attraction exerted by the spirit of Cynicism. Both of the satire's protagonists, Moi and Lui, quote Diogenes as their authority. Moi, the narrator, represents a Cynicism faithful to the ancient tradition, while Lui, the Nephew, the incarnation of a parasite who despises society and voluntarily chooses a kind of ethic of abjection, already heralds cynicism in the modern sense of the term.

The 19th century had its own version; it witnessed the flowering of what Ludwig Stein called Nietzsche's "Neocynicism." In fact, the *Umwertung der Werte*, the inversion of values extolled by Nietzsche, was deliberately rooted in "the Diogenean counterfeiting of money." Today the word *cynicism* conveys a rather different reality from the ancient *kunismos*. We use the term *cynics* for those who deliberately flaunt an attitude of impudence, of bold contempt for propriety and systematic immorality. Today cynics care nothing about helping their contemporaries on the way to happiness; their provocation is purely negative, and the mere idea of asceticism has no part in their way of life. If there is any link connecting the philosophy of Diogenes to the present cynicism, it seems to be only superficial, external. Even when the attitude is identical, the underlying motives and aim are not at all the same. It is worth noting that the German language, in an attempt to avoid confusion—at least since the 19th century—has used two distinct terms: *Kynismus*, designating the ancient Cynic philosophy, and *Zynismus,* specifying the modern attitude. German philosophers have focused recently on resemblances and differences between the two notions; pertinent here are Heinrich Niehues-Pröbsting's *Der Kynismus des Diogenes und der Begriff des Zynismus* and Peter Sloterdijk's *Kritik der zynischen Vernunft.* The latter text, which has been extraordinarily successful in Germany, explains why *Kynismus* liberates while *Zynismus* oppresses, why the one warrants respect while the other should be condemned, and it proposes *Kynismus* as the only alternative to the generalized *Zynismus* of the present day.

THE PRINCIPLES OF THE CHALLENGE

Diogenes makes a point of asserting difference. "He was going into a theatre, meeting face to face those who were coming out, and, being asked why: 'This,' he said, 'is what I practise doing all my life'" (*Lives* VI.64). "When people laughed at him because he walked backward beneath the Portico, he said to them: 'Aren't you ashamed, you who walk backward along the whole path of existence, and blame me for walking backward along the path of the promenade?'" (Stobaeus, III.iv.83).

Diogenes had taken up "counterfeiting money" as a slogan, perhaps as the result of a personal experience of counterfeiting for which he (or his father) may have been responsible. The phrase referred to the idea of reversing the currently respected values in all realms of human activity, individual and collective, and replacing these false values with new ones based on the Cynics' view of humankind and of life—an undertaking of systematic subversion.

For the Cynic, only the individual matters, with all his singularity: to ensure his happiness, he must be shown the way to individual revolution. From this perspective, the Cynic rejects all the prohibitions that ordinary social life requires and urges a radical return to nature. Emboldened by a heightened lucidity, he understands that man's unhappiness derives from his intrinsic weakness, which is attributable to his passions, to pride, fear, and the attraction to pleasure, and also to the aggressions of the world around him that lead him to sacrifice to illusory values. A slave to fame, to social obligations, and to wealth, which leaves him insatiable, man spends his life engaged in feverish activity directed toward the emptiest of goals. Thus Diogenes points out an athlete who trains like a madman in the stadium in order to triumph in the Olympic games, or a politician prepared to make any sacrifice to win power, not to mention rich men, or committed gourmets who expend great energy so that their table can provide countless pleasures for the most delicate palate. For such men, prey to all sorts of desires and anguish, Diogenes, like a doctor with his patient, wants to make him understand that the real struggle does not lie where he thinks it does, and that a conversion is in order. Given that the ultimate goal is happiness, man must create three indispensable conditions in himself to achieve it: autarchy, that is, the ability to be self-sufficient and completely independent; apathy, which allows him to be impassible under all circumstances; and, finally, freedom. Whereas people traditionally deem a man happy when he is provided with abundant material goods, Diogenes shows on the contrary that happiness is achieved when one manages to limit one's needs to the maximum degree and to reach a total serenity that makes it possible to face the whims of fortune without any difficulty. From this perspective, the Cynic proposes animals as concrete models of autarchy, for animals are able to support themselves with what nature offers, and God as a theoretical model, according to the principle that "it was the privilege of the gods to need nothing and of god-like men to want but little" (*Lives* VI, 105). In one of his poems, Crates proclaimed: "Far be it from me to pile up fabulous treasures! I scheme only to achieve the happiness of the beetle, and the ease of the ant" (Julian, *Discourse* VII.9.213c).

THE SOCIAL CHALLENGE

The most obvious form is the social challenge Diogenes posed in his everyday lifestyle. Its symbol was his dress: the cloak *(tribōn)*, folded in two, generally filthy, which served as a wrap in all seasons and also as a blanket at night; the staff, at once a voyager's staff, beggar's rod, and royal scepter; the double sack into which the cynic put everything he needed for daily life. To complete the picture, the philosopher had a long beard, his hair was long and dirty, and he went barefoot. This negligent appearance was one of the components of the practice of asceticism: it showed a deliberate intent to practice social nonconformity and also an ardent desire to return to nature. Perhaps it was derived from tragedy, since the Cynics had taken as models not only Heracles, but also Telephus, his son, whom Euripides put on stage in the tragedy that bears his name, and who arrived at Aulis dressed in rags, carrying a little basket.

The Cynic opposed the society of his own time by hurling invectives and using frankness to the point of insult. He took to task those around him who tried to avoid him at all cost for fear of his sarcasm. Everything in which his contemporaries took pride was systematically belittled: Olympic victories, the exercise of power, intellectual success. Moreover, Diogenes did not hesitate to play the parasite and beg for alms, thinking he was reclaiming in this way only what was his due. But what most shocked the people who encountered him was his shamelessness. It was more than distasteful to see Diogenes in the public square, unembarrassed, doing anything he wanted to do: eating, urinating, masturbating. For their part, Crates and Hipparchia created a scandal by consummating their union in the sight of all, to the great embarrassment of poor Zeno, the Stoic philosopher, who tried as best he could to hide them from prying eyes with an old cloak (Apuleius, *Florides* 14).

THE POLITICAL CHALLENGE

Diogenes, who lived at the time Alexander went off to conquer the world, declared himself *a-polis* (without a city), *a-oikos* (homeless), and *kosmopolites* (a citizen of the universe), and Crates declared: "Not one tower has my country nor one roof / But wide as the whole earth its citadel / And home prepared for us to dwell therein" (Diogenes Laertius, *Lives* VI.9). Yet their contemporaries were not yet ready to give up the traditional markers of civic and political life, especially as cynical cosmopolitanism appeared rather negative: in being a citizen of the world, the philosopher is a citizen nowhere, and Diogenes advocated abstention with regard to all political commitment; the very notion constituted an impediment to individual liberty, in his eyes. In keeping with this stance, as he explained in his *Republic*, he rejected the law that was the cornerstone of the city-state, and he opposed to it the law that rules the universe, otherwise called natural law. His work, as one might well imagine, created a scandal, for he encouraged people to drop all taboos, to reject every impediment to individual freedom, and thus potentially to practice anthropophagy and incest, to hold women and children in common, and finally to practice complete sexual liberty. In the Cynic republic, there would no longer be room for weapons, and knucklebones would take the place of money. Diogenes' text produced such a scandal that some Stoics, contemporaries of Philodemus, an Epicurean philosopher of the 1st century B.C.E., judged it too brash and declared, to avoid being tainted by such theories, that it was not by Diogenes.

THE RELIGIOUS CHALLENGE

It should come as no surprise that Diogenes challenged the religious practices of his time in just as radical a manner. He relentlessly called attention to the lack of morality his contemporaries displayed in their way of honoring the gods and in the demands they made on them; he showed that popular religion came from custom and convention, not from nature, and that it was in fact an obstacle to the apathy he sought, because of the fears it inspired in people, particularly the fear of death and infernal punishment. Diogenes rejected all anthropomorphism and criticized religious institutions and traditional forms of the cult, notably the mysteries, prayer, interpretation of dreams, and ritual purifications. It was unacceptable to him that human happiness should depend on practices that have nothing to do with man's moral disposition. But his challenge went even further. He had no rational image of the world, no providential concept of nature. He did not think that the universe was made for man or that there was a mystery of the world to penetrate. His vision of things showed the gods to be, in a sense, insignificant. By imitating animals, man would come to know only animal happiness and would be able to accept the inevitable. Thus the Cynic drew his strength from his impassibility in the face of destiny, not because he accepted its superior or mysterious rationality, but simply because he himself asserted his will to be impassible. Noting the artificiality of the world in which we live, he resigned himself to it. His realism and his desire to refuse all illusions required him to submit to the laws of nature and to refrain from making pronouncements on questions that were beyond him. Thus one could define the Cynic's overall position as an agnosticism that allowed him to preserve his apathy and to achieve his own happiness, day after day, by willpower alone.

THE PHILOSOPHICAL CHALLENGE
AND ITS CONSEQUENCES

Perhaps it was with regard to the traditional notion of philosophy that Cynicism offered its most radical challenge. When a new philosophy offered solutions, these were generally formulated in opposition to the ones offered by existing schools. Cynicism was no exception. It was not an improvised reaction; it proceeded to evaluate the choices offered by contemporary philosophies, all of which it grouped together into an overall stance whose inefficacy and intellectualism it denounced. But at the same time, Cynicism was not purely and simply a denunciation of philosophy, since it proposed a new kind of philosophy, one deemed more authentic and more effective at ensuring human happiness. Cynicism represented itself, indeed, as a "short-cut" (Diogenes Laertius, Lives VII.121), accessible even to those who lacked education, those who had not had the means to frequent the renowned schools of philosophy. It did away with the notion of an intellectual elite that took itself too seriously. Diogenes was aware of the pretension it takes to proclaim oneself a philosopher, and "to one who says to him, 'You know nothing and yet you philosophize,' he replies: 'Even if I am but a pretender to wisdom, that in itself is philosophy'" (Lives VI.64). To counterfeit traditional philosophy, that is, to philosophize without claiming to know anything, was, from the Cynic's standpoint, the only legitimate practice.

In a period when speculative philosophy was in the process of acquiring its elitist credentials, Cynicism played the spoilsport with its distrust of study, reason, and debate. While the Platonic dialogues were offering a dazzling demonstration of superior intelligence, while Aristotle was broadening his research into all fields of learning and the Stoics were about to work out a vast systematic construction, the Cynics threw themselves into provocation, deliberately breaking with the intellectual component of philosophy and insisting on existential experience. Why this rejection of paideia? First because, in their eyes, virtue depended on actions, and then because the disciplines traditionally taught—music, geometry, astronomy, and so on—were not useful for the acquisition of virtue. What is the use of tuning the strings of one's lyre if one leaves untuned the temper of one's soul? As a general rule, the Cynics did not value book learning; they far preferred practice to study. One day when Hegesias begged him to lend him one of his works, Diogenes replied: "You are a simpleton, Hegesias; you do not choose painted figs but real ones; and yet you pass over the true training and would apply yourself to written rules" (*Lives* VI.48).

The path to virtue recommended by Diogenes was thus that of a purely corporeal asceticism, based on daily training, and its aim was the health of the soul. This asceticism was conceived as a preventive method: anyone who practices *ponoi* (suffering) daily, by drinking only water, eating very frugally, sleeping on the bare ground, and enduring the cold and heat of the seasons, feels no fear, because he knows that one day when suffering is imposed on him by *Tuche* (Fortune) in the form of exile, poverty, or dishonor, he will be trained to bear it and will be able to meet it with serenity. Thus poverty appears to be "an instinctive support for philosophy." If one submits to the law of Cynic asceticism, that is, to a lifestyle based on frugality and to satisfying only life's bare necessities, one becomes autarchic, apathetic, free, and therefore happy, like Diogenes, "a homeless exile, to his country dead, / A wanderer who begs his daily bread" (*Lives* VI.38). "Nothing in life, . . . he maintained, has any chance of succeeding without strenuous practice; and this is capable of overcoming anything. Accordingly, instead of useless toils men should choose such as nature recommends, whereby they might have lived happily. Yet such is their madness that they choose to be miserable" (VI.71). If happiness is the result of such strenuous asceticism, we may suspect that Diogenes also falsified the idea of pleasure. For him, true pleasure came from contempt for pleasure and had nothing to do with the way civilized life commonly defines it. This is why, even as a prisoner of pirates, Diogenes continued to be happy, for owing to his asceticism he was able to preserve a sphere within himself that no external aggression could disturb. Whereas philosophers such as Plato and Aristotle sought truth through the intermediary of learning, the Cynic philosopher sought internal peace and serenity by training his will and submitting his body to the harsh law of asceticism.

Such a conception of philosophy could not help but seem provocative and give rise to criticism. In fact, Cynic philosophy seems to have been challenged fairly early, perhaps as early as the period of classical Cynicism. In any event, it was challenged in the 2nd century by one Hippobotus, the author of *On the Sects*, who explicitly excluded the Cynic sect from his list. Among the complaints leveled against Cynicism, the absence of coherent dogmas and of a specific end, of a clearly defined *telos*, seem particularly noteworthy. Certain critics, as Diogenes Laertius recalls (*Lives* VI.103), thus thought they could reduce the Cynic movement to a simple way of life, and they refused to grant it the status of a *hairesis* (school).

The antiestablishment positions of the Cynics aroused discomfort among the Stoics, though not among those of the earliest generations. For Zeno of Citium, a disciple of Crates of Thebes, and probably also for Chrysippus, Stoicism seemed in fact to be Cynicism's heir. One can nevertheless perceive a considerable divergence, for as some of the Cynic attitudes were reinterpreted within Stoicism, they took on quite different meanings from the initial inspiration. For Zeno and Chrysippus, the overturning of customs and taboos, scandalous as it was, would serve to affirm a natural law valorized in itself insofar as it expressed the rationality of the universe. For the Cynic, however, these attitudes marked a break with society and its laws, without going beyond this critique to manifest an idealization of the order of nature.

Later on, certain Stoics influenced by Panetius, hoping to avoid being linked to the scandalous positions of the Dogs, declared that Diogenes did not write the *Republic* attributed to him; others also saw Zeno's *Republic* as an inauthentic work (Diogenes Laertius, *Lives* VII.33–34), or else as an error of his youth (Philodemus, *De Stoicis* col. IX). One approach was as good as another to wipe out the scandal. The procedure could be less flagrant, more subtle. Epictetus, for example, rejected the Cynicism of his contemporaries and admired that of the past. It was certainly easier to refer to a Diogenes remote in time, by then a quasi-legendary figure, than to address the Dogs who were very much alive, dirty, biting, "barking," and begging.

THE LITERARY CHALLENGE

It may well seem surprising that the Cynics produced an abundant body of literary work (which has unfortunately been lost), given that they rejected every form of learning. But here again, in order to understand their position, we must fall back on the notion of "falsification." Diogenes and his followers succeeded in practicing subversion at the very heart of writing itself. While they borrowed the framework of traditional genres, they marked these with their own imprint. We attribute dialogues, letters, and tragedies to Diogenes, and to Crates letters and tragedies as well; however, the latter won fame especially in the poetic genre, with elegies such as his *Hymn to the Pierian Muses*, in which he parodied Solon, and poems such as *Pera (The Beggar's Sack)*, in which he imitated Homer. Crates' poetry, especially his Homeric parodies, seems to have had a decisive influence on Timon of Phlius, author of *Silloi*. Moreover, the Cynics invented new literary genres that achieved great success later on: these included diatribe (Bion of Borysthene), satire (Menippus of Gadara), and the *chreia* (Metrocles, and perhaps before him Diogenes), generally rather short philosophical remarks often accompanied by a flash of wit. Above all, the Cynics practiced a new style, so characteristic of their writing that it was called the *kunikos tropos* (Demetrius, *De elocutione* 259); one of its compositional principles is the *spoudaiogeloion*, a mixture of humor and seriousness honored in the light verse of Monimus of Syracuse and Crates of Thebes. Despite their preference for acts, these philosophers knew how to use words in new ways, practicing humor and making skilled use of piercing sallies or multilayered wordplay. Their writing had playful elements, even as it remained, paradoxically, powerfully serious.

THE PEDAGOGICAL CHALLENGE

A doctor of souls, like every philosopher of the Hellenistic period, the Cynic, though in many respects a misanthrope, was a man of crowds and assemblies; he needed a public receptive to his "barkings." A missionary in his own way, he sought to convince, to get his message across. To this end, he used three weapons: frankness, which led him to scold and use biting words; humor, or, rather, sarcastic sallies that could take the form of derision, light joking, or buffoonery, and that were designed to force the interlocutor to react; and, finally, provocation, gratuitous only in appearance, which allowed the Cynic to bring his interlocutor to ask himself questions directly, to emerge from his lethargy. Diogenes was at once the guilty conscience of his time and the midwife of scandal.

Not only have Cynics not disappeared from view, as we can tell from the numerous publications devoted to them in recent years, but they seem be undergoing a revival. Why? Cynicism can be reproached for proposing a reductive morality that offers a totally negative happiness consisting in experiencing no sorrow and acknowledging no difficulties. One can also stress that this happiness is offered to truncated human beings, mutilated in their aspirations, who practice an attitude of retreat with regard to engagements of all kinds and who renounce every project of an intellectual nature. One can finally judge that the morality in question is too narrow, too centered on the individual, and that the tribute paid to independence and to happiness is too great. Still, the Cynics continue to exert their fascination. Among these philosophers, lived experience entails such dynamism, such passion for life and happiness, that one remains captivated even if one does not share their manner of "making life wild."

Cynicism challenges the historian of philosophy in particular, for it reveals that philosophy, contrary to all expectations, is not just an exercise of reason. Diogenes was said to be "a Socrates gone mad." With the Cynics, one is always at the limit of madness, on the line between laughter and sobriety, between comedy and tragedy: in other words, in an uncomfortable, ambivalent position. Thus it was more convenient to ridicule them or to forget them. But for all that, Diogenes has not put down his stick or put out his lantern. He continues, and will continue, to stroll backward through porticoes.

MARIE-ODILE GOULET-CAZÉ
Translated by Rita Guerlac and Anne Slack

Bibliography

Texts and Translations

Billerbeck, Margarethe, ed. *Epiktet: Vom Kynismus.* Philosophia Antiqua 34. Leiden: E. J. Brill, 1978.

———. *Der Kyniker Demetrius: Ein Beitrag zur Geschichte der frühkaiserzeitlichen Popularphilosophie.* Philosophia Antiqua 36. Leiden: E. J. Brill, 1979.

Diogenes Laertius. *Lives of Eminent Philosophers.* Trans. R. D. Hicks. Loeb Classical Library.

———. *Vies et doctrines des philosophes illustres.* Ed. Marie-Odile Goulet-Cazé. Paris: Librairie Générale Française, 1999.

Dorandi, Tiziano. "Filodemo: Gli stoici (PHerc 155 e 339)." *Cronache Ercolanesi* 12 (1982): 91–133. (In particular, Dorandi edits, translates, and comments on the accounts of Diogenes' *Politeia* preserved in Philodemus's *De Stoicis.*)

Giannantoni, Gabriele. *Socratis et Socraticorum Reliquis,* 2nd ed., expanded. 4 vols. Naples: Bibliopolis, 1990. Vol. 2, pp. 135–589; commentary in vol. 4, nn. 21–55, pp. 195–583.

Kindstrand, Jan Fredrik. *Bion of Borysthenes: A Collection of the Fragments with Introduction and Commentary.* Acta Universitatis Upsaliensis—Studia Graeca Upsaliensia 11. Uppsala: University of Uppsala, 1976 (distributed by Almquist and Wiksell International, Stockholm).

Malherbe, Abraham J., ed. *The Cynic Epistles: A Study Edition.* Society of Biblical Literature, Sources for Biblical Study, no. 12. Missoula, Mont.: Scholars Press, 1977.

Paquet, Léonce. *Les Cyniques grecs: Fragments et témoignages.* Philosophica 4. Ottawa: Editions de l'Université d'Ottawa, 1975; Philosophica 35, new ed., rev. and expanded, Ottawa: Les Presses de l'Université d'Ottawa, 1988; shortened version with foreword by Marie-Odile Goulet-Cazé, Paris: Librairie Générale Française, 1992.

Studies

Billerbeck, Margarethe, ed. *Die Kyniker in der modernen Forschung: Aufsätze mit Einführung und Bibliographie.* Bochumer Studien zur Philosophie 15. Amsterdam: B. R. Grüner, 1991.

Brancacci, Aldo. "I *koine areskonta* dei Cinici e la *koinōnia* tra cinismo e stoicismo nel libro VI (103–105) delle *Vite* di Diogene Laerzio." *Aufstieg und Niedergang der Römischen Welt (ANRW)* II, 36, no. 6 (1992): 4049–4075.

———. *Oikeios logos: La filosofia del linguaggio di Antistene.* Elenchos 20. Naples: Bibliopolis, 1990.

Branham, R. Bracht, and Marie-Odile Goulet-Cazé, eds. *The Cynics: The Cynic Movement in Antiquity and Its Legacy.* Berkeley: University of California Press, 1997.

Döring, Klaus. "Sokrates, die Sokratiker und die von ihnen begründeten Traditionen." In *Grundriss der Geschichte der Philosophie: Die Philosophie der Antike,* vol II. 1. Ed. Helmut Flashar. Basel: Schwabe, 1998.

Dudley, Donald R. *A History of Cynicism: From Diogenes to the 6th Century* A.D. London: Methuen, 1937; repr. New York: Gordon Press, 1974.

Goulet-Cazé, Marie-Odile. *L'ascèse cynique: Un commentaire de Diogène Laërce VI*

70–71. Histoire des doctrines de l'Antiquité classique 10. Paris: Librairie Philosophique J. Vrin, 1986.

———. "Le Cynisme à l'époque impériale." *ANRW* II, 36, no. 4 (1990): 2720–2833.

———. "Le Livre VI de Diogène Laërce: Analyse de sa structure et réflexions méthodologiques." *ANRW* II, 36, no. 6 (1992): 3880–4048.

Goulet-Cazé, Marie-Odile, and Richard Goulet, eds. *Le Cynisme ancien et ses prolongements*. Actes du colloque international du CNRS (Paris, 22–25 July 1991). Paris: Presses Universitaires de France, 1993.

Niehues-Pröbsting, Heinrich. *Der Kynismus des Diogenes und der Begriff des Zynismus*. Humanistische Bibliothek I, 40. Munich: Wilhelm Fink Verlag, 1979.

Onfray, Michel. *Cynismes: Portrait du philosophe en chien*. Paris: Grasset, 1990.

Sloterdijk, Peter. *Critique of Cynical Reason*. Trans. Michael Eldred. Minneapolis: University of Minnesota Press, 1987.

HELLENISM AND
CHRISTIANITY

To STUDY THE RELATION between Christianity and Hellenism is to think simultaneously of harmony and contrast. This ambivalence is perfectly illustrated by Paul's sermon to the Areopagus: a missionary sermon addressed to the Athenians and a reflection of the Hellenistic approach to true knowledge of God, it combines a Stoic conception of the relation of man to God with the doctrine of salvation by the resurrected Christ. The scene also sets in place the roles of partners and antagonists: in their approach to a new form of doctrine, the Greeks are torn between mocking rejection and curiosity; the disciple of Christ contrives to pour his preaching into the mold of their culture, to minimize the differences while at the same time contriving to draw his audience into a movement of radical conversion. On the Christian side, there will be no end, in the following centuries, to the alternation of conciliation and rupture. Paul himself will not persevere in his pacifism. He knows how to proclaim brutally the incompatibility between the wisdom of the Greeks and his message, "A crucified Christ: to the Jews an obstacle that they cannot get over, to the pagans madness" (1 Corinthians 1:23).

Still, one fact must be stressed. Christianity has had a strong tie with Hellenism from the beginning, in that it was spread by means of Greek. The oldest Christian writings, the authentic letters of Paul, were written in Greek. Whatever may have been the linguistic form of the oral traditions and underlying sources of the canonical Gospels, these, too, were composed in Greek. The choice of this language is not limited to the mission of the "Apostle to the Gentiles." It is inherent in the usage of the communities that produced the texts that were later canonized as a coherent set, the New Testament. The Jews of the Diaspora were speakers of Greek. They adopted the *koine*, the language of communication throughout the Orient from the time of Alexander's conquests. Galilee was strongly marked by Hellenistic civilization, and even in Judaea, Greek was widespread.

Koine left its imprint on the religious expression of the authors of the New Testament, who used as their Bible the Septuagint, that is, the Greek translation of the Bible begun in Alexandria in the 3rd century B.C.E. and followed up largely in Palestine. It is also the language in which revisions were made, and in which various writings called "intertestamentary" were produced, forming the multiple Jewish traditions well known to the first Christian authors.

It is precisely these Jewish origins of Christianity that draw our attention toward Hellenism in the larger sense, in its cultural and intellectual dimensions. The mindsets, the ways of thinking, the literary products of the first Christian centuries bear witness to the meeting that had already taken place between Hellenism and Judaism. A process of Hellenization began with the Greek translation of the Torah, the Pentateuch, and continued with the works written directly in Greek, like the Book of Wisdom. It grew more vigorous in Alexandrian Judaism, owing to contributions by authors such as Aristobulus and especially Philon; the latter consciously adapted Greek philosophical concepts to his understanding of the Bible by means of allegory, producing a theology, a cosmology, and an anthropology that profoundly influenced the first church fathers.

This Hellenized Judaism plays an important role starting with the earliest Christian missions, as attested by the figure of Apollos, born in Alexandria, who definitively joined the new faith at Ephesus, before preaching the "Way of the Lord" to the Jews of Corinth (Acts 18). The exegesis of the Letter to the Hebrews shows some resemblance to Philon's style. The horizon of thinking found in John's Gospel is clearly apparent in the religious and philosophical writings of the same Philon. It also has some affinity with the intellectual universe of the properly Hellenistic current that produced the hermetic writings. This literature dates from the 2nd and 3rd centuries, but it reveals a more ancient religious trend and, in its way, the reciprocal fruitfulness of Greek and oriental thought.

Among the so-called apostolic works of the Fathers, the *Letters* of Ignatius of Antioch take their place in the tradition of Johannine theology. Barnabus's *Epistle* makes use, in his exegesis of Moses' dietary prescriptions, of the moral allegories already suggested by Hellenized Judaism. The *Epistle to the Corinthians* of Clement of Rome, who witnessed the variety of intermingling currents in the Christian community of Rome at the end of the 1st century, abounds in traces of Hellenistic culture. Clement was well versed in the methods of contemporary rhetoric. At the same time, he had access to the images and themes of what has come to be called the Cynico-Stoic argument; he drew on these to invoke the combat of virtue, to recommend voluntary exile out of devotion to the group, and to give examples of self-sacrifice among the Gentiles. Some of his ideas recall Stoic notions about divinity, as being exempt from anger, or the harmony of the world, a model for human concord. In his writings, one can find echoes of the Pythagorean theme of friendship and communion among men and between humankind and the divine. Still, all these turns and motifs derive only indirectly from Hellenism. They are rooted first of all in Jewish homiletic, which had already absorbed them, and they were modified by specifically biblical concepts.

Starting in the middle of the 2nd century, the confrontation between Christianity and Hellenism, provoked by the expansion of the new religion into a pagan milieu and by the resistance of Greco-Roman philosophers and governors concerned with political control, led, among Christian apologists, to explicitly formulated problematical questions that are related to Paul's sermon to the Areopagus. The first to confront the difficulty with the requirement of thinking as a philosopher and as a Christian was Justin Martyr. In his *Apologia*, written around 153 to 155 C.E. on the pretext of defending his religion against slander, he sought to transform the Greco-Roman world following the model of his own intellectual and spiritual itinerary, which had led him from philosophy to Christianity, according to the narrative he offered at the beginning of another work, *Dialogue with Tryphon*. In reference to Plato, the Stoics, the poets, and prose writers, he dared to proclaim: "Whatever good they taught belongs to us Christians" (*II Apologia* 13.4). This triumphal gesture implies a favorable judgment on Greek thought. Justin saw Greek thought as capable of presenting real entities, at least confusedly. According to him, there is a kinship between the partial generation of the Logos in the intelligence of the philosophers and the Logos born of the unbegotten and ineffable God. A Platonist by training, Justin remained one, appearances notwithstanding, after his conversion. His knowledge of Plato did not depend simply on doxographic collections or anthologies. He makes precise references in his work to the texts of Plato himself. In his exchanges with the Christian master who is thought to have led him to the faith, he carries over the critical method set forth by Plato in his dialogues. And having become a Christian, he refuses to grant any propositions except those that could be deduced rationally. His system even seems very close to that of the most original Platonist of his time, Numenius.

This did not prevent Justin from borrowing from the Jewish apologetics of the Alexandrian tradition the theory that the teachings of philosophy proceed from the prophets of the Bible, or from affirming, in particular, that Plato found his material in Moses. This theory was not without parallel on the Greek side in this period of infatuation with "barbaric wisdom," as we learn from Numenius's famous remark: "Who is Plato, if not Moses speaking Greek?" The coexistence of a rational explanation and a myth of plagiarism affirming that Christian revelation fulfills Greek philosophy is found again at the end of the 2nd century in the writings of Clement of Alexandria, who praises the progress achieved by the Greeks in learning, all the while excoriating their "larceny."

Clement is certainly the most "Greek" of the church fathers. In his *Hortatory Address*, exhorting Greeks to conversion, he transforms the language of Homer, Pindar, and the Euripides of *Bacchantes*. In *Pedagogue*, he presents Christian virtue as the perfection of the successful man, as modeled by the rules for good living in a well-regulated society and the ethical ideal of the philosophers. *Miscellanies* leads toward the "aphorism," which brings Platonic contemplation to its culmination in the illumination dispensed by the divine Logos, the Son, mediator between a transcendent God the Father and man. In the first stage of this progression, Clement puts into play an idea of the unity of learning, subordinated to real philosophy, that is typically Platonic, and that has already been adopted by Philon. An "encyclical education" thus consists in four mathematical sciences and dialectic. These are auxiliaries that contribute to awakening the soul and exercising it in view of grasping intelligible matters. As for the alteration that must transform Hellenism into Christianity, it begins with philosophical eclecticism. No more than "Middle Platonism," a vigorous movement of which Clement is a good representative, is the "eclecticism" of the author of *Miscellanies* to be taken in a pejorative sense. It is not a question of combining heterogeneous elements in the confusion of flabby thinking. Clement took unequivocal responsibility for the eclectic course of his method: "When I speak of philosophy, I do not mean Stoic philosophy, or Platonic philosophy, or Epicurean or Aristotelian, but all that has been well said in each of these schools, through the teaching of justice accompanied by pious knowledge: it is this whole ensemble resulting from pious choice that I call philosophy" (*Miscellanies* I).

To be sure, Greek philosophy is conceived as propaedeutic. Still, if it appears inferior to "real philosophy," Christian wisdom, it is what determines Clement's doctrinal program (dominated by the tripartite division of philosophy), which provides a large part of the instruments of his research (for example, the rules of argument, the theory of causes, the path of abstraction leading to the incorporeal principle) and which characterizes even the content of his Christian gnosis. In fact he discovers in the Bible the message of the "best of the Greeks" in his eyes, Pythagoras and Plato.

Even when he claims to contrast the virtues of the "barbarian" wisdom of the prophets and the Apostles with the defects of Hellenism, Hellenism preserves a preponderant importance. Clement wants to reduce "Greek speech" to the style of artifice, which distracts, by way of "tropes," from the propriety of sense. The "dialect of the Hebrews," on the contrary, whose emblematic form is the "parable," is set forth as a model of truthful expression because it is first of all obscure: setting out to identify, through resemblance, it leads to the thing itself. Now this dialect of the Hebrews was in fact "prophecy in Greek," the Septuagint. The displacement brought about thus has the effect of justifying a double movement of translation, which has allegory as its driving force: the cryptic language of the Bible contains statements that can be expressed in philosophical terms, and the "best of the Greeks" use the same veiled diction as "prophecy."

This attempt at assimilation does not go as far in the writings of other apologists. For Athenagoras, who addresses his *Petition* to Marcus Aurelius and Commodus in 177, the recourse to Greek accounts and the philosophical formulation of Christian dogma has as its chief aim the defense of the rationality of Christianity against attacks from the outside, without minimizing the differences between Christianity and Hellenism. This moderate attitude is found again in the *Contra Celsum* of Origen, whose ample and powerfully erudite response to the pagan pamphleteer Celsus attests to an acute sense of the singularities of civilization and systems of thought.

Not all Christians, not even all educated Christians, were sympathetic to Hellenism. Clement had to fight against those who represented philosophy as an invention of the devil. If he often takes up the myth, grafted onto the interpretation of Genesis 6 in the Book of Enoch, that associates philosophy with the union of angels and the daughters of men, he is more prone to speak about reflection and imitation. Tatian, on the contrary, indulges in a violent polemic against Hellenism in his *Oration to the Greeks*, produced around 165. Not content with condemning—along with other apologists—the pagan religion as idolatrous, or with denouncing the immorality of Greek myths and affirming the anteriority and superiority of Moses, he accuses the Greek philosophical systems of inanity; he deems them absurd, owing to their internal contradictions.

The variety of opinions held by the Fathers on the subject of Hellenism, and also the ambiguity of the relations between Christian thought and Greek tradition, surface again in the internal controversies of Christianity. Justin invented the idea of heresy, to combat tendencies considered deviant. It was a major part of the procedure devised to control dissension, and was borrowed from the heresiography of the time, which defined a school in terms of allegiance to doctrines ascribed to the patronage of a great thinker of the past, and not as an organized institution endowed with rules of succession. The malleability of the concept makes it easy to define a sect, and to trace a doctrinal filiation from tenuous indications. The effectiveness of the system is strengthened by another factor, the Christian tradition of the demonic origin of quarrels, built around the figure of the false prophet. Still, in Justin, the comparison with trends in Greek thought does not go beyond analogy. His entire offensive strategy lies in his ability to hold in check the tactic ascribed to his adversary, in denying him the attribution of "Christian." Other heresiologists handle Justin's weapon quite differently: Greek philosophy becomes the source of heresies. This is already the case with Irenaeus of Lyon, and the polemic reaches its height and approaches absurdity in the *Refutation of All Heresies*, attributed to Hippolytus of Rome, who likens the doctrine of such and such a heresiarch to the system of a Greek philosopher. Thus Marcion is viewed as depending on Empedocles, Basilides on Aristotle, and Noetus on Heraclitus. Still, for the historian of Hellenism, the author deserves credit: not only does he preserve fragments of the Presocratics, but also his knowledge allows him to bear witness to ancient Greek doxography, which he exploits with great skill.

Christians borrowed the instruments of allegory from the Greeks and put them to use in their understanding of Moses and the Bible as a whole. Here again, they had been preceded by Alexandrian Judaism. Still, the New Testament writings also provided decisive rules and models. The church fathers exploited to the maximum the exegetic devices that were at work in these texts: the story of Jesus and his followers brings to fruition the figures sketched by the institutions, events, and individuals referred to by the law and the prophets; Paul gives examples of the method and specifies its purpose; the veil that hid Moses' face was removed through conversion to Christ (2 Corinthians 3:12–16). The Christians appropriated the Bible, which became an immense allegory whose meaning was reserved for them. The two wives of Abraham, Hagar and Sara, represent two covenants and are thus thought to stand on the side of slavery and freedom, respectively. "This can be regarded as an allegory," writes Paul (Galatians 4:24). The parables of the synoptic Gospels, beyond their narrative content, have a symbolic meaning to unveil. In the Gospel according to John, too, Jesus's language is presented as enigmatic. Moreover, Paul uses the term *type;* this term will be the focus of lengthy developments in the "typology" of the church fathers, who stripped it of its literal meaning and discovered in every element of the Old Testament the "figure" of an element of the New and, by extension, of the church. The question of the Greek legacy comes up again here, but it bears more directly on the Jewish hermeneutic that dominates the writings of the New Testament and that continues, despite the break, to nourish the interpretation of the Fathers. However, the role of Hellenism is hard to appreciate in the rabbinical traditions and in the conventional methods of the adepts of Qumran, whose similarities with Christian "typology" and "allegory" are striking.

Moreover, a major difference separates Greek allegory from that of the Christians. As found in Homer and other poets, Greek allegory is devoid of the historical aim that characterizes Christian allegory, which sees prophetic signs realized in the recent past or in the present time. This sense of progress, related to a divine plan, is often reinforced by the eschatological perspective, which gives hope for the perfect fulfillment of promises at the end of time.

The fact remains that certain features of Christian allegory depend directly on Hellenism. Recourse to etymological meaning, in the style of Plato's inventions in *Cratylus,* the taste for Neopythagorean numerology, the quest for the moral meaning and for the cosmological and theological significance of the stories all go back to the Greek allegorism of the period. For Clement of Alexandria, the symbolic exegesis of the Greeks was the way to uncover the secret meaning of the messages handed down by the great civilizations. He consciously transposed these procedures to the study of the Bible, a divine perquisite of the most noble of the "barbarian" cultures.

A number of apologists, on the contrary, considered Greek allegory a ruse to mask the noxiousness of pagan fables. As for the writings of the Pseudo-Clement, which retain, well into the 4th century, the expression of a Christianity close to Judaism, they go so far as to reject the "typology" of the Pauline tradition, because in wishing to prove the divinity of Jesus, that typology compromises monotheism and multiplies rival interpretations. For other reasons, from the 4th century on, the Fathers of the Antiochian tradition differentiate typology from allegory: they disapprove of the latter but recognize the validity of the former. The separation is thus expressed in their vocabulary, which had been rather vague before: the terms *image, type, symbol,* and *enigma* were used indiscriminately, and the technique of allegory had a very wide range.

One other attitude appears that seems contradictory. Origen used the procedures of Greek allegory abundantly in his biblical exegesis, but rejected it when it applied to his own subject, the texts and myths of Hellenism. We can find a similar approach among adversaries of Christianity, such as Celsus, Porphyry, and the emperor Julian. It must be said that Origen's scorn for the allegory practiced by the Greeks stems from his condemnation of the pagan myths, taken literally, while he always finds the literal meaning of the Bible useful. As for his personal hermeneutic, it brought together the traditions stemming from Judaism, Hellenism, and the earlier church fathers so forcefully that it mapped out the paths Christian interpretation would follow for centuries to come. The Greek part of his theory and practice is important, even if it does not play the preponderant role with which it has too often been credited. The reasons Origen gives for the obscurity of the Scriptures (to stimulate research, to protect the unprepared from dangerous illusions) have their equivalents in the Greek pedagogical practice of reading the great texts. The images he uses to describe the articulations among the historical, "psychic," and "spiritual" meanings do not refer to Scripture alone. They also refer explicitly to the tripartite division of philosophy and the composite structure of human beings. The comparison between the harmony of the Scriptures, which is hard to perceive at first glance, and the coherence of the world, which is often invisible, is grafted onto Greek representations of the cosmos. The fundamental principle according to which the Bible is to be explained by way of the Bible corresponds to the "golden rule," formulated quite late by Porphyry but followed by the first masters of Alexandrian philology, decreeing that "Homer is to be explained by way of Homer." When Origen finds gaps in the historico-legislative record inviting a search for spiritual meaning, he falls back on a precept illustrated by Greek exegesis of poets, oracles, and myths: absurdities and contradictions are signs calling for allegorization. The fact that Origen refers to these breaks in continuity as "impossibilities" may even be evidence that the encounter must have taken place, in the Greek tradition, between the allegorical justifications of Homeric passages that had been judged unbecoming and an examination of "impossibilities" in poetic texts—an operation like the one Aristotle carried out for a different purpose in *Poetics* and in his *Homeric Problems*.

Origen also adapts to his commentaries the rules used in the schools to explicate Aristotle and Plato. The prologue to his treatise on the Song of Songs contains certain elements of schemas that would become known in a later period as introductions to the works of the two philosophers. This evidence shows that the establishment of such schemas began in the 3rd century in the Platonic commentaries. Furthermore, this ingenious allegorist is a proven "grammarian." Origen is one of the best representatives of his time of the discipline of textual explication. This discipline is divided into four parts: lexical and syntactic decoding of the text, explanation of its contents (history, topography, physical data, and so on), textual criticism, and examination of the text's aesthetic and moral value. He demonstrates complete mastery of the rules and concepts relevant to these fields. The same knowledge is put to work, in the 4th century, by the Christian interpreters of the Antiochian movement, who are for their part hostile to allegorization. The Cappadocian Fathers—Basil of Caesaraea, Gregory of Nazianzus, and especially Gregory of Nyssa—reflect, on the contrary, all the dimensions of the Origenian hermeneutic.

For Origen the strenuous work of hermeneutics ultimately conflates his understanding with the very inspiration of the Scriptures; this is for him the highest, and probably the only, mystical experience. A similar alliance of rational urgency and affective tension appears in Christianity through another form of spiritual exercise, which also bears the mark of Hellenism, the way of thinking that defines Christianity as a philosophy. It is a question of the way the church fathers understood "ascesis" in the philosophic sense: as an internal activity of thought and will that leads to a life conducted according to reason. From Justin to John Chrysostomos, by way of Clement, Origen, and the Cappadocians, we see Christianity conceived as "true philosophy" and as lived wisdom. It appropriates the spiritual practices of ancient philosophy, substituting the divine Word for universal Reason. The techniques of introspection, attention to the self, concentration on the present moment, and examination of one's conscience, along with continual practice of the presence of God and constant recourse to the principles of life (which are always available), are aimed at attaining tranquillity of soul and self-mastery. The Greek heritage is thus imprinted on Christian behavior and goes as far as monachism, where reference to the fundamental "dogmas" of the philosophic schools is replaced by constant reference to the ancients' words and "commandments," which were preserved in the *Apophthegmata* and *Kephalaia*. These exercises undoubtedly included properly Christian features: they always presuppose the help of God's grace, and humility, penitence, and obedience on the part of the sinner; renunciation is experienced as a way of participating in Christ's suffering and divine love. But they also contribute to the partial Hellenization of Christianity, especially when Christian "philosophy" becomes a rehearsal for death, in view of separating the soul from the body and liberating it from the "passions," in the Platonic manner.

If we limit our inquiry to the role of Hellenism in the development of Christian doctrines, two fields in particular stand out, anthropology and theology. Meditating on human nature and destiny, the church fathers spun out endless versions of the analogy between the biblical motif of creation "in the image and likeness" of God and the Platonic theme of identification with God (*Theaetetus* 176b). They also rediscovered in Genesis 2:7 Greek theories on the quickening of the embryo and various classical descriptions of the way human beings are constituted. However, the passage from Genesis 2, associated with other scriptural formulas (Wisdom 15:11, Joel 3:1, John 20:22), is related by some exegetes to the gift of the Spirit and to baptism as a second creation. Similarly, the focus on redemption transforms the Greek representations when it brings the Adam-Christ typology into play. Faith in the resurrection of the body, furthermore, never ceases to assert its singularity. Its apologists strive, at best, to prove that it is not unreasonable. But Origen's attempt, employing Greek concepts to imagine the permanence of corporeal "form," was not well received by the church, because it was suspected of diminishing the reality of the resurrected body. It was quite probably the reflection on free will and human responsibility that most advanced the influence of Hellenism. To refute the determinism attributed to the gnostics, first of all, and, more generally, astral fatalism, the church fathers borrowed Aristotle's analysis of free will, or the Stoics' doctrine of "assent." A leitmotiv of this reflection is also found in the famous line from Plato's myth of Er (*Republic* X): "Virtue is free . . . the responsibility lies with the one who chooses—God is justified." It is a principal reference for Gregory of Nyssa, later on. To be sure, the church fathers took on the task of harmonizing the importance of human choice with divine omniscience and foreknowledge, but their insistence on the capacity of reason distances them from Paul's teaching and gives their doctrine of salvation an entirely different cast from the doctrine of occidental Augustinianism.

In theology, the question of the relations between Christianity and Hellenism is particularly controversial. At least since the Reformation, the debate has centered on the "Platonism of the Fathers," which has been viewed as the pinnacle of Christian "Hellenism." Ecclesiastical positions and differing ideas on the essence of Christianity have interfered with scientific examination of the facts. Historians of dogmas have oscillated between partial inquiries, which set forth the use the early church fathers made of the concepts of Greek philosophy, and interpretations that reopen the controversy over the compatibility of the two systems. Heinrich Dörrie has sought to reduce "Christian Platonism" to a means of propaganda for the apologists: at worst metaphorical, at best a correction that renewed the model in question from top to bottom. Even as he has helped identify borrowings, Dörrie has deemed the Christian doctrine of grace and revelation contrary to the Platonic hierarchy of being. Endre von Ivánka, more sensitive to the complicities between

Platonic and Christian theology, ends up reaching similar conclusions, stressing the unassimilable singularity of the concepts of creation and grace. He has even given new life, paradoxically, to the old slogan "Plato purveyor of heresies," by purporting to indicate just how far the theologian can follow Platonism without falling into error. On the opposing side, the learned research of John Whittaker and others tends to blend the ancient Christian doctrines with the moral and intellectual ambiance of the Hellenistic culture of the time.

It is undeniable that the Fathers, to think through their faith and construct their doctrine conceptually, turned toward Platonic "theology," the most prestigious of their era. In so doing, they did not cease to confront a crucial difficulty: how to reconcile the biblical notion of a God endowed with will and acting in a contingent fashion, going so far as to incarnate himself, with an ontology that assumes God's immutability? One of the historian's tasks is to study the successive solutions found by the ancient scholars, or to note the aporias in their work. Contemporary studies, based on a critical knowledge of the sources used by the church fathers, have brought to light the kinship between the latters' hypotheses about the relations between Father and Son, up to the beginning of the 5th century, with Platonic propositions concerning the relations between the demiurgic intellect, the intelligible world, and the transcendent One. The Christian theologians who went farthest along the path to Platonism, far enough to sketch, as Origen did, the disjunction between the supreme principle and the Intellect that was imposed by Plotinus, continue to attribute intellective and voluntary activity to the Father. And, according to Rowan Williams, if Arius radicalizes the difference between the Father and the Son, in terms that the Plotinian decision best illuminates, it is to affirm the perfect independence of God's will. The Arian crisis marks the culmination of the theology of the Logos, which implicated the Son in the cosmic process while subordinating him to the Father. But the new problematic, based on the consubstantiality of the Father and the Son, raises the question of the divine will once again. If the Father is the cause of the Son, and if his will intervenes in the eternal generation of the Son, how can this causality include equality between Son and Father? Such is the difficulty envisaged by Gregory of Nazianzus.

The development of trinitarian theology led the Fathers, from Eusebius of Caesaraea to Cyril of Alexandria, to seek in the Platonists the equivalent of the doctrine of the "three hypostases." Their efforts succeeded so well that a number of commentators on Plotinus, even among the moderns, carried over into philosophical works the Christian sense of "hypostases" (existing persons, and not "substantial products" of a transcendental reality), and wrongly applied these terms to the Good, the Intellect, and the Soul, terms that have been misused in their turn by the title given to treatise V.1.10: "On the Three Hypostases That Have the Rank of Principles."

We obviously cannot reduce the encounters between Christian and Hellenistic theology to misunderstandings, nor can we conclude, as Adolf Harnack did, that the springtime of the alliance between orthodoxy and philosophy was followed not by a summer but by devastating storms. Far from making any value judgment, we would do well to recognize that the development of Christian dogma took place in a Hellenistic context, and that the questions raised by philosophy and by Greek ideas about God, man, and the world have influenced the system of Christian thought in a decisive manner.

ALAIN LE BOULLUEC
Translated by Rita Guerlac and Anne Slack

Bibliography

Texts and Translations

Justin Martyr. *An Early Christian Philosopher: Justin Martyr's Dialogue with Trypho, Chapters 1 to 9.* Ed. J. L. M. Van Winden. Leiden: Brill, 1971.

──────. *The First and Second Apologies.* Trans. and ed. Leslie William Barnard. New York: Paulist Press, 1997.

──────. *The Works Now Extant of S. Justin the Martyr.* Oxford and London, 1861.

Sources chrétiennes. Paris: Editions du Cerf, 1940–. Numerous works by the church fathers translated into French, with the Greek or Latin texts, introductions, and notes.

Wiles, Maurice, and Mark Santer, eds. *Documents in Early Christian Thought.* Cambridge: Cambridge University Press, 1975.

Studies

Armstrong, Arthur Hilary. *Hellenic and Christian Studies.* London: Variorum, 1990.

Aubin, Paul. *Plotin et le christianisme: Triade plotinienne et Trinité chrétienne.* Paris: Beauchesne, 1992.

Brown, Peter. *The Making of Late Antiquity.* Cambridge, Mass.: Harvard University Press, 1978.

Chadwick, Henry. *Early Christian Thought and the Classical Tradition: Studies in Justin, Clement, and Origen.* Oxford, 1966, 1984.

Dodd, Charles Harold. *The Interpretation of the Fourth Gospel.* Cambridge: Cambridge University Press, 1953, 1970.

Dorival, Gilles. "L'originalité de la patristique grecque." In *Las humanidas grecolatinas e a civilicao do universal,* Congresso internacional, Coimbra, 1988. Pp. 383–420.

Dörrie, Heinrich. *Platonica minora.* Munich: W. Fink, 1976.

Festugière, André-Jean. *L'idéal religieux des Grecs et l'Evangile.* Paris: Gabalda, 1932.

Gnilka, Christian. *Chresis: Die Methode der Kirchenvater im Umgang mit der antiken Kultur.* Vol. 2, *Kultur und Conversion.* Basel: Schwabe, 1984–.

Hadot, Pierre. *Philosophy As a Way of Life: Spiritual Exercises from Socrates to Foucault.* Trans. Michael Chase. Oxford: Blackwell, 1995.

————. *Porphpyre et Victorinus.* Paris: Etudes augustiniennes, 1968.

Ivánka, Endre von. *Plato Christianus.* Einsiedeln: Johannes Verlag, 1964.

Mansfield, Jaap. *Heresiography in Context: Hippolytus' Elenchos as a Source for Greek Philosophy.* Leiden: E. J. Brill, 1992.

Meijering, E. Peter. *God Being History.* Amsterdam: North-Holland Publishing Company, 1975.

Pépin, Jean. *Mythe et allégorie: Les origines grecques et les contestations judéo-chrétiennes.* 2nd ed. Paris: Etudes augustiniennes, 1981.

————. *De la philosophie ancienne à la théologie patristique.* London: Variorum, 1986.

————. *La tradition de l'allégorie: De Philon à Dante.* 2nd ed. Paris: Etudes augustiniennes, 1987.

Rist, John M. *Platonism and Its Christian Heritage.* London: Variorum, 1985.

Whittaker, John. *Studies in Platonism and Patristic Thought.* London: Variorum, 1984.

Williams, Rowan. *Arius: Heresy and Tradition.* London: Darton, Longman and Todd, 1987.

HELLENISM AND JUDAISM

THE ENCOUNTER BETWEEN Hellenism and Judaism, a complex phenomenon that is sometimes difficult to pin down, will be discussed here from two different perspectives. The Greeks—or *some* Greeks—were able to discover a people, a culture; we may wonder what they really knew and thought about it. But these Greeks were also bearers of a body of learning, which spread (without the Jewish world being necessarily eager to receive it). We shall try to gauge the effects of this process.

It is in the Hellenistic period that contacts between Greeks and Jews are most significant, in Judaea and Egypt; thus our search will take us to Paul of Tarsus, to Philon of Alexandria, and later to Flavius Josephus. It was Christianity that recovered the work and intellectual heritage of these three Jews.

Did the Greeks know anything about the Jewish people? Were the Jews worthy of attention and interest in their eyes? We would search in vain for an unambiguous mention of any exchange with Jews in a Greek text from the archaic period. The poet Alcaeus cites the exploits of his brother Antimenidas of Lesbos, who went off to offer his services to the Chaldaean armies. Antimenidas may have been a mercenary under Nebuchadnezzar: he may have besieged Ashquelon (604 B.C.E.) and even Jerusalem (598–597). But we are already in the realm of historical fiction: Alcaeus does not mention the Jews, nor do his contemporaries. What meaning could there be for them in a small, crushed, vassal kingdom lacking even access to the sea during this period? The picturesque voyage was as yet an unknown genre.

Still, in the early 1960s, archaeologists in the neighborhood of Yavne (between Jaffa and Ashdod) uncovered the remains of a military fortress. The garrison that lived there used a great quantity of Greek pottery, exclusively from the Orient, all of it dating from the last third of the 7th century. This is enough to allow us to infer the direct presence of Asian Greeks. The architecture and masonry of the place offer no evidence of restoration; it seems logical to suppose that the pottery is contemporary with the walls. One hesitates to identify these Greeks as mercenaries in the service of the pharaoh, since no trace of Egyptian equipment has been found. Were they not rather in the service of Josiah (king of Judah from 640 to 609)? One shard found on the site apparently bore a Hebraic character. If this was the case, the Greek garrison was probably powerless to prevent the raid by the pharaoh Nekaon in 609. If the first hypothesis is correct, the garrison was swept away in 605 or 604 by Nebuchadnezzar's army. These Greeks, whichever their faction, unquestionably knew of the Jews' existence (and may have been acquainted with their culture). But of the Greeks who survived, it is likely that a certain number settled in Egypt or Phoenicia and that very few returned home; they were not numerous enough to spread knowledge of the Jewish people and their culture in Greece.

Writing in the second third of the 5th century B.C.E., Herodotus discusses the dissemination of the Egyptian people and their customs in the Orient. Speaking of circumcision, he asserts in particular that "the Colchians and Egyptians and Ethiopians are the only nations that have practised circumcision from the first" (II.104). Thus the Phoenicians and the Syrians of Palestine allegedly owe this practice to these three groups, through imitation. The historical validity of such reasoning is not important here; still, we can ask what the term "Syrians of Palestine" may have meant to a Greek traveler. Circumcision is known to be a Jewish practice, but it is not limited to Jews. The Greek term for Palestinians corresponds to the term *Philistines* in the Bible, though the Bible calls them uncircumcised, like the Phoenicians. Did Herodotus confuse Jews and Philistines? Possibly, but according to our sources, the term *Philistines* was politically outdated in the 5th century. Is it a reference to circumcised Nabataean immigrants? The term *Palestine*, which is ordinarily used for the Syrian coast, comes up again in Herodotus (VII.89), when the historian indicates that "the Syrians of Palestine" (the same ones?), together with the Phoenicians, supplied ships for the Persian army. It is hard to imagine the Judaeans furnishing a battle fleet, even as a tributary obligation. Here, the term can only mean the cities of the coast, once known as Philistia. None of this is very clear. But we can hardly expect Herodotus, who had apparently never gone into Syria, to think in terms of a cultural mosaic in describing a region and peoples that he had been led—by the Persian administration, as well as by the atavistic contempt of the Egyptians (his informants) for Asiatics—to call Syria. It is highly probable that Herodotus knew nothing at all of the existence of a Jewish people.

Moreover, in the Bible Isaiah seems to indicate that this general lack of knowledge was reciprocal (66:19). There are numerous traces of active commerce—direct or indirect—between Greeks and Jews, starting in the 7th century B.C.E. and continuing more or less indefinitely thereafter; but this by no means signifies that Jews and Greeks were acquainted except in the vaguest way.

Writing in the second half of the 4th century, Aristotle refers in his *Meteorologica* to the properties that the Dead Sea owes to its high salinity. But he warns his reader that the anecdotal account is to be taken, as it were, *cum grano salis:* "If there were any truth in the stories they tell about the lake in Palestine . . ." (II.iii.359a18–19). Such a reservation tells us not only that Aristotle is not personally acquainted with the region and does not know the term *Judaea*, but also that no really reliable source has gone to see it. In the framework of Greek ideas, this means that the author has collected (directly or indirectly) the tales of some merchant, one of a breed notoriously given to exaggeration and falsehood in the eyes of the ancient geographers and scholars. Furthermore, this informant, if he himself has seen the Dead Sea, may well have seen it from the east bank, following the route of Nabataean commerce, rather than from the Jewish oases. A Greek of that period would have no reason to associate the Dead Sea with Jews rather than with Nabataeans (this is the connection the historian Jerome of Cardia makes at the end of the 4th century). However that may be, we still have no trace of Jews in Greek literature.

It is thus surprising and interesting to come across the following anecdote. Clearchus of Solis reports that his master Aristotle told him one day of his encounter in Asia Minor with a Jew from Coelo-Syria. His exceptional people, whose capital city bore the "tortuous" (sic) name of Jerusalem, is somewhat comparable to Brahman sages from India (!). This man, in any case, "was Greek, not only in language but also in soul." It must be said unequivocally that this testimony, which dates from the beginning of the 3rd century, is inadmissible for historical reasons: according to what is known about his life, Aristotle lived at Atarneus, in Asia, between 347 and 342. Now it is very unlikely that there was a Jewish community settled in Asia Minor, in Pergamum (neighboring city of Atarneus) or elsewhere, at this time. The first Jews of the Diaspora did not appear much before the beginning of the 3rd century, and they lived more to the south, toward Sardis and Ephesus. The first attested communities in Asia Minor go back to Antiochus II (261–247), who ensured a collective migration of his Jewish subjects, since he granted them citizenship in the cities of Ionia, where they settled. Furthermore (for one might object that a given Jew could have traveled independently, coming from Judaea), the notion of a perfectly Hellenized Jew is completely anachronistic with regard to the period to which the anecdote is thought to refer. Clearchus's account is equally unacceptable on literary grounds: the passage includes numerous devices meant to alert readers to the dreamlike and prodigious nature of such an encounter (reported in a treatise on sleep), or to make them laugh at this awkward people with philosophical pretensions. It shows only that Clearchus was aware that Jews existed as a separate people, and that he had enough (or little enough) understanding of their customs to see them as a people as exotic as the Indians.

Until the end of the 4th century, then, the Jews were neither within the scope of the Greeks' acquaintance nor of concern to them. In Arnaldo Momigliano's formula, "The Greeks lived happily in their classical age without recognizing the existence of the Jews" (p. 78). The converse is also true, and even more so: Jewish isolationism must be taken into account. Unquestionably, individual adventurers must have encountered Jews at least as early as the 7th century, and Clearchus himself, who may well have been a great traveler, could have known some in the Orient, in Ionia, or in his native Cyprus. But up to that point, such an encounter had never produced any hint of a collective preoccupation, not even an interest limited to a circle of educated men. In this respect, Clearchus marks a turning point.

Indeed, not long before, in 332, an event occurred that was fundamental in many respects, and certainly for the question at hand: the conquest of the Orient by Alexander the Great. The Greeks and Jews really discovered each other at this point. If Alexander's voyage to Jerusalem stems from legend, it is nonetheless true that Judaea came to be administered by Macedonia and that its inhabitants had to learn, if not to speak Greek, at least to recognize the existence of the language and to acknowledge a new institutional reality. The Greeks, for their part, were to discover this small vassal nation (among many others), and they were to learn of the Jews' unshakable attachment to strange customs. But they also encountered a prodigiously rich culture and an unexpected field of knowledge that was to spread throughout the Orient.

At this point in our study, it is time to pause. For as the contacts between Hellenism and Judaism developed under quite particular geographical conditions (in Palestine and Egypt principally; probably in Mesopotamia as well, but these contacts are more difficult to estimate) and in specific chronological circumstances (after the Macedonian victory over the whole of Greece), Hellenism now looked quite different from the way it had appeared half a century earlier. Hellenism as a vital force was no longer a phenomenon bound up with Greece itself. The conquerors did not come from all of Greece: they were for the most part Macedonians. The men who had won control of the known world were the grandsons of those whom the rest of the Greeks regarded as semibarbarians. Now, in the course of a few short years, they burst open the geographical and mental confines of Hellenism to an extraordinary extent. They displaced the core of its activity, principally toward Lagid Egypt and its new city-state, Alexandria (the great intellectual center of the epoch), and toward the Seleucid Orient to a lesser degree. Palestine was at the heart of this "new world." But they did not bring Hellenism to the Orient as a museum piece, unalterable and frozen in its classical grandeur. The Hellenism they offered had been renewed, profoundly modified, often by the conscious and voluntary action of the king. The model of the city-state, which was never the only viable political form in Greece but which constituted the norm for most Greeks, with its system of assemblies in which the government—whether democratic or oligarchic—took shape through the ongoing practice of verbal exchanges, was replaced by the hegemonic model of monarchy, incontestable but familiar in the Orient. Absolute, the embodiment of power, monarchy soon extended its reach over vast territories, blending countless peoples in a common subjection. United in a shared dependence on the same sovereign, these peoples and lands came to be ruled by written laws, in a process that fostered the juridical unity of the great kingdoms that emerged as Alexander's successors divided up the realm. Administration and war (which had remained essentially the duty of citizens, thus of amateurs) were already becoming professionalized. Cults and supplicants' pleas came to be addressed to the person of a monarch, who looked more and more like a god, greatly scandalizing most Jews, whose intransigent monotheism was viewed as an oddity, and gaining ground on the old civic or regional cults.

In the intellectual domain, too, things changed: intensifying a development initiated by the Sophists, the educated man, the scholar, also became a professional and at the same time a specialist. Science, pure or applied, was most often dissociated from philosophy. Unlike Plato, Euclid and Archimedes did not mix philosophy, and still less political philosophy, with their work as mathematicians. Astronomy, geography, and agronomy, as well as philology, gave rise to technical treatises written by specialists. To grasp the originality of the (often conflicted) relations between Hellenism and Judaism, it is important to understand that this new culture, which we call Hellenism, is not "a Greek surface plastered onto a non-Greek base" (even though, elsewhere, mechanisms for segregating Greeks from indigenous peoples were also present). This new culture was the original fruit of an epoch, of circumstances, of the actions of some great men, but especially of the encounter—not uniformly successful or far-reaching, but always complex—between a Greek model in full mutation and oriental milieus capable of changing in the same direction: in Jerusalem itself, in the 2nd century B.C.E., an aristocratic minority (?), although it originated in the priesthood, sought to transform the traditional theocratic Jewish state into a Greek city-state (a polis).

The primordial vehicle for learning is language, and it was the local populations who had to learn Greek, not the other way around. This relation was to determine the direction of cultural transmission. Until the Christian mission got under way in the course of the 1st century C.E., it was essentially Greek culture that spread throughout the Oriental world—which happened to be Jewish. There was very little movement in the opposite direction; what there was corresponded to an infatuation with the exotic. The Greeks were not interested in the Jews until fairly late, and even then their audience was Roman (Posidonius and Strabo, for example).

No more than it had in Egypt did Greek ever become the language of exchange common to all levels of the Jewish population. In any case, the Greeks had no tradition of "cultural missionaries." Ordinary people used Aramaic. But the religious milieus, though often hostile to the culture of the new masters, did not necessarily remain apart from the Greeks. The new language spread, by and large, through aristocratic urban environments: yesterday's masters, if they wanted to conserve any part of their privileged status, had to be in a position to approach the masters of the day and earn at least some respect. Little by little, a whole class of administrators and educated men, including the priestly circles, absorbed the Greek language; they became fully bilingual, even trilingual, starting in the 2nd century B.C.E. at least, and in some cases as early as the end of the 3rd century.

In fact, while the author of Ecclesiastes (or Quoheleth) still wrote in Hebrew during the 3rd century, he was nourished on Greek culture. Jesus ben Sirach, the cultivated scribe of Jerusalem, wrote—also in Hebrew—at the beginning of the 2nd century; but (if we are to believe the preface attached to his work) his grandson translated him into Greek at the end of the 130s. Shortly afterward (around 124), an abridger rewrote the second book of Maccabees, by Jason of Cyrene (a Jew with a Hellenized name), directly in Greek. This flowering implies that at least a core of educated men had given their children a Greek education of high quality, sometimes motivated by the stamp of nobility and purity conferred by its Atticizing tint. "Supplementary education" at first, it often became the only education, to the point that Philon of Alexandria, on the threshold of the Christian era, is thought not to have known Hebrew. Without the existence of such a Hellenized class, we could not understand an enterprise like the Septuagint Bible, the translation into Greek of the Hebrew text of the Pentateuch, perhaps starting in the second quarter of the 3rd century, then later the other books, by scholars working in Egypt and more precisely in Alexandria. If the sacred text was translated, counter to the entire Near Eastern tradition, it was surely because a not inconsiderable segment of Jewish society, principally in the Diaspora, felt the need for a Greek text, for want of being able to read the Hebrew one (the curiosity of learned Greeks and the mistrust of the Lagid power with regard to a text capable of governing a community may have played a supporting role). Now translation itself, by obliging its authors to approach it from philological and religious standpoints simultaneously, fixed the text, increased its importance at the expense of the living practice, and made it known in this new form; hence Elias Bickermann's remark that Judaism became the religion of the Book when the Bible was translated into Greek.

The existence of a strong Jewish Diaspora, especially in Alexandria, a city-state created by the Greeks, is a primordial factor in the diffusion of Greek thought and knowledge in a Jewish milieu and in Judaea. We know that in the Hellenistic period Alexandria became the principal center from which Hellenism radiated, and we know of its famed Library, which was thought to have brought together all literature written in Greek or translated into Greek. The Hellenistic epoch represents the high point of the empirical and technical sciences: it is scarcely possible to imagine that this library and the centers of intellectual activity that comprised the glory of the Egyptian city-state failed to have repercussions, in Judaea and elsewhere. Moreover, Judaea does not seem to have been exempt from the economic expansion that stemmed from the logical and technical enrichment characterizing this period. The problem lies in the difficulty of measuring these repercussions. Varro lists some fifty authors of technical treatises, a specifically Greek genre; a treatise on agronomy by a certain Bolos of Mendes, for example, enjoyed great renown throughout antiquity and even later; there were also treatises on gardening, farming, and so on. Yet it seems quite impossible to find a trace of any of these where Judaea is concerned. We can only note that Apollonius, minister of finances under Ptolemy II, who was passionately interested in agricultural and arborial experimentation, owned a vineyard in Galilee. It would be indeed astonishing if this had not had some impact on the growing techniques of the local peasantry, especially in this region scorned by pious Judaeans for its lack of attachment to Jewish formalism and traditions. But we know virtually nothing about this. The same could be said about botanical treatises, those dealing with zoology, medicine, architecture, and especially treatises on manufacturing techniques. At most, we could mention the probable introduction by the Greeks of artificial irrigation in the 3rd or 2nd century B.C.E., attested in Ecclesiastes (2:6), in Ecclesiasticus (24.30–32), and in the use in the Talmudic language of the word *ntly,* Greek *antlia* (irrigation wheel); or, in the text of the Greek Bible of the Septuagint, the distinctions made among the various stages of fetal development, unknown in the Hebraic lexicon.

In contrast, it is easier to follow the introduction by the Greeks of technologies related to the exercise of power: in particular to warfare, administration, and tax collection. The overwhelming, crushing, universal victory of the Greek armies offers the best proof of the excellence of their technologies. The Hellenized aristocracy of Jerusalem not only had a gymnasium built in order to conform to a cultural model, it also recognized the superiority conferred by the premilitary or paramilitary training acquired there. Syria bristled with fortresses constructed in conformity with Hellenistic techniques, built through the good offices or on the order of the Hellenistic powers, first Lagid, then Seleucid. But although neither Polybius nor the Books of the Maccabees describe for us the tactics used by the Jewish armies in the Hellenistic period, most of the Jewish mercenaries who enlisted in the Hellenistic armies, and who came to constitute a not inconsiderable vehicle for Greek values and knowledge, also offered the Maccabees, when the time came, an abundance of skills that were decisive for the Maccabees' ability to hold the Greek armies in check (even if their revolt also allowed them to develop guerrilla techniques specifically adapted to the Jewish situation).

In the interim before these periods of crisis, thanks to tax farming (a typically Greek system), the rise of the Tobiades family proves that from the Lagid period (the 3rd century) on the Jewish aristocracy had integrated Hellenistic techniques into its tax collecting and administrative practices. In the absence of a manual of ancient fiscal practices, it is difficult to evaluate the innovations with any precision. But it is certain that the Hellenistic monarchies were responsible for constructing a bureaucratic system—a ponderous one, certainly, but also, as it developed through elaboration, one capable of real efficiency. We can judge the value of these innovations by observing the progressive replacement of tribute in natural goods by tax revenue in cash, and also, probably, by the relative satisfaction of the Jews—at least the urban Jews—with a system that was sufficiently rational to function without major difficulty until the Romans arrived. Thus, according to Artapanos, a 2nd-century Judaeo-Egyptian author, the biblical Joseph and Moses are known as the "first financial ministers" of Judaea: this is a way of legitimizing the new fiscal techniques both by biblical precedent and by the antiquity that such a precedent confers on them.

The discretion of our sources about the contributions of Greek technical knowledge may, at least for the Jewish sources, have to do with an intellectual tradition. For we clearly cannot refer to the encounter between Hellenism and Judaism without mentioning the source par excellence of their collective survival: their historical, moral, and religious productions.

The problem posed by the conjunction of these two cultures is first of all epistemological. Greek knowledge is divided into several domains that, in the period that concerns us, are quite distinct. Traditional myths provide the key to certain fundamental revealed bodies of knowledge, for example, agricultural myths such as that of Eleusis, or the myth of Prometheus; other areas of knowledge and skill have an intermediary status that one might call "patronage": the Muses inspire the poet—without them, there would be no poetry—but they do not reveal or "inspirit" texts as the Holy Spirit does for Pope Gregory; finally, even if they are theoretically under the patronage of the Muses, history, geography, astronomy, politics, the various intellectual *technai,* and even philosophical speculation are bodies of knowledge produced or acquired by the human spirit: they lend themselves more and more to a dual movement of theorization and empirical verification (thus Hipparchus will do his best to measure the dimensions and the distances of the Moon and Sun to verify the heliocentric system posited theoretically by Aristarchus of Samos). Eratosthenes is the teacher of a pharaoh who subsidized the scholarly and literary life; Archimedes frequented the palace of the king of Syracuse; Hellenistic scholars have much more to do with the circle of temporal power than with the realm of the sacred. In contrast, "Jewish knowledge" stems from God and from revelation—all the more so because the scribes and the priestly hierarchy are historically its only vehicles in Judaea, and we do not see in the Diaspora any writer who could be called secular (not even—especially not—Flavius Josephus).

If these two cultures had anything in common intellectually, it is that they each constructed a long historiographical tradition, one that was particularly lively among the Greeks of the Hellenistic period (even though in this matter Alexandria probably did not play a major role) and very ancient among the Jews, since its first elements may go back to the 11th century B.C.E. However limited literary diffusion in antiquity may have been, both cultures also distinguished themselves from the annalistic Egyptian and Mesopotamian traditions, in that they did not limit the use of texts to the powerful monarchies and their clergy.

Between the two, not much had to change for the Books of the Maccabees and then, at the end of the 1st century C.E., Flavius Josephus to appear as examples of a historiography that could be called Judaeo-Hellenistic. Even though it retained phraseology of a prophetic type (the epiphany of a god is not foreign to Greek historical literature), from that point on the Jewish chronicle, like that of the Greek historian, produced justificative texts, diplomatic in particular (1 Maccabees 10:25ff). The traditional practice of dialogue or discourse (often brief, except for Isaiah 36:4–10) leads quite naturally to its rewriting according to the canons of Greek rhetoric.

Willingly or not, Jewish authors had to come to terms with the idea that even the divine manifests itself in history, through institutions that had developed more or less gradually and that were to take on a given secular form at a given time; thus the law of Moses was a codification of principles, an ancient one to be sure, and yet Abraham and the generations that followed him before Moses had had to act without the support of such a code. This question of historical evolution is an "import." The Talmudic treatise *Pirke Abot* is meant to show the triumph of rejection, of rigidity: "Moses received the Torah from Sinai and handed it on to Joshua . . . and Hillel and Shammai took over from them" (in Bickermann, p. 299). But such a citation also shows, on the contrary, the religious and epistemological malaise that arose in the Hellenistic period from contact with Greek historical thought.

This led, then, to the integration of the Bible with the renewed historical genre; the process was completed by the end of the 3rd century by a certain Demetrius (a Samaritan?), then by Flavius Josephus. Paradoxically, this literary convergence adapted itself to a fundamental divergence in the philosophy of history that each of the two cultures professed. To differing degrees, depending on the authors, the Greeks attributed to history a double driving force: human action on the one hand, either destiny or fortune *(tyche)* on the other (this distinction is particularly characteristic of Polybius, but it is a banality in Greek thought). If such a conception is discernible in the high Hellenized sacerdotal aristocracy (which wagered on a solely political and later military but purely *human* dimension when, in the 2nd century, it attempted to integrate the Jewish world with the Greek), the Jewish tradition as a whole recognized as the driving force of history nothing but God and the piety of the human actor. Jesus ben Sirach, in the 2nd century, is no exception. Whereas in Hellenistic historiography the divine sign, consulted by soothsayers, is merely indicative, and moreover scantily reported by the authors, in the Jewish world history is driven by the conformity of human action to the teaching of the prophets and the covenant concluded by God with man; in his preamble to *Jewish Antiquities*, Josephus still holds this view. We can speak, then, of a consciously accepted competition between two visions of the world.

Itinerant "sages" in the Greek mode began to appear, devoting themselves to spreading their moral and religious views (on this point, Jesus is their heir). Perhaps this is the way the mysterious title Quoheleth, the Hebrew title of Ecclesiastes, should be translated: he who stirs up a crowd (of listeners). Like their Greek counterparts, such sages dispensed their wisdom in public, in a highly logical discourse that did not share in what was characterized as biblical discourse up to that point. Whether their moral philosophy was marked by Greek influences or nourished by more or less universal principles remains a controversial question. Nevertheless, the celebrated "All is vanity" has been compared with an identical apothegm of Minumus of Syracuse (4th century); his morality of "Carpe diem" and his skepticism about the morality of retribution have brought to mind Euripides, Archilochus, and Theognis. Even his major opponent, Jesus ben Sirach, professed a morality in conformity with Aristotle's ethics and cited the fable of the two routes that, through Prodicos of Ceos and Xenophon, supposedly came from Pythagorean circles. The historical analysis of this evolution is complicated. On the one hand, the tradition of Jewish exclusivity probably slowed it down; on the other, it was considerably facilitated, first, by the almost monotheist option of Platonic philosophy (which in *Timaeus*, for example, calls to mind the creation of the cosmos by a single, demiurgic god), then by the convergent evolution of oriental thinking and Greek philosophies. These latter could be compared in some respects with the "sects" (the different currents of Judaism); Stoicism was the most influential, if only through the idea of a cosmos organized by a rational power that merges with divinity. The idea of a hidden, incomprehensible God, closely related to an impersonal force like Destiny, could then circulate at the same time as dualist notions, such as the allegories of time and fortune used by Quoheleth, or divine personifications of Wisdom and Science, auxiliary hypostases of God. The convergence of the reflections was given vigorous expression by a gnostic of the 2nd century C.E., Numenius of Apamaea: "Who is Plato, if not Moses speaking Greek?" The god of the Greek philosopher blended, for some, with the God of the Jews.

And in fact Philon was very familiar with Plato's work (*Timaeus*, in particular) and with the Presocratics (Heraclitus, for example); his Moses was every bit a match for the Greek physicists, those scholars who studied nature and its laws. Others openly professed a philosophical ecclecticism in which the Stoa often remained the dominant component: thus Aristobulus defined wisdom as "the knowledge of things human and divine" (ca. 160 B.C.E.). It is Aristobulus who inaugurated the reading of the biblical text according to the allegorical method (taken up again by Philon). They practiced *interpretatio Graeca*: Yahweh was a local form of a great universal divinity worshipped elsewhere under the names of Pan (the All) or Dionysus. Enoch was nothing but an avatar of Atlas, also the inventor of astrology; Kronos crystalized the figures of Noah and Nimrod, the founder of Babylon and the builder of its tower. These associations may conceivably point to the influence of Euhemerism, for which the figure of the gods perpetuates the transfigured memory of particularly eminent and beneficent men. Presenting the patriarchs as teachers of humanity, as Triptolemus did, is a clear sign of Hellenization.

But we must not be misled: this intellectual attitude, mostly limited to certain intellectual circles, carried with it new ways of thinking, but they always served to glorify Judaism as the true philosophy. Greek philosophy was only a way of rereading the testamentary revelation: the Jews remained the only ones who truly "know God." Pythagoras, Socrates, and Plato were sometimes portrayed as Moses' disciples in monotheism; the Jewish religion had to retain its primacy.

The Greek influence was nevertheless sufficiently powerful that, from this period on, the figure of the Hellenistic king strongly influenced that of the Messiah to come. The Greeks, for their part, remained full of disdain for what they saw as one more oriental superstition, about which they knew essentially nothing (only the Romans would violate the *soreg*, the sacred enclosure that marked off the Square of the Gentiles at the entrance to the Temple).

In every realm, it is clear that evaluating the Greeks' knowledge of Judaism, like assessing the diffusion and reception of the branches of learning the Greeks conveyed, remains a delicate task. As a model, Hellenism was ignored by the great majority and adopted by a numerically weak but socially powerful minority, and even among those who approached it, a certain number did so to infiltrate the enemy. The practical disciplines presumably spread more readily. Be that as it may, after the destruction of the Temple in 70 C.E., the principal authorities of the pharaonic faction rebuilt a crushed Judaism while abandoning the Neoplatonist heritage, and on the basis of an ahistorical line of thinking. The divorce was to be more or less gradual, and it allowed etymologically Greek terms to become established in the Talmudic language. But it was not through Judaism that Greek culture would live outside of Greece: it was through Christianity, by way of Rome and the labyrinth of gnostic sects, until the Arabs took it to Spain, where Jewish intermediaries translated it in turn for Roman Europe.

Serge Bardet
Translated by Rita Guerlac and Anne Slack

Bibliography

Texts and Translations

Aristotle. *Meteorologica*. Trans. H. D. P. Lee. Loeb Classical Library.
Herodotus. *Histories*. Trans. A. D. Godfrey. Loeb Classical Library.

Studies

Bickermann, Elias Joseph. *The Jews in the Greek Age.* Cambridge, Mass.: Harvard University Press, 1988.

Genot-Bismuth, Jacqueline. *Le Scénario de Damas: Jérusalem hellénisée et les origines de l'essénisme.* Paris: F. X. de Guibert, 1992.

Hengel, Martin. *Judaism and Hellenism: Studies in Their Encounter in Palestine during the Early Hellenistic Period.* Trans. John Bowden. 2 vols. Philadelphia: Fortress Press, 1974.

Isaac, Jules. *Genese de l'antisémitisme.* Paris: Calmann-Lévy, 1956.

Michaud, Robert. *Qohélet et l'hellénisme.* Paris: Le Cerf, 1987.

Momigliano, Arnaldo. *Alien Wisdom: The Limits of Hellenization.* Cambridge: Cambridge University Press, 1976.

Rostovtzeff, Michel. *The Social and Economic History of the Hellenistic World.* 3 vols. Oxford: Clarendon Press, 1953.

Vidal-Naquet, Pierre. "Du bon usage de la trahison." Pp. 7–115 in *Flavius Josèphe, La Guerre des Juifs.* Paris: Editions de Minuit, 1977.

———. "Les Juifs entre l'Etat et l'Apocalypse." Pp. 846–848 in Claude Nicolet, *Rome et conquête du monde méditerranéen,* vol. 2: *Genèse d'un empire.* 2nd ed. Paris: PUF, 1989.

Will, Edouard, and Claude Orrieux. *Ioudaismos-Hellenismos: Essai sur le Judaïsme judéen à l'époque hellénistique.* Nancy: Presses Universitaires de Nancy, 1986.

THE MILESIANS

THREE CITIZENS OF MILETUS in the 6th century B.C.E.—Thales, Anaximander, and Anaximenes—are conveniently grouped together under the
term *Milesians*. They were apparently approximate contemporaries, as well as
sharers (and rivals) in a new intellectual enterprise: the science of nature.

This brief description rests principally on the interpretation due to Aristotle. The writings of the Milesians themselves have not survived (apart from
one or two possibly authentic quotations). The scanty reports by later ancient
authors derive almost entirely from Aristotle or from the tradition of doxography (writing about philosophers' doctrines) established by Aristotle's
pupil Theophrastus. The first step toward understanding the Milesians therefore consists in understanding Aristotle's own conception of physical science,
within which his interpretation of the Milesians is framed. The next is understanding the method of dialectical examination of previous opinions that Aristotle applied to help establish and clarify the principles of his own physics.

Once Aristotle's interpretation of the Milesians is understood, it must next
be subjected to critical examination. Here there is other evidence to be taken
into account—indirect evidence, it is true, but not negligible. The Milesians
were at the fountainhead of the study of "natural science," which was continued into the 5th and 4th centuries by others (both cosmologists and medical
theorists), and which was criticized by philosophers (notably Heraclitus, Parmenides, Plato, and Aristotle) who reflected on its underlying assumptions.
The historians Herodotus and Thucydides show traces of its influence. Even
in the tragedies of Euripides and the comedies of Aristophanes, some echoes
of the scientific enterprise can be heard. Enough is known to allow us to grasp,
at least in outline, the aims and methods of natural science, as it was understood and practiced in the 200 years *after* the Milesians. With due caution, it
is legitimate to argue backward from this later evidence to the Milesians
themselves.

The path toward an understanding of the Milesians is therefore, unavoid-
ably, a tortuous one. It is also beset by the danger of unconscious anachronism. Here as elsewhere, it is only too easy to import into the study of ancient Greece mistaken assumptions derived from our own era. In particular, it
is necessary to examine with caution both the similarities and the dissimilarities between Milesian science and modern science. By calling the enterprise of
the Milesians physical science, we do not imply that they shared all the aims,
methods, and programmatic assumptions of modern physics. Rather, it is

meant that their activities are best understood, when allowances are made for differences in knowledge and conceptual tradition, as something closely akin in some essential respects to the modern natural sciences.

Aristotle recognized the Milesians as his first true predecessors in natural science. For him, Thales, the pioneer of this kind of investigation, marks the boundary before which there were only theologians and writers of stories. He recognizes in the Milesians a new respect for *system*. Aristotle was well aware that Hesiod, and other earlier cosmogonical authors, had general ideas governing their constructions. But they used them "in a storylike way" *(muthikōs):* that is, their aims, guiding concepts, and substantive theses were not stated clearly and explicitly, and were not used systematically. By contrast, Aristotle implies, the Milesians professedly inquired into *phusis,* the nature of individual things and of things collectively. They aimed at a system of knowledge that would cover that realm completely and systematically.

There is no reason to doubt the correctness of Aristotle's account thus far; no evidence exists that would support an attempt to undermine it, and there is a good deal to confirm it. Much more difficult to evaluate is Aristotle's report on the substance of the Milesian theories. This hinges on the Aristotelian concept of "cause" *(aition* or *aitia),* of which the interpretation is perennially controversial. It is at least clear that the four types of cause serve to identify the types of relationship within the structure of physical processes and the types of understanding of such processes by the human intellect. The close tie between structure and understanding is, as will be suggested later, already implicit in the Milesian concept of *phusis.*

In *Metaphysics* I Aristotle seeks to show historically that physics has always consisted in the search for these causes. But he himself is forced to admit that the evidence is not straightforwardly in favor of his reading. He therefore sees the Milesians and their successors as beginners; they were like children who cannot pronounce their words distinctly, or amateur boxers who sometimes land good punches by chance. They do not make clear and conscious use of any of the four causes, but they do in a way use all four.

With these qualifications, Aristotle identifies the Milesians as using the "material cause," and that type of cause alone. He gives examples: Thales said that everything was made of water; Anaximenes, of air. Some skepticism is required here. Like all philosophers, Aristotle is constantly pressed in the direction of anachronism when he interprets earlier thinking. Only a full examination of all the other evidence for Presocratic science can, in the end, tell us how far Aristotle is correct. But it is very important to note that even if Aristotle's testimony is accepted in full, it does not have the implications that have often been supposed. In particular, it does not imply that the Milesians were materialists, or that they employed anything like any modern concept of *matter.* It does not imply that they excluded from consideration other kinds of explanation that correspond to Aristotle's other causes. It implies only, in that respect, that Aristotle could not find in their writings an *explicit* recognition of such "causes." In *Metaphysics* I, Aristotle is in fact judging his predecessors, not like a physicist judging earlier physicists but like a philosophy professor judging his own students. For the purposes of the Aristotelian dialectic, all interlocutors are considered to be contemporary, and what is not said clearly and explicitly does not count as having been said at all.

Aristotle's testimony in *Metaphysics* I turns out, therefore, to be much less certain and positive than it may appear. Fortunately, Aristotle's own evidence in other places may be combined with the indirect evidence already mentioned to produce a reasonably consistent picture of Presocratic science in general and (if some backward inferences are permitted) of the Milesians in particular.

The Milesians took, as the object of their thinking, "all things" *(ta panta)* or "the universe" *(to pan, to holon)*. This in itself was, it seems, a novelty. Earlier cosmologies (those of the ancient Near East and Hesiod's *Theogony*) do aim at some kind of completeness in their coverage; they give accounts of the origins and functioning of the whole of the presently observable world order. But they do not seem to raise explicitly the question of whether that order is "everything there is"; correspondingly, the spatial and temporal boundaries of the world order, and whatever may lie beyond, are left ill-defined or wholly unspecified.

The Milesians' search for an account of "everything"—that is, of whatever there may be—led them to push back the boundaries of thought. The conscious intent to consider everything leads immediately to the question of whether the limits, in space and in time, of human observation, are also the limits of the universe. One of the most significant facts about the Milesians (attested by Aristotle) is that they asked this question, and answered it by postulating the spatial and temporal infinity of the universe. For, as Aristotle observes, given any limited space or stretch of time, one can always conceive of a space or a time stretch outside of it and containing it; and why should one stop anywhere in particular?

It might seem hopeless, though, to aspire to knowledge of anything about the universe generally, particularly if it is infinite in space and time. What guarantee could there be that this vast totality is knowable or intelligible as a whole to human minds? Such epistemological doubts were expressed explicitly as early as Xenophanes, in the late 6th century B.C.E. It is not certain how the Milesians met them, but what must be true is that they held their theorizing to be probable and in some sense an advance toward the truth: it was not meant as an idle game.

Necessarily, then, they assumed not only that the universe was a possible object of study but also that it was, at least in principle and in outline, knowable and intelligible *as a whole*. This assumption is implicit in the concept of natural science that Aristotle attributes to them. It is another powerful assumption, and a revolutionary step in contrast to what had preceded. Earlier cosmologists, like Hesiod, normally specified a unified *origin* for the observable world order, but no kind of unity beyond that.

The Milesian enterprise was constituted by "the rules of the game." By this is meant both the rules governing the construction of theories and the corresponding rules of argument by which those theories were criticized and justified. Once again, the scanty earlier evidence has to be supplemented from the practice of the late 5th and the 4th century, so that there is always the danger of reading too much back into the Milesians.

The foundation of each Milesian theory was the single "fundamental entity" (what Aristotle wished to see as the "material cause"), the entity of which, ultimately, the universe consisted, and in terms of which it was to be understood. It was also implicit that this fundamental entity was of necessity essentially *uniform*, in the large scale and the long term.

Closely linked to this functional unity of the theory was its explanatory economy and power. Everything had to be explained, and explained easily, in terms of the fundamental entity and its essential properties.

But how was such explanatory power to be achieved? The aim was to represent many diverse phenomena as variations on one underlying theme, and many complex entities as the result of intelligible complications of a single one. The theory's merit was to be judged by how well it functioned explanatorily as a whole. The systematic effort to achieve explanatory economy and power by these means is evident in the Milesians, as in their successors.

The demand contained in the "principle of sufficient reason"—namely, that there should be no unexplained asymmetries or ad hoc features—was just one particular facet of the demand for explanatory efficiency. It finds extensive application in a maximally uniform universe, and it was connected to the demand for "equality" and "justice" in nature. These may have been partly intended as analogies with human political systems. They can also be understood as recognitions of the importance of symmetry and efficiency of explanation. Here symmetry is meant in its widest mathematical sense (including not only reflection symmetry but also radial symmetry and uniformity in space and time generally).

The argumentative form of the principle of sufficient reason is the question, Why this particular thing/time/place rather than any other? The most striking early application is Anaximander's explanation of why the Earth rests in the middle of the cosmos: it stays at rest because the symmetry of its position within the cosmos gives it no reason to move one way rather than another (Aristotle, *Cael.* 2.13.295b11–16). But the essential overall uniformity of the Milesians' whole universe, in both its spatial and its temporal extensions, is even more important structurally.

According to the interpretation followed here, the Milesians postulated a universe not only infinite (as already mentioned) but also filled at any time with an infinite number of "worlds" *(kosmoi)*. The word *kosmos* here (although the usage is not directly attested for the Milesians) signifies an ordering of the world (of Earth, atmosphere, celestial bodies and outer heavens) like that which is observable by humans on Earth. If the universe is infinite, it is obviously contrary to the principle of sufficient reason to assume that the particular *kosmos* that happens to contain us is in a privileged position. Therefore there must be infinitely many *kosmoi*, scattered approximately uniformly throughout the infinite extent.

These formal requirements are only one aspect of the constraints on Milesian theorizing. The other aspect, the appeal to experience, is represented by the use of analogies and by the concept of nature *(phusis)*. For in the end it was "ordinary experience" that the theories (however abstract and intellectually elegant their construction) had to look to, to command understanding and assent.

Here, one must always recognize the inherent indeterminacy of the notion of ordinary experience. It is doubtful whether "our" notion of ordinary experience corresponds at all closely or unambiguously to that of Ionians in the 6th century B.C.E. A naive appeal to common sense as a source or touchstone of Milesian theories is unilluminating. It must be true, of course, that Milesian theorists felt themselves constrained by what they took to be "the facts." But they will have found, as scientists always do, that what the facts are, and how they should be appealed to, is already an ambiguous and contestable matter. Even the most basic aspects of everyday life, and the results of the most careful experiments, are always open to reinterpretation.

The Milesians used analogies from ordinary experience. But their intentions are not self-explanatory, and are not reliably reported. We can imagine that analogies might be used in justifying and expounding the theoretical setup and the account of the total system, or in giving accounts of particular phenomena. In either case, the analogy might be a substantive part of the *justification* for the theory, or it might be a *heuristic*, theory-building, explanation-suggesting device; or it might be no more than an *expository* device, a way of supplementing the lack of technical terminology. Mixed and intermediate cases are also, obviously, possible.

It is reasonable to assume that, in theorizing about the universe as a whole, overall analogies were used heuristically, and as argumentative supports. In any case, what the Milesians aimed at was certainly not an *explanation* meeting modern scientific (or even Aristotelian) standards of explanation, but an intelligible and plausible outline that fitted into the chosen overall framework. The three types of Greek cosmic "model" apparently used by the Milesians—the living organism, the artifact, the political entity—all have obvious appeal to a cosmologist. Living organisms, artifacts, and political structures are complex things but as a rule fairly predictable, and with a distinct overall individuality and unity.

To complete the understanding of Milesian theorizing, what is needed is the concept of nature *(phusis)*. The Ionian enterprise was, in the 5th and 4th centuries, often referred to as speaking (or writing or inquiring) about the *phusis* of everything, of the universe. So it is no far-fetched hypothesis that the concept of *phusis* was central.

The nontechnical early usage of the word *phusis* makes it correspond systematically to the uses of the verb *be (einai)*. The *phusis* of anything is what supplies the answer to the question "What is it?"—in any sense of "is." The concept of *phusis*, for the Milesians, involved a compound of empirical content and theoretical interpretation. The *phusis* of any (type of) thing comprised all those properties that were observed in nature to be its invariable properties. These were then theoretically "baptized," i.e., they were specified, within the theory, as being (all of) its essential properties.

This notion of *phusis*, though it was a constraint, did not determine by itself the specific form that the theories took. It did not determine the number and the identity of the fundamental entities, nor the general nature of their interaction within the (usually infinite) universe. Yet if explanations were required to be given in terms of *phusis*, that demand already severely limited the possibilities for ultimate entities. They had to be either (1) directly observable things, (2) "enriched" entities combined out of observables, or (3) entities formed by "impoverishment" of observables. The Milesians' ultimate entities, water, the infinite, and air, are examples of case 2: combinations from observables. Thus, Thales' water and Anaximander's air were not just ordinary water and air, but water and air enriched by the properties of life and intelligence. Anaximander's infinite was not just "something infinite" but something infinite that was also living and intelligent.

In this way the notion of *phusis* gives Milesian theorizing its empirical anchorage. The essential properties of the fundamental entities were understood to be those that are known to belong to the *phusis* of the entity in question. At the same time, the concept of *phusis* grounded a notion of natural *necessity*, for the "nature" of a thing was always understood as a constraint upon it.

Naturally, this notion of *phusis* was never unproblematic. It remained, of necessity, a concept of debatable application. It was originally intended to indicate the aspects of the external world that we seem to be able to grasp immediately as objectively regular in their behavior. But it is always debatable what should count as "external" or as "regular." Are colors, for example, or rainbows, part of the external world? Is the stability of the earth something "regular"? The notion of *phusis* was bound to focus debate on the questions (scientific and philosophical) of the nature and reliability of sense perception. These questions become, in fact, steadily more prominent after the Milesians.

Like modern science, the Presocratic enterprise tended to transform the understanding and delimitation of its own empirical basis, and to generate philosophical questions in the process.

The concept of *phusis* was also the structural tie that held together and balanced the demands of formal theorizing and those of empiricism. There was, as there always is, a natural *internal* tension between the "top-down" and the "bottom-up" approaches, between the exhilarating generalities and the awkward particular facts. It is possible, for example, even with the wretchedly incomplete evidence we have, to trace the Milesians' efforts to reconcile their grand theoretical vision of the unity of the universe with the apparently irreducible multiplicity of everyday experience. In so doing, they invoked the *phusis* of everyday things—water and air, animals, human societies—and made it carry a heavy theoretical load.

There is no reason in principle why Milesian cosmology should not have operated with a notion of god or the divine, provided of course that that notion satisfied the rules of the game set out above. In particular, if the divine was to be fundamental in the explanatory setup, it had to be both genuinely unified and well defined, and its *phusis* had to contain essential properties having a clear connection with ordinary experience. Also, to be functionally efficient, it would have to be in principle wholly intelligible to human minds. Therefore it had to be rather unlike any traditional Greek conception of a god or of the gods collectively.

In fact, a "scientific theology," in which the divine formed part of the natural world, was seen, at least from the late 5th century on, as characteristic of the Milesians and their successors in natural philosophy. Later commentators, from Plato and Aristotle onward, found the scientific theology of the Milesians difficult to understand. In modern times it has often been treated with skepticism or discussed in anachronistic terms.

The concept of nature *(phusis)* and the rules of the game, as explained above, can provide insight into this theology without the danger of anachronism. Yet it must be admitted that the evidential basis for this reconstruction consists almost entirely of the reports of Aristotle, with some help from Plato and other incidental indications. (The post-Aristotelian doxographic reports about the Milesians' theology are probably worthless.)

The essence of Milesian "natural theology" is that the basic item (or one of the basic items) in the explanatory setup is taken to have, among its basic properties, those of being alive, intelligent, purposeful, and able to act with infinite power on the contents of the universe, including itself. It seems further to have been taken to be omniscient and (within the limits imposed by the theory itself) omnipotent. Hence this, the divine and its purposes, is the ultimate explanation of the large-scale spatial and temporal structure of the universe, insofar as that, too, is not dictated by the explanatory setup itself. There is therefore a form of teleology inherent in this kind of theory.

The explanatory economy of this type of theory is fairly obvious. It enabled the Milesians to give a kind of explanation for certain centrally important phenomena:

1.   The existence in our cosmos of living, intelligent, and purposive beings. To explain this, it is easier to begin with something living and intelligent, from which the other beings are derived.

2.   The existence of change and movement generally. The divine was, as a living thing, naturally a source of movement.

3.   The existence of order and apparent purposefulness in the cosmos. This was derived from the purposeful planning of the divine.

(The assertion of an *overall* teleology of this kind must be sharply distinguished from the assertion of a divine providence directly involved in the planning of *particular* features of the world.)

Hence this concept of the divine unites everything that is needed to complete the explanatory task. It may have seemed to the Milesians that it promised the only kind of unity reasonably to be hoped for in the universe. The unity of living beings, and the unity of minds, are impressive kinds of unity. Animals unite dissimilar components, and involve change and yet stability through change. So too with the conscious mind, which also unites dissimilars and involves change and stability, and therefore may seem more promising as a model to explain the universe than mere material unity. This is particularly so if the lawlike behavior of the contents of the universe is taken not only as part of the explanation but also as one of the things to be explained. Thus the divine, with its intelligence and justice, is meant as a substantive and functional part of the whole theoretical construction. (This does not imply that Milesian theorizing was substantially continuous with any earlier theology. Nor does it imply that Milesian theorizing was a priori, or *dictated* by theological or teleological considerations.)

Such a theology obviously has its difficulties. It may be asked, in particular, how one is supposed to understand the idea of, say, "intelligent water" or "purposive air." But to put the question thus is to look at matters the wrong way round, from the point of view of a theory based on *phusis*. The claim is that the *phusis* of (e.g.) water includes life and intelligence, a claim that in itself is no more and no less difficult to understand than the observed fact of life and intelligence inhabiting animal bodies. The difficult question that the theorist faces is, rather, the following one: Why then are there no signs of life and intelligence in ordinary everyday water or air? And on this question there is room for argument; perhaps in fact there are such signs, but they are overlooked or misinterpreted.

Milesian theorizing turns out to have been like modern science in important respects, and unlike it in other important respects. There is no simplistic, one-dimensional story to be told. It is often claimed that rationality (as opposed to the alleged irrationality of myth or of "mythical thinking") is the principal characteristic of the Milesians as against their predecessors. Yet the concept of rationality is elusive and contested, and it is not clear that prescientific thinking is in any sense irrational. It is clear that 6th-century Miletus produced something that was genuinely and strikingly new. Whatever influences there may have been from the ancient Near East (and none have been firmly proved), it is not possible to claim that the Ionians were merely continuing ancient Near Eastern or other cosmologies by other means.

It has been suggested that the Milesians had: (1) a notion of "objective reality," (2) a programmatic demand that it should be intelligible as a whole, and (3) the outlines of a method for finding and representing it as intelligible. It cannot be stated dogmatically that no one before them had had this combination of aims and methods. Apart from the obvious point that our evidence for earlier thinking is excessively scanty, it might plausibly be argued that some of the speculative cosmogonies and theologies of the ancient Near East are products of a similar program. Yet the fact remains that the ancient Near East saw no explosive outburst of theorizing like the one seen in 6th-to-4th-century Greece, nor did it produce philosophy or anything like science, apart from specialized accumulations of knowledge in restricted areas.

What seems different in 6th-century Miletus is not the activity of the theoretical intellect as such, but its adoption of a naturally "self-developing" program of investigation. Can we identify the decisive ingredient of such a program? The freedom enjoyed by the Greeks in the face of traditional and generally accepted ideas must be relevant. The Presocratics are clearly associated with frank and radical criticisms of the most revered authorities known to the Greeks on religious matters: Homer and Hesiod. Such freedom, however, is only a negative matter, and in any case there cannot be forthright criticism of tradition unless one is already sure enough of an alternative "Archimedean point" from which to criticize. We may see the achievement of freedom in the face of tradition, as well as the advent of literacy, as the removal of external obstacles.

The positive new ingredient was presumably closely connected with (and almost defined by) the adoption of the *formal* demands on theories, as listed above. To give a central place to completely formal, abstract, logically absolute properties of theories and theoretical entities (for example, essential unity or universal uniformity of behavior) creates a new kind of freedom from the phenomenal world. This is not, of course, inconsistent with *respect* for the phenomena as such.

The formal demands are the product of an *abstract* manner of conceiving of reality as a whole. This is not the same as conceiving of reality as itself entirely abstract (which the "natural philosophers" obviously did not). It means going behind the phenomena to a "hidden structure" that is postulated as something abstract, such as, for example, the structure shown by a geometrical diagram. It is no accident that this period also sees the beginnings of mathematics as a systematic and abstract study.

We do not, then, need to assume any polarity between myth or mythical thinking, on one side, and rationality or rational/logical thinking, on the other. The transition was rather between less and more abstract styles of theorizing. It was a reform of thinking, a freeing of the mind from traditional habits. It also implied a new self-awareness of the abstracting theoretical mind as something autonomous, recognizing no court of appeal higher than itself, and as something universal, capable in principle of investigating anything whatever.

The application of the rules of the game led to abstract accounts of the concrete realities of nature. The underlying abstract structure was, perhaps, guessed rather than fully grasped. It was modeled by the behavior of a mind or a city, or by that of a pebble or a wheel. Such teleology as was involved did not exclude "mechanical" explanations, which did most of the detailed work. Though there was little or no systematic experiment, a corpus of ideas about the mechanical workings of the material world began to be accumulated.

The rules of the game also necessarily led to critical debate of the most fundamental kind. As noted above, they already contained, like every scientific and philosophical enterprise, tensions, circularities, and ambiguities that led to conflict and dissension: about methods and aims, about the appeal to "reasonableness" and to "experience," about the dual commitment to both overall simplicity and respect for the detail of the phenomena. By the very nature of their enterprise, the Presocratic natural philosophers were led, from the Milesians onward, further and further into debates about first principles with their colleagues. Their bare, abstract style of theorizing made the existence and the nature of disagreements more obvious than before, while at the same time the shared appeal to intrinsic reasonableness or explanatory efficiency (rather than authority or tradition) made disagreements less theoretically tolerable. It is in these self-developing theoretical tensions that we can recognize the forerunner of modern science and philosophy.

EDWARD HUSSEY

Bibliography

Barnes, Jonathan. *The Presocratic Philosophers.* London: Routledge, 1982.

Fränkel, Hermann. *Dichtung und Philosophie des frühen Griechentums.* Munich: Beck, 1962.

Furley, David, and R. E. Allen, eds. *Studies in Presocratic Philosophy,* vol. 1. London: Routledge, 1970.

Gadamer, Hans-Georg, ed. *Um die Begriffswelt der Vorsokratiker.* Darmstadt: Wissenschaftliche Buchgesellschaft, 1968.

Guthrie, W. K. C. *A History of Greek Philosophy,* vol. 1: *The Earlier Presocratics and the Pythagoreans.* Cambridge: Cambridge University Press, 1962.

Heidegger, Martin. "Der Spruch des Anaximander." In *Holzwege.* Frankfurt: Klostermann, 1950.

Hölscher, Uvo. "Anaximander und der Anfang der Philosophie." In *Anfängliches Fragen.* Göttingen: Vandenhoeck and Ruprecht, 1968. Pp. 9–89.

Jaeger, Werner. *The Theology of the Early Greek Philosophers.* Oxford: Clarendon Press, 1947.

Kahn, Charles. *Anaximander and the Origins of Greek Cosmology.* New York: Columbia University Press, 1960.

Kirk, G. S., J. E. Raven, and M. Schofield. *The Presocratic Philosophers: A Critical History with a Selection of Texts,* 2nd ed. Cambridge: Cambridge University Press, 1983.

Lloyd, G. E. R. *Magic, Reason, and Experience: Studies in the Origin and Development of Greek Science.* Cambridge: Cambridge University Press, 1979.

———. *Polarity and Analogy: Two Types of Argumentation in Early Greek Thought.* Cambridge: Cambridge University Press, 1966.

Maddalena, Antonio. *Ionici: Testimonianze e Frammenti.* Florence: Nuova Italia, 1963.

Snell, Bruno. *Die Entdeckung des Geistes.* 3rd ed. Hamburg: Claasen Verlag, 1955.

Stokes, Michael C. *One and Many in Presocratic Philosophy,* Cambridge, Mass.: Harvard University Press, 1971.

Vernant, Jean-Pierre. *Mythe et pensée chez les Grecs.* Paris: La Découverte, 1985.

———. *Les origines de la pensée grecque.* Paris: Presses Universitaires de France, 1962.

Vlastos, Gregory. "Equality and Justice in Early Greek Cosmologies." In *Studies in Presocratic Philosophy,* vol. 1: *The Beginnings of Philosophy.* Ed. D. J. Furley and R. E. Allen. London: Routledge and Kegan Paul, 1970. Pp. 56–91.

PLATONISM

In antiquity, and especially in the Hellenistic period, a Platonist *(Platonikos)* was either a commentator on Plato or one of his disciples. Members of the first group, such as Panaetius of Rhodes, a Stoic commentator on *Timaeus,* may well not have shared the Platonic positions. Whether they claimed the critical heritage of the early dialogues or presented what they viewed as the doctrines developed in the other dialogues, Plato's followers pursued their activity primarily within the framework of schools, where reading and explanation of the master's works, along with commentary on them, were based on an exceptionally strong manuscript tradition and were closely linked with the practice of virtue. As a school-based phenomenon that took its inspiration very early from the Pythagorean tradition, Platonism showed an astonishing diversity through the ages; innovation did not appear to be irreconcilable with true fidelity.

This diversity originated in the Platonic corpus itself. After an initial critical period during which, with Socrates as spokesperson, Plato called into question his contemporaries' opinions and values, he adopted a more dogmatic approach, staking out a certain number of positions in the fields of ethics, epistemology, and ontology. In all these domains, one idea was stressed above all others: that of transcendence, implying on the one hand the division of reality into two realms—the sensible, the realm of individuals that is continually changing, and the intelligible, the realm of the absolutely immutable—and on the other hand the distinction, within each human being, between a mortal body endowed with five senses and an immortal soul that can grasp the intelligible.

PLATO

In the early dialogues, up to *Meno,* Socrates makes use of the method called *elenchos:* a thesis is refuted if, and only if, its negation is deduced from the interlocutor's opinions. In fact, the *elenchos* presents four essential features: (1) from a formal point of view, this method is negative: Socrates does not defend a thesis of his own but limits himself to examining a thesis advanced by his interlocutor; (2) since Socrates seeks to discover the truth while realizing he knows nothing, he must derive this truth from premises his interlocutors hold to be true; (3) he must accept as provisionally established that truths are involved; and (4) it follows that the *elenchos*, as a tool for seeking out the truth, cannot guarantee certainty.

To arrive at certainty, that is, at the confidence that results from possessing truth, Plato will, in view of the overwhelming success of the geometrical method, use mathematics, considered as a paradigm of all methods. A truly demonstrative method should present the following logical structure: to link the truth of a proposition to the truth of a hypothesis, one must try to prove the proposition true (or false) because it is a necessary consequence of the hypothesis in question, which is considered true (or false) in the final analysis, for the latter (or its contrary) is the necessary consequence of the axioms of the system—that is, of the propositions whose truth is immediately and incontrovertibly self-evident within the framework of the system.

Plato's use of this method suggests that the philosopher had a "doctrine," even though it was subject to a continuous and significant process of elaboration. Now the doctrine in question is paradoxical, characterized as it is by a double reversal. First, for Plato, things perceived through the senses are only images of intelligible Forms, which themselves conceal the principle of their existence and constitute true reality. Second, man is not reduced to his body; his true identity coincides with the soul, an incorporeal entity that explains every movement, whether material (growth, locomotion, and so on) or spiritual (emotions, sense perceptions, intellectual knowledge, and the like).

The hypothesis of the existence of intelligible Forms, which Plato never defines and which he evokes only in terms of their negative features, allows him to lay the foundations for an ethics, a theory of knowledge, and an ontology.

Given the confusion that reigned in Athens, where the classical city-state was crumbling under the assaults of its adversaries and where citizens spoke in diametrically opposed terms about common values, Plato, in an effort to prolong Socrates' activity, sought to establish a different political order based on absolutely sound moral principles; this explains why the early dialogues deal with ethical questions. It was a matter of defining the essential virtues of the perfect citizen, a requirement that implies the existence of absolute norms depending neither on the tradition transmitted by the poets nor—as the Sophists claimed—on arbitrary conventions, norms that could serve as reference points for evaluating the human condition.

But this hypothesis, which makes an ethical system possible, refers back to the epistemological sphere, as *Meno* in particular makes clear. To grasp the absolute norms that ethics requires, we must hypothesize the existence of a faculty distinct from opinion: the intellect. Now a distinction between intellect and opinion implies a distinction between their respective objects; whereas opinion has as its domain sensible entities immersed in becoming, the intellect can grasp immutable and absolute realities. In short, to provide a foundation for the epistemology required by his moral system, Plato is led to hypothesize the existence of realities that he calls intelligible Forms.

Intelligible Forms account for the processes of intellectual knowing; still, perceptible reality does not depend on these processes. If, in the sensible world, objects and their features are reduced to transitory results of compound movements, no ethics or epistemology can be developed, and from this standpoint the hypothesis of the existence of a world of intelligible Forms presents itself as empty and gratuitous. Accordingly, independently of the needs that ethics and epistemology impose, an ontological foundation must be found that will allow us to take into account sensible phenomena, which, left to themselves, would dissolve in an incessant becoming. We can only know these sensible phenomena, we can only speak of them, if they present a certain stability, which derives from their participation in the intelligible. In short, in creating the universe while keeping his eyes fixed on intelligible Forms, the artificer or demiurge guarantees the existence, in the sensible world, of a certain stability that allows us to know the world and to talk about it, and in the city-state, the existence of norms serving to orient both individual and collective human conduct. This indeed must have been Plato's intention in writing *Timaeus* in particular.

THE OLD ACADEMY

This doctrine, which is formulated more or less explicitly in the dialogues from *Meno* on, must have been the object of intense discussion in the context of the Academy that Plato is believed to have founded in 387 B.C.E. He had just returned from his first tour of Magna Graecia (southern Italy), where he had met some Pythagoreans, among them Archytas, and Sicily, where he had been received at the court of Dionysius the Elder, tyrant of Syracuse, and had made the acquaintance of Dion. Plato established his school in Athens, at his own expense, in a tree-shaded setting freshened with springs, a park devoted to the hero Academos. The park was on the road to Eleusis, near the Cephissus River and not far from Colonos; a gymnasium stood at its center. The school was intended above all to prepare young people to play an active role in politics by giving them a philosophical education according to the program set forth in Books VI and VII of *The Republic*. The Academy rapidly achieved great success; it soon became the principal rival of Isocrates' school, which focused on teaching rhetoric.

Plato seems to have been surrounded by friends and associates, each responsible for a particular discipline. The best known are Aristotle of Stagira, Speusippus of Athens, Xenocrates of Chalcedon, Philippus of Opus, Hermodorus of Syracuse, Heraclides of Pontus, Eudoxus, Hestiaeus of Perinthus, and Theaetetus. We should also include in this group a certain number of other mathematicians and astronomers, such as Menaechmus, his brother Deinostratus, Amphinomus, Amyntas, Athenaeus, Hermotimus, Callipus (who is thought to have refined the system of the spheres), and Theodius of Magnesia, to whom *Elements* in the style of Euclid are generally attributed. Other persons mentioned in the *Letters* include Euphraius (*Letter V*), Erastus, and Coriscus of Scepsis (*Letter VI*).

From the outset, the Academy seems to have been a place of intense discussion rather than an instrument for the dogmatic transmission of a body of privileged doctrines. It is important to keep this in mind: neither Aristotle nor any of Plato's successors as head of the Academy maintained the core of the founder's thought in its orthodoxy, that is, the doctrine of intelligible Forms. If we consider the relations Plato and Speusippus maintained with Dion, who, after listening to Plato's talks and even frequenting the Academy, returned to Sicily to try to seize power, political action must have occupied an important place, along with the development of astronomical theories and geometry.

Moreover, we have every reason to believe that, as the geometric method prescribed, a search for the highest principles was undertaken within the framework of the Academy. This quest, of which *Philebus* may have supplied an early sketch, could well have given rise to the system of principles that, according to some modern authors and some contemporaries, constitutes the heart of the "esoteric doctrines." In this esoteric context, the true Plato is the one Aristotle criticized, a Plato whom only his closest disciples knew. The figure of Plato conveyed by the Platonic tradition was thus from the beginning an "Aristotelized" Plato, a Plato whose doctrine had already been discussed within the framework of the Academy and in terms that in many instances were fixed once and for all by Aristotle.

This school, which defined itself neither by the possession of the property bought by Plato nor by a particular status as an association, existed institutionally only through the election of a scholarch, or head, an Academic named by his peers who thus became a successor to Plato. The Academy remained faithful to the directions set by its founder; however, the heart of the Academy's activity seems to have been the systematization and diffusion of the master's thought, as opposed to the competing views professed by other schools. Aristotle's philosophy was taught in the gymnasium of the Lyceum; that of Antisthenes, who was viewed as the founder of Cynicism, was expounded in the Cynosarges gymnasium. Later, two new schools were established, also in Athens: Zeno's Stoic school, and the Epicurean school.

If, for the Sophists and for Plato, philosophical training was intended to prepare young men for life as citizens, by teaching them to master their external discourse and their internal dialogue by dialectic or rhetorical methods and to understand all the rational principles that these could involve, later philosophical instruction was designed instead to prepare for life in general, either public or private; still, in one way or another, mastery of discourse was always involved.

This means that the method of teaching consisted, above all, at least among the Platonists, Aristotelians, and Stoics, in dialectical exercises by means of which the interlocutors learned to carry on a dialogue with others and also with themselves. Although master classes did exist in these schools, probably resembling the classes that resulted in Aristotle's *Physics* and *Metaphysics,* the philosopher's monologue was not the presentation of an entire system, for the speaker was always responding, if not to a listener's question, at least to a specific problem. The teaching generally included three distinct areas, thought to have been introduced by Xenocrates, the Academy's second *diadoch* (successor to Plato). The first area might be said to correspond both to logic and epistemology, in the sense in which these terms are used today; it was called logic by the Stoics, canonics by the Epicureans, dialectics by the Platonists and by the Aristotelians, though these two schools had given a very different content to dialectics; all the schools called the second area physics and the third ethics.

THE NEW ACADEMY

With Arcesilaus of Pitane, who succeeded Crates as diadoch in 268/264, the Academy transformed itself into the "New" Academy, in that all effort at systematization was abandoned. Suspension of judgment became the cardinal principle of philosophy; the refusal of certainty led to universal questioning. Arcesilaus symbolizes this crucial shift in his own person. He began by studying mathematics with Autolycus, and spent some time at the school of Theophrastus before becoming acquainted, at least through their writings, with some of the dialecticians of Megara and Eretria. Turning away from Xenocrates' grandiose system, which was largely inspired by the dialogues of Plato's maturity, Arcesilaus went back to the practice of Socrates, which the earlier dialogues illustrate. This is why he gave primacy to critical dialogue and to the affirmation of ignorance; this is the sense in which he understood Plato's dubitative formulas and mythical narratives. His principal target was quite naturally Stoicism, the most widespread dogmatism of the period; starting from overall conceptions based on certainty and extending to the universe, Stoicism presented itself as the necessary precondition of wisdom.

Like Socrates, Arcesilaus wrote nothing and never dogmatized; he engaged his interlocutors in lively conversation and asked them for advice. His students were to be guided not by the master's authority but by their own reason; Arcesilaus's replies were in turn new questions. The spirit of Arcesilaus's teaching was perpetuated by Carneades, who sought to establish a hierarchy of representations according to their degree of verisimilitude, since he maintained that one cannot assert with certainty of any given representation that it is true.

At all events, the history of the Academy seems to have ended in 88 B.C.E., when Philo of Larissa fled Athens, under siege by Mithridates, to seek refuge in Rome. But even before Philo's exile, the Platonic school had undergone a major schism with the departure of Antiochus of Ascalon, who claimed to find the inspiration of the Old Academy outside of this New Academy, which he himself finally wrote off as an aberrant parenthesis in the history of Platonism. He had a dual purpose: to reestablish a dogmatic interpretation of Platonism, and to demonstrate the preeminence of the Academy over the Lyceum and the Stoa, making Aristotle and Zeno epigones of Plato. Thus his Platonism was strongly influenced by Aristotelianism and especially by Stoicism. Antiochus was never recognized as head of the Academy, whose institutional lineage had been disrupted. The school taken over by Antiochus outlived its founder by nearly a century.

MIDDLE PLATONISM

The period just described, which lasted from the 4th to the 1st century B.C.E., is characterized by two features: the presence of philosophical institutions in Athens and teaching intended as training in the arts of speaking and living. The major schools—Platonic, Aristotelian, Epicurean, and Stoic—had been set up in different parts of the city of Athens. Instruction consisted in dialectical exercises and discussions designed to train students for political action enlightened by knowledge (Platonism), for a life devoted to science (Aristotelianism), or for moral life (Epicureanism and Stoicism).

On their last legs during the final years of the Roman republic, these philosophical institutions were virtually defunct in the early years of the principate. The disappearance of the philosophical schools of Athens and the formation of numerous philosophical institutions throughout the Mediterranean basin inaugurated a new phase in the history of philosophy.

To affirm their loyalty to the tradition from which each took its inspiration, the four philosophical schools—which by that time were spread among various oriental and occidental cities—could no longer turn for support to the Athenian institutions created by their founders; thus they carried on an oral tradition. Platonic philosophy, in particular, became essentially textual commentary, focusing on *Phaedo, Alcibiades* I, *Gorgias, Phaedrus, Symposium, Theaetetus, The Republic, Laws, Statesman,* and, especially, *Timaeus.*

The existence of philosophical commentaries had its origins in the remote past; indeed, Crantor very probably commented on Plato's *Timaeus* around 300 B.C.E. But at the beginning of the Roman empire, this practice took on a newly systematic character. In the past, students had learned to speak, and in learning how to speak they had learned how to live. Now, they learned not so much to speak as to read, even if, in learning how to read, they were still learning how to live. The philosophic enterprise thus became exegetic. If one were to inquire, for example, what relations pertain among "the Living Thing," the intelligible Forms, and the intellect, one would be seeking to grasp the meaning of the following phrase from *Timaeus:* "Reason perceives

Forms existing in the Living Thing" (39e). Reflection bears directly not on a given problem, but on the problem as it is addressed by Aristotle and Plato.

From the end of the 1st century B.C.E. and during the early stages of the Roman empire, the dominant philosophy continued to be Stoicism, which permeated even a cultivated, eclectic, relatively undogmatic Platonism that was strongly influenced by Aristotle. But gradually the need for a more religious philosophy made itself felt. Platonism then appeared as a means to accede to another order of reality, that of the divine, which only the soul could grasp. This is the context that produced, among the Platonists, a renaissance later known as Middle Platonism.

In the middle of the 1st century C.E., Potamon is considered to have been the father of eclectic Platonism, following the model of Philo Judaeus (first half of the 1st century C.E.), the most prolific and most intelligent representative of a syncretism in which Platonism played a decisive role. Plutarch of Chaeronaea (ca. 50–125) has his place within this new stream of thought; after him, in the second half of the 2nd century, came the Sophists Maximus of Tyre and Apuleius of Madaurus, and a little later Galen the physician, who may have studied with Albinus (the latter, in turn, may have been a disciple of Gaius in Smyrna), Celsus (the virulent refutation of whom by the Christian Origen allows us to reconstruct in part his *Real Discourse*), Numenius of Apamea (who rediscovered Moses behind Plato), and also Alcinous in his *Didaskalikos* (The Handbook of Platonism). All these Platonists either interpreted Plato in a theosophic spirit, using the allegorical method without hesitating to invoke astrology, demonology, and even magic, or else, at the very least, they compared Platonism with Aristotelianism, with Stoicism, or—as did the first apologists—with Christianity.

One institutional sign of this renaissance, which also touched the other schools, is Emperor Marcus Aurelius's establishment in Athens in 176 of four chairs of philosophy: Platonic, Aristotelian, Stoic, and Epicurean. Atticus, who may have belonged to the family of Herod Atticus, may have been the first chair of the Platonic school; this would explain his openly anti-Aristotelian attitude.

The Pythagorean influence, which had already been exerted over Platonism in the Old Academy by Speusippus and Xenocrates, became decisive at this point, although the details of its historical transmission remain obscure. This tendency is clearly discernible in Eudorus, who is thought to have lived in Alexandria during the 1st century B.C.E., and who may have commented on *Timaeus*, and in his compatriot Philon. Pythagorean thought, significant in the work of Thrasyllus (an astrologer under Tiberius and a philosopher at the court of Nero), is transformed in Plutarch's writings into a philosophical presupposition.

The Pythagorean influence made itself felt not only on the level of doctrine but even on the material level. The order in which Plato's writings were presented reflects the order adopted by Thrasyllus, who may himself have written about the principles of Plato and Pythagoras. In fact, this rearrangement of Plato's works into nine groups of four (tetralogies), which can perhaps be attributed to Dercyllides, may go back to the annotated edition that Cicero's friend T. Pomponius Atticus arranged to have produced in Rome. This edition may already have had the benefit of the work of revision carried out in Alexandria by Aristophanes of Byzantium (271–180 B.C.E.). And the Alexandrian edition, in which Plato's works were organized in groups of three (trilogies) is thought to have been based on the Academic edition published while Xenocrates was scholarch, some thirty years after Plato's death.

The Pythagorean influence on Platonism had many facets, but one of them, secrecy, took on crucial importance. Secrecy applied to two elements that came into play in the communication of Platonism: the means of transmission, and coding. The privileged means of transmission of fundamental truths was supposed to be the spoken word, for writing put information within everyone's reach, at least in theory. Whence the use of the term *akousmata* to designate the Pythagorean doctrines; writing was used only to produce memoranda *(hupomnēmata)*, or memory aids. As the relation to writing never ceased to be problematic in the Platonic tradition, the ties between Platonism and Pythagoreanism were strengthened. And this first restriction bearing on the means of transmission was accompanied by another, one that concerned the symbolic and enigmatic fashion in which these doctrines were formulated; indeed this is why they were described as *sumbola* and *ainigmata*.

Timaeus and *The Republic* were the key dialogues used initially to construct this new dogmatism. In the early stages at least, they were not the object of extensive commentary, but their interpreters looked to them for viewpoints on divinity, the world, man, and society, in the context of a system articulated around three principles: God, the Model, and Matter.

For Atticus as for Plutarch and Alcinous, the God in question has to be identified with the Good of *The Republic* and with the demiurge, the Constructor of the Cosmos, of *Timaeus*. Since this God is first among all gods, and the supreme principle, nothing can be superior to him. Such supremacy determines the type of relation that this God maintains with the second principle: the paradigm, or Model.

The Middle Platonists were accustomed to envisaging the problem by recalling the passage in *Timaeus* where "the artificer of any object . . . keeps his gaze fixed on that which is uniform" (28a.6–7). This led them to the conviction that, in a way, the intelligible Forms were God's "thoughts," which did not prevent them from having existence in themselves, apart from the Intellect. Consequently, the Model, which corresponded to the Intelligible, was, as the object of God's thought, at once external and internal to the Intellect, that is, to the first God.

Atticus declares that Plato was merely perpetuating the opinions of his predecessors and that, like them, he recognized only four elements, from which all the other bodies were formed as a consequence of transformations and combinations according to clearly defined proportions. These elements are earth, water, air, and fire, and the positions they occupy in space are determined by the very constitution of the universe. They emerged from a single, homogeneous, and undifferentiated matter—probably what Plato, in *Timaeus*, called the third principle, an extended, wandering cause, a receptacle. He was probably referring here to that in which or upon which figures and bodies are outlined, but he never views this reality as corporeal matter. Atticus had been to a school other than Plato's. He must have studied with Plutarch, from whom he took this very idea (unless it was from Alcinous). Atticus in fact understood the third principle in the sense of a corporeal and sensible reality, a sort of undifferentiated chaos, in which all the elements of the universe are merged: like Plato, he still called it "a receptacle, nurse, mother, substratum, elusive to the senses, having as a property only the power to receive forms, all the while being itself without quality, without form; matter, which is neither corporeal nor incorporeal, which is only potentially a body"; but he definitely regarded it as "matter," a notion that Plato never adopted. Atticus could have been influenced on this point by Posidonius or Galen the Aristotelian, who, like Posidonius, also recognized a universal matter in which all the elements are resolved, a "primal substance that provides the basis of all bodies born and perishable." The fact remains that in making a material reality of the third principle, Atticus seems to have gone far beyond his master Plato.

Beyond this doctrine of the three principles, the representatives of Middle Platonism interpreted the soul of the world in *Timaeus* in a quite original manner. Probably in reaction against the Stoics' material monism, they hypothesized that the world has an irrational soul. Having made the distinction between a transcendent divinity and a totally indeterminate primary matter, these interpreters of *Timaeus*, who were seeking in this way to account for the chaos and the irregularity of the movement that permeates corporeal nature, considered that the soul of the world, irrational at first, would later be set in order, insofar as possible, by the demiurgic intelligence. In Middle Platonism, the constitution of the universe thus took on the aspect of a drama, while in Neoplatonism it would be considered within the framework of a system in which the Intellect deployed, without intentionality, all the possibilities inherent within it.

The best way to get a sense of this interpretative strategy is to read Alcinous's *Didaskalikos* (ca. 150 C.E.). The author was closely linked with the branch of Middle Platonism that interpreted Plato in the light of Aristotle; it has recently been established that he must be distinguished from Albinus, another Middle Platonic philosopher and the author of *Introduction to the Dialogues of Plato*, with whom Galen the physician may have studied. The title *Didaskalikos* designates a more or less well defined principle of philosophical

Introduction

Development

discourse consisting in the account of a philosophy that had previously been reduced to a body of doctrine.

The accompanying outline of Alcinous's work in *Didaskalikos* highlights the principal vectors that allow us to define Middle Platonism. Grounded in the opposition between the Philosopher and the Sophist thematized in *Sophist*, which extends into an opposition between being and nonbeing, truth and error, this account of the Platonic doctrine is developed in terms of the three major components of philosophy in the Hellenistic period: dialectical, physical integrated with theoretical, and practical. Theoretical philosophy actually includes three areas: mathematics, as a method; theology, which concerns first causes; and physics, which deals with the universe and its contents. Theology is in fact concerned with the three principles that structure the Middle Platonic interpretation: God, the Model, and Matter; these account for the macrocosm and the microcosm alike.

The passage from Middle Platonism to Neoplatonism, illustrated by the polemic launched by Porphyry at Plotinus's school in Rome, is played out in the relation between God and the Model, that is, more precisely, in the question of knowing whether the Model, the Intelligible, is at the same level as the Demiurge, at the same level as the Intellect, before it or after it. In his *Commentary on the Timaeus of Plato,* Proclus recapitulates the positions of Plotinus, Porphyry, and Longinus on this: "For among the Ancients, some, like Plotinus, have represented the Demiurge as containing the Forms of all things, while others, rejecting that view, have situated the Forms either before the Demiurge, as Porphyry did, or after him, as Longinus did" (II.1.322c). Longinus thus defended a position in conformity with the Middle Platonists' doctrine on God and the Model; since the Demiurge was the supreme principle, the Model could only be inferior to him.

At the same time, positions like that of Plotinus and Porphyry result from an approach to interpreting Platonic doctrine that apparently goes back to Numenius. In identifying the Good with the first Intellect, Numenius construed it as a principle superior to the Demiurge, which he identified with a second Intellect. From that point on, as the Demiurge was no longer the ultimate principle, the Model could be situated either prior to it, as Porphyry maintained, or in it, as Plotinus affirmed. Porphyry, who had just arrived from Athens, went on to defend Longinus's doctrine in Rome in Plotinus's school. In the ensuing polemic, Amelius, Plotinus, and of course Longinus all had their say. Longinus reaffirmed his positions, but in vain, for Porphyry joined forces with Plotinus. The story of Neoplatonism was beginning.

But this story was paradoxical from the very outset, for in separating the ultimate source of being from being itself, the Neoplatonists raised a redoubtable problem. If the Absolute is determined by nothing but itself, if it transcends being and reason, it can intervene at any level it chooses, independently of any preexisting rational order. Moreover, the Absolute is free to reveal itself to human beings, independently of their behavior and their efforts in the field of reason. That was the problem Plotinus raised in his fascinating treatise *On the Freedom and Will of the One* (*Enneads* VI.vi.39). Hermeticism, Gnosticism, and the Chaldaeans would offer a soteriological answer to this problem that the Neoplatonists would try, for better or worse, to solve by appealing to reason.

NEOPLATONISM

The story thus begins with Plotinus, who was inspired by Ammonius, his teacher in Alexandria (about whom we know very little). Plotinus undertook to explain Plato's principles, which had previously been identified with those of Pythagoras; he took his inspiration from what we now call the later dialogues, and primarily from *Parmenides,* a difficult text that had either been neglected until then or interpreted superficially. This vast enterprise led to a renaissance that would leave a decisive stamp on Platonism.

Plotinus founded a true school of philosophy in Rome that functioned on a strictly private basis for twenty-five years, from 244 until 269. Porphyry, who attended this school for less than five years (from 263 to 268), describes its operations succinctly in his *Life of Plotinus*, which he wrote as a preamble to his edition of the master's treatises collected in six *Enneads*, or groups of nine. (The number six was obtained by multiplying the first uneven number by the first even one, and the number nine, by multiplying the first uneven number by itself; all these numbers and operations presented a profound metaphysical meaning in the framework of Neopythagoreanism.)

Probably born to a family of high Roman officials in Egypt, Plotinus settled in Rome, after a misadventure at the court of the emperor Gordian (to which he belonged during an unfortunate campaign against the Persians), to take advantage of the opportunities his family ties afforded him. The school, which he founded shortly after his arrival in Rome, met in the home of a noblewoman who may have been the widow of the emperor Trebonianus Gallus. Senators sat in on the courses, during which Plotinus discussed problems raised by Plato and Aristotle in a polemical anti-Stoic context; he eschewed rhetorical staging and paid close attention to the major commentators. Two of the master's pupils soon became his favorite disciples and collaborators: Amelius, who functioned as his assistant before leaving to take over Numenius's school in Apamaea, and Porphyry, who later prepared a systematic edition of Plotinus's writings.

In metaphysics, Plotinus brought the break with Middle Platonism to its culmination on the level of principles, by extracting all the consequences of the position held by Numenius. As we have seen, Numenius identified the Good with the first Intellect and made it a principle superior to the Demiurge, which he considered a second intellect. Since Aristotle's divine intellect did not suffice to explain the world of beings, Plotinus maintained that there must be a principle beyond being, which is the One, and which must be identified with the Good. In Plato's *Parmenides*, which for this reason supplants *Timaeus* as Platonism's key dialogue, Plotinus found not only the theory of the One but also theories of the Intellect and of the Soul. This led him to oppose the Gnostics as well, by elaborating an entire architecture of the intelligible world that accounts, in a different way, for the presence of the intelligible in the sensible world. But in the case of Plotinus, as well as all the other philosophers who followed, the effort to maintain a rationalistic attitude within the framework of a system whose principle is located beyond reason constituted a source of inexhaustible difficulty.

So far as the soul is concerned, Plotinus held a view that he himself described as paradoxical. One part of the soul—and even a part of the human soul—remains on the divine level of intelligible realities. It is thus through only a part of itself that the human soul is united with the body. A thesis of this sort leads, moreover, to the view that there is also an intermediate part of the soul between the two extreme parts; its task is not only to resolve conflicts between soul and body but also to allow knowledge of Forms, for it is an intermediate part of the soul that becomes conscious of what the superior part contemplates eternally. This intermediate part is in fact self-awareness. This thesis is also related to problems concerning the movement of the soul, its immortality, its purification through virtues, and its mystical life, which consists in making our empirical "I" coincide with the transcendent "I," without falling back on grace or ritual. Supreme wisdom can thus operate on a purely philosophical level.

In Rome itself, Plotinus's teaching remained without influence. Even before the end of his life, his two best disciples had already abandoned their master: Porphyry had gone to Lilybaeum in Sicily, and Amelius to Apamaea in Syria. Nevertheless, Plotinus had established the foundation for all of Neoplatonism and had initiated its evolution: the preference for *Parmenides* over *Timaeus* as the key Platonic dialogue; the Platonic One taken as the very first principle beyond the Aristotelian Intellect; all the degrees of being set forth in a hierarchy starting from the One. What is more, Plotinus had inquired into the nature and the structure of the soul. And above all, as we know from Porphyry, it was Plotinus who reread the principal texts of the great philosophers, giving them new currency and commenting on them in relation to his own fundamental project: to achieve an original synthesis between the Platonic and the Pythagorean principles.

Porphyry was the agent of transmission of Plotinus's philosophy. His work, which must have been immense, is largely lost. Born in Tyre, he studied at first in Athens with Longinus, a Middle Platonist who made no distinction between philosophy and literature. Then he went to Rome to study at Plotinus's school. From the start he had to repudiate Longinus's typically Middle Platonic doctrines concerning the relations between the Intellect and the Intelligible in favor of Plotinus's views. Plotinus used his polemical skills against the Gnostics and, according to Porphyry—who was thereby justifying his own work as editor of the *Enneads*—entrusted Porphyry with the revision of his work. But five years after his arrival in Rome, Porphyry suddenly broke with Plotinus, perhaps because of the latter's anti-Aristotelian outlook.

This is the hypothesis that comes readily to mind if we assume that it is in Sicily that Porphyry plunged into the production of commentaries on Aristotle. He wrote on *Categories*, *Peri hermeneias*, *Physics*, and *Metaphysics* (XII); he also wrote *Isagoge* and, in particular, *That the Schools of Plato and Aristotle Are Only One*, a treatise that proclaims Aristotle's agreement with Plato. He also drafted an enormous treatise called *Against the Christians*, which earned him the wrath of the Christian emperors. Of course, he dedicated himself to the study of Platonic philosophy by composing commentaries on *Timaeus* and *Parmenides*. He even commented on Plotinus and based the manual called *Sentences* on his work. He was also a historian of philosophy *(Life of Pythagoras, On the Soul)*, and he took part in controversies on several subjects *(On Abstinence, Letter to Anebo)*.

Porphyry seems not to have had a school. Visitors spent limited periods of time with him. The most famous of these is Iamblichus, the originator of Syrian Neoplatonism. But Porphyry also influenced the rhetor Marius Victorinus in Rome, and Chalcidius, whose translation and Latin commentary on part of *Timaeus* had a critical impact throughout the Middle Ages. Having become a Christian, Marius Victorinus was to be the intermediary between Plotinus and the Christian Neoplatonism illustrated by St. Ambrose and St. Augustine.

Porphyry's essential contribution to the history of Neoplatonism is a double one. He reintroduced the literary genre of commentary—on Aristotle first of all, then on Plato—into Neoplatonism. He also spread Plotinus's doctrine through his own works, in particular in 301, when he produced a standard edition of Plotinus's treatises in the form of the *Enneads,* which have survived. Porphyry commented on the *Enneads* in *Sententiae,* a work of which only fragments remain, but in which Porphyry develops for the first time the doctrine of levels of virtue (civic, purificatory, contemplative, and paradigmatic), a doctrine that played an essential role in later Neoplatonism. In fact, the way the *Enneads* were organized in three volumes ensured a progressive order of reading designed within a pedagogic perspective to elevate the soul to knowledge of the highest realities.

Volume One
Ennead I: treatises with a moral focus
Ennead II: treatises on physical reality
Ennead III: treatises relating to the world

Volume Two
Ennead IV: treatises on the soul
Ennead V: treatises on the intellect

Volume Three
Ennead VI: treatises on the One

Also, Porphyry went on to defend what he took to be his master's doctrine against what he viewed as Iamblichus's deviations.

We know practically nothing about Iamblichus's family (the name comes from a transcription from the Syriac or Aramaic *ya-mliku,* "he is king" or "let him be king"). Iamblichus was born in Chalcis in Syria-Coele, probably Chalcis ad Belum, the present Quinnesrin, around 240. He studied first with

Anatolius, then with Porphyry. He probably founded a school in Syria at Apamaea. His best-known pupil is Sopater. After Sopater was executed by order of Constantine, Iamblichus was succeeded by Aidesius, who is thought to have settled in Pergamum, then by Eustathius. Theodorus of Asine and Dexippus were also among his disciples.

No clear-cut criterion allows us to propose a chronology of Iamblichus's works. His most significant production seems to have been a collection of ten books on Pythagoreanism, only four of which have survived. The first, intended to serve as an introduction, is *Life of Pythagoras*. This book is followed by three others: *Exhortation to Philosophy, On Common Mathematical Science*, and *On the Introduction to Nichomachean Arithmetic*. The missing books dealt with physics, ethics, theology, geometry, music, and astronomy. Psellus preserved excerpts from Books V through VII, of which two fragments survive: "On Physical Number" (Book V), and "On Ethical and Theological Arithmetic" (Books VI–VII). In the same vein there is a curious book called *The Theology of Arithmetic*, which turns out to be a compilation of passages from a work with the same title by Nicomachus of Gerasa and from a work by Anatolius (probably Iamblichus's teacher), *On the Decade and the Numbers Contained in It*. After such a massive effort, Platonism could no longer be dissociated from Pythagoreanism.

Iamblichus's most original work nevertheless remains his response to Porphyry's *Letter to Anebo*, which, in the manuscripts, bears the title *Abammo's Reply to Porphyry's Letter to Anebo and Solution of the Difficulties Inherent in It*. This work comprises two volumes that appeal to Chaldaean and Egyptian wisdom to promote the "true" theurgy.

Stobaeus preserved lengthy fragments of *On the Soul*, a treatise that deals with the nature of the soul, its powers, and its peregrinations, whether it is in a body or separated from it; in this text, Iamblichus evokes the positions of several other contemporary and more ancient philosophers. He commented on the *Chaldaean Oracles* in a work comprising twenty-eight books, of which only fragments remain; we also have fragments from *On the Gods*, a treatise that became the basis for two discourses (IV and V) by the emperor Julian and for *On the Gods and on the Universe*, a book by Sallustius.

In the area of commentary, Iamblichus seems to have developed the doctrine according to which each dialogue has a single theme, which is its end, its design *(skopos)*, and to which everything else must be related (Anon., *Prolegomena* 26; Westerink, pp. 13–44). On the strength of this conviction, he proposed an order for reading the Platonic dialogues that takes the student through the three traditional divisions of philosophy, ethics *(Alcibiades* I, *Gorgias, Phaedo)*, logic *(Cratylus, Theaetetus)*, and physics *(Sophist, Statesman)*, to lead him to the height of these studies, theology *(Phaedrus, Symposium)* and even to bring him to the summit of theology, the Good *(Philebus)*. *Timaeus* and *Parmenides* come last, recapitulating all of Plato's teaching in the fields of physics and theology. This approach to reading Plato, which Iamblichus must have followed in his teaching, remained the rule for all later Neoplatonists.

A fairly large number of fragments of Iamblichus's *Commentary on Timaeus* survive, along with several fragments of a *Commentary on Parmenides* and a *Commentary on Phaedo*. We find exegetic remarks on specific points in passages from *Alcibiades* I, *Phaedo*, and *Philebus*. And, in a scholium on *Sophist*, we find an allusion to the *skopos* that Iamblichus attributed to this dialogue. Iamblichus occupied a unique position in the interpretation he proposed of the hypotheses of *Parmenides*, into which the Neoplatonists read the organization of the first principles. To ensure a position—very high up in the hierarchy of the gods—for the actors in the theurgy whom Iamblichus called "superior beings" (archangels, angels, demons, and heroes), he shifted the entire hierarchy of the gods up a notch and even went beyond *Parmenides*, since he was obliged to posit an ineffable god not included among the hypotheses found in that dialogue; Damascius later adopted this crucial interpretive detail.

At bottom, Iamblichus's philosophical system resulted from an elaboration of Plotinus's, carried out within the framework of an original interpretation powerfully influenced by Neopythagoreanism and the *Chaldaean Oracles*. Iamblichus postulated a totally ineffable principle prior to the One. In addition, between the One and the Intelligible he imagined a pair of principles, the limited and the unlimited. Thus the One-Being, which is at the summit of the intelligible triad, is a mixture resulting from these two principles. In this manner Iamblichus may have opened the way to the doctrine of units *(henads)*, which played an important role in later Neoplatonism.

After the domain of the One, we find the domain of Being, that is, that of the Intelligible and the Intellect. At this level, according to Proclus (*On Timaeus* I.308.17ff), Iamblichus hypothesized seven triads: three triads of intelligible gods, the first being that of the One-Being (*hen on*), three triads of the intelligible and intellective gods, and one triad, the seventh, of intellective gods. This last triad may have included Kronos, Rhea, and Zeus, who was the Demiurge for the Neoplatonists. There is reason to doubt that this was the case, however, because Proclus introduces this development to show that Iamblichus expressed himself too summarily when he gave the entire intelligible world the name of Demiurge in his controversy against Porphyry (*On Timaeus* I.307.14–308.17ff).

Then comes the domain of the Soul, the hypostasis of the Soul as well as all other sorts of souls. Concerning particular souls, Iamblichus distanced himself from Plotinus and Porphyry on one essential point. He refuted the thesis according to which a higher part of the soul dwells at the level of the Intelligibles. For him, the soul was completely one with the body. This was the Aristotelian position, and it implies that salvation of the soul must necessarily come from elsewhere. The gap between Porphyry's position and Iamblichus's on this specific point widened: while Porphyry remained faithful to Plotinian rationalism, Iamblichus gave priority over philosophy to theurgy, understood as a spiritual movement through which one appeals directly to the gods according to well-established rites in order to obtain the union of the soul with the gods. Hence the importance of the *Chaldaean Oracles* in Iamblichus's works.

As far as nature is concerned, Iamblichus, who was less optimistic than Plotinus on the capacities of the Intellect, nevertheless maintained that destiny exercises its power only over the inferior (nonrational) soul, and that the superior soul can liberate itself through the practice of theurgy.

Finally, matter, which can perhaps be traced back to the dyad in the realm of the One, should be viewed as that which introduces otherness into the *logoi,* which are the manifestations of Forms in the soul and in the sensible.

Iamblichus taught in Apamaea during the first quarter of the 4th century, and his school flourished. One of his disciples, the highly talented Theodorus of Asinaea, set himself up as a rival of his master. Iamblichus remained under the influence of Numenius and Porphyry, and continued to maintain the Plotinian thesis according to which one part of the soul is not transmitted through generation. After his death (around 326), Sopater succeeded him in Apamaea, and Aedesius founded a new school in Pergamum that was to have special historical importance, since the future emperor Julian had his first contact with Neoplatonism there in 351.

Aedesius's disciples went in three different directions: Maximus left to teach in Ephesus, Chrysanthius went to Sardis, and Priscus to Athens. The emperor Julian turned to these philosophers to ensure his restoration of the pagan cult: he brought Maximus to his court and he named Chrysanthius high priest of Lydia, while Priscus, who had refused to come with Maximus to join the emperor, preserved the Iamblichean tradition of Neoplatonism in Athens. It was to Priscus that Julian wrote: "I entreat you not to let Theodorus and his followers deafen you too by their assertions that Iamblichus, that truly godlike man, who ranks next to Pythagoras and Plato, was worldly and self-seeking" (letter to Priscus, 358–359, from Gaul). Thus the respective merits of Iamblichus and Theodorus were debated in Athens in the 350s. Priscus's presence in Athens ensured a victory for Iamblichus in the second half of the century.

Neoplatonism was given a powerful impetus in Athens, where a Platonic school could quite naturally claim the legacy of the Academy. Iamblichus's successors ensured the establishment of a new dynasty of philosophers who, more than any other group, could view themselves as Plato's successors: Plutarch, Syrianus, Proclus, and Damascius. We know that, every year, Proclus took it upon himself to go to the Academy to celebrate the memory of his philosophical ancestors, Plato and all his successors.

Under the reigns of the emperors Theodosius (379–395) and Justinian (527–565), two waves of antipagan legislation gradually put in place increasingly repressive measures directed against non-Christians. Centers of cult practices had to be destroyed or transformed into Christian churches, and their rites were banned. Philosophers felt that they were the last custodians of a religious tradition that had been practiced in the Greek Orient for nearly a thousand years.

Athenian Platonists reacted by initiating a return to the sources of their religious spirituality, the *Orphic Rhapsodies* and the *Chaldaean Oracles* (which were viewed at the time as testimony to a fabled antiquity), and also by undertaking a theological rereading not only of the ancient poets Homer and Hesiod but also of Plato, construing the second half of *Parmenides* as a systematic theological treatise that described the hierarchy of classes of gods by means of "hypotheses." For these philosophers, *epopteia* was no longer the result of the Eleusinian initiation, but rather of the reading of Plato's *Parmenides*. From this point on, the entire Neoplatonic school in Athens took up the task of reconciling these theological traditions with one another. To this end, the Athenian masters wrote a work, unfortunately lost, called *The Harmony of Orpheus, Pythagoras and Plato with the Chaldaean Oracles*, which was based on the following "myth": "All Greek theology is the progeny of the mystic tradition of Orpheus; Pythagoras first of all learned from Aglaophamus the initiatory rites providing access to the gods; then Plato received the all-perfect science of the gods from the Pythagorean and Orphic writings" (Proclus, *On the Theology of Plato* I.5.25–26). The Platonic school in Athens went as far as it was possible to go in associating Platonism with Pythagoreanism, a Pythagoreanism that claimed to be the repository of the Orphic mysteries.

We do not know very much about the Athenian philosopher Plutarch, who is viewed as the founder of the Neoplatonic school in Athens. None of his writings has been preserved, and we are aware of his importance only through the respect in which he was held by his successors. He set up his school in a large house, discovered by archaeologists south of the Acropolis, which remained its site to the end. He deserves particular credit for training Syrianus—probably the most prolific mind in the school—as a teacher.

Syrianus offered his students the following program of study. During the first two years, they would read all of Aristotle. They would then study Plato's dialogues in turn, in the order established by Iamblichus; finally, they would be shown the harmony between the Orphic and Chaldaean theologies. This was achieved through detailed commentary on *Timaeus*, for the philosophy of nature, and on *Parmenides*, for the theology.

Traces of this teaching have been preserved in Syrianus's commentary on four books of Aristotle's *Metaphysics* (III, IV, XIII, and XIV), and in his commentary on *Phaedrus*, which is known only via notes made by Hermias, one of his pupils. Syrianus had time to carry out only part of his program, for he limited himself almost entirely to establishing harmony between Plato, Pythagoras, and the Orphic texts. He did not take the *Chaldaean Oracles* into account to the same degree, and he died before he could undertake a scholarly presentation of the Oracles.

But Syrianus is famous above all for his exegesis of the hypotheses of *Parmenides*. In studying the structure of the hypotheses, he had noticed a perfect correspondence between the negations of the first hypothesis and the affirmations of the second. He concluded that the first hypothesis contained the negative theology of the first god, the One, while the second enumerated, in order, the characteristic properties of each degree in the hierarchy of the gods. He reached fourteen conclusions that matched the fourteen classes of the transcendent and cosmic gods. Proclus, who adopted this remarkable result, always attributed it to Syrianus. Proclus presented his master as the one "who, as our guide in all that is beautiful and good, had received in its purest state the most genuine and pure light of truth in the bosom of his soul. He made us partaker in Plato's philosophy as a whole, he made us his companions in the traditions he had received in secrecy from his predecessors, and he brought us into the group of those who sing the mystic truth of divine realities" (*On the Theology of Plato* I.1.7).

Of all the Neoplatonists, Proclus is certainly the best known, because a large part of his work has been preserved. Syrianus had foreseen this and named him as his successor; Proclus led the school in Athens for more than fifty years. As Marinus relates: "without stint did he give himself up to his love for work, daily teaching five classes, and sometimes more, and writing much, about 700 lines. Nor did this labor hinder him from visiting other philosophers, from giving purely oral evening lectures, from practicing his devotions during the night, for which he denied himself sleep; and further, from worshipping the sun at dawn, noon, and dusk" (*The Life of Proclus* 22). Under Proclus's leadership, the school experienced a period of intense activity.

Considerable portions of Proclus's commentaries on *Alcibiades*, *Timaeus*, *The Republic*, *Cratylus*, and *Parmenides* have been preserved. These texts show with what rigor Proclus practiced scientific commentary. He divided each text into pericopes (excerpts), subjected it to a general explanation by discussing the opinions of his predecessors, and produced a word-for-word exegesis. This procedure had two phases, *theoria* and *lexis*. The school produced commentaries composed in this way on all the canonical Platonic dialogues, and the same method was applied to the end. In fact, the method outlived the Athenian school, as it is found in Simplicius's commentaries on Aristotle, and in medieval Arabic and Latin commentaries.

But Proclus's importance lies essentially in the fact that he achieved the most important synthesis of late Neoplatonism, in a vast work titled *On the Theology of Plato*. This text contains, first of all, the formula for what we must call "theology as science," a Neoplatonic creation. Indeed, Proclus wrote: "Plato alone, as it appears to me, of all those who are known to us, has attempted to make correct distinctions in the regular progression of all the divine classes, and to describe their mutual differences and the properties common to all these classes and those which are peculiar to each one" (*On the Theology of Plato*, I.4.20). And it is in *Parmenides* that he finds this result. Proclus also wrote: "If it is necessary to have an overview, in a single Platonic dialogue, of the entire series of the gods from first to last, my formulation will perhaps appear paradoxical; it will be self-evident only to those of our own persuasion. We ought to dare, however, since we have begun to use such arguments, to affirm against our opponents: the *Parmenides* is what you need, and you have in your mind the mystic revelation contained in this dialogue" (*On the Theology of Plato* I.7.31). Here is a very schematic representation of this divine hierarchy:

The One, first god
The monads
The intelligible gods
The intelligible-intellective gods
The intellective gods
The hypercosmic gods
The hypercosmic-encosmic gods
The encosmic gods
The universal souls
The intelligible souls: demons, angels, heroes
The partial souls: those of men and beasts
Bodies
Matter

This gigantic construction thus sums up the tripartite scheme inaugurated by Plotinus: the One, Intellect-Intelligible, Soul. But it multiplies the intermediaries while introducing, on the one hand, the monads between the One and the simultaneous multiplicity of the Intellect-Intelligible, and on the other, the reign of the hypercosmic divinities, hypercosmic-encosmics, and encosmics between the Intellect-Intelligible and the Soul. Moreover, it makes very clear how even matter emanates from the One; this produces an optimistic vision of the sensible world and all it contains. Indeed, all reality is thus integrated into this metaphysical continuum that proceeds from the One to matter, and that for this reason construes even the sensible world and matter as participating to some degree in the Good.

Starting with the conclusions of *Parmenides*, then, Proclus confirmed them by turning to parallel texts drawn from the other Platonic dialogues or from other traditions: those of the Theologians, the Orphics, and the *Chaldaean*

Oracles: in six books he offered a reasoned explanation of the whole of Platonic theology. At the same time, he designed, in the geometrical manner, the architecture of the first principles in the short work titled *The Elements of Theology;* in *The Harmony of Orpheus, Pythagoras and Plato with the Chaldaean Oracles,* a treatise whose paternity he attributed in part to Syrianus, he argues that these theologies are in concord. Indeed, the final impetus that Proclus gave Syrianus's theology consisted in confronting it systematically with the *Chaldaean Oracles,* of which he also offered a complete interpretation in an extensive commentary (more than a thousand pages) that has unfortunately been lost.

The work of Proclus can be characterized as the culminating point of Neoplatonism. Damascius, who succeeded him, was the last head of the Athenian school. Damascius came from Alexandria, where another Platonic school defended virtually the same doctrine as that of the Athens school, but in a different style. Hermias, who had studied in Athens with Syrianus, and who included notes on the latter's course on *Phaedrus* in his own *Commentary on the Phaedrus,* had introduced the doctrines of the Athens school to Alexandria several decades earlier.

Ammonius, one of the sons of Hermias and his wife, Aidesia (who was also related to Syrianus), wrote a commentary on Aristotle's *De interpretatione.* His successor as head of the school was a certain Eutocius, none of whose writings has survived. But it was Philoponus, who seems not to have had any official function in the school, who published notes on Ammonius's course, and all the evidence suggests that there was a connection between the publication of his most important work, *Against Proclus on the Eternity of the World,* and the closing of the Athenian school in 529. The last pagan *diadoch* of the Alexandria school was Olympiodorus, three of whose commentaries on Plato—on *Alcibiades, Gorgias,* and *Phaedo*—and two on Aristotle—on *Categories* and *Meteorologica*—have survived. His Christian successors were Elias, David, and Stephen, all of whom commented on Aristotle.

As head of the Athenian school, Damascius preserved the essential elements of the Platonic doctrines as represented by Proclus, although Damascius's works are filled with endless discussions of Proclus's teaching, in most cases marking a return to Iamblichan theses. Taking his cue from Iamblichus, in his own key work, which is a commentary on Plato's *Parmenides,* Damascius demonstrates his originality, especially by establishing a principle prior to the One, the Ineffable, which is totally buried in an abyss of silence. Although derived from the Ineffable, the One remains extremely close to it. But in removing itself from all distinctions, the One projects itself on the near side of the Ineffable in three monadic principles: the One-All, the All-One, and the Unified. In addition, Damascius is the only Neoplatonist to prolong the procession across the negative hypotheses of the *Parmenides;* they constitute for him the structure of the sensible. In all other respects, Damascius remains faithful to the system set forth by Proclus.

The closing of the school in Athens by Justinian in 529 brought to a definitive end this specifically Greek attempt to assert and maintain authentic transcendence both in reality and in human beings. In all antiquity, Platonism alone proved to offer an escape outside the universe, thus offering one of the rare glimmers of hope traversing philosophy.

The idea of transcendence was of course maintained by Christianity, which had institutionally eliminated Neoplatonism, even while appropriating the principal elements of its doctrine. But this transcendence was put within the reach of all and no longer reserved for a small group of thinkers leading a specific way of life in the context of a school. Moreover, transcendence was now no longer based on the use of reason in search of certainty in the application of a method inspired by the one used in mathematics; instead, it was based on recourse to such emotions as love. And above all, it no longer had as its "end" (telos) the dissolution of the individual within an absolutely universal Unity; its end lay in individual immortality.

Luc Brisson
Translated by Rita Guerlac and Anne Slack

Bibliography

Texts and Translations

Alcinous. *The Handbook of Platonism*. Trans., introduction, and commentary John Dillon. Oxford: Clarendon Press, 1993.

Atticus. *Fragments*. Ed. and trans. Edouard Des Places. Paris: Les Belles Lettres, 1977.

Damascius. *Traités des premiers principes*. 3 vols. Ed. L. G. Westerink. Trans. Joseph Combès. Paris: Les Belles Lettres, 1986–1991.

Iamblichus. *Iamblichi Chalcidensis in Platonis dialogos commentariorum fragmenta*. Ed. and trans. John Dillon. Leiden: E. J. Brill, 1973.

———. *On the Pythagorean Way of Life*. Ed., trans., and notes John Dillon and Jackson Hershbell. Atlanta, Ga.: Scholars Press, 1991.

———. *Vie de Pythagore*. Ed. and trans. Luc Brisson and A. Ph. Segonds. Paris: Les Belles Lettres, 1996.

Julian. *Letters; Epigrams; Against the Galileans; Fragments*. Trans. Wilmer C. Wright. Loeb Classical Library.

De Laodamos de Thasos à Philippe d'Oponte. Ed. and trans. François Lasserre. La Scuola di Platone 2. Naples: Bibliopolis, 1987.

Marinos of Neapolis. *The Life of Proclus*. In *The Extant Works*. Ed. A. N. Oikonomides. Chicago: Ares, 1977.

Plato. *Complete Works*. Ed. John M. Cooper. Indianapolis: Hackett, 1997.

Der Platonismus in der Antike: Grundlage, System, Entwicklung. Vol. 1: *Die Ge-*

schichtlichen Wurzeln des Platonismus. Ed., trans., and commentary Heinrich Dörrie (posthumous work published under the direction of Annemarie Dörrie). Vol. 2: *Der hellenistische Rahmen des kaiserzeitlichen Platonismus.* Ed., trans., and commentary Heinrich Dörrie (posthumous work published under the direction of Matthias Baltes and Annemarie Dörrie). Vol. 3: *Der Platonismus im 2. und 3. Jahrhundert nach Christus.* Ed., trans., and commentary Matthias Baltes. Vols. 4 and 5: *Die philosophische Lehre des Platonismus.* 2 vols. Ed., trans., and commentary Matthias Baltes. Stuttgart and Bad Cannstatt: Frommann-Holzboog, 1987–1998.

Plotinus. Trans. A. H. Armstrong. 7 vols. Loeb Classical Library.

Porphyry. *Life of Plotinus.* In *Plotinus,* vol. 1. Trans. A. H. Armstrong. Loeb Classical Library.

———. *La vie de Plotin.* Vol. 1: *Travaux préliminaires et index complet.* Luc Brisson, Marie-Odile Goulet-Cazé, and Denis O'Brien et al. Vol. 2: *Etudes d'introduction, texte grec et traduction française, commentaire, notes complémentaires, bibliographie.* Luc Brisson et al. Paris: Vrin, 1982, 1992.

Proclus. *Commentaire sur le Timée.* Trans. and notes A. J. Festugière. 5 vols. Paris: Vrin/CNRS, 1966–1968.

———. *Commentary on Plato's Parmenides.* Trans. G. R. Morrow and J. Dillon; introduction and notes J. Dillon. Princeton: Princeton University Press, 1987.

———. *Elements of Theology.* Rev. text, trans., introduction, and commentary E. R. Dodds. Oxford: Clarendon Press, 1933; 2nd ed., 1963.

———. *In Timaeum.* Ed. E. Diehl. Leipzig: Teubner, 1903–1906; repr. Amsterdam: Hakkert, 1965.

———. *Proclus's Commentary on the Timaeus of Plato.* Trans. Thomas Taylor. London, 1820; repr. Frome, Somerset: Prometheus Trust, 1998.

———. *The Six Books of Proclus . . . on the Theology of Plato.* Trans. Thomas Taylor. London, 1816.

———. *Théologie platonicienne.* 6 vols. Ed. and trans. H. D. Saffrey and L. G. Westerink. Paris: Les Belles Lettres, 1968–1997.

Prolégomènes à la philosophie de Platon. Ed. L. D. Westerink. Trans. J. Trouillard with A. Ph. Segonds. Paris: Les Belles Lettres, 1990.

Speusippus. *Frammenti.* Ed. and trans. Margherita Isnardi Parente. La Scuola di Platone 1. Naples: Bibliopolis, 1980.

Speusippus of Athens: A Critical Study with a Collection of the Related Texts and Commentaries. Ed. Leonardo Tarán. Leiden: E. J. Brill, 1981.

Xenocrates and Hermodoros. *Frammenti.* Ed. and trans. Margherita Isnardi Parente. La Scuola di Platone 3. Naples: Bibliopolis, 1982.

Studies

Dillon, John. *The Middle Platonists.* Ithaca, N.Y.: Cornell University Press, 1977; rev. ed., 1996.

Görler, Waldemar. "Älterer Pyrrhonismus, Jungere Akademie, Antiochus aus Askalon." In *Die Philosophie der Antike,* vol. 4: *Die hellenistische Philosophie.* Basel: Schwabe, 1994. Pp. 717–1168.

Krämer, Hans-Joachim. "Altere Akademie." In *Die Philosophie der Antike,* vol. 3: *Die hellenistische Philosophie.* Basel: Schwabe, 1983. Pp. 1–174.

Lévy, Carlos. *Cicero Academicus: Recherches sur les Académiques et sur la philosophie cicéronienne*. Rome: Collection de l'Ecole française de Rome, no. 162. 1992.

O'Meara, Dominic. *Plotinus: An Introduction to the Enneads*. Oxford: Clarendon Press, 1993.

Rosán, L. J. *The Philosophy of Proclus: The Final Phase of Ancient Thought*. New York: Cosmos, 1949.

Saffrey, Henri Dominic. *Recherches sur le Néoplatonisme après Plotin*. Paris: Vrin, 1990.

Siorvanes, Lucas. *Proclus: Neo-Platonic Philosophy and Science*. New Haven: Yale University Press, 1996.

Smith, Andrew. *Porphyry's Place in the Neoplatonic Tradition: A Study in Post-Plotinian Neoplatonism*. The Hague: Nijhoff, 1974.

PYTHAGOREANISM

PYTHAGORAS IS THE MOST WIDELY KNOWN of the Presocratic philosophers, yet modern scholars often view Pythagoras and Pythagoreanism with considerable suspicion. Instead, the history of Presocratic philosophy is told in terms of the great figure of Parmenides, his rejection of earlier accounts of reality, and the response to his challenge by figures such as Anaxagoras and Democritus. This ambivalent attitude toward Pythagoras is mirrored in the ancient evidence as well. Plato and Aristotle, writing one hundred to one hundred fifty years after his death, hardly mention Pythagoras himself. Aristotle is famous for reviewing the work of his predecessors in each field of philosophy before presenting his own views. Yet, although he discusses at some length the Pythagoreans of the 5th century, who were active fifty years after Pythagoras's death, he never in his extant works mentions Pythagoras himself as an important figure in any branch of philosophy. Aristotle did write a treatise on the Pythagoreans, surviving only in fragmentary form, in which he deals directly with Pythagoras himself, but only as a wonder-working religious teacher. Plato likewise shows influence from 5th- and 4th-century Pythagoreanism but mentions Pythagoras himself only once, as a famous teacher who left a way of life for his followers. However, if we jump six hundred years to the Neoplatonist Iamblichus writing in the 2nd century C.E., we find Pythagoras presented as a semidivine figure who brought all true philosophy from the gods to men and from whom Plato and Aristotle stole all their best ideas. So by 300 C.E. Pythagoras is viewed in some circles as the philosopher par excellence, while in the 4th century B.C.E. Plato and Aristotle could discuss the important philosophical issues of the day with no reference to Pythagoras.

Recent scholarship (most notably the work of Walter Burkert) has made enormous progress in unraveling the complex tradition about Pythagoras and Pythagoreanism, but inevitably much remains uncertain and controversial. Before giving a detailed assessment of Pythagoras and specific Pythagoreans, it is necessary to give a brief overview of the whole Pythagorean tradition, to identify the unique problems in arriving at an accurate portrayal of Pythagoras and his philosophy. Pythagoras spent his early years on the island of Samos off the coast of Asia Minor; probably around the age of forty (ca. 530 B.C.E.), he emigrated to Croton in southern Italy, and he spent the rest of his life there, dying around 490 in the town of Metapontum. One of the crucial things to remember about him is that he wrote nothing. It is true that by the

2nd and 3rd centuries C.E. books were attributed to him, and the seventy-one lines of the *Golden Verses* were confidently accepted as his on into the Renaissance, but these forgeries were part of the phenomenal growth of the Pythagoras legend. The first book written in the Pythagorean tradition was by Philolaus of Croton (ca. 470–390 B.C.E.). Fragments of this book survive, and it seems to have been the primary basis for Aristotle's reports on the Pythagoreans. The other important name in early Pythagoreanism was Archytas (fl. 400–350 B.C.E.), who was a contemporary of Plato and who is connected to serious mathematical work, particularly in relation to music theory.

Aristotle is careful to distinguish the Pythagoreans from Pythagoras himself and refers to them as the "so-called Pythagoreans," probably to show that this is the name commonly given them but to express doubts about the exact connection between their thought and Pythagoras himself. However, among the immediate successors of Plato in his school the Academy, Speusippus and Xenocrates, an important new attitude toward Pythagoras arises. Many of Plato's most mature ideas, and particularly his positing of the One and the indefinite dyad as the basic principles of reality, come to be regarded as simply developments of ideas that Pythagoras had originated. It is not completely clear why Plato's followers should want to see his philosophy as simply a development of Pythagoras's thought, but it seems to be part of a mind set that sees philosophy as a divine revelation given to a chosen man (Pythagoras). Such a view, of course, gives the authority of divine revelation to the philosophy of Plato insofar as it unfolds ideas of Pythagoras.

This attitude toward Pythagoras comes to dominate the entire later tradition, and Aristotle's distinctions both between Pythagoras and later Pythagoreans and between the Pythagoreans and Plato are ignored. One important result of this dominant attitude toward Pythagoras is that by the 2nd century C.E. a very large collection of writings had been forged in the name of Pythagoras and early Pythagoreans. These pseudepigrapha are full of Platonic and Aristotelian ideas and terms and are clearly meant to provide the "early" texts from which Aristotle and Plato supposedly derived their whole philosophy. A few short treatises survive intact; the most famous is the purported original of Plato's dialogue *Timaeus,* supposedly written by Timaeus of Locrus. It is largely a précis of Plato's *Timaeus,* and like most of the pseudepigrapha it adheres very closely to the doctrine of its model while possessing little of its literary merits. Plato's own dialogue *Timaeus,* with its powerful description of the structuring of the cosmos by a divine craftsman, was more frequently quoted but regarded as simply a report of Pythagorean doctrine. Many more fragments from spurious Pythagorean works survive than fragments that are likely to be from genuine works by early Pythagoreans.

It is not until the 3rd century C.E. that we have the appearance of the first detailed accounts of the life of Pythagoras and the Pythagorean way of life that have survived intact. These lives by Diogenes Laertius (fl. 200–250), Porphyry (232–ca. 305), and Iamblichus (ca. 250–325) are the sources that were used in the Renaissance and by many later scholars to provide a picture of Pythagoras and his accomplishments. They drew heavily on sources from the 4th century B.C.E. that have not survived. In particular they drew on Aristotle's two-volume work on Pythagoreanism and on works on Pythagoras by Aristotle's pupils Aristoxenus and Dicaearchus, as well as works by the Platonist Heraclides and the historian of southern Italy, Timaeus. Since these lives are rather uncritical compilations of earlier sources, they must be used with utmost caution. However, it is their portrait of Pythagoras as a philosopher of almost divine status that dominates the late antique world and carries over even into many modern interpretations.

The present overview of the Pythagorean tradition is necessarily drastically simplified and selective. However, the crucial lesson to be learned is that from the time of Plato's successors in the Academy onward (ca. 350 B.C.E.), the Pythagorean tradition is dominated by a school of thought that assigns back to the divine Pythagoras all that is true in later philosophy. If we want to get behind that view to gain an appreciation of the actual significance of Pythagoras's thought in the late 6th century B.C.E., we must begin by looking only at the early evidence for Pythagoras. Initially, then, we must look only at the evidence of authors up to and including Plato and Aristotle, but not their pupils.

By modern standards there is not much evidence from this early period, a collection of twenty or so brief references in works of early philosophers, poets, and historians, apart from the fragments of Aristotle's book on the Pythagoreans, but this is in fact much more evidence than we have for many other early thinkers, and to some extent it is a reflection of Pythagoras's fame. What emerges most clearly from this evidence is that Pythagoras was famous for his knowledge of the soul and its fate after death, and more specifically for his belief in metempsychosis, the doctrine that our soul is reborn in another human or animal form after our death. Even these early reports about Pythagoras often have a polemical tone, either attacking some aspect of his doctrine or portraying him as possessing superhuman wisdom. Thus his contemporary Xenophanes (ca. 570–480) is clearly having fun at Pythagoras's expense when he reports the story that Pythagoras pitied a puppy that was being beaten by a man and said to the man, "Stop, don't keep beating it, for it is the soul of a friend of mine, I recognize his voice" (frg. 7). On the other hand, Ion of Chios (b. ca. 490 B.C.E.) is clearly serious in his praise of Pythagoras for his knowledge of the fate of the soul after death (frg. 4).

Heraclitus attacks Pythagoras, among others, for being a polymath without having attained any real understanding (frg. 40), calls him "the chief of swindlers" (frg. 81), and says that he practiced inquiry beyond all other men, making a wisdom of his own by picking things out of the writings of others, a wisdom that was in fact "a polymathy and evil trickery" (frg. 129). Some

scholars have thought that since Heraclitus links Pythagoras with Xenophanes and Hecataeus as polymaths (frg. 40), Heraclitus must have regarded
Pythagoras as being engaged in the same sort of rational inquiry about the
world that they pursued and that had arisen around the city of Miletus in
Asia Minor, close to Pythagoras's home of Samos, in the 6th century. However, the fragment of Heraclitus in fact joins him more closely to Hesiod the
poet, who was famous for his mythical account of the origin of the gods in
Theogony. Nevertheless, the overall tone of Heraclitus's reports is clear. He
regards Pythagoras as a charlatan of some sort. Empedocles (ca. 493–433),
in a fragment that most agree refers to Pythagoras (frg. 129), adopts the exact opposite tone toward Pythagoras and begins by praising him in general
terms as a man who knew "extraordinary things" and possessed "the greatest
wealth of wisdom." He then goes on to praise him specifically for "wise
deeds" and says that "whenever he reached out with all his intellect he easily
beheld all the things that are in ten and even twenty generations of men." It
is not necessary, but it is tempting, to see this last phrase as a reference to the
idea of rebirth, and the mention of "wise deeds" calls to mind the image of a
wonder-worker of some sort who here is venerated but who might well also
elicit Heraclitus's description of him as a charlatan.

Other early evidence about Pythagoras shows a close connection to religious ritual. His connection with Orphism in Ion of Chios and Herodotus un-
derlines his close connection to ritual (initiations) and his expertise on the
soul and the afterlife. Plato's contemporary Isocrates says (*Busiris* 28) that
Pythagoras journeyed to Egypt and makes the vague point that "he first
brought other philosophy to the Greeks" before going on to say that he was
particularly zealous about the matters of sacrifice and rites of the temple.

Other early evidence suggests that in connection with his interest in the
soul and its afterlife and religious ritual Pythagoras showed a broader interest
in how we should live our lives. Thus the atomist Democritus (b. 460) is reported as having been very influenced by Pythagorean ideas and as perhaps
having studied with Philolaus. However, it seems clear that this influence was
on his ethical views, since we are told that he wrote a book on Pythagoras and
that this book was classified with Democritus's ethical works. Isocrates in the
passage mentioned above said that Pythagoras's reputation was so great that
young men wanted to be his pupils and that their parents were happier to
have them associate with him than to attend to family affairs. Isocrates comments that even in his day, Pythagoreans were more marveled at for their silence than great orators for their speech. This statement suggests that the
later tradition of a rule of silence among Pythagoras's pupils has some foundation. The 4th-century rhetorician Alcidimas gives what is probably an
apocryphal report, but which nonetheless represents early 4th-century attitudes, that Empedocles studied with both Pythagoras and Anaxagoras, and
that while he got knowledge of nature from Anaxagoras, he got the dignity of

his bearing from Pythagoras. Once again it is striking how consistently Pythagoras is associated with the manner in which we live our lives rather than with theoretical knowledge.

The most famous evidence for Pythagoras as an influential teacher and founder of a way of life is Plato's only reference to him, which is found in *The Republic*. Pythagoras is not included in the list of those who have contributed to the good government of a city, as the lawgivers Lycurgus and Solon did, nor among the good generals, nor among the men wise in practical affairs and the producers of ingenious inventions, such as Thales. Instead Plato places Pythagoras's activity in the private sphere and presents him as the model of the sort of figure who was particularly loved as a teacher and whose followers even now are famous for their Pythagorean way of life (600a9–b5). Thus, the early evidence consistently portrays Pythagoras as a figure with an extremely loyal following who can tell you how to live your present life to best satisfy the gods and to ensure the best fate for your soul in the next life. At the same time, outsiders such as Heraclitus and Xenophanes could well view his pretensions to knowledge about ritual and the fate of the soul, as well as the glorification of him by his followers, as foolishness or even quackery.

Particularly problematic for nonbelievers would have been the "wise deeds" to which Empedocles refers and which may well be the miraculous actions that Aristotle assigns to Pythagoras. Aristotle reports that Pythagoras was supposed to have appeared in both Croton and Metapontum at the same hour on the same day; that when he crossed a river it gave him the greeting, "Hail, Pythagoras"; that he bit and killed a poisonous snake; and that he had a golden thigh. This last report probably picks him out as the favorite of the god and is tied to initiation rites in which a part of the body is dedicated to the divinity. Indeed, Aristotle reports that the people of Croton called him the Hyperborean Apollo. The other reports stress his special control over the animal and natural world. Often these miraculous stories are rejected as useless in understanding the historical figure of Pythagoras, but this attitude is mistaken because the stories show how he was conceived by his early followers and are thus crucial in understanding the type of figure he was.

The biggest lacuna in the picture of Pythagoras presented in the early evidence is the precise nature of the way of life he handed on to his followers. Once again some details can be filled in from Aristotle and other later 4th-century witnesses, but these sources contradict each other in important ways; accordingly, the following description of the Pythagorean life is very problematic. Particularly important are the many Pythagorean maxims preserved by Aristotle. Some of these are likely to go back to Pythagoras himself because they fit well with the picture of Pythagoras derived from the earliest evidence. These maxims are called *acusmata* (things heard) or *symbola* (passwords, or things to be interpreted) in the later tradition. Iamblicus gives a very large collection of them in his work *On the Pythagorean Life* (82–86), which is surely based primarily on Aristotle.

In Iamblichus's collection the maxims are broken up into three classes, corresponding to the three questions: (1) What is it? (2) What is best? (3) What must be done? Of the first sort are the maxims reported by Aristotle: "The ring of bronze when it is struck is the voice of a daimon trapped in it" or "The planets are the hounds of Persephone." Of the second sort Iamblichus lists, "What is wisest? Number"; "What is the most just? To sacrifice"; "What is the loveliest? Harmony." But the biggest number of maxims are of the third sort, which often have clear ties to rules of religious ritual. Aristotle is given as the authority for maxims against eating certain fish (red mullet and black tail) and certain parts of animals (heart and womb). Iamblichus gives a long list, including the injunctions that one must beget children, one must put the right shoe on first, one must not sacrifice a white cock, one must not use public baths. As early as 400 B.C.E. a tradition sprung up according to which these maxims were not to be taken literally but interpreted to find a deeper meaning. Thus the prohibition not to eat the heart is interpreted as meaning that one should not grieve. However, this is likely to be the attempt of later generations to explain away seemingly bizarre rituals rather than the original import of the maxims. Their connection with ritual and magical practices elsewhere in Greece shows that they were probably meant to be taken quite literally and also that many of them were hardly original to Pythagoras but were adopted by him.

One of the most famous of the maxims is the one that prohibits the eating of beans. All the early evidence supports the authenticity of this maxim except Aristotle's student Aristoxenus, who reports in his book on Pythagoras that "Pythagoras especially valued the bean among vegetables saying that it was laxative and softening. Wherefore he especially made use of it." This is probably an attempt on Aristoxenus's part to eliminate the stranger aspects from early Pythagorean doctrine, and it is likely that we should follow Aristotle's report that the eating of beans was prohibited. Aristotle gives several obscure explanations for the prohibition: that beans were like the genitals, or the gates of Hades, or the universe, or connected to oligarchy. It is also plausible that the problems beans cause for digestion, or indeed the fact that many people are allergic to a certain amino acid that is in this type of bean, was behind the prohibition.

Slightly more complicated is the issue of vegetarianism. There would seem to be a natural connection between the belief in metempsychosis and vegetarianism; the philosopher Empedocles writing in the generation after Pythagoras made the connection clear in graphically condemning the eating of all animal flesh as cannibalism. Moreover, Eudoxus of Cnidus, a famous mathematician and member of the Academy in Plato's day, reports that Pythagoras not only did not eat any meat but also even avoided the company of butchers and hunters. Aristoxenus, however, takes the iconoclastic view again and asserts that although Pythagoras avoided plow oxen and rams, he was particularly fond of young kids, suckling pigs, and cockerels. Moreover, in this case there is considerable support for Aristoxenus's view that Pythagoras was not a strict vegetarian. Some *acusmata* reported by Aristotle only ban eating specific parts of animals. Moreover, there is the maxim mentioned above that says that the most just thing is to sacrifice, and Iamblichus reports among the *acusmata* one to the effect that souls do not enter into sacrificial animals. Some scholars have argued that to reject animal sacrifice totally would be such a complete overturning of traditional ways as to be unthinkable, while others have tried to argue that sacrifice was acceptable but that the Pythagoreans limited themselves to a simple sacramental tasting of the victim. The fact that Pythagoreans were recognized as so distinctive in their way of life suggests that a prohibition on animal sacrifice is not so unthinkable and that, with Empedocles as the model, we should believe that Pythagoras was a strict vegetarian. This issue is an excellent example of the complexity of determining the actual nature of the Pythagorean way of life and shows the already contradictory nature of the evidence even in the 4th century B.C.E.

One way of trying to reconcile the contradictions in the testimony about vegetarianism both in the ancient world and among modern scholars has been to suppose that there were different grades among the followers of Pythagoras, as the later tradition suggests, and to argue that vegetarianism was practiced to different degrees by members of different grades. This explanation raises directly the broader question of whether Pythagorean societies in a strict sense ever existed at all. Some have suggested that the notion of a community separated from regular society and governed by a strict rule along the lines of a monastery would be an anachronism in the 6th century B.C.E., and that such an idea was introduced into the tradition at a later point and perhaps even by Iamblichus. However, some of our early evidence, the reports of Plato and Isocrates, make it very clear that Pythagoras attracted a loyal following and showed them a way of life that made them easily distinguishable from ordinary citizens even as late as the 4th century. How strict the way of life was and how the community was related to the rest of society may remain open questions, but this evidence surely justifies our talking about Pythagorean communities as groups of people who lived a way of life that clearly set them apart from other people.

A number of reports from the 4th century B.C.E. indicate that Pythagoras and his followers had significant impact on the politics of the Greek city-states in southern Italy. It is difficult to derive any coherent Pythagorean political views out of these reports, which contradict one another on a number of points. Since Plato seems to clearly distinguish Pythagoras from lawgivers and other public figures, it seems most likely that there were not many specific Pythagorean political policies. Rather it was probably the case that many of the talented and prominent members of the communities became followers of the Pythagorean way of life while at the same time participating in the government of the city-state. Of course the Pythagorean societies may have looked like political organs to their opponents, and we know that there were two major attacks on them. One seems to have occurred in the lifetime of Pythagoras himself and to have led to the deaths of many of his followers in a fire set in the house where they were meeting in Croton, and to the flight of Pythagoras himself to Metapontum. Another attack on the societies seems to have occurred in the mid-5th century and to have led once again to many deaths and to the apparent dispersal of many of the communities.

A common feature of an exclusive society is some sort of secrecy associated with initiation and grades of membership. Isocrates' report lets us know that the Pythagoreans were famous for their silence, but it is unclear whether this refers simply to their self-restraint in not speaking too much, or to a sort of novitiate in which new members were not allowed to speak for the first five years, as mentioned already by the historian Timaeus in the 4th century. It is also possible that it refers to some sort of specifically secret doctrine. Both Aristotle and Aristoxenus give evidence that at least some doctrines were not for all ears. Aristotle reports that among their very secret doctrines was the division of rational animals into three groups, men, gods, and beings like Pythagoras. Aristoxenus says that the Pythagoreans used to say that not all of Pythagoras's doctrines were for all men to hear, which suggests both secret doctrine and perhaps grades of initiates. All the same, neither Aristotle nor Plato hints that the Pythagorean philosophy of the 5th and 4th centuries was in any way secret. The most likely scenario is that the Pythagoreans, like most exclusive societies, did have secrets such as Aristotle and Aristoxenus suggest. However, these were limited to a certain group of maxims, without putting any restriction on the publication of philosophical ideas such as we find in the book of Philolaus, or on mathematical proofs such as those that appear in Archytas. It is true that Hippasus, a Pythagorean active in the generation after Pythagoras, is supposed to have been killed for the impious act of publishing a construction of a dodecahedron. However, in terms of the history of mathematics it is unlikely that Hippasus gave a strict construction of the dodecahedron at this date; the story may instead relate to the dodecahedron as a cult object.

Hippasus is also connected to the problem of the existence of different sects of Pythagoreans. A report in Iamblichus that seems to go back to Aristotle suggests that in the 5th century there were two groups referred to as the *acusmatici* and the *mathematici*. The *acusmatici* were clearly connected with the *acusmata* and were said to be recognized as genuine Pythagoreans by the *mathematici*. However, the *acusmatici* argued that the *mathematici* were not true Pythagoreans but in fact stemmed from Hippasus rather than Pythagoras. The *mathematici* in turn argued that Pythagoras himself had presented his views to some people in simple commandments, while to others who had time for more study (young men), he had given the explanations. Hippasus, as they presented him, was publishing views that were originally Pythagoras's own, only for his own aggrandizement. Thus it is clear that by Aristotle's time, and probably earlier, there was already debate about what ideas in fact went back to Pythagoras himself, with the *mathematici* seeming to adopt the view found among the successors of Plato, that all ideas really go back to the master.

At this point we must confront the most controversial of all issues regarding Pythagoras: Was he a natural philosopher and mathematician as well as the founder of a way of life and expert on the gods, ritual, and the afterlife? After all, he is most famous among the educated public for his connection to the so-called Pythagorean theorem (see below). However, it should be clear from the evidence given above that, up to and including Plato and Aristotle, there is no direct evidence that shows him to be either a mathematician or a natural philosopher. The example of Empedocles shows that the roles of religious wonder-worker and natural philosopher can well be combined in 5th-century Greece, but were they so combined in the figure of Pythagoras? Pythagoras grew up on Samos, which was the site of great technological achievements involving the application of mathematics (most notably the tunnel of Eupalinus, which went under a mountain and was dug from both sides, missing only slightly in the middle). Samos was an easy journey from the city of Miletus, on the coast of Asia Minor, which was home to a series of early natural philosophers, such as Anaximander and Anaximenes. Accordingly some scholars argue that it is impossible to imagine that Pythagoras was not aware of such work or that he could have become famous in such a milieu if he were simply a wonder-worker. However, this argument fails spectacularly since, however probable it may be that Pythagoras knew of the natural philosophy that grew up at Miletus, this argument says nothing about whether or not he was interested in that sort of inquiry himself. Surely an expert on the fate of the soul after death might achieve as much or more fame as someone who speculates about whether water or air is the original state of the cosmos.

The strongest reason for believing that Pythagoras had special interest in mathematics and the structure of the natural world is that Aristotle's evidence and Philolaus's book make clear that in the 5th century people called Pythagoreans gave an account of the natural world that showed it to be structured according to pleasing mathematical relationships. Furthermore, Archtyas, the contemporary of Plato, who is also identified as a Pythagorean, was a distinguished mathematician. We must remember that Philolaus and Archytas may have been Pythagoreans only insofar as they followed a Pythagorean way of life, and that their views on the natural world and mathematics may have been primarily influenced by non-Pythagorean writers such as Anaxagoras, or Hippocrates of Chios. However, it is legitimate to ask if the seeds of this interest in mathematics and the mathematical structure of the world were planted by Pythagoras himself.

The connection between Pythagoras and proposition 1.47 of Euclid's *Elements* (ca. 300 B.C.E.), popularly known as the Pythagorean theorem, is based on the commentary on Euclid written by Proclus in the 5th century C.E. It is reported that Pythagoras, on making a geometric discovery of some sort, sacrificed an ox. This tradition seems to rest on an epigram by an obscure Apollodorus: "When Pythagoras found the famous figure, for which he carried out the noble ox-sacrifice." This Apollodorus might date back to the 4th century, which would give the story considerably more authority, but this dating is far from certain. The story was actually as famous in the ancient tradition for the apparent contradiction with vegetarianism represented by the ox sacrifice as it was for its connection to a geometrical theorem. However, even if we accept the story as genuine 4th-century tradition, there are serious problems. First, it is clear from the history of Greek mathematics that it is unlikely that Pythagoras could have proven the theorem. A strict proof would have required some sort of structure of theorems and definitions, and the first hint of such a structure that we have is connected to Hippocrates of Chios in the later 5th century. However, it is known that the Pythagorean theorem had been part of Babylonian arithmetical technique for centuries, although the Babylonians had given no general proof of it. One might say that Pythagoras was the first Greek to discover the truth of the theorem or the first Greek to bring the knowledge from Babylon to the Greeks, but the truth of the theorem is likely to have come to Greece through several sources. Indeed the reports about Pythagoras do not stress that he was the one who discovered the theorem, and it is tempting to take the reports to emphasize the value he put on knowledge of the theorem. He was so impressed when he found out that the sides of the right triangle were related according to this precise mathematical rule that he sacrificed an ox, something that an ordinary Greek might do to celebrate a more material success, such as a safe voyage home.

Another set of late stories associated Pythagoras with the discovery that the basic musical concords of the octave, fourth, and fifth could all be expressed in terms of whole-number ratios of string lengths (1 : 2, 3 : 4, and 2 : 3, respectively). Supposedly he heard the musical concords in the sounds made by a blacksmith's hammers and discovered that hammers whose weights were in the ratios given above produced the musical concords when struck one after the other. He is also said to have hung weights equal to the hammers by strings so that the strings also produced the concords. However, none of these observations or experiments correspond to physical reality. The earliest full versions of the stories come from Nicomachus in the 2nd century C.E., but in the 4th century B.C.E. Xenocrates had already reported that "Pythagoras discovered that the musical intervals did not arise without number" (frg. 9). At the same time, there is a report that ascribes an experiment to Hippasus that does in fact work and thus may well be true. It is important to note that another report associates Lasus of Hermione with such an experiment. Lasus is in fact a contemporary of Pythagoras, although he is not a Pythagorean. In conclusion, it seems best to say that Pythagoras himself did not discover the whole-number ratios that underlie the musical concords, but that the knowledge may well have been available in his day and that Hippasus may have demonstrated it with a valid experiment in the next generation. As in the case of the Pythagorean theorem, it may well be that what was important was the value Pythagoras attached to this information when he learned of it from others.

What then can we conclude about Pythagoras's connection to mathematics? The key may be found in the maxims attested for the early Pythagoreans. One says that the wisest thing is number, and yet another reports that the oracle of Delphi is "the tetractys which is the harmony in which the Sirens sing." In the later tradition the "tetractys," the tetrad consisting of the numbers one through four whose sum equals the "perfect" number ten, was central to Pythagoreanism but clearly had become contaminated with ideas derived from Platonism. The Pythagoreans were supposed to have sworn oaths by Pythagoras as "the one who handed on to our generation the tetractys, which has the source and root of everflowing nature." It is doubtful that the oath in this form can go back to the time of Pythagoras, but the tetractys itself as mentioned in the *acusmata* might. The connection of the tetractys to the Sirens, who were famed for their singing, suggests a connection to music, and it becomes just possible that the tetractys was in part venerated because its four numbers were all involved in the whole-number ratios that govern the musical concords. If we connect the Sirens in turn with the famous doctrine of the harmony of the spheres, which says that the heavenly bodies produce musical concords as they move (as Plato does in *The Republic*), then Pythagoras starts to emerge as someone impressed with the power of number— particularly as embodied in the first four numbers, which seem to be the basis of the musical concords, which in turn seem to structure the cosmos. The doctrine of the harmony of the spheres is discussed by Aristotle in *De caelo* but once again is ascribed only to Pythagoreans and not to Pythagoras himself; it remains quite possible that it too belongs to 5th-century Pythagoreanism and not to Pythagoras. It was never worked out in any mathematical detail by the early Pythagoreans but was, rather, a very general conception.

It should be clear that the evidence does not support the conclusion that Pythagoras was any sort of serious mathematician or that he was a natural philosopher or scientist. Instead he is to be seen as a charismatic teacher who attracted a large group of followers for whom he prescribed a way of life that included instruction about the future life of the soul, the gods, ritual, and a bewildering variety of rules that applied to many aspects of daily life, including what foods to eat and how to dress. Some of this instruction encouraged certain moral virtues (such as silence) and probably included the memory training and emphasis on friendship attested in the later tradition. It may be that it also instilled a certain attitude toward the cosmos and promoted reverence for the concept of number and particularly for certain significant numbers. The followers of Pythagoras stood out in the communities of which they were a part, attracting both praise and ridicule as well as having some influence on the politics of southern Italy.

The real significance of Pythagoras, as Walter Burkert points out, is that he was the first person to establish a set of rules that apply not just to the special moments of life that are marked by religious ritual but that give direction as to how each day of our life ought to be lived, as well as how our life in this world relates to the life in the next. It is in this sense that he is a great moral teacher and a true precursor of Socrates and Christ, however bizarre to modern sensibility some of the teachings of the *acusmata* may seem to be. It is with the so-called Pythagoreans of the 5th century B.C.E., and in particular with Philolaus of Croton, that we see the important contributions of Pythagoreanism to natural philosophy.

We know virtually nothing about Philolaus's life (ca. 470–390) except that he came from Croton (or perhaps Tarentum) in southern Italy and visited Thebes in mainland Greece sometime before 399. Nonetheless he is the central figure in early Pythagoreanism, since his book was the first to be written by a Pythagorean. The book was still available in the late 4th century B.C.E. to Aristotle's pupil Meno, who reports Philolaus's medical views in his history of medicine. The whole book has not been handed down to us, although more than twenty fragments and a number of secondhand reports (testimonia) have survived. A consensus has emerged that, although more than half of the fragments that survive in his name are from spurious works, a central core of fragments from his genuine book survive (1–7, 13, 17). These fragments show that, although Philolaus's book was the primary source for Aristotle's account of Pythagoreanism, Aristotle recast Pythagoreanism in important ways to fit his own purposes, and that Aristotle's evidence thus must be used with caution. In addition it becomes clear that Philolaus's book was a significant influence on Plato's *Philebus*.

The book appears to have followed a typical Presocratic pattern in that it presents an account of the natural world, beginning with a cosmogony, and goes on to present astronomical, psychological, and medical theories. It is striking that in the fragments there is no discussion of morality or how to live one's life, although Philolaus is mentioned in Plato's *Phaedo* as arguing that suicide is not permissible. Philolaus explains the cosmos in terms of two basic types of things, limiters and unlimiteds. Unlimiteds include the elements, such as water and air, that had been used by earlier Presocratics to explain the natural world, but Philolaus does not focus on any one specific element or group of elements of this sort. Instead he argues simply that a supply of such unlimiteds (continua that are in themselves without any limit, including water, air, earth, and also things like void and time) must be presupposed in order to explain the world that we see. But Philolaus's most noteworthy innovation is his claim that earlier thinkers had been mistaken to think that the world could be adequately explained in terms of such unlimiteds alone. He argues that limiters, things that set limits in a continuum—e.g., shapes and other structural principles—must also be regarded as basic principles. Objects that we observe in the world, such as a tree, are manifestly combinations of continua that are unlimited in their own nature (the wood) and structural principles (the shape and structure of the tree). Thus individual objects in the world and the cosmos as a whole are combinations of limiters and unlimiteds.

However, limiters and unlimiteds alone are still not sufficient to explain the world. Limiters and unlimiteds are not combined in a chance fashion but are instead held together by a *harmonia,* a fitting together in accordance with pleasing mathematical relationships. The first sentence of Philolaus's book sets out his basic view of the world: "Nature in the cosmos was fitted together both out of limiters and unlimiteds, both the cosmos as a whole and everything in it" (frg. 1). Philolaus gives as the model of this fitting together a musical scale. The unlimited continuum of sound is limited by certain notes picked out in that continuum. However, these notes are placed not at random intervals but in accord with the whole-number mathematical ratios that govern the basic intervals of the diatonic scale. Thus, to really understand the world or anything in it, we must not only observe the limiters and unlimiteds that make it up but also the number in accordance with which those limiters are fitted together. Writes Philolaus, "And indeed all things that are known have number. For it is not possible that anything whatsoever be understood or known without this" (frg. 4). Of course he is putting forward a grand scheme here and was unable to specify many of the numbers that governed the structure of individual things. It is to his credit that there is little evidence that he tried to postulate an arbitrary set of numbers that governed all things.

Aristotle recasts this emphasis on number as giving us knowledge of things into the claim that the Pythagoreans thought that things were made up of numbers in some way, but Philolaus says nothing of the sort. In trying to distinguish the Pythagoreans from Plato, who thought that numbers had existence separate from things, Aristotle supposed that the Pythagoreans must have identified numbers with things. However, this anachronistically supposes that the Pythagoreans had asked the questions, what sort of existence do numbers have, and how are they related to things? These questions probably first directly arose in the 4th century in Plato's Academy. Philolaus was content to argue that numbers give us knowledge of things in the world, without focusing on the ontological status of numbers. What is crucial is the insight that, in principle, both the cosmos as a whole and also everything in it are knowable with the determinacy of perspicuous numerical relationships.

The cosmos began with a fire (an unlimited) in the center of a sphere (a limiter). This central fire then breathed in another group of unlimiteds (time, void, breath), which were fitted together with limiters to produce Philolaus's famous astronomical system. With this theory, for the first time the Earth is made a planet, and Copernicus refers to Philolaus as one of his precursors. However, rather than orbiting around the Sun, the Earth orbits around the central fire along with the Sun, the Moon, the five planets, the fixed stars, and a counter-Earth that was evidently introduced to bring the number of orbiting bodies up to the perfect number ten. The system thus combines a reverence for principles of order that fly in the face of observation with a desire to accommodate the basic observable facts. Night and day are explained by the Earth's moving around the central fire in one twenty-four-hour period, while the Sun takes a year, thus turning our side of the Earth away from the Sun for a portion of the twenty-four-hour period. The Earth rotates so that our side of the Earth is always turned away from the central fire and counter-Earth, explaining the fact that we never see them. This is also the first astronomical system that identifies a set of five planets and arranges them in proper order according to observations of their periods.

After presenting his view of the generation of the cosmos as a whole, Philolaus turned to a discussion of life. Just as he was interested particularly in the structure of the cosmos, so he emphasizes the structure of the animate world, in ways that prepared for the later Platonic and Aristotelian systems. He regarded all life as ordered in the hierarchy of plant, animal, and human beings, where each higher level shares the abilities of the lower but has a unique ability of its own. All life shares the ability to reproduce itself; plants have the ability to send out roots (which is paralleled by the human umbilical cord), animals can move and have sensation, but humans alone have reason. Philolaus saw a clear analogy between the birth of the cosmos and the birth of individual human beings. Humans were seen as initially consisting of just the hot, which then at birth naturally breathes in the cold, just as the central fire breathed in to generate the cosmos. The health of the human body seems to have depended on the proper limitation of the hot by cooling breath. Philolaus is said to have explained disease in terms of the three humors, bile, blood, and phlegm, which are also prominent in the contemporary theories of medicine found in the Hippocratic writings.

Philolaus's view of the cosmos is recognizably Presocratic, just as his medical views employ the same concepts as the early Hippocratic writings. However, the thematic emphasis on the structural features of the cosmos (limiters) and on the role of number in making the cosmos intelligible are important original steps that had influence on both the great philosophers of the next century, Plato and Aristotle. Indeed, Philolaus is the first philosopher to present a coherent view of the natural world that calls for its explanation in terms of mathematical relationships. However, the growth of the Pythagoras legend that began in Plato's Academy made it imperative that the Pythagorean cosmos appear to be not merely an important precursor of Plato and Aristotle but the true revelation of reality. Hence, Philolaus's system, after being relatively faithfully represented by Aristotle, was pushed aside and neglected, and Plato's mature presentation of the cosmos in *Timaeus* came to be regarded as in reality the work of Pythagoras; accordingly, the term *Pythagorean* in the Renaissance usually in fact refers to the Platonism of *Timaeus*.

Archytas (fl. 400–350), who belonged to the generation after Philolaus and who was a contemporary of Plato, is the Pythagorean who comes closest to matching the modern stereotype of a Pythagorean as the master mathematician. Whereas there is no evidence that Philolaus made any contribution to the advancement of Greek mathematics, Archytas is primarily known for important mathematical proofs and as the founder of the discipline of mechanics. There are in fact only three fragments (1–3) that can with some confidence be regarded as coming from genuine works, amid a much larger group of fragments that derive from spurious works. We know of his mathematical achievements through secondhand reports.

Archytas came from Tarentum in southern Italy, and the details of his life are largely unknown to us. He has tended to be better known than Philolaus because he is closely associated with Plato in several Platonic letters, whose authenticity, however, is controversial. He sent a ship to rescue Plato from the clutches of the tyrant Dionysius II of Syracuse in 361. However, even if we accept the Platonic letters as providing accurate information, the exact relationship between Plato and Archytas and the nature of their influence on one another is unclear. He is never mentioned in the Platonic dialogues.

As in the case of Philolaus, and in contrast to the tradition about Pythagoras himself, we have little information about Archytas's views on moral issues or the proper way to live one's life. Two anecdotes suggest that he emphasized the importance of acting solely on rational judgments and never in anger or under the influence of the enticements of pleasure. When Archytas came back from war to find his lands neglected, he reportedly told his slaves that they were lucky that he was angry, because otherwise they would have been punished. In another case, when someone had argued that pleasure was the ultimate good, Archytas responded that reason was the greatest gift of the gods to human beings, but that in the throes of pleasure we are unable to use it. In fragment 3 he praises "correct calculation" as the source of political harmony.

It is not unlikely that Archytas did have something to say about the basic principles of the cosmos, but we have very little evidence about his views on this topic. There is nothing in the tradition about Archytas that mentions limiters and unlimiteds. However, Aristotle does say that Archytas gave definitions that appealed to both form and matter. Thus, calm weather is defined as "lack of movement in a mass of air," where the air is the matter and the lack of movement is the form. Such a definition could well have arisen out of the Philolaic distinction between unlimiteds and limiters. Again it is unclear whether Archytas accepted Philolaus's view of the structure of the cosmos or not. He is reported as arguing that what is outside the cosmos is unlimited in extent, by asking, "If I were at the extremity, for example at the heaven of the fixed stars, could I stretch out my hand or my staff into what is outside or not?" The study of such sciences as astronomy, geometry, arithmetic, and music is for him crucial to the understanding of reality. His reference to these sciences as "sisters" may have influenced Plato (*Republic* 530d). But the fragment goes on to present a theory of acoustics rather than discussing the cosmos as a whole.

It is for his work in the specific sciences that Archytas is particularly famous. Ptolemy (2nd century C.E.) in his *Harmonics* reports that Archytas was the most dedicated of all the Pythagoreans to the study of music and then presents Archytas's mathematical accounts of the diatonic, enharmonic, and chromatic scales. Archytas's proof that numbers in a superparticular ratio $(n + 1/1)$ have no mean proportional is important for ancient musical theory in that it shows that neither the whole tone $(9 : 8)$ nor the central musical intervals of the octave $(2 : 1)$, fifth $(3 : 2)$, and fourth $(4 : 3)$ can be divided in half. Fragment 2 shows Archytas working with the arithmetic, geometric, and harmonic means that are also important in music theory.

He was regarded as the founder of mechanics and was said to have given method to the discipline by applying mathematical principles to it. This interest is manifested in the charming reports of his making toys for children, including a flying wooden dove. It is also reported that he was the first to use mechanical motion in geometrical constructions. Thus, in his proposed solution to the famous problem of doubling the cube, which was supposedly first posed by inhabitants of the island of Delos, who were commanded by the god to double the size of an altar, he used a striking construction in three dimensions that determined a point as the intersection of three surfaces of revolution.

After Archytas there are no prominent Pythagoreans. Aristotle's pupil Aristoxenus says that the Pythagoreans of the first half of the 4th century were the last Pythagoreans. However, this is not in fact the end of Pythagoreanism in the ancient world, although it is probably the end of the Pythagorean societies. As has been mentioned above, there was a strong revival of what were regarded as Pythagorean ideas in the 2nd and 3rd centuries C.E., although there were some important figures even earlier. The revival was connected with Neoplatonism to such an extent that it is sometimes hard to know whether to call an individual thinker a Neopythagorean or a Neoplatonist.

Some Neopythagoreans focused primarily on Pythagoras's special connection to the gods, his wonder-working, and his way of life. Most prominent is Apollonius of Tyana (1st century C.E.), whose writings are largely lost but whose way of life is described in Philostratus's *Life of Apollonius*. Apollonius was a wandering ascetic wonder-worker who claimed a divine wisdom derived from Pythagoras. Some of his miraculous achievements were clearly modeled on stories about Pythagoras, such as his ability to be in two places at one time and the ability to speak the language of animals. Most Neopythagoreanism, however, focused on Pythagoras as the archetypal philosopher to whom the divine revelation of the true philosophical doctrine had been given. Two figures will serve as central examples of this tradition, Nicomachus and Iamblichus.

Nicomachus (ca. 50–150 C.E.), who wrote a very influential *Introduction to Arithmetic*, is a good example of the tendency to treat Platonism as if it were in fact Pythagoreanism. Nicomachus begins his book with Pythagoras and presents him as the first person to correctly define philosophy as knowledge of the immaterial and unchangeable reality that lies behind the flux of bodily existence. He is thus ascribing to Pythagoras Plato's central distinction between the world of unchanging forms and the constantly changing phenomena. Nicomachus then illustrates Pythagoras's supposed philosophy by quoting from Plato's *Timaeus*, thus exemplifying a pattern that will be repeated many times in the later tradition. While some authors do quote the Pythagorean pseudepigrapha to illustrate Pythagorean doctrine, it is more common to treat Plato's *Timaeus* as the central text for Pythagorean doctrine. Nicomachus also portrays Pythagoras as the master mathematician and scientist who instituted the quadrivium of mathematical studies that must be mastered to understand reality. These are the studies of arithmetic, music, geometry, and astronomy. Nicomachus himself wrote works on at least three of the sciences in the quadrivium.

The Neoplatonist Iamblichus (ca. 250–325 C.E.) wrote a ten-volume work entitled *On Pythagorean Doctrine*. The first volume, *On the Pythagorean Life*, was, as its title suggests, more than a biography of Pythagoras. Iamblichus's goal was to show Pythagoras as the archetype of the sage who had close contacts with divinity, and to present the way of life that he handed on to his followers. Many scholars have suggested that it would not be inappropriate to call Iamblichus's work a gospel, and it may be that Pythagoras was consciously set forth as a competitor to Christ. Iamblichus went on to write a volume on each of the four sciences in the quadrivium and then a volume each on the role of mathematics in physics, in ethics, and in theology. These last three works are lost and known only secondhand. But a later treatise of uncertain authorship entitled the *Theologumena arithmeticae* seems to have drawn extensively on Iamblichus's and Nicomachus's work on the theology of number and comprises a discussion of the properties of each of the first ten numbers, including their connection with various divinities. Iamblichus had a number of important predecessors in his work on Pythagoreanism, including Nicomachus and a 2nd-century Neopythagorean named Numenius. Iamblichus's teachers Porphyry, who was the pupil of the great Neoplatonist Plotinus, and Anatolius, who wrote a work titled *On the Decad,* also fostered his Pythagoreanism. But Iamblichus himself is a crucial figure insofar as he appears to be responsible for the Pythagoreanizing and mathematizing of Neoplatonism that is still prominent in the important Neoplatonists Proclus and Syrianus in the 5th century C.E.

Neopythagoreanism has some connections to early Pythagoreanism: the inspiring figure of the semidivine sage is based to some extent on the historical Pythagoras; the picture of the cosmos ordered according to number does go back, in spirit at least, to Philolaus; and the notion of a set of sciences necessary to understand reality is found in Archytas. However, it was only in Platonism that these general ideas were given a sophisticated metaphysical foundation and a compelling literary embodiment. Neopythagoreanism is not so much a revival as a transformation of Pythagoreanism.

CARL HUFFMAN

Bibliography

Barker, A. D., ed. *Greek Musical Writings,* vol. 2. Cambridge: Cambridge University Press, 1984.

Barnes, Jonathan. *The Presocratic Philosophers,* rev. ed. London: Routledge & Kegan Paul, 1982.

Burkert, Walter. *Lore and Science in Ancient Pythagoreanism.* Trans. E. L. Minar, Jr. Cambridge, Mass.: Harvard University Press, 1972.

Guthrie, W. K. C. *A History of Greek Philosophy.* 6 vols. Cambridge: Cambridge University Press, 1962–1981.

Huffman, Carl. "The Authenticity of Archytas Fr. 1." *Classical Quarterly* 35, no. 2 (1985): 344–348.

———. *Philolaus of Croton.* Cambridge: Cambridge University Press, 1993.

Iamblichus. *On the Pythagorean Way of Life.* Ed. and trans. John Dillon and Jackson Hershbell. Atlanta, Ga.: Scholars Press, 1991.

Kahn, Charles. "Pythagorean Philosophy before Plato." In *The Pre-Socratics: A Collection of Critical Essays,* rev. ed. Ed. A. P. D. Mourelatos. Princeton: Princeton University Press, 1993.

Kirk, G. S., J. E. Raven, and M. Schofield, eds. *The Presocratic Philosophers: A Critical History with a Selection of Texts.* 2nd ed. Cambridge: Cambridge University Press, 1983.

Lloyd, Geoffrey E. R. "Plato and Archytas in the Seventh Letter." *Phronesis* 35, no. 2 (1990): 159–174.

O'Meara, Dominic J. *Pythagoras Revived: Mathematics and Philosophy in Late Antiquity.* Oxford: Oxford University Press, 1989.

Thesleff, Holger. *An Introduction to the Pythagorean Writings of the Hellenistic Period.* Åbo: Åbo Akademi, 1961.

————, ed. *The Pythagorean Texts of the Hellenistic Period.* Åbo: Åbo Akademi, 1965.

Zhmud, Leonid. *Wissenschaft, Philosophie und Religion im frühen Pythagoreismus.* Berlin: Akademie Verlag, 1997.

SKEPTICISM

LIKE MANY PHILOSOPHICAL TERMS that end in "-ism," the word *skepticism* does not exist as a word in ancient Greek, even though it combines a Greek root and a Greek suffix. There was indeed a group of thinkers who called themselves *skeptikoi*, among other things; however, when they wanted to designate their "school" (in which nothing was taught), they used the word *skepsis*, with a suffix evoking an activity and not a doctrine. "Skeptics" did not profess a system that we might call Skepticism; they practiced an activity known as *skepsis*.

The philosophical positions of the *skeptikoi* were not unrelated to what we call Skepticism, but they were not identical to the modern version, either. Many philosophers whom we would describe as skeptics were not viewed in the same light by the *skeptikoi*; indeed, it was enough to adopt certain positions, which for us are characteristic of Skepticism (for example, to say that one cannot know anything), to distinguish oneself from the *skeptikoi*. Any introduction to classical Skepticism consistent with the ancient criteria would be incomplete from today's standpoint; if it were consistent with modern criteria, it would be historically unfaithful. The most delicate issue, in this regard, would be how to situate the New Academy, that phase of the school Plato founded during which, under the leadership of teachers such as Arcesilaus and Carneades, it adopted positions that we would classify as skeptical: the *skeptikoi*, for reasons whose validity has been controversial since ancient times, did not view them in the same way. Still, it is generally acknowledged today that the two tendencies were mutually influential; most modern historians argue at the very least that the "external analogies" between them "suffices to make it impossible to write a history of Skepticism without speaking of the New Academy" (Victor Brochard).

If we restrict ourselves to the vocabulary of the ancients, however, we may be tempted to concentrate here on so-called Pyrrhonist Skepticism—which means not so much on Pyrrhon himself as on later thinkers who claimed to be his heirs and who should rather be called Neopyrrhonists. This means dealing essentially, on the one hand, with two great philosophers whose texts have been lost and whose lives and personalities are obscure, but whose work is relatively well known: Aenesidemus (active toward the middle of the 1st century B.C.E.) and Agrippa (probably active at the end of the 1st century C.E. and at the beginning of the 2nd), and, on the other hand, with Sextus Empiricus (probably active at the end of the 2nd century and at the very begin-

415

ning of the 3rd), a prolific writer whose works, largely intact, constitute the richest and most influential source of information about ancient Skepticism.

But adopting this approach would still not solve all the problems. Nothing in the activity of *skepsis* itself necessarily associates it with what we mean by Skepticism. First of all, *skepsis* designates the activity of looking attentively at something, of observing, examining with the eyes: the verb *skeptesthai*, the frequentative form of the verb *skopein*, refers to the idea of seeing and looking (as in the words *microscope* and *telescope*); then, through a metaphor that is a familiar one in the vocabulary of epistemology, it designates the activity of examining with the mind, reflecting, studying. The terms in question are thus not the exclusive property of Skeptics; they characterize all philosophers as such. Who could in fact claim to be a philosopher in ancient Greece and say that he did not reflect, that he did not examine things, that he accepted a system of belief without testing its claims? In one sense, all Greek philosophy is skeptical, and words from the *skepsis* family regularly appear in the work of philosophers whom the Skeptics do not count among their own, such as Plato and Aristotle. The philosophers of the New Academy represented themselves as faithful to Plato, and their arguments in favor of Plato as a Skeptic could not be discounted out of hand; the *skeptikoi* themselves, although they did not agree that the New Academy was skeptical, were willing to consider the possibility that Plato may have practiced skepticism. As for Aristotle, his theory and his practice of dialectical discussion "for" and "against" provided the Academics with a model that they appropriated as their own.

SKEPTIC NOMENCLATURE

What, then, constitutes the specifically skeptical method of practicing *skepsis*? To answer this question, let us examine the other names the Skeptics gave themselves. One in particular warrants attention: *zetetikoi* (zetetics, or seekers: *zetesis* designates the activity of seeking). Sextus Empiricus does not hesitate to acknowledge that all philosophers are seekers. But at the very beginning of his *Outlines of Pyrrhonism*, he specifies the properly skeptical manner of seeking as follows: "The natural result of any investigation is that the investigators either discover the object of search or deny that it is discoverable and confess it to be inapprehensible or persist in their search. So, too, with regard to the objects investigated by philosophy, this is probably why some have claimed to have discovered the truth, others have asserted that it cannot be apprehended, while others again go on inquiring" (I.i.1–2).

The first group is that of the Dogmatics (not the authoritarian teachers who propound their doctrines dogmatically, in the contemporary sense of the term, without providing any supporting arguments, but philosophers who hold doctrines that they deem perfectly reasoned and rationally teachable);

this group is represented, in Sextus, by Aristotle, Epicurus, the Stoics, "and certain others."

The second group is that of the philosophers who despair of searching and declare truth to be inherently ungraspable. This "negative metadogmatism" (Jonathan Barnes) consists in proffering second-order dogmatic assertions (having to do not with the real itself, but with the possibility of knowing the real), and assertions that are negative (the real is not knowable). Logically, there is nothing unacceptable in negative metadogmatism: if one specifies the degree of what is unknowable, or the type of statements that one rules out presenting as true or false, nothing precludes one from saying that one knows that something is unknowable, unverifiable, or unfalsifiable. However, a good part of the history of classical Skepticism stems from the fact that it was considered self-contradictory to say, "I know that nothing is knowable"; philosophers thus always tried to attribute this contradiction to their adversaries, and to demonstrate that they themselves made no such claim. Sextus (after Aenesidemus) thus associates philosophers who renounced all inquiry with the New Academy, the better to differentiate himself from them.

As for true Skeptics, they do not say that truth is ungraspable, and they do not give up its pursuit; they profess "to pursue the quest." Those whom we would probably call Skeptics, because they do not believe in the possibility of reaching truth, are thus the ones whom Sextus, for this very reason, refuses to call by that name. As for those who, like Sextus, say neither that truth is unattainable nor that it is not, we would be more likely to call them open-minded agnostics. The zetetic is therefore not simply someone who seeks or who has sought: he is someone who up to this point has done nothing but seek without finding, and who has the intention of continuing to seek, without giving up hope of finding. The label Skeptic can be explained in the same way: all philosophers devote themselves to inquiry, or have done so; only Skeptics "go on inquiring" because they have so far found no good reason to adopt any one position rather than another, and thus no good reason to break off their inquiry to settle on some particular position.

The Skeptics gave themselves two other labels as well: "aporetic" and "ephectic." An aporia, literally, is an impasse, a dead end, an "embarrassing" situation that one can experience oneself in the face of an obstacle that one has taken into account, or that one can produce in others by raising obstacles that one brings to their attention. An aporetic philosopher is thus, one might say, both embarrassed and embarrassing. The term is not the exclusive property of the Skeptics. With his questions, Socrates led his interlocutors into aporias; when they complained, he said that he reduced them to this situation only insofar as he himself was reduced to it; most of Plato's early dialogues, traditionally called aporetic, end with the acknowledgment of failure, at least on the surface. But aporia can be fertile, whether because it provokes reflection, because it eliminates ignorance unconscious of its own existence and

reinvigorates the investigation, or even because it makes possible its own sur-
passing. All of Plato's philosophy is, in one sense, the result of Socratic
aporias. And Aristotle was careful, before resolving a given problem, to review all the difficulties that earlier considerations of the problem, and his own
reflections, brought to the fore: he trusted that "diaporia," the systematic examination of all relevant aporias, would finally lead to "euporia," a way out of
the impasse.

What is unique to the skeptical aporia is that it is unacquainted with this
outcome, or even with the hope of finding in itself the possibility of such an
outcome. The Skeptic is aporetic, it seems, in a double sense: he experiences
passive aporia in a lasting way (he presents himself as more sensitive than
anyone else to conflicts of appearances, to the contradictions and anomalies of
all kinds that the world offers us), and he simultaneously cultivates active
aporia (he identifies *skepsis* with the power of making these contradictions
appear, by developing arguments capable of counterbalancing, "with equal
force," arguments that support any given position). Is it inconsistent on his
part to claim that he "goes on inquiring" while he is doing everything in his
power to perpetuate the aporia in which he encloses himself and in which he
wants to enclose others? Probably not: he freely admits that nothing keeps
him from possibly stumbling onto the truth one day; but in the meantime,
whenever a candidate for "truth" comes along, he examines it carefully to see
if he can shoot it down, and experience shows him that, in any event up to the
present moment, none has stood up to the shock. If ever some truth were to
end up imposing itself on his mind, it would not be because the maieutic practice of aporia had "given birth" to it, but because it had been unexpectedly
spared by the infanticidal practice of aporia.

The label "ephectic," for its part, is related to the only outcome that the
Skeptic expects from his aporetic attitude, and the only one that he does hope
for it: not an advance in his knowledge, not a positive step forward in the
search for the truth, but rather the state of suspension of judgment *(epochē)*
from which the word *ephectic* comes. *Epochē* is not to be confused with doubt
(despite the association usually made today between doubt and skepticism), if
one views doubt as a state to which, according to the current expression, one
"is prey"—which means that one is its passive victim, in a state of indecision
or even anguish, wavering endlessly between a belief and its opposite. If
epochē resembles doubt, it would be the deliberate and methodical doubt
through which Descartes, taking up on his own account and carrying to the
extreme "all of the Skeptics' most extravagant suppositions," tried to see if
there were anything undoubtable that could hold up against it. Historically,
in fact, it is probable that the word *epochē* and the corresponding attitude
originated, independently of the Pyrrhonist tradition, in the course of a fundamental debate between the Stoics and the Academics. The former maintained that the sage must abstain from giving his assent to any representation

that is not absolutely self-evident, but the latter retorted that no representation possesses such self-evidence, and that thus the sage must always, and in all matters, abstain from giving his assent. On this point, the *skeptikoi* seem to be indebted to the Academics, even if they disguise this by accusing them of a metadogmatism that is incompatible with the generalized *epochē*. This latter is, in sum, a state of immobile equilibrium: there is no topic at all on which the Skeptic is inclined toward affirmation or denial, and he finds in this equilibrium not only intellectual tranquillity but also the peace and happiness of his soul.

This ethical stake in the skeptical approach leads us to examine one last name that the *skeptikoi* gave themselves (the only one, along with the label Skeptics, that has withstood the test of time): the label Pyrrhonists. Unlike the others, this designation is not drawn from the Skeptics' manner of philosophizing, or from the methods they used, or from the results they claimed they had achieved, but from history, and from a precise and crucial moment of history, since Pyrrhon lived at the turning point between two historical eras, the classical and the Hellenistic, periods separated by the expedition of Alexander the Great and all the accompanying upheavals. Even if the coincidence is accidental, it is symbolic that Aristotle, the last of the great classical Dogmatics, and Pyrrhon, officially the first of the Skeptics, had each had a personal relationship with Alexander: the former was the prince's preceptor before Alexander's accession to the throne, while the latter was an obscure member of the conqueror's intellectual entourage. Since Pyrrhon wrote nothing, as it happens, and since he was manifestly an extraordinary individual, all the conditions were at hand to enhance his place in history—or in legend.

PYRRHON AND NEOPYRRHONIST SKEPTICISM

Does Greek Skepticism really begin with Pyrrhon? This question, which seems simple enough, nevertheless raises several others. The first is whether we can consider Pyrrhon as the first of the Pyrrhonists; the next questions are whether, when, and why he was considered a Pyrrhonist by the ancient Skeptics themselves.

As to the first question, one can say briefly that the accounts of those closest to him (in particular, that of his disciple Timon, a brilliant poet-philosopher who spent some twenty years in Pyrrhon's circle of intimates, and that of Cicero) present Pyrrhon first and foremost as a master of happiness, as a moralist for whom the surest ways to achieve happiness are through insensitivity *(apatheia)* and imperturbability *(ataraxia)*. Plausibly enough, Pyrrhon did not view the problem of knowledge as fundamental, and he was not primarily concerned with refuting the claims of scientists and philosophers; "human instability, vain concerns, and puerility," which he denounced with the help of citations from Homer, were his chief targets. There are reasons to believe that Timon was the first person responsible for the shift in his master's thought toward a questioning of cognitive powers. The alliance between the search for happiness and the critique of knowledge, which is found in Pyrrhon in a preparatory stage at most (and which seems to be absent, on the contrary, from the preoccupations of the Neoacademics), is in any case clearly confirmed in Timon.

This alliance will subsist among the later Skeptics, including those indefatigable collectors of antidogmatic arguments, Aenesidemus and Sextus; in this sense, Pyrrhon's ethical message survives in the Neopyrrhonists. But we can identify several shifts of emphasis showing that determining the exact nature of the link between cognitive Skepticism and the conquest of happiness remains problematic. According to Timon (as reported by Aristocles), the attitude Pyrrhon recommended—that is, "life without beliefs," the absence of any inclination toward a given opinion rather than its opposite, as well as any absence of wavering between the two—has as its effects, first, abstention with respect to any assertion (aphasia) and, second, imperturbability, or ataraxia. As these effects are expected and desired, ataraxia seems to coincide with the ethical goal pursued by Skeptics, and with respect to which Skeptics knowingly make use of the means recognized as most appropriate.

In other texts, where Timon is associated with Aenesidemus, epochē is designated as being itself the end (telos) sought by Skeptics; ataraxia is said to follow "like its shadow." This image seems intended to disconnect cognitive Skepticism from ataraxic happiness: by setting himself a goal of an intellectual nature, epochē, the only goal in view of which the deployment of appropriate means depends on the Skeptic himself, the latter achieves a different goal of an ethical nature, ataraxia; but he achieves it as a supplement, as it were, and by a stroke of good luck. (In this connection, Sextus tells the story of the painter Apelles: one day, furious that he was not managing to portray a horse's foam, he threw his sponge at the canvas and in so doing produced the very result that he had given up hope of achieving.) This development is completed by Sextus himself, who differentiates clearly between two separate goals, one having to do with matters of judgment, ataraxia (taken here in a strictly intellectual sense), and the other concerning affectivity: the latter goal no longer entails complete insensitivity (apatheia) but rather moderation of affect(s) (metriopatheia). Ataraxia is what makes moderation possible: in fact, if the Skeptic cannot escape the inevitable perturbations to which external needs give rise, at least, thanks to his intellectual ataraxia, he can avoid making them worse by ill-considered judgments. One suffers more from pain when, not content with experiencing it, one deems it an evil in itself; Sextus notes astutely that observers have more difficulty tolerating a surgical operation than the patient does.

As for the Skeptics' own opinion of Pyrrhon's thought and its originality, there are distinctions to be made. Timon, Pyrrhon's direct disciple, uses his full poetic powers to present his master as a unique and peerless man whose example is comparable to that of the sun-god, man's eternal guide. To enhance his teacher's prestige even further, in a kind of jovial parody of Homer, in a poem titled *Silloi*, Timon indulges in lively attacks on virtually all philosophers past and present, although he makes a few exceptions or near exceptions (Xenophanes in particular). Let us also note that a figure about whom we know nothing, Ascanius of Abdera, attributed Pyrrhon's radical originality in the context of the Greek tradition to his experiences in the East: in Ascanius's view, Skepticism is an import, brought back by Pyrrhon from India and Persia. Not all modern scholars dismiss this hypothesis; but the fact that Timon says nothing about it, whereas his testimony on this point would presumably have been preserved if it had existed, is an invitation to try to do without it.

The fragments of *Silloi* that have survived allow us to suppose that the poem's message was not completely destructive. In the scenario Timon offers, Xenophanes may have played the role of an intercessor of sorts, soliciting indulgence for some of his colleagues; this would explain why some philosophers who are treated very badly in one fragment receive better treatment in another. Thus Timon's partial amnesties may have paved the way for the construction of a portrait gallery of the ancestors of Skepticism.

SKEPTICISM BEFORE PYRRHON

The ancients' effort to insert Pyrrhon into a plausible genealogy took several forms. The most serious consisted in introducing him into one of the "successions" *(diadochai)* of masters and disciples that scholars at the end of antiquity constructed, more or less artificially, to create some order in the burgeoning field of Greek philosophy. Timon's suggestions may have been used, among other materials, to construct the succession given in the structure of Book IX of Diogenes Laertius's *Lives of Eminent Philosophers*. The book's headings appear in the following order: Xenophanes, Parmenides and the Eleatics, the atomists Leucippus and Democritus, then, after several more obscure intermediaries, Anaxarchus, Pyrrhon's teacher and Alexander's friend, Pyrrhon himself, and, finally, Timon. This succession established a filiation between Pyrrhon and Democritus, whose complex and still-controversial theory of knowledge presented some skeptical aspects; the relationship was probably both an effect and a cause of the interpretation of Pyrrhon's thought in gnoseological terms.

Another trend, probably less "scientific" in its claims, sought to show that Skepticism was less the distinctive feature of a specific philosophical line of thinking than a diffuse and very old tradition characteristic of virtually all Greek thought. This approach thus challenged Pyrrhon's right to be viewed as the "founder" of Skepticism; however, it did not necessarily stem from an intent to denigrate him (novelty was rarely taken as a positive value in antiquity, and it was thought to be more useful to a philosophy to endow it with prestigious ancestors than to underscore its revolutionary character). Once again it is Diogenes Laertius who provides us with a list of "honorary Skeptics" (*Lives* IX.71–73) along with one or two citations apiece by way of justifying their inclusion: Homer, the Seven Wise Men, Archilochus, Euripides, Xenophanes, Zeno of Elea, Democritus, Plato, Euripides again, Empedocles, Heraclitus, Hippocrates, and Homer once more (the repetitions may indicate that the list results from an amalgam of several sources).

If we think solely about the desire for and the intoxication with knowledge that are so manifest in the Greeks, the attempt to portray Greek thought as a generalized Skepticism, through several of its seminal figures, may seem absurd. And yet it is not completely so, for we also have to take into account the sort of gnoseological pessimism that in some ways constituted the terrain out of which Greek dynamism (or, more precisely, the dynamism of certain Greek thinkers) was extracted, and onto which that dynamism collapsed on more than one occasion.

Thus, for some of the ancients, Skepticism began with Homer. This affirmation seems eccentric to us, and the arguments that have been offered in its defense are unquestionably weak. However, in the Homeric poems we can readily find a strong sense of the limitations of human knowledge as contrasted with the extent and quality of divine knowledge, and this sense is unquestionably characteristic of the most ancient Greek wisdom (the dogmatic thinkers understood that that sentiment had to be reckoned with, and that they had to overcome it). In a celebrated invocation, the poet beseeches the Muses to inform him about the distant past that he is preparing to describe: "For you are goddesses and are present and know all things, but we hear only a rumor and know nothing" (*Iliad* II.484–486). The human mode of knowledge is made fragile by our enclosure within a narrow space and an ephemeral time: considered individually or even collectively, human beings have a field of vision that is necessarily linked to, and therefore limited by, a particular point of view.

Countless echoes of this call to order run through Greek thought: man is not God, and to seek to ignore the fact is a culpable and dangerous excess (the celebrated hubris). There is probably not yet any skepticism here, even in the broadest sense of the word. If it is imprudent to want to gain access to the knowledge the gods keep for themselves (for example, what goes on in heaven and in the underworld), this does not rule out the possibility that such knowledge is in principle attainable: quite to the contrary, indeed, since we must be warned of its dangers. A seed of practical skepticism, as it were, appears when transgression of the forbidden is presented as useless: the famous anecdote about Thales falling in a well while looking at the stars is only one illustration of a widespread antitheoretical theme according to which scientific knowledge of nature adds nothing—indeed, quite the opposite—to the modest knowledge needed for daily life. A metadogmatic form of skepticism is finally attained when the desire for knowledge appears not only dangerous or useless but impossible to satisfy, and above all when arguments in support of this thesis are provided, instead of mere assertions that man is not God.

This path was quickly followed to its end. The proliferation of theoretical research in the pre-Socratic era had given rise almost as rapidly to skeptical reactions. Several limited experiments and some bold arguments had led thinkers of that era to construct ambitious doctrines on the broadest and most difficult subjects: "nature," the origin and foundation of reality; the principles of being and becoming; the genesis and structure of the world; the origin of the elements, stars, and living beings—for them nothing seemed inaccessible to the enterprises of knowledge, and they did not hesitate to present their results in solidly self-assured tones. The trouble was that these doctrines were numerous, and mutually incompatible; in a very short time and with staggering theoretical imagination, the principal options had been tested and confronted with their competitors (the one and the multiple, the finite and the infinite, the continuous and the discontinuous, movement and rest, mechanism and finality). Aristotle sought to discern signs of progress in this proliferation, but more superficial ears heard in it only discordance and cacophony (*diaphonia*), which were well suited to give rise to Skepticism.

However, it is one thing to take note of cacophony, quite another to prove that it is inevitable. On this point, we need to reckon with a famous fragment by Xenophanes of Colophon, a poet-philosopher and a powerful personality whose long life spanned the late 6th and early 5th centuries. We need to do so for several reasons. Remarkably precocious in terms of its date, the fragment may prefigure a famous argument against the very possibility of the search for truth; this argument was presented as "eristic" by Plato in *Meno*, and it played an essential role in the later history of theories of knowledge. In addition, Xenophanes' fragment unquestionably explains the particular position that Timon had attributed to the Colophonian in his *Silloi*; finally, the question of whether it contains a skeptical argument, and if so, just which one, gave rise to many debates in late antiquity and continues to do so in our own day. Here is an approximate translation: "The clear and certain truth no man has seen nor will there be anyone who knows about the gods and what I say about all things. For even if, in the best case, one happened to speak aptly of what has been brought to pass, still he himself would not know it. But opinion [*dokos*] is allotted to everybody (Greek *epi pasin*: maybe "to everything")" (Xenophanes, in Diels-Kranz, frg. 21.B.34). In the absence of context, it is difficult to know what scope Xenophanes assigned to the domain in which he claims, for his discourse, only the status of true belief and not that of exact knowledge, but he seems to endow it with this status thanks to an argument according to which, in the domain under consideration, no verification criterion is available. One might happen on a truth by chance, but one would have no way to know whether it was a truth or not. One would then be in possession of a belief that could happen to be true, but what would be missing, not by chance but of necessity, is the justification that alone would transform it from belief to knowledge.

Xenophanes thus brought himself to the attention of the future Skeptics. For those who were less demanding about the criteria for filiation, the search for the ancestors of Skepticism became even easier. The most extreme dogmatic thinkers could figure in the genealogical tree. Not only were their violently counterintuitive theses about "the nature of things" contradictory among themselves, but in addition, taken in isolation, their theses exploited the conflicts between perceptible appearances (this was the case for Heraclitus, the Eleatics, and Democritus); thus they made it possible to nourish the aspect of skeptical thought that also made use of these conflicts. For their part, the Sophists—Protagoras and Gorgias, for example—each in his own manner and with arguments that the Skeptics could also put to good use, had undermined the notions of objective truth and absolute knowledge. The candidates for the status of precursors to Skepticism were rapidly presenting themselves in serried ranks. Sextus Empiricus himself, who was not overly interested in Pyrrhon and who obviously knew little about him, grants him only relative and comparative originality: others, Sextus admits, had devoted themselves to *skepsis* before Pyrrhon's time, but "Pyrrhon appears to us to have applied himself to Scepticism more thoroughly and more conspicuously than his predecessors" (*Outlines* I.iii.7). Once Neopyrrhonist Skepticism had succeeded in defining itself clearly, well after Pyrrhon's day, it was no longer urgent for it to find guarantees of historical authenticity; on the contrary, it was necessary to keep authentic Skepticism from being confused with the "neighboring philosophies" that seemed to resemble it.

NEOPYRRHONISM AND THE "NEIGHBORING PHILOSOPHIES"

Sextus Empiricus undertakes the confrontation between Skepticism and other philosophies in a long and important section of *Outlines of Pyrrhonism* (I.xxix–xxxiv), where he studies in turn Heraclitus, Democritus, the Cyrenaics, Protagoras, the Middle Academy (Arcesilaus) and the New Academy (Carneades), and the empiricist physicians. In each case, he attempts to determine, along with the reasons that might have led to the idea that these philosophers were Skeptics, the differences that proved to him that they were not. His criterion for differentiation is quite strict: "The man that dogmatizes about a single thing, or ever prefers one impression to another in point of credibility or incredibility, or makes any assertion about any non-evident object [that dogmatic philosophers claim to know] assumes the dogmatic character" (*Outline* I.xxxiii.223).

The Skeptic thus appears to present himself as more "radical" than those from whom he wishes to be distinguished. This description is not completely accurate, however. Without examining each of the "neighboring philosophies" that Sextus summarizes, we shall choose one of them, the philosophy of the Cyrenaic school (developed by one of Socrates' direct disciples, Aristippus), because its theory of knowledge, less well-known than its moral hedonism, is of great philosophical interest.

If, among the ancient theories of knowledge, it were necessary to choose one that was "radically skeptical" in the sense in which we are using the term, Cyrenaic theory would probably be an even better candidate than Neopyrrhonist Skepticism. Its sole text is contained in a single formula: "Our affects (pathe) alone are graspable." These "affects" are the impressions of all sorts—tinged with pleasure or pain, according to circumstances—that we experience in an entirely passive manner. As we do not produce them ourselves, agents outside of ourselves that produce them in us must exist. But we can know nothing about the identity or nature of these agents; nothing guarantees that they actually and intrinsically have the properties that correspond to the feelings that they make us experience, or that the affects they produce on people other than ourselves are identical to ours. I am "affected whitely," says the Cyrenaic; but is what affects me this way something white or not? I cannot know, since I would have to go look, and this is by definition impossible: I have no relation with the things that affect me except by way of the affects that they produce in me. To seek to grasp them independently would be to seek to leap over my own shadow; as Plutarch says about this theory, we are in a city under siege, cut off from the rest of the world.

The Cyrenaics do not seem to have identified the positive side of their thesis, namely, the infallible, incorrigible, and indubitable character with which we "grasp" our own affects (in antiquity, it seems, only St. Augustine had the already Cartesian idea that this thesis can lead to an argument against Skepticism rather than for it); this is probably because the idea of knowledge, for the ancients, implies grasping an object that (at least before its cognitive appropriation) is other than the knowing subject. By stressing the fact that the causes of affects are ungraspable, rather than the fact that affects themselves are graspable, Cyrenaic theory thus developed a remarkably powerful argument. Though many philosophers up to our own day have sought to refute it in various ways, it readily springs back to life from its own ashes, drawing as needed on resources appropriate to each era (including those of science fiction: how can I be sure, for example, that I am not a brain in a jar, covered with electrodes, through which an army of scientists supplies me with precisely the impressions that I have?). This argument tends to establish that, as a matter of principle, anything other than my own modifications is radically inaccessible to me.

To distinguish them from the Skeptics, Sextus criticizes the Cyrenaics, first, for their dogmatism in ethics. For the Skeptic, nothing is good by nature; pleasure is no more so than anything else. On the gnoseological level, the same argument holds up against most of the "neighboring philosophies": Cyrenaic theory asserts, and even claims to demonstrate, that external things are unknowable; the Skeptic says only that he knows nothing about that, and he denounces the manifestation of negative metadogmatism in the Cyrenaics' assertion. There may appear to be very little difference between the Cyrenaic who takes note of his own modifications and declares their causes unknowable and the Skeptic who denies suppressing appearances *(phainomena)* by saying that he does no more than ask whether things are as they appear to be. However—and in this sense, Skepticism is less "radical" than Cyrenism—it would be hard to say about the Skeptic, even with ill will, that he is locked up in a fortress under siege. The *phainomenon*, the subject of the verb *appear*, is still a sort of object for the consciousness to which it appears, and this distinguishes it subtly but clearly from affect *(pathos)*, which is only a modification of the subject itself. There is an eloquent difference between typically Cyrenaic statements, such as "I am affected whitely," and typically Skeptical statements, such as "a certain thing appears white to me." This difference allows us to understand another, crucial difference: while it would appear absurd to speak of assent given by a subject to his own modifications, it is not absurd (at least not for a Skeptic) to speak of a weak form of assent that the subject can give to what appears in front of him: assent without deep-seated commitment, a kind of instinctive adherence that Sextus compares to a pupil's distracted acceptance of his master's discourse. According to the Skeptics, *epochē* is not at all incompatible with this weak form of assent.

NEOPYRRHONISM AND STOICISM

To determine how and why the specifically skeptical position was able to define and maintain itself, it is at least as necessary to give an account of the opposing philosophies as of the neighboring ones. Negative metadogmatism is one reaction, comprehensible enough, to positive dogmatism: whether one takes a position on the level of the certainties of naive consciousness or on the level of the arrogance of scientific theories, the fact that appearances conflict and that doctrines contradict one another readily gives rise to the idea that the reality of the world is, in its very nature, inaccessible to human knowledge. For something like a Skepticism that is itself exempt from negative metadogmatism to appear, a little higher up on the scale of reflection what could be called a positive metadogmatism had to appear in the meantime, that is, a doctrine tending to justify, on a theoretical level and in a closely argued fashion, the possibility of knowing the external world. In other words, just as, in the first degree, the opposition of positive and negative dogmatisms (for example, "Everything is in movement," "Not everything is in movement") favors the appearance, in the second degree, of negative metadogmatism ("It is impossible to know whether everything is in movement or not"), so the opposition to this negative metadogmatism by a positive metadogmatism ("It is possible to know whether everything is in movement or not") favors the appearance, in the third degree, of a Skepticism that is careful to stay out of the traps of each of the two opposing metadogmatisms. This Skepticism has to take pains not to assert, for its part, either that it is possible or that it is impossible to know whether everything is in movement or not and, more generally, whether the real is knowable or not.

From this point on, it is not Pyrrhon's existence that ought to be seen as the crucial event in the history of Neopyrrhonist Skepticism; it is rather the appearance of a dogmatism that was refined and reflective enough to have created a metadogmatic theory of the foundations of its own certainties. This dogmatism that deemed itself capable of establishing itself on its own has a name: Stoicism. In fact there is no better candidate to be found. Plato could not play this role: the Academies of Arcesilaus and of Carneades, both of which were inclined toward Skepticism, claimed Plato, no less than Socrates—not without cause—as their founding father. Aristotle may well be placed, by Sextus Empiricus, in the first rank of dogmatic philosophers, but he is not one of Sextus's habitual interlocutors, and in any case, his most important works were not well known during the period in which Neopyrrhonism emerged. Epicureanism had long been marginalized by its hedonist ethic, by its requirement of political abstention, by its affectation of lack of culture, and by several doctrines viewed as logically scandalous (the theory of the *clinamen*); it does not have the appearance of a respectable partner, and Sextus is careful to stress his distance from it when he touches on points against which Epicureanism and Skepticism are waging war in common (for example, against the traditional mode of education).

Stoicism, on the other hand, inaugurates a new type of thought in which dogmatism no longer seeks to be excused but declares itself and shores itself up with arguments. For what is probably the first time in so decisive a manner, the Stoics free themselves from the ancient fear of arousing the jealousy of the gods; in this view, human reason is homogeneous with the divine reason that governs the world, and the sage is Zeus's equal. The only vestige the Stoics retain of the ancient divisions is the distance they put between the sage, a phoenix nowhere to be found, and the rest of us, ignorant fools all. However, philosophically speaking, this factual difference does not count: however rare he may be, the Stoic sage is a man; to draw his portrait, as the Stoics never tired of doing, is to describe what man can be when he is fully human.

Now, the base on which this unprecedented dogmatism stands is the famous "cognitive impression" *(phantasia kataleptike)*, the essential characteristic of which, from the standpoint that interests us, is that it contains its own self-certification. According to the Stoics, among the "impressions" that affect us, some have the privilege both of being causally produced by the external states of things and at the same time of representing these states of things, in their content, with absolute precision and exactitude, to the point that these impressions cannot arise from any state of things other than the one from which they have arisen. In other words, a cognitive impression caused by a given state of things is inherently distinguishable from any impression caused by a different state of things; it cannot be false. As Cicero says when he is describing Stoic theory, cognitive impressions possess "a sort of inherent power to bring to full light the things that are manifested in them"; they include an intrinsic "note" that guarantees their truth. Such is, indeed, the most heroic element in the Stoic solution: some of our impressions certify by themselves that they are not merely our impressions, but that they also allow us to know what is.

Over several generations, the early Stoics argued against contemporary adversaries, the members of the New Academy, on the subject of cognitive impressions; the early Pyrrhonists were not involved. In these disputes, the Stoics made out fairly well, since the successive Academics had an increasing tendency to moderate their Skepticism; they even ended up thinking, as did Antiochus of Ascalon (1st century B.C.E.), that the two schools differed in form alone. The disputes had several consequences that concern Neopyrrhonist Skepticism.

On the historical level, we know very little about what went on between Timon and Aenesidemus. Ancient scholars evoked either an uninterrupted succession of masters and disciples, whose names mean nothing to us, or else an eclipse brought to an end by a predecessor of Aenesidemus. We have very little information about Aenesidemus himself. It was thought for a long time (though some scholars question this today) that he had started out as a member of the Academy, and that owing to his disagreement with the school's dogmatic drift, he had sought to resuscitate a pure, hardline Skepticism with Pyrrhon as his patron, Pyrrhon being a shadowy, legendary figure at the time. In any event, Photius, patriarch of Constantinople in the 9th century C.E., who was a reader of Aenesidemus's *Pyrrhonian Arguments*, attests that, according to Aenesidemus, it was necessary to renew the struggle against Stoic dogmatism: the Academics had watered down the doctrine to such an extent that in the final analysis it was a matter of "Stoics fighting against Stoics." The formula eloquently reveals to what extent, for Aenesidemus, the philosophic landscape had been literally invaded by Stoicism.

The whole effort of Aenesidemus's Neopyrrhonism was thus aimed at forging an apparatus capable of destroying the Stoics' self-certifying mechanism. It was not enough to deny the existence or the possibility of cognitive impressions, as the Academics had done with tireless ingeniousness: to do that was once again to pit one metadogmatism against another. To refute a dogmatism that claimed to justify itself by including itself in its own field of application, Aenesidemus presented Pyrrhonist thought, with a symmetry that was perhaps deliberate, as a Skepticism that succeeded in eliminating itself by including itself in its own domain. Although Aenesidemus was probably not the originator of this approach, Photius's testimony shows rather touchingly that he was still aware of submitting language and thought to an acrobatic test: "For the Pyrrhonist determines absolutely nothing, not even this very claim that nothing is determined. (We put it this way, he says, for lack of a way to express the thought)" (Long and Sedley, *The Hellenistic Philosophers*, I:469). When he says: "I determine nothing" (that is, I answer no question in the affirmative or in the negative), the Skeptic professes not to "determine" further the question of whether he determines anything or not.

This way of turning the typical formulas of Skepticism ("in no way more," "all things are indeterminate," "for every argument there is an opposing argument of equal weight") back on themselves becomes systematic with Sextus Empiricus; to the extent that Sextus expresses less circumspection than Aenesidemus toward his own language, the difficulties of the skeptical position are manifested more clearly in his case. The Skeptic, we are told, for example, gives his assent "in no way more" *(ouden mallon)* to *p* rather than to non-*p*; but if this formula is applied to itself, it is also necessary to understand that the Skeptic "in no way more" privileges the attitude over the attitude expressed by the opposite formula, "in some way more," which is the very negation of the Skeptic *epochē*. Would Skepticism be condemned by its very logic to refuse to choose between itself and dogmatism? Some of Sextus's well-known images attempt to make arguments out of comparisons: Skepticism is like a fire that consumes itself as it consumes its fuel; it is like a ladder that one tosses aside after climbing a wall (this image will be passed along all the way to Wittgenstein); finally (less poetically, but very much in the spirit of a late Skepticism that had forged an alliance with medical empiricism), it is like a purgative that evacuates itself along with the matter that it is intended to evacuate. Whatever logical and psychological difficulties these images may dissimulate (and what if a purgative eliminated itself *before* eliminating what it was supposed to eliminate?), Neopyrrhonism considered that it was freed, through this device that was a mirror image of the Stoic mechanism, from the risks of contradiction that negative metadogmatism entails.

THE STATUS OF SKEPTICAL DISCOURSE

This benefit implies several others, first of all in the theoretical realm. By protecting himself from dogmatism at all levels, the Skeptic believes he has found a way of speaking without asserting anything, a way of being "aphasic" without remaining silent. He thus expresses weak assent, which allows him to avoid extravagance. He gives this sort of assent to his bodily sensations: it is not a problem for him to say that he is hot. He also gives weak assent to his inferences, triggered by an association of ideas: if he sees smoke without seeing fire, he concludes that there is fire, because he has already seen the two things associated; he has no objection to the use of such "commemorative" signs, whereas he does object to the use of "indicative" signs, by means of which dogmatics believe they can infer, on the basis of observable phenomena, the existence of realities that are in principle unobservable. The same type of assent is valid for his own philosophic utterances: at the beginning of his *Outlines,* Sextus Empiricus takes pains to warn his readers that nothing in what he is about to say is to be taken as "affirmed," nothing is presented decisively as expressing exactly the way things are; the Skeptic only "records" facts as they have appeared to him *(phainetai)* up to the present moment. As he does not record just anything at all, however, one may argue that he has "beliefs," in an appropriate sense of the term. The beliefs he avoids are not those that our nature leads us to maintain but the artificial and hasty beliefs that dogmatics think they can profess on their own behalf and instill in others, and that claim to reach beyond appearances to the hidden nature of things themselves.

Several recent publications have distinguished between two varieties of Skepticism: a "rustic" Skepticism, which submits all beliefs to *epochē,* including those that govern ordinary people's daily lives, and an "urbane" Skepticism, which condemns only the dogmatic beliefs of scientists and philosophers. In this respect, and even if some more or less legendary aspects of Pyrrhon's personality (which Aenesidemus contests, moreover) have placed him at the origin of a tradition of rustic Skepticism, we may say that Neopyrrhonism is on the whole an urbane Skepticism.

There is not enough room here to examine all the means the Skeptics used to arouse and justify *epochē:* Aenesidemus's ten "tropes" or devices; his eight specific tropes against the possibility of knowing the causes of phenomena; and finally Agrippa's five tropes, which form an admirable network in the form of a spider's web in which dogmatics can be caught. We shall look briefly to see whether any belief incompatible with urbane Skepticism is presupposed by one of these devices and arguments or another.

Aenesidemus's tropes do not pose too many problems in this regard, because they lead precisely to not taking what appears as the criterion for what is. They draw attention to the diversity presented by phenomena, chiefly perceptible ones, according to a whole series of dimensions that involve either the subject or the object or the relation between the two. The diversity of phenomena is itself, in some cases, a phenomenon that can be observed directly; in other cases, it can be inferred on the basis of commemorative signs, that is, signs of the type that Skeptics allow themselves to use. To take just one example (this is Aenesidemus's first trope), the sensory organs of many animals are not the same as ours; now, we observe that when our own organs are modified in one way or another, our perceptions are likewise modified; we may thus infer, without claiming to know what animals different from our-selves perceive, that they do not perceive in the same way we do. And there is no reason to think that our perceptions discover the nature of things "in any way more" than theirs do.

Agrippa's tropes raise other, quite fundamental questions. They presuppose that a certain number of intellectual situations are intolerable: first, contradic-tion (Pyrrhon is sometimes thought to have rejected the principle of noncon-tradiction, but it is clear that the Neopyrrhonists do not do this); next, all for-mal defects (infinite regression, circular reasoning, arbitrary hypotheses) to which the demonstration procedures that attempt to escape from contradic-tion are condemned, according to Agrippa. What is the epistemological status of these logical interdictions? Let us take the example of infinite regression: we may suppose that the Skeptics would justify its interdiction by invoking either the empirical impossibility, for the human mind, of going back in-definitely from each statement to the one that proves it, or else the logical im-possibility, for every possible mind, of considering as proved a statement whose proof would require an infinite series of prior statements.

THE PRACTICAL QUESTION

It is necessary to go back to the empirical component of Skepticism to de-scribe the gist of its response to an objection that is constantly raised, among the ancients as well as the moderns, against all forms of Skepticism: the charge of "making life impossible." According to this view, Skeptics are con-demned, unless they are inconsistent, to inaction *(apraxia):* is it not impos-sible to live "without beliefs" *(adoxastos)*, as Skeptics claim they can live? To live in the world of things and of people, can one do without a certain number of beliefs having to do either with the state of things here and now or with the values that make it possible to choose between various possible courses of action? Neopyrrhonism does not consider itself to be affected at all by these criticisms; quite the contrary. The phenomenon, to which it gives the weak assent it permits itself, appears to Neopyrrhonists to be a sufficient cri-terion for action, and an effective guide for "nonphilosophic" life. Must we say that Skeptics, like Sartre's *salauds,* act like everyone else and think like no one else? But do ordinary people themselves adhere dogmatically to the be-liefs that govern their behavior? The Skeptic does not think so, and he would prefer to say that he acts and thinks like everyone else, except for the small, stubborn core of dogmatists. By giving in to his natural reflexes, he meets his own needs and keeps himself out of danger; giving up the illusory quest for universal and objective values, he obeys the laws and follows the customs of his country. He is capable of not remaining professionally inactive, so long as we do not imagine that technical action requires objective knowledge of the area in which he operates.

The Skeptic's conception of technical action owes a great deal to the model of so-called empirical medicine. As early as the 3rd century B.C.E., a school of empiricist physicians appeared; in opposition to rationalist physicians, the empiricists thought they could base effective practice on experience alone, without any recourse to a supposedly scientific knowledge of the human body, its hidden mechanisms, the objective causes of illness and health, or the intrinsic reasons why remedies and treatments are effective for one illness and not for another. The medical field is probably the one in which a balanced rivalry between empirical and rational practices was established in the most clear-cut and well thought out way (in other areas, the struggle was more uneven: the successes of reason were manifest in mathematics, and the experience of a sailor or a farmer was hard to challenge when it came to predicting the weather). The debate between the schools of medicine thus took on an epistemological and philosophical significance whose importance the philosophers were quick to measure: the Skeptics could see in medical empiricism a model for renouncing dogmatism that did not imply renouncing action, and that could even justify the idea of a nondogmatic form of practical knowledge.

Between Skepticism and the assorted variants of medical empiricism, not only did there exist a sort of preestablished harmony, but also, starting from a date that is difficult to pin down, both philosophies ended up being embodied in the same individuals, such as Menodotus (probably active in the 2nd century C.E.) and several of his successors. Sextus Empiricus himself, as his nickname indicates, was a physician as well as a philosopher; he presented himself as a therapist dealing with illnesses of both mind and soul; he wrote works on medicine that have been lost. Other texts, those of Galen in particular, allow us to clarify the interferences and the debates over epistemological problems that took place between physicians and philosophers of the various schools.

Should we be disappointed that the waters of Skepticism ended up mingling with those of medical empiricism? All this, for such an outcome? A centuries-long effort aimed at critical reflection, at vigilance against illusions, at mastery of the mind over itself, only to end up advocating renunciation of all intellectual ambition, acceptance of a life of dull conformity and the weary exercise of a routine trade? Before giving in to disappointment, we should perhaps ask ourselves whether medical empiricism was as woefully sterile as one might think. The method of empiricist physicians, according to Galen, does not rely only on direct personal observation ("autopsy," in the strict sense of the term); it also calls on the testimony of predecessors (history), a source of enrichment of experience and also an instrument of critical reflection, and on an operation of "passage from like to like," which probably does not purport to explain the similarity of particular cases through a common cause, but which, motivated and governed by experience, can succeed in establishing laws of regular association between the similar cases. If it is difficult to expect therapeutic progress from a purely empirical medicine, in our sense of the term, we may readily expect progress from experimental medicine; and the empiricist medicine of the ancients came to resemble experimental medicine more and more closely.

What is certain is that Skepticism itself, at least as a thought experiment, has not been sterile in the history of Western philosophy. Rarely taken up again as such (it would hardly be very skeptical to adopt Skepticism as a received doctrine) but frequently revisited and rethought, sometimes attenuated, sometimes radicalized, sometimes taken up as a challenge, it has proved capable, by way of Montaigne, Descartes, Pascal, Bayle, Hume, Kant, Nietzsche, and many others, of arousing thought from its "dogmatic slumber." Perhaps it would succeed, if needed, in arousing it from its antidogmatic slumber as well. Let us say that it can lead to anything, on the condition that, if one leaves it behind, one does not do so too quickly.

JACQUES BRUNSCHWIG
Translated by Emoretta Yang and Catherine Porter

Bibliography

Texts and Translations

Diogenes Laertius. *Lives of Eminent Philosophers*, book 9, vol. 2. Trans. R. D. Hicks. Loeb Classical Library.

The Hellenistic Philosophers. Ed. Anthony A. Long and David N. Sedley. Cambridge: Cambridge University Press, 1987.

Sextus Empiricus. *Works*. Trans. R. G. Bury. Loeb Classical Library.

Studies

Algra, Keimpe, Jonathan Barnes, Jaap Mansfeld, and Malcolm Schofield, eds. *The Cambridge History of Hellenistic Philosophy*. Cambridge: Cambridge University Press, 1999.

Annas, Julia, and Jonathan Barnes. *The Modes of Skepticism: Ancient Texts and Modern Interpretations*. Cambridge: Cambridge University Press, 1985.

Barnes, Jonathan. "The Beliefs of a Pyrrhonist." *Proceedings of the Cambridge Philological Society* 28 (1982): 1–28; *Elenchos* 4 (198): 5–43.

———. "Diogenes Laertius IX 61–116: The Philosophy of Pyrrhonism." In W. Haase, ed. *Aufsteig und Niedergang der römischen Welt* II, 36, no. 6 (1992): 4241–4301.

———. *The Toils of Scepticism*. Cambridge: Cambridge University Press, 1990.

Bett, Richard. *Pyrrho: His Antecedents and His Legacy*. Oxford: Oxford University Press, 2000.

Brochard, Victor. *Les sceptiques grecs.* 1887; repr. Paris: Vrin, 1981 and Le Livre de Poche, 2002.

Burnyeat, Myles. "Conflicting Appearances." *Proceedings of the British Academy* 665 (1979): 69–111.

———. "The Sceptic in His Place and Time." In *Philosophy in History: Essays on the Historiography of Philosophy.* Ed. Richard Rorty, J. B. Schneewind, and Quentin Skinner. Cambridge: Cambridge University Press, 1984.

Burnyeat, Myles, ed. *The Skeptical Tradition.* Berkeley: University of California Press, 1983.

Castagnoli, Luca. "Self-Bracketing Pyrrhonism." *Oxford Studies in Ancient Philosophy* 18 (2000): 263–328.

Dal Pra, Mario. *Lo scetticismo greco.* Repr. Rome-Bari: Laterza, 1975.

Flashar, Hellmut, ed. *Die Philosophie der Antike, Bd. 4: Die Hellenistische Philosophie. Zweiter Halbband* (W. Görler, *Älterer Pyrrhonismus—Jüngere Akademie—Antiochos aus Askalon*). Basel: Schwabe, 1994.

Frede, Michael. *Essays in Ancient Philosophy.* Minneapolis: University of Minnesota Press, 1987.

Giannantoni, Gabriele, ed. *Lo scetticismo antico.* 2 vols. Naples: Bibliopolis, 1981.

———. "Sesto Empirico e il pensiero antico." *Elenchos* 13 (1992): 1–366.

Hankinson, R. J. *The Sceptics.* London: Routledge, 1995.

Lévy, Carlos. *Les Philosophies hellénistiques.* Paris: Le Livre de Poche, 1997.

Robin, Léon. *Pyrrhon et le scepticisme grec.* Paris: Presses Universitaires de France, 1944.

Schofield, Malcolm, Myles Burnyeat, and Jonathan Barnes, eds. *Doubt and Dogmatism.* Oxford: Clarendon Press, 1980.

Stopper, M. R. "Schizzi Pirroniani." *Phronesis* 28 (1983): 265–297.

SOPHISTS

In the Presocratic dawn of philosophy, the intellectual movement known as sophistic seduced and scandalized all Greece. Indeed, the sophists were the "masters of Greece," according to Hegel's apt expression. Instead of reflecting on being, like the Eleatics, or on nature, like the Ionian physicists, they elected to be professional educators, through whom "culture itself came into being." They were itinerant foreigners who traded on their wisdom and skills like courtesans trading on their charms. However, they were also men of power who knew how to convince judges, sway an assembly, lead a successful embassy, give a new city its laws, build democracy—in short, they were engaged in politics. This dual mastery was rooted entirely in their command of language, from linguistics (the morphology, grammar, and synonymy that made Prodicus famous) to rhetoric (the study of tropes, sonorities, and opportuneness, at which Gorgias excelled); above all, according to Hegel's diagnosis, the sophists were "masters of eloquence."

This type of connection to language constituted, for better or for worse, the line separating the "sophist," *sophistēs*, an expert in wisdom, from the "philo-sophe," who loves his subject but dares not claim to possess it completely. Consider the following example that shows, in symptomatic fashion, the double meaning of the word *sophistic* as found in one of the most current dictionaries of philosophy (translated from André Lalande, *Vocabulaire technique et critique de la philosophie*): "Sophistic: A. Collection of doctrines, or, rather, the intellectual attitude shared by the principal Greek sophists (Protagoras, Gorgias, Prodicus, Hippias, etc.). B. Said of a philosophy of verbal reasoning that is neither sound nor serious." The first meaning situates the Greek sophists of the 5th century B.C.E. within the framework of intellectual history: powerful personalities who constituted something like a movement. In this sense, sophistic is a way of thinking that, with increasing appreciation, we define today as relativist, progressivist, concerned with phenomena and the human world, even humanistic. By contrast, in the second definition, in a way that is timeless and somewhat mysterious, the name serves to designate one of the nonphilosophical modes within the field of philosophy, that of "verbal reasoning." And so we are obliged to conclude that sophistic came into being, and has been constituted, as philosophy's alter ego: it is not only a historical fact but also a structural effect.

The evidence for this duality is found first of all in the texts. Owing to the vagaries of transmission, only a few original fragments have survived. Almost all of these are contained in statements or interpretations that sought to discredit them.

Hermann Diels and Walther Kranz, and later Mario Untersteiner, assembled the fragmentary writings of the sophists. By looking at this collection, we can measure the sparseness of the authentic works, those that can be attributed *expressis verbis* to the sophists. There are two clear tendencies: on the one hand, the work of Gorgias, with the ontology, or "meontology," of his *Treatise of Non-Being* and the rhetoric of his *Encomium of Helen* and *Defense of Palamedes;* on the other hand, the work of Antiphon, new fragments of which have recently been discovered, with its focus on ethics and politics in the papyrus *On Truth* and with the model speeches presented in the *Tetralogies.* The surviving fragments are insignificant, however, compared with the number of accounts and dramatizations that they generated. Reconstructing these theses and doctrines resembles a kind of paleontology of perversion, since the same texts supply both reliable knowledge and distorted representations of sophistic.

The starting point, and Plato's point of fusion of history and structure, is as follows: sophistic is a historical reality and at the same time an artifact, a by-product of philosophy, which always represents it as the worst of the alternatives. Let us take the example of Protagoras, who is said to have been the first sophist. We possess only two statements made by him. One refers to the gods: "I can neither know that they are, nor that they are not" (Diogenes Laertius, IX.51); the other, the more famous, deals with the *khrēmata*, normally translated as "things": "Man is the measure of all things: of those that are, that they are, of those that are not, that they are not" (Plato, *Theaetetus,* 151e–152e). It is significant that the context for the transmission or interpretation of this phrase is none other than Plato's *Theaetetus* and Book IV of Aristotle's *Metaphysics,* as well as Book VII of Sextus Empiricus's *Adversus Mathematicos.* The dialogue between Socrates and Theaetetus alone doubtless suffices to give credence once and for all to the relativist and subjectivist meaning of "Protagoras's proposition," and to strip it of all pretension: if truth is reduced to what each person feels it to be, Protagoras might just as well have said that "a pig or a baboon is the measure of all things."

The now traditional image of sophistic first appears in Plato's dialogues. It is discredited on all grounds: ontological, because the sophist is not concerned with being but takes refuge in nonbeing and the accidental *(Sophist);* logical, since he does not seek truth or dialectical rigor but only opinion, superficial coherence, persuasion, and victory in oratorical jousting *(Euthydemus);* and on ethical, pedagogical, and political grounds, since he does not strive for wisdom and virtue, either for the individual or for the city, but aims at personal power and money *(Gorgias).* Sophistic is discredited even on literary grounds, since its stylistic devices are nothing more than the swelling of an encyclopedic emptiness (as illustrated throughout *Protagoras,* for example). If measured by the yardstick of being and truth, sophistic must be condemned as pseudophilosophy: a philosophy of appearances and the appearance of philosophy. Plato invents the sophist as the alter ego of the philosopher, continually imitating and pretending to be a philosopher. They resemble one another, according to the remark of the Stranger in *Sophist*, "as the wolf resembles the dog, the fiercest resembles the tamest." Yet from the use of grammatical cases alone we understand that resemblance is "the slipperiest of genres," for (although this normally goes unnoticed) in the exchange between Theaetetus and Socrates, the dative case clearly puts the sophist in the position of the dog, thus putting the philosopher in the position of the wolf. They resemble one another so closely that, even when you grasp them with both hands, whenever you think you have caught one, you find yourself holding the other: Socrates' cathartic maieutics, his method of refutation, thus constitutes the *genei gennaia sophistikē* ("the authentic and truly noble sophistics"), and generates the possibility of Socrates as a sophist or quasi sophist. Conversely, when all the dichotomies that have served to trap the sophist and construct a definition of him are recapitulated at the end of the dialogue, the final branch leaves us on the same side, opposite the demagogue, with the alternative "sage or sophist?" (268b10), and the answer is determined by just one thesis: "But we have posited"—says Theaetetus—"that he knows nothing." The sophist is not only an imitator but also a paronym of the "sage," designated by a word of the same family, neither more nor less than the philosopher himself. Consequently—and this is of course what surfaces in *Sophist* and completely disrupts its tight organization—the artifact is, conversely, a producer of philosophy; it leads inevitably to parricide and prompts a reflection on being and nonbeing, the major genres, and syntax.

Aristotle, in turn, refutes those who use Protagoras's "man is the measure" to claim that "all phenomena are true," and who believe that they can thus escape the principle of noncontradiction: like Heraclitus and in fact like all the Presocratics, they simply confuse thought with feeling, and feeling with alteration (*Metaphysics* IV). To trust exclusively in the perceptible and in feelings, and to seek to translate faithfully this perpetual becoming in words, is like trying to catch a bird in midflight, and it means condemning oneself to silence, like Cratylus who, simply by moving his finger, designates the river that is never the same and that no one can ever enter (Aristotle, *Metaphysics* IV.5.1010a10–15). If the sophist perseveres with consistency in his so-called phenomenology of all that is fleeting and relative, he condemns himself to silence and disqualifies himself single-handedly. But what if he prefers to continue speaking, and knowingly contradicts himself? Unlike Plato, Aristotle cannot be content to reduce sophistic to a shadow cast by philosophy—a harmful one, since it is both misled and misleading: he has to elaborate a veritable strategy of exclusion. This time, the impossibility of subverting the principle of noncontradiction lies in the proper demonstration of the principle itself, since this demonstration is a refutation. Starting with what the adversary of the principle maintains, if only to deny it, the demonstration reveals the surprising consequence that the adversary is obeying the principle at the very moment he is contesting it. Sophistic taken at its word is Aristotelian, and if Protagoras speaks (which sophists ordinarily do), he can speak only as Aristotle does. The core of the refutation depends on a series of equivalencies that, once articulated, are as obvious as ontology itself: to speak is to say something, something that has a single meaning, the same for everyone, speaker and listener alike. Therefore, all I have to do is speak; the principle of noncontradiction is thereby proven and established. The same word cannot simultaneously have and not have the same meaning. All I have to do is speak, or, to quote Aristotle, have "the adversary say something." Aristotle seals the argument by incorporating that necessary and sufficient condition in the very definition of man as an animal endowed with *logos*: this excludes a priori from humanity all those who choose not to participate in the demonstration, since then "such a man, inasmuch as he is [such], is from the outset equal to a plant" (*Metaphysics* IV.4). Those who refuse to accept this condition are thus reduced to a prelinguistic stage: silence or noise. They are free to take an interest in "what is in the sounds of the voice and in words," such as the barbarian's bla-bla-bla; they are left to focus on the signifier, inasmuch as it does not signify. The need for meaning, thus confused with the goal of univocity, can then become, throughout Aristotle's *Sophistical Refutations*, a formidable weapon against homonymy (a single word with several meanings) and amphiboly (homonymy in syntax, when a single phrase may be construed in several ways). But, more radically, by making the necessity of noncontradiction, the necessity of meaning, and the goal of univocity equivalent, Aristotle marginalized the resisters, equating them with "talking plants," and relegated them to the fringes not only of philosophy but also of humanity.

If the sophist is the philosopher's other, and if philosophy systematically excludes sophists from its own field, the philosopher can only define himself as the sophist's other, an other that sophistic never stops pushing further into a corner. Philosophy is the daughter of wonder, and, according to the first sentence of *Metaphysics*, "all men by nature desire understanding" (Aristotle, *Metaphysics* I.980a). However, "those who feel doubt about whether or not the gods ought to be honoured and parents loved, need castigation, while those who doubt whether snow is white or not, [just need to have a look]" (Aristotle, *Topica* I.xi). The sophist (Protagoras on the gods, Antiphon on the family, Gorgias on what is) exaggerates: he always asks one question too many, draws one conclusion too many. This insolence (*hybris*, shameless excess, and *apaideusia*, the ignorance of the ill-bred, are the two Greek terms that characterize the sophist's philosophical perception) succeeds in putting philosophy literally outside itself; it forces the love of wisdom to transgress the limits that it assigns itself and to perform a certain number of gestures—to come to blows—that are definitely not of the same order as the rest of its approach. Sophistic marks the boundaries of philosophy.

In this light, we can understand the value of studying the repeated resurfacing of sophistic, the way in which it constantly outwits philosophical censure, particularly with the movement that called itself, at the height of the imperial period five centuries after Protagoras and Gorgias, the second sophistic. It is something other than philosophy, different from the metaphysics extending from Plato and Aristotle to Hegel and Heidegger, and yet there is nothing purely and simply irrational in it. This is why sophistic remains very much an issue today.

SOPHISTIC AND THE CRITIQUE OF ONTOLOGY: THE PRIMAL SCENE, OR GORGIAS VERSUS PARMENIDES

If philosophy seeks to silence sophistic, it is probably because, conversely, sophistic produces philosophy as an artifact of language. Witness, first and foremost, a remarkable little treatise by Gorgias, a Sicilian born at Leontium around 485 B.C.E. (We have two versions of this text, one transmitted by Sextus Empiricus, *Adversus mathematicos* VII.65–87, the other constituting the third part of an anonymous doxographic text, *On Melissus, Xenophon and Gorgias [M.X.G.]*, traditionally published within the Aristotelian corpus.)

On Nonbeing, or On Nature: the title of Gorgias's treatise, passed on by Sextus, is provocative. It is precisely the title given to the works of almost all Presocratic philosophers who wrote treatises on nature. But it is also the exact opposite, since what these physicists, or physiologues, especially Parmenides, call *phusis*, or "nature," as Heidegger will insist, designates whatever grows and hence comes into presence: being. Gorgias's treatise, emblematic of sophistic in this respect, must be understood as a secondary discourse, as the critique of a previous text—in this case, Parmenides' poem, which potentially contains the ontology.

"Nothing is." "If it is, it is unknowable" (or, as Sextus puts it, "it cannot be grasped by man"). "If it is and if it is knowable, it cannot be communicated to others" (or "formulated and explained to one's fellow man"). In addition to the title, Gorgias's discursive gesture, in its very form, runs counter to the poem's development. Instead of the self-unfurling of the "is" in the circular fullness of its very present and represented identity, instead of "nature" as progress, as a self-revelatory accretion, the treatise offers a structure of retreat, setting forth the main thesis at the outset, then dwindling according to the characteristics of antilogy, of defense, of discourse that remains forever secondary. This structure is illustrated quite masterfully by Freud, who refers to the sophists in *Jokes and Their Relation to the Unconscious* and is often invoked by their interpreters: A has borrowed a copper pot from B; when A returns it, B complains that the pot has a large hole that makes it useless. A's defense: (1) I never borrowed the pot from B; (2) it had a hole when I borrowed it; (3) I returned the pot intact.

Each of Gorgias's three theses appears to be an ironic or crude overturning of the conventional reading of Parmenides that everybody since Plato must have learned by heart: first, that there is being because being is and nonbeing is not; next, that being is by nature knowable, since being and thinking are the same. This means that philosophy, and more precisely the primary philosophy we call metaphysics, has been able quite naturally to follow its own course: to know being as such, and to trade in doctrines, disciples, and schools. To be, to know, to transmit: not to be, to be unknowable, to be untransmissible.

With his first thesis, Gorgias's whole strategy is to make us understand that Being, Parmenides' hero just as Ulysses is Homer's hero, is never anything but the effect of the poem. By following the way the key word *Is* at the beginning of the poem suffices through a series of infinitives and participles to conceal the entire subject, *being* (in Greek *to on*, "the being," fully identified by means of the definite article), the sophist dissects the way syntax creates semantics. Such a reading is sufficient to overturn the evidence of the poem, for nonbeing can be expressed in a sentence just as well as being. Plato's Stranger will return to this Wittgensteinian argument: Parmenides should not have spoken of nonbeing, should not have pronounced the word or even thought it, for unless it accomplishes the inhuman feat of making sounds like a chiming bell, language propels us, and whoever says *ouk esti* ("is not") will, before he knows it, borne by the very syntactic force of the language he is speaking, reach the point of saying *ta me eonta* (literally, "the nonbeings"; *Sophist* 237a–239b). Gorgias explains it perfectly: "If Not-being is Not-Being, Not-Being IS no less than being. For Not-Being IS Not-being, and Being IS also Being, so that things exist no more than not exist" (*M.X.G.* 979a). Hegel suggests, in *The Science of Logic*, that "those who insist on the difference between being and nothingness ought to *tell* us what the difference is." But Gorgias reveals something else again, in a way that leads this time rather more from Aristotle to Kant and Benveniste: not only can nonbeing be expressed in a sentence just as being can, it can be expressed better than being: better in the sense of being less "sophistic," because it allows less room for ambiguity between the copula and existence. In fact, when someone says "the being is being," the two meanings of the verb *to be* are confirmed in one another and risk becoming indistinguishable; conversely, the proposition of identity applied to nonbeing ("the non-being is non-being") does not lead one to conclude, in the absence of error or bad faith, that nonbeing exists; it simply leads to a distinction between the two meanings of "is": the ontologist is, as it were, more sophist than the sophist.

The catastrophe is complete with the second premise of the poem—"being, thinking: the same," to borrow the paratactic translation that Heidegger occasionally proposes for the controversial Fragment 3—where truth as unveiling, and then as adequacy, finds its moorings. It suffices in fact to think something, and, a fortiori, to say it, for that thing to be; if I say, "Chariots are fighting in the middle of the sea," then chariots are fighting in the middle of the sea. This series of reversals does not belong to rhetorical—hence external—virtuosity, but to catastrophe, in the etymological sense of the word: it is a radical internal criticism of ontology. If it is impossible to say what is not, then anything one says is true. There is no room for nonbeing, nor any room for error or lies; it is Parmenides' ontology alone, taken at its word and pushed to its limits, that guarantees the infallibility and the efficacy of speech, which is thereby sophistic. Gorgias's procedure, his treatise against Parmenides' poem, thus simply consists in drawing attention, somewhat insolently, to all the maneuvers (even those of language and discursive strategies themselves) that allow the relationship of unveiling between being and saying to occur. The effect of limit or catastrophe thus produced consists in showing that, if the ontological text is rigorous, in other words if it does not constitute an exception with regard to the rules it lays down, then it is a sophistic masterpiece.

In place of ontology, which is now only one discursive possibility among others, quite patently self-legitimated, the sophist proposes something like a "logology" by his "performances" (as early as in Plato's dialogues, *epideixeis* designates the lectures and presentations characteristic of the sophistic style). The term *logology* is borrowed from Novalis, to indicate that being, inasmuch as it is, is first produced, performed, by speech. This is readily verified in *Encomium of Helen*, which is the model for epideictic oratory, the rhetorical genre par excellence: *epideixis* again, but this time in the rhetorical terminology adopted by Isocrates and especially by Aristotle, in the narrower sense of "eulogy." Far from giving us an adequate picture of Helen of Troy, the "dog face," a traitress twice over—to her first and second homelands—who left Greece scorched and bloodied, both in actual wars and in Homer's poems, Gorgias fabricates for future generations (from Euripides, Isocrates, and Dio Chrysostom to Offenbach, Claudel, and Giraudoux) an innocent Helen who will make him famous. He imagines four scenarios: Helen is innocent, obviously, if "she did what she did" owing to the will of fortune, the whim of the gods, and the decrees of necessity—"fatality," as Offenbach will have her say; she is innocent again if, as a weak woman confronted by male strength, "she was taken violently" (*Encomium of Helen* 6–7). But Gorgias adds that she is also innocent if—his third hypothesis—she was persuaded by words, or if—in the fourth case—she was simply in love. How can her crime itself—letting herself be seduced—make her blameless? Very simply because it is not Helen's fault if she has eyes and ears. Just as her eyes beheld Paris's beautiful body, her ears heard his speech. Now "speech is a great master [lo-

gos dunastēs megas estin] which, [by the means of] the smallest and most imperceptible bod[ies] achieves the most divine acts, for it has the power to end fear and banish pain, to produce joy and increase pity" (ibid. 8). Gorgias goes on to analyze the results of discursive tyranny in different areas of speech and its deep causes, anchored in human temporality. In the end, Helen's innocence depends on just that power of the *logos:* seduced by Paris's words, Helen is not guilty because words are, in the strictest sense, irresistible, and the encomium becomes both a hymn to the *logos,* and an encomium of the encomium itself. Gorgias deploys the eulogy like a toy (*emon de paignion,* "my game" or "my toy," as the final words of the *Encomium* crudely state): it is a matter finally of a performance, both codified and creative, that enables the orator not only to strengthen the consensus but also to create it. Appealing to opinion, starting with banalities, those things everyone agrees on (everyone says "with a single voice and a single heart" that Helen is the guiltiest of women [ibid.]), he plays with the *logos* to make these objects exist differently, to produce them as different, to produce different ones ("in every case she escapes accusation": Helen is worthy of praise). Or again, there is a moment in every encomium when language overtakes the object, when language becomes the maker of objects, when description, commonplace statements, open up. This is the moment of creation, including the creation of values: the moment of rhetorical convergence between critique of ontology and institution of politics.

If being is an effect of speaking, then the immediacy of nature and the evidence of words that have the duty of expressing it adequately disappear together: *phusis*—nature—revealed by words, gives way to politics created by speech. Here, thanks to the sophists, we reach the political dimension: the city appears as the continual creation of language. If it is a game, sophistic is a game that produces the world just as the game of the Heraclitean child does.

ETHICS AND POLITICS: PROTAGORAS, ANTIPHON

Once confidence in Plato's artifact is lost, it is difficult to speak of sophistic, especially with regard to politics: taken individually, according to all accounts, the sophists held very contradictory views. The first generation, that of Protagoras of Abdera (ca. 490–421 B.C.E.), a friend of Pericles and legislator of Thourioi who was finally exiled for impiety, is sometimes thought to have consisted of democrats and freethinkers. The second generation, that of Critias, who was allied with the Thirty and conspired with Sparta to turn Attica into "a desert left to the sheep" (Philostrates, *Lives of the Sophists* I.16), is thought to have turned away from this sort of equality. Sophistic seems to value contradiction, not just in logic or ontology, but throughout the political and social domain. The sophists somehow managed to appear both as the "new wise men" who sought to do away with prevailing ideas and traditional values, and as promoters of orthodoxy in the city-state, champions of the most conventional and stereotypical behavior.

The difficulty is most pronounced in the case of Antiphon. Projecting contemporary contradictions, some scholars have believed, based on their reading of the doxographers and biographers, that there must have been several Antiphons, and in fact, for many years a distinction was made between two Antiphons in particular (and some still make the distinction today). Antiphon of Rhamnus, born around 470 B.C.E. and known as an oligarchic aristocrat, was condemned to death in 411 for high treason following his involvement in the affair of the Four Hundred; he was a logographer and mainstream orator of whom Thucydides gives a highly favorable portrait. The second Antiphon, whom Hermogenes, relying on Didymus of Alexandria, introduces for stylistic reasons as "the other Antiphon" (*De ideis* II), was the author of *Peri aletheias* and *Peri homonoias*. A later tradition identified him as Antiphon the Sophist, who, as an anarcho-democrat, was able to maintain that Greeks and barbarians were of the very same nature.

The paradox is partially explained if we agree to return to a position that antedates our own antitheses (democracy/conservatism, revolution/reaction): to the very constitution of the polis that signals the "Greek miracle" of the 5th century. Polis, *logos*, sophistic: the eminently political character of sophistic is first of all a matter of *logos*, a term that in Greek ties together thinking and speaking. The sophists would certainly not have existed without the city-state par excellence, Pericles' Athens, where they could establish their reputation, and where they could recruit their wealthy students from the assembled crowds. But, for better or worse, the Greek city-state itself could not have existed without these troublesome strangers—the city-state that Aristotle defines as composed of animals who are simply more political than the others because they can speak.

We can verify the strength of the bond between *logos* and politics through Protagoras's statement, the one that forced Socrates, as if he were ashamed of his relativistic interpretation, to make an "apology" for its author. Protagoras does not simply mean that a phenomenon is only what it appears to be to those to whom it appears, man or pig, but also that from that point on there can be no distinction between being and appearance, opinion and truth. Hence, the wise man will not be in the right, nor will he ever persuade anyone to give up a false opinion in favor of a true one, but he will, like a physician with his medications or a sophist with his speech, produce "inversions" or "reversals" and bring his interlocutor from an inferior state to a better one. Thus "the wise and good orators make the good [things that are useful to their states], instead of the evil [harmful ones], seem to be right" [Plato, *Theaetetus* 167c]. In perfect agreement with *Encomium of Helen*, the *logos* of the sophists is not an *organon*, a tool needed to show or demonstrate what is, but a *pharmakon*, a remedy for improving souls and cities—even if, follow-

444 ❖ CURRENTS OF THOUGHT

ing Plato, no one can forget that *pharmakon* means, indissolubly, poison. Like Gorgias's so-called nihilism, what is called Protagoras's relativism takes its meaning only if interpreted in light of political life when related to eloquence as its very foundation.

Thus, instead of an opposition between true and false, there emerges a question of value; and not in the form of a new alternative between good and evil, but, according to the plurality inherent to the comparative, as a quantification of "the best," understood as useful and, more exactly, useful for. It is on this basis that we must understand, in the phrase about man the measure, the meaning of *khremata*, which Protagoras uses to designate exactly that of which man is the measure. *Khrema*, from the same family as *khrē* (it is necessary, it must) and *khraomai* (to desire, to lack, to use), is understood as linked to *kheir*, the hand. In contrast to *pragmata* (things as resulting from action, the state of things) and *onta* (things inasmuch as they are there, present, as beings), it designates what one needs and uses—a "deal," an event, and, in the plural, wealth and money. This key word of sophistic launches, in the face of an accumulation of being as presence, the temporalized spread of usage, of usury, of expenditure. "Whatever someone has not used, nor will not use, whether or not it belongs to him, will have neither more nor less effect," says Antiphon (frg. 87B.54, *Die Fragmente des Vorsokratiker* 2, p. 362), for example, to console the miser in the fable who, instead of "pouring as much as possible," like Callicles, into his punctured vessels, had buried his treasure (thus *khremata*) in the garden and was robbed. Some interpreters, like Aristotle, will link this notion to the infinite evil of the chrematistic, where money, just by circulating, produces money independently from any need; they may even read into it a model for a general economy in which accumulation and exchange yield to flux and to what Georges Bataille calls "consumation." Whether it is a matter of *logos* or of *khremata*, we understand in any case that sophistic chooses time and flux over space and presence.

While calculating what is best, "the line between good and evil disappears: there is where the sophist is found" (Nietzsche, *Posthumous Fragments* 87–88). Yet Protagoras claims that he teaches "virtue" (at least that is how *arete* is normally translated), despite Socrates' protestations in *Protagoras* and in *Gorgias*. Socrates never stops fighting that claim, using examples drawn from fathers and statesmen celebrated for their virtue but unfortunately surrounded by unworthy sons and compatriots. The famous myth of Protagoras would seem to give credence to this goodwill on the part of the sophist, and to make it plain that a politics worthy of the name, in the stable form of a city-state, depends on ethics, for politics is inconceivable without the participation of all in *aidōs* and *dikē*, two fundamental virtues usually translated as respect and justice. This interpretation of a major text of political philosophy, which offers the conventionally minded a good Protagoras to redeem the insufferable Callicles or Thrasymachus, warrants a more serious reexamination, starting with the literal text of the myth and of the sustained speech that explicates it (Plato, *Protagoras* 320c–328d).

We know that Prometheus, to compensate for Epimetheus's carelessness, steals "knowledge of art along with fire" from Hephaestus and Athena, and that these gifts are enough to procure for men "all the abilities they need to live": not only can they build houses, clothe themselves, and cultivate the land, but they can also honor the gods and speak words; faced with aggressive beasts, they even try to "gather together" and "build cities." Yet they need the art of politics for two reasons: to triumph over animals, and to stay together without letting the injustices they commit against one another divide them from the start. Hence the intervention of Zeus, worried about our species' survival, who sends Hermes bearing *aidōs* and *dikē*, "so that the cities might have the structures and bonds of friendship necessary for [gathering people together]" (Plato, *Protagoras* 322c3), with instructions to divide them up among all men, and to destroy all those incapable of sharing in *aidōs* and *dikē* as constituting a "disease of the city" (ibid., 322d5).

If we take the terms more literally, *aidōs*, respect, represents the feeling produced by others' scrutiny and expectations, a respect for public opinion and, as a result, self-respect; similarly, *dikē*, before it meant justice, hence trial and punishment, signified rule, custom, everything that one might "display" *(deiknumi):* a standard of public behavior. *Aidōs* is thus simply the reason to respect *dikē*, and *dikē* is strong insofar as human beings feel *aidōs:* in this combination of respect and custom there is nothing suggesting an ethical intention, and even less the autonomy of a moral subject; the terms refer only to the rules of public action, always mediated by the gaze of the other. What is more, this kind of behavior necessarily demands hypocrisy: when Protagoras comments on his myth, he reinterprets the "disease" condemned by Zeus, and stresses that "all men must call themselves just, whether they are or not, and anyone who doesn't feign justice is a fool" (*Protagoras* 323b). Such a myth cannot be purely and simply the ethical basis for politics.

If we read closely, it becomes apparent that the model for political "excellence" (the most literal translation of *arete*) is once again nothing other than *logos* itself. The two teachings converge when the child begins to practice the convention represented by words, later when he learns to read, write, and make music, and finally through the written texts of the laws (indeed, a magistrate, on finishing his term, has to submit a report to show that he has copied the laws well). To seek a teacher of virtue is the same as to seek someone who teaches one to *hellenizein:* "Why, you might as well ask who is a teacher of Greek," concludes Protagoras (327e–328a): politics and language, or more exactly teaching the Greek language, thus make common cause. This is just what Aelius Aristides, a sophist of the second sophistic, will demonstrate forcefully, rewriting the myth seven centuries later and substituting for *aidōs* and *dikē* the single term *rhetorical virtue* (*Orations* II.394–399). While human beings in the Prometheus myth had the means "to articulate sound and words" (*Protagoras* 322a), according to Aristides, they obviously did not know either Greek or the art of speaking well: the myth of Protagoras, reread in light of Protagoras's explication in Plato's *Protagoras*, makes the institution of politics an *analogon* of discursive excellence.

The paradox inherent in Protagoras's teaching as well as in his myth thus appears very clearly. Everyone in the city teaches virtue, just as everyone teaches Greek, and everyone is an expert; however, some students are more gifted than others, and some teachers, like Protagoras, ask to be paid. Without exception, they all participate in politics, just as they all speak: Protagoras's myth is clearly the founding myth of democracy. But certain people are differentially "better," are recognized as such, and therefore must be listened to, so the same myth is after all a founding myth of aristocracy—which means that democracy and aristocracy are linked by pedagogy, by paideia. To prefer to be a teacher who is paid rather than a philosopher-king who subjugates is perhaps the truly sophistic—and surprisingly modern—way to separate ethics from politics while reinforcing democracy.

Logos produces the continuous creation of the city-state, because it is the crafter of the *homonoia* (literally, identity of spirit, of feeling) to which both Gorgias and Antiphon, among others, devote a treatise. In Plato's *Republic*, where politics and ethics are one and the same, subjected to the same idea of the Good, *homonoia* determines one of the four virtues that characterize the individual's soul as well as the expanded soul that constitutes the city-state: it is defined as a sense of hierarchy, and, along with justice, is a virtue of structure, determining the proper function of each class within an organic whole. In contrast, a consensus of the sophistic type is always the precarious result of a rhetorical exercise of persuasion, which produces, time after time, an instantaneous unity made entirely of dissension, of differences (this opportunity, *kairos*, is represented in the guise of a young man who is balding in back and who must be seized by the front hairs). The model of the city-state, unified only as a plurality in progress (*homonoia:* consensus), extends to the way in which each individual, in order not to be "at war against himself," relates to himself (*homonoia:* "accord of the self with the self" [Stobaeus, II.33.15; 87B.44a Diels-Kranz]). The unity implied by "with" becomes the matrix of singularity.

The scraps of *Peri homonoias, On Consensus* (on concord, on agreement, as we might say) that have been attributed to Antiphon are too fragmentary to allow us to make much progress: often in the form of a proverb or a fable (that of the miser, discussed earlier, for example), they lead us to take time and usage into account when actual behavior is at stake, but in the surviving fragments the term *homonoia* appears only in the title.

In contrast, Antiphon's *On Truth*, which has to be reevaluated in light of some recently discovered fragments, constitutes the longest authentic text we have on the political thought of a Sophist. The object of a multitude of interpretations (it has been associated with the names of Hobbes, Rousseau, Kant, Sade), it establishes the opposition between nature and law, probably for the first time—an opposition taken up again later, with contradictory evaluations, by Plato's Socrates and Callicles in *Gorgias* and by Thrasymachus in *The Republic*. In Antiphon's text, nature and law are differentiated not by the ideas on which they are based but by the way they are used, their utilization and their usefulness, and in particular by the consequences their transgression entails. The transgression of natural necessity does harm "according to truth" (*di alētheian*, frg. B, col. II and III; 87B.44, Diels-Kranz frg. A): as the etymology suggests, one cannot "escape" (*lāthei*, from *lanthanō*, to be hidden) nature, and punishment always follows. By contrast, the transgression of a conventional rule produces only an effect "according to opinion"; thus the effect is radically different depending on whether one is acting under public scrutiny or in the secrecy of the private realm. With secrecy, clearly, we come back to the natural, but nature is then no longer primary: it is a simple break—which Antiphon describes in a tone sometimes evocative of Sade—with the imperialism of the legality that claims to limit even our senses and to prescribe, for example, "what the eyes may and may not see." But the laws that define the city-state in which one lives are themselves "the result of an agreement" or "consensus" (*homologethenta*): such is the role of *homonoia*, in all the force of its novelty and its separation from the natural order. Antiphon even invents a neologism to say that man, from the beginning, is no longer a creature of nature but of culture: "one is citizenized" (*politeuetai tis*, behaves like a citizen), in other words, one is immersed in a "there is" of politics. Hence man-as-citizen is confronted with laws from the outset, although it might be in his interest, yet again, to have as little to do with them as possible, especially if the laws are powerless to defend him against ensuing violence. Thus, in a manner that allows criticism of the law once its effectiveness has been overwhelmingly established, politics again substitutes for physics as it typically does in sophistic, and the definition of political legality is simply sharing, agreement, and even—in the true meaning of *homologia*—linguistic agreement.

Antiphon, in the very controversial and conjectural fragment A (44, Diels-Kranz frg. B, col. II) is quite probably the inventor of another neologism: to barbarize. "The laws of those who live far away are unknown to us and we do not respect them. In this behaviour we have become like barbarians [*bebarbarometha*] to one another, whereas, by nature, we all find ourselves in all respects naturally made to be both Barbarian and Greek." This simple sentence has contributed to the view of Antiphon as a subversive and modern partisan of absolute equality among all men. It is a matter of replacing the natural basis for the difference between Greek and barbarian—a difference invalidated by the universality of the characteristics of the species ("we all breathe air through the mouth and nostrils" (44, Diels-Kranz frg. B, col. II)—with a cultural basis, even a political one: Greeks and barbarians have a different way of relating to laws. We know that the term *to barbarize* will later come to mean (and it is the irrefutable sign of ethnocentrism) to speak in an unintelligible manner, to commit barbarisms. We should understand that, for Antiphon, we "barbarize" and lose our identity as "Greeks" whenever we relate to the law in a manner that is purely idiosyncratic and thus renounce the intelligibility and universality of both the *logos* and the *homologia*. This view is confirmed by, among other things, the relationship between Antiphon and certain texts of sophistic learning, including Euripides' *Orestes* (to barbarize is to reject, like Orestes, the "common law"—which happens to be precisely that of the Greeks, who are thus champions of the universal—and to fall back into bestiality as a result) and the dialogue between Socrates and Hippias as reported by Xenophon (*Memorabilia* IV), in which Socrates distinguishes Greece from the rest of the world because one law, valid for all, demands that the citizens "take an oath of *homonoia*." If we sought to find something of Kant in Antiphon, as all the major interpreters have attempted to do, it would have to be not the Kant of the autonomy of moral conscience but rather the Kant of the typic of pure practical reason, who recommends acting as if the law were universal, that is to say, as universal as a natural law.

But we must always keep in mind this "as if," which has to do with the fabrication of the universal and the legal. Apart from the historical and philological reasons, this is no doubt the best argument for believing that the two Antiphons are in fact only one. Indeed, *Tetralogies* provides textbook cases for the fabrication of law. For example, in the second *Tetralogy* a young man has killed his friend while practicing with the javelin. A specialist in Athenian law such as Glotz cannot comprehend why Antiphon fails to invoke that law, which provides for acquittal in precisely such a case of involuntary murder. Instead, in what happens it is as if the law, and not just jurisprudence, had to be invented, along with both the meaning and the understanding of the concepts that define and delimit causation *(un état de cause)*. Thus the father of the javelin thrower stipulates that his son acted voluntarily, in throwing, but suffered involuntarily, by being prevented from reaching his target; the agent responsible for the involuntary murder turns out to be the victim himself, whose fault *(hamartia)*, with respect to himself, has already been punished by death (*Tetralogies* III.B.7–8). *Nomimon* and *dikaion*, that which conforms to the law and to justice, are nothing more than the effect of a convention whose judgment will provide the ultimate content until the next trial. To the surprise of jurists, but not of readers of Aristotle's *Rhetoric*, the orator only shows the elaboration that suits the *kairos:* he can call on the *jus sacrum* (religious law), miasma and revenge, to reestablish purity, or upon *jus civile* (civil law), which he can apply in one direction or another ("the law that serves to pursue me absolves me," *Tetralogies* IV). Aristotle will elaborate without scruples on this practice, under the name of "nontechnical proof" *(atekhnos pistis)*, in chapter 15 of the first book of his *Rhetoric*. Laws, like witnesses' accounts, conventions, confessions under torture, and oaths, must be used with skill. One must be able to determine their "spirit"; one can and must play written law against common law, the legal against the equitable, one text against another, one interpretation against another. In short, it is all a matter of discourse.

Thus we measure the sophistic power that *Tetralogies,* a series of four speeches, possesses as a model of judicial rhetoric: an accusation, a defense, a new accusation that takes into account the first defense, then a final defense, each offering its own narrative and its own version of the same event, according to the immediate tactical demands. The identity of the individuals and of the behaviors in question is diffracted in a perfect illustration of the fact that "truth" always comes second. Just as, in the papyrus *On Truth,* the immediate is nothing other than the legal, in view of which the primacy of nature is only secondary, in the same way the *Tetralogies* immerse us in the *eikos,* the probable, the plausible, so that the true becomes a simple trope of the *eikos.* On the one hand, both *eikos* and *nomos* are first and foremost the product of a discourse that succeeds in obtaining agreement about what it presents, thus constructing the public sphere. On the other hand, truth *(alētheia)* does not exist any more than nature *(phusis)* does: whether logical or physical, *alētheia* and *phusis* can only appear as hollow, as a break or a way out, as a secret for which, by definition, no public proof can ever be definitively given.

So it is for solid theoretical reasons, linked to sophistic as a starting point for politics and to a definition of the conventional and the legal as logic or language, that a single Antiphon is at least capable of having been both orator and sophist, without our having to search history for a pretext to split him in two.

The thematic order of sophistic offers the best means of understanding the rift—a rift that sheds light on a number of contemporary antagonisms—between the two major political philosophies of classical antiquity, those of Plato and Aristotle. Hannah Arendt is especially sensitive to this rift when, bent on distinguishing herself from the tragic Platonism of Heidegger and his political philosophy, she attempts to characterize in her own way the *bios politikos* (the political "type of life") and the "Greek solution" to the fragility of human affairs. It is easy to see that the Platonic *theōria,* along with the total submission of politics to philosophy that it implies, is wholly developed against a politics of the sophistic type and its Athenian practice; on the contrary, several fundamental principles of Aristotle's *Politics* constitute, de facto, an anti-Platonic rehabilitation of traditional sophistic themes. We can readily recapitulate the features by which Aristotle, in one of his guises, in order not to be a Platonist, makes himself a sophist: the city-state, which implies a distinction between economics and politics, private and public, defines itself as a "plurality of citizens" whose diversity or "symphonic" quality must be maintained—it is far from being a "homophonic" unity of an organic or hierarchic type that does away with the specifically political dimension. This is why the flaws or anomalies of individuals become—as in the case of a contest judged by the public, or a potluck supper—more qualities to go into the mix; and democracy is the only system finally to be awarded the unqualified name of "Constitution" (cf. *Politics* II.5; III.1; III.4; III.11; IV.2). Armed with the critical and doxastic virtue known as prudence, citizens are thus trained in the Agora, with Euripides, Isocrates, or Thucydides, in the school of the sophists (among whom one could legitimately include one version of Socrates), where they learn the place of appearances, the combative plurality of speech, the exchange and criticism of different points of view—what Arendt calls judgment.

One's assessment of the sophists' politics obviously depends on the position one occupies. And if today we all call ourselves democrats, the sophists can still be called—by writers ranging from Grotius to Finley—precursors of the Enlightenment; or, on the contrary, by such writers as Croiset in his *Démocraties antiques,* and by more than one connoisseur of Plato, they can be called demagogues who need to be eliminated to preserve a healthy democracy, that is, a nonrhetorical one. But the process of conceptualizing politics and democracy has always involved the sophists.

FIRST AND SECOND SOPHISTICS

The first sophistic lost the philosophical war: Plato and Aristotle reduced it to *pseudos* (nonbeing, fake, falsification) and relegated it to the status of bad rhetoric, whether it usurps the status of true rhetoric, which is philosophy (this was Plato's thesis in *Phaedrus*) or is a combination of recipes incapable of amounting to theory (this was Aristotle's opinion at the end of *Sophistical Refutations*). It was a successful expulsion: the second sophistic, so called by Philostrates in the 3rd century C.E., belongs not to the field of philosophy but to that of oratory. If no one quibbles today about whether or not the second sophistic has a real, separate existence, we must nevertheless acknowledge that the importance attributed to it, particularly among Anglo-Saxons, has never been anything but literary, or even merely historical.

However, the second sophistic demands, like the first, to be evaluated, or reevaluated, by the yardstick of philosophy. Its first gesture, with Philostrates, who signals its birth, is to turn the accusation of *pseudos* against philosophy itself. For Philostrates, answering Plato's *Phaedrus,* the old sophistic is a "philosophizing rhetoric" (*Lives of the Sophists* I.480) and only the best philosophers can attain the name and status of sophists: while sophistic defined itself in *Metaphysics* as "[looking] like philosophy, without being so"

(III.2.1004b.26), it is now the philosophers "who are not sophists, but just [look like them]" (*Lives of the Sophists* I.484). Thus, in the palimpsestic replies of the second sophistic to Plato and Aristotle, sophistic becomes both a model for and an eponymous genre of philosophy. The first sophistic, as Philostrates presents it with Gorgias as its founder, covers the gamut of themes that philosophy only attempts to broach, whether with cunning or caution. But the second sophistic—which is as old as the first, for traces of it go back as far as Aeschines—produces "hypotyposes" instead; that is, it describes types (the poor, the noble, the tyrant) and composes case studies. It has more to do with *historia,* as inquiry and narrative, than with philosophy.

Under the Roman empire, sophistic triumphed: if in the early pages of the *Protagoras* Hippocrates blushed with shame at the very idea of being called a sophist, the emperor Trajan in his victory chariot leaned over to Dio Chrysostom and whispered: "I don't understand what you are saying, but I love you as myself," while in the chapel of Alexander Severus there were four portraits, representing Christ, Orpheus, Abraham, and Apollonius of Tyana, the hero of Philostrates' "biography." The triumph of sophistic is rooted in the hegemony of paideia, i.e. of sophistic education, and the development of a literary culture: in schools where the director was a sophist, "rhetorical imitation" encouraged appropriation of all the works of classical antiquity throughout the curriculum. This generalized rhetoric is above all creative: the palimpsest displaces, diverts, changes the meaning and even the literary genre of the texts it appropriates. Alongside a multitude of ancient genres, new genres were gradually identified, in particular one that was to become for us literature par excellence: the novel.

In fact, we can argue that the novel constitutes a completely original response to the philosophical prohibition against fiction. For the novel is a *pseudos* that acknowledges and claims its status as *pseudos,* speech that renounces any ontological equivalency to follow its own "demiurgy": it speaks not to mean something but for the pleasure of producing a "world-effect," a novelistic fiction. The popularity of novels, restoring a link with the founding tradition of Homeric poems, ends up constituting the cultural avatar of a political consensus that has spread, by virtue of the Pax Romana, throughout the inhabited world. As Dio said, not everyone sees the same sky, but even the Indians know Homer.

The paradigm of truth has thus been transformed. Sophistic is no longer judged by the yardstick of philosophical authenticity, but rather by that of the accuracy of the historical facts. Now the historians, in their turn, are the ones accusing sophistic, and its philosophical and literary kin, of being *pseudos.* Evidence of this new conflict is seen in Lucian's text, *How to Write History:* the historian, whose judgment must be a "clear mirror, unblemished and well-centered" (50.1), is the complete opposite of the poet, who, unlike Thucydides, has the right to "overturn the fortress of Epipolae with a stroke of the pen" (38.27). In other words, the historian defines himself as having nothing to do with fiction. However, Lucian is being sophistic about sophistic itself: his irony, in *The True History*, ultimately calls his own practice into question: "I decided to lie, but with greater honesty than others, for there is a point on which I will tell the truth, and [it is] that I am lying" (1.4.8). "True" history thus returns to the paradox of the liar, and it counters the history of the chroniclers and the faithful account of events with the incomparable power of fiction *(plasma)* and invention. The first sophistic, when confronted with philosophy, preferred consensus-building speech to speech in conformity with reality, or with the substance of reality. This very shift, from conformity to political and cultural consensus, parallels a shift in the relevant opposition: the second sophistic can be understood through its difference from history and not, like the first, through its difference from philosophy. We have moved from ontology to the human sciences, and from sophistic to literature.

We can understand—as Gorgias asserts in connection with tragedy—why "he who seduces [i.e., he who deceives, *ho apatāsas*] is more just than someone who does not seduce," and why "he who is seduced [i.e., he who agrees to be deluded, *ho apatētheis*] is wiser than someone who is not seduced." *Apatē* is, in short, the sense of the power of speech, in all its forms: ontological, political, and cultural. What sophistic may, in its own way, help to bring to light in philosophy, politics, and literature is the loss and gain constituting such a discursive autonomy, in other words, constituting a *logos* that is an alternative to the Platonist-Aristotelian logic that has always been ours.

BARBARA CASSIN
Translated by Elizabeth Rawlings and Jeannine Pucci

Bibliography

Texts and Translations: First Sophistic

Antiphon. *Corpus dei papiri Filosofici Greci e Latini*. Ed. and trans. G. Bastianini and Fernanda Decleva-Caizzi. Florence: Olschki, 1989. Vol. 1, 1, pp. 176–236.
———. *Tetralogies*. In *Discours*. Trans. Louis Gernet. Paris: Les Belles Lettres, 1923.
Aristotle. *Metaphysics*. Trans. H. Tredennick. Loeb Classical Library.
———. *On Sophistical Refutations*. In *On Sophistical Refutations; On Coming-to-be and Passing Away*. Trans. E. S. Forster. Loeb Classical Library.
———. *Topica*. Trans. E. S. Forster. Loeb Classical Library.
Cassin, Barbara. *Si Parménide: Le traité anonyme De Melisso Xenophane Gorgia*. Lille: Presses Universitaires de Lille, Maison des Sciences de l'Homme, 1980.
Diels, Hermann. *Die Fragmente des Vorsokratiker*, vol. 2. Berlin: Weidmann, 1903; 6th ed. rev. Walther Kranz, 1952. Pp. 252–416, 425–428.
———. *The Older Sophists*. Columbia: University of South Carolina Press, 1972.

Plato. *Euthydemus* and *Protagoras*. In *Laches; Protagoras; Meno; Euthydemus*. Trans. W. R. M. Lamb. Loeb Classical Library.

———. *Gorgias*. In *Lysis; Symposium; Gorgias*. Trans. W. R. M. Lamb. Loeb Classical Library.

———. *Greater Hippias* and *Lesser Hippias*. In *Cratylus; Parmenides; Greater Hippias; Lesser Hippias*. Trans. H. N. Fowler. Loeb Classical Library.

———. *Theaetetus; Sophist*. Trans. H. N. Fowler. Loeb Classical Library.

Untersteiner, Mario. *Sofisti: Testimonianze e frammenti*. 4 vols. Florence: Nuova Italia, 1949–1962.

Texts and Translations: Second Sophistic

Aelius Aristide. *Orations I, Orations I–II*. Ed. and trans. C. A. Behr. Loeb Classical Library.

Dio Chrysostom. Ed. and trans. J. W. Cohoon and H. Lamar Crosby. Loeb Classical Library.

Lucian. Ed. and trans. A. H. Harmon, K. Kilburn, and M. D. Macleod. Loeb Classical Library.

Philostratus. *Lives of the Sophists*. Ed. and trans. W. C. Wright. Loeb Classical Library.

Romans grecs et latins. Ed. and trans. Pierre Grimal. Paris: Gallimard, 1958.

Studies

Anderson, Graham. *The Second Sophistic: A Cultural Phenomenon in the Roman Empire*. London: Routledge, 1993.

Bowersock, G. W. *Greek Sophists in the Roman Empire*. Oxford: Clarendon Press, 1969.

Cassin, Barbara. *L'effet sophistique*. Paris: Gallimard, 1995.

Cassin, Barbara, ed. *Le plaisir de parler*. Paris: Minuit, 1986.

———. *Positions de la sophistique*. Paris: Vrin, 1986.

Classen, C. J. "Bibliographie zur Sophistik." *Elenchos* 6, no. 1 (1985): 75–140.

Classen, C. J., ed. *Sophistik*. Darmstadt: Wissenschaftliche Buchgesellschafts, 1976.

Détienne, Marcel. *The Masters of Truth in Archaic Greece*. Trans. Janet Lloyd. Cambridge, Mass.: Zone Books, 1996.

Dupréel, Eugène. *Les Sophistes*. Neuchâtel: Ed. du Griffon, 1948.

Gomperz, Heinrich. *Sophistik und Rhetorik: Das Bildungsideal des eu legein in seinem Verhältnis zur Philosophie des V. Jahrhunderts*. Leipzig and Berlin: Teubner, 1912; repr. Darmstadt: Wissenschaftliche Buchgesellschaft, 1965, and Aalen: Scientia, 1985.

Grote, George. *History of Greece*, vol. 8. New York: Harper, 1850. Pp. 151–204.

Hegel, G. W. F. *Lectures on the History of Philosophy*, vol. 2. Trans. E. S. Haldane and Frances H. Simson. London: Routledge and Kegan Paul; New York: Humanities Press, 1974.

Kerferd, George B. *The Sophistic Movement*. Cambridge: Cambridge University Press, 1981.

Perry, B. E. *The Ancient Romances: A Literary-Historical Account of Their Origins*. Berkeley: University of California Press, 1967.

Reardon, B. P. *Courants littéraires grecs des IIème et IIIème siècles après J.-C.* Paris: Les Belles Lettres, 1969.

Rhomeyer Dherby, Gilbert. *Les Sophistes,* 5th ed. Paris: PUF, 2002.

Rocca-Serra, G. "Bibliographie de la seconde sophistique." In *Positions de la sophistique.* Ed. Barbara Cassin. Paris: Vrin, 1986. Pp. 301–314.

Untersteiner, Mario. *The Sophists.* Trans. Kathleen Freeman. Oxford: Blackwell, 1954.

STOICISM

If Zeno of Citium (ca. 334–262 B.C.E.), Cleanthes of Assos (ca. 331–230), and Chrysippus of Soli (ca. 280–208) were to return among us today, they would probably have mixed feelings on seeing what has become of their thought and their work. They would not be displeased to see that the name of the *Stoa poikile* (Porch of Paintings), the Athenian portico where they taught and that gave its name to their school, has gloriously survived, not only in academic terminology, where it designates Stoic philosophy, but also in the vernacular, where it refers to the "stoic" attitude, which for many is identical with philosophy itself. They would rejoice to see that study of their thought is not strictly limited to specialists, and that their philosophy has formed a sort of ideal type in the Western tradition; it has continued to play a powerful role in the self-definition of doctrines, particularly in ethical philosophy. They would be flattered and intrigued by the title of Michel Spanneut's book, *Permanence du Stoïcisme: De Zénon à Malraux* (1973).

But aside from these reasons to be pleased, the first Stoics would also find some cause for melancholy. They wrote a great deal, Cleanthes more than Zeno, and Chrysippus even more than Cleanthes; they would find to their dismay that almost all of their works have disappeared in the turbulence of the centuries. Apart from Cleanthes' famous *Hymn to Zeus* (whose survival could provide an argument for those among the early Stoics who actively valued the educational role of poetry), we have access today only to lists of titles and some short textual citations, accompanied or not by a more or less precise reference. They would realize that to inform ourselves about them, we have to resort to the texts of much later writers who may well be their adversaries (such as Cicero and Plutarch), and we must often turn as well to the texts of more or less intelligent and well-informed compilers, authors of manuals, résumés, or collections of opinions (called doxographies, of which the best-known surviving example is the work of Diogenes Laertius).

Adversaries and doxographers alike tend to speak of Stoics in general, without going into detail concerning the thought of individuals. The risk in this approach is that it may give an exaggerated idea of the homogeneity of the Stoic school. The extended and lasting success of that school in antiquity surely rests in part on the fact that it was governed by a spirit of liberty along with fidelity (in the eyes of its partisans), of dissension and of competition (in those of its adversaries). Those who are often described as dissident Stoics were not shunted aside because of their lack of orthodoxy; they were considered unorthodox because their competitors within the school had prevailed. Besides, the doxographic literature tends to hold on to theses without reproducing the arguments that uphold them. Stoic philosophy, undeniably dogmatic in the antique sense of the term (in the sense that it had "dogmas," positive doctrines that it thought itself in a position to prove and to teach), thus runs the risk of appearing, despite its passionate rationalism, just as dogmatic in the modern sense of the word, that is to say, authoritarian, rigid, little concerned with arguing.

Another surprise would await our long-lost friends. They would learn that the works of their successors have known quite contrasting destinies. Those of the 2nd- and 1st-century Stoics, like Panaetius of Rhodes (born around 185) and Posidonius of Apamea (born around 135), have been swallowed up in the same shipwreck as theirs (which is particularly unfortunate in the case of Posidonius: if his numerous scientific works had been preserved, we would have a different image of the Stoic contribution to Greek knowledge). But still today we find some famous Stoics in bookshops; they differ considerably from philosophy's founding fathers, and also from one another. No longer intellectual heads of schools, teaching in Athens, passing along the official direction of the Stoa, they include a member of the imperial Roman court, Seneca (ca. 8 B.C.E.–65 C.E.), Nero's teacher and minister; a freed slave, Epictetus (ca. 50–130), exiled in Epirus, where he taught before an audience that fortunately included a competent stenographer; and, for a beautiful finish, the master of the world in person, Emperor Marcus Aurelius (121–180). In contemplating these very dissimilar descendants, the first Stoics might well feel a certain pride: their diversity bore witness to the universality of Stoicism, its capacity to give an intellectual and moral frame to a wide range of vocations. But if they were to read their successors' works, in the form in which we have received them, the earliest Stoics might also be rather astonished, if not scandalized.

Why so? Because if there is anything in their philosophy of which Stoics have been proud, it is surely its systematic unity, which reflects in the register of discourse the very unity of the great system we know as the world. Of course everything cannot be explained all at once; thus it is inevitable that the exposition of Stoic philosophy is spread among several chapters or "places," the most extended of which are logic, physics, and ethics. Plato's successors had probably already used the same classification to put their master's teaching in order; indeed, it will dominate all Hellenistic philosophy. But this categorization does not affect the philosophy itself, the organic unity of which is such that nothing in it could be changed or withdrawn, the Stoics claim, without overthrowing the whole system.

Now imperial Stoicism, at least at first glance, puts its entire emphasis on ethics—its theoretical principles and its practical applications. The earliest Stoics could thus complain that their descendants, more favored than they by the accidents of history, have transmitted to posterity only a deformed or truncated image of Stoicism. They themselves certainly did not fail to teach a moral theory, to which they attributed great importance, nor did they fail to practice it to the best of their ability. Nevertheless, they wanted to make that theory inseparable from the rest of their doctrines: they thought they had anchored it solidly to a dogmatic system with a high level of coherence and technical adequacy. And now these distant successors, however respectable they may have been personally, were turning Stoic morality into spiritual counseling, popular philosophy, or solitary meditation.

Zeno and Chrysippus might have remembered, in this context, that they had already encountered philosophers who, believing they held fast to the lesson of Socrates, had scorned theoretical research, and who had adopted "ethics only" as their motto. The Cynics were the radical representatives of this tendency; now, Zeno had had among his masters the Cynic Crates, and the influence of the *Republic* of the Cynic Diogenes had been sufficiently strong on his own *Republic* to have embarrassed certain of his successors, so much so that they sometimes suppressed it, declared it inauthentic, or represented it as a youthful error. The slogan "ethics only" was taken up by one of Zeno's disciples, Ariston; a 2nd-century Stoic, Apollodorus of Seleucia, described Cynicism as "a shortcut to virtue." But if Zeno and Chrysippus were the founders of Stoicism and not simply Cynics succeeding other Cynics, it was to the extent that they refused this shortcut and adopted a "long path" toward virtue, implying not only physical and moral asceticism but also intellectual effort, the critical acceptance of the legacy of earlier philosophies, the development of techniques of language and reason, knowledge of the physical world, and the elaboration of a theology. Was this immense work, recorded in the veritable library that issued from the fertile pen of Chrysippus, forgotten in the imperial era? We might well think so, seeing that a small, practical, portable selection of Epictetus's maxims was in circulation under the title *Manual*—a title that Simplicius justified, when he annotated the work, by saying "that it should be always at hand for those who want to live well, as we call the short swords of soldiers 'daggers' or 'manuals,' because they must always be at hand for those who want to fight."

But given a closer look, the founders of Stoicism might well perceive that they had not been betrayed by their successors. Even if the latter admired Diogenes the Cynic, they did not imagine the primacy of ethics according to the model he established. Despite the disdain he showed for the subtleties of the school, Seneca put together an austere collection of physical and meteorological studies, the *Quaestiones naturales*. Epictetus's *Discourses*, transcribed by Arrian and handed down to posterity in this form, reproduce only the part of his teachings in which, after a course of a more scholarly nature (Chrysippus would have been happy to learn that the students did exercises in logic and explicated his own texts), the master exhorted his followers in a familiar manner to put their philosophy into practice; even these "diatribes," with their supple and often digressive air, are based on a more rigid doctrinal framework than it would appear. As for Marcus Aurelius, who wrote down his famous *Meditations* for his own use (such is the most commonly accepted translation of their title), he had internalized the fundamental spirit of Stoic physics and theology, even though he made no display of it, and even though he dared consider the possibility that the Stoic principles might be incorrect. Were they to read his sublime reaction to this hypothesis ("If there is a Providence, all is well; and if the world operates by chance, do not you, yourself, behave by chance") would not Zeno and Chrysippus, harsh schoolmasters though they were, be won over?

Moreover, if the Stoic ethic had evolved into a relative autonomy, they would not have anyone but themselves to blame. In the person of Zeno, despite his exotic demeanor and his flirtation with Cynicism, the Athenians, good judges in the matter since Socrates' trial, recognized a perfectly respectable master of morals: they awarded him official honors because he had "for many years been devoted to philosophy in the city and ha[d] continued to be a man of worth in all other respects, exhorting to virtue and temperance those of the youth who come to him to be taught, directing them to what is best, affording to all in his own conduct a pattern for imitation in perfect consistency with his teaching" (Diogenes Laertius, *Lives* VII.10–11). The Stoics used many different images to symbolize the various aspects of their doctrine and their intimate unity (the white, yolk, and shell of an egg; the fences, trees, and fruits of an orchard); in most of these images, if not all, ethics held the place of honor. Chrysippus himself, undoubtedly the most theoretical head of the whole school, certainly brought his teaching to its climax with the most speculative parts of the doctrine, physics and its theological culmination; he professed nonetheless, in terms Epicurus would not have rejected, that "physical speculation is to be undertaken for no other purpose than for the discrimination of good and evil" ("On Stoic Self-Contradictions," *Plutarch's Moralia* 1035d). This instrumental relation between physics and ethics contained the seeds of a potential split, for if some other instrument should appear as a basis for Stoic ethics—one more economical than the vast detour by way of knowledge of the world, one less tightly bound, at least for the centuries to come, to a specific state of science—it could enter into competition, or at least into coexistence, with the instrument of physics.

This rapid sketch of the history of ancient Stoicism, from its founders to its last representatives, is intended to shed light on a structural characteristic of Stoic philosophy: the factors of systematic unification of the doctrine and the factors of relative autonomization of its elements coexist in a relatively unstable equilibrium. This tension among centripetal and centrifugal forces (similar to the type of unity that the Stoics discovered in living organisms, in the world, which is itself a living organism, and in their accounts of the world) is not necessarily a weakness: on the level of historical longevity and philosophical seductiveness, it has allowed Stoicism to offer "a big tent," as we say today of ideologies flexible enough or comprehensive enough to adapt themselves to the needs of quite varied clienteles. It is this tension that will serve here as our guideline.

Having decided, as they left their Cynic inheritance behind, that they would have something to teach, and not just rely on provocative examples or edifying exhortations, the Stoics needed an infallibly solid pedestal on which to base their dogmatism. According to an authorized and justly famous account, "'The Stoics agree to put in the forefront the doctrine of impression *(phantasia)* and sensation, inasmuch as the criterion by which the truth of things is tested is generically an impression, and again the theory of assent *(sunkatathesis)* and that of cognition *(katalepsis)* and thought, which precedes all the rest, cannot be stated apart from impression. For impression comes first; then thought, which has the power of talking, expresses what it experiences by the agency of the impression'" (Diogenes Laertius, *Lives* VII.49). On a first reading, this text argues in favor of the primacy of the theory of knowledge over all knowledge of any domain of objects whatsoever: before offering any dogma at all as true, we must know whether we possess a "criterion," a means of access to "the truth of things." By giving priority to their strongly affirmative reply to this crucial question, the Stoics exposed their response to vigorous polemical attacks, but they defended their position with all their might.

The Stoics' principal criterion is not named in the text just cited; we are told only that it belongs to the genus *phantasia*. This first specification leads us to identify the criterion with a psychophysical event, described in material terms as the action of external bodies on the soul, itself a body, with the soul playing a purely passive role. The order of the account thus reproduces the very genesis of the human mind, which is a tabula rasa at birth and is bombarded thereafter with sense impressions whose sedimentation eventually produces speech and reason, both of which are expressed by the key word *logos*. When we analyze the mechanism of perception, however, we find that the passivity of the initial moment leaves room for an active moment, that of the acceptance or "assent" through which the perceiving subject adheres to the content of the impression. Subjects can do this more or less decisively, some to a lesser extent than they might, others to a greater extent than they should. From Zeno on, assent is held to "reside within us and be a voluntary act" (Cicero, *Academica* I.xi.40): this means not that it results from a deliberate and conscious choice (certain impressions are "so obvious and striking they almost grab us by the hair and impel us to assent"), but that it is attributable to us, and that if, owing to haste or bias, we give or refuse our assent unwisely, the responsibility is ours, as well as the responsibility for the consequences of our mistake. It is up to us to organize our entire set of beliefs in a more or less coherent way; it is up to us to make a good or bad "use of our impressions," to use one of Epictetus's favorite expressions; and we are morally accountable for that.

Moreover, this is not the only moral dimension of the theory of knowledge. Indeed, the very notion of impression is not limited to the reception of perceptible qualities: things give us the impression not only of being white, or sweet tasting, but also of being worthy of choice or not. Our assent to such impressions results in a belief, and also in an action, in which we express both the kind of person we are and the responsibility that is ours for having assented to the impression.

Since on the dual levels of knowledge and action we can thus see that assent can be given or refused, and since we can also judge whether it has been given or refused wisely or unwisely, it should respond, well or ill, to the intrinsic characteristics of the impression. In this connection, the type of impression that stands out among all others is the one the Stoics call cognitive or comprehensive *(phantasia kataleptike)*. This kind of impression has three distinctive features: it comes (causally) from a real object; it reproduces the relevant particular characteristics of the object adequately; it is such, finally, that it could not come from any object that is not exactly the one from which it comes. This last provision, added by Zeno to stave off an objection (drawn from the alleged indiscernibility of impressions provoked, for example, by a pair of twins), is crucial: if no impression fulfilling this condition existed, there would be no possibility, either theoretical or practical, of an infallible knowledge of reality. Hence the Stoics' determined efforts to defend this point against all objections. With the theory of cognitive impressions, they had found a philosophical goose laying golden eggs: something self-evident that carries in itself the unfalsifiable certificate of its own truth. On this theory the very foundation of their dogmatic system was to stand or fall.

Once assent is given, as it should be and normally is, to a cognitive impression, the result is cognition, a grasping or comprehension *(katalepsis)*. Although such a grasping cannot be erroneous, what is important is that at this stage Stoicism refuses to speak of knowledge or of science *(episteme):* if we are to situate the grasping "between science and ignorance," and consequently are not to count it "among either goods or evils," it is because the cognitive impression is a grasping of only an isolated state of affairs; hence it runs the risk of being "shaken" by some seductive argument or some unexpected occurrence, while science can be only unshakable. There is no knowledge until the precarious morsels of what is "true," picked up here and there, are integrated into a "truth," into a coherent system of rational convictions where they support one another like the stones of an arch.

To say and think the "true" is thus accessible to every human being, but the "truth," for which the standards of satisfaction are much higher, is found only in an ideal human being, which no Stoic claimed to incarnate: the *sophos* (at once learned and wise), a perfect figure of human beings such as they can be. In contrast, people as they really are, are all equally "worthless" (*phauloi*, of no use, both ignorant and mad). The whole analysis of the cognitive process and its stages—impression, assent, comprehension, science—as Zeno represented it, accompanied by a famous series of gestures in which a hand closes little by little, had the explicit function of showing that no one "except the wise man *knows* anything" (Cicero, *Academica* II.xlvii.145).

This is a decisive strategy, it seems, that allows Stoicism to remain flexible: instead of setting the bar of human knowledge at a single height, the Stoics set up a range of levels, while ensuring the possibility of passing from one to another. This is probably why their philosophy has sometimes seemed contradictory. Thanks to its idea of *katalepsis*, a cognitive moment accessible to the mad as well as to the wise, it claims that our perceptual and rational equipment gives us direct access to knowledge of reality. We are not fallen souls, exiled in a world that is not our true homeland; we are the inhabitants of a world made for us, parts of a world that is a living being, sensitive and rational as we are, made of the same substances as we are. Thus Stoicism can be a popular philosophy, universal by right, intent on presenting itself as the simple "articulation" of the "common notions" that nature implants in everyone. Rejecting the symmetrical paradoxes of Epicureanism and Skepticism, the Stoics believe that there are hosts of things that are clear as day, and on which we can lean as we attempt to shed light on the realm of those that are not clear. It is no accident that "There is daylight" (literally, there is light, *phōs esti*) is their favorite example of an elementary statement, for through an etymological figure they find this light *(phōs)* again in the very name *phantasia*, which "shows itself at the same time as the object that produces it," exactly as light "shows itself simultaneously with the objects on which it shines" (Aetius IV.12.2).

What benefit, then, does the doctrine derive from having reserved for the wise man, a bird "rarer than the phoenix," the privilege of science? More generally speaking, in a philosophy that is opposed by its materialism and its nominalism to all aspects of Platonic "idealism," what is the use of invoking the chimerical figure of the wise man at every turn, and accumulating with respect to him the famous "Stoic paradoxes"? Not only does the wise man "know everything," but he also has all virtues, all skills, and he enjoys perfect happiness under all circumstances; he is "the equal of Zeus." But the important point is that he is never presented as the favorite of Zeus, as a man permitted by a special gift to transcend the limits of the human condition. He remains a man, the only man, indeed, who is wholly human, the only one in whom man's rational nature is fully developed. On these grounds, we other *phauloi* can benefit from the lesson he teaches, even if we do not run into him on the street: through the intermediary of teachers who are no less *phauloi* than we are, even though they may be less remote from wisdom than we are, the wise man teaches us that it is not owing to some inherent defect that we are not what we should be, nor what we could be if we had not let our natural development be impeded or perverted. Plato and Aristotle invited us to imitate God "insofar as possible": they implied that no one is expected to do the impossible. In showing us what a perfect man would be like, if such a man existed, the Stoics implied that no one is authorized to renounce the possible. From his own viewpoint, then, Pascal is right to find in Epictetus not only the marks of man's greatness but also, for want of a counterpart on the side of man's misery, the marks of a "diabolical pride." This is perhaps why Stoic philosophy was able to exalt the most exacting consciences of antiquity, yet without discouraging in the process men of goodwill.

Let us look, now, in the field of logic to begin with, at how the articulation between factors of unification and factors of autonomization is worked out. The Stoics identified two disciplines in this field: dialectic, the art of argumentation through questions and answers, and rhetoric, the art of continuous discourse. They devoted by far the most energy to dialectic. In the time of the earliest Stoics, dialectic had already undergone remarkable developments at the hands of subtle and willfully paradoxical "dialecticians." Far from thinking, like the Cynics (whose work on this point will be developed by Ariston), that logic is "nothing that concerns us," Zeno joined the dialectic school. But he did not cultivate it for its own sake. Ever faithful to his gestural approach to teaching, he summed up his own conception of dialectic by comparing it to a closed fist (as opposed to rhetoric, symbolized by an open palm): in other words, dialectic was to serve to protect his mind, and his disciples', against the risk of being shaken in their theoretical or practical convictions by some fallacious argument. This defensive function of logic, like a remedy one would not have to use if the malady for which it is the antidote did not exist, turns up in several of the images that symbolized the unity of Stoic thought: logic is like an eggshell, like a fence around an orchard, like a rampart protecting a town.

Once the Stoics were launched on this path, however, there was no turning back. Zeno, enamored of "laconic" formulas, left the core of the school's characteristic doctrines to his successors; however, many of these doctrines remained indefinite in their meaning and uncertain in their argumentative foundations. Zeno's principal adversaries, the skeptical Academics of the period, set out to exploit all the school's weaknesses. Thus Zeno's successors had to make the meaning of their master's formulas explicit (without always agreeing among themselves on their proper interpretation), and they had to strengthen their rational foundations. Cleanthes, a faithful disciple but a mediocre debater, put the legacy at risk. Chrysippus took it upon himself to restore the school's foundations, to be a second founder, as it were ("But for Chrysippus, there had been no Porch"; Diogenes Laertius, *Lives of Eminent Philosophers* VII.183—or so the saying went). He is said to have told his master Cleanthes, with some condescension, "that all he wanted was to be told what the doctrines were; he would find out the proofs for himself" (*Lives* VII.179). This is a fine example of *ben trovato:* the saying makes clear that the dogmas, specific truths that, in the aggregate, sum up the doctrine, can doubtless be transmitted without proof (they have a meaning that everyone can grasp), but that it is possible and useful to demonstrate them (they have a content of objective rationality that permits them to be logically linked with a network of other statements).

Chrysippus put all his genius into strengthening the logical framework of the doctrine, so much so that he is like an architect who is as absorbed by the construction of the scaffolding as by the straightening up of the building. Through the scarce remnants of his work, we can still see him as one of the three or four great names in the entire history of logic, and we can understand why it was said that "if the gods took to dialectic, they would adopt no other system than that of Chrysippus" (*Lives* VII.180). It is a matter not simply of a logic, in the narrow sense of a theory of formally valid reasoning, but of a grand theory of the *logos*. In brief, it consists of an effective and subtle theory of signification, a stratified analysis of the signifiers of language (whose development exercised a considerable influence on the theories of the ancient grammarians); a theory of signifieds, incomplete or complete (the most fundamental of these last being the proposition, the bearer of truth or falsity); a theory of propositions, simple or composite (here we find in particular a remarkable analysis of interpropositional connectors *and, or, if . . . then,* an analysis that is essential for the construction of a propositional logic, which is itself logically anterior to the Aristotelian logic of terms), assertoric or modalized according to possibility or necessity (notions whose manipulations entail profound consequences with respect to the contingency of the future and the moral responsibility of the agent); an analysis of lines of reasoning and the different properties they can or cannot have (validity, truth, demonstrativity); a thorough reflection on sophisms and paradoxes, which are powerful motors of logical and philosophical creativity. In the hands of the Stoics, logic becomes a full-fledged discipline. It is no longer, as it was in the Aristotelian tradition, an *organon*, an instrument for science, something such that one knows nothing so long as one knows nothing else; it is an integral part of science, and when one knows it, one knows something.

The rigor and the "formalism" with which this grand theory is constructed have long been considered defects, justifying the scorn in which Stoic logic was held. However, these defects turned into assets for those who succeeded in rehabilitating it in the light of modern logic—to the point that many have felt the need to react, more recently, against a too anachronistically assimilative enthusiasm. In these debates we find again the effect of our axial problematic. Might Chrysippus (who led the studious life of an "academic," even if he felt a little guilty about it) have been caught in his own game? In constructing a timelessly true logic, might he not have forgotten that he was a philosopher, and a Stoic philosopher? The definition of dialectic as the "science of statements true, false, and neither true nor false" (Diogenes Laertius, *Lives* VII.42), which was probably his, is curiously ambiguous: at first sight, it seems to identify the dialectician with the wise man who "knows all things, divine and human," but it should most probably be read in a different sense, that is to say, as the science of what is capable of being true or false (propositions) and what is not (nonpropositional and incomplete signifieds). In this second sense, dialectic corresponds well with the logical enterprise as it was in fact undertaken by Chrysippus.

Yet we must not overestimate the independence of Stoic logic, even for Chrysippus, with regard to the doctrine as a whole. It is worth pointing out, in any case, that after a brief series of dialecticians succeeded Chrysippus, Posidonius, although a Stoic inclined to empirical research rather than pure logic, criticized images that attributed to logic a role of external protection with regard to the doctrine as a whole: he preferred to compare philosophy to an animal, in which logic was symbolized by the bones and tendons, the internal parts responsible for the body's solidity and movement. The fact is that dialectic, whatever the scope and rigor of its formal architecture, does not constitute a closed system. In exploring the structures of language and reason, dialectic explores not only the structures of the thinking and acting human mind but also, and quite legitimately, those of the divine mind, and those of the world, which is not really distinct from God. Nor are the ties between dialectic and ethics lost from sight. The virtues required by the dialectical exercise of reason—the absence of haste, the rigorous control of terms and connections, the mastery of internal order—are the same as those presupposed by moral virtue ("Let us strive to think well: that is the principle of morality"; this saying of Pascal is very Stoic), and Diogenes Laertius concludes his account of Stoic logic by saying that the fundamental objective of the school, in this sphere, was to show that "the wise man is the only dialectician," including when he applies himself to physics or ethics, because he considers all things "by means of logical study" (Diogenes Laertius, *Lives* VII.83).

Epictetus, too, warned his students against the dangers of an insularization of logic, of which the beginner can be a victim in two opposite ways: either he prides himself on "knowing how to analyze syllogisms like Chrysippus" (Epictetus, *Discourses* II.xxiii.44), or else he minimizes the importance of his mistakes in logic, suggesting that they are not tantamount to parricide (I.vii.31). Questioning a student of the first sort, who is led by the delights of logical virtuosity to forget the primacy of ethics, Epictetus asks: "What prevents you from being wretched, mournful, envious—in a word, bewildered and miserable?" As for the second, who forgets the ethical signification of the practice of reason itself, Epictetus teaches him a concise lesson with the famous paradox of the "equality of errors": "You have committed the one error which was possible in this field" (I.vii.32). Thus, far from being abandoned (and even if it does not benefit from any more technical improvements), logic remains firmly anchored in the ethical totality of Stoicism.

Stoic physics also reveals a paradoxical alliance between the accessibility of *katalepsis,* which is a matter of fact, and that of *episteme,* which is a matter of right. What the Stoics meant by physics has little relation with modern physics. What would come closest is what they called etiology, the search for and knowledge of the causes that account for natural phenomena. The Stoics did not hesitate to engage in this, but it was not their most characteristic activity: Posidonius, the most expert among them in this type of study, was labeled an "Aristotelizer" for this reason. In their era, one could not escape from the "philosophical" agenda as it had been drawn up long before by the Presocratics: a self-respecting school had to have not only a theory of the principles and elements of nature and a theory of the structure of matter, but also a cosmology, an astronomy, a meteorology, a zoology, an anthropology, a psychology, and even a theology, since the gods were not "supernatural." Still, one of the striking features of Hellenistic culture is that many branches began to detach themselves from the philosophic tree. More and more specialized scientists, mathematicians, astronomers, physicists, medical doctors, scholars, and philologists began to appear—learned men who were not philosophers and did not wish to be considered as such.

The Stoics took note of this tendency even while trying to control it. In the realm of explanations of specific phenomena, a field that requires observation and experience, the collection of facts, and the recognition of signs, they were willing to leave the detailed work to "experts"; but as they saw it, philosophers could qualify as experts, and had to keep themselves abreast of the others' work. Above all, it is the philosopher's task to determine the principles that establish the framework in which the expert's work is to be developed, and to reflect on the methodological conditions of this work. The Stoics made important contributions (in collaboration or in polemic with Epicureanism, empiricist medicine, and Skepticism) to debates over the acceptability of intellectual acts that, starting from observable effects, trace back to the causes that these effects may signify—debates that in the last analysis raise the problem of the degree to which knowledge of nature can be scientific. To avoid modernizing these reflections too much, we must nevertheless keep in mind that one of the disciplines to which the Stoics most readily turned to illustrate their thinking was divination, the prediction of the future through the interpretation of signs supplied by the gods—a subject on which we are likely to share the skepticism of their adversaries.

This division of roles between philosophers and experts makes it possible to say that there is, all things considered, a kind of immanent justice in the selection made over the centuries among the works of authors of the Stoa. We can regret having lost Chrysippus's *Logical Inquiries,* while the elementary dialectic doxography of Diogenes Laertius survives; in the same way, we can regret having lost Posidonius's treatises on winds, tides, and the flooding of the Nile, while Cicero's *De natura deorum* lives on, which makes clear the theological resonances of his conception of a universe tied together by cosmic "sympathy." But what survives is, in one sense, what was destined to survive: the fundamental, elementary core.

The heart of Stoic physics, then, consists of principles whose determination depends on conceptual decisions rather than empirical considerations. At the center of their ontology the Stoics, taking Plato's analyses in *Sophist* literally and turning them inside out like a glove, equate with being, body, the ability to act and the ability to be acted upon. Only what is capable of acting and being acted upon exists, properly speaking; only what is tangible and corporeal has these capabilities. The principles that are necessary and sufficient to account for the totality of being are thus, once isolated in their pure polarity, a wholly active principle, identifiable with God, and a wholly passive principle, identifiable with matter stripped of all qualities. The object of the science of being is therefore the object of physics, that is, the entire set of bodies, for which forming a totality and acting and reacting one on another amount to one and the same thing. Nevertheless, pairing once again the sturdy assumption of common notions and the paradoxical subtleties of the technical apparatus, the Stoics carve out a special ontological niche for a collection of "incorporeals" (the void, time, place, and also, for reasons that are not at all foreign to physics, the *lekta*, immaterial significations of the vocal signs of language), which do not fulfill the necessary conditions for being actual beings, although they cannot be said to be nothing, either; they are "something." This two-level ontology finds a cosmological translation in the representation of a world that fully exists, a finished and unified totality of bodies, and that is surrounded to infinity by a "something" that "is not," the void. This void is not philosophically superfluous: too perfectly empty to make room for the innumerable worlds of the atomists, or to harbor the extra-worldly residence of the Epicurean gods, it metaphorizes the exclusion of any "intelligible place" of the Platonic type, as it does that of any transcendent God. In Stoicism, no object offers itself to a "first philosophy" in relation to which physics would be, as it is for Aristotle, a "second philosophy."

The Stoic image of the world, even in its details, derives from this strong intuition of the *kosmos,* which precedes all proofs and finds as many as it needs in the moral and religious impetus that never ceases to support it. The litanies of the world, in the rhetoric of the Stoa, are like the litanies of the wise man: in effect, they are the same, for there are not two different ways to be perfect, one for man and one for the universe. From the starting point of this intuition, Stoicism takes to the logically coherent extreme one of the two great worldviews that characterized ancient thought, the other being perfectly represented by atomistic and mechanistic Epicureanism. The skein of attributes of the Stoic world is so closely woven that it comes all together no matter on which strand one tugs: this world is a totality, not a simple sum; it is one, finite, spherical, geocentric, full, continuous, ordered, organized. The events that take place in this world are not mutually independent; this world's temporal and causal unity is summed up in the notion of fate, an orderly and inviolable arrangement of causes, a notion to which the Stoics held no less than to that of moral responsibility, which the notion of fate seemed to put at risk. To articulate their physics and their ethics, they elaborated a complex and differentiated theory of causes that made Chrysippus "sweat," according to Cicero, who relates this discussion in his treatise *De fato*.

The parts of the world are not more foreign to one another than are the events that take place in it; quite to the contrary, the Stoics recognize the possibility of a "total mixture" among bodies, a notion that explicitly transgresses the principle according to which two bodies cannot occupy the same space. The Stoics can consequently conceive of the parts of the world as connected by a vertical and horizontal network of complicities and "conspiracy" (from corespiration, *sumpnoia*), the agent of which is seen as a sort of energetic substance, or substantial energy, penetrating bodies and passing through the whole universe, for which various physical models have been tried, including fire, principally represented by vital heat, and the breath of life *(pneuma)*, a mixture of fire and air. The composition of the *pneuma*, in particular, makes it possible to attribute to it a control of the forces of expansion and contraction, whose result, called *tonos* (tension), accounts in accordance with its varying degrees for the qualities that differentiate natural beings (inanimate, vegetable, and animal substances). From this standpoint, the cosmic picture is clothed in biological and vitalist colors: the differences between natural beings are of degree rather than of nature, and the world itself is imagined, according to the ancient analogy of the microcosm and the macrocosm, as possessing the properties that its most perfected parts possess: life, to begin with, but also the sensitivity characteristic of an animal and the rationality characteristic of man. It would not be contrary to the spirit of the Stoa to say that man is "at home" in this great warm cocoon that resembles him, where everything that is not man is made for him, where evil is but an illusion, a detail, or an inevitable ransom for the good. Still, we must add that man himself, a rational but mortal animal, does not achieve fulfillment except by acknowledging the whole of which he is a part, a great, perfect, rational living being—that is, God. Fate is a form of providence, and at the last stage of initiation to the mysteries (the image is from Chrysippus), physics turns out to be a theology.

The Stoic ethic, a total part of the doctrine, shows in an exemplary manner the dual structure that serves us here as guiding thread, to such an extent that this ethic has often been accused of incoherence or contradiction. In identifying not only human nature but also universal nature with reason, the Stoics still gave themselves the means to give ethics both a natural and a rational foundation. Cicero, in his account of Stoic ethics (*De finibus* III), provides an admirably telling image: nature gives us a letter of recommendation addressed to wisdom and, as often happens, we become more closely attached to the letter's addressee than to its sender.

To pull the rabbit of a singularly powerful moral rigor out of the hat of nature, the Stoics found, both in experience and in theory, a remarkably ingenious instrument. Contrary to what a superficial observation would suggest to their Epicurean adversaries, natural instinct does not lead the small living being, either animal or human, toward the search for pleasure or the avoidance of pain: it leads it to self-preservation and the development of inborn possibilities, even at the cost of effort and pain. This process makes manifest the somewhat maternal providence (foresight or preintelligence, *pronoia*) of a nature that would not put a being in the world without endowing it with this "adaptation" to itself, this "familiarity" with itself, this "attachment" to itself, which is called *oikeiōsis* in Greek, and which makes all the values distributed among external objects, among other individuals, among specific acts of choice or rejection, depend on the contribution they make to the agent's own maintenance and fulfillment. This reading of natural behavior makes it possible to see in it something like the primitive model of a unified organization of the active life.

One must add, nevertheless—and here we see how the paradoxical alliance occurs, in Stoicism, between the legacy of Cynicism and conformity—that the notion of *oikeiōsis* is not, appearances to the contrary, strictly egocentric. The living being, originally "appropriate" to itself, is also appropriate to the parts of which it consists; it has the "feeling" of its own constitution. Now, when it reproduces, its own parts take on autonomous life, but it remains attached to them, as the parental behavior of animals already shows. By this expedient the Stoics thought they could lay the foundation in nature, by a progressive movement of expansion whose outline outlasted many objections and many refutations, of a familial and civic altruism and, to top it off, a cosmopolitan philanthropy supported by the idea of a natural human justice. In this respect, I must at least mention in passing the way Stoicism was grafted onto Roman law, particularly with regard to the idea of an international *ius gentium* ("law of nations"); it was a Roman jurist, Marcian, who transmitted the Chrysippian definition of the law, "queen of all things divine and human," "rule of the just and unjust, which lays down for naturally political animals what they must do, and forbids what they must not do" (*Stoicorum veterum fragmenta* III.314).

But let us return to the primitive model of unified organization of practical life that *oikeiōsis* provides. This model is accessible to the observer, not to the agent itself; the agent is aware only that he is seeking his own preservation and his own maintenance in his natural state, as well as the things and actions that promote those ends. Still, as man develops and as his activity of choosing and refusing progresses in assurance and systematicity, he comes to see (and here I am paraphrasing Cicero, who explains the meaning of the image of the letter of recommendation) that the order and harmony of actions have more value than the actions themselves, that they are the end to which the actions are only the means. To act in accordance with nature, but *in a certain manner* (finalized, selective, regular), *is* to act in accordance with reason, the specific nature of man. *Homologia,* the unification of practical life under the rule of a unique and dominating *logos,* the formal consistency and rational coherence of activity, is thereby qualified as the sovereign good or ultimate end *(telos),* as that in view of which is sought everything that is sought. The rationalist rabbit was not hidden in the naturalist hat; the rabbit is the hat itself, turned neatly inside out, seen from an entirely new and different perspective; there is a reversal of relations between the matter and form of behavior, between what one does and the manner in which one does it, between the verb and the adverb, just as, in certain optical games, there is a reversal of relations between figure and background.

The historical and theoretical gains of this well-conducted operation turned out to be considerable. First of all it made it possible to conceive of the notion of the good in strictly moral terms: if Stoicism preserves the idea, common in Greek morality, that what is good is what is good for the agent (what is "beneficial" or useful to him), it also defends the idea, a much more paradoxical one (when it is compared, for example, to the Aristotelian ethic, which deliberately focuses on making ordinary common moral intuitions explicit), that the only thing that is good for the agent himself is what is morally good (the beautiful, the honorable, *to kalon* in Greek, *honestum* in Cicero's Latin), that is, the perfection (or virtue, *arete*) of his practical reason, unchangeable and unshakable through all the choices it brings about and all the acts it controls, its absolute nonconflictuality, its infallible constancy. Virtue thus understood suffices for happiness, because being happy is less a subjective state of satisfaction than an objective state of "success," of full efflorescence of the nature of the agent in what is specific to that nature. This is a paradox that nourishes many others, and the Stoics never tired of developing them. The thesis rests not only on the model of the god, in whom is displayed, for anyone who has followed the Stoic teaching of physics and theology through to the end, a complete coincidence between reason, beneficence, and happiness, but it also claims to be in accord with the innate intuitions of good and evil such as they would develop naturally in common humanity, if they were not perverted or obscured by society and its false values. In spite of everything, these intuitions retain enough strength to subsist in the form of moral concepts, which we all have even if we do not apply them; the philosopher has only to gather them up in our common sense and "disarticulate" them to find his theory again. In characteristic fashion, the Stoics justify a very paradoxical thesis (virtue is enough for happiness) paradoxically, by saying that that is really what everyone has thought all along.

Thus defined by its formal characteristics of rational coherence, moral perfection nevertheless does not leave in its wake the matter it needs to be practiced and made manifest. Strictly speaking, everything that is neither virtue—which is the only good—nor vice—which is the only evil—is precisely "indifferent"; this is the case for everything that is valorized by ordinary behavior and commonly governs it: life and death, health and illness, pleasure and pain, wealth and poverty, liberty and slavery, power and submission. Nothing in all this, however intensified, contributes to or alters moral perfection. However—and here is where Stoicism parts company with Cynicism, relayed in vain by Ariston—these "indifferent" states are such only from the point of view of morality, which is not the only view from which they can and should be considered; from the point of view of natural tendencies, which morality transcends without abolishing them, they maintain a value of selection, that is to say, a relative value: other things being equal, it is reasonable to prefer the ones that are "in conformity with nature," like life or health, to their opposites; as for those—for example, death or illness—it is preferable to avoid them, because they are "contrary to nature." Only a small category of things that are neither in conformity with nor contrary to nature, such as having an odd or even number of hairs, are indifferent from the double viewpoint of virtue and nature. Epictetus quotes a statement by Chrysippus that sums up very well the Stoic attitude toward the things "in conformity with nature," which are pursued "with the reservation" (hupexairesis) that they not show themselves contrary to the providential plan of Zeus: "As long as the future is unknown to me, I always cling to what is most naturally apt to help me obtain what is in conformity with nature: it is God himself who has made me capable of making these choices. But if I knew that my fate was now to be ill, my inclination would be to give way to illness; in the same way my foot, if it were intelligent [if it could understand that it is, for the man of whom it is a part, the means of arriving at his end] would have a tendency that would lead it to get dirty." The Stoic notion of fate leaves no room for the "lazy argument" (it is useless to see the doctor or take medicine if in any case it is written that I shall die from this illness or that I shall recover): in the book of fate are written not only isolated sentences, but also connected sentences (I shall recover if I see the doctor), conjugations of events that are conjointly subject to fate (confatalia), in which my own initiatives are implicated.

In the capacity of raw material for moral behavior, "things in conformity with nature" are thus explicitly introduced into Stoic formulations of the *telos*, starting with Chrysippus and continuing with his successors Diogenes of Babylon and Antipater. These formulations are continually reworked to ward off the ceaseless criticism, and they always strive to preserve the essential: what counts is not to obtain these things but to choose those that it is reasonable to choose, and to do everything in one's power to obtain those. Without going into the detail of the complex polemics these formulations elicited, I shall simply recall the famous image by which the spokesman of Stoicism in Cicero's *De finibus* sums up the connection between the absolute value of the good and the relative value of "things in conformity with nature": the image of the archer whose *aim* is doubtless to hit the target, but whose *end* is to do all in his power (more precisely, in his power as an expert in archery) to hit it. Let us develop the image somewhat freely: it is preferable to hit the target rather than to miss it, but as this result does not depend entirely on the archer, expert though he is, we may say quite precisely that the only end that unquestionably lies within his power is to do everything he can to hit the target that it does not unquestionably lie within his power to hit. The archer who thinks only of being successful risks being unhappy; the one who thinks only of trying his best and aiming with the greatest precision holds his happiness in his own hands.

Our archer is a hypocrite: he seems to want something other than what he really wants. The Stoic is also a hypocrite, at least in the sense of the Greek word *hypokrites*, which means "theatrical actor." Stoics could not reject this image, which they themselves often use. Ariston (in no way heterodox in this respect) compares the wise man to a good actor who plays his role to perfection, whether he is playing Thersites or Agamemnon. The theoretical translation of this alliance between the actor's professional conscience and his refusal to identify completely with his character can be found in the interplay between two crucial and difficult notions of the Stoic ethic, *katorthōma*, a rigorously right and correct action, and *kathekon*, an action that it is appropriate (to the nature of the agent) to accomplish, and that can therefore be reasonably justified if this nature is that of a rational being—the word has been translated fairly well in Latin by *officium*, less well in French and English, often, by *devoir*, duty. It is not a question of two materially different classes of action. The relation between the two notions is more like the one just noted between the "grasping" of the true, which belongs to the wise and the nonwise man alike, and its integration into a "science" of the truth, which belongs only to the wise man. An action of a given type, such as honoring one's parents, is in itself neither good nor bad. In conformity with the animal and social nature of man, as it is, such an action is a *kathekon*, and only a *kathekon*, when it is the nonwise man who carries it out. But an action of the same type becomes a *katorthōma* when it is the wise man who carries it out, because he does it in a different way, purely owing to his virtuous disposition, solely on the basis of his own wisdom. The wise man is like a moral genius in whom reason, fully in charge, finds at its own level the infallibility of animal instinct. If this moral genius can be put to work in the "perfect" accomplishment of the ordinary functions of natural and social man, it is still not bound by a conventional list of these functions: for certain men and under certain circumstances, it is reasonable to act otherwise than is reasonable for other men, under ordinary circumstances, to act. This distinction creates a new bridge between the seductions of nonconformism and concessions to conformism. The extreme example is that of suicide, which the theory justifies in terms of expediency, and which was practiced in a spectacular way by several masters or disciples of the school.

With its supple force, and owing to its very ambiguities, the contours of Stoicism allowed it not only to spread throughout broad layers of the Hellenistic and Roman world but also to survive over the centuries. It has been reproached for painting resignation in the colors of fervor, for sublimating human powerlessness by transforming it magically into a purely inner liberty. An image attributed to Zeno and Chrysippus seems to justify this interpretation: the figure of a dog attached to a cart, the animal's only choice being to trot along behind the cart willingly or to be dragged along by force. As Seneca puts it more nobly, "The willing soul Fate leads, the unwilling it drags along" (Seneca, *Ad Lucilium Epistulae Morales* CVII.11). Stoicism thus gained its reputation as a philosophy for hard times: in private distress and public calamities, it offers the impregnable help of the "interior citadel" of which Marcus Aurelius spoke. The description of the dog and cart is not quite right: the dog follows the cart of his fate, but it can also be his fate to have his own little cart to draw. Stoicism is not a school of inaction; rather, it teaches man to live and to act with adverbs, so to speak: in a certain manner, serious and detached at the same time, with the conviction that his intentions are pure, and with a relative indifference to results that may eventually belie his intentions. We have the right to dream of a humanity that would no longer have any need of the smallest scrap of Stoicism. But we are not likely to see our dream come true tomorrow.

JACQUES BRUNSCHWIG
Translated by Rita Guerlac and Anne Slack

Bibliography

Texts and Translations

Arnim, Hans von, ed. *Stoicorum veterum fragmenta*. 4 vols. Stuttgart: Teubner, 1903–1924.

Bréhier, Emile, and Pierre-Maxime Schuhl, eds. *Les Stoïciens*. Paris: Gallimard (Pléiade), 1962.

Cicero, Marcus Tullius. *De finibus*. Trans. H. Rackham. Loeb Classical Library.

———. *De natura deorum; Academica*. Trans. H. Rackham. Loeb Classical Library.

———. *De officiis*. Trans. Walter Miller. Loeb Classical Library.

———. *Tusculan Disputations*. Trans. J. E. King. Loeb Classical Library.

Diogenes Laertius. *Lives of Eminent Philosophers*. Trans. R. D. Hicks. 2 vols. Loeb Classical Library.

Epictetus. *The Discourses and Manual, Together with Fragments of His Writings*. Ed. and trans. P. E. Matheson. 2 vols. Oxford: Clarendon Press, 1916.

———. *The Discourses As Reported by Arrian; The Manual, and Fragments*. Trans. W. A. Oldfather. Loeb Classical Library.

Inwood, Brad, and L. P. Gerson, eds. *Hellenistic Philosophy: Introductory Readings*, 2nd ed. Indianapolis: Hackett Publishing Company, 1957.

Long, Anthony A., and David N. Sedley, eds. *The Hellenistic Philosophers*. 2 vols. Cambridge: Cambridge University Press, 1987.

Marcus Aurelius. *The Communings with Himself of Marcus Aurelius Antoninus, Emperor of Rome*. Trans. C. R. Haines. Loeb Classical Library.

Plutarch's *Moralia*. XIII.2. Trans. H. Cherniss. Loeb Classical Library.

Plutarque. *Oeuvres morales XV.2: Traité 72: Sur les notions communes contre les Stoïciens*. Ed. and French trans. M. Casevitz and D. Babut. Paris: Les Belles Lettres, Collection des Universités de France, 2002.

Seneca. *Epistulae morales*. Trans. R. M. Gummere. Loeb Classical Library.

———. *Moral Essays*. Trans. J. W. Basore. Loeb Classical Library.

Sextus Empiricus. Trans. R. B. Bury. Loeb Classical Library.

Studies

Alesse, Francesca. *La Stoa e la tradizione socratica*. Naples: Bibliopolis, 2000.

Algra, Keimpe, Jonathan Barnes, Jaap Mansfeld, and Malcolm Schofield, eds. *The Cambridge History of Hellenistic Philosophy*. Cambridge: Cambridge University Press, 1999.

Annas, Julia. "Stoic Epistemology." In *Epistemology*. Ed. Stephen Everson. Companions to Ancient Thought, 1. Cambridge: Cambridge University Press, 1990. Pp. 184–203.

Barnes, Jonathan. *Logic and the Imperial Stoa*. Leiden-New York-Köln: Brill, 1997.

Barnes, Jonathan, et al., eds. *Science and Speculation*. Cambridge: Cambridge University Press, 1982.

Bobzien, Susanne. *Determinism and Freedom in Stoic Philosophy*. Oxford: Clarendon Press, 1998.

Bréhier, Emile. *Chrysippe et l'ancien Stoïcisme*. Paris: Presses Universitaires de France, 1910.

Brunschwig, Jacques, ed. *Les Stoïciens et leur logique*. Paris: Vrin, 1978.

Flashar, Hellmut, ed. *Die Philosophie der Antike, Bd. 4: Die Hellenistische Philosophie. Zweiter Halbband* (P. Steinmetz, *Die Stoa*). Basel: Schwabe, 1994.

Frede, Michael. *Die stoische Logik*. Göttingen: Vandenhoeck & Ruprecht, 1974.

Goldschmidt, Victor. *Le système stoïcien et l'idée de temps*. Paris: Vrin, 1953.

Hadot, Pierre. *La citadelle intérieure: Introduction aux pensées de Marc Aurèle*. Paris: Fayard, 1992.

Ierodiakonou, Katerina, ed. *Topics in Stoic Philosophy*. Oxford: Clarendon Press, 1999.

Inwood, Brad. *Ethics and Human Action in Early Stoicism*. Oxford: Clarendon Press, 1985.

Lévy, Carlos. *Les Philosophies hellénistiques*. Paris: Le Livre de Poche, 1997.

Long, Anthony A. *Hellenistic Philosophy: Stoics, Epicureans, Sceptics*. Berkeley: University of California Press, 1971.

———, ed. *Problems in Stoicism*. London: Athlone, 1971.

———. *Stoic Studies*. Cambridge: Cambridge University Press, 1996.

Mates, Benson. *Stoic Logic*. Berkeley: University of California Press, 1953.

Rist, John, ed. *The Stoics*. Berkeley: University of California Press, 1978.

Schofield, Malcolm, Myles Burnyeat, and Jonathan Barnes, eds. *Doubt and Dogmatism*. Oxford: Clarendon Press, 1980.

Schofield, Malcolm, and Gisela Striker, eds. *The Norms of Nature*. Cambridge: Cambridge University Press, 1986.

Sharples, R. W. *Stoics, Epicureans and Sceptics: An Introduction to Hellenistic Philosophy*. London: Routledge, 1996.

Spanneut, Michel. *Permanence du Stoïcisme: De Zénon à Malraux*. Gembloux: Duculot, 1973.

Striker, Gisela. "Kritèrion tès aletheias." In *Nachrichten der Akademie der Wissenschaften in Göttingen*. Philologische-historische Klasse 1. Göttingen: Vandenhoeck & Ruprecht, 1974. Pp. 51–110.

CHRONOLOGY

HISTORY	CULTURE	SCIENCE
1270(?)B.C.E.: Trojan War		
~1200: First Greek colonization (Asia Minor)		
	Composition of Homeric poems (~850–750 B.C.E.)	
753: Founding of Rome		
750: Second Greek colonization (Western and Eastern)	Hesiod (~700?)	
593: Solon's reforms in Athens	"Milesians": Thales, Anaximander and Anaximenes (~600–550). Anaximander writes the first Greek treatise in prose ~546	~585 B.C.E.: Eclipse predicted by Thales
540: Founding of Elea	Pythagoras teaches (~532?)	
509: Founding of Roman Republic	Heraclitus (~545–480)	510–490: Voyages of Hecataeus of Miletus
508–507: Cleisthenes' reforms in Athens		
490: Battle of Marathon, defeat of the Persians		
481: Alliance between Athens and Sparta (second Persian War)		
480: Battle of Salamis, Greek naval victory	Parmenides of Elea teaches (~478)	
	Aeschylus, *The Persians* (472); *Oresteia* (458)	
	~454: Anaxagoras (500–428) tried for impiety in Athens	
	Empedocles (~492–432)	
	Protagoras (~492–421)	
	Zeno of Elea (~490–454)	
443: Pericles General of Athens. Alcibiades (450–404), Athenian political leader, student of Socrates	~450: Herodotus (~484–425), *Histories*. Sophocles, *Antigone* (443)	~440: Leucippus, first expression of the theory of atomism

HISTORY	CULTURE	SCIENCE
	~435: Socrates (469–399) teaches in Athens	Hippocrates of Chios (~470–400), *Elements of Geometry*
	Democritus (~460–?)	
	Thucydides (~455–400)	
Peloponnesian War (431–404)	427: Gorgias (~480–376) teaches rhetoric in Athens	
	~423: In *The Clouds*, Aristophanes ridicules the teaching of Socrates	
404: Rule of the Thirty Tyrants in Athens	Antisthenes (~445–360)	Hippocrates (~460–380)
	~405: Euclid of Megara founds the Megarian school	
403: Restoration of democracy	399: Trial of Socrates; death penalty. Aristippus founds a school at Cyrene	
	~390: Isocrates opens a school at Athens and teaches "philosophy" to a large audience	
	Xenophon (~428–354)	
	387: Plato (429–347) founds the Academy	Mathematical works of the Academy (Theaetetus, Eudoxus, Archytas, Leodamas)
		388–315: Work of Heraclides Ponticus (rotation of the earth)
384–322: Demosthenes	Diogenes of Sinope (400–325)	381: Observations of Eudoxus of Cnidus (400–347) in Egypt; epicycloidal movement of the planets (370)
343: Aristotle tutors Alexander the Great	347: Death of Plato; Speusippus succeeds him as head of the Academy	
340: War between Philip of Macedon and Athens		
338: Defeat of Athens at Chaeronea		

HISTORY	CULTURE	SCIENCE
336: Accession of Alexander the Great, King of Macedonia	335: Aristotle (385–322) founds the Lyceum in Athens. Pyrrhon (~365–275) accompanies Alexander to Asia	Aristoxenes' theory of harmonics
332: Founding of Alexandria		
323: Death of Alexander at Babylon; formation of separate Hellenistic monarchies	322: Death of Aristotle; Theophrastus succeeds him	
	306: Epicurus (~342–271) founds the Epicurean School	
	~301: Zeno of Citium founds the Stoic School	~300: Euclid's *Elements*
	~295: Ptolemy I founds the Library at Alexandria	
	283–239: Antigonus Gonatas, King of Macedonia, protects philosophers, especially the Stoics	~281: Aristarchus of Samos and heliocentrism
		~270: Herophilus (physician) practices in Alexandria
	268–264: Arcesilaus succeeds Crates as head of the Academy and gives the school a skeptical orientation	~260: Erasistratus practices medicine
	262: Cleanthes succeeds Zeno as head of the Stoic school	
	The Septuagint	250: Teaching of Diophantus (mathematician)
		~245: Eratosthenes (~275–194) librarian in Alexandria

HISTORY	CULTURE	SCIENCE
	~232: Chrysippus (~280–207) succeeds Cleanthes as head of the Stoic school	
218: Second Punic War 217: First War of Macedonia		Archimedes (~287–212) killed by a Roman soldier during the siege of Syracuse ~200: Work of Apollonius (theory of conics)
169: War between the Seleucids and the Jews of Palestine	Polybius (208–118) 167–166: Carneades, Scholarch of the Academy	161–126: Teaching of Hipparchus (origins of trigonometry, excentric and epicyclic systems theory)
	155: Carneades becomes Ambassador to Rome; accompanied by Diogenes of Babylon (Stoic) and Critolaos (Peripatetic)	
148: Macedonia becomes a Roman Province 146: Greece becomes a Roman Province. Destruction of Carthage by Rome		~150: Hipparchus's geographical map
	110–109: Philon of Larissa becomes Scholarch of the Academy; in 88, flees Athens and seeks refuge in Rome	
~88–86: War of Mithridates		
	~79: Antiochus of Ascalon, Scholarch of the Academy, opens his own school at Athens and moves away from the "skeptical" orientation that lasted from Arcesilas to Philon of Larissa	Posidonius (~135–51) works in geography and astronomy

History	Culture	Science
	Lucretius, *De Natura Rerum* (~54–53)	
	Cicero, *De Republica* (54–52)	
	Philodemus of Gadara founds a center of Epicurian studies in Naples	
	48: First fire in the Library of Alexandria	
	~40: Andronicos of Rhodes publishes the works of Aristotle	
30: Battle of Actium; Egypt becomes a Roman Province. End of the Hellenistic period	30(?): Epicurian inscription of Diogenes of Oenoanda (dated by some scholars to ~125 C.E.)	
27 C.E.: End of the Republic; beginning of the Roman Empire	29(?)C.E.: Death of Jesus of Nazareth	10–25 C.E.: Strabo, *Geography*
	37–41: Embassy of Philon of Alexandria to Caligula	
54–68: Nero's reign; burning of Rome (64); persecution of Christians	48–65: The Stoic Seneca becomes tutor, then advisor to Nero, before being forced to commit suicide; *Letters to Lucilius*, 63–64	
	60: Teaching of Ammonius, a Platonist in Athens	~60: Heron of Alexandria, *Mechanica*
70: Titus takes Jerusalem	64(?): Death of Saint Paul	
	93–94: Expulsion of the philosophers from Rome by Domitian. Epictetus (55–135) founds a school at Nicopolis, on the Greek coast of the Adriatic	~100: Nicomachus of Gerasa (theory of numbers) and Menelaus (on spheres)
	~110: Plutarch (~46–~120) advisor to Trajan, then Hadrian, for Greek affairs	

History	Culture	Science
	~120: Christian apologists begin to present Christianity as philosophy	~125: Theon of Smyrna (numbers theory)
135: Jewish Diaspora	~133: Earliest evidence of gnosticism (Basilides)	
	~150: *Didaskalikos* (summary of Platonism) of Alcinous	Teaching of Ptolemy at Alexandria: *Almagest* (150); *Geography* (155)
161–180: Reign of Marcus Aurelius in Rome	176: Marcus Aurelius founds chairs in the four principal schools of philosophy at Athens: Platonic, Aristotelian, Stoic, Epicurian	
	~177: Celsus, Platonist and anti-Christian polemicist	Galen (129–200)
	~180: *Stromates* by Clement of Alexandria	
	~190: *Outlines of Pyrrhonism* by Sextus Empiricus, source of information on the arguments of early Skeptics (Agrippa and Aenesidemus)	
	~198: Teaching of Alexander of Aphrodisias (Peripatetic) in Athens	
	200: *Lives and Doctrines of the Philosophers* by Diogenes Laertius	
	244: Plotinus (205–269) opens a school in Rome	Diophantus: *Arithmetica*
	~260: Founding of the School of Antioch	
	263: Porphyry becomes a student of Plotinus; publishes the *Enneads* ~301	
312: Conversion of Emperor Constantine		

History	Culture	Science
313: Edict of Milan allows Christianity in Roman Empire	~313: Iamblichus (250–325) founds a Neoplatonist school at Apamea	
314: First partition of Roman Empire		~320: Pappus of Alexandria writes a commentary on Ptolemy and Euclid
	Writings of Basil of Caesarea, Gregory of Nazianzus, Gregory of Nyssa	Theon of Alexandria succeeds Pappus as professor of mathematics
361–363: Reign of Julian the Apostate, Neoplatonist philosopher; reaction against the Christians		
380: Christianity becomes official religion of Roman Empire	386: Conversion of Augustine; writes *Confessions*, 400; *The City of God*, 413–426	
410: Sack of Rome by Alaric		415: Death of Hypatia, daughter of Theon, scholar and a key figure in Neoplatonist philosophy
	~438: Proclus succeeds Syrianus as head of the Neoplatonist school	
476: Fall of the Western Empire		
	520: Damascius succeeds Zenodotus as head of the Neoplatonist school	
	529: Justinian closes the school of Athens. Seven Neoplatonist philosophers flee to Persia (including Simplicius and Damascius)	

CONTRIBUTORS

Julia Annas, University of Arizona

Serge Bardet, Université de Versailles—Saint-Quentin

Enrico Berti, Università di Padova

Henry Blumenthal, University of Liverpool

Luc Brisson, Centre National de la Recherche Scientifique, Paris

Jacques Brunschwig, Université de Paris I

Monique Canto-Sperber, Centre National de la Recherche Scientifique, Paris

Barbara Cassin, Centre National de la Recherche Scientifique, Paris

Maurice Caveing, Centre National de la Recherche Scientifique, Paris

Armelle Debru, Université de Paris V

Fernanda Decleva Caizzi, Università di Milano

Françoise Frazier, Université de Montpellier III

David Furley, Princeton University

Marie-Odile Goulet-Cazé, Centre National de la Recherche Scientifique, Paris

François Hartog, Ecole des Hautes Etudes en Sciences Sociales, Paris

Carl Huffman, De Pauw University

Edward Hussey, All Souls College, Oxford

Christian Jacob, Ecole des Hautes Etudes en Sciences Sociales, Paris

Jacques Jouanna, Université de Paris IV

Wilbur Knorr, Stanford University

André Laks, Université de Lille III

Alain Le Boulluec, Ecole Pratique des Hautes Etudes, Paris

Carlos Lévy, Université de Paris XII

Geoffrey E. R. Lloyd, Darwin College, Cambridge

Donald Morrison, Rice University

John David North, University of Groningen

Martin Ostwald, Swarthmore College

Pierre Pellegrin, Centre National de la Recherche Scientifique, Paris

Gilbert Romeyer Dherbey, Université de Paris IV

R. W. Sharples, University College London

INDEX

Academy, 277–298; and Aristotle, 52; Early (Old), 278–287, 373–375; founding of, 150; and Lyceum, 52; New, 375–376, 415, 416; and Skepticism, 415, 416

Aelius Aristides, 445

Aenesidemus, 287, 288, 428–429, 430–431

Agrippa, 430, 431

Alcaeus, 348

Alcibiades, 249–250

Alcinous, *Didaskalikos*, 379–381

Alexander of Aphrodisias, 175, 305–306, 307, 308, 310–311, 312, 314, 315–316

Alexander the Great, 33–34, 351

Alexandria, 353

Ammonius Saccas, 171

Anaxagoras, 3–12, 58

Anaximander, 363, 365

Antiochian Fathers, 342

Antiochus of Ascalon, 295–296, 376

Antiphon, 443, 444; *On Consensus*, 446; *Tetralogies*, 448–449; *On Truth*, 446–447. *See also* Sophists

Antisthenes, 14–20, 47, 322, 323

Anytus, 227

Apollonius of Tyana, 412

Arcesilaus of Pitane, 287–290, 291, 375

Archimedes, 22–31

Archytas, 404–405, 410–411

Areius Didymus, 305

Aristobulus, 357

Ariston of Ceos, 302

Aristophanes, 228, 230

Aristotelianism, 300–319; and Neoplatonism, 180; and Plotinus, 176, 178; and Stoicism, 463

Aristotle, 32–52; and the Academy, 278, 279; and Anaxagoras, 5, 6, 7, 10; and Antiphon, 444, 448–449; and aporia, 418; and biology, 60; and Democritus, 54, 55, 56, 58, 60; and emotion, 317; and Epicurus, 64–65, 77; and Forms, 280–281; and Galen, 101, 102; and Hippocra-

tes of Cos, 127; and intellect, 315; and Jews, 349–350; and logic, 307; and metaphysics, 309, 310; and Milesians, 360, 361; and Neoplatonism, 306, 318–319; and Parmenides, 142, 144–145, 148; and physics, 308, 309; and Plato, 34–35, 37, 41, 47, 48, 49, 51, 159, 280–281, 374, 449–450; and Plotinus, 174, 175, 306, 318; and Porphyry, 384; and Protagoras, 437; and providence, 310, 311; and Pythagoras/Pythagoreanism, 396, 397, 400, 401, 407, 408, 410; reputation of, 303, 304; and rhetoric, 38; and Socrates, 224, 230, 234, 236; and Sophists, 437–439, 449, 450, 451; and soul, 313, 314; and Speusippus, 281, 282, 283; and Stoicism, 41, 51; and Theophrastus, 301, 302; and void, 58; and Xenocrates, 283, 284, 285; and Zeno of Elea, 270, 271; *Categories*, 39; *Generation of Animals*, 45–46; *History of Animals*, 46; *Metaphysics*, 48–49; *Meteorologica*, 43; *Parts of Animals*, 45; *Physics*, 44, 45; *Poetics*, 38; *Politics*, 50; *Posterior Analytics*, 40; *Prior Analytics*, 39; *Rhetoric*, 38; *On the Soul*, 49–50; *Topica*, 37–38. *See also* Lyceum

Aristoxenus, 402

Arius, 345

Ascanius of Abdera, 421

Asclepiades, 99

Asclepius, 104, 128

Aspasius, 317

Athenagoras, *Petition*, 339–340

Athens, 247–248

Atomism, 148

Atticus, 310, 378–379

Babylon, 211, 405

Bible, 337, 341, 353, 354, 356–357

Carneades, 290–292, 295, 375. *See also* Skepticism

483